Advances in the Creation and Revision of Writing Systems

Contributions to the Sociology of Language

8

Editor

Joshua A. Fishman

MOUTON · THE HAGUE · PARIS

Advances in the Creation and Revision of Writing Systems

Edited by

Joshua A. Fishman
Yeshiva University

MOUTON · THE HAGUE · PARIS

ISBN 90 279 7552 3

Jacket design by Jurriaan Schrofer

Printed in the Netherlands

דודלען
ווײַל עס גייט אים
אין לעבן שרײַבן
ייִדיש אָן גרײַזן

Contents

SECTION III: THE REVISION OF CLASSICAL WRITING SYSTEMS

SECTION IV: THE REVISION OF MODERN WRITING SYSTEMS ASSOCIATED WITH NATIONAL POLITICAL ESTABLISHMENTS

SECTION V: THE REVISION OF MODERN WRITING SYSTEMS NOT ASSOCIATED WITH NATIONAL POLITICAL ESTABLISHMENTS

Preface

JOSHUA A. FISHMAN

Advances in the Creation and Revision of Writing Systems*

The sophistication of phonological theory, both that of the early part of this century as well as that of recent years, and the recent linguistic interest in theories of writing systems and in the relations between such systems and spoken language are, and have long been, powerful linguistic contributions to the world-wide efforts to create writing systems for pre-literate peoples. However, the very sophistication of the linguist's professional skills in code description and code creation (e.g. Pike 1947; Ray 1963) merely intensified the separation trauma when it became increasingly obvious that it was necessary to go outside the code and to confront the real world if writing systems were not only to be devised but employed. The first steps in this direction were moderate indeed. These consisted of Vachek's (1945-1949; 1948) and Bolinger's (1946) protests (among others) that the writing system must be viewed separately from the spoken code, i.e. that it could not properly be viewed as merely the phonetic transcription of the spoken code, and that it was basically a 'visual system' with regularities all its own.

The reverberations of these early protests are still with us. As Berry has pointed out (1958), new alphabets have merely become less purely phonemic and more inclined to the 'use of reason and expedience' (rather than to rely on phonemicization alone) in their pursuit of acceptance. Indeed, the latter concern, that of acceptance, has tended to replace the

* This preface is a revision and expansion of my 'The Uses of Sociolinguistics' which first appeared in G. E. Perren and J. J. M. Trim (eds.), *Applications of Linguistics. Selected Papers of the Second International Congress of Applied Linguistics, 1969* (Cambridge: Cambridge University Press, 1971), 19-40, and subsequently, in my *Language in Sociocultural Change*, ed. by A. Dill (Stanford: Stanford University Press, 1972), 305-330.

former, that of 'reduction to writing', and, as a result, arguments pertaining to intra- (writing) code phenomena have tended to recede evermore into the background. While 'phonetic ambiguity' is still considered a 'bad' thing and while it is generally agreed that 'words pronounced differently should be kept graphically apart' (Bradley 1913-1914), it is considered to be an even 'worse thing' if alphabets of exquisite perfection remain unused or unaccepted. More and more the creation of writing systems has shown awareness of the fact that such nonacceptance is only to a relatively minor degree governed by intra-code ambiguities, inconsistencies or irrelevancies (all of these being rampant characteristics of the most widely used writing systems today and throughout history). Time and again in recent years the greater importance of extra-code phenomena has been hinted at (Gelb 1952; Bowers 1968), pointed to (Sjoberg 1964; 1966), and, finally, even catalogued (Smalley 1964).

DESIRED SIMILARITY AND DISSIMILARITY

Perhaps because their attention is basically directed toward intra-code factors, linguists and applied linguists were quickest to notice those extra-code factors in the adoption or rejection of writing systems which indicated societal preferences or antipathies for writing conventions associated with some other language or languages. Thus, among the 'practical limitations to a phonemic orthography' Nida (1953) discussed the fact that both the Otomi and the Quechua 'suffer from cultural insecurity' and want their writing systems not only to 'look like Spanish' but to operate with the same graphematic alternances as does Spanish, *whether these are needed or not* in terms of their own phonemic system.[1] In a related but crucially different vein Hans Wolff (1954) recommended that Nigerian orthographies be created not only in terms of tried and true technically linguistic criteria (such as 'accuracy, economy and consistency') but that 'similarity to the orthographies of related languages' also be used as a guide. Of course, Wolff was merely following in the footsteps of the Westermann Script, of the late twenties, which, in its fuller, more generally applicable form, became the All-Africa Script of the International African Institute (Anon. 1930). However, he was also following in the tradition that placed the linguist or other outside expert in the position not only of judging *which languages* were sufficiently related in order to deserve a common writing system, but also of deciding whether such similarity in writing system was or was not a 'good thing' and whether it was or was not desired by the speech communities involved.

However, once having stepped outside of the charmingly closed circle of intra-code considerations, Pandora's box had been opened never again to be shut. In recent days, to mention only such examples, Serdyuchenko has assured us that the Cyrillic alphabet is used as the model in 'the creation of new written languages in the U.S.S.R.' only because of the widespread and still growing interest in subsequently more easily learning Russian. More recently the Bamako Meeting on the Use of the Mother Tongue for Literacy (February 28-March 5, 1966, UNESCO sponsored) went a step further. It not only recommended that new writing systems be similar to those of *unrelated but important languages for the learners* (Bowers 1968) but it also warned of 'possible repercussions of a technical and economic nature' following upon the adoption of non-European diacritics and special letters in the standard transcriptions of West African languages (Ferru 1966). Such letters and diacritics, it is pointed out, increase the cost of printing and typing, as well as the cost of manufacturing printing and typing equipment, and do so at the time when the *per capita* cost of printed or typed material is already likely to be troublesomely high in view of the limited number of consumers available for them in newly literate societies.

The reverse case has been less fully documented, namely, that in which newly literate communities have desired a more *distinctive* writing system, one that they could call *their own* or one that would more effectively differentiate their language from others with which they did *not* seek similarity but rather *dissimilarity*. Dickens' (1953) discussion of the Ashante rejection of the Akuapem-based writing system for standard Twi (in the late thirties and early forties) is one such case. Another is Ferguson's reference (1967) to the fact that St. Stefan of Perm (fourteenth century) purposely created a separate alphabet for the Komi (giving 'some of the letters an appearance suggestive of the Tamga signs in use among the Komi as property markers and decorations') 'so that the Komi could regard the writing system as distinctively theirs and not an alphabet used for another language'. There must be many examples of this kind, e.g. St Mesrop's creation of the Armenian alphabet in the fifth century (Ferguson 1967), but little detailed evidence concerning them is available in the scholarly literature dealing with contemporary societies.[2] The reluctance to document such cases is probably not unrelated to the more general reluctance of those who practice applied linguistics upon others to recognize the frequent desires of nonliterate peoples to be themselves (albeit 'in a modern way') rather than merely to be imitative copies of *ourselves* (whether we be Chinese, Russian, French, British, American, Spanish, or Portuguese).

'A little more complicated than that'

If economics answers all questions with 'supply and demand', and psychology with 'it all depends', then the first contribution of sociolinguistics to linguistics is doubtlessly to make us aware of the fact that the relations and interpenetrations between language and society are 'a little more complicated than that', whatever *that* may be. Indeed, although it is nearly half a century since Radin first implied that the adoption (actually, the borrowing) of an alphabet by an aboriginal people was a fascinatingly complex and internally differentiated chain of social processes, we have not to this day seriously followed up this seeming complexity, let alone tried to reduce it to some underlying set of basic dimensions. Our technical expertise and theoretical sophistication lead us more readily to agree with Burns' (1953) early conclusion, based on sad experience with the failure of 'linguistics without sociology' in Haiti, that the choice of an orthography has widespread social and political implications. They also lead us to continually admire Garvin's accounts (1954; 1959) of his attempts to achieve consumer consensus and participation in the creation of a standard orthography for Ponape, and to share his disappointment that even this was not enough to assure the use of that orthography. Beyond such agreement and admiration, however, we can only suggest that the process of gaining acceptance for technically sound writing systems is even 'a little more complicated than that'.

Basically what is it that sociolinguistics could contribute to future studies of the acceptive creation of writing systems? As I see it, being almost entirely an outsider to the area of endeavor, modern sociolinguistics can contribute most by linking this branch of applied linguistics with the body of theory and practice that has grown up in connection with the acceptance of other systematic innovations, the planning of social change more generally, and the amelioration of the inevitable dislocations that follow upon the introduction of innumerable innovations and changes of which new writing systems are merely symptomatic.

The creation of writing systems is itself necessarily an outgrowth of culture contact, if not of political and economic domination from outside. Thus, the creation of a writing system is singularly unlikely to be viewed dispassionately and its propagation and acceptance by indigenous networks are necessarily viewed as having implications for group loyalty and group identity. Latinization, Cyrillization, or Sinoization are not merely far-going indications of desired (and frequently of subsidized or directed) social change and cognitive-emotional reorganization, but they have immediate consequences for the relevance of traditional elitist skills and implications for the distribution of new skills and statuses related to literacy and to the philosophy or ideology which is the carrier of literacy.

The creation of writing systems is significant only insofar as it leads to the acceptance and implementatoin of writing systems. The latter are revolutionary rather than narrowly technical acts. They succeed or fail far less on the basis of the adequacy of their intra-code phonological systems or on the basis of their fidelity to model systems than on the basis of the success of the larger revolutions with which they are associated: revolutions in the production and consumption of economic goods (leading to new rural-urban population distributions, new jobs, new training programs, new avocations, new pastimes, and new purposive social groups) and revolutions in the distributions of power and influence. All of these both lead to and depend upon an increasing number of new texts and new written records. Thus, when sociolinguistic attention is finally directed to the creation of writing systems it will be focused upon the organization, functioning, and disorganization of an increasingly literate society. This is potentially a useful addition to the linguist's disciplinary focus because even more than writing changes speech (via 'spelling pronunciations'), literacy changes speakers and societies. It is this perspective on the creation of writing systems – as always, a perspective which is outside of the linguistic system alone – that is part of the programmatic promise of the sociolinguistics of writing systems.

Such attention will improve or alter the creation of writing systems precisely by relating the problem of creation to the problem of acceptance, of impact, of possible dislocation, of possible manipulation, of possible exploitation, of possible redistribution of power, and of studied awareness of the interdependency of the best writing system on revolutionary processes at their most pragmatic as well as at their most symbolic. Of course, it will require a far greater liberation of sociolinguistics from disciplinary linguistics and its far greater immersion in societal processes and problems before sociolinguistics can be broadly useful in these respects rather than merely descriptively 'helpful' on the one hand or diffusely 'stimulating' on the other.

Orthographic Reform

To some extent such liberation and immersion are more advanced with respect to the study and planning of orthographic *reforms*, perhaps because the truly vast amount of technical linguistic effort invested in these reforms has yielded such meager results. Even though orthographic reform may be so sweeping as to involve the complete replacement of one writing system by another (and, in that sense, it may be viewed as a subcategory of the topic just reviewed), it deals with *already literate networks* and, as a result, more clearly reveals the societal ramifications and reverberations of seemingly technical linguistic adjustments.

If the introduction of a newly created writing system easily threatens to change established lines of relative advantage and disadvantage, practical and symbolic, the revision of traditional orthographies often *attempts* to do so. Orthographic change represents the abandonment of written tradition and as such it *must* cope with the gatekeepers of written tradition, the poets, priests, principals, and professors, with the institutions and symbols that they create and serve, or be destined to oblivion. Indeed, the greater and grander the tradition of literacy, literature, and liturgy in an orthographic community, the less likely that even minor systematic orthographic change will be freely accepted and the less likely that any orthographic change will be considered minor.

In this connection we have a larger number of rather detailed and, to some extent, *sociolinguistically oriented* descriptions, than is the case for the creation of writing systems, but, as yet we have no sociolinguistic analyses or hypotheses *per se*. The socioculturally contextualized descriptions of orthographic reforms in the U.S.S.R. (Orenstein 1959; Quelquejay and Bennigsen 1961; Serdyuchenko 1965; Weinreich 1953; Winner 1952), Turkey (Rossi 1927; 1929; 1935; 1942; 1953; Heyd 1954; Ozmen 1967; Gallagher 1967; 1969), Norway (Haugen 1966, which contains an exhaustive bibliography of other studies), and Vietnam (Haudricourt 1943; Sheldon 1946) again point to the literally revolutionary nature of the societal processes that have often accompanied system-wide orthographic change. On the other hand, the available descriptions of less successful attempts to bring about orthographic changes under less dramatic circumstances, e.g. in Japan (DeFrancis 1947; Holton 1947; Meyenberg 1934; Scharshmidt 1924), Haiti (Valdman 1968; Burns 1953), and Israel (Rabin 1969), or to bring about the orthographic unification of closely related languages in the absence of accompanying societal unification, e.g. in

India (Anon. 1963; Jones 1942; Ray 1960), Africa (Dickens 1953; Ward 1945), and Indonesia-Malaysia (Alisjahbana 1969; 1972), all indicate the difficulties encountered and the failures experienced thus far.

However, there is no justification for interpreting the above cited investigations as implying 'revolutionary success and non-revolutionary failure' as the proper summation of experience with orthographic reform. In earlier centuries a great deal of orthographic reform seems to have been accomplished both quietly and successfully, essentially without the involvement of mobilized populations or, indeed, of any population segments other than 'the authorities' whose business it was to make wise decisions for the community. The initial orthographic distinctions between Serbian and Croatian or between Ruthenian (Ukrainian) and Polish were decided upon by representatives of God and Caesar who sought to cultivate *ausbau* differences between speech communities that were 'in danger' of religious, political, and linguistic unification. The restoration of written Czech (and Slovak) in Latin script was engineered by Count Sednitzsley, the administrative director of the Austro-Hungarian police and one of the most influential officials under the Emperor Francis (early nineteenth century), by subsidizing the publication of the Orthodox prayer book in Latin letters as 'an important device to fight the political danger of the Pro-Russian Pan-Slav movement' (Fischel 1919: 57). The Roumanian shift from Cyrillic to Latin script in 1863 was accomplished by a painless edict which sought to further that nation's self-defined Latinizing and Christianizing role in the heathen 'Slavo-Moslem' Balkans (Kolarz 1946). In more recent days Irish orthography has been changed without arousing great interest (Macnamara 1969) – indeed, the ease of the change is a reflection of the lack of widespread Irish interest or concern for the Revival – as have the orthographies of other small speech communities.

Not only *has* there been much successful orthographic reform without revolutionary change (particularly where mass mobilization along language-related lines was absent for one reason or another), but there has also been a good bit of unsuccessful orthographic reform even when these have been accompanied by revolutionary social changes. Thus, the Soviet 'rationalization' of Yiddish orthography initially aimed at both the *phonetization* of words of Hebrew-Aramic origin, as well as at the *discontinuation* of the special final letters of the traditional Hebrew alphabet. However, forty-five years after the October revolution, the names of the grandfathers of modern Yiddish literature were neither spelled:

שאָלעמ אַלייכעמ, ייִצכאָק לייבוש פערעצ אונ מענדעלע מויכער ספאָרימ

(as they *had* been throughout the twenties and thirties), nor were they spelled:

שלום עליכם, יצחק לייבוש פרץ און מענדעלע מוכר־ספרים

(as they *had* been before the Revolution and continued to be everywhere outside of the Soviet Union). Rather, in an attempt to reach a compromise that would maximize the propaganda value of the few permitted Yiddish publications primarily distributed to and published for readers outside of the U.S.S.R., they were spelled:[3]

שאָלעם אַלייכעם, ייִצכאָק לייבוש פערעץ און מענדעלע מויכער ספאָרים

However, even in its heyday the Soviet revolution in Yiddish orthography could not entirely overcome the visual traditions of the orthographic community. The initial silent aleph at the beginning of words that would otherwise begin with the vowels י and ו was *never* dropped, regardless of its phonemic uselessness, perhaps because the initial silent aleph in such cases was considered to be too strong a visual convention to be tampered with (Hebrew writing itself – i.e. the visual precursor to Yiddish – never begins words with vocalic י or ו).

A far more widely renowned revolutionary attempt at orthographic reform which has failed (certainly thus far) is the once promised phonetization of (Northern Mandarin) Chinese. While the basic sources available to us in English (DeFrancis 1950; 1968; Mills 1956; Hsia 1956) all agree that the Latinized New Writing was abandoned sometime late in the fifties, the reason for this abandonment can still only be surmised. By 1956 it had become necessary to defend the 'Han (Chinese) language phonetization draft plan' as being concerned with an alphabet (Latin) which was truly progressive and international rather than necessarily related to any antiproletarian class (Chinese Written Language Reform Committee 1956; Wu Yu-chang 1956). By 1959 Chou En-lai had officially demoted phonetization from its original goal of immediate 'liberation and development of the whole Chinese language from the shackles of the monosyllabic Chinese characters' (Ni Hai-shu 1949, cited by DeFrancis 1968) to third place and the indefinite future, after both simplification of the traditional characters and adoption of a spoken standard for

'Common Speech' had been attained (Chou En-lai 1965). While work on the first two tasks is constantly going on in a direct fashion (see Anon. 1964; Wu Yu-chang 1965), work on the latter is primarily nominal (i.e. phonetization is kept alive as a distant goal but is not substantively advanced) and indirect (i.e. phonetization is utilized for subsidiary purposes, such as annotating novel or complex Chinese characters in technical texts, furthering instruction in the Common Speech among speakers of other regional languages, or creating 'initial alphabetic scripts' for illiterate non-Chinese-speaking minorities). Indeed, while phonetization has recently been reported to be superior for such special purposes as telegraphic communication (Wu Yu-chang 1964) and minority group initial literacy (Li Hui 1960), the traditional characters have again been proclaimed as superior in connection with general education for the bulk of the population among whom these characters are viewed as symbolic of education and the standard pronunciation (Serruys 1962). The goal of phonetization is, seemingly, still a long way off and may or may not be reached any more rapidly than the withering away of the state.

From the foregoing examples it is clear that if we but dichotomize 'success' (acceptance) and 'revolutionary social change', we have examples of all four possible types of co-occurrences: successful orthographic revision with and without revolutionary social change, and revolutionary social change with and without successful follow-through of planned orthographic revision. The discussions of revolutionary social change thus far encountered in studies of either the creation of writing systems or the revision of orthographies is still far too crude to be considered as more than rough labeling. As sociolinguistic description it is regrettably out of touch with the sizable modernization literature in economics, political science, sociology, and anthropology. It lacks either the concepts or the technical data collection methods and data analysis skills needed to inquire into intensity, extensity, or continuity of the change forces and processes or counterchange forces and processes that it notices.

It is also unfortunate that there are *so few* localized case studies of *variation in subgroup reactions* to new writing systems or to revised orthographies and, conversely, proportionally *so many* commentaries, studies, evaluations, and recommendations that deal with entire countries, continents, and even the world at large. The result is an imbalance with respect to the usual mutual stimulation between microanalysis and its emphases on process and function concerns, on the one hand, and macroanalysis and its emphases on structure, quantification, compositing, and weighting of parameters on the other hand. Either type of study, when pursued too long without correction from the other, becomes myopic and, therefore, dangerous for theory as well as (or even more so) for application.

REMEMBRANCE OF THINGS PAST

The above prefatory remarks have constituted an IOU to myself during the past few years. With the present collections I hope, at least in part, to liquidate the debt that I assumed and to fill some of the gaps that I initially recognized. However, in all truth, my current interest in the creation and revision of writing systems goes back much further than would appear to be the case from the foregoing remarks alone. Indeed, as with most of my sociolinguistic interests, it is an intellectualization and generalization of concerns and experiences that were part and parcel of my growing up as a native speaker of Yiddish in America, in a milieu in which cultivation of the language was regarded as the supreme commandment. This milieu prompted me to ask, first of myself and then of others, whether the writing system problems of minorities were, indeed, different than (severer than, qualitatively other than, more prolonged than) those of majorities with more effective control or enforcement potential in the sphere of implementation. This milieu, brim-full of loyalists though it was, also prompted me to wonder whether writing systems did not engender a special breed of language problem, in view of the fact that even the most committed often found it more difficult to change or revise their writing-system habits than, for example, their lexical habits. Finally, in connection with an early paper (1948) on the problems of transliterating from Yiddish to English, I pondered the apparent need to set up sociopolitical antimodels and sociopolitical rationales in conjunction with what was superficially no more than a technical question of commensurability between two phoneme-grapheme conventions.

Returning to these issues a quarter century later, I have taken pains to locate studies that deal with 'majority', well-established writing systems, as well as studies that deal with writing systems that are brand new, relatively recent, or of clearly 'minority' power status. I have also sought studies that contrasted successes and failures in the planning of writing systems (whether these be *de novo* or revisions of prior systems) with successes and failures in the planning of other aspects of language. Finally, I have sought studies in which sociopolitical circumstances were clearly the predominant forces influencing the acceptance or rejection of writing system innovations and alterations, as well as studies in which such factors appeared to be (or 'still to be') secondary to the technical competence or intra-corpus concerns of the writing system planners and their immediate associates.

Three Concerns

The papers selected or commissioned for this volume also reflect the three more recent major concerns that I have had in connection with this field of endeavor. First of all I have been concerned that this field should become more mature in terms of technical and theoretical social science sophistication. Frankly, I hope and expect that the greatest growth in this connection still lies ahead, since few investigators are yet to be encountered whose social science training and orientation equals their investment in linguistics or language pedagogy. Nevertheless, it is obvious that even in this most difficult respect of fruitful interdisciplinary depth there has been great progress relative to the research on the creation and revision of writing systems of even a decade ago. Gone, I believe, are the days of linguistic innocence and linguistic imperialism in this domain. Even when no obvious sociopolitical problems loom on the horizon, the social-process planning needed for gaining acceptance and use of a new or revised writing system is often both crucial and endless, and the implementation and evaluation skills needed for gauging differential progress in these respects are clearly far too complicated to be left to autodidactive catch-as-catch-can.

A second major concern that I have tried mightily to keep in mind while putting together this volume is that of a balance between macro- and microanalysis, both on the linguistic and on the societal fronts. Here, I do believe, we can register appreciable satisfactions. I continue to believe that we must struggle – against errors, against biases, against gaps in the data – to macrolevel generalizations with as much sociohistorical depth as possible. There are papers in this collection which do exactly that, and which must be congratulated for doing so, even though they are probably mistaken with respect to one detail or another. On the other hand, surrounding and undergirding all attempts at macroconceptual integration, there must be the constant accretion of confirmed microlevel details. Here too, we are far more fortunate than ever before, although we are still far from the number of studies, the degree of detail, or the variety of internetwork or inter-method comparisons that the field requires if its micro level analyses are ever to be of real value theoretically and practically.

The practical or applied concern is the third one that I have sought to pursue – not only in connection with the creation and revision of writing systems but in the entire decade and a half of my practically full-time involvement in the sociology of language. As I have envisaged and experimented with graduate programs in the sociology of language – at Yeshiva University in New York, at Hebrew University in Jerusalem, and at the several other Universities at which I have been involved in summer sessions, institutes, workshops, and conferences – I have come to favor a three-year sequence of course and research work in both linguistics and the social sciences. Each of these three years involves two integrating course-and-research experiences in the sociology of language proper, and one of these, toward the end of the entire sequence, is devoted to the applied sociology of language. I have attempted three different concentrations in the latter connection, namely, the sociology of bilingual education, guided language maintenance and language shift (at times, in conjunction with 'English as a second language'), and finally, the creation and revision of writing systems. While the last-named topic has not elicited as much interest among my American students as it has among students from other corners of the world, probably because my American students are less likely to foresee their own involvement in the creation and revision of writing systems, it has, nevertheless, given them a world perspective and an applied sensitivity that they would otherwise have lacked. It is my hope that the current collection will provide the types of materials through which yet other instructors and students will be able to more fully realize both the great potential and the great need for an ethically and effectively applied sociology of language.

My deep appreciation and gratitude toward the authors who have permitted me to reprint their papers is only second to that toward those who have revised them or specially written them at my request. I take their cooperation as a note of confidence in the future of the sociology of language as a whole, in the future of efforts directed toward creating and revising writing systems in particular, and toward myself as the servant of both of these trends.

NOTES

1. The unpopularity of 'hooked letters' in written Hausa (ɗ, ɓ, ƙ) is said to reflect a

desire among its users that it looks as much like English as possible. A similar desire has led to several other orthographic differences between modern Hausa as written in Nigeria and as written in Francophone Niger. The Yiddish Scientific Institute's recommendations that the conventional װ for /v/ be written V and that the conventional בּ, ב and פּ, פֿ distinctions be rendered as ב̄ , ב and פ̄, פ have found little acceptance, largely on the ground that no change is needed but, in part, also on the ground that it would tend to make Yiddish 'look different' than the current traditional alphabet for Hebrew (an attempt which is also associated with Soviet attempts to 'de-clericalize' Yiddish).

2. Kolarz (1967) refers briefly to the reformed Arabic alphabet adopted by the Volga Tatars in the early twenties prior to central Soviet concern for their writing system. Henze (1956) comments that 'the practicality and popularity of this reformed alphabet made the Soviet introduction of the Latin alphabet among the Tatars very difficult. Even Tatar Communists at first opposed it.' As with many other brief references it is difficult to determine whether the creation and adoption of a *new* writing system or the reform of an *existing* one was primarily involved, or if both problems were involved for various segments of the population, and when and for whom the problem ceased to be primarily the former or the latter or shifted from being one to being the other. The Chinese government's claim (Anon. 1964: 67-68) that it would 'help create written languages for those nationalities having no written languages of their own and improve existing written languages of others' is another example of the lack of detail that makes sociolinguistic documentation in this area difficult.
3. A parallel example of retreating from the internal Soviet orthography for the purposes of external propaganda has occurred in conjunction with Uiger (Vigur). Whereas publications for the Uigers living in Soviet Central Asia have been completely Cyrillicized since 1941, the Uiger-Russian and Russian-Uiger dictionaries of 1955 and 1956 employ the Arabic script. The impression that these publications are intended for the Uigers in Sinkiang is reinforced by the fact that the textbook includes a short dictionary of 'new words' encountered in Soviet political and economic writings (Najip, 1954).

BIBLIOGRAPHY

Alisjahbana, S. Takdir (ed.)

1969 'Some Planning Processes in the Development of the Indonesian/Malay Language', *Consultative Meeting on Language Planning Processes* (Honolulu: EWC-IAP). Reprinted in Rubin and Jernudd, *Can Language be Planned?* (Honolulu: University Press of Hawaii, 1971).

1972 *The Modernization of the Languages of Asia* (Kuala Lumpur: University of Malaysia).

Anon

1930 *Practical Orthography of African Languages* (= *International Institute of African Languages and Cultures, Memorandum* 1), revised edition (Oxford: Oxford University Press).

1953 *Policy Towards Nationalities of the People's Republic of China* (Peking: Foreign Language Press).

1963 *A Common Script for Indian Languages* (Delhi: Ministry of Scientific Research and Cultural Affairs).

1964 'Continue to Promote Reform of the Written Language', *Selections from Mainland China Magazines* 411 (April 6).

Berry, Jack

1958 'The Making of Alphabets', in *Proceedings of the Eighth International Congress of Linguists* (Oslo, 1957) (Oslo: Oslo University Press), 752-764. Reprinted in J. A. Fishman (ed.), *Readings in the Sociology of Language* (The Hague: Mouton, 1968), 737-753.

Bolinger, D. L.

1946 'Visual Morphemes', *Language* 22, 333-340.

Bowers, John

1968 'Language Problems and Literacy', in J. A. Fishman, C. A. Ferguson, and J. Das Gupta (eds.), *Language Problems of Developing Nations* (New York: Wiley), 381-401.

Bradley, Henry

1913-1914 'On the Relation between Spoken and Written Language', *Proceedings of the British Academy* 6, 212-232.

Burns, Donald

1953 'Social and Political Implications in the Choice of an Orthography', *Fundamental and Adult Education* 5: 2, 80-85.

Chinese Written Language Reform Committee

1956 'Several Points concerning the Han Language Phoneticization Plan (Draft) Explained', *Current Background* 380 (March 15), 4-13.

Chou En-lai

1965 'Current Tasks of Reforming the Written Language', in *Reform of the Chinese Written Language* (Peking: Foreign Language Press).

DeFrancis, John

1947 'Japanese Language Reform: Politics and Phonetics', *Far Eastern Survey* 16: 19, 217-220.

1950 *Nationalism and Language Reform in China* (Princeton: Princeton University Press).

1968 'Language and Script Reform [in China]', *Current Trends in Linguistics* 2 (The Hague: Mouton), 130-150.

Dickens, K. J.

1953 'Unification: The Akan Dialects of the Gold Coast', in *The Use of the Vernacular Languages in Education* (Paris: UNESCO), 115-123.

Ferguson, Charles A.

1967 'St. Stefan of Perm and Applied Linguistics', in *To Honor Roman Jakobson* (The Hague: Mouton). Reprinted in J. A. Fishman, C. A. Ferguson, and J. Das Gupta (eds.), *Language Problems of Developing Nations* (New York: Wiley, 1968).

Ferru, Jean Louis

1966 'Possible Repercussions of a Technical and Economic Nature of the Adoption of Particular Letters for the Standard Transcription of West African Languages', *Bamako* [*Mali*] *Meeting on the Standardization of African Alphabets February 28-March 5, 1966* (Baling: UNESCO/CLT).

Fischel, A.
1919 *Der Panslawismus bis zum Weltkrieg* (Stuttgart and Berlin: Cotta).
Franke, Wolfgang
1935 'Die Möglichkeiten einer Schriftreform in Japan', *Ostasiatische Rundschau* 16.
Gallagher, Charles F.
1967 'Language Rationalization and Scientific Progress', paper prepared for Conference on Science and Social Change, California Institute of Technology, October 18-20.
1969 'Language Reform and Social Modernization in Turkey', *Consultative Meeting on Language Planning Processes* (Honolulu: EWC-IAP).
Garvin, Paul L.
1954 'Literacy as Problem in Language and Culture', *Georgetown University Monograph Series on Language and Linguistics* 7, 117-129.
1959 'The Standard Language Problem – Concepts and Methods', *Anthropological Linguistics* 1: 3, 28-31.
Gelb, I. J.
1952 *A Study of Writing* (Chicago: University of Chicago Press).
Haudricourt, A. G.
1943 'De l'origine des particularités de l'alphabet Vietnamien', *Dan Vietnam* 3.
Haugen, Einar
1966 *Language Conflict and Language Planning: The Case of Modern Norwegian* (Cambridge: Harvard University Press).
Henze, Paul B.
1956 'Politics and Alphabets', *Royal Central Asian Society Journal* 43, 29-51.
Heyd, Uriel
1954 *Language Reform in Modern Turkey* (= *Oriental Notes and Studies* 5) (Jerusalem: The Israel Oriental Society).
Holton, Daniel C.
1947 'Ideographs and Ideas', *Far Eastern Survey* 16: 19, 220-223.
Hsia, Tao-tsi
1956 *China's Language Reforms* (New Haven: Yale University Press).
Jones, D.
1942 *Problems of a National Script for India* (Hartford: HSF).
Kolarz, Walter
1946 *Myths and Realities in Eastern Europe* (London: Lindsay Drummond).
1967 *Russia and her Colonies* (Hamden, Conn.: Archon Books).
Li Hui
1960 'The Phonetic Alphabet – Short Cut to Literacy', *Peking Review* 13: 28 (July 12).
Macnamara, John
1969 'Successes and Failures in the Movement for the Restoration of Irish', *Consultative Meeting on Language Planning Processes* (Honolulu: EWC-IAP). Reprinted in Rubin and Jernudd, *Can Language be Planned?* (Honolulu: University Press of Hawaii, 1971).
Meyenberg, Ervin
1934 'Der heutige Stand der Romazi-Bewegung in Japan', *Forschungen und Fortschritte* 10, 23-24.

Mills, H.
1956 'Language Reform in China', *The Far Eastern Quarterly* 15, 517-540.
Najip
1954 *Uigurski Yazyk* (Moscow).
Nida, Eugene
1953 'Practical Limitations to a Phonemic Orthography', *Bible Translator* 5.
Orenstein, Jacob
1959 'Soviet Language Policy: Theory and Practice', *Slavic and East European Journal* 17, 1-24.
Ozmen, Yucel
1967 'A Sociolinguistic Analysis of Language Reform in Turkey 1932-1967, with Special Reference to the Activities of the Turk Dil Kurumu', unpublished MS Thesis (Georgetown University).
Pike, Kenneth L.
1947 *Phonemics: A Technique for Reducing Languages to Writing* (Ann Arbor: University of Michigan Press).
Quelquejay, C., and A. Bennigsen
1961 *The Evolution of the Muslim Nationalities of the USSR and Their Linguistic Problems* (London: Central Asian Research Centre).
Rabin, Chaim
1969 'Spelling Reform: Israel, 1968', *Consultative Meeting on Language Planning Processes* (Honolulu: EWC-IAP). Reprinted in Rubin and Jernudd, *Can Language be Planned?* (Honolulu: University Press of Hawaii, 1971).
Radin, Paul
1924 'The Adoption of an Alphabet by an Aboriginal People', *Cambridge University Reporter* (*Proceedings of the Cambridge Philological Society*) (November 25) 27-34.
Ray, Punya Sloka
1960 'A Single Script for India', *Seminar* (July).
1963 *Language Standardization* (The Hague: Mouton), ch. 9: 'Comparative Description and Evaluation of Writing Systems', pp. 106-120.
Rossi, Ettore
1927 'La questione dell'alfabeto per le lingue turche', *Oriente Moderno* 7, 295-310.
1929 'Il nuovo alfabeto latino introdotto in Turchia', *Oriente Moderno* 9, 32-48. (Note: for text of the statute changing the alphabet for various types of publications by specific dates, see pp. 41-42).
1935 'La riforma linguistica in Turchia', *Oriente Moderno* 15, 45-57.
1942 'Un decennio di riforma linguistica in Turchia', *Oriente Moderno* 22, 466-477.
1953 'Venticinque anni di rivoluzione dell'alfabeto e venti di riforma linguistica in Turchi', *Oriente Moderno* 33, 378-384.
Rubin, Joan
1969 'Evaluation and Language Planning', *Consultative Meeting on Language Planning Processes* (Honolulu: EWC-IAP). Reprinted in Rubin and Jernudd, *Can Language be Planned?* (Honolulu: University Press of Hawaii, 1971).
Rubin, Joan, and Bjorn Jernudd
1971 *Can Language be Planned?* (Honolulu: University Press of Hawaii).

Russell, J. K.
1948 'Starting a Literacy Campaign', *Books for Africa* 18: 2, 17-20.
Scharshmidt, Clemens
1924 'Schriftreform in Japan: Ein Kulturproblem', *Mitteilungen des Seminars für Orientalischen Sprachen* 26/27: 1, 183-186.
Serdyuchenko, G. P.
1962 'The Eradication of Illiteracy and the Creation of New Written Languages in the USSR', *Intern. J. of Adult and Youth Education* 14: 1, 23-29.
1965 *Elimination of Illiteracy among the People who had no Alphabets* (Moscow: U.S.S.R. Commission for UNESCO, Ministry of Education, RSFSR), 16 pp.
Serruys, Paul L-M.
1962 *Survey of the Chinese Language Reform and the Anti-Illiteracy Movement in Communist China* (= *Studies in Communist Chinese Terminology* (Berkeley: Center for Chinese Studies, Institute of International Studies, UC-B).
Sheldon, George
1946 'Status of the Viet Nam', *Far Eastern Survey* 15: 25, 373-377.
Sjoberg, Andrée F.
1964 'Writing, Speech and Society: Some Changing Interrelationships', in *Proceedings of the Ninth International Congress of Linguists* (The Hague: Mouton), 892-897.
1966 'Socio-Cultural and Linguistic Factors in the Development of Writing Systems for Preliterate Peoples', in William Bright (ed.), *Sociolinguistics* (The Hague: Mouton), 260-276.
Smalley, William A., et al.
1964 *Orthography Studies: Articles on New Writing Systems* ('*Help for Translators*' 6) (London: United Bible Societies).
Vachek, Josef
1945-1949 'Some Remarks on Writing and Phonetic Transcription', *Acta Linguistica* 5 (Copenhagen), 86-93.
1948 'Written Language and Printed Language', *Recueil Linguistique de Bratislava* 1, 67-75. Reprinted in J. Vachek (ed.), *A Prague School Reader in Linguistics* (Bloomington: Indiana University Press, 1964), 453-460.
Valdman, Albert
1968 'Language Standardization in a Diglossia Situation: Haiti', in J. A. Fishman, C. A. Ferguson, and J. Das Gupta (eds.), *Language Problems of Developing Nations* (New York: Wiley), 313-326.
Ward, Ida C.
1945 *Report of an Investigation of Some Gold Coast Language Problems* (London: Crown Agents for the Colonies).
Weinreich, Uriel
1953 'The Russification of Soviet Minority Languages', *Problems of Communism* 2: 6, 46-57.
Winner, T. G.
1952 'Problems of Alphabetic Reform among the Turkic Peoples of Soviet Central Asia', *Slavonic and East European Review*, 132-147.
Wolff, Hans
1954 *Nigerian Orthography* (Zaria: Gaskiya Corp.).

Wolfram, Walter A.
1969 *A Sociolinguistic Description of Detroit Negro Speech* (Washington: CAL).
Wu Yu-chang
1956 'Concerning the Draft Han Language Phonetization Plan', *Current Background* 380 (March 15), 14-20.
1964 'Widening the Use of the Phonetic Script', *China Reconstructs* 13: 6, 29-31.
1965 'Report of the Current Tasks of Reforming the Written Language and the Draft Scheme for a Chinese Phonetic Alphabet', in *Reform of the Chinese Written Language* (Peking: Foreign Language Press).

Section One

Theoretical Overviews

JACK BERRY

1

'The Making of Alphabets' Revisited

This paper is intended to bring my earlier 'The Making of Alphabets' up to date by reviewing the more important literature published since 1958 on the design of writing systems and on other related and pertinent topics. New literature directed specifically to writing systems is not abundant. By far the most comprehensive study of orthography design published in the last fifteen years is Smalley's and we may as well begin with that.

Orthography Studies (Smalley et al. 1964) is a collection of fifteen previously published articles, some of which deal with the principles underlying the preparation and structure of devised scripts and the rest of which describe in great detail the applications of these principles with the different solutions worked out in different scripts. Smalley, as well as editing the volume, has contributed two further articles – the first by way of general introduction to the volume and the other to resume discussion of the many problems connected with devising non-roman scripts. Somewhere in the volume he proposes five criteria of an adequate new writing system. These are, in the order of importance assigned to them by Smalley:

(1) maximum motivation for the learner
(2) maximum representation of speech
(3) maximum ease of learning
(4) maximum transfer
(5) maximum ease of reproduction

Smalley's list is reasonably comprehensive; it covers most aspects – political, sociocultural, psychological, and pedagogical – of orthography design. No one would wish to quarrel with it on that score. And the individual criteria taken separately are unlikely to meet any serious objection, given that (2) is suitably defined. What is debatable, of course, is Smalley's weighting of the criteria. Here there is wide scope for disagreement. Recently, for example, Venezky (1970) has suggested that 'while socio-cultural factors [i.e. Smalley's (1)] must be considered at some point in the design of practical writing systems, these are subordinate to the linguistic, psychological and pedagogical variables [i.e. Smalley's (2) and (3)] which determine the optimal system or range of systems for the language and speakers involved.' In devising orthographies, as Smalley himself is well aware, the problem is not to decide what features are good for our purposes, which is after all a fairly easy business. The difficulty is that features which seem to be good for most purposes are often mutually conflicting, and in the actual situations in which the orthographies are to be used, the relative weights assigned to the various features will have to be different.

We shall now take each of Smalley's criteria in turn (since this seems as good a way into the literature as any), and examine its implications for orthography design against the background of recent theory in the relevant disciplines.

(1) Maximum motivation for the learner recognizes that 'the creation of writing systems is significant only insofar as it leads to the acceptance and implementation of writing systems' (Fishman 1972). Fishman's point is not a new one. As early as 1947 Nida, for example (*Bible Translating*, p. 113), writing on the practical adaptations of a 'scientific' alphabet admits that 'once the translator has made a scientific analysis of the language and has reached a satisfactory one-to-one correspondence between the symbols and the psychologically significant sound units, it is sometimes necessary because of practical circumstances to make certain modifications of the scientific alphabet.' Among the factors which may force changes, he lists 'the language attitudes of the local elite, the government and the educational authorities'.

Since then evidence has been accumulating – rapidly in the last few years as the interest in sociolinguistic phenomena has quickened – which shows that acceptance or rejection of an orthography has little to do with its linguistic adequacy, however we define that term. The primacy of the extralinguistic factors has been stressed most recently by Sjoberg (1964; 1966) and Bowers (1968) among others, as well as Gudschinsky (1959) and the earlier writers cited in my 'The Making of Alphabets' (Berry 1958).

Smalley himself cites examples from Northern Laos, Africa, Haiti, and Latin America where the influence of educated bilinguals, identification with a prestige culture, and elements of transfer value (his fourth criterion) have all united to make new literates want to learn a system as close as possible to the prestige language around them. It is presumably for the same reasons that the Cyrillic alphabet is used as the model for 'the creation of new written languages' in the U.S.S.R. (Serdyuchenko 1962; 1965). Smalley also mentions the rarer (or less well-documented?) instances where nationalistic opposition to a dominant language or a colonial language may produce the entirely opposite effect: in Cameroun, tribal groups stoutly opposed writing their language with symbols based upon the values given them in French, and in Thailand, different segments of the same Yao tribe have different attitudes which would govern their motivation to reading different kinds of scripts.

Ferguson (1968) has an interesting example from history of St. Stefan of Perm who, in the fourteenth century, invented an alphabet for the Komi called Abur. The alphabet was clearly based on his knowledge of Greek and Church Slavonic but he deliberately made the forms of the letters sufficiently different from both so that the Komi could regard the writing system as distinctively theirs and not an alphabet used for another language. Ferguson also mentions the example of St. Mesrop's creation of the Armenian alphabet in the fifth century which has striking parallels with the inventions of the indigenous scripts of West Africa many hundreds of years later (Dalby 1967). These latter instances evidence the desire of nonliterate peoples to be themselves.

The practical implications of all this are obvious. In planning to introduce a writing system in a nonliterate society, there is a succession of choices to be made. Beyond the fundamental choice between syllabary and alphabet, there is the choice between the use of an existing system and one specially invented for the language. Within these major choices are a host of minor questions such as whether to employ digraphs or diacritics or both, how much grammatical information should be incorporated, and what features of punctuation are desirable. None of these choices can be made arbitrarily by the planner. He, rather, must consult at all stages of the planning not only governments and other controlling groups but also what Pike once called 'the naive native speaker's reaction' and Garvin has since rephrased as 'the sophisticated native speaker's reaction' (Garvin 1954). Recent attempts to derive a writing system experimentally are encouraging evidence of the growing awareness of this fact among missionaries and others involved in literacy work. Walker (1969) describes an experiment in which Zuni speakers were asked to indicate spelling preferences for Zuni words dictated by the experimenter. The results seem to indicate a bias in favor of English sound-letter correspondences as against a more 'phonemic' spelling probably due to the fact that all the subjects were literate in English.

Venezky (1970) has discussed experimental approaches to the making of orthographies suggesting refinements such as tests for reading as against spelling preferences and for testing the learning rates of illiterates for alternate writing systems. He thinks such attempts to derive a writing system experimentally must be viewed as a major step forward, however difficult the experiments are to design and laborious and expensive to execute. It is worth mentioning perhaps that concern with the native speaker's reactions to a proposed writing system is well in line not only with present sociolinguistic thinking but also with the influential theories in linguistics of the transformational-generative grammarians who give a central importance to the native speaker's intuitions about the structure of his language and who have reverted in the area of phonology to a view of the phoneme similar to Sapir's 'abstract' view (see below).

It is more convenient to consider Smalley's fourth criterion next, since it has already been mentioned and since in some senses the two principles of 'motivation' and 'transfer' are interrelated. Many of the orthographies devised by missionaries and others are for use in multilingual societies. Some, perhaps the majority, are 'transitional' orthographies (Venezky 1970) intended only for the initial acquisition of literacy in some minor first language after which it is expected that the learner will be transferred into reading in the national language or language of wider communication in his area. An example of a somewhat different type of transitional orthography is the ITA or Initial Teaching Alphabet which has been used experimentally in schools in England and the United States for about ten years (Downing 1967).[1] Smalley's fourth principle is the principle that 'having learned to read his native language, a reader should be able to read the trade or colonial language of the area with as little difficulty as possible in the transference of the value of the symbols'. A good deal more is implied, of course, than simply choosing to write 'ou' for sound /u/, say, in a language of Francophone Africa (Houis 1958). The problem is more complicated than that, especially where non-roman scripts are used. Maximum transfer means following all the conventions associated with a writing system including the less desirable features: the Thai manner of writing vowels around the consonants or the vowel pointings and other difficulties of the Arabic script.

But just how serious a psychological problem is transfer? There is not much experimental evidence one way or another on this question in the psycholinguistic literature. (Venezky does mention some.) On the other hand, there is empirical evidence enough to suggest that once literacy is obtained in one language, there is rarely trouble in obtaining it in another language with a similar type of writing system, provided the reader has already acquired the second language.

And given a certain view of the writing process there will always be difficulties in following the principle of maximum transfer if only because no two languages are that alike. Take the case of nasalized vowels in French, for example. These are written with a following *n*. The letter sequence is relatively unambiguous in French. This spelling convention has been followed in a number of West African languages for reasons of motivation and transfer. But in these languages, the letter sequence *vowel* + *n* then becomes a source of potential confusion because there are also sound sequences of a vowel followed by an alveolar nasal consonant in places where these do not occur in French (Smalley 1964; Houis 1958; Bamgbose 1965; Awobuluyi 1966).

Another problem exists with regard to the spelling in the transitional orthography of loanwords from the target language. In most languages written in the Arabic script, Arabic loanwords traditionally are spelled as they are in Arabic regardless of their pronunciation in the borrowing languages, 'a procedure that facilitates the study of Arabic or other Islamic languages but causes trouble for the monolingual person learning to read his own language' (Ferguson 1968). This was also the earlier Russian practice when using the Cyrillic alphabet for the minority languages of the U.S.S.R., but Soviet linguists now seem to prefer to spell Russian loanwords in a manner consistent with the pronunciation and orthographic conventions of the borrowing languages. As to which of the two is the better practice, it can only be said that the answer depends crucially on what view is taken of the relationship between spoken and written language. This brings us back to Smalley's second (and, possibly, third) criterion.

It is obvious that for Smalley the optimal writing system for any language would be something like a phonemic transcription of the language giving 'maximum representation of speech' but tempered perhaps by certain concessions to practicality especially where a particular phonemic distinction has low functional load. This is an attitude to writing not far removed from the typical attitude of the Bloomfieldian era which is marked by such features as a rather rigid insistence on the derivative character of writing as against speech, a 'functional' or 'physical' view of phonemics, and, reflecting in a rather general way the positivistic intellectual climate of the period, a strict adherence to inductive discovery procedures in analysis.

There were dissenting views, of course: some are cited in my earlier paper. Vachek (1945-1949) and Bolinger (1946) asserted the mutual independence of the phonic and graphic systems though they both attest the same thing. (See also Pulgram 1951; 1965; Gleason 1965: 108-111; and others.) And in phonology, Firth questioned the 'once a phoneme, always a phoneme' position, preferring a 'polysystemic' approach which gave theoretical recognition to the fact that features of a sound which are distinctive in one position may not be distinctive when that same sound is in another position; and to the fact that there may be significant phonological differences between various divisions of a language, between, say, different elements of the lexicon or between the parts of speech. Firth also advocated the use of deductive procedures in analysis. These procedures operate in essentially the reverse order from the inductive discovery procedures and hence grammatical information is always available if needed in the phonological part of the description (Fudge 1970).

These dissentients apart, it would still be true to say that in the twenty-five year period which ended in 1957, the dominant view of language, in the United States at least, was that of the structural school of linguistics, associated primarily with the name of Leonard Bloomfield.

Under the influence of transformational-generative theories in linguistics, attitudes have changed dramatically since 1957. Recent work in phonological theory within the framework of transformational grammar is, like Firth's, grammatically oriented. In contrast to the many structuralists' descriptions, generative treatments begin by stating syntactic structure and only then pass on to phonology which can make use of any syntactic facts which are relevant. In *The Sound Pattern of English* (Chomsky and Halle 1968), the two authors provide a description of English phonology which postulates an abstract level of representation of words and then provides general rules which operate on the abstract underlying forms within their syntactic context to convert them to their surface phonetic realizations. A particular consequence of this recent work of special relevance to the design of writing systems is that it has provided a respectable theoretical basis for a reappraisal of English spelling. Chomsky has recently pointed out that insofar as it corresponds in essentials to the abstract lexical representations postulated in his 1968 work, the conventional orthography represents 'a near optimal system for representing the language' (N. Chomsky 1970).

Carol Chomsky (1970) has examined the implications for reading and writing of this new, positive view of English spelling. In favor of 'lexical spelling' and the conventional orthography which corresponds so closely to it, she finds, first, that lexical spellings represent meaning-bearing items directly, without introducing phonetic detail irrelevant to their identification, and so permit reading with more efficiency. Second, she believes that in a real sense, the lexical level of representation and the corresponding aspects of English orthography have a psychological reality for the language user. Third, she is of the opinion that the abstract lexical level is highly resistant to change over time and in space. Pronunciation shifts stem from adjustments of phonological rules rather than differences in lexical spellings. It is for this reason that English orthography remains effective over time and is a reasonably adequate system of representation for British and American English and for the vast range of dialects that exist within each country and around the world.

There are several implications of this view of English orthography for reading. It implies, first, that what the mature reader seeks and recognizes when he reads is not grapheme-phoneme correspondences but rather the correspondence of written symbols to the abstract lexical spelling of words. The child beginning reading, on the other hand, may assume that the orthography is in some sense 'regular' with respect to pronunciation. But in order to progress, he must abandon this early hypothesis, and come eventually to interpret written symbols as corresponding to the more abstract lexical spellings. Failure to make this transition successfully is probably at the heart of the difficulties 'the poor reader' experiences.

The Chomskian influence in linguistics has undoubtedly been responsible for parallel approaches in the rapidly expanding field of psycholinguistics. And with this new cognitive approach in psycholinguistics has come a greater attention to reading.[2] The early applications of linguistics to reading were narrow. Bloomfield (1942), for example, concentrated almost exclusively on phonemics, going only so far as to seek regularity of phoneme-grapheme correspondence in the materials. He did not study the process of reading nor make a full application of linguistics to it.

Fries (1964) looked at reading theoretically but he also focused on a narrowly defined linguistic principle of minimal contrast (Goodman 1969). Indeed, a basic assumption of these early applications would appear to be that linguistics can be applied to reading *only* to explain phoneme-grapheme correspondence. And given the prevailing theories of linguistics of the time, this may well have been true. Much recent work in psycholinguistics has challenged this assumption from a number of different angles and presents a different view of the reading process from that which generally obtained in 1958 (if it is possible at all to speak of a general view of reading at that time). The recent literature on reading from the psycholinguistic point of view is already extensive. To attempt even a cursory survey of all the pertinent books and papers would be beyond the scope of this review. It will be sufficient for present purposes to outline a few of the more widely held assumptions about reading that have been propounded in recent psycholinguistic works on the subject.

There seems to be general agreement among most writers on the mutual independence not only of writing and speech but of writing and reading. And for purposes of pedagogy, reading is held to have priority over writing (Fries 1964; Venezky 1967).

Some (e.g. Chall 1967) see reading as matching oral units with written units, an operation they have frequently called 'decoding'. But this view of reading as decoding to spoken language has been challenged vigorously by Goodman (1971) and Smith (1971) among others, who assert in their different ways that reading is not primarily visual; only a small part of the information comes from the printed page. Words are identified on a basis of visual feature relationships in the configuration as a whole not by synthesis of information about individual letters or letter sequences. Comprehension must precede the identification of words because it reduces uncertainty and permits identification on minimal visual information.

If these assumptions are correct it would appear that the way in which a fluent reader identifies words has little or nothing at all to do with phonology; the sound-spelling relationship is not of critical importance. An extreme conclusion to be drawn from this view is that the alphabetical principle is irrelevant for reading. The fluent reader reads English or French or German efficiently only insofar as he treats the written language as if it were ideographic: '*Kun*-reading', rather than '*on*-reading', as it were (Makita 1968). Writing, of course, is another matter. In writing, the alphabet has the edge if only because it is easier to reproduce words that are made up of a relatively few letter elements than the thousands of say, Chinese ideograms. And it would appear that words written alphabetically are easier for the beginner to copy and to learn (Smith 1971; Kolers 1969).

The mention of reproduction returns us to Smalley's last criterion. For him, the fact that it provides maximum ease of reproduction is the least important desirable feature of an orthography. On this point, he would seem to be against the consensus of present-day opinion. However distasteful, the fact has to be accepted that it is the typewriter and typesetting machines that call the tune today (Ferru 1966).

The design of letters and alternative symbols for writing was considered in some detail in my earlier paper. The subject continues to attract attention: Smalley (1964), Ray (1963), Malkiel (1962), Pulgram (1965), MacCarthy (1964), Chao (1968), Venezky (1970).

There is by no means general agreement on every aspect. Smalley, for example, sees the linearity of roman as an advantage. Others would disagree. It seems largely because of its linear nature that our writing carries so little visual information as compared with, say, multidirectional and two-dimensional ideograms of Chinese. Quite simply English words do not stand out so prominently in a text as do the Chinese characters (Chao). Making roman type larger is out of the question both economically and visually because words in roman are so much wider than they are deep. MacCarthy discusses some recent proposals to improve the readability of roman without basically changing the alphabet. These proposals include an ingenious suggestion that texts might be printed in overlapping lines of print in alternate colors to be read with complementarily colored glasses. Roman is considered by some to have another advantage over some alphabets in the small number of characters it employs. If this is an advantage, it is an advantage only from the printing point of view: English in roman is easier to print than Devanagari, say, which requires four cases to accommodate it, while English needs only two. But it is possible to look at this another way: if roman had a thousand characters, no word in English need be more than two characters wide. Chao (1968) makes two guesses at what the balance between number of symbols and size of symbol complexes might be in an ideal writing system and in each case arrives at a figure for symbols substantially in excess of the number of letters in roman. He believes somewhere between one hundred and seventy and two hundred monosyllabic symbols would be about right.

The problem in all of this, of course, is the same problem that is encountered in other aspects of orthography design: different features are desirable for different purposes and sometimes these purposes conflict. In written language, ease of production seems opposed to ease of discrimination, so that we find rapid cursive harder to read than more careful hand. Sometimes ease of production is opposed to what is desirable on sociolinguistic grounds, as in the suggested use of roman capitals to replace nonroman letters in the alphabets of Francophone West Africa. To use capital letters in this way might be expedient since they are already on most typewriters, but to do so would be culturally ridiculous. The PBA[3] has no provision for capitals and proposes that letters be disjoined in both print and handwriting on the assumption that disjunctive writing discourages the proliferation of cursive forms and so promotes legibility. This assumption may well be true. Legibility will be promoted through uniformity. But what of the special hands and types for special purposes? Writing has many uses: religious, academic, ornamental . . . (Rudolf van Larisch frequently attacked what he called 'brutal legibility'.)

Fortunately, there is usually some scope for compromise between conflicting demands. If, for example, some letters have to be given greater complication of line and greater width, then these can be relegated normally to the less frequent sounds. When capitals are provided, they need not be very different from their lower-case counterparts but only, perhaps, larger. Or 'blacker'? (MacCarthy 1964) Or both? And so on.

We have now completed our discussion of Smalley's criteria against the background of supporting and conflicting views in the literature of the subject and have reached a point where an attempt can be made to reach a few conclusions. A first conclusion which can be safely drawn is that neither modern linguistics nor modern psycholinguistics require that a writing system should be phonetic or phonemic or even one-to-one. This once popular theory is now outdated. In the new view of reading there seems little to choose between phonemic, morphophonemic, or even paraphonemic[4] systems of spelling. If anything, a morphophonemic spelling facilitates reading better than the reverse.

From this first conclusion, a number of supplementary conclusions follow. It should be apparent that we need not be unduly concerned to mark all contrasts especially where these have low functional load. And we need not be unduly 'purist' in our attitude to mixing systems. If competent readers do process function words differently from content words[5] then, as Venezky says, that is all the more the reason for these functional words to be short and rapidly distinguishable in their written forms. As indeed they are in the PBA,[6] for example. Or again, transfer may be a less important problem than it was once thought to be, if English spelling is really as efficient as it is now claimed to be, since English spelling is largely paraphonemic due to its overwhelming latinity.

Dialect problems can also be seen in a new perspective as depending more on political, sociocultural and economic factors than upon psychological and linguistic ones (Wolff 1959). If one of the great virtues of English spelling, for instance, is its uniformity across dialects and if, as Chomsky and others have suggested, English spelling is a near optimal system, then, rather clearly, the difficulties speakers of some dialects have in learning to read must be for other reasons than the way they speak. Sociolinguists who have worked on these problems in the urban ghettos of the United States are inclined to see the difficulties in terms of cultural rather than linguistic differences (Labov 1969).

Much of this could have been said in 1957. (Some of it I tried to say.) But it can be said with greater conviction today, and from a sounder theoretical base. What seems to me now the most crucial aspect of orthography design lies in the area of applied sociolinguistics. Chao's tenth requirement for good symbols is 'universality', which can be interpreted as wide acceptance over space and time. Sociolinguistics is at present only a descriptive science but it offers some promise for better research and understanding of this problem, of what is involved in acceptance, and of how acceptance is obtained.

NOTES

1. Another example is mentioned in Halliday, McIntosh, and Stevens (1964: 290): the use of a phonological script as a bridge to literacy in Chinese characters.
2. A second important factor contributing to the new interest in reading is the recognition that even in 'advanced' societies a reading problem exists on a massive scale. HEW's Targeted Research and Development Program on Reading comes in the United States at a time of general apathy in the developing societies as far as literacy is concerned (Foster 1971).
3. Early in the 1960's, Kingsley Read's design for a new (i.e. non-roman) script for English, which had been one of the four prize winners in the George Bernard Shaw Alphabet Competition, was chosen, after considerable recasting, as the Proposed British Alphabet and was used to transliterate Shaw's play *Androcles and the Lion* in an edition published by Penguin Books Ltd.
4. This term I believe is Ray's (1963: 96).

5. Venezky cites experimental evidence adduced by Shapiro and Palermo (1967) that suggests that this is so.
6. The PBA provides four unilateral signs for 'the', 'of', 'and', and 'to', saving, it is estimated, 10 percent of space by this device alone. Provision is made for extensive use of abbreviation but the percentage saving falls off sharply as the frequency of occurrence reduces.

BIBLIOGRAPHY

Abercrombie, David
1967 *Elements of General Phonetics* (Edinburgh University Press), Ch. 7: 'Notation'.

Awobuluyi, A. O.
1966 'Review of A. Bamgbose, *Yoruba Orthography*', *Word* 22: 1-2-3, 344-348.

Bamgbose, Ayo
1965 *Yoruba Orthography: A Linguistic Appraisal with Suggestions for Reform* (Ibadan: Ibadan University Press).

Berry, Jack
1958 'The Making of Alphabets', in Eva Siversten (ed.), *Proceedings of the VIII International Congress of Linguists* (Oslo: University Press), 752-764.

Bloomfield, Leonard
1942 'Linguistics and Reading' *Elementary English Review* 19:4, 125-130; 5, 183-186.

Bloomfield, Leonard, and Clarence L. Barnhart
1961 *Let's read: A Linguistic Approach* (Detroit: Wayne State University Press).

Bolinger, D. L.
1946 'Visual Morphemes', *Language* 22, 333-340.

Bowers, John
1968 'Language Problems and Literacy', in J. A. Fishman, C. A. Ferguson, and J. Das Gupta (eds.), *Language Problems of Developing Nations* (New York: Wiley).

Chall, Jeanne
1967 *Reading: The Great Debate* (New York: McGraw-Hill).

Chao, Yuen Ren
1968 *Language and Symbolic Systems* (Cambridge University Press).

Chomsky, Carol
1970 'Reading, Writing and Phonology', *Harvard Educational Review* 40: 2, 287-309.

Chomsky, Noam
1970 'Phonology and Reading', in H. Levin (ed.), *Basic Studies in Reading* (New York: Basic Books).

Chomsky, Noam, and Morris Halle
1968 *The Sound Pattern of English* (New York: Harper and Row).

Dalby, David
1967 'A Survey of Indigenous Scripts of Liberia and Sierra Leone', *African Language Studies* 7, 1-51.

Downing, John
1967 *Evaluating the Initial Teaching Alphabet* (London: Cassell).

Ferguson, C. A.
1968 'St. Stefan of Perm and Applied Linguistics', in J. A. Fishman, C. A. Ferguson,

and J. Das Gupta (eds.), *Language Problems of Developing Nations* (New York: Wiley).

Ferru, J. Louis

1966 'Possible Repercussions of a Technical and Economic Nature of the Adoption of Particular Letters for the Standard Transcription of West African Languages', *Bamako Meeting on the Standardization of African Alphabets* (UNESCO).

Fishman, Joshua A.

1972 'The Uses of Sociolinguistics', in J. A. Fishman, *Language in Socio-Cultural Change*, ed. by Anwar S. Dil (Stanford: Stanford University Press).

Foster, Philip J.

1971 'Problems of Literacy in Sub-Saharan Africa', in T. A. Sebeok (ed.), *Current Trends in Linguistics* 7, 587-617.

Fries, Charles C.

1962 *Linguistics and Reading* (New York: Holt, Rinehart and Winston).

Fudge, E. C.

1970 'Phonology', in John Lyons (ed.), *New Horizons in Linguistics* (Harmondsworth: Penguin), 76-95.

Garvin, Paul L.

1954 'Literacy as a Problem in Language and Culture', in Hugo J. Mueller (ed.), *Report of the Fifth Annual Round Table Meeting on Linguistics and Language Teaching* (Washington, D.C.: Georgetown University Press), 117-129.

1959 'The Standard Language Problem – Concepts and Methods', *Anthropological Linguistics* 1: 3, 28-31.

Gleason, H. A., Jr.

1965 *Linguistics and English Grammar* (New York: Holt, Rinehart, and Winston).

Goodman, Kenneth J.

1969 'Analysis of Oral Reading Miscues', *Reading Research Quarterly* 5, 19-30.

1971 'Decoding, from Code to What', *Journal of Reading* 14: 7, 455-462.

Gudschinsky, Sarah

1959 'Recent Trends in Primer Construction', *Fundamental and Adult Education* 2, 67-96.

Halliday, M. A. K., Angus McIntosh, and Peter Stevens

1964 *The Lingistic Sciences and Language Teaching* (London: Longman, Green and Co.).

Houis, M.

1958 'Comment écrire les langues Africaines? Nécessité d'un humanistic Africain', *Présence Africaine*, 76-92.

Kolers, Paul

1969 'Reading is Only Incidentally Visual', in K. Goodman and J. Fleming (eds.), *Psycholinguistics and the Teaching of Reading* (Newark, Delaware: Int. Reading Assoc.).

1970 'Three Stages of Reading', in H. Levin and J. P. Williams (eds.), *Basic Studies in Reading* (New York: Basic Books).

Labov, William, and Clarence Tobins

1969 'A Note on the Relation of Reading Failure to Peer Group Status in Urban Ghettos', *The Teachers College Record* 70: 5.

MacCarthy, P. A. D.
1964 'Criteria for a New Orthography for English', in D. Abercrombie et al. (eds.), *In Honour of Daniel Jones* (London: Longmans, Green and Co.), 156-170.
Makita, K.
1968 'The Rarity of Reading Disability in Japanese Children', *American Journal of Ortho-Psychiatry* 38: 4, 599-614.
Malkiel, Yakov
1962 'Review of Leonard Bloomfield and Clarence L. Barnhart, *Let's Read: A Linguistic Approach*', *Romance Philology* 16: 89.
Pulgram, E.
1951 'Phonome and Grapheme: A parallel', *Word* 7, 15-20.
1965 'Graphic and Phonic Systems: Figurae and Signs', *Word* 21, 208-224.
Ray, Punya Sloka
1963 *Language Standardization: Studies in Prescriptive Linguistics* (The Hague: Mouton).
Serdynchenko, G. P.
1962 'The Eradication of Illiteracy and the Creation of New Written Languages in the USSR', *International Journal of Adult and Youth Education* 14: 1, 28-29.
1965 *Elimination of Illiteracy Among the People Who Had No Alphabets* (Moscow: USSR Commission for UNESCO).
Shapiro, S. T., and C. A. Palermo
1967 'The Influence of Part of Speech on Paired-Associate Learning', *Psychonomic Science* 8, 445-467.
Sjoberg, A. F.
1964 'Writing, Speech, and Society', in Horace Lunt (ed.), *Proceedings of the Ninth International Congress of Linguists* (The Hague: Mouton), 892-897.
1966 'Sociocultural and Linguistic Factors in the Development of Writing Systems for Preliterate People', in W. Bright (ed.), *Sociolinguistics* (The Hague: Mouton), 260-276.
Smalley, William A., et al.
1964 *Orthography Studies: Articles on New Writing Systems* (= *Helps for Translators* 6) (London: United Bible Societies).
Smith, F.
1971 *Understanding Reading* (New York: Holt, Rinehart and Winston).
Vachek, Josef
1945-1949 'Some Remarks on Writing and Phonetic Transcription', *Acta Linguistica* 5, 86-93.
Venezky, Richard
1967 'English Orthography: Its Graphical Structure and Its Relation to Sound', *Reading Research Quarterly* 2: 3, 75-105.
1970 'Principles for the Design of Practical Writing Systems', *Anthropological Linguistics* 12, 256-270.
Walker, Willard
1969 'Notes on Native Writing Systems and the Design of Native Literacy Programs', *Anthropological Linguistics* 11, 148-166.
Wolff, Hans
1959 'Intelligibility and Inter-Ethnic Attitudes', *Anthropological Linguistics* 1: 3, 34-41.

VALTER TAULI

2

Speech and Spelling

The important role of writing in modern society makes rational orthography planning of great importance. As in other branches of language planning, so also in orthography planning it is necessary to distinguish between theory and practice. Equally essential is the difference between TELEOLOGY, based on the ideal of orthography as an efficient instrument, and the TACTICS (strategy or sociology) of orthography planning, which must take into account the tradition as well as the social and other conditions of the language community. Unfortunately, language planners and linguists have often not been sufficiently aware of these distinctions. The teleological problems are mainly linguistic, the tactical problems mostly sociological. Due to practical experiences and the growth of sociolinguistics, the tactical aspect has for some time overshadowed the teleological one.

THEORY AND TELEOLOGY

In theory and teleology a pronounced change of view and confusion have become manifest. Not long ago the authors who discussed orthography planning held in general the view that a 'scientifically' or 'linguistically justified spelling' 'is based on the phonemic system and structure of the language'.[1] Now they base their standpoint on the new 'scientific' doctrine: 'the mutual independence of speech and writing'.[2] I will discuss this doctrine of independence briefly.[3]

An early pioneer of the doctrine of independence in the twentieth century was the Finnish linguist Aarni Penttilä, who in 1932 maintained that the grapheme language is an independent symbol system. But he added that this does not mean that the grapheme and the phoneme languages would be foreign to each other. First, there is an extensive correspondence between graphemes and phonemes, and, second, there is a mutual influence.[4] Other advocates of the doctrine of independence have not been able to ignore the correspondence between speech and writing.[5] The stressing of the doctrine of independence became fashionable in linguistics in the sixties.[6]

There are some linguists who are regarded as representatives of the doctrine of independence but who do not use the word 'independent'. They hold the view that writing and speech 'express' or 'manifest' the same language. Now the question arises: what does the term 'language' mean in this connection?

The most often cited authors of this group are H. J. Uldall and Josef Vachek.[7] The first represents the glossematic view. According to Louis Hjelmslev, writing and speech are different manifestations or EXPRESSION SUBSTANCES of the same expression form.[8] Uldall is not so clear in this respect.[9] First, he says that 'our something, that which is common to sounds and letters alike, is a form' and that 'The substance of ink has not received the same attention on the part of linguists that they have so lavishly bestowed on the substance of air'. But further on he discusses the question: 'what is meant by saying that pronunciation and orthography express the same language?' His answer (p. 14) is: 'we mean simply that the orthographic units and the units of pronunciation correspond to, or, better, are functions of the same units of content: the fact that both *kat* [the speech unit] and "cat" [spelling] are functions of the idea *felis domestica* . . .' But here Uldall forgets that the orthographic units *c*, *a*, *t* also correspond to phonemes /k/, /a/, /t/. In Uldall's opinion, neither speech nor writing is primary. In fact we may interpret the relation so that both the sound [k'] and the grapheme *c* represent the phoneme /k/, but according to the general unsophisticated interpretation the letter *c* represents the phonic unit /k/.

Angus McIntosh expressed in 1956 the view that 'the spoken language system' and 'the written language system' stand 'in some sort of filial relation to "the language system"' and that the difference between them lies in expression substance.[10] In a paper delivered in 1961, McIntosh maintains that 'written language and spoken language *both* symbolize mental experience but that written language, by virtue of its graphological system, *also* symbolizes spoken language'.[11]

One who most strongly has emphasized the doctrine of independence, but, like other linguists, has not been able to ignore the correspondence between writing and speech, is John McLaughlin. Due to this discrepancy, several contradictory statements occur in his work.[12]

Penttilä tackles the relation of speech and writing once more.[13] Having pointed to the spread of the doctrine of independence, he tries to answer the question: what exactly is meant by the independence of written language? Penttilä argues rightly that written language is not independent of spoken language, although such an optic language is possible (and in fact in the history of interlinguistics there have been proposals for such purely graphic languages). In Penttilä's opinion the written language is independent mainly because of its material nature, that its symbols are optic and visual, not acoustical and auditive. But if the different material of the written symbols proves the independence of writing, then transcription, too, would be independent of speech. Further, Penttilä maintains rightly that it is not clear what is meant by the SAME language if one says that writing and speech are the manifestations of the same language. According to Penttilä, the essential precondition for speaking about the same language is an extensive correspondence between the spoken and the written languages – structural similarity or isomorphism. As a matter of fact, Penttilä's discussion does not answer the question: what is this 'the same language' whose manifestations are speech and writing?

Theoretically it is of course possible to maintain that a speech unit S and the corresponding writing unit W both manifest a third unit – a 'language' unit L. But from where do we take 'the language'? Shall we here construct an 'underlying' L? We cannot derive S and W from an abstract L. We can only compare S and W with one another. When S and W differ regarding a component we cannot say that S and W express the same L in a different way (the substance is here of course irrelevant). We can only say that here W differs from S, or vice versa. The interpretation of unsophisticated persons and perhaps most linguists is that S is primary, and W represents (more or less faithfully) S.

We can not interpret 'the language' as mere meaning, and say that the similarity or correspondence between speech and writing lies only in meaning, content, 'mental experience', or thought[14] the different expressions of which are speech and writing. In fact the morphemes, words, and sentences express meaning, but the individual letters or graphemic units do not express meaning, but phonemes or sounds, i.e. concrete speech units. If correspondence between speech and writing lay only in meaning, the existence of exactly corresponding absolute synonyms (words with identical meaning used in identical contexts) would be inexplicable. For example, in Estonian the synonyms *osastav* and *partitiiv* both express in speech and writing the meaning 'the partitive case'. Why such a correspondence? Why do we sometimes have in writing just the form *osastav*? Because it represents the phonemic speech form /osastav/. Analogously we have in writing just the form *partitiiv*? Note also the grapheme *ii* which represents the long phoneme /i/. It is meaningless to speak of 'independent' writing, for the spelling of these words depends on the speech form of the words. One often feels that some new words correspond well to the meaning they express while other words do not. When one comes across a new word in a text, one does not ask whether its graphic form corresponds to the meaning or thing it expresses, but whether its phonic form corresponds well to the meaning.

A new variant of the doctrine of independence is represented by W. Haas who interprets the phonographic correspondence as translatability.[15] Such an interpretation is scarcely illuminating. Between speech and writing of the same language there is an extensive correspondence or isomorphism as far as matching of phonemes and graphemes is concerned. But two languages may differ in various respects at all levels. The relation of speech and writing is not that of mutual independence, as Haas claims.[16] He admits that phonemic analysis is demanded of the users of an alphabetic script (p. 29); however, no graphemic analysis is demanded in speaking.

Haas' translation theory has been accepted by C. V. Taylor who maintains: 'The fact that, so far as we know, writing systems have not appeared without being based in some way upon speech, does not mean they could not do so.'[17] Nonetheless, no natural language is based on another language, even though Taylor regards speech and writing as two 'languages'. Fortunately the doctrine of independence has not influenced Taylor's discussion of orthography planning, in spite of his 'translation' view, involving 'the mutual independence of speech and writing'.[18]

One may point out more differences in the relations between speec hand writing on one hand and between two translatable languages on the other hand. A translation renders mainly the meaning of another language and only partly the syntactic structure (various structural features are untranslatable), whereas writing renders most syntactic, morphological, and phonological features of speech.

If the doctrine of independence belonged exclusively to language philosophy and terminology without relevance in orthography planning and the problems of this volume – the creation and revision of writing systems – I would not have devoted so much space to it. Unfortunately things are not so innocent. From the supposition that writing is independent of speech some (but not all) advocates of the doctrine of independence and their uncritical followers have inferred that spelling need not consider speech at all. The opponents of spelling reform have found in the doctrine of independence support for their view. As McIntosh[19] maintains, Bradley's paper 'has been cited again and again (sometimes quite unfairly) as an argument against spelling reform'. Uldall reached the drastic conclusion: 'From a theoretical point of view it is therefore nonsense to talk about for instance the English graphic system being inadequate: we might just as well turn it around and say that the English phonic system is inadequate . . . Another thing is that for practical purposes it is probably more convenient to have one system than two, and as it is less difficult to change the orthography than the pronunciation, it might be an advantage to bring the graphic system into harmony with the phonic system'.[20] I would rather use the label 'nonsense' for the theory which is in conflict with such practical purposes.[21] However, it must be granted that Uldall sees rightly the practical problem of orthography planning. Therefore, he cannot be blamed for opposing the revision of orthography. One of Vachek's statements is confusing: 'Thus writing should not be blamed for being inaccurate in recording the phonic make-up of spoken utterances – it lies outside the scope of its function to do this.'[22] Later he admits that those demanding spelling reforms show that '*something* is wrong with the written norm' and that 'too complicated co-ordinations may (and most probably should) be replaced by simpler ones, if external factors make such replacements feasible'.[23]

The doctrine of independence has also been used as an argument against spelling reform in Sweden. For example, Tor G. Hultman maintains that the current written Swedish language is an independent manifestation of Swedish. He admits that spelling and pronunciation causes difficulties because of discrepancies between writing and speech, and that the current spelling is rather irrational. But in discussing spelling reform he also points to the 'viewpoint of principle': 'Our present written language is an independent system, a system which is not subordinate to spoken language, but co-ordinate with it. Thus there is no reason to change spelling referring to the things in the spoken language.' Fortunately, Hultman has not lost his common sense and surrendered to the doctrine of independence. He maintains: 'It is neither desirable that the linguistic, theoretical speculations lead to widening of the split between the two systems in absurdum.' He adds that if writing does not give clues to pronunciation, we get as the result wrong pronunciation and social complications.[24] A theory of the doctrine of independence which in principle is against revision of spelling is absurd indeed. Hultman's argumentation is one proof that something is wrong with the doctrine of independence.[25]

It goes without saying that the above does not contradict the fact that writing is an important means of communication, equal to speech. In discussing the relation of speech and spelling, some misunderstandings and wrong conclusions are a result of confusing the concepts WRITING or WRITTEN LANGUAGE with WRITING SYSTEM, ORTHOGRAPHY, or SPELLING. It sometimes happens that one makes a statement about writing which may be right in some sense, and then infers from it something nonsensical about orthography. Writing is the process or result of recording language in graphic signs. Written language can be defined as one of the 'modes of linguistic communication', whereas writing system is 'a code of conventional graphic signs representing speech'.[26] Orthography or spelling can be defined as representation of speech in graphic signs by means of standardized rules. One can say that the purpose of writing or written language is to convey meaning, but this is not true of orthography. It is the orthography that is relevant in orthography planning. We are concerned only with the alphabetic writing system in this paper. Archibald A. Hill has clearly defined the purpose of orthography: 'A speaker of the language should be able to pronounce correctly any sequence of letters that he may meet, even if they were previously unknown, and secondarily, to be able to spell any phonemic sequence, again even if previously unknown.'[27] Ability to pronounce correctly an unknown sequence of letters is essential, for example, when new words are introduced in writing.That writing is not independent of speech is proved also by fact that in introducing new words one should avoid sequences of graphemes which are difficult to pronounce and that often in constructing a new word one tries to use a sequence of phoneme which well symbolizes the meaning.

Regarding orthography, it is not the fact that writing can be read without voice or even without knowledge of how it is pronounced that is essential, but the fact that it can be read aloud. Nor should one forget that many texts are written mainly for the purpose of being rendered aloud, e.g. speeches and dramas. Should such texts be written in another transcription than the standardized spelling?

The theoretical possibility of designing writing independent of speech is irrelevant in orthography planning. A great sociological and pedagogical problem of our day is to teach children over the world to read and write. One need not point to the well-known fact that learning to read and write is a difficult task in some old written languages due to complicated orthography, i.e. rules for representing speech in writing. In this connection it is meaningless to speak of writing independent of speech. It may be true that somewhere someone has taught reading by a method which ignores the fact that writing corresponds to speech, but probably no one has designed a writing independent of speech for a preliterate people.[28]

Linguistics and orthography planning cannot ignore the fact that to unsophisticated people, spelling represents pronunciation, and a letter is associated with a sound.[29] This is, among other facts, proved by numerous spelling pronunciations which are spreading, especially in recent times, in several languages.[30] Most of the complaints regarding language addressed to Swedish Radio concern pronunciation. People think it is unreasonable that the pronunciation in broadcasting differs from the spelling.[31] Contrary to the view of some purists and linguists,[32] spelling pronunciation is to be regarded as the expression of a sane intuition and of the natural conception that spelling reflects the correct speech form.[33] The Swedish linguists are in favor of spelling pronunciation. Carl Ivar Ståhle maintains that it is essential from the social and pedagogical point of view that spoken and written language resemble each other so much as possible.[34] According to Gun Widmark, the adaptation of speech to writing is so well documented that there is no doubt that this facilitates the task of the brain.[35]

Regarding the intuitive view that spelling represents pronunciations, one cannot ignore the viewpoint of all grammarians and spelling reformers and their supporters,[36] and the numerous spelling reforms that have been carried out in several languages with the aim to adjust spelling better to speech. It is superfluous to point to the viewpoint of older and modern linguists,[37] still less to that of orthography planners. This intuition is not discredited by the circumstance that the current orthography in many languages fulfills this function in a rather unsystematic, uneconomic, complicated, or irrational way. According to several orthography planners 'the fullest, most adequate representation of the actual spoken language, is by and large, the ideal'.[38] This fundamental function of orthography is not disproved by the fact that many features of speech are ignored in writing and in the latter there occur purely 'visual morphemes', signs that have no correspondence in the vocal-auditory process. Even Bolinger, who has insisted that 'writing can exist as a series of morphemes at its own level, independent of or interacting with the more fundamental (or at least more primitive) vocal-auditory morphemes', and who is regarded as the representative of the doctrine of independence, admits that 'most writing is the graphic representation of vocal-auditory processes'.[39] Further, the fundamental function of orthography is not disproved by the fact that in many countries the vocabulary and grammar of the written language differ in several points from those of the spoken language (cf. diglossia). This fact is a matter of spelling; as such a written language is also read aloud and often spoken.[40]

If we accept Hill's definition of the purpose of spelling – that the function of orthography is to represent speech – then the question is: which units of speech are to be symbolized by graphemes? It should be obvious that the most economic system is the symbolizing of phonemes on the ground of the simple fact that it employs the fewest symbols and rules to represent speech.[41] Such a system is certainly easier in learning to read and write.[42] Thus the most efficient orthography is phonemic. It is essential to stress this simple BASIC, phonemic principle of orthography, in spite of practical difficulties in applying it in many languages.[43]

By definition a phonemic orthography cannot represent more than one dialect at the same time if the differences are on the phonemic level. Thus a standard orthography must inevitably be based on one speech form, be it the standardized speech or a culturally or politically dominant dialect. Sometimes it is necessary to represent phonemically different dialect speeches in standard orthography, whether in literary works written entirely in dialect or in rendering isolated words or phrases of a dialect or substandard pronunciation. This can be more or less adequately done only in a phonemic or phonetic orthography, but not in an unsystematic or historical orthography. Teaching and learning to read standard writing in a nonphonemic historical orthography causes additional difficulties for children who do not speak the standard language. The difficulties of the child increase proportionately with the degree of difference between the child's dialect and the standard dialect and with the complexity of the orthography. The difficulties and problems to be surmounted in such a situation are illustrated by several papers in the collection *TeachingBlack Children to Read*.[44] Such problems do not exist in languages with phonemic orthography, for example, Estonian or Finnish.

Stressing the basic phonemic principle of orthography does not mean that it should be implemented 100 percent. Thus it may sometimes be expedient to omit some phonemic features, particularly prosodic ones, because of the principles of economy and simplicity. This is possible especially because of language redundancy.[45] But every deviation from the phonemic principle must be carefully calculated. Haas maintains that every deviation from phonemic orthography will be some sort of loss and that in every case 'we shall have to ask whether or not the loss of phonological economy is made good by non-phonological advantages'.[46]

In recent years some linguists, although hesitating, have been in favor of the morphological or morphophonemic orthography. Weir maintains: 'An orthography then should be basically morphophonemic, and account for both the phonemic and morphemic structures'.[47] But she asks: 'should the singular-plural relationship between *Apfel* and *Äpfel* or *Baum* and *Bäume* be obscured in writing?' And answers: 'Probably not, or at least we should defer any decision in this regard until we know more about the variables which are important to the reading process.' Bertil Malmberg thinks that 'there is no doubt that morphemics has to be reflected, in some way, in spelling'. And that 'there is a definite advantage in having the same vowel symbol in, say *write* and *written* . . .'[48] For a person whose native language has roughly phonemic orthography, such an argument is incomprehensible. In my opinion it would be a definite advantage if English had something like *ai* or *ay* in *write;* cf. *profound: profundity*; *hale: health*; *lead: led*; *crisis: critical* (instead of *critis*); *delude: delusion*; in French there is *loi: légal*; in Swedish *vinna: vunnit*; in Estonian *tege-ma* 'do, make' (infinitive)*: tee-n* (first p. sg); *teh-ku* (imperative)*: tei-nud* (participle); *aitama: aidanud* (cf. *paitama: paitanud*).

It seems that the advocates of morphophonemic orthography have taken notice only of some morphophonemic spellings in English and some other languages, ignoring the opposite spellings, without pondering over the consequences of a consistent morphophonemic orthography. It is obvious that morphophonemic orthography cannot be recommended as a universal principle for all orthographies. Application of morphophonemic orthography in a language with extensive allomorphism would make the reading of such a language impossible, not to speak of learning to read. This would mean that reading presupposes a knowledge of the entire morphophonemics and even of a great part of the lexicon of a language. Discussing 'the optimal orthography for a language', Klima presupposes that the learner and the user of the orthography 'knows the language'. By this he means that the speaker-hearer knows not only the phonological and grammatical rules, but also the vocabulary (or a representative vocabulary) and the 'underlying' forms, e.g. that '*giraffe* has an underlying representation with, in some abstract sense, a double continuant and a final vocalic segment'.[49] This obviously exceeds a child's skill in learning to read.[50]

It may be expedient in only a few exceptional cases to deviate from phonemic orthography in favor of morphophonemic orthography. It would be valid mainly in cases where there is a phonically conditioned automatic change of a phoneme on a morpheme boundary (e.g. in compound words).[51] But even in such cases it is mostly expedient to employ phonemic orthography. For example, in Estonian there occurs the following automatic change: when a stem ends in /m/ and the following suffix begins with /t/, /m/ is replaced by /n/, e.g. (*lumi* 'snow':) *lum-* + *d* = *lund* (partitive), cf. *meri: merd.* It would look strange in the eyes of an Estonian to write *lumd* instead of *lund.* The morphophonemic exceptions often cause trouble in writing. Haas reports that a child may learn fairly quickly to read *-ed* of *jumped* as required, but may continue for a long time to write *jumpt.*[52] There is no doubt that a general phonemic orthography is easier to read and to write than a morphophonemic one, even in languages with relatively slight allomorphism.

PRACTICE AND TACTICS

As in other fields of language planning, so also in the practical orthography planning, i.e. in creating and revising orthographies, there arise conflicts between linguistic or intra-code (Joshua A. Fishman's term) considerations and nonlinguistic or extra-code elements, mainly various sociocultural factors.[53] The last factors are often emotional and passionate. 'Indeed the pressure of social groups within the community may make it difficult if not impossible to secure the acceptance of the linguist's choice, however evident its advantages may appear to be.'[54] Several linguists and orthography planners have stressed the need for compromise between linguistic and sociocultural considerations. In the fifties and sixties the sociocultural considerations received more attention at the expense of linguistic ones in devising or recommending orthographies for languages of formerly preliterate peoples, as is evident, for example, from Smalley, et al., *Orthography Studies.*

Sociocultural factors in language are the domain of sociolinguistics. Fishman asks: 'What is it that sociolinguistics could contribute to future studies of the acceptive creation of writing systems?' In his opinion 'modern sociolinguistics can contribute most by linking this branch of applied linguistics with the body of theory and practice that has grown up in connection with the acceptance of other systematic innovations, the planning of social change more generally....' Fishman correctly declares that this 'will require a far greater liberation of sociolinguistics from disciplinary linguistics and its far greater immersion in societal processes and problems'.[55] In fact such a sociolinguistics would have little to do with linguistics. This does not mean that it would not contribute to language planning. So far sociolinguistics has been largely a descriptive science. If 'applied sociolinguistics'[56] could really tackle the problems of language planning tactics, it would be a great gain for language planning in general and for orthography planning in particular. The purpose of language planning tactics as a branch of the theory of language planning is to help find the most efficient ways to implement the ends of language planning. What does this imply for orthography planning?

First, one should be aware of the difference of a linguistically efficient orthography and a socially acceptable orthography. A linguistically trained orthography planner must not forget that the goal is to implement a linguistically efficient orthography, and this can be 'scientifically' established for any language. But it is doubtful whether one can work out scientifically based instructions on how to act in all sociocultural situations in devising, launching, or revising an orthography, although a more developed sociolinguistics would be a certain help here. Tactics and strategy are to a great extent an art rather than a science.

Besides being affected by the attitudes of the community, the success of orthography planning depends on the skill of the orthography planners to convince and influence the community and its leaders. Propaganda is also an important factor in language planning. Creation of an orthography must be viewed in a wider perspective. An orthography planner must be farsighted, especially in view of the fact that it is difficult to revise an established orthography later on. As in social and technical planning, language planners have often to combat with various prejudices. It is scarcely wise of a linguistically trained orthography planner always to surrender immediately, e.g. to yield to pressure to make a writing system 'look like' Spanish, French, or English. A language planning expert would render a disservice to a people by introducing the rather 'chaotic orthographic patterns of English wherever possible'.[57] Instead one should explain to the natives that their orthography is superior to French or English or Spanish. The use of foreign inefficient graphic patterns may in the long run become unpleasant even for the people themselves, when their national self-confidence strengthens and the anticolonial feelings become manifest. Thus we cannot approve of Smalley's orthography principles of maximum motivation in the direction of the prestige language and maximum transfer to the colonial language[58] if these principles imply acceptance of irrational symbolizations of a foreign language.[59] The language planning experts should also try to suggest to the people a rational attitude towards language and writing as means.

It is curious that while one carefully considers the irrational suggestions of recent preliterate peoples regarding their writing systems, one entirely ignores the rational views and proposals of intellectuals, educators, scientists, writers, politicians, etc. – among them the most outstanding intellects of the nation, including distinguished linguists – of nations with long literary traditions. Typical is the case of English. Ben D. Wood, director of the Bureau of Collegiate Educational Research, Columbia University, has recently summarized the situation in the English-speaking world as follows:

> 'While English is already the nearest to a world-wide *spoken* language, our traditional orthography not only handicaps English as a world *written* language, but in our own and other English-speaking nations puts an intolerable and too often traumatic burden on beginning learners. Even among those of our children and adults who do not become nonreaders, the traumas of an irrational alphabet often continue as hidden or unconscious antipathies for, and roadblocks to, effective reading habits, and even more effective roadblocks to writing. Nonreaders not only feel declassé, but also too frequently become victims of frustration leading to delinquency, crime, and the self-destructive violence associated with political infantilism and susceptibility to demagoguery.'[60]

In recent years some scholars have tried to prove that English orthography is quite satisfactory. The most 'counter-intuitive and incredible' viewpoint has been launched by the well-known representatives of the transformational generative school, Noam Chomsky and Morris Halle, who maintain that English orthography 'comes remarkably close to being an optimal orthography system for English'.[61] How this conclusion is reached is described by Göran Hämmarström: 'The authors establish underlying forms, which are often closer to orthography than to the spoken forms. Then they invent rules that change these underlying forms to forms which suitably describe the spoken language. This is always possible in all languages (although on many points one will have to include long lists of words the form of which is just accidental) and cannot possibly be taken as a proof of the suitability of English orthography.'[62]

A conclusion just as incredible has been reached by Richard L. Venezky: 'There is no valid basis, either diachronic or synchronic, for claiming that the current orthography should be anything in particular other than what it is.'[63] Venezky based his research on the 20,000 most common words with the purpose to show the patterning in the English orthography. This research resulted in complex rules with exceptions and listing of words. Z. Šaljapina and V. Ševoroskin,[64] who have commented on and criticized Venezky's model (in a positive review) maintain that a spelling-sound model should include as its vital part a dictionary of morphs or morphemes. This is necessary for dividing graphical words into allomorphs, which is a precondition for the operation of the system. Venezky himself maintains that from his patterns of graphemic, morphemic, syntactic, and phonotactical processes a model can be constructed from which the rules to predict the pronunciation can be found. But he adds: 'What relationship this model has to the reading process of literates or to the teaching of reading is at present unknown.' And he admits that 'many of the patterns in the model have no counterparts in reading habits'.[65] Furthermore, Venezky's model is meant only for converting writing into speech, but not the opposite conversion.

Venezky's and Chomsky's and Halle's models and rules have not disproved, but rather proved again that English orthography is a highly irregular and uneconomic alphabetic convention, which, among other drawbacks, causes great difficulties in learning to read for children during several school years.[66] The burden which English orthography imposes on children and teachers becomes drastically evident if we take note of experiences in languages with phonemic orthography, where reading problems are unknown.[67] Is it not curious that detection of this 'optimal' English orthographic system and its rules demands long years of research by several scholars and computers? The whole Estonian orthographic system is described in a few rules and the exceptions to phonemic orthography in a few lines. The counter-intuitive declarations of the efficiency of English spelling show how far away some modern linguists have moved from reality. Unfortunately such declarations are not irrelevant in orthography planning. First, they encourage the opponents of spelling reform. As a matter of fact one may oppose spelling reform on several grounds and one may admit that it is unrealistic, but one cannot maintain that English orthography is optimal or just as it should be.[68]

The situation of French is analogous to English, although the defects of French orthography are partly of a different kind. The situation of French may be illustrated by some passages from René Thimmonnier's recent book.[69] All know that French orthography is difficult. The majority of Frenchmen have difficulty in learning it. All – physicians, lawyers, writers, professors included – make mistakes. A most used method for orthography presents 116 rules for initial syllables and 167 rules for final syllables. Psychologists and pedagogues have studied the problem of orthography. One scholar has reached the conclusion: '*Il n'y a pas de méthode orthographique* digne de ce nom'. One of the peculiarities and difficulties of the French written language is that it has a grammatical system different from that of the spoken language, so that spoken and written French are in fact two different languages.[70] Nevertheless the written language is considered to correspond to the spoken language, as it is read as the spoken language. According to a questionnaire of the Institution of Sociology Solvay in 1953, 63 percent wished for a simplification of French orthography.[71] After fifteen years of work Thimmonnier has 'discovered and demonstrated' that the French orthography is less aberrant than the ignorants and the scholars think. The result of this work has been that it is no longer necessary to assimilate the graphic peculiarities of 35,000 words, but of 4,500 (sic!) series. But even these 4,500 series comprise only 95 percent of the dictionary, whereas the remaining 5 percent constitute the real but the most redoubtable difficulty of the French orthography.[72] After all Thimmonnier proposes a spelling reform comprising 228 words (the project being approved in principle by the Ministry of Education and the French Academy).[73] Chomsky's and Halle's method and evaluation concerning English orthography has its French counterpart in S. A. Schane, but he does not consider the French orthography as optimal, but 'in general as entirely satisfactory'.[74]

Really, sociolinguistics should investigate not only the orthographic planning problems and the attitudes of peoples in developing countries, but also those in industrialized societies with old literary traditions.[75]

NOTES

1. Cf. J. Voorhoeve in William Smalley, et al., *Orthography Studies: Articles on New Writing Systems* (=*Helps for Translators* 6) (London: United Bible Societies, 1964), 61.
2. Cf. C. V. Taylor, 'Notes on Transcription of Natural Languages', *Linguistic Communications* 2 (1970), 48.
3. For references on earlier scholars see A. McIntosh, *Transactions of the Philological Society* (1956), 40 note. McIntosh's citation of Bradley does not do justice to Bradley's view. McIntosh cites the following passage of Bradley: 'Speech and writing are two organs for the expression of meaning, originally co-ordinate and mutually independent' (*Proceedings of the British Academy* 6 [1913-1914], 227). The emphasis is here on the word *originally*, by which Bradley means ideographic writing. Bradley continues: 'This dual system involved an intolerable burden on the memory. It was needful that the two organs should be put into mutual relation, so that the spoken and the written symbol of every idea could be inferred from each other. This ideal could be realized only through phonetic spelling: by making writing the bondslave of speech.' For later views see S. Allén, *Grafematisk analys som grundval för textedering* (Göteborg, 1965), 13 ff.
4. *Virittäjä* 36, 19 ff.
5. For example, Ruth H. Weir in *Papers in Linguistics in Honor of Léon Dostert* (The Hague, 1967), 170. After considering 'the orthographic representation as an independent system' she proceeds to discuss the phonetic and morphophonemic spellings. One wonders what cognitive value this doctrine has, and why at all compare spelling with speech if the former is an 'independent' system.
6. Cf. Ernst Pulgram, *Word* 21 (1965), 208.
7. Regarding Vachek, cf. *Acta Linguistica* 5 (1945-1949), 86 ff.; *Brno Studies in English* 1 (1959), 7 ff.; *Folia Linguistica* 6 (1973), 47 ff.
8. Hjelmslev, *Prolegomena to a Theory of Language* (Baltimore, 1953), 67 ff.
9. Uldall, *Acta Linguistica* 4 (1944), 11 ff.
10. McIntosh, *Transactions of the Philological Society* 1956, 45.
11. McIntosh, *Patterns of Language* (London, 1966), 99 ff.
12. McLaughlin, *A Graphemic-Phonemic Study of a Middle English Manuscript* (The Hague, 1963). Cf. 'There should be no real question, it seems to me, of one kind of expression revealing something significant about the other' (p. 28). 'One of the most interesting features of an alphabetic writing system is, of course, that as a system of signs it provides the basis for assumptions about the structure of the spoken system when that system is no longer available for direct observation' (p. 36). This discrepancy is due to the circumstance that McLaughlin 'hopes to maintain a distinction between a writing system as an independent mode of language expression and as a system of signs representing segments in the spoken system' (p. 32, note 23).
13. Penttilä, *Acta Universitatis Tamperensis* A26 (1969), 123 ff.; *Acta Societatis Linguisticae Upsaliensis* 2: 2 (1970).
14. Cf. R. A. Crossland, *Proceedings of the University of Durham Philosophical Society* B 1 (1957), 13. According to David W. Read, writing and speech are actualizations of 'linguistic forms' and neither represents the other. 'Linguistic

form' is defined as 'a linking of a meaning to a physical representation in terms of a conventional system such as speech or writing' (Mark Lester [ed.], *Readings in Applied Transformational Grammar* [New York, 1970], 292). According to Vachek, 'writing refers to "things", just as speech does' (*Language* 49 [1973], 193).

15. Haas, *Phono-Graphic Translation* (Manchester, 1970).
16. Cf. also David Abercrombie, *Elements of General Phonetics* (Edinburgh, 1967), 17 ff.
17. Taylor, 'Notes on Transcription . . .', 47. It should be noticed that Taylor's paper deals with how various writing systems represent phonic features. In the beginning he employs once the term 'translation' of phonological features, but in the rest of the paper he uses the term 'transcription' (!) with the same meaning. Finally he discusses the problems in devising new orthographies.
18. Taylor, 'Notes on Transcription . . .', 3.
19. McIntosh, *Transactions of the Philological Society* 1956, 41, note.
20. Uldall, *Acta Linguistica* 4 (1944), 16.
21. Another thing is the situation when the practical purposes cannot be implemented. Cf. below.
22. Vachek, *Acta Linguistica* 5 (1945-1949), 90. Vachek warned already in 1939 against mixing up written language and orthography (*Travaux de Cercle linguistique de Prague* 8, 95), but actually he himself commits the same mistake.
23. Vachek, *Brno Studies in English* 1 (1959), 16 ff.
24. These quotes from Hultman are in *Språket i blickpunkten* (Lund, 1969), 137, 146.
25. I do not touch here the question, irrelevant to orthography planning, whether it is possible and useful to investigate and describe the structure of an alphabetic system apart from any reference to the phonic system of the language it expresses, assuming that the writing system does not represent the spoken system (cf. McLaughlin, *A Graphemic-Phonemic Study* . . ., 27, 36, 41). According to McLaughlin (p. 43) who is an advocate of such a graphic linguistics, its value remains hypothetical.
26. Cf. R. R. K. Hartmann and F. C. Stork, *Dictionary of Language and Linguistics* (London, 1972), 258.
27. Hill, in *Papers in Linguistics in Honor of Léon Dostert* (The Hague, 1967), 98. Cf. Robert D. King, *Historical Linguistics and Generative Grammar* (London, 1969), 204.
28. Cf. J. Berry, in *Proceedings of the Eighth International Congress of Linguists* (Oslo, 1958), 753 ff.
29. Cf. McLaughlin, *A Graphemic-Phonemic Study* . . ., 27. Cf. also Leonard R. Palmer: 'This naive attitude to writing persists with most uneducated people. They write as they speak, and very often speak as they read' (*Descriptive and Comparative Linguistics* [London, 1972], 266).
30. For the latest developments in English, cf. Dwight Bolinger, *Aspects of Language* (New York, 1968), 96 ff.; Fred Householder, *Linguistic Speculations* (Cambridge, 1971), 252 ff. For the latest developments in French, see Jesse Levitt, in *Linguistics* 42 (1968), 19 ff. For the latest developments in Hebrew, see Chaim Rabin in J. Rubin and B. H. Jernudd (eds), *Can Language be Planned?* (Hawaii, 1971), 102.
31. Bertil Molde, in *Språk i Norden* (1970), 131.
32. Bolinger calls the influence of most spelling pronunciations 'reactionary' or 'subversive' (*Aspects of Language*, 96 ff.).

33. Cf. Lewitt in *Linguistics* 42 (1968), 27. Householder interprets spelling pronunciation the other way round, that the naive speakers 'intuitively feel that speech is rendition of writing, not vice versa' (*Linguistic Speculations*, 253). This is an improbable supposition.
34. Ståhle, *1900-talsvenska* (Stockholm, 1970), 71.
35. Widmark, *Om uttal och uttalsnormering* (Lund, 1972), 23.
36. Regarding English, cf. W. Haas, *Alphabets for English* (Manchester, 1969).
37. Of recent discussions, cf. John Lotz: 'Script refers directly to speech in literal script systems', (in *Language by Ear and by Eye* [Cambridge, Mass., 1972], 123).
38. Smalley, et al., *Orthography Studies*, 34.
39. Bolinger in *Language* 17 (1946), 333.
40. In French, where the written language manifests an entirely different grammar from the spoken language, the graphemes representing morphemes which are never spoken nor read aloud (cf. *ils chantent*, *chantées*, etc.) are considered a matter of spelling.
41. Cf. Haas, *Phono-Graphic Translation*, 4; Smalley, et al., *Orthography Studies*, 7.
42. Lotz in *Language by Ear and by Eye*, 22. This is also realized by Pulgram, who stresses the doctrine of independence (*Word* 21, 210).
43. Cf. Andrée F. Sjoberg in William Bright (ed.), *Sociolinguistics* (The Hague, 1966), 265.
44. Edited by Joan C. Baratz and Roger W. Shuy (Washington, 1969). Cf. especially pp. 7, 14 ff., 25 ff., 29 ff., 60 ff., 92 ff., 184 ff., 191 ff. Cf. also George A. Miller in *Language by Ear and by Eye*, 125.
45. Cf. Smalley, et al., *Orthography Studies*, 11; E. A. Nida in *Orthography Studies*, 26 ff.
46. Haas, *Phono-Graphic Translation*, 4.
47. Weir in *Papers in Linguistics in Honor of Léon Dostert*, 172.
48. Malberg in *Applications of Linguistics* (Cambridge 1971), 14.
49. Klima in *Language by Ear and by Eye*, 61 ff., 67.
50. Cf. Ralph W. Fasold in *Teaching Black Children to Read*, 76; William A. Stuart in *Teaching Black Children to Read*, 193. Regarding English phonology, Wayne O'Neil (in *Language by Ear and by Eye*, 115) has come to the conclusion that 'the child's phonology seems to be quite separate from his morphology, whereas the orthography reflecting adult phonology relates them in nearly optimal ways. And this difference may in fact be where the difficulties (insofar as they are linguistic) in children's learning to read may lie.' The solution of this problem, according to O'Neil, may be to teach children to read in a more 'superficial' orthography or to delay the teaching of reading until the children 'have developed the phonological perceptions of an adult'.
51. Cf. Smalley, et al., *Orthography Studies*, 7.
52. Haas in *Phono-Graphic Translation*, 4 ff. In Estonian a frequent spelling mistake is (*leidma:*) *leitsin* vs. *leidsin;* cf. *peitma: peitsin.*
53. Cf. Sjoberg in Bright (ed.), *Sociolinguistics*, 260; Smalley, et al., *Orthography Studies*, 13 ff.
54. Donald Burns, *Fundamental and Adult Education* 5 (1953), 80.
55. Fishman in *Applications of Linguistics*, 26 ff.
56. Cf. Fishman, *Sociolinguistics, a Brief Introduction* (Rowley, Mass., 1970), 107 ff.

57. Cf. Sjoberg in Bright (ed.), *Sociolinguistics*, 267 ff., 271 ff.
58. Cf. also Willard Walker in *Anthropological Linguistics* 11 (1969), 163. Cf. on opposition to symbolizations based on the colonial languages, *Anthropological Linguistics*, 35; Fishman in *Applications of Linguistics*, 24 ff.
59. Cf. also Richard L. Venezky, 'Principles for the Design of Practical Writing Systems', reprinted in this volume.
60. Quoted in Godfrey Dewey, *English Spelling: Roadblock to Reading* (New York, 1971), VII. Regarding recent research in reading difficulties, cf. Kenneth S. Goodman (ed.), *The Psycholinguistic Nature of the Reading Process* (Detroit 1968); and *Teaching Black Children to Read.*
61. Chomsky and Halle, *The Sound Pattern of English* (New York, 1968), 49.
62. Hämmarström, 'The Problem of Nonsense Linguistics', *Acta Societatis Linguisticae Upsaliensis*, Nova series 2: 4 (Uppsala, 1971), 107. For criticism of *The Sound Pattern of English* regarding English orthography see also Geoffrey Sampson in *Language* 46 (1970), 621 ff.; and Lotz in *Language by Ear and by Eye*, 121 ff. Cf. also Haas, *Phono-Graphic Translation*, 68 note. Chomsky has described his method of 'lexical representation' and his view on orthography in more detail in Harry Levin and Joanna P. Williams (eds.), *Basic Studies in Reading* (New York, 1970). Cf. also W. Nelson Francis's critical remarks on Chomsky's views about orthography in *Basic Studies in Reading*, 50 ff.
63. Venezky, *The Structure of English Orthography* (The Hague, 1970), 122.
64. Šaljapina and Ševoroskin in *Linguistics* 84 (1972), 97.
65. Venezky, *The Structure of English Orthography*, 127 ff. cf. also the rules discovered by D. W. Read, *Readings in Applied Transformational Grammar*, 295, who studied 225 monosyllables containing no more than one postvocalic consonant and one of the three vowels /a: ɔ: ɔ/. He found that in his idiolect twenty-nine rules are needed to convert the graphemes to vowel phonemes, and thirty-six rules to convert vowel phonemes to graphemes. The conversion goes via so-called 'linguons' ('the smallest linguistic unit such as actualized by phonemes in speech and by graphemes in writing'). Observe that these rules are needed only for three vowels in certain monosyllabic words mentioned above! Another attempt to construct 'a workable set of phonic rules for English' (by Betty Berdiansky et al.), comprising 166 rules and 661 exceptions for 6092 words, has been described by Frank Smith in *Understanding Reading* (New York, 1971), 169 ff.
66. Lotz (in *Language by Ear and by Eye*, 122) maintains that if the English orthography were a near optimal system 'the teaching of reading would not cost the Anglo-Saxon world billions of dollars a year simply to maintain classrooms and instruction for reading'. Halle himself (in *Language by Ear and by Eye*, 125) has now admitted that English spelling 'indeed has many difficulties and inconsistencies' and if it were possible to eliminate them many problems of reading would also be eliminated. Unfortunately Chomsky's and Halle's declaration on English orthography (in *The Sound Pattern of English*) is uncritically accepted by many as a new scientific truth. The practical value of their hypothesis is anecdotically illustrated by Halle's declaration (in *Language by Ear and by Eye*, 127) that one of his colleagues (linguists?) has claimed that his spelling had improved as a result of reading *The Sound Pattern of English.* This means that even scholars do not master English orthography, and to improve one's skill one must be acquainted with

the knowledge in *The Sound Pattern of English*!

67. Cf. also Haas, *Phono-Graphic Translation*, 43, 52; Lotz in *Language by Ear and by Eye*, 122. Venezky maintains: 'That *homo sapiens* is somehow more at ease with a one-letter one-sound system has often been assumed, but no evidence has ever been produced to substantiate this limitation on men's mental capacities' (*The Structure of English Orthography*, 120). Actually this theoretically simple fact which underlies the system is substantiated not only for men, but also for other beings and machines. In another paper Venezky maintains: 'It may be true that children who learn to read with highly phonemic orthographies, like Finnish, learn to relate specific letters to specific sounds quite quickly, but this is not itself reading. When attempts are made to compare reading abilities across cultures, one of the few valid observations that can be made is that regardless of the phonemic regularity of the orthography, a significant percentage of children in all countries will be classed as remedial readers, and within this group most will come from lower socio-economic environments' (*Anthropological Linguistics* 12 [1970], 263; reprinted in this volume. The fact remains that a reading problem such as some have with English or French is unknown with Finnish or Estonian.
68. For the latest positive discussion of English spelling reform cf. W. Haas, *Alphabets for English*, 8 ff.; and *Phono-Graphic Translation*, 52, 83, 84.
69. Thimmonnier, *Le système graphique du français* (Librairie Plon, 1967).
70. Cf. Claire Blanche-Benveniste and André Chervel, *L'orthographie* (Paris, 1969), 184, 199, 215. According to these authors the majority of young people forget the orthography within some years after they have left the school.
71. There were 433 participants, of whom 379 had at least secondary education (Eric Buyssens, *La communication et l'articulation linguistique* [Bruxelles, 1967], 79 ff.).
72. Thimmonnier, *Le système graphique du français*, 13, 26.
73. Thimmonnier, *Le système graphique du français*, 32, 370 ff. For a recent positive discussion on the French spelling reform by a linguist, cf. Aurélien Sauvageot in *Vie et langage* 205 (1969), 266 ff.
74. Schane in *Languages* 8 (1967), 58.
75. Above I have discussed some arguments which have been advanced in recent years and which are relevant in the creation and revision of orthographies. For more discussion on orthography planning see Tauli, *Introduction to a Theory of Language Planning* (Uppsala, 1968), 127 ff.

RICHARD L. VENEZKY

Principles for the Design of Practical Writing Systems*

0. INTRODUCTION

The design of new writing systems is being undertaken today either to bring about literacy in a language that previously was unwritten or to reform or replace an existing writing system. While each of these goals requires unique considerations, both are concerned with the more general problem of developing an orthography that is (1) mechanically suited for the language it is to reflect, (2) compatible with, or at a minimum, not alien to its social-cultural setting, and (3) psychologically and pedagogically appropriate for its speakers. In the last twenty years the linguistic, political, and sociocultural aspects have been discussed widely, especially by Pike (1947), Burns (1953), Gudschinsky (1959), and Sjoberg (1966). Only recently, however, have the psychological problems, or to be more specific, problems of learning, been considered seriously.[1] While conflicts between the linguist's phonological classifications and the native speaker's perceptions have been noted in the past, no attempt has yet been made to explore these systematically, and consequently the design of new orthographies is still derived primarily from the linguist's systemization, based upon the highly suspicious principle that 'the ideal orthography is a one-letter, one-sound system'.[2] The purpose of this paper is to explore the psycholinguistic basis for the design of new writing systems, drawing especially upon recent research on the reading process.

The focus of this paper will be on the development of writing systems for languages which have no prior literacy experience; the reform or replacement of an existing orthography will not be considered, except as

* From *Anthropological Linguistics* 12: 7 (1970), 256-270. Reprinted with permission.

it applies to the design of totally new systems.[3]

Furthermore, while sociocultural factors must be considered at some point in the design of a practical writing system, these are subordinate to the linguistic, psychological, and pedagogical variables which determine the optimal system or range of systems for the language and speakers involved, and will not be discussed here.

1. BACKGROUND

The earliest publication showing serious concern for accurate representation of speech was by Sir William Jones (1788). Jones, who was also the first to formulate the fundamental postulate of Indo-European comparative grammar, developed a system heavily laden with superscripts to represent the 'primary elements of articulation', which he described as the '. . . soft and hard breathings, the spiritus lenis and the spiritus asper of the Latin Grammarians'.[4] Following Jones' lead, Volney in Europe and Pickering in the United States devised systematic orthographies using Roman letters. While Volney, like Jones, was concerned with scientific accuracy in writing Asiatic languages, Pickering was concerned with the practical writing of American Indian languages: '. . . it never was my plan to give a *universal* alphabet on strict philosophical principles for the use of the learned, but merely a *practical* one, to be applied to the Indian languages of North America . . . .'[5] Nevertheless, Pickering made little improvement on Jones' work. The vowels, for example, were viewed as a continuum of sounds to be represented by the letters *a, e, i, o, u, y*, plus a bevy of diacritics, including numbers, that were to be written both above and below the linear units.

The first guide lines for the design of a universal writing system were developed by Lepsius (1855). Lepsius, a world-renowned Egyptologist, had developed a set of orthographic principles for the Church Missionary Society in 1848 in collaboration with philologists from Cambridge and London. The new system, which was based upon the earlier principles, was sponsored jointly by almost a dozen missionary societies from England, the United States, and the Continent and resulted in a clumsy procedure for recording all known speech sounds according to articulatory movements, regardless of their functional value within any single language. The vowel system began with the three primary vowels (represented by *a, i, u*) which Lepsius likened to the three primary colors, and then expanded into the other Latin vowel letters plus an extensive set of superscripts and subscripts, much like Pickering had suggested. The consonants were no less burdensome. As a phonetic transcription system it made little headway, being superseded in time by Sweet's Broad Romic and the International Phonetic Alphabet. As a writing system for pre-literate languages, however, it was widely employed, especially in Africa, where the missionary societies which had sponsored it were the most active.

Concern over the difficulties encountered in teaching reading with Lepsius' system led to the design of a new set of principles for orthographic design, set forth in 1930 by the International African Institute. The basis of the new system was a phonemic representation of speech, using single letters, digraphs, and a minimal number of diacritics. For the first time in print, psychological and pedagogical factors were considered, derived primarily from Huey's research on reading (Huey 1908). One innovation was the suggested deviation from pure phonemic representation for some instances of tones, a suggestion which had been anticipated by Westermann a year earlier.[6]

> 'In books for Africans, tones . . . may sometimes be omitted when the context makes it quite clear which word is intended' (International African Institute 1930: 11).

This attention to human factors in the design of orthographies for African languages precedes by almost twenty years any similar concern in the United States. The Institute's recommendations were accepted for several dozen African languages and continue to be used today by both missionaries and educators.

The current attitudes in the U.S.A. toward orthographic design were developed primarily by workers of the Summer Institute of Linguistics, and in particular by Pike (1947), Gudschinsky (1953), and Nida (1954), beginning with a one symbol per phoneme concept which has been modified slowly as experience has demonstrated its nondesirability in particular situations. Pike's original position was clearly stated in *Phonemics:*

> 'A practical orthography should be phonemic. There should be a one-to-one correspondence between each phoneme and the symbolization of that phoneme' (Pike 1947: 208).

Within a few years after this position was stated, it was seriously challenged by Nida (1954) who distinguished between the technical use of an orthography by linguists and the practical use by speakers of the language. Both psychological and cultural factors were cited for deviating from the one-letter, one-sound basis, but even more important for the development of design principles was the description of reading as a 'complex series of reactions to visual symbols' and the resulting emphasis on preserving the 'unity of visual impressions'.

Nevertheless, the belief that the ideal orthography (not just 'transcription' system) should be a one-letter, one-sound system was still tenaciously guarded.

> 'In an ideal orthography there is a one to one correspondence between the symbols and the phonemes of the language' (Gudschinsky 1959: 68).

This attitude appears to be derived from three implicit, but generally unstated assumptions:

(1) that the reading process involves little more than producing sounds from symbolic stimuli,

(2) that human language processing is isomorphic to the descriptions of language which structural linguists produce, that is, proceeds from one discrete level to the next in the order of phonology, morphology, syntax, and semantics,

(3) that there is a psychological reality to the phonemic system which a linguist derives.

The first of these assumptions dates in American linguistic writing from Bloomfield (1933); the second and third are somewhat older; none, nevertheless, is unquestionably valid.

Other exceptions to the one-letter, one-sound approach to practical orthographies have been expressed by Daniel Jones (1950), DeFrancis (1950), and Hockettt (1951). Jones assumes a one letter per phoneme basis for an orthography, but then gives a variety of reasons for departing from this principle, the most important being:

(1) to distinguish homophones,

(2) to show popular alternative spellings,

(3) to avoid cumbrous spellings.

Jones, to the horror of most spelling reformers, even countenanced the inclusion of certain silent letters:

> 'It may even at times be found advisable to introduce unpronounced

letters into orthography in order to show relationships between words or to distinguish homophones' (Jones 1950: 232).

In a discussion of alphabet reform in China, DeFrancis (1950) devoted an entire chapter to the question of whether or not to include indicators for tone in an alphabetic writing system. He concluded that the amount of graphic ambiguity resulting from their omission in Chinese would be small enough to justify such a procedure. This, in essence, is what Westermann stated in 1929 (see footnote 6). Hockett concurs with DeFrancis, but goes one step further:

> 'So far as possibility is concerned, it can be shown that any established omission of some sufficiently small number of [the operative phonological contrasts] produces a nevertheless workable notation, whether the omission is systematic or haphazard' (Hockett 1951: 444 ff.).

Walker (1969) cites examples of writing systems now used for North American Indian languages which deviate from the one-letter, one-sound principle. Foremost among these are the syllabic alphabets now used for Cherokee, Cree, Ojibiwa, Chipewyan, Slave, and Eastern Eskimo. Walker also cites an experiment in which twenty-eight speakers of Zuni indicated their spelling preferences (multiple choice) for Zuni words which were dictated by the experimenter. Although there were systematic preferences for some nonphonemic spellings, all of the subjects were literate in English and therefore may have been biased by English sound-letter correspondences. Furthermore, even if these results could be shown to be valid for spelling preferences, they could not automatically be assumed to represent reading preferences, especially since they were derived from words in isolation. Nevertheless, this attempt to derive a writing system experimentally must be viewed as a major step forward in the design of practical orthographies.

2. PRELIMINARIES TO DESIGN

In the remainder of this paper it is assumed that the primary motivation for any writing system is obtaining literacy, and that ornamental, academic, or religious uses of writing systems are relatively unimportant compared to this need. Furthermore, it is assumed that new writing systems will be phonologically based and that reading holds priority over spelling.[7]

The design of a practical system should be based upon three considerations:

(1) the intended function of the orthography,
(2) the process of acquiring literacy,
(3) the structure of the language it is to reflect.

2.1. Function

While the basic function of an orthography, as stated above, is to promote literacy, a separation must be made between transitional orthographies and permanent orthographies, that is, between those systems which are meant only for the initial acquisition of literacy, usually in a 'native language', after which the learner is transferred to reading in some other language (here called the TARGET LANGUAGE), and those systems which will become the primary medium for written expression in a heterogeneous society.[8]

A transitional orthography should be designed in relation to the target orthography, although transfer from one system to the other is probably not a major problem (see section 3, below). More importantly, a transitional orthography is concerned primarily with the initial stages of reading, while a permanent orthography must be concerned with both initial and advanced stages. In the initial stages, the reader is perfecting the mechanics of oral reading, with emphasis on relating writing to speech. In the advanced stages, on the other hand, the reader is rarely engaged in oral reading, but instead is doing rapid, silent reading in which whole words, or groups of words rather than individual letters are processed as single units. For the beginner, the orthography is needed as an indicator for the sounds of words (*inter alia*), but for the advanced reader, meanings, not sounds, are needed. This conflict between the needs of beginning and advanced readers forces certain compromises upon the design of a practical writing system, depending upon the intended function of the system.

2.2. Teaching Reading

In all methods now in use for the teaching of reading, the following tasks are encountered, either overtly or covertly:

(1) discrimination of letters and linking them to sounds,

(2) pronunciation of words, either in isolation or in phrases and sentences,

(3) reading aloud connected discourse,

(4) acquisition of a sight vocabulary, consisting chiefly of high frequency function words,

(5) silent reading for comprehension.

Although these are not the only tasks involved in learning to read, they are the most important for the present discussion. The first, that of discrimination, places limits on the number and shapes of the symbols selected for any system. Whether or not to employ digraphs, for example, is not simply a matter of aesthetics; it may be more difficult to learn to discriminate a totally new symbol from an existing repertoire than it is to learn that a sequence of two existing symbols has a special significance. There are, however, two drawbacks to the employment of digraphs: one is that the average word length (in letters) increases and the other is that ambiguities may occur, as in the English words *gopher* and *haphazard*, where *p* and *h* function as a digraph in one, but as independent units in the other.

Besides digraphs, a second technique is available for reducing the number of unique forms in an orthography, and that is to have certain forms related to two or more sounds, depending upon adjacent letters or some other environmental feature. In English, for example, *i* has two major pronunciations. [ɪ] or [ai] as in rip: ripe, and dinner: diner, depending in part upon the letter or letters which follow. Similarly, in the Dutch, German, Danish, Spanish, and in a few other writing systems, *c* has two values, depending upon the following letter.[9] Where the spelling of the following sound would indicate the wrong pronunciation of *c*, a MARKER is often inserted to indicate the correct correspondence. Thus, in Romanian writing an *h* is inserted after *c* or *g* to indicate /k/ or /g/ in environments that would otherwise indicate /č/ or /ǰ/. Similarly in German, *h* is employed to mark vowel quantity. (On the concept of markers, see Venezky 1970: 49 ff.) The designer of an orthography must balance the difficulty of discriminating additional forms against the potential ambiguity and added word length of digraphs, and the practicality of relating single letters to more than one sound. (The latter alternative will in general depend upon the morphophonemics of the language. We would not, for example, consider representing /d/ and /p/ in English by the same letter. Where frequently occurring morphophonemic alternations are involved, however, there is a potential use for bi-valued forms.)

Linking letters to sounds is one of the hardest tasks which children encounter in learning to read, yet we do not know whether this difficulty is inherent in the task itself or in the procedures commonly employed in teaching it.[10] One known source of difficulty, however, is the segmentation of sounds within words. The sound value for a letter – especially a consonant letter – is generally presented in the teaching of reading as a component of a real word. For example, the correspondence of *b* to /b/ might be presented as a correspondence between *b* and the first sound in *boy*, with the assumption that the learner will abstract the concept of the /b/ either from the word *boy* or from the teacher's attempt to pronounce /b/ in isolation (/b^{ə}/). Young children, and especially culturally deprived children, do not make such generalizations with ease, although there is a limited amount of evidence that shows that proper training tasks can overcome this problem (McNeill and Stone 1965; Zhurova 1963-1964). In a syllabic writing system, this difficulty can generally be avoided, but unfortunately syllabic writing systems tend to have relatively large symbol repertoires and, furthermore, can not be utilized efficiently with languages whose phonological structures deviate markedly from a CV or a VC base.

In the design of the actual letter forms for an orthography, the similarity of letters which represent 'similar' sounds should be controlled, but whether such letters should be maximally distinct or minimally distinct has never, to my knowledge, been investigated. (We can determine fairly easily the relative discriminability of both letters and sounds, but this information by itself does not allow prediction of the interaction between the two scales.)[11]

The second and third tasks, pronouncing words seen in isolation and reading aloud connected discourse, require some semblance of order in relating spelling to sound, but do not demand a one-letter, one-sound system. Where, for example, phonotactical restrictions limit the selection of phones in a particular environment, the writing system may be selective. In English for example, the regular plural may have three different sounds, as in *clumps*, *monsters*, and *horses*, yet all may be spelled with the same letter since the selection of the proper sound is part of the speech habits of children by the age that reading instruction begins.[12] What the child must learn to respond correctly is that *s* at the end of certain forms indicates plurality – the proper pronunciation of the plural he already knows. Spelling the plural with the same form regardless of its sound is an aid toward meaning in that it allows a more rapid translation from spelling to meaning than would a pure phonemic system. This same principle should be considered in the design of new orthographies, especially where frequently occurring affixes serve grammatical functions.

The consistent spelling of the plural is one of several morphemic spellings in English which facilitate translation from spelling to meaning. Most prominent among the other morphemic devices are the primary vowel spellings *a*, *e*, *i*, *o*, and *u*, each of which represents two sounds which alternate in particular environments: *sane: sanity*, *meter: metric*, *wild: wilderness*, *cone: conic*, *reduce: reduction*. In each pair, the graphic identity of the base is retained even though the vowels alternate from *free* to *checked*.[13] A similar device is employed in Hebrew orthography where two spellings exist for /k/; one, *koph*, is invariantly /k/; where the other, *kaph* may alternate to /x/: thus, /kotev/ *write* (pres. ind. m. sg.), but /lixtov/ *to write* (inf.). Similarly the letter *vav* is always pronounced /v/, but *bet* may be either /v/ or /b/, depending (for the most part) upon the phonological environment. There is no evidence that these alternations are a barrier for learning to read, even though they have been abhorred by linguists who tend to view reading as a strictly phonological process.

The acquisition of a sight vocabulary (task 4 above) is important for reading connected discourse smoothly. In oral reading there is a distance between the word being pronounced at any given time and the word being observed by the reader. This distance, called the eye-voice span, depends upon the structure of the material being read, reading ability, and position in the printed line.[14] All of these factors, in turn, depend in part upon high-speed word recognition, especially of function words which aid in establishing relationships among words and in defining syntactic/semantic boundaries. (There is experimental evidence which shows that competent readers tend to process function words differently from content words.)[15] It is important, therefore, that these forms be short and rapidly distinguishable – a criterion which may conflict with the one-letter, one-sound notion. (Throughout the history of English spelling there has been a tendency to restrict the shorter spellings – especially the two letter ones to function words. This led, for example, to the addition of the final *e* to words like *doe*, *toe*, and *roe*, as well as the doubling of the final consonants in *ebb*, *add*, *odd*, and *egg*.)

Silent reading, the final task listed above, is facilitated by anything that aids in the rapid segmentation of words into syntactic/semantic groups. For a permanent orthography, some compromises should be made, therefore, for morphemic identification, although it is clear that the phonological component must be given priority. Those who have reached this stage of literacy have acquired more than the ability to translate from symbols to meaning; they have learned what the game of reading is all about – the nature of written symbols, their relation to meaningless sounds, the blending of these sounds into meaningful words, scanning symbols for logical groupings, relating these groupings to each other while at the same time searching for new groups, and so on.[16] For the accomplished reader, these processes are highly integrated and are carried out without conscious direction. For such a person to learn a writing system for a second language he knows is a relatively trivial task of acquiring new relationships for symbols, assuming that the two writing systems in question are based upon the same principles. For the uninitiated, however, these habits either do not exist, or are not yet available for the reading process. Acquiring the actual symbol-sound or symbol-meaning relationships is only one part – and probably by itself not the most crucial part – of learning to read. This point should not be ignored if the real goal of developing an orthography is to teach reading.

2.3. *Language Structure*

2.3.1. Considerations of the language which an orthography is to reflect must be directed towards the entire language structure, and not just its phonology, although in most instances the phonology will be given priority over the other features. The importance of morpheme and word identity to the reading process were discussed above, as was the potential desirability of morphophonemic spellings. The graphemic distinction of homophones and foreign words – considerations which could lead to further deviations from a one-letter, one-sound system – has been suggested elsewhere (Jones 1950). The most crucial decisions, however, are those concerning which phonemic distinctions to differentiate graphemically. While it is clear that an alphabetic system must give unique representations to all major segmental units, there is little justification for retaining low functional load contrasts, especially if the contrasts are those that tend to be recorded with superscripts (that is, suprasegmental contrasts). To do so is to burden the graphemic repertoire with forms that increase the difficulty of word recognition and spelling while benefiting no one aside from those linguists who confuse reading with phonemic transcription. Justification for the retention of all phonemic contrasts is usually based upon the argument that children learn to read much more quickly with a regular (i.e. phonemic) writing system, than they do with a system which deviates in any way from this ideal.

For this contention there is no supporting evidence; in fact, experiments with the I.T.A. system for almost ten years in America and England have produced, at best, equivocal results.[17] On one issue, that of its effects upon the slow learner, both proponents and opponents tend to agree. 'The slower-learning children do begin to show some benefit from I.T.A. at the end of the third year, but the poorest 10 percent show negligible improvements in test results' (Downing 1967: 293). It may be true that children who learn to read with highly phonemic orthographies, like Finnish, learn to relate specific letters to specific sounds quite quickly, but this is not in itself reading. When attempts are made to compare reading abilities across cultures, one of the few valid observations that can be made is that regardless of the phonemic regularity of the orthography, a significant percentage of children in all countries will be classed as remedial readers, and within this group most will come from lower socioeconomic environments. It has been observed in practice, furthermore, that certain deviations from a one-letter, one-sound system do not have a significant effect upon learning to read (Feitelson 1965: 4 ff.). Reading is a complex task, requiring a variety of skills, among which is translating from letters to sound. Success in this process is, for normal learners, a necessary, but not sufficient, condition for acquiring literacy. Those who experience difficulties in letter-sound learning are troubled more by the manipulation of meaningless sounds in memory than they are by the irregularities of the writing system.

2.3.2. In the design of new orthographies, dialect differences appear to pose a greater problem in theory than they do in practice. In English, for example, there is no evidence that dialect differences per se are a barrier to learning to read, even though some dialect differences are nonsystematic. In theory, systematic phonological differences between dialects should have no effect upon orthographic design, assuming that the orthography is to be based upon a single dialect. If all occurrences of phone A in one dialect correspond to phone B in another, then the correspondence rules for the two dialects are isomorphic. If, however, phone A has two reflexes in the second dialect, depending upon environment or some other feature which native speakers can observe, then the correspondence rules are no longer isomorphic, but are still predictable for both dialects. This is the situation in English for *r*. In postvocalic positions before consonants and juncture it corresponds to /ø/ in some dialects; in all other positions it is /r/ uniformly.

We might predict reading problems when a phone in the dialect which an orthography is based upon has two or more reflexes in another dialect, and where this distribution is not totally predictable. This occurs in English for Upper Midwestern [æ] which corresponds unpredictably to either [a] or [æ] in Eastern New England (cf. *mass* and *grass*). But no reading problem has ever been attributed to this misalignment. Gudschinsky [1959: 71] reports a similar distributional situation encountered in the design of an orthography for Cashibo and where, similarly, no reading problem appears to have resulted. Although we can imagine dialects so divergent that no practical common orthography could be devised, such situations are rare in practice. Dialects, by nature, are characterized by systematic phonological differences. Where major differences do occur, the designer can resort to either a common core representation (which is probably undesirable in practice), or to different systems for each dialect. This decision, however, probably will depend more upon political and economic considerations than it will upon linguistic and psychological ones.

3. TRANSFER

The effect that learning a transitional orthography might have on learning the target orthography has been a concern of a number of linguists. Walker (1969: 163) in discussing transitional orthographies for American Indian languages, says 'The new orthography should have maximal transference with written English and reflect the predilections of the target population.' Gudschinsky (1959: 69) has suggested the introduction of nonphonemic elements in a writing system to facilitate transfer, but concludes that 'The evidence for the effects of inconsistent orthography on transition to the major language is not clear.' In discussing transfer it is necessary to qualify first what is to be transferred. To do this it is convenient to define three levels of skills that are acquired in learning to read with an alphabetic writing system:

(1) general concepts related to the function of an orthography, its orientation on the writing surface, and the notion that the symbol sequences relate to an already acquired system, i.e. language;

(2) general concepts about the types of relationships in the writing

system: one-letter, one-sound; two-letters, one-sound; one-letter, two-sounds; one-letter, one meaning,

(3) specific correspondences for the letters; e.g. *c* corresponds to /k/, /s/, or /š/.

The more general concepts (class 1 above), of course, are the most important ones to transfer, and if literacy is obtained in one language, there is rarely any trouble obtaining literacy in another language with a similar writing system, assuming that the new language has already been acquired. Experiments by Levin and Watson (1963) and Levin, Baum, and Bostwick (1963) indicate that concepts about the types of relationships within a writing system (class 2) may also effect transfer to a new system. In these studies, the effects of variant and invariant letter-sound correspondences in another language were studied. It is not clear from these experiments, however, how important this form of transfer is.

The third class of transfer, that of specific relationships, is the least important of the three classes and should be considered only to minimize negative effects.

Regardless of the importance attributed to transfer, it should not be invoked to justify the marking of nonphonemic contrasts in a writing system simply because such contrasts are phonemic in the target language. On purely psychological grounds such a procedure is indefensible, in that it has a negative effect upon the most difficult of the two reading tasks, that of the initial acquisition of literacy. In this task the learner must acquire a concept of what reading is – of how symbols relate to meaning, as well as the specific bonds between spelling and sound. For reading a second language, only the specific relationships between the orthography and sound must be learned; the nature of the game is already known. The only positive result of this practice, that of aiding the learner to hear new contrasts, can be achieved much less harmfully through proper language training.

4. DESIGN BY EXPERIMENTATION

Experimental approaches to the formation of new orthographies are difficult to design due to the nature of the reading task. People who read an orthography well can continue to read this same orthography under extreme distortions and deletions. For example, one can read English fairly rapidly even when all of the vowels are deleted or when the bottom halves of the letters are covered over. The illiterate, on the other hand, if he is truly an unbiased subject, is not only unfamiliar with letter forms, but does not know yet that they can relate to sounds and words which he already produces. To obtain his preferences, or to test his learning rate for alternate writing systems is laborious and expensive. (To use subjects who are literate in one language for judgments about a writing system for a different language is highly suspect – unless most of the people who will be reading the new system are at the same level of literacy.) Preference tests, if they are employed, should involve preferences for reading, not for spelling. This might be done by preparing paragraphs of varying semantic complexity in each of the alternate systems, and obtaining preferences for readability on each pair. These same materials might also be used for testing differences in reading speed and comprehension for alternate systems. For testing the need for marking a particular contrast, two approaches should be considered. In one, two groups receive identical reading instructions, one using an orthography which retains the contrast, the other without it. After one or two years, the reading levels of the two groups are compared.

In the second approach, learners are tested for oral reading errors, comprehension, and reading speed on the two alternate forms at various times after they begin to learn reading with the full system. This should be done before a full-scale experiment on learning the alternate systems is tried. If within a few years after reading instruction begins, the reduced system can be handled with ease, then the first approach above is justified. If, however, only advanced readers can handle the reduced system such an experiment is not justified.[18]

NOTES

1. Fries and Pike (1949) used native speakers' reactions to different transcription systems to justify a particular phonemic solution to Mazateco, a Mexican Indian language. 'The Mazatecos seem to learn to read and write [nd] as 'nt' more easily than as 'nd', which implies that [nd] is phonemically /nt/.' But no attempt was made to apply this procedure to the development of writing systems until the last ten years. Notes on the use of native speakers' reactions to different orthographic systems can be found in Nida (1954), Gudschinsky (1959), and Walker (1969).
2. This statement has been made by a number of linguists over the last twenty years, including Pike (quoted in section 1, below) and Gudschinsky. One of the more recent restatements was made by Lado (1957: 96): 'Ideally a writing system should have a one-to-one relation between its symbols and the language units they

represent. That is, an alphabetic system should have one letter for each phoneme of the language, and no more.'

3. The desirability of native literacy programs, for which almost all new writing systems are being designed, will not be an issue here. The case for such programs is advanced in *The Use of Vernacular Languages in Education* (1953). Some cogent arguments against the recommendations of the Unesco report are offered by Bull (1955) in his review of the document, and in Gorman (1968).
4. Jones (1788: 183). Jones' system is apparently derived from one designed by Halhead for his Bengal Grammar and was motivated strongly by the gross distortions made by Classical Greek and Latin writers in writing foreign terms. 'The ancient Greeks', wrote Jones, 'who made a voluntary sacrifice of truth to the delicacy of their ears, appear to have altered by design almost all the oriental names which they introduced into their elegant, but romantick Histories' (Jones 1788: 175 ff.).
5. Pickering (1820: 32).
6. Westermann (1929) suggested the omission of nasalization marks where ambiguity (within context) would not result.
7. The relative importance of spelling compared to reading is discussed by Charles C. Fries (1962: 189).
8. Fishman (1969) uses the more explicit but clumsier 'language of wider communication' where I am using *target language*; Gudschinsky (1959: 68, fn. 2) prefers *major language* (official national language, or trade language), and *minor language* ('the language of a relatively small group within a major speech community').
9. For a summary of relationships between spelling and sound in a variety of languages, see Edward Gleichen and John H. Reynolds (1933).
10. Regardless of how reading is taught – whole word method, phonics, or some combination thereof – the better readers acquire letter-sound generalizations. For experimental evidence on this point, see Carol Bishop (1964: 215-221) and Robert Calfee, R. Venezky, and R. Chapman (1969).
11. The design of letters for an orthography is discussed by J. Berry (1958: 752-764). On the visual discrimination of letter forms, see E. J. Gibson, et al. (1963).
12. This has been demonstrated by Berko (1968), among others.
13. The relationship of English spelling to English morphophonemics is detailed in Venezky (1970: *passim*).
14. The eye-voice span in reading was first studied by Quantz (1897). More recent studies are reported by Schlesinger (1968) and Levin and Turner (1966).
15. See Shapiro and Palermo (1967).
16. A more detailed analysis of reading skills is given in Venezky, Calfee, and Chapman (1969).
17. It should be noted, however, that I.T.A. is not strictly a one letter per phoneme system, but contains deviations from this for facilitating transfer to traditional orthography. Furthermore, both political and economic restrictions have made experimentation with this system difficult and consequently it has not been fairly evaluated.
18. There are other possible experimental techniques for comparing alternate writing systems, such as measuring response times for word or phrase recognition under

tachistoscopic presentation, but it is difficult to determine whether or not these techniques require exactly the same skills as reading.

BIBLIOGRAPHY

Berko, J.
1968 'The Child's Learning of English Morphology', *Word* 14, 150-177.

Berry, Jack
1958 'The Making of Alphabets', in Eva Siversten (ed.), *Proceedings of the VIII International Congress of Linguistics* (Oslo: University Press), 752-764.

Bishop, C. H.
1964 'Transfer Effects of Word and Letter Training in Reading', *Journal of Verbal Learning and Verbal Behavior* 3, 215-221.

Bloomfield, Leonard
1933 *Language* (New York: Holt, Rinehart and Winston).

Bull, William E.
1955 'Review of: *The Use of Vernacular Languages in Education*' (= *Monographs on Fundamental Education* No. 8) (Paris: Unesco, 1953), *IJAL* 21, 288-294. Reprinted in Dell Hymes (ed.), *Language in Culture and Society* (New York: Harper and Row, 1964).

Burns, D.
1953 'Social and Political Implications of the Choice of an Orthography', *Fundamental and Adult Education* 5, 80-85.

Calfee, Robert C., Richard L. Venezky, and Robin Chapman
1969 *Pronunciation of Synthetic Words with Predictable and Unpredictable Letter-Sound Correspondences* (= *Technical Report* 71, *Wisconsin Research and Development Center for Cognitive Learning*) (Madison, Wis.: University of Wisconsin, February).

DeFrancis, John
1950 *Nationalism and Language Reform in China* (Princeton: Princeton University Press).

Downing, John
1967 *Evaluating the Initial Teaching Alphabet* (London: Cassell).
1969 'I.T.A. and Slow Learners: A Reappraisal', *Educational Research* 11, 229-331.

Feitelson, Dina
1965 'The Alphabetic Principle in Hebrew and German Contrasted with the Alphabetic Principle in English', paper presented at the International Reading Association Preconvention Workshop.

Fishman, Joshua
1969 'National Languages and Languages of Wider Communication in Developing Nations', *Anthropological Linguistics* 11, 111-135.

Fries, Charles C.
1962 *Linguistics and Reading* (New York: Holt, Rinehart and Winston).

Fries, Charles C., and Kenneth L. Pike
1949 'Co-existent Phonemic Systems', *Language* 25, 29-50.

Gibson, E. J., et al.
1963 'An Analysis of Critical Features of Letters, Tested by a Confusion Matrix', in Harry Levin (ed.), *A Basic Research Program on Reading* (Ithaca, N.Y.: Cornell University).

Gleichen, Edward, and John H. Reynold
1933 *Alphabets of Foreign Languages*, 2nd ed. (London: Edward Stanford).

Gorman, T. P.
1968 'Bilingualism in the Educational System of Kenya', *Comparative Education* 4 (June), 213-221.

Gudschinsky, Sarah
1953 *Handbook of Literacy* (Norman, Okla.: Summer Institute of Linguistics).
1959 'Recent Trends in Primer Construction', *Fundamental and Adult Education* 11, 67-96.

Hockett, Charles
1951 'Review of: John DeFrancis, *Nationalism and Language Reform in China*' (Princeton: Princeton University Press, 1950), *Language* 27, 439-445.

Huey, Edmund B.
1908 *The Psychology and Pedagogy of Reading* (New York: Macmillian). Reprinted with an introduction by Paul A. Kolers (Cambridge, Mass.: M.I.T., 1968).

International African Institute
1930 Memorandum 1: *Practical Orthography of African Languages* (London: Oxford University Press). Reprinted in 1962.

Jones, Daniel
1950 *The Phoneme* (Cambridge: W. Heffer and Sons).

Jones, Sir William
1788 'A Dissertation on the Orthography of Asiatick Words in Roman Letters', *Asiatick Researches* I, 1-56. Reprinted in Captain John Towers (ed.), *The Works of Sir William Jones* 1 (London, 1799), 175-228.

Lado, Robert
1957 *Linguistics Across Cultures* (Ann Arbor: University of Michigan Press).

Lepsius, C. R.
1855 *Standard Orthography for Reducing Unwritten Languages and Foreign Graphic Systems to a Uniform Orthography in European Letters* (London and Berlin: Seeleys, Fleet Street, and Hanover Street).

Levin, Harry, Esther Baum, and Susan Bostwick
1963 'The Learning of Variable Grapheme-Phoneme Correspondences: A Comparison of English and Spanish Speakers', in Harry Levin (ed.), *A Basic Research Program on Reading* (Ithaca, N.Y.: Cornell University).

Levin, Harry, and Elizabeth Turner
1966 'Sentence Structure and the Eye Voice Span', *Project Literacy Report* 7 (Ithaca, N.Y.: Cornell University), 79-87.

Levin, Harry, and John Watson
1963 'The Learning of Variable Grapheme-Phoneme Correspondences', in Harry Levin (ed.), *A Basic Research Program on Reading* (Ithaca, N.Y.: Cornell University).

McNeill, L. D., and J. Stone
1965 'Note on Teaching Children to Hear Separate Sounds in Spoken Words', *Journal of Educational Psychology* 56, 13-15.

Meinhof, Carl
1928 'Principles of Practical Orthography for African Languages-I', *Africa* 1, 228-239.
Nida, Eugene A.
1954 'Practical Limitations to a Phonemic Alphabet', *The Bible Translator* 15 (Jan., April), 35-39, 58-62. Reprinted in William A. Smalley, et al. (ed.), *Orthography Studies* (London: United Bible Societies, 1964), 22-30.
Pickering, John
1820 *An Essay on a Uniform Orthography for the Indian Languages of North America* (Cambridge: University Press).
Pike, Kenneth L.
1947 *Phonemics: A Technique for Reducing Language to Writing* (Ann Arbor: University of Michigan Press).
Quantz, J. O.
1897 *Problems in the Psychology of Reading* (= *Psychological Review Monograph Supplements* 2) (Dec.).
Schlesinger, I. M.
1968 *Sentence Structure and the Reading Process* (The Hague: Mouton).
Shapiro, S. I., and D. A. Palermo
1967 'The Influence of Part of Speech on Paired-Associate Learning', *Psychonomic Science* 8, 445-446.
Sjoberg, Andree F.
1966 'The Development of Writing Systems for Preliterate Peoples', in W. Bright (ed.), *Sociolinguistics: Proceedings of the U.C.L.A. Sociolinguistics Conference, 1964* (The Hague: Mouton), 260-274.
Use of Vernacular Languages in Education
1953 *The Monographs on Fundamental Education* 8) (Paris: Unesco).
Venezky, Richard L.
1970 *The Structure of English Orthography* (The Hague: Mouton).
Venezky, Richard L., Robert Calfee, and Robin Chapman
1969 'Skills Required for Learning to Read: A Preliminary Analysis', *Education* 4, 298-302.
Volney, Count
1819 *L'Alphabet européen appliqué aux langues asiatiques*, 8 vol. (Paris).
Walker, Williard
1969 'Notes on Native Writing Systems and the Design of Native Literacy Programs', *Anthropological Linguistics* 11, 148-166.
Westermann, D.
1929 'The Linguistic Situation and Vernacular Literature in British West Africa', *Africa* 2, 337-351.
Zhurova, L. E.
1963-1964 'The Development of Analysis of Words into their Sounds by Preschool Children', *Soviet Psychology and Psychiatry* 2 (Winter), 17-27. Translated.

S. I. A. KOTEI

4

The West African Autochthonous Alphabets: An Exercise in Comparative Palaeography*

INTRODUCTION

Culture is transmitted by symbols, and the most prevalent and predominant symbol is oral language, but oral language has never at any time or place sufficed all the needs of communication. Man began to express himself quite early by means of cave drawings, rock engravings, wood carvings, and various other inscriptions, depending on the available material and the content and purpose of communication. From these crude beginnings were evolved ideographs and pictographs of a more or less flexible form, adequate for certain kinds of long distance communication.

The Voegelins[1] claim that although these prealphabetic forms were universal, their development into self-sufficient systems, capable of extended discourse, occurred only among the Plains Indians. Jack Goody[2] also asserts that the achievement of a system of prealphabetic writing completely based upon the 'representation of phonemes' (the basic units of meaningful sound) was left to the Near Eastern syllabaries, which developed between 1500 and 1000 B.C., and finally to the introduction of the alphabet proper in Greece. In the following pages, it will be shown that at least one West African syllabary was developed to the same degree of flexibility as the Plains Indian and Near Eastern alphabets.

What needs to be noted at this point is that graphic communication is a universal and timeless phenomenon; therefore literacy, in its most elementary sense, has flourished in every human society, though some societies were more literate than others. When Europe made its first con-

* From *Ghana Social Science Journal* 2: 1 (1972), 98-110. Reprinted with permission.
S. I. A. Kotei is lecturer of the Department of Library Studies, University of Ghana, Legon.

tact with West Africa in the fifteenth century, certain primitive forms of writing had been developed but were not used widely enough for Africa to make any pretensions to literacy in the modern sense.

The terms 'oligoliterate' or 'protoliterate' have been used to describe societies in which literacy is restricted, for technical or cultural reasons, to a closed hierarchy of persons, usually the administrative and religious elite, for example among the Sumerians, Hittites, and Chinese before they developed democratic scripts. Because of their restricted use, all pre-alphabetic scripts remained fundamentally unchanged for a long time.[3] As writing became more common, 'protoliterate' societies moved into various stages of 'stunted', 'special', 'neo', or 'conditional' literacy.[4]

Until recently – more than 400 years after contact was made with the Roman alphabet – an oral culture in which prealphabetic symbols were used existed side by side with a fully literate culture in many European communities. The Teutonic peoples were using the Runic alphabet and the Irish were still writing in Ogam at a time when several communities on the European continent had adopted pure alphabetic forms.[5] Certain West African societies also employed the dual mode of communication until the early part of this century, and yet, with the exception of Diringer's sketches together with a few other isolated comments, Western historians, palaeographers, and alphabetologists have on the whole been regrettably silent on the contribution of African systems of writing to the collective cultural heritage of mankind. These scripts, like others elsewhere, are important, not only for 'our understanding of the mental capacity of the natives themselves but also for our knowledge of the history of writing in general'.

It is a historical fact that in most places where the alphabet had been invented, written documents had also been produced and in course of time had been accumulated in some repository. That being the case, one would expect that the West African alphabets also should have brought into being their own libraries and archives. That this did not happen to any marked extent was due to a number of historical and natural factors, including certain inherent strictures of the alphabets themselves, an environment of predominant illiteracy, the imposition of the Roman alphabet, and the colonial factor.

Whichever was the more regressive factor is not particularly important, but it is of considerable palaeographic interest to West Africa at least to trace the evolution and uses of alphabets which may well have become the medium of written communication, book production, and eventually library formation in the areas concerned. One must assume that if indeed libraries had been built on books written in local languages from local alphabets, they would have made a greater impact on reading habits. For one thing, the literature would have had all the linguistic advantages of comprehension. Until 1848 when Commodore Forbes[6] first published the Vai syllabary, it was assumed that the continent south of the Sahara was totally without a literate culture. Discounting the Egyptian hieroglyphic and Arabic script, there had in fact been developed a number of autochthonous 'alphabets' in scattered areas of Negro Africa. The oldest such alphabet was created in the early Ethiopian or Nubian Kingdom. Although the Kingdom at first was subjected to Egyptian political and cultural domination, it eventually became independent in every sphere of activity. By the second century B.C., Nubia had developed a distinctive non-Arabic script of its own in the form of a quasi-alphabet known as the Meroitic.[7]

For the rest of the continent, West Africa holds a position of pre-eminence both with regard to the sophistication and to the variety of indigenous script inventions. They include the Vai syllabary of Liberia, the Mende syllabary of Sierra Leone, the Nsibidi ideograph of Eastern Nigeria, the Bamoun alphabet of Cameroons, the Bete alphabet of the Ivory Coast, and the neo-Arabic of Northern Ghana. Ghana did not invent an indigenous alphabet of its own, but, in so far as no country in West Africa is a linguistic or cultural isolate, it is reasonable to expect that some others, in particular the Bete of Ivory Coast,[8] would eventually have diffused themselves into Ghana.

Although the oldest of the scripts are said to have been invented in the middle of the nineteenth century, other critics are of opinion that their initial inspiration came from pre-Roman and Arabic alphabets.[9] It would be rewarding to test both assumptions by means of a comparative analysis of styles and use between the older Roman and Arabic scripts and the indigenous ones of West Africa. It is useful also to trace the development of these scripts in order to show the potential which they had for writing books, and by inference, for library and archival formation, and to investigate why the alphabets failed to reach their ultimate potential.

In a recent historicolinguistic treatment of the West African scripts, Dr. David Dalby[10] of the School of Oriental and African Studies, University of London, raised a number of other significant questions with which a library or literary historian of this region should be concerned. What social forces inspired these inventors to devise new and exceedingly complicated scripts for each of their own languages? What elements contributed to their design and construction? What encouraged the Vai of Liberia in particular to make active use of their scripts as soon as it was invented, in spite of the greater simplicity of the Roman alphabet, and what factors have led to the widespread survival of the Vai for over 130 years, as well as the Ogam among the Irish for a much longer period?

THE VAI SYLLABARY[11]

When exactly the Vai syllabary was invented is a matter of wild conjecture. Indeed it is hard to explain how the Vai people came to their position of primacy among other West African tribes in regard to the invention and finesse of their syllabary. The only plausible explanation that can be offered is that they may have experienced a literate culture sometime in the distant past. Vai legend[12] itself believes that several centuries ago an adventurous faction of their people (Mandingos) were enticed to migrate from their Sahel[13] homeland in search of the gold which was said to be available in abundance on the West African littoral. There is ample historical evidence to confirm that the Mandingo exodus was in full swing in the twelfth century A.D., and that the West African gold fields were the El Dorado which the emigrants sought. It is also quite certain that there are ethnolinguistic affinities between the Vai and the original Mandingo peoples. However, present diversities in vocabulary and structure of language are so vast that the transformation must have taken several centuries. Mande settlement in Vai country may have ended by the middle of the seventeenth century.[14] But evidence as to when exactly the syllabary came into being is scanty, tenuous, and controversial.[15]

The first philologist to take an academic interest in the Vai script was the Reverend S. W. Koelle, a German missionary who in the 1830's was attached to Fourah Bay College, Sierra Leone, on research work in African languages. In his account of an expedition which he made into Vai country, Koelle gave all credit for the invention to its first and only claimant, a forty-year old illiterate called Momoru Daulu Bukara (Momolu Duwalu Bukele).[16]

According to this testimony, a venerable old man had appeared to Bukele in a vision fifteen years before Koelle's arrival and had shown him the mysteries of recording thought in symbolic language. With the help of some friends and the patronage of chief Goturu (also called Fa Toro),

Bukele was able to design and refine his syllabary to such a state of perfection that it could be used in translating Psalm 23, 'The Lord is my Shepherd', and other documents! It is a curious fact that most other 'inventors' of the alphabet in West Africa were evasive or reticent about their inspiration, or else said that they had been inspired by a dream or vision.

If the historical evolution of writing in other parts of the world is anything to go by, then it seems more likely that the Vai syllabary must have evolved from pictograms and ideograms. Massaquoi says that before 1840 'there were a few rude signs which did not express, but merely suggest ideas'. Therefore the best that Bukele could have done was to give phonetic values to an existing ideogram probably of great antiquity.

Delafosse casts further doubts on the credibility of both Koelle and Bukele by denying that the former ever set foot in Bandakoro, capital of Vai country.[17] In further attempts made to determine the age of the Vai syllabary and probably to deny its autochthonous origins, several writers have been convinced that the characters were plagiarized from other, older alphabets, and have taken great pains to prove that the exception makes the rule. Delafosse for example claims to have recognized the following Greek and Roman letters – B, E, H, I, S, T, and the Arabic numerals 5, 6, 8, among others.[18] However, he noticed that the phonetic values of the corresponding Vai syllables bear little resemblance to the 'originals'.[19] Klingenheben, on the other hand, has shown by comparative analysis that there is not the remotest connection between the Vai on the one hand and the Greek or Roman on the other.

Steinthal, who supposedly had treated the whole investigation in the most scientific manner, maintained that 'it would hardly be due to chance that the syllable *be* is like the Latin P, and *gba* like B'. But on the other hand Steinthal concedes a number of irreconcilables, e.g. that 'N' = *po*, H = *re*, E = *to*, 8 = *so*, 5 = *fa*, and K = *mbe*'. Finally he contradicts his basic theory by admitting that the *majority* of the Vai signs consist of arbitrary figures – rectangles, circles, etc.[20]

Writing from a time perspective when a more detached view of the whole mystery would have been better, Sir Harry Johnston,[21] then Governor of Sierra Leone, should perhaps have been more objective in his judgment. But he also was quite certain that there were foreign influences on the Vai, although most of the characters were of indeterminate origin. The figures 2 and 3, he says, were definitely derived from the Arabic. On the further evidence that Greek, Carthaginian, and Phoenician traders had sailed round to the West Coast of Africa (several centuries before), Sir Harry concludes that the Vai syllabary is most likely an adulteration of these older scripts. Indeed there is corroborative evidence that the ancients sailed round the West Coast,[22] but none to indicate literary contact with the inhabitants. As regards the possibility that the script already existed on the coast before the Vai came down, none of the available sources show any traces of writing among those they displaced on the coast.[23]

Speaking in more realistic terms, Diringer says that most people developed their civilization, including writing, more or less independently. That being the case, there is no reason why the Vai also should not have designed the alphabet without foreign aid. Surely, it would have saved them a great deal of trouble to adopt these other alphabets in their entirety than to copy the few freaks which Steinthal and Delafosse have so ingeniously contrived to decipher.

A more objective assessment of the originality of the Vai script would consider the cultural forces which could have caused invention of an indigenous script. First, as the Vai were ethnically different from the original settlers, they naturally were anxious to protect their identity. One way of doing this and of consolidating their own culture was to invent a system of communication that was unique to themselves and excluded all others. That the Vai held on to their script long after the Roman alphabet had been established would help support this view. Sir Harry Johnston's own hypothesis[24] for this behaviour is further evidence of Vai desire for cultural exclusiveness. He saw the syllabary as a symbol of protest against Christian infiltration, added to the 'desire to carry on correspondence not readily deciphered by the American Negroes who rule their country'. Sir Harry suggested that the Liberian Government should break such recalcitrant behaviour by enforcing the Roman alphabet on the Vai through secular and Christian education. This suggestion was apparently not heeded for a long time. However, it was the first example of various overt attempts made to suppress dissemination of the indigenous alphabets.

Dalby holds the view that the reason why the Vai and other West African scripts were retained after the introduction of the Roman and Arabic scripts was born of the desire to compete with the civilizations implicit in these older alphabets.[25] All the inventors were men of intellect and imagination, well aware of the gulf which existed between their peoples and foreigners, especially Europeans, and thought that this was primarily due to the latters' genius for literate communication. All lived in areas where Christian missions were active; they were aware that the esoteric spiritual associations of the written word, as symbolised by the Bible, not to speak of the Koran, were a means of enforcing authority over their subject, ignorant, tribal peoples. For the moment, the Vai alphabet would be the most effective means of counteracting such influences, hence the stubborn tenacity with which they preserved their script in spite of its relative inflexibility.

To conclude the Vai controversy, it would seem that the resemblance between their syllabary and the older scripts was accidental rather than contrived. All inventors of writing are limited to a number of strokes and flourishes. Within these limits characters are likely to be similar if the objects described (e.g. water in the case of pictographs) and to a lesser extent the ideas (ideographs) or sounds represented are also identical. The idea of 'water' has been represented in the same, wavy lines by different ideographs in different parts of the world. Where writing materials are the same, calligraphers produce symbols which bear a strong resemblance to each other although they may have different symbolic and sound qualities.

In terms of primogeniture, the Vai script deserves special merit, but it was not unique in West Africa. Some of the alphabets which were discovered afterwards were more ingeniously designed and proved more versatile than Vai in the writing of books. The Nsibidi and Bamoun (Bamun) are briefly described in the following pages mainly to show contrasts in their bookish promise. These scripts were invented in the Eastern extremities of West Africa; it is therefore difficult to conceive of any means by which their respective inventors could have known of the Liberia-Sierra Leone cluster of syllabaries. This means that each type was an independent invention.

THE NSIBIDI IDEOGRAPH

The Nsibidi ideograph was not known to the outside world until 1904 when T. D. Maxwell, then District Commissioner for Calabar in the Eastern Province of Nigeria, suddenly came upon it. A year later, and quite independently of Maxwell, the Rev. J. K. McGregor of the Church Missionary Society also came to know of its existence.[26]

The writing apparently was the sole property of the Nsibidi Secret Club until much later when it had become more stylised and had been adopted for purposes other than secret communication. These secret societies were quite prevalent in West Africa, and come into existence before the seventeenth century. Each society designed its own symbolic means of communication; Butt-Thompson gives evidence of the prevalence of graphic symbols for secret communication prior to the dates at which the West African scripts are said to have been invented.[27]

As to the exact origin of the Nsibidi script, the Club itself says that it was adopted from the Uyanga Ibos. The Ibos disclaim any knowledge of its source, except that it is of great antiquity. To add to all this obscurity, the Ekoi of the Efik tribe say that it was their forefathers who developed it from symbols which they had learned from the *idiok*, a specie, of the baboon/monkey family.

Talbot and other contemporary researchers claim to have detected certain resemblances between Nsibidi and the earliest Egyptian hieroglyphics.[28] McGregor denies this on the grounds that by 4000 B.C., hieroglyphics had already begun to develop hieratic and demotic versions. In other words, if Nsibidi was derived from hieroglyphics then it must be over 4000 years old, which is unlikely. To prove his theory, Talbot delved into the ethno-history of the Ekoi, and concluded that they must have originated from the lower end of the Nile, judging not only from their mixed Hamitic and Negroid features,[29] but also from archaeological evidence. He refers to Keith's excavations in Nigeria and the Congo where there are 'some very old, roughly carved (wooden) figures curiously like some ancient Egyptian burial masks discovered by Dr. Hugh Baker in the sands of the Egyptian oasis of Kharga'.[30] Whatever the truth of the matter, the fact remains that Nsibidi, unlike Vai and hieroglyphics, never reached the syllabary stage, nor was it used for recording anything elaborate.

THE BAMOUN ALPHABET

Among West African alphabets that can be dated with any accuracy is that which was designed by Njoya, Sultan of the Bamoun tribe of the Cameroons. The invention was discovered by yet another missionary, the Reverend Goehring, during the time of German occupation of the Cameroons. Like Koelle, Goehring attributes the invention to the genius of one man only, who by a process of 'diffusion' had borrowed, not the example, but the idea of writing from other cultures.[31]

Curiously enough, Njoya, like Bukara claimed to have got his inspiration from a dream. He, too, was assisted by 'courtiers' who eventually were to become a high-powered, governing bureaucracy among their people. Together, they designed about 100 symbols representing material and abstract ideas in current circulation. From 1907 onwards the symbols were systematically altered from ideographs, to phonographs, and finally to a neoalphabet. By the time Njoya died in 1932, the script had been used for a large variety of purposes, although most of the actual writing was done in Njoya's capital at Foumban by palace officials.

It is a matter for some speculation why, despite Germany's occupation of the whole of the Cameroons for the previous several decades, and despite the fact that some of Njoya's subjects could read and write Arabic, he still found it necessary to invent his own alphabet. Such speculations may be of academic interest generally, but they are of direct relevance to us because it was the Bamoun alphabet in particular which came nearest to book production and library formation in West Africa.

By 1899 German colonial administration was firmly established in most parts of the Cameroons. Bamoun territory however was among the few districts which were not much affected by the German presence. For one thing Bamoun was situated behind a curtain of mountains away from the Colonial administrative capital at Bamenda, and so remained effectively insulated from political interference and the literate culture of the Germans.

Apparently Njoya had posted a consul at Bamenda quite early in the colonial era; this made it possible for him to govern his territory free from direct German control. The long and short of these arrangements was that Bamoun never had its full share of the evils, or benefits, of Western literate culture.

As regards other influences, although many Bamouns could read and write Arabic by 1907, Arabic literature, as is the case in most Islamic communities, appeals only to a small fraction of the population. Its highly esoteric structure and enormous vocabulary makes it suitable only for religious and literary texts, but not for commercial or general purposes. Consequently the majority of the people were illiterate in Arabic.

It is reasonable then to expect that, having thus been denied both Western and Eastern literacy, an enlightened monarch would wish to find a substitute for his people. Njoya seems to have thought along these lines. From all accounts he occupied a position that was unique among West African rulers; he assumed the uncommon role of priest-king and sought to establish a paternalist kind of government. With respect to his literary activities, his position may be compared to that of the Assyrian monarchy who, by documenting the traditions of their people, tried to achieve stability and continuity in the society.[32]

Anxious to preserve the religious customs of his people, and yet unable to discard altogether their newly acquired Islamic and Christian faiths, Njoya proceeded to propound a strange amalgam of Moslem, Christian and 'pagan' philosophy of life and nature. This and other more mundane matters were carefully written down in his new alphabet. He directed that schools be established to teach both the alphabet and the subject matter of his books so that their contents may be the better assimilated and more widely disseminated.

PROTOLITERACY IN WEST AFRICA

The Chadwicks are of the opinion that as soon as a new alphabet had reached the utilitarian stage it was first of all employed in recording the legal and administrative documents of the land.[33] The Bamoun and Ekoi people seem to have conformed with this general rule.

Njoya established chanceries and appointed officials with special responsibility for maintaining public records on administrative, commercial, diplomatic, and judicial matters. The more important of these documents were deposited in his palace archives. Crawford discovered hundreds of legal decisions and reports of meetings carefully preserved in embroidered skin bags and hung on walls in Njoya's palace.

Thus, following an ancient tradition first introduced by the Assyrian monarchy, notably Hammurabi (c.1950 B.C.), both Njoya and Goturu of the Vai codified their edicts. Goturu, according to Koelle,[34] further recorded the oral history of his people and a chronology of past rulers. By 1899, according to Dalby,[35] most Vai adults could read books written in the syllabary, for example, the *Book of Rora*, by Kali Bara, available in the British Museum, the Royal Commonwealth Society Library, London, and the School of Oriental and African Studies, University of London.

Njoya also is said to have presented copies of his reminiscences and the folklore of his people to the national museums of France; they survive as living testimonies to the genius of a 'noble savage'.

Both scripts were used also for aphoristic texts, traditional tales, and translations from the Bible and Koran. However, the most common use was for letter writing. The Vai script appears to have been even more elastic than the Bamoun with regard to its allusive use of language, imagery, and vocabulary. Massaquoi translated Homer's *Iliad* and extracts from the Koran into Vai with apparent ease.[36] He also issued grammatical works including a 'phonetic chart' published by the Board of Missions of the Protestant Episcopal Church in their journal *Missionary Herald.* This chart became the standard text for teaching throughout the Vai country from 1899 onwards. It is therefore not quite correct for Westermann, writing as recently as 1952, to say that the Vai had 'hardly been used for literary or educational purposes'.[37]

The Nsibidi ideograph was the least developed of the scripts. Nevertheless, McGregor discovered an advanced form which had been used to record the proceedings of a court hearing in a town on the Emon Creek, near Calabar. Every detail is ingeniously recorded by means of a few strokes of the pen: the dilemma of the trial judge and, more important, the judgment of the court are ideographically and imaginatively described.

It appears that the scripts also had a potential for commercial and allied purposes. In Liberia during the 1930's, Loma foremen of the American Firestone rubber plantations used Vai to register names of plantation workers,[38] and at least one person is known to have kept a diary and financial records of his personal business transactions. We should recall that the first domestic libraries unearthed in ancient Egypt consisted of similar commercial records, albeit inscribed on clay tablets.

Every attempt was made by the originators of these scripts to popularise their invention. Koelle tells us that within a comparatively short space of time all adults in Bandakoro could read and write Vai.[39] It has also been estimated that by 1907, 600 persons in the Calabar Province were literate in Nsibidi. Njoya, as already said, established schools to teach the Bamoun alphabet. Since the literates so produced formed only a tiny minority of the population, the indigenous alphabets could not have made any significant change in the traditional mode of communication of West African society, except as an instrument of administrative and religious control by the minority over the majority. This, however, is characteristic all over the world during the early years of the spread of indigenous literacy. More is the pity, then, that the West African scripts were not given the chance to survive and develop into a medium for book production, education, and library formation. The following paragraphs enquire into the endemic and alien causes of the early demise of the black art in West Africa.

WHY THE WEST AFRICAN ALPHABETS DID NOT SURVIVE

Proportionate blame should be given to natural causes, human factors, and social change in ascending order of culpability.

NATURAL CAUSES

Of the natural causes, the most destructive was undoubtedly the tropical climate. The palm fronds upon which Nsibidi characters were inscribed[40] would have had a short span of life in the hot and humid climate of Eastern Nigeria. Without proper precautions being taken for their preservation hardly any vegetable writing materials can survive for more than four or five decades; neither Talbot nor McGregor could find any Nsibidi of more than sixty years of age. The Vai took to paper, probably after a long period of experimentation with raw vegetable substances. But even with paper, the profusion of predatory insects, in particular termites, would have taken their toll on what the climate had left.

Dalby's findings confirm these observations. Only three years after the death of Kisimi, inventor of the Mende script of Sierra Leone, no more than fifteen fragments of a collection which was probably quite voluminous could be unearthed; the extant paper fragments had been badly decayed by damp and damaged by cockroaches. In appearance they 'resembled ancient crumbling papyri rather than records of modern script'.[41] Papyrus, as is well known, also had a vegetable base, but the Egyptians had taken care to preserve their documents against the vicissitudes of nature. Similarly Chinese handmade paper, manufactured several centuries ago, has survived to this day, partly owing to a favourable climatic environment and to the use of chemical-free raw materials.

In contrast, the 'ink-leaves' from which the Vai are said to have extracted ink for writing could well have contained natural chemicals which accelerated deterioration of paper, and made permanent legibility most improbable.

The combined effect of the above natural causes has destroyed not only the literature, but also evidence as to the exact time when the older scripts were invented and first used for communication. Thus the three basic elements making for book production on a large scale, namely, preservation, accumulation, and dissemination were lacking. The earliest known original manuscript, according to Dalby, is that held by the

British Museum's Department of Printed Books; it is a fragment of Vai documentation dating to the middle of the nineteenth century. But in view of Dalby's own observations on the state of Kisimi's archives, we must expect the probability of other, older, but now extinct, documents.

With the exception of Njoya's chanceries where the records were stored in skin bags, all other local 'repositories' were exposed to the destructive effects of the elements. Njoya's storing of records in skin bags made him come nearest to founding a book-conscious society.

HUMAN FACTORS

Natural causes and acts of negligence apart, one other important reason why the life expectation of written documents was so short was the fact that there was no strong incentive to preserve them.

It is characteristic of oral societies, because of their total reliance on memory for recall of social and historical events, to regard written documents as redundant and cumbersome commodities to be discarded as soon as they had served their immediate purpose. The rationale for this behaviour, which is to be found also in literate societies, is that where there is no prospect of using particular documents for reference it is pointless to conserve them.

As was the case with most of the tribes concerned, there was constant fear of their writings falling into alien hands, especially those of foreign missionaries and administrators. The use of these scripts as secret media of communication precluded their dissemination even among the indigenous population. Most literature was composed in 'revealed language'; the bulk of Nsibidi documents consisted of proscribed material meant for the eyes of an inner circle of initiates of the Nsibidi cult and no others.[42] Members were in the habit of using pantomimic codes incomprehensible to the outsider. Although a standard vocabulary might be used among secret societies in the same area, their meaning was peculiar to each sect. The more abstruse words were not known to the neophytes because younger members were sometimes taught by signs and gesture mostly and only occasionally by writing and reading.

Writing was often impressionistic, in the sense that there was no fixed order of verbal succession. Besides, a word may be written vertically, horizontally, or obliquely, depending on the style of the calligrapher and probably the writing instruments he employed. The Sumerian cuneiform also suffered from this peculiarity.

To crown all these difficulties, there were far too many characters to be memorised by learners. Dayrell collected no less than 363 Nsibidi signs; Koelle identified 215 Vai syllabaries, and Njoya could not go beneath 350 signs.[43] All things being normal, the sheer weight of numbers alone would have suppressed growth of literacy, although the Chinese seem to have overcome the constraints of their enormous logogram of 50,000 characters!

It should be said, in passing on to other causes of failure, that a serious hindrance to diffusion of the alphabet was the difficulty of cultural communication across tribal boundaries. Neighbouring tribes were suspicious of, and often hostile to, each other, and therefore had little social or cultural intercourse. The dense tropical forests surrounding tribal units also made communication extremely tedious. Until a money economy was introduced, each tribe was economically self-sufficient. Without the need to exchange goods there was no opportunity to exchange ideas. Only the Vai were an exception to this rule. Between 1700 and 1830 they were undergoing a phase of mental activity and acquiring a considerable amount of wealth from trading with the Spanish slave raiders.[44] As middlemen, they themselves were left in comparative peace to develop their culture. The effect of slavery on other tribes was most regressive. It disrupted cultural development and so demoralized the people that they felt no urge to create anything of lasting value. Nor is there a strong motive for intellectual development in a state of human and economic exploitation. On the other hand it has been shown in other societies that a vigorous peaceful commercial existence is among the greatest stimulants for literary and intellectual development. This was absent in West Africa during the period under review.

THE COLONIAL FACTOR

More recent events in the colonial history of the territory have also taken their toll on cultural development. Colonial policy contrived to subdue native institutions. In the cultural context the *mission civilisatrice* philosophy interpreted African traditional institutions, and their artifacts of culture as barbaric, and therefore to be destroyed, suppressed, or adapted. It is revealing that although the first persons to discover the indigenous alphabets were mostly administrators (Talbot, Migeod, Maxwell, Dayrell, and Delafosse), they made no attempt to revive them. Sir Harry Johnston, who, as Governor of Sierra Leone, was in a position of influence enough to encourage development of Vai, sought to check its popularisation.[45] The main reason, of course, was that the Western alphabet was already firmly entrenched, but an additional factor was the supercilious attitude which the colonial administrators adopted to every artifact of 'primitive' culture.

Milburn also was Director of Education in Sierra Leone at the most critical stage in the development of local scripts; he thus had the unique opportunity of adopting either the Vai, based on Koelle's *Grammar*, for the mass literacy campaign which he introduced, or, alternatively the Mende script invented by a native Sierra Leonean. Instead, Milburn uncharitably reminded Kisimi that even he, the inventor, had not succeeded in teaching his own children to write his alphabet intelligibly, how much less outsiders.[46] This argument was patently illogical. Apart from a few inconsistencies, Milburn continued, the Roman alphabet was by far superior to the Mende script.

Following this tradition of denigration, native-born administrators in more recent times have refused to consider their own indigenous scripts for modern usage. Take, for example, the Dita alphabet which was developed between 1958 and 1966 by Dembele, a native of Mali and a graduate of Koranic schools with some competence in French. Apparently he tried to get Mali officials to adopt his script for vernacular literature instruction, but was rebuffed.[47] The officials concerned would much prefer the Roman script. He was pointedly told in 1965 to desist from further attempts to popularise his alphabet. Apart from having written in his own Bambara language, Dembele transcribed other languages into his script; if this was true, and given the possibility that the script could be developed, it would have been ideal for literacy programmes in other Mali languages. Doob has shown how use of the Roman alphabet has led to curious verbal gymnastics among the Bambara,[48] which should lead one to suggest that an indigenous medium may have had greater advantages in mass literacy campaigns.

It is not sufficient to argue, as most other administrators must have done, that the scripts had only reached their ideographic or syllabic forms and were therefore unsuitable for most modern purposes. At the time when the Phoenician alphabet was adopted for popular use, it had itself only reached the syllabic stage. All that needed to be done was to extend its vocabulary in a technical direction by word borrowing, coining of new words, and giving new meanings to old words. This is of course easier said than done, but all the same worthy of consideration in principle. Admittedly the angular form of the scripts would have presented problems in cursive writing and printing type design, far greater than problems presented by Roman and Greek alphabets. For example, the tedious *serie continua* style in which Vai and Bamoun were written would have made them much too rigid for modern typography, although the addition of a few serifs could have made considerable difference. If the Greek manuscript of the New Testament was written in a *serie continua* style similar to the Vai script, so also could the traditional religion of West Africa. Egypt, China, and Japan have overcome the strictures of their own national alphabets by selective publishing. Most technical works are printed in the Roman alphabet but the humanities are printed in Arabic or logographs, as the case may be. The scripts' mechanical defects were therefore not sufficient excuse for their neglect.

Among those who took the keenest interest in the alphabets were the missionaries Koelle and Goehring. In the initial stages some missions appeared anxious to utilise the new invention for mass book production. The preface to Koelle's *Narrative*, written by the head of the Church Missionary Society in London, specifically expressed the hope that the Vai alphabet would become the main vehicle for spreading the Gospel. Encouraged by this prospect, Koelle in due course produced a grammar of the Vai language in 1853.

It is regrettable that this initial enthusiasm was not carried forward. The missionaries soon found to their cost that literal translation of certain passages from the English Bible into the vernacular often resulted in ridiculous distortions of meaning. Even in their vernacular versions certain passages in the Bible completely lost their meaning when read with the wrong inflexion. This is because the Roman alphabet's tone system is not wholly suited to the highly tonal structure of the *Kwa* West African languages. Certainly these mistakes could have been avoided if the correct syllabaries had been used in translating the scriptures.

Lastly, the alphabets failed to develop because the function of communication was not complex enough to necessitate their development into more expansive forms.

NOTES

1. C. F. Voegelin and F. M. Voegelin, *Typological Classification of Systems with Included and Self-Sufficient Alphabets* (= *Anthropological Linguistics* 3) (1961).

Cited from J. Goody and I. Watt, *Literacy in Traditional Societies* (C.U.P., 1968), 34.

2. J. Goody and I. Watt, *Literacy in Traditional Societies*, 35.
3. D. Diringer, *The Alphabet, A Key to the History of Mankind*, 2nd ed. (London: Hutchinsons, 1953), 607.
4. J. Goody and I. Watt, *Literacy in Traditional Societies*, 33-34.
5. H. M. Chadwick and N. K. Chadwick, *The Growth of Literature* 3 (C.U.P., 1968), 697.
6. F. E. Forbes, *Despatch Communicating the Discovery of a Native Written Character at Bohmar on the West Coast of Africa, Near Liberia, Accompanied by a Vocabulary of the Vahie, or Vai Language* (London: E. Norris, 1849). It should be noted that the discovery of the Vai alphabet is also credited to two American missionaries, J. L. Wilson and S. R. Wijnkoop (1834), of the American Board of Foreign Missions.
7. J. Garstang, *Meroe: The City of the Ethiopians* (O.U.P., 1911).
8. Th. Monod, 'Un nouvel alphabet quest-africain', *Bull. de l'I.F.A.N.*, Ser. B., 20.
9. D. Dalby, 'The Indigenous Scripts of West Africa and Surinam: their Inspiration and Design', *African Language Studies* 9 (1968).
10. D. Dalby, 'The Indigenous Scripts . . .'; see also D. Dalby, 'A Survey of the Indigenous Scripts of Liberia and Sierra Leone: Vai, Mende, Loma, Kpelle, and Bassa', *African Language Studies* 8 (1967); and 'Further Indigenous Scripts of West Africa: Manding, Wolof and Fula Alphabets and Yoruba "Holy" Writing', *African Language Studies* 10 (1969).
11. The Vai syllabary is treated in more detail than the rest because of its primacy in West Africa and because it shows a pattern of development that could be applied to the other scripts.
12. M. Massaquoi: 'The Vai People and their Syllabic Writing', *Journal of African Society* 10 (1911). The author claims direct descent from the original settlers.
13. Sahel refers to the southern fringe of the Sahara and includes much of the Republic of Mali. The Mandingo are also known as Mande or Malinke.
14. For evidence of their ethnic, linguistic, agricultural, and historical origins, see G. P. Murdock, *Africa, Its People and Their Culture History* (New York: McGraw-Hill, 1959), 261; D. Westermann and M. A. Bryan, *Languages of West Africa* (London, O.U.P. for Int. Afr. Inst., 1952), 35; J. F. A. Ajayi and I. Espie (eds.), *A Thousand Years of West African History* (Ibadan, U.P.: Nelson, 1965), 153 ff.
15. D. Dalby, 'A Survey of the Indigenous Scripts . . .', fixes the date of invention at 1833; M. Delafosse, 'Les Vai, leur langue et leur système d'ecriture', *L'Anthropologie* 10 (1899), 129-151, 294-314, fixes the date at the sixteenth or seventeenth century. The Oberi Okaime script of eastern Nigeria is allegedly much older, being 'derived directly from the Minoan Linear'. See Kathleen Hau, 'The Ancient Writing of Southern Nigeria', *Bull. de l'I.F.A.N.* 29:1-2 (1967), 150-191.
16. S. W. Koelle, *Narrative of an Expedition into the Vy Country of West Africa, and the Discovery of a System of Syllabic Writing Recently Invented by the Natives of the Vy Tribe* (London: Seeley, 1849), 30.
17. A. I. Klingenheben, 'The Vai Script', *Africa* 6: 2 (1933), 158-171.
18. M. Delafosse: 'Les Vai . . .', 129-151, 294-314. He concludes his hypothesis of origin as follows: 'L'alphabet Vai a dû etre, inventé au debut du XVIe siècle au

moment de la découverte de L'Amerique provoquait les premiéres expéditions des marchands d'esclaves à la côte d'Afrique', cited from Klingenheben, 'The Vai Script', 306.

19. It is, of course, conceivable, if there is any borrowing at all, that an illiterate people would copy signs arbitrarily and attach their own phonetic-symbolic values to them.
20. Klingenheben, 'The Vai Script', 160.
21. Sir H. Johnston, *Liberia* (London 1911), 114 ff.
22. A. A. Kwapong, 'Africa antiqua', *Trans. Gold Coast and Togoland Historical Society* 2: 1 (1956), 1-11. The author is inclined to the 'by no means novel conclusion that Hanno came as far down as Sierra Leone, and most probably Liberia also.'
23. But Johnston reports Captain d'Ollone, in his *De la cote d'Ivoire*, as saying that there were Greek and Roman characters on the walls of huts in Palube country, 150 miles from the coast. Even if this were so, it is highly improbable that the Vai were exposed to these alphabets to the extent that they would adopt them as models.
24. Johnston, *Liberia*, 115.
25. D. Dalby, 'The Indigenous Scripts . . .'.
26. J. K. McGregor, 'Some Notes on Nsibidi', *Jnl. Roy. Anth. Inst.* 39 (1909), 209-219.
27. F. W. Butt-Thompson, *West-African Secret Societies, Their Organization, Officials and Teaching* (London: Witherby, 1929), 18 ff.
28. P. A. Talbot, *In the Shadow of the Bush* (London: Heinemann, 1912), 217.
29. See plate opposite p. 318 in Talbot, *In the Shadow of the Bush*, which shows that Ekoi facial features are neither Negroid nor Hamitic, but bear some resemblance to both.
30. Talbot, *In the Shadow of the Bush*, 217.
31. D. Diringer, *The Alphabet* . . ., 151.
32. E. D. Johnson, *A History of Libraries in the Western World* (Scarecrow, N.Y. 1965), 418.
33. Chadwick and Chadwick, *The Growth of Literature* 3.
34. Koelle, *Narrative of an Expedition* . . ., 14-30.
35. Dalby, 'A Survey of the Indigenous Scripts . . .'.
36. Massaquoi, 'The Vai People . . .'.
37. Westermann and Bryan, *Languages of West Africa*, 35. The University of Liberia's Institute of African Studies is currently working on the standardization of Vai under Prof. Fahnbulleh-Massaquoi, daughter of M. Massaquoi.
38. Dalby, 'A Survey of the Indigenous Scripts . . .'.
39. Koelle, *Narrative of an Expedition* . . ., 25. Teaching was concentrated at Dsondy and Bandakoro, both of which were attacked and burned by a neighbouring tribe. Consequently, all the 'book men' were scattered, which event aided the diffusion of the script.
40. 'For a long time messages have been sent in Nsibidi script, cut or painted on split palm stems' (see Talbot, *In the Shadow of the Bush*, 309).
41. Dalby, 'The Indigenous Scripts . . .'.
42. E. Dayrell, 'Further Notes on the Nsibidi Signs with their Meanings from the Ikom District, S. Nigeria', *Jnl. Roy. Anth. Inst.* 41 (1911), 521-540. The story is

recounted of a man who refused a large sum of money offered as tuition fee by Maxwell on the grounds that if he taught the D.C. 'he would know all the Egbo signs and the secrets of the animals'.

43. According to Dalby's estimation, Bamun was finally reduced to eighty signs; Mende had 195, Loma 185, Kpelle eighty-eight and Bete 401 characters.
44. F. E. Migoed, 'The Syllabic Writing of the Vai People', *Jnl. African Society* (*African Affairs*) 9 (1909), 46-58.
45. T he Vai script was also used in neighbouring Sierra Leone.
46. S. Milburn, 'Kisimi Kamara and the Mende Script', *Sierra Leone Language Review* 3 (1964), 20-23.
47. Dalby, 'Further Indigenous Scripts . . .'.
48. L. Doob, *Communication in Africa, A Search for Boundaries* (Yale University Press, 1961).

Section Two

The Creation of Writing Systems

KEITH H. BASSO AND NED ANDERSON

A Western Apache Writing System: The Symbols of Silas John*

In a lengthy essay published in 1886, Garrick Mallery, a retired military officer employed as anthropologist by the Bureau of American Ethnology, invited explorers, missionaries, and ethnographers to provide him with information pertaining to systems of graphic communication then in use among the Indian tribes of North America. Expressing his conviction that these '. . . primitive forms of writing provide direct and significant evidence upon the evolution of an important aspect of human culture', Mallery also warned that they were rapidly disappearing, and that unless those in existence were studied immediately the opportunity would be lost forever.[1] Unfortunately for anthropology, Mallery's invitation went largely unheeded and his prophesy came true. In the closing decades of the nineteenth century, a number of native graphic systems went out of existence and a fledgling social science, occupied with more urgent concerns, scarcely took note of their passing.

The lack of enthusiasm that greeted Mallery's early call for research set a precedent which was destined to continue, for to this day the ethnographic study of so-called 'primitive' writing systems – including those stimulated by contact with Europeans – has failed to engage the sustained interest of either linguists or cultural anthropologists. The result, I. J. Gelb has observed, is that 'Some of these writings are known very inadequately, others are known only from hearsay and still others must exist in obscure corners of the globe as yet unnoticed by scholars.'[2]

Under these circumstances, it is with marked enthusiasm that we greet the opportunity to report upon a previously undescribed writing system which is in active use today among Western Apache Indians living on the Fort

* From *Science* 180 (June 8, 1973), 1013-1022. Reprinted with permission.

Apache and San Carlos Reservations in east-central Arizona. This system has persisted essentially unchanged since its invention in 1904 by Silas John Edwards, a preeminent Western Apache shaman who was also the founder and leader of a nativistic religious movement which established itself on both Western Apache reservations in the early 1920's and subsequently spread to the Mescalero Apache in New Mexico.[3]

Mr. Edwards is ninety-one years old, almost blind, but still very much alive. Known to Apaches and Anglo-Americans alike simply as Silas John, he created a writing system so that an extensive set of prayers expressing the ideological core of his religion could be recorded in permanent form and disseminated among his followers. Although the content of these prayers is deeply influenced by Christian symbolism, a result of Silas John's early association with Lutheran missionaries on the Fort Apache Reservation, the written script was entirely his own invention, initially conceived in a 'dream from God' and later developed without assistance from Anglo-Americans or Apaches. An ability to read and write English, acquired by Silas John as a young man, undoubtedly accounts for his exposure to the idea of writing. However, it does not account for the graphic form of his script or its underlying structural principles, which depart radically from those of the English alphabet. Like the Cherokee syllabary invented by Sequoyah around 1820, the writing system of Silas John represents a classic case of stimulus diffusion that resulted in the creation of a totally unique cultural form.[4] As such, we believe, it ranks among the significant intellectual achievements by an American Indian during the twentieth century.

METHODOLOGICAL PROBLEMS

Since Garrick Mallery's day and before, American Indian writing systems have been described with a set of time-honored concepts that were originally devised by European epigraphers to classify distinct types of graphic symbols and, by extension, to classify whole systems.[5] For example, if all the symbols in a particular system were identified as pictographs the system itself was classified 'pictographic'; on the other hand, if stylized ideographs existed side by side with pictographs the system was termed 'pictographic-ideographic'. In this way, different systems were compared on the basis of what types of symbols composed them and, in conjunction with historical data, arranged sequentially in order of their presumed chronological appearance.

The typologies constructed for these purposes, almost all of which classify graphs according to attributes of external form, are strictly etic in character, the products of a long tradition of Western scholarship that often lacked access to native informants and was chiefly concerned with the formulation of broad-scale comparative strategies.[6] Although no one would dispute the importance of such strategies nor deny the fact that adequate typologies are basic to their development, it is essential to point out that serious problems may arise when etic concepts are applied a priori to the description of individual writing systems. Unless it is first established that the distinctions and contrasts imposed by these concepts coincide with those considered meaningful by users of the system, the resulting description is almost certain to suffer from bias and distortion.[7] In the great majority of American Indian studies no such evidence is adduced.

The fact that the symbols in a writing system may be submitted to classification by some existing etic scheme should not be taken to mean that the classification is automatically, or even necessarily, relevant to an understanding of how the system works. It would be a simple task, for example, to classify every symbol in the Silas John script according to whether it is pictographic or ideographic. Yet, as we shall see, this distinction has no significance for the Western Apache, who classify these symbols on the basis of different criteria. An account of the Silas John script that ignored these native – or emic – distinctions, and proceeded instead in terms of the pictographic/ideographic contrast, would fail to reveal the basic principles that impart structure to the system as a whole. Simultaneously, and equally damaging, such an account would suggest that the system's operation was predicated on rules which, in fact, are irrelevant to it and altogether absent from Western Apache culture.

Methodological problems of this kind cannot be dismissed as inconsequential, nor can they be ignored on the supposition that their occurrence has been infrequent. To the contrary, a recent survey of the literature on American Indian graphic systems reveals the use of unverified etic concepts to be so pervasive that in all but a few cases it is impossible to determine the kinds of conceptual skills that were actually required to produce and interpret intelligible written messages.[8]

The adequacy of an ethnographic description of a writing system should be judged by its ability to permit someone who is unfamiliar with the system – but who has a knowledge of the language on which it is based –

to read and write. It should provide him, in other words, with an explicit formulation of the knowledge necessary to become literate. Among other things, this requires that the basic units in the system be identified and defined in accordance with criteria that persons already literate recognize as valid, necessary, and appropriate. If these criteria are not disclosed, or if they are arbitrarily replaced with criteria derived from the investigator's own culture, the knowledge necessary to use the system correctly will remain hidden.

Ward Goodenough[9] has observed that an adequate etic typology must be sufficiently sensitive '. . . to describe all the emic distinctions people actually make in all the world's cultures in relation to the subject matter for which the etic concepts are designed'. This requirement applies as much to typologies of writing as it does to those for any other cultural phenomena. Goodenough also emphasizes that the emic and etic enterprises are not mutually exclusive, but complementary and logically interrelated. Emic concepts provide us with what we need to know to construct valid etic concepts, while the latter, besides determining the form and content of comparative propositions, assist in the discovery and description of the former.

Studies of American Indian writing systems contain so few emic analyses that the basic materials needed to construct adequate etic typologies are all but absent. Consequently, the few etic concepts that have been proposed are open to serious question. On the one hand, it has not been shown that these categories describe '. . . all the emic distinctions people actually make . . .'; on the other, they are so all-encompassing that their utility for comparative purposes is seriously impaired.[10] Obviously, these difficulties cannot be overcome through the creation of more arbitrary categories. The surest solution lies in the continued investigation of individual writing systems which, if properly described, will contribute to an inventory of demonstrably relevant emic distinctions and thus assure that subsequent etic typologies have a more secure grounding in cultural fact. Our account of the Silas John writing system is intended as a contribution in this direction.

DEVELOPMENT OF THE WRITING SYSTEM

In 1904, when Silas John Edwards was twenty-one years old and living in the community of East Fork on the Fort Apache Indian Reservation, he experienced a vision in which he was presented with a set of sixty-two prayers and an accompanying set of graphic symbols with which to write them. Silas John recalls his vision as follows:

> There were sixty-two prayers. They came to me in rays from above. At the same time I was instructed. He [God] was advising me and telling me what to do, at the same time teaching me chants. They were presented to me – one by one. All of these and the writing were given to me at one time in one dream . . .
> God made it [the writing], but it came down to our earth. I liken this to what has happened in the religions we have now. In the center of the earth, when it first began, when the earth was first made, there was absolutely nothing on this world. There was no written language. So it was in 1904 that I became aware of the writing; it was then that I heard about it from God.

Silas John used his writing system for the sole purpose of recording the sixty-two prayers he received in his vision. The script was never applied to the large body of traditional Apache prayers already in existence by 1904, nor was it ever employed as a vehicle for secular speech. This is important to keep in mind because the merits of the script, as well as its limitations, stem directly from the fact that it was purposely designed to communicate information relevant to the performance of ritual and NOT to write the infinitude of messages capable of expression in spoken Western Apache.

In 1916, a full twelve years after Silas John experienced his vision, he publicly proclaimed himself a messiah and began to preach. At the same time, he wrote down each of his prayers on separate pieces of tanned buckskin, using paints made from a mixture of pulverized minerals and the sap of yucca plants. This technique of writing soon was replaced, however, and by 1925 prayer texts rendered in ink were appearing on squares of cardboard. Today, many (and possibly all) of the original painted buckskins have been lost or disposed of, and Silas John's script is preserved in paper 'prayer books' (*sailiš ǰaan biʔokąąhi*) belonging to Apaches living on the San Carlos and Fort Apache Reservations.

By 1920, when it was apparent to Silas John that his acceptance as a religious prophet was assured, he selected twelve 'assistants' (*sailiš ǰaan yiłnanałseʔhi*) to circulate among the Apache people, pray for them, and encourage them to congregate. The assistants were given instruction in how to read and write and, after acquiring these skills, went through an initiation ritual in which they were presented with painted buckskins of their own. Thus equipped, they were placed in charge of carefully prepared sites known as 'holy grounds' and urged to perform ceremonials on a regular basis, using their buckskins as mnemonic aids. As time passed and members of the original group of assistants began to die, Silas John appointed new ones who in turn were taught the script, formally initiated, and given the texts of prayers. This process, which has continued unmodified up to the present, accounts for the fact that even among Apaches knowledge of Silas John's writing system is not widespread. From the very beginning, access to the system was tightly controlled by Silas John himself, and competence in it was intentionally restricted to a small band of elite ritual specialists. Commenting on this point, one of our informants observed:

> Silas John just let a few people know what the writing meant. He once told my father that it had to be kept just like it was when he heard about it from God. If some person ever tried to change it, he said, God would stop listening to the people when they prayed. He knew that if he let it out for all the people to know some wouldn't know about this, some wouldn't take it seriously. Maybe some would try to change it. So he just gave it to a few people, men and women who would learn it right – just the way he taught them – and leave it alone. It has been that way for a long time, and it [the writing] is still the way it was when it came to this earth from God.

DESCRIPTION OF THE WRITING SYSTEM

The following account of Silas John's writing system is based upon an analysis of six texts that were copied from a prayer book belonging to one of his youngest assistants on the San Carlos Reservation. This was the only prayer book we were permitted to see, and, although it contained several additional texts, instruction in these was prevented by the sudden and unexpected hospitalization of our chief informant, a much older assistant whom Silas John had recommended as a particularly well-qualified teacher. The fact that we were unable to enlarge our sample hindered our analysis at certain points.[11] However, it did not prevent us from discovering the underlying principles according to which the system operates, the kinds of information it conveys, or the concepts Apaches must learn to become literate. Our description should enable anyone with a knowledge of spoken Apache to read fully and correctly the six prayer texts that constitute our corpus. No more can honestly be claimed since these were the only texts in which we ourselves received adequate training and developed an acceptable measure of competence by Western Apache standards.

A 'Silas John prayer text' (*sailiš ǰaan biʔokąąhi*) may be defined as a set of graphic 'symbols' (*keʔeščin*) written on buckskin or paper whose members are arranged in horizontal lines to be read from left to right in descending order (Figure 1). Each symbol is separated from the one that follows it by an empty space and corresponds to a single line of prayer which may consist of a word, a phrase, or one or more sentences.

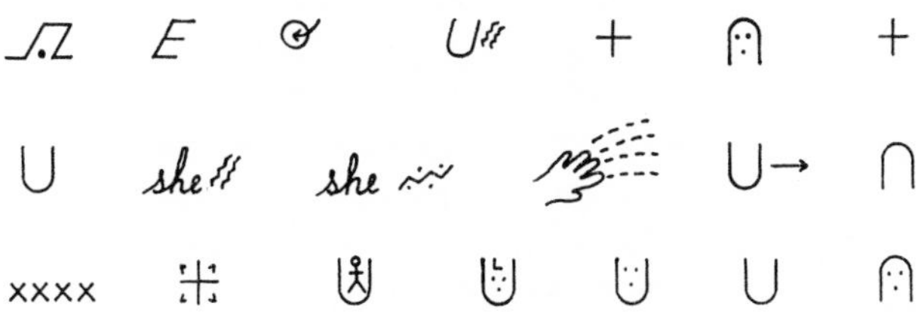

Figure 1: Text of 'prayer for life' in correct reading form from left to right in descending order.

The sixty-two prayers authored by Silas John are partitioned into three major categories:

1. 'prayers for life' (*ʔindee biʔokąąhi*), which promote health, longevity, and the maintenance of tension-free social relations;

2. 'prayers for man and woman' (*ʔindee keʔistsane biʔokąąhi*), which are invoked to combat and resolve marital discord;

3. 'prayers for sickness' (*ʔidaʔan biʔokąąhi*), which are employed to relieve physiological and mental illnesses caused by witchcraft, snakebite, or supernatural forces that have been antagonized by disrespectful behavior.

Prayers belonging to the same category are virtually identical in linguistic structure with the result that the number and sequential arrangement of their written symbols exhibit little variation. Consider, for example, the three 'prayers for life' whose texts are presented in Figure 2; note that each text contains the same number of symbols (twenty) and

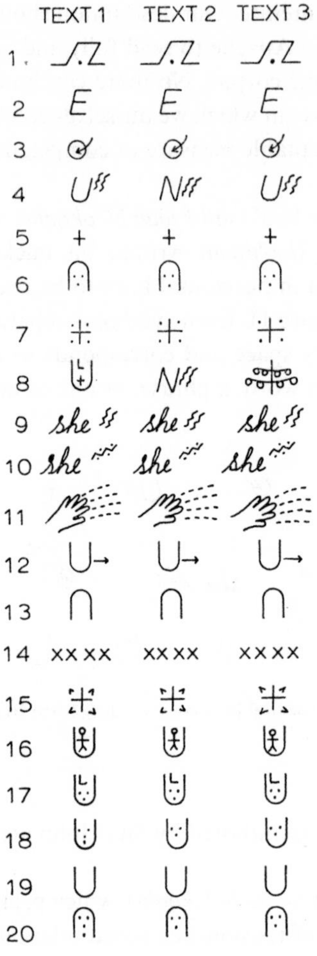

Figure 2: Three texts of 'prayer for life' arranged in vertical order for ease of comparison.

that their serial order is disturbed at only two points (4 and 8). Because this kind of uniformity is typical, the texts in each prayer category manifest a characteristic pattern. Two of these patterns can be readily discerned by comparing the 'prayers for life' in Figure 2 with the three texts of 'prayers for sickness' that appear in Figure 3.

Western Apaches assert that symbols in the Silas John script are composed of isolable 'symbol elements' (also termed *keʔeščin*), and they

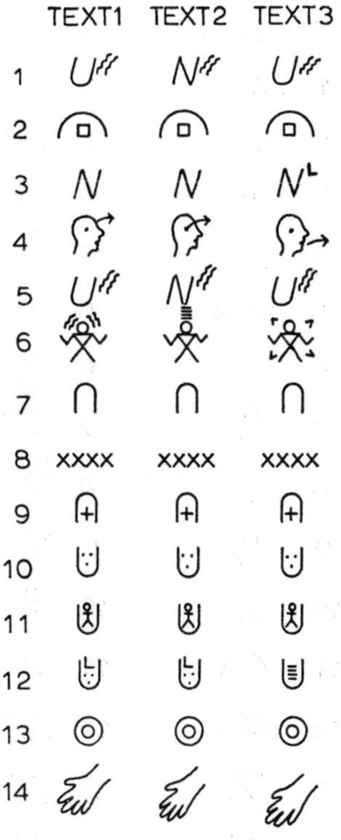

Figure 3: Three texts of 'prayer for sickness' arranged in vertical order for ease of comparison.

emphasize that to write and read a prayer text properly it is essential to discriminate among symbols that consist of two or more elements and those that consist of only one. The former class, whose members we shall refer to as COMPOUND SYMBOLS, is labeled by the Western Apache expression *keʔeščin łeedidilgoh* 'symbol elements put together', while the latter, whose members we shall refer to as NONCOMPOUND SYMBOLS, is termed *keʔeščin dołeedidildaahi* 'symbol elements standing alone'. Figure 4 presents the Apache classification of the symbols in our corpus into these two categories.

Symbol elements are not to be equated with discrete graphic components, for as a glance at Figure 4 will show, noncompound symbols may consist of more than one component. For example, the symbol ↵,

Figure 4: Noncompound and compound symbols.

which might suggest itself to an outsider as having two graphic components – ○ and ↵ – is not construed as such by Apaches, who consider it a noncompound symbol that cannot be dissected. The reason, our informants explained, is that by themselves neither ○ or ↵ has meaning and, as a result, must always occur in association with each other. In other words, they become semantically viable only as a unit, and in this respect contrast sharply with the components of compound symbols which, besides having meaning in combination, also have meaning in isolation. Thus we arrive at an important insight: the classification of compound and noncompound symbols is based upon other than visual criteria and cannot be deduced solely from the inspection of a symbol's outer form.

When requested to identify and define the individual symbol elements in our corpus, our informants sorted them into three classes. One class (A) is made up of elements that only occur in isolation and function exclusively in the capacity of noncompound symbols. Elements in the second class (B) also occur alone, but in addition can be combined with other elements to form compound symbols. The third class (C) consists of elements that occur only in compound symbols and never in isolation. In Figure 5 each of the twenty-eight symbol elements that appear in our corpus has been assigned to one of these three classes.

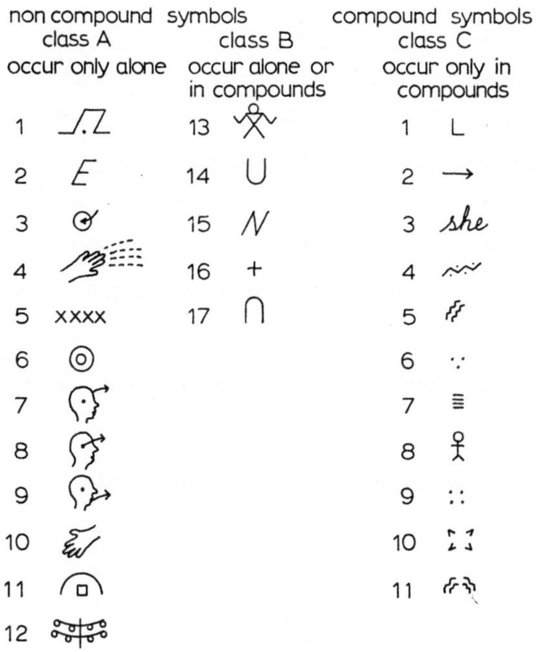

Figure 5: Symbols grouped into classes A, B, and C.

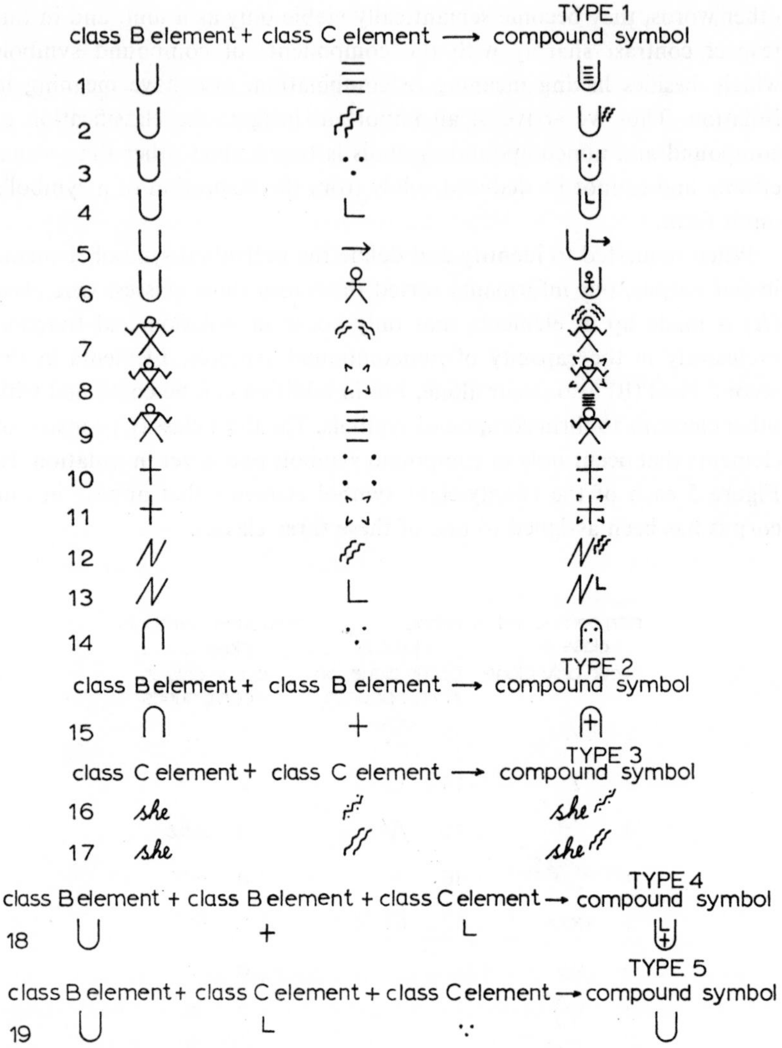

Figure 6: Formulas for the formation of types of compound symbols.

Compound symbols may be divided into five structural types according to the number of elements they contain (two or three) and the classes (B and/or C) to which these elements belong. For the sake of convenience and economy, the members of each type are expressed in Figure 6 as the outcome of simple formulas that operate on individual elements and specify the manner in which they are combined. We make no claim for the psychological reality of either the typology or the formulas; they are employed here simply as descriptive devices that allow us to make formally explicit the knowledge an Apache must possess in order to form the compound symbols that appear in the prayer texts at our disposal.

Compound Symbol Type 1: one element from Class B is combined with one element from Class C.

Compound Symbol Type 2: one element from Class B is combined with one other element from Class B.

Compound Symbol Type 3: one element from Class C is combined with one other element from Class C.

Compound Symbol Type 4: two elements from Class B are combined with one element from Class C.

Compound Symbol Type 5: one element from Class B is combined with two elements from Class C.

A striking feature of the Silas John script is that it encodes information relevant to the production of nonverbal behavior as well as speech. This is made explicit in a distinction Apaches draw between 'symbols that tell what to say' (*keʔeščin hantʔe ndii*) and 'symbols that tell what to do' (*keʔeščin hantʔe ʔanleʔ*). All symbols 'tell what to say' in the sense that each one signals the vocalization of some particular prayer line. However, a few symbols – those that 'tell what to do' – function simultaneously to signal the performance of key ritual actions without which the prayer, no matter how correct in its linguistic details, is considered incomplete.

In essence, then, a prayer text consists of a set of highly detailed instructions that specify what an individual must say and do to perform ceremonials in a manner that satisfies the standards held by Silas John and the members of his religion. So fundamental is the knowledge necessary to read these instructions, Apaches claim, that any attempt to execute the role of 'ceremonial leader' (*diiyin*) without it is certain to be flawed and unacceptable. One of our informants commented on this as follows:

> It's all in here [pointing to a prayer text], how to pray in just the right way. That's why he Silas John made them like this, so the ones who pray can be sure they know how to do it right. Only the ones who can read can pray .... I heard of a man at Whiteriver who wanted to be a ceremonial leader like the ones who work for Silas John. So he went to many ceremonials and tried to watch everything they did. After a long time he thought he knew what to do and got ready to try it out .... The people came to where he was and he started up. But pretty soon they knew he didn't really know it .... This was because no one had taught him to read buckskins; he couldn't do it without them. When he [Silas John] chooses you to be a ceremonial leader, first you learn what the symbols say, then, after that, what the symbols mean for you to do. You must know both because if you don't you will make mistakes like that Whiteriver man I was telling you about before.

MEANING OF THE SYMBOLS

The process of learning what the symbols in a prayer text represent may be considered complete when the linguistic referent of each symbol – that is, the prayer line it serves to recall in the performance of a ceremonial – has been committed to memory. The process begins, however, with the memorization of expressions that define the meaning of symbol elements. These expressions are termed 'symbol elements names' (*keʔeščin biži*ʔ) and are held by Apaches to constitute the basic semantic units of the Silas John writing system.

The 'names' of elements that function as noncompound symbols are identical to the prayer lines these symbols elicit in ritual contexts. Consequently, the linguistic referent of a noncompound symbol is always isomorphic with the meaning of the element that forms it and can be learned in a single operation. The linguistic referents of the noncompound symbols that appear in our corpus (those symbols formed by elements in class A and, when occurring in isolation, elements in class B) are presented below. The numbers refer to the symbols in Figure 5.

NONCOMPOUND SYMBOLS

Class A Elements (occur only alone)

1. *ni? ?ayolzą̨ąną?* 'earth, when it was made'
2. *?iiyaa? ?ayolzą̨ąną?* 'sky, when it was made'
3. *daitsee dagoyą̨ąną? ni??iłdįįžę̨?* 'first, when it all began in the center of the earth'
4. *šilagan hadaaže? dįįgo bihadaa?istįįgo* 'my fingers, from their tips, like four rays, power emanates'
šilagan hadaažę̨? biha?dit?iigo 'my fiingers, from their tips, power illuminates all'[12]
5. *nagowaahi nagoščǫǫdi nagołdiihi behegozini* 'sinful things occurring, bad things occurring, sickness and evil occurring, together with harmful knowledge'[13]
6. *bij̆ii hadndin* 'his heart, sacred pollen'
7. *ya?itsii košyo* 'from where his thoughts dwell'
8. *ya? ?odišyo* 'from where he looks out'
9. *ya? ?iiyałtii?yo* 'from where he speaks out'
10. *yoosn bihidaahi yoosn binadidzool behe?ndzili yedaaholdi tsiyaago daadoldi niką?žę̨?* 'with his life, his breath, his power, God extends his hand and blesses you'
11. *yoosn bigoyą̨ą* 'God, his dwelling'
12. *hadndin ła?ašniidn* 'he who is decorated with and enriched by pollen'[14]

Class B Elements (occur alone or in compounds)

13. *hadndin ?iškiin* 'sacred pollen boy'[15]
14. *yoosn* 'God'
15. *naalezgane* 'Jesus'[16]
16. *hadndin ?ilna?aahi* 'sacred pollen, that which is crossed'
17. *nagostan biyalatažę̨?* 'world, on the surface of it'

The 'names' of elements in class C must also be memorized since a knowledge of these constructions, together with those that label class B elements, is basic to the interpretation of compound symbols. The numbers refer to the symbols in Figure 5.

COMBINING SYMBOLS

Class C Elements (occur only in compounds)

1. *hidaa* 'life'
2. *ʔintin* 'path'; 'trail'; 'road'
3. *šii* 'I'; 'me'; 'mine'
4. *ʔokąąhi* 'prayer, that which is'
5. *hadndin* 'sacred pollen'
6. *hadndin* 'sacred pollen'
7. *hadndin* 'sacred pollen'
8. *ʔindee* 'man'; 'men'[17]
9. *dįįyo* 'four places'
10. *dįįžę?* 'in'; or 'from four directions'
11. *dįįʔįį* 'four times'

When an Apache learns the expressions that label elements in a compound symbol, he does not simultaneously learn that symbol's associated prayer line. This is because the linguistic referents of compound symbols are never isomorphic with the 'names' of the class B and/or C elements that form them. Consider, for example, compound symbol 2 (Figure 6). The meaning of class B element 14 is *yoosn* 'God' and the meaning of class C element 5 (Figure 5) is *hadndin* 'sacred pollen'. The prayer line evoked by compound symbol 2 is *yoosn bihadndin* 'God, his sacred pollen' which, while replicating exactly the meanings of its elements, is not identical to either one because of the addition of the possessive pronoun *bi* 'his'. It should be emphasized that the degree of correspondence between the referent of a compound symbol and the expressions that define its elements is not always this high. In the case of compound symbol 5 (Figure 6), for example, whose referent is *dašižǫ? beišgaał čʔidii* 'it is said that I alone go forth with this power', the meaning of class B element 14 (Figure 5) is *yoosn* 'God' and that of class C element 2 *ʔintin* 'path'; 'trail'; 'road'.

Because the prayer line associated with a compound symbol is structurally and semantically more complex than the 'names' of its elements it cannot be inferred from them and, as a consequence, must be memorized separately. However since the 'names' either form some part of the prayer line or allude metaphorically to key concepts embedded within it, the elements serve as indispensable aids for bringing the prayer line to mind.

The linguistic referents of the compound symbols in our corpus are as follows. The numbers refer to the symbols in Figures 5 and 6.

Compound Symbol Type 1

1. Class B element 14 (*yoosn* 'God') plus class C element 7 (*hadndin* 'pollen') produces compound symbol 1 (*yoosn bihadndin* 'God, his sacred pollen')[18]
2. Class B element 14 (*yoosn* 'God') plus class C element 5 (*hadndin* 'pollen') produces compound symbol 2 (*yoosn bihadndin* 'God, his sacred pollen')
3. Class B element 14 (*yoosn* 'God') plus class C element 6 (*hadndin* 'pollen') produces compound symbol 3 (*yoosn bihadndin* 'God, his sacred pollen')
4. Class B element 14 (*yoosn* 'God') plus class C element 1 (*hidaa* 'life') produces compound symbol 4 (*yoosn bihidaa* 'God, his life')
5. Class B element 14 (*yoosn* 'God') plus class C element 2 (*ʔintin* 'path'; 'trail'; 'road') produces compound symbol 5 (*dašižǫʔ beišgaał čʔidii* 'it is known that I alone go forth with this power')
6. Class B element 14 (*yoosn* 'God') plus class C element 8 (*ʔindee* 'man'; 'men') produces compound symbol 6 (*bitʔla nabąąžeʔ yoosn biyiʔ siziįhi* 'following this, God entered into man')
7. Class B element 13 (*hadndin ʔiškįįn* 'sacred pollen boy') plus class C element 11 (*dįįʔįį*; 'four times') produces compound symbol 7 (*dįįʔįį hadndin ʔiškįįnihi* 'four times, that which is sacred pollen boy')
8. Class B element 13 (*hadndin ʔiškįįn* 'sacred pollen boy') plus class C element 10 (*dįįžęʔ* 'from four directions') produces compound symbol 8 (*hadndin ʔiškįįn dįįžęʔ nadiyoołhi* 'sacred pollen boy, he who breathes in four directions')
9. Class B element 13 (*hadndin ʔiškįįn* 'sacred pollen boy') plus class C element 7 (*hadndin* 'sacred pollen') produces compound symbol 9 (*ʔizidadasdil hadndin ʔiškįįn* 'from above it cures, pollen boy')
10. Class B element 16 (*hadndin ʔiłnaʔaahi* 'sacred pollen, that which is crossed') plus class C element 9 (*dįįyo* 'four places') produces compound symbol 10 (*hadndin ʔiłnaʔaahi dįįyo nadiyooł* 'sacred pollen, that which is crossed, breathing in four places')
11. Class B element 16 (*hadndin ʔiłnaʔ aahi* 'sacred pollen, that which is crossed') plus class C element 10 (*dįįže* 'in four directions') produces compound symbol 11 (*dįįžeʔ bilhadaagoyaa* 'these things dispersed in four directions')

12. Class B element 15 (*naalezgane* 'Jesus') plus class C element 5 (*hadndin* 'sacred pollen') produces compound symbol 12 (*naalezgane bihadndin* 'Jesus, his sacred pollen')

13. Class B element 15 (*naalezgane* 'Jesus') plus class C element 1 (*hidaa* 'life') produces compound symbol 13 (*naalezgane bihidaa* 'Jesus, his life')

14. Class B element 17 (*nagostsan* 'world') plus class C element 6 (*hadndin* 'sacred pollen') produces compound symbol 14 (*hadndin hidaahi* 'sacred pollen, that which is alive')[19]

Compound Symbol Type 2

15. Class B element 17 (*nagostsan* 'world') plus class B element 16 (*hadndin ʔiłna'aahi* 'sacred pollen, that which is crossed') produces compound symbol 15 (*hadndin ʔiłnaʔaahi nagostsan bikažęʔ* 'pollen, that which is crossed, on the surface of the world')

Compound Symbol Type 3

16. Class C element 3 (*šii* 'I'; 'me'; 'mine') plus class C element 4 (*ʔokąąhi* 'prayer') produces compound symbol 16 (*šii siʔokąąhi* 'mine, that which is my prayer')

17. Class C element 3 (*šii* 'I'; 'me'; 'mine') plus class C element 5 (*hadndin* 'sacred pollen') produces compound symbol 17 (*šii šihadndinihi* 'mine, that which is my sacred pollen')

Compound Symbol Type 4

18. Class B element 14 (*yoosn* 'God') plus class B element 16 (*hadndin iłnaʔaahi* 'sacred pollen, that which is crossed') plus class C element 1 (*hidaa* 'life') produces compound symbol 18 (*yoosn bihadndin ʔiłnaʔaahi hidaahi* 'God, his sacred pollen, that which is crossed, that which is alive')

Compound Symbol Type 5

19. Class B element 14 (*yoosn* 'God') plus class C element 6 (*hadndin* 'sacred pollen') plus class C element 1 (*hidaa* 'life') produces compound symbol 19 (*yoosn binadidzoołhi* 'God, that which is his breath')[20]

CODING OF NONVERBAL BEHAVIOR

We have already drawn attention to the fact that certain symbols in the Silas John script call for the performance of specific types of nonverbal behavior as well as the utterance of a prayer line. To cite an example, compound symbol 2 (Figure 6) requires that simultaneous with the vocalization of its linguistic referent, which is *yoosn bihadndin* 'God, his sacred pollen', the speaker bless the ritual paraphernalia that identify him as a ceremonial leader by sprinkling each item with a pinch of cattail pollen. Actions of this kind, which constitute what we shall henceforth describe as a symbol's KINETIC referent, consistently involve the manipulation of material culture, and for this reason a brief description of the physical settings in which ceremonials take place is essential.

All rituals connected with the Silas John religion are conducted within the perimeters of what both monolingual and bilingual Apaches call 'holy grounds'. These are small areas of land, usually about fifteen feet square, whose corners correspond to the four cardinal directions and are marked by upright wooden crosses (*ʔilnaʾaahi ʔindeez* 'long crosses'). Each cross is approximately seven feet tall, painted a different color – east (black), north (yellow), west (green), south (white) – and decorated with the breastfeathers of eagles.

Other objects of material culture which assume importance in ceremonial activities include:

(1) 'wooden hoops' (*bą̨ąse*). Used only in rituals held for the purpose of curing the sick, hoops are made in sets of four and suspended on the crosses that define the corners of 'holy grounds'. Each hoop is roughly a yard in diameter, painted to match the color of the cross on which it hangs, and adorned with eagle feathers or strips of colored ribbon.

(2) 'painted buckskins' (*ʔepan keʔeščin*). Every ceremonial leader is the owner of one or more buckskins which he spreads on the ground before the start of a ceremonial. Roughly square or rectangular in shape, these buckskins are inscribed with nonorthographic symbols that represent 'sand paintings' (*niʔkegoščiʔ*), and, unless the ceremonial is of a particular type that requires the creation of these designs, the buckskins serve no mnemonic purpose.

(3) 'personal crosses' (*ʔindee biʔilnaʔaahi*). Every ceremonial leader also owns a personal cross, which he displays at ritual gatherings by placing it on top of his buckskins. Between ten and fourteen inches long and six to ten inches wide, these objects are fashioned from wood and are some-

times enclosed in an outer covering of buckskin. An eagle feather and at least one turquoise bead are attached to the center of personal crosses with a strand of sinew, and it is not unusual to see specimens whose arms have been painted yellow.

(4) 'Sacred pollen' (*hadndin*). All ceremonials involve the use of cattail pollen, which is kept in an open container (usually a shallow basket) that is placed on the ground near the ceremonial leader's buckskins and personal cross.

We may now return to our prayer texts and discuss in greater detail 'symbols that tell what to do'. Ten symbols of this type occur in our corpus. Each is a compound symbol and is listed below with a description of the actions that collectively comprise its kinetic referent. In keeping with the verbal style of our Apache informants, these descriptions are phrased as instructions to be followed by ceremonial leaders.

1. Compound symbol 17 – Face toward the east. Extend fully the right arm, fold the left arm across the chest, and bow the head. After remaining in this position for a few moments, drop the left arm and trace the sign of a cross on one's chest.
2. Compound symbol 1 – Face toward the east. Take a pinch of sacred pollen in the right hand and hold it directly over the ritual paraphernalia, which are lying on the ground.
3. Compound symbol 3 – Take a pinch of sacred pollen in the right hand and trace four circles in the air directly over the ritual paraphernalia.
4. Compound symbol 2 – Take a pinch of sacred pollen in the right hand and place a small amount on each item of ritual paraphernalia.
5. Compound symbol 12 – Same as No. 4.
6. Compound symbol 10 – Take a pinch of sacred pollen in the right hand and place a small amount on each arm of the ceremonial cross that marks the eastern corner of the holy ground.
7. Compound symbol 11 – Same as No. 6.
8. Compound symbol 9 – Take a pinch of sacred pollen in the right hand and place a small amount on the head of the person (seated on the ground) for whom the ceremonial is being given.
9. Compound symbol 8 – Take a pinch of sacred pollen in the right hand and with the same hand trace the sign of a cross on the chest of the person for whom the ceremonial is being given.
10. Compound symbol 7 – Remove the wooden hoop from the cross that defines the eastern corner of the holy ground and pass it four times over the head and shoulders of the person for whom the ceremonial is being given.

'Symbols that tell what to do' appear to be the only ones in the Silas John script which sometimes lack unique linguistic referents. We have seen, for example, that the referent of compound symbol 1 (*yoosn bihadndin* 'God, his sacred pollen') is identical to that of compound symbols 2 and 3. Neither is it the case that all symbols of this type possess unique kinetic referents; the actions associated with compound symbol 10 are exactly the same as those associated with compound symbol 11. It should be noted, however, that symbols with identical linguistic referents never possess the same kinetic referents, and vice versa. In other words, two symbols may be kinetic allographs or they may be linguistic allographs, but they are never both at once and consequently complete redundancy is avoided.

According to one of our informants, the kinetic values of 'symbols that tell what to do' are indirectly expressed by their linguistic referents. In some instances, this seems plausible, as when compound symbol 17 (*šii šihadndinihi* 'mine, that which is my sacred pollen') calls for the ceremonial leader to bless himself with cattail pollen. However, in other cases, the relationship is more obscure, as with compound symbol 2 (*yoosn bihadndin* 'God, his sacred pollen') which requires the ceremonial leader to perform a blessing on his ritual paraphernalia.

What is significant is not that symbols vary in the extent to which their kinetic values can be inferred from their linguistic referents, but rather that they encode both types of information. Silas John might easily have chosen to convey kinetic instructions with one set of symbols and linguistic instructions with another. Instead, he created a script in which single symbols function in both capacities, thereby reducing the total number of symbols in the system and endowing it with added economy.

It should now be possible for the reader of this essay to translate into speech and action any and all of the prayer texts in our corpus. At this stage, of course, he will not have memorized the referent(s) of every symbol element and therefore will not be able to read spontaneously. However, he has been provided with a complete inventory of these referents as well as an explicit formulation of the rules that govern their combination and interpretation.

In general terms, the reader of a prayer text must be able to distinguish compound symbols from noncompound symbols, associate each with a particular linguistic construction, and pronounce that construction in Western Apache. In addition, he must be able to recognize symbols that call for nonverbal behavior, assign to each of these a particular kinetic referent, and transform that referent into the appropriate set of ritual gestures. With these skills and an ability to apply them swiftly and flawlessly in the physical context of a 'holy ground', our newly literate reader should be able to give a total performance that comes satisfactorily close to those expected of experienced Apache ceremonial leaders.

TRANSLATION OF 'PRAYER FOR LIFE'

As an illustration of what these performances consist of, we now present a detailed account of the 'prayer for life' which appears in Figure 1. The Apache text is accompanied by full kinetic instructions and a free translation of the linguistic material which attempts to capture some of the drama and dignity of Silas John's ritual poetry. Numbers refer to symbols in Text 1, Figure 2.

1. *ni??aɣolzą̨ąną?* 'when the earth was first created'
2. *?iiyaa? ?aɣolzą̨ąną?* 'when the sky was first created'
3. *daitsee dagoyą̨ąną? ni??iłdį̨įžę̨?* 'in the beginning, when all was started in the center of the earth'
4. *yoosn bihadndin* 'God's sacred pollen' (Take a pinch of sacred pollen in the right hand and place a small amount on each item of ritual paraphernalia.)
5. *hadndin ?iłna?aahi* 'a cross of sacred pollen'
6. *hadndin hidaahi* 'living sacred pollen'
7. *hadndin ?iłna'aahi dį̨įyo nadiyooł* 'a cross of sacred pollen breathing in four directions' (Take a pinch of sacred pollen in the right hand and place a small amount on each arm of the ceremonial cross that marks the eastern corner of the holy ground.)
8. *yoosn bihadndin ?iłna'aahi hidaahi* 'God's cross of living sacred pollen'.
9. *šii šihadndinihi* 'My own, my sacred pollen' (Face towards the east, extend fully the right arm, fold the left arm across the chest, and bow the head. After remaining in this position for a few moments, drop the left arm and trace the sign of a cross on one's chest.)
10. *šii ši?oką̨ąhi* 'my own, my prayer'
11. *šilagan hadą̨ąže? dį̨įgo bihadaa?istį̨įgo* 'like four rays, power is flowing forth from the tips of my fingers'

šilagan hadą̨ąže? biha?dit?į̨įgo 'power from the tips of my fingers brings forth light'

12. *dašižǫʔ beišgaal čʔidii* 'now it is known that I go forth with power'

13. *nagostsan biγalatažęʔ* 'on the surface of the world'

14. *nagowaahi nagoščǫǫdi nagołdiihi beheʔgozini* 'sinful things are occurring, bad things are occurring, sickness and evil are occurring, together with harmful knowledge'

15. *dįįžęʔ biłhadaagoyaa* 'in four directions, these things are dispersed and fade away' (Take a pinch of sacred pollen in the right hand and place a small amount on each arm of the cross that marks the eastern corner of the holy ground.)

16. *bitlʔanabąąžę yoosn biyiʔ siziįhi* 'following this, God came to live with man'

17. *yoosn binadidzoołhi* 'the breath of God'

18. *yoosn bihadndin* 'God's sacred pollen' (Take a pinch of sacred pollen in the right hand and trace four circles in the air directly over the ritual paraphernalia.)

19. *yoosn* 'God Himself'

20. *hadndin hidaahi* 'living sacred pollen'.

SUMMARY AND CONCLUSION

At the outset of this essay it was observed that the adequacy of an etic typology of written symbols could be judged by its ability to describe all the emic distinctions in all the writing systems of the world. In conclusion, we should like to return to this point and briefly examine the extent to which presently available etic concepts can be used to describe the distinctions made by Western Apaches in relation to the writing system of Silas John.

Every symbol in the Silas John script may be classified as a PHONETIC SEMANTIC SIGN. Symbols of this type denote linguistic expressions that consist of one or more words and contrast as a class with PHONETIC NONSEMANTIC SIGNS, which denote phonemes (or phoneme clusters), syllables (or syllable clusters), and various prosodic phenomena.[21]

Phonetic semantic signs are commonly partitioned into two subclasses: LOGOGRAPHS, which denote single words, and PHRASEOGRAPHS, which denote multilexemic constructions. Although every symbol in the Silas John script can be assigned to one or the other of these categories, such an exercise is without justification.[22] We have no evidence to suggest that

Apaches classify symbols according to the length or complexity of their linguistic referents, and therefore the imposition of distinctions based on these criteria would be inappropriate, irrelevant, and misleading.

A far more useful contrast, and one we have already employed, is presented in most etic typologies as an opposition between COMPOUND (or composite) and NONCOMPOUND (or noncomposite) symbols. Used to partition the category of phonetic semantic signs, these two concepts enable us to describe more or less exactly the distinction Apaches draw between 'symbol elements put together' (*keʔeščin łedidilgoh*) and 'symbol elements standing alone' (*keʔeščin doledidildaahi*). The former may be defined as consisting of COMPOUND PHONETIC SEMANTIC SIGNS, while the latter is composed of NONCOMPOUND PHONETIC SEMANTIC SIGNS.

Up to this point etic concepts have served us well. However, a deficiency appears when we search for a terminology that allows us to describe the distinction between 'symbols that tell what to say' (*keʔeščin hantʔe ndii*) and 'symbols that tell what to do' (*keʔeščin hantʔe ʔanleʔ*). As far as we have been able to determine, standard typologies make no provision for this kind of contrast, apparently because their creators have tacitly assumed that systems composed of phonetic semantic signs serve exclusively to communicate linguistic information. Consequently, the possibility that these systems might also convey nonlinguistic information seems to have been consistently ignored. This oversight may be a product of Western ethnocentrism; after all, it is we who use alphabets who most frequently associate writing with language.[23] On the other hand, it may simply stem from the fact that systems incorporating symbols with kinetic referents are exceedingly rare and have not yet been reported. In any case, it is important to recognize that the etic inventory is not complete.

Retaining the term PHONETIC SIGN as a label for written symbols that denote linguistic phenomena, we propose that the term KINETIC SIGN be introduced to label symbols that denote sequences of nonverbal behavior. Symbols of the latter type which simultaneously denote some unit of language may be classified as PHONETIC-KINETIC signs. With these concepts the contrast between 'symbols that tell what to say' and 'symbols that tell what to do' can be rephrased as one that distinguishes phonetic signs (by definition nonkinetic) from phonetic-kinetic signs. Pure kinetic signs – symbols that refer solely to physical gestures – are absent from the Silas John script.

The utility of kinetic sign and phonetic-kinetic sign as comparative concepts must ultimately be judged on the basis of their capacity to clarify and describe emic distinctions in other systems of writing. However, as we have previously pointed out, ethnographic studies of American Indian systems that address themselves to the identification of these distinctions – and thus provide the information necessary to evaluate the relevance and applicability of etic concepts – are in short supply. As a result, meaningful comparisons cannot be made. At this point, we simply lack the data with which to determine whether the kinetic component so prominent in the Silas John script is unique or whether it had counterparts elsewhere in North America.

The view is still prevalent among anthropologists and linguists that the great majority of American Indian writing systems conform to one or two global 'primitive' types. Our study of the Silas John script casts doubt upon this position, for it demonstrates that fundamental emic distinctions remain to be discovered, and that existing etic frameworks are less than adequately equipped to describe them. The implications of these findings are clear. On the one hand, we must acknowledge the possibility that several structurally distinct forms of writing were developed by North America's Indian cultures. Concomitantly, we must be prepared to abandon traditional ideas of typological similarity and simplicity among these systems in favor of those that take variation and complexity into fuller account.

NOTES

1. G. Mallery, *Annual Report, Bureau of American Ethnology* (1886).
2. I. J. Gelb, *A Study of Writing* (Chicago: University of Chicago Press, 1963), 210. We have adapted Gelb's (p. 12) broad definition of writing as 'a system of human intercommunication by means of conventional visible marks'. The Silas John system is a script because it consists of phonetic signs.
3. K. H. Basso, *The Cibecue Apache* (New York: Holt, Rinehart, and Winston, 1970), 92; G. Goodwin and C. R. Kaut, *Southwestern Journal of Anthropology* 10 (1954), 385-404; W. La Barre, *Current Anthropology* 12 (1971), 26; M. Opler, *An Apache Odyssey* (New York: Holt, Rinehart and Winston, 1969), 191; E. H. Spicer, *Cycles of Conquest* (Tucson: University of Arizona Press, 1962), 259-260, 532, 534. References to the impact of the Silas John movement upon Western Apache and Mescalero Apache religion are not infrequent, but a systematic appraisal of the cultural and historical factors that precipitated its appearance and acceptance has yet to be made. The earliest example of the Silas John script consists of two prayer texts recorded by Harry Hoijer on the Mescalero Reservation in New Mexico during the summer of 1931. A number of symbols that occur in

Hoijer's Mescalero texts are absent from those we collected at San Carlos (and vice versa), but at present we do not know whether these symbols represent innovations by the Mescalero or whether they originally appeared in Western Apache texts not included in our sample.

4. A. L. Kroeber, *Anthropology* (New York: Harcourt, Brace, 1948), 369-370.
5. P. E. Cleator, *Lost Languages* (London: R. Hale, 1959); M. Cohen, *La grande invention de l'écriture et son evolution* (Paris: Imprimeur National, 1958); D. Diringer, *The Alphabet* (London: Hutchinson's Scientific and Technical Publications, 1949) and *Writing* (New York: Praeger, 1962); J. Février, *Histoire de l'Ecriture* (Paris: Payot, 1948); I. J. Gelb, *A Study of Writing* (Chicago: University of Chicago Press, 1963); A. L. Kroeber, *Anthropology* (New York: Harcourt, Brace, 1948); G. Mallery, *Annual Report, Bureau of American Ethnology* 4 (1886) and 10 (1893); A. C. Moorhouse, *The Triumph of the Alphabet* (New York: H. Schuman, 1953); C. F. Voegelin and F. M. Voegelin, *Anthropological Linguistics* 3 (1961), 55-96.
6. The terms 'etic' and 'emic' are used in this paper to refer to contrasting types of anthropological description. A description of a linguistic or cultural system is emic to the extent that it is based on distinctions which are demonstrably meaningful and functionally significant for competent users of the system. A description is etic to the extent that it rests upon distinctions (typically drawn from cross-cultural typologies) whose meaningfulness for a particular system's users has not been demonstrated and whose functional significance within the system is therefore open to question. For an extended treatment of the etic/emic distinction and its implications, see W. H. Goodenough, *Description and Comparison in Cultural Anthropology* (Chicago: Aldine, 1970). Other general discussions of this topic include W. H. Goodenough, *Culture, Language and Society* (Reading, Mass.: Addison-Wesley, 1971); D. H. Hymes in P. L. Gavin (ed.), *Method and Theory in Linguistics* (The Hague: Mouton, 1970); K. Pike, *Language in Relation to a Unified Theory of the Structure of Human Behavior* (The Hague: Mouton, 1967); W. C. Sturtevant, *American Anthropology* 66 (1964), 99-131.
7. As a general methodological premise in cultural anthropology, this point has been made repeatedly in recent years. However, its relevance to the study of writing systems has not been explicitly noted. We are inclined to attribute this to two major factors. On the one hand, cultural anthropologists have not been accustomed to view the description of writing systems as an exercise in ethnographic theory construction. On the other, students of writing seem only rarely to look to modern anthropology for theories and methods that might enhance their own investigations.
8. K. H. Basso, 'An Annotated Bibliography of American Indian Writing Systems', manuscript (University of Arizona, Tucson: Arizona State Museum Library, 1971).
9. W. H. Goodenough, *Description and Comparison in Cultural Anthropology*, 129.
10. C. F. Voegelin and M. F. Voegelin, *Anthropological Linguistics*, 3 (1961), 55-96.
11. For example, we were unable to record the full inventory of symbols used by Silas John to write his sixty-two original prayers.
12. 'Power' is the power God confers upon those who truly believe in Him.
13. 'Harmful knowledge' refers to the body of techniques employed by 'witches' (*ʔilkašn*) to cause sickness and misfortune. For a description of some of these

techniques see K. H. Basso, *Western Apache Witchcraft* (Tucson: University of Arizona Press, 1969).

14. This is the ritual name of Silas John. It is spoken only during the performance of ceremonials.
15. In all rituals associated with the Silas John religion, the phrase *hadndin ʔiškįįn* 'sacred pollen boy' refers metaphorically to male ceremonial patients. If the patient is female, the phrase is modified accordingly to *hadndin nailin* 'sacred pollen maiden'.
16. In traditional Western Apache myths and prayers, the term *naalezgane* is the name of a prominent male figure who with a twin brother rid the earth of much that was evil and made it a suitable dwelling place for man. See G. Goodwin, *American Folklore Society, Mem.* 39 (1939). Silas John uses the term in an extended sense to refer to Jesus.
17. In all the prayers we collected, the term *ʔindee* 'man'; 'men' is used in the more general sense of 'all men' or 'mankind'.
18. Cattail pollen is the foremost cultural symbol of God and Jesus and their spiritual presence upon this earth.
19. Like God and Jesus, pollen is construed as having life.
20. Pollen, a symbol of God, has life; to live is to breathe; hence the equation of pollen with the breath of God.
21. I. J. Gelb, *A Study of Writing*, 248, 2.
22. Written symbols that denote single phonemes (alphabetic graphs) and single syllables (syllabic graphs) are absent from the Silas John script. Four symbols in our corpus (class A-2; class B-14, 15; class C-3; all in Figure 5) represent clear borrowings from the English alphabet, but all of these denote specific words or sentences, and, as such, would have to be classified as logographs or phrase-ographs.
23. In this connection, it is interesting to note that etic concepts for the classification of alphabetic and syllabic systems have received far more attention – and have proven far from adequate – than those used to classify simpler forms of writing. See, for example, the classification of alphabetic systems by C. F. Voegelin and F. M. Voegelin, *Anthropological Linguistics* 3 (1961), 55-96.
24. We thank the following Western Apaches, whose understanding, cooperation, and friendship made this study possible: Silas John Edwards, for permission to undertake the study, to publish the results, and for providing us with essential information about the origin and history of his writing system; Marshall Miller, for gifted instruction in how to read; John Nolene, for his generous loan; Mr. and Mrs. Marion Zahgotah who allowed us to disrupt the daily routine of their household and never once complained; and Mrs. Maggie Anderson, who opened her home to us as a base of operations and whose advice, warmth, and sheer goodwill made everything that much better. We also thank David Schneider who brought the Silas John script to our attention by pointing out the presence of Harry Hoijer's Mescalero texts in an unpublished manuscript by the late Jules Henry. Henry had given Schneider access to the manuscript, and the latter supposed, quite correctly, that it would be of singular interest to us. We are grateful to Harry Hoijer for allowing us to examine his original fieldnotes. Finally, we thank Bernard Fontana, Dell Hymes, William Sturtevant, and Sol Tax who urged us not to delay our

investigation and took steps that enabled us to begin.

Our field research was sponsored by the Center for the Study of Man, Smithsonian Institution, Washington, D.C., and the Doris Duke American Indian Oral History Project, Arizona State Museum, University of Arizona. Finally, we thank the following scholars whose comments on an earlier draft of this paper were especially helpful: Ellen Basso, Roy D'Andrade, Harold Conklin, Regna Darnell, Bernard L. Fontana, I. J. Gelb, Erving Goffman, McGuire Gibson, Philip Greenfeld, Kenneth Hale, Harry Hoijer, Dell Hymes, Morris Opler, Alfonso Ortiz, Joel Sherzer, William Sturtevant, and Richard Thompson.

JAMES R. JAQUITH

Ayn Plotdiytshet Obaytsay: A Practical Alphabet for Plattdeutsch in Spanish-Speaking Areas*

The people who are the subject of this report are Mennonite farmers in northern Mexico. The primary issue to be discussed herein is the complex literacy status of these people. Some explication of the even more complex history and functioning of Mennonite multilingualism (Jaquith 1969) and general culture seems necessary, for in its absence the cultural significance of the points to be discussed below will not be appreciated.

Historically, Mennonites spring from the Anabaptist phase of the Reformation. (For detailed accounts of Mennonite background, and of their immigration to and experiences in Mexico, see Fretz 1945, Redekop 1969, Sawatzky 1967, Schmiedehaus 1948.)

Mennonite behavior generally is best understood as relating to two themes. The first is a profound objection to the baptism of infants on grounds that only adults have the knowledge, wisdom, and disposition to be effective church members. The second is that what Mennonites call 'the world' inevitably is contaminating in a ritual sense and is to be avoided. Thus, Mennonites began early to display avoidance behaviors toward institutions in the nations in which they resided. Indeed, the direct ancestors of Mennonites in contemporary Mexico demanded – and received in advance – guarantees from representatives of Catherine the Great that when Mennonites colonized the Vistula delta they would remain exempt from certain obligations that Russians faced. They must never, for example, be obliged to do military service. Nor must they be required to attend schools other than their own, to take oaths, or to involve themselves in nation-linked economic institutions. By 1870 the Russian government had already begun to erode these original exemp-

* From *Anthropological Linguistics* 12: 8 (1970), 293-303. Reprinted with permission.

tions. Resulting anxiety and the hard economic fact that – since the religion positively sanctions large families – their lands were overpopulated stimulated more conservative Mennonite leaders to seek out a new home to colonize, a home where the social concessions they demanded would be available along with sufficient reasonably priced and reasonably productive lands.

It is here worth pointing out that this kind of migration dynamic, more than anything else, has generated the different kinds of Mennonites who are in the world today. That is, those who migrate are selected primarily on either one or both of two bases. The first is ideological reaction to threats by host governments to revoke social concessions which Mennonites hold dear and which many Mennonites hold to be necessary. The second is a consequence of the overpopulation referred to above. After a few generations in a given scene there simply has not been enough land for everyone. Since farming is regarded by the leadership as the only really appropriate way to make a living, there comes a time, inevitably, when some people must move on in order to fulfill both ideological and economic needs. And those who go are the most conservative from the perspective of the apartness or avoidance theme referred to above. It is a fact, however, that some Mennonites have always been willing to pay a higher price in worldly involvement than others for long term economic success. These are the ones who have made it in some important social sense and who opt to make concessions to national pressures when migration is made an open alternative. National pressures have often taken the form of compulsory attendance of the children in national schools or of compulsory participation in national economic or other social programs. World Mennonites today constitute a broad spectrum of conservatism vis-à-vis involvement with 'the world'.

The most conservative of all the Mennonites in Russia were known as the Old Colony (from Hochdeutsch Altkolonie). Old Colony officials, seeing their traditional ways threatened by the Russian government, sent scouts in various directions to seek a new home. An agreement was finally reached with the Canadian government which made lands and social concessions available in that country, particularly in Manitoba and Saskatchewan. Beginning in 1874, many members of the Old Colony made the difficult and expensive move. By the end of World War I the seemingly inevitable cycle of government pressure and internal overpopulation was upon Canadian Mennonites. Unsuccessful efforts were made to find land in several South American countries. Finally, stimulated by the government's decision to Canadianize all ethnic minorities except the Québécois, Old Colony officials came to an agreement with the government of then President Alvaro Obregón of Mexico. In 1922 the migration began. As in the Russian experience, a combination of the most conservative and the most landless constituted the majority of those who pioneered the agricultural exploitation of the high, arid, northern Mexican intermontane. After an indifferently successful period of adaptation to strange soil and strange climate, the Old Colony began to prosper. And it still does, or, more precisely, those who own land still do.

In differing ways and degrees four languages are functionally involved in the Mexican Old Colony (Jaquith 1969). These are Hochdeutsch, Plattdeutsch, English, and Spanish. Briefly, their functions are as follows: Plattdeutsch (in Plattdeutsch it is called Plotdiytsh and will be so called hereinafter) is the routine ingroup vernacular; Hochdeutsch is the ritual language; English functions to reduce dependency on Mexico as a nation by facilitating the continuing exploitation of Canadian- and U.S.-based resources; Spanish is the Old Colony's current host language and is, ipso facto, the language of commerce.

Ideally, no Old Colony member should learn host languages, since their use constitutes one kind of traffic with 'the world' and facilitates still more such traffic. As a matter of practical necessity, however, men must learn sufficient of a host language to conduct buying and selling operations. This is a consequence of the fact that the Old Colony has a cash-crop economy rather than a subsistence economy. Since the traditional division of labor does not require that women participate in the market, they do not learn host languages.

Plotdiytsh, even though it is the most pervasive and frequent vehicle of expression in the Old Colony, is never written. Few Old Colony Mennonites are even aware, for example, of the existence of a rather small body of fiction (e.g. Dyck 1948) in their language. Some have gone so far as to assure the writer that Plotdiytsh cannot be written.

Hochdeutsch is the language of religious life. This is consistent with the fact that Mennonite sacred writing – the Luther Bible, the Märtyrer-Spiegel (an account of Mennonite martyrs to the Counter-Reformation), the traditional hymnal (*gesangbuch*) – are in this language. In fact, the most important single purpose of Old Colony schools (children never attend schools of the host society) is to inculcate sufficient Hochdeutsch so that when baptized as young adults they will be able to participate effectively in the religious life of the community. The correspondence that Old Colony Mennonites do is in Hochdeutsch. More than one Mexican merchant in the nearby service town has sought to increase his trade by advertising in this language.

Among other things, Old Colony culture in Mexico is notable in that it illustrates rather clearly the gap between what Kluckhohn (1945) has called 'ideal' and 'behavioral' patterns. On the 'ideal' side, for example, the following are some of the things which have been proscribed by church leaders as too much of 'the world': wheeled vehicles with rubber tires, automobiles, trucks, synthetic fertilizers, radios, phonographs, all secular music, instrumental music in church, wrist watches (pocket watches are acceptable), pictures on the walls of houses, the use of electricity in the home (acceptable only when used in ways directly concerned with working, e.g. to operate machinery used to repair farm equipment), and attendance of other than Old Colony schools. Among prescribed patterns are distinctive dress (overalls for men and boys; full dresses, hats and scarves for women and girls) and the writing of Hochdeutsch in Gothic script. It is clear that among other manifest and latent functions, the nonwriting of Plotdiytsh and the writing of Hochdeutsch in Gothic has contributed to the perpetuation of separation between the Old Colony and its Mexican hosts. From the Old Colony 'ideal' point of view this is good. On the 'behavioral' side, however, detailed ethnographic observation reveals a broad range of adherence to Old Colony ideals as promulgated by the *preydyash* 'ministers' and the *aeltesta* 'bishop'. That some Old Colony people do use radios, for example, is apparent from the fact that the local (Mexican) radio station broadcasts paid 'dedications' of songs from Mennonite young men to Mennonite girls. And one of the writer's informants not only owns three radios but repairs radios for other Mennonites. It is the same with clothing, the use of electricity in the home, and ideas about education and writing.

It is the case that a small percentage of Old Colony Mennonites knows and reads the *Koop enn Bua* series in Plotdiytsh (e.g. Dyck 1948). A larger percentage has expressed considerable positive interest to the writer in having a vehicle more practical than that available in the Dyck literature for reading and writing Plotdiytsh.

One way to approach the understanding of this interest is in terms of the Old Colony migration cycle. While pressure from the Mexican government is at this time minimal and latent, overpopulation has plagued the Old Colony for some time. A small percentage of the Mexico colony has already sold out and gone to Bolivia. An even smaller percentage has gone to Paraguay. There is no indication, however, that this migration will ever attain the proportions of the Russia-to-Canada or the Canada-to-Mexico moves. It has been argued elsewhere (Jaquith 1967; 1969) that the complex of conditions demanded by conservative Mennonites – the right kinds of lands and favorably disposed host governments – may well be unavailable and that more and more young Old Colony Mennonites will prefer to remain in the Mexican scene. The only way this can be done with much hope of success is through increased industrialization. Already there are Mennonite cheese plants, a print shop, an oats processing plant, farm machinery plants, box factories, etc. The only way to attain maximal industrialization is through a generalized rapprochement with pertinent facets of the host society. Although this runs directly counter to Old Colony ideals, it is in fact being pursued by an increasing number of Mennonites who see industrialization – with the implied partial accommodation to Mexican culture – as preferable to migration or poverty. In general these Mennonites are dissatisfied with traditional Old Colony schools and the numerous and often arbitrary proscriptions of the *preydyash.*

While there seems to be sufficient capital within the Old Colony for considerable industrial expansion, not to mention technical skills and motivation, there continue to exist significant obstacles, notably opposition from the *preydyash* and from the conservative core of the older generations.

The relations among excommunication (principle negative sanction of the church and at this time the inevitable price Old Colony members pay for industrialization), economic adaptation, and religious alternatives to the Old Colony are beyond the scope of this report. It seems appropriate, nonetheless, to draw attention to a fundamental aspect of this complex dynamic. The disposition of religious leaders to invoke excommunication (a fairly powerful sanction) is moderated de facto by two considerations. The first is that if too many are excommunicated it would be tantamount to the members having excommunicated their leadership (which in any case is elected). The second is that there is a legitimately Mennonite alternative to the Old Colony already operating on the scene. It represents a relatively liberal branch of the total church which has the reputation among Old Colony young of deriving its message from 'the commandments of God' (i.e. the Bible) rather than from 'the commandments of men' (i.e. the *preydyash*). Some have already gone to it from the Old Colony, either at the cost of excommunication or after being excommunicated for industrializing or some equivalently 'excessive' traffic with the Mexican 'world' which surrounds them. Thus, a potential for considerable culture change has developed – something new for the Old Colony. It is in this context that the following discussion of the Dyck and the Jaquith-Feya (Owbrom P. Feya was the writer's principal informant and collaborator) alphabets must be understood.

Chart I contains a fragment of some 420 words from Dyck (1948). The graphic units (letters, punctuation) are from the Gothic Hochdeutsch tradition: to a considerable extent Dyck has followed Hochdeutsch patterns of fit. These include not only such obvious phoneme-grapheme correspondences as /v/ = ⟨w⟩ and /y/ = ⟨j⟩, but specifying vowel by following consonant, e.g., ⟨enn⟩ = /en/ while ⟨en⟩ = /æn/. Moreover, Hochdeutsch patterns of allographic distributional complementarity have been followed where applicable.

Chart I: *Fragment from Koop enn Bua Faore nao Toronto, Dyck Alphabet*

	Words Numbered
2. Tweschen Kenora enn Fort William	1-4
„Daut heet, daut's weet de leewen Tiet," schult Bua dän	6-15
aundre Morje, aus se wada losläde, „je tjlanda soone	16-24
Staudt es, je leijhta vebiestat eena dôabenne!"	25-31
Daut scheen wertjlich, Ohmtje Bua wurd ut Kenora	32-39
nijh 'rutfinje. Wann hee nijh woa aum Bôaj pralld,	40-48
mußt'a woa ver'm Wôta bräke. Enn dôabi jinje dôa doch,	48-57
nijh väl mea aus een Wajh en'e Staudt'nen enn eena 'rut.	49-58
Schließlich holp am ôba eene Fru tôschetj, de so tiedig aul	59-70
Wôta tô de Däa 'rutgoot, vermutlich haud see sitj jrôds	71-81
jewosche. Aus se donn eascht de Jebieda hinja sitj, eenen	82-91
hôaden Wajh unja sitj enn daut blanke Sonntie ver siti	92-101
haude, wißte de Toronto-Fôarasch, daut se op'm rajhten	102-111
Wajh nôm Oste weere. Uck nô Wiens sine Koat stemmd	112-120
daut, wiels sea bold head daut Päwment op enn daut	121-130
Jauma fung aun. Daut jing bôajop enn bôajauf, de Wajh	131-140
wea jegrewelt, daut jô, ôba Côare enn Trucks haude dôavon	141-150
'ne Wauschriew jemôakt, so daut daut tetjad enn rätad	151-160
enn stuckad enn deed, enn daut Elend jing dann uck bold	161-169
los. Ohmtje Toewse flautad so de Haund, daut hee lang ziele	170-180

mußt, ear'a de Piep twesche Täne haud, emma wada 192-200
pôakst hee vebi enn trôff dann bold aune Tjenn, bold aune 201-211
Räs, enn eenmôl sogôa en'e Räs, daut'a meisttjis jepruft 212-220
haud. Wienße deed daut Stuckre von bute nijh waut, 221-229
dôafäa oba von benne, am tjitteld daut dôavon em Buck, 230-239
enn so saut hee dann enn sine Atj enn lacht. Bua, dee daut 240-252
väre em Speajel sach, jleewd, Wiens lacht äwa sine Backe, 253-262
de mau so op'n dôl daunzte. „Waut jibbascht, „fôat hee nu 263-273
Wienße aun, „eena mott seene, daut eena nijh gaunz 274-282
utenaundajeit enn dôabi noch nô de Côa oppauße, enn hee 283-292
sett enn lacht." Hee wull sest noch mea saje, ôba am word 293-304
angst, daut am meteens noch de Tung twesch'ne Täne 305-313
stuckre kunn. Aus ôba sin Bletj op Koope foll, raunzta uck 314-324
däm aun: „Waut hast du dann noch tô piepe!" Daut 325-334
wea ôba gôanijh aun däm, daut Ohmtje Koop piepe deed. 335-344
Am wea man daut Jebiß ut'm Mul jestuckat, enn hee 345-354
haud'et sitj en'e Fupp jestoppt enn saut nu en môak'n 355-364
speßet Mul. Aundre oole Mensche ône Täne tratje de 365-373
Leppe nô benne, Koop schoof se 'rut enn daut sach dann 374-384
so, aus wann hee piepe deed ôda wäm ,n Kuß jäwe wull. 385-396
Jenoag, jieda haud met sitj tô doone, enn Bua 397-405
bôwenen noch met aundre, enn eene Reisefreid wull nijh 406-414
rajht opkôme, wann daut sest rundom uck wundascheen wea. 415-423

Chart II illustrates that for the thirty-five segmental phonemes of the Plotdiytsh spoken in the Mexican Old Colony, Dyck's alphabet employs a total of eighty-three allographs. One of the significant problems with this scheme is that in several cases a given graph specifies more than one phoneme, e.g. ⟨e⟩ = /e, æ, iy, ey, ay/. Moreover, in other cases a given phoneme is graphed in a variety of ways, e.g. /t/ = ⟨t, dt, d, tt⟩. In one case a graph (') which is most usually thought of as punctuation (i.e. that it normally has referents other than segmental phonemes) becomes in effect a letter in that ⟨'⟩ = /e/.

That the Dyck alphabet is relatively inefficient in terms of fit and reversibility (phoneme-grapheme interpredictability) is clear and not really at issue. Put somewhat abstractly, the question is: if the Old Colony is to transform its culture to the extent of incorporating a viable alphabet, what kind of alphabet should it be? Obviously, one possibility would be to use Dyck's alphabet in its present form. This would have the advan-

Chart II: *Comparison of Jaquith-Feya and Dyck Alphabets*

	Plotdiytsh Phonemes	Jaquith-Feya Alphabet[1]	Arnold Dyck Alphabet	Illustrative Words (See Chart No. 1)
1.	a	a	a o	13, 76
2.	æ	æ; ae	e	1
3.	ay	ay	ee e aj oe	6, 18, 40, 129
4.	aw	aw	o oo Oh ô	20, 22, 31
5.	b	b	b bb	26, 174
6.	k	c, qu; c	k ck g C	84, 95, 108, 116
7.	d	d	d	9
8.	e	e	e i a '	1, 25, 77, 90
9.	ey	ey	ä e	14, 104
10.	ə	ə	o u ô	16, 117, 142
11.	f	f	v ſ ſſ	26, 35, 142
12.	g	g, gu; g	g	70
13.	h	h	h	6
14.	iy	iy	ie i e	11, 47, 77
15.	x	j	ch g	50, 218
16.	ky	k	tj k g	21, 45, 110
17.	l	l	l ll	10, 41
18.	m	m	m mm	31, 100
19.	n	n	n nn	1, 3
20.	ŋ	ŋ; ng	n ng	80, 132
21.	o	o	au ô	5, 17, 64
22.	ow	ow	ô o au oo	28, 99, 107, 194
23.	p	p	p pp	41, 183
24.	r	r	r	15
25.	s	s	s ſ ß ſch z	7, 26, 42, 77, 133
26.	š	š; sh	ſch ſ S	1, 100, 151
27.	t	t	t dt d tt	5, 23, 74, 157
28.	u	u	u a	12, 140
29.	ü	ü	u ô o	13, 140, 208
30.	uw	uw	o	38
31.	v	v	w	1
32.	ç	x	jh ch g	25, 30, 66
33.	y	y	j	16
34.	z	z	ſ	18
35.	ž	ž; zh		
	/eya/	eya	ä	165
	/ts/	ts	tz	209

1. Semicolons separate original from current versions of certain letters. Changes are discussed in the text.

tages (1) that a certain body of Plotdiytsh literature already exists in this alphabet and (2) that it uses Gothic letters in a way which parallels Hochdeutsch-Gothic fit fairly closely, a significant point since Gothic Hochdeutsch is taught in Old Colony schools. Another possibility would be to clean up Dyck's alphabet so that it would have but thirty-five letter graphs. This would result in a Gothic-based, highly efficient device which could be learned easily, although, to be sure, a considerable amount of the traditional Hochdeutsch fit would be obliterated.

Both of these possibilities, for all their short-term advantages, have a particular disadvantage which argues against the use of Gothic at all. This relates to the larger cultural context of increasing Old Colony industrialization, one major consequence of which would be a degree of rapprochement (some Mexicans call it 'acercamiento') between Mennonites and Mexicans. That the potential applications of Plotdiytsh literacy are not solely intra- but also intercultural argues against the use of Gothic for two reasons. The first is that the host language uses Roman letters. The second is that using Roman letters for a Plotdiytsh alphabet implies the possibility of building in features which will facilitate subsequent acquisition of written Spanish by Mennonites. The fact is that no fewer than nineteen (54 percent) of Plotdiytsh phonemes have allophones which are interpretable as allophones of Spanish phonemes as well. These are numbers 1, 3, 5, 6, 7, 8, 9, 11, 12, 15, 17, 18, 19, 21, 23, 24, 25, 27 and 33 on Charts II and III. The strategy here was to use, insofar as other factors allowed, traditional Spanish graphing for these Plotdiytsh phonemes. This adaptation of Spanish orthographic resources has worked out as follows: /a/ = ⟨a⟩; /ay/ = ⟨ay⟩; /b/ = ⟨b⟩ (but /b/ ≠ ⟨v⟩, as it does in Spanish, since Plotdiytsh /v/ = ⟨v⟩); /k/ = ⟨c⟩ (however, although Spanish ⟨qu⟩ = /k/ before ⟨e, i⟩ as well, this usage was dropped from the Plotdiytsh alphabet); /d/ = ⟨d⟩; /e/ = ⟨e⟩; /ey/ = ⟨ey⟩; /f/ = ⟨f⟩; /g/ = ⟨g⟩ (Spanish ⟨gu⟩ = /g/ before ⟨e, i⟩ was dropped); /x/ = ⟨j⟩ (Spanish ⟨g⟩ = /x/ before ⟨e, i⟩ was dropped); /l/ = ⟨l⟩; /m/ = ⟨m⟩; /n/ = ⟨n⟩; /o/ = ⟨o⟩; /p/ = ⟨p⟩; /r/ = ⟨r⟩; /s/ = ⟨s⟩ (Spanish ⟨z, c, sc, x⟩ = /s/ were all dropped); /t/ = ⟨t⟩; /y/ = ⟨y⟩.

As originally formulated, the alphabet provided that Plotdiytsh /æ/ = ⟨æ⟩, /ŋ/ = ⟨ŋ⟩, /š/ = ⟨š⟩, /ž/ = ⟨ž⟩. Because Mexican printers do not carry these graphs and because they have up until now resisted the notion of ordering sufficient of each to do a printing job, the following modifications were made: /æ/ = ⟨ae⟩, /ŋ/ = ⟨ng⟩, /š/ = ⟨sh⟩, /ž/ = ⟨zh⟩. The current version has the advantage that Mexican printers are already equipped to use it. They stock ⟨ü⟩ since in certain graphic environments Spanish ⟨ü⟩ = /w/. ⟨ə⟩ is nothing more than inverted ⟨e⟩. Moreover, with one modification – ⟨ə⟩ – Plotdiytsh can be written on any typewriter equipped to write Spanish.

Chart III: *Jaquith-Feya plotdiytshet obaytsay*

	Kliyne Latren	Grawte Latren	Nowmen Fe day Latren	Viyed fe Deyn ütdruc
1.	a	A	a	han (han)
2.	ae	AE	ae	aek (etj)
3.	ay	AY	ay	zay (ſe)
4.	aw	AW	aw	gawt (got)
5.	b	B	bay	büuc (buak)
6.	c	C	cay	cəp (kopp)
7.	d	D	day	düuc (duak)
8.	e	E	e	vet (witt)
9.	ey	EY	ey	ney (nä)
10.	ə	ə	ə	nəj (uoch)
11.	f	F	aef	faya (vea)
12.	g	G	gay	gawt (got)
13.	h	H	ha	hont (haunt)
14.	iy	IY	iy	viy (wi)
15.	j	J	jət	daj (dach)
16.	k	K	kay	kowak (tjoatj)
17.	l	L	ael	leyven (läwen)
18.	m	M	aem	maensh (menſch)
19.	n	N	aen	yana (jana)
20.	ng	NG	aeng	shlang (ſchſang)
21.	o	O	o	mon (maun)
22.	ow	OW	ow	mown (mon)
23.	p	P	pay	piyet (piat)
24.	r	R	aer	frü (fru)
25.	s	S	aes	hüs (hus)
26.	sh	SH	aesh	shlownen (ſchlonen)
27.	t	T	tay	tiya (tia)
28.	u	U	u	hunt (hunt)
29.	ü	Ü	ü	hüs (hus)
30.	uw	UW	uw	vuwa (woa)
31.	v	V	vaeev	viy (wi)
32.	x	X	ex	vax (wajh)
33.	y	Y	iy iy	yow (jo)
34.	z	Z	zaet	zaya (ſea)
35.	zh	ZH	zhaet	cruzhel (kruſjel)

Letters were named (Chart III, Nowmen fe day Latren) following Hochdeutsch practice where applicable, since Old Colony Mennonites already know these names. Vowel letters not already named in Hochdeutsch were assigned their phonemic values as names, e.g. ⟨ae⟩ = /æ/, ⟨ay⟩ = /ay/, ⟨ü⟩ = /ü/. Plotdiytsh consonant phonemes which have no Hochdeutsch analogues were provided analogous names, e.g. ⟨sh⟩ = *aesh* by analogy with the already existing ⟨s⟩ = *aes*; ⟨zh⟩ = *zhaet* by analogy with the already existing ⟨z⟩ = *zaet*; ⟨ng⟩ = aeng by analogy with the already existing ⟨n⟩ = *aen*.

Chart IV: *Fragment from Koop enn Bua Faore nao Toronto, Jaquith-Feya alphabet*

2. Tvaeshen Kenora en Fort William

'Dot hayt, dot's vayt de layven tiyt,' Shult Büa deyn ondre mərye, os zay vada lawsleyde, 'yeklanda zawne shtot aes yelaeexta febiystat ayna dowabaene!'

Dot shayn vaerklex awmtye Büa vurd üt Kenora nex 'rütfengye. Van hay nex vuwa om boway prald, must'a vuwa fer'm vowta breyke. Aen dowabiy yengye dowa dəj nex feyl maya os ayn vax aene shtot naen en ayna rüt. Shliyslex həlp am owba ayne frü toshaek, day zaw tiydex ol vowta taw de deya rütgawt, femütlex hod zay zek yrowts yevəshe. Os zay dan iyesht day yebiyda hengya zek, aynen howaden vax ungya zek en dot blangce zəntye faer zek hode, veste day Toronto-fowarash, dot zay əpem raxten vax nowm awste viyere. Uc no Viyns cowat shtaemd dot, viyls zaya bawld heyad dot peyv-maent əp en dot yowma fungc on. Dot yengk bowayəp en bowayof, day vax viya yegraevelt dot yow, owba coware on trocs hode dowafan ne voshriyv yemowact, zaw dot dot taekad en reytad en shtucad en dayd en dot eylaent yengk dan uc bawld laws. Awmtye Tayvze flotad zaw de hont, dot hay lang siyle must, ayara de piyp tvaeshne teyne hod, aema vada püucst hay febiy en trəf dan bawld one kaen, bawld one neyz, en aynmowl zogowa aene neyz, dota maeesttyes yeprüst hod. Viynse dayd dot shtucre fən büte nex vot, dowafeya owba fan baene, am keteld dot dowafən aem buc, en zaw zot hay dan aen ziyne ak en lajt. Büa, day dot feyare aem shpiyeyel zaj, ylayvd, Viyns lajt eyva ziyne bace, day mo zaw əpendowl donste. 'Vot yebasht,' fowat hay nü Viynse on, 'ayna mət zayne, dot ayna nex gons ütenondayaeet en dowabiy nəj now de cowa əpose, en hay

> zaet en lajt.' Hay vul zaest nəj maya zaye, owba am vərd angst dot am maetayns nəj de tung tvaeshne teyne shtucre cun. Os owba ziyn blek əp Cowpe fəl, ronsta uc deym on: 'Vot hast dü dan nəj taw piype!' Dot viya owba gowanex on deym, dot awmtye Cowp piype dayd. Am viya mo dot yebes ütem mül yeshtucat en hay hodet zek aene fup yestəpt en zot nü en müucen shpaetset mül. Ondre awle maenshe teyne trake de laepe now baene, Cowp shawf ze erüt en dot zaj dan zaw, os van hay piype dayd owda veymen cus yeyve vul.
>
> Yenüuj yiyda hod maet zek taw dawne, en Büa bowvenaen nəj maet ondre, en ayne raeezefraeed vul nex raxt əpcowme, van dot zaest runtəm uc vundashayn viya.

As an empirical test of the ability of the obaytsay to account for a considerable amount of more or less random text, the entirety of Dyck (1948) was transliterated from the Gothic to the alphabet herein proposed (Charts I, IV). Considerable discussion between the writer and his collaborator Feya and with several other Plotdiytsh-speaking informants failed to disclose any problems. That is, the graphic units of this obaytsay would appear to fit Plotdiytsh segmental phonemes perfectly, with no internal contradictions and relatively little interference from outside sources – Spanish or Hochdeutsch.

Thus, the primary technical resource for Plotdiytsh literacy in the Mexican Old Colony (and other Spanish-speaking areas with Mennonite populations, e.g. Bolivia, Paraguay) is now available. The implementation of this resource is a different sort of problem and is, in principle, beyond the scope of this report. Briefly, however, the following can be said. While the introduction of literacy is not viewed by the *preydyash* as evil or sinful per se, those with whom the writer has talked profess to see no value in it, 'since we have never written our language'. Thus, they are unwilling to support, say, the teaching of the obaytsay in the schools. The school operated by the liberal Mennonite group referred to earlier may well experiment with it in the future, however. The most promising approach at this time would seem to be external and passive, i.e. by introducing Plotdiytsh materials into the already existing and intensive commercial relations between the Old Colony and Mexican merchants in the nearby service town. To date several advertising flyers have been printed and distributed to Mennonites. Plans are now underway to print the Jaquith-Feya version of Dyck (1948) and to distribute it within the Old Colony. In conjunction with this project, the entire text has been recorded on magnetic tape and will be broadcast on the local radio station on a prearranged basis in twenty weekly segments. This pedagogic reinforcing of the printed with the spoken version will be maximally effective with the young, since it is they who own most of the radios. Finally, plans are under way to establish a Plotdiytsh newspaper located outside the Old Colony but staffed by Mennonites. There are aspects of the communications resources commanded by the Old Colony which argue strongly that such a newspaper would be welcomed by a significant proportion of the Old Colony. Once it is accepted, Plotdiytsh literacy in the Mexican Old Colony will have been established.

BIBLIOGRAPHY

Dyck, Arnold

1948 *Koop enn Bua faore nao Toronto* (North Kildonan, Man.: Gelbstverlag des Verfaffers).

Fretz, J. Winfield

1945 *Mennonite Colonization in Mexico* (Akron, Penn.: The Mennonite Central Committee).

Jaquith, James R.

1967 'Language Factors Bearing on Culture Change among Mennonites in Mexico', paper delivered at the Sixty-Sixth Annual Meeting of the American Anthropological Association.

1969 'The Role of Multilingualism in Old Colony Culture', *Mennonite Life* 24: 3, 137-142.

Kluckhohn, Clyde

1941 'Patterning as Exemplified in Navaho Culture', in Leslie Spier (ed.), *Language, Culture and Personality* (Menasha, Wis.: Sapir Memorial Publication Fund).

Redekop, Calvin Wall

1969 *The Old Colony Mennonites: Dilemmas of Ethnic Minority Life* (Baltimore, Md.: Johns Hopkins).

Sawatzky, Harry Leonard

1967 'Mennonite Colonization in Mexico: A Study in the Survival of a Traditionalist Society', doctoral dissertation (Berkeley: *University of California*).

Schmiedehaus, Walter

1948 *Ein feste Burg ist unser Gott* (Cuauhtémoc, Chih., Mexico: G. J. Rempel).

Section Three

The Revision of Classical Writing Systems

JOHN DEFRANCIS 7

Language and Script Reform in China*

1. BACKGROUND

Present developments in the area of language and script reform in China represent a further stage in a movement which goes back to the nineties of the last century. The views advanced, the proposals made, and the decisions reached can best be understood if placed against the perspective of similar activities during the past three-quarters of a century.

Chinese activities in the area of script reform were initiated by the publication in 1892 of a book by Lu Kan-chang. The author, a native speaker of the Amoy dialect, presented a system of fifty-five semi-Western, semi-Chinese symbols together with the following views:

(1) In order to increase literacy and speed up the educational process, China should adopt a phonetic system of writing.

(2) Separate phonetic scripts should be created for each of the various dialects of China (e.g. Mandarin, Amoy) by selecting from among his fifty-five symbols those needed to represent the dialect.

(3) After illiterates have learned the system for their own dialect, they should all go on to study the nationwide standard language.

Lu Kan-chang's pioneer work was followed by similar activities of other would-be reformers in the dying years of the Manchu empire. Despite varying degrees of local success, none of the schemes was taken up officially and all eventually faded out.

Renewal of interest in the subject after the establishment of the Republic of China led to the calling of a Conference on Unification of Pronunciation in 1913 and to the creation of what came to be known as

* From *Current Trends* 2 (The Hague: Mouton), 130-150. Reprinted with permission.

the National Phonetic Symbols, a set of simple symbols having the same general appearance as Chinese characters. The name of the conference indicates clearly the limited scope envisaged for the symbols. They were to be used only to represent the sound of the national language, and then only as adjuncts to characters, as a means of representing the sounds of the characters. What little use was ever made of the symbols as an independent script was largely confined to the national language. In their primary function of indicating the pronunciation of characters, the symbols have had a modest success and continue to be used in dictionaries and other places where phonetic annotation is needed.

The next important development occurred in the twenties with the creation, largely by Y. R. Chao, of the National Language Romanization. The most distinctive feature of this system was the indication of tones by what was called 'tonal spelling'. The scheme was devised chiefly as a means of writing the national language, as the name indicates, and was not intended to be used in creating independent scripts for the various dialects. Despite its official acceptance in 1928 as the Second Pattern of the National Alphabet (the first being the above-mentioned Phonetic Symbols), the scheme did not receive official encouragement and was not widely used.

In the thirties a further stage in the reform movement came about with the creation of still another system variously known as *Latinxua* 'Latinization' or *Sin Wenzi* 'New Writing' or *Latinxua Sin Wenzi* 'Latinized New Writing'. The scheme was originally developed in the Soviet Union as part of its anti-illiteracy program for use by the approximately one hundred thousand Chinese within its confines. Subsequently it spread into China itself. Here it was taken up in the Communist-controlled areas, where it received the support of some of the top Communist leaders, in foreign-controlled cities like Shanghai, and even in areas under the control of the central government. The Latinized New Writing was distinctive chiefly in two ways: it did not provide for indication of tones, and it reverted to the idea initially advanced by Lu Kan-chang of devising separate scripts for the various dialects with Mandarin accepted as the national common language provided that it was not imposed on dialect speakers as the exclusive standard.

The appearance of the New Writing on the Chinese scene engendered a sharp debate. The scheme was attacked by those who objected to any thought of the characters giving way to an alphabetic system of writing. It was also criticized by supporters of the National Language Romanization on technical grounds for its failure to indicate tones, and on political grounds for what was considered a threat to national unity by the provision of separate scripts for the various dialects.

The Latinization movement reached its height in the middle and late thirties, died out toward the end of World War II,[1] but began to display some sparks of life again in the years immediately following the defeat of Japan, years marked by the outbreak of civil war and the final victory of the Communists in 1949. This seemed to foreshadow still another stage in the movement for reform of Chinese writing. In a postscript dated February 23, 1949, to his *Rebirth of the Chinese Language*, a collection of articles on the Latinization movement, Ni Hai-shu, one of the leading supporters of the New Writing, spoke of the future in the following terms:[2]

> 'Today and from now on the movement for phonetic writing will no longer be merely a superficial change in the written symbols but will be the liberation and development of the whole Chinese language from the shackles of the monosyllabic Chinese characters.'

The language policies actually instituted by the new government from its inauguration in 1949 down to the present can be summarized as follows:[3]

(1). simplification of the Chinese characters by reducing the number of strokes in complicated characters;

(2). promotion throughout the country of a standard language based on the Peking dialect;

(3) creation of a phonetic system as a means of (a) annotating Chinese characters, (b) promoting the common language, (c) creating alphabetic scripts for the non-Chinese-speaking minorities of China, and (d) possibly at some unspecified date in the future replacing the traditional characters with a phonetic system of writing.

This then, in broad outline, is the background against which the discussions within China on various aspects of the reform will be examined. Such an examination, in addition to taking up the things which were discussed in this latest phase of the reform movement, also needs to take up some important matters which were NOT discussed or were touched upon only in passing. For example, though the preceding outline makes clear that the policies of the Communist regime today are at variance with those advocated during the Latinized New Writing period, on the basis of current publications one is hard put to learn much about what prompted the change in attitude. There is a tantalizing dearth of information about some of the key issues involved in the whole reform program. This must be borne in mind in the following discussion of the main policies of simplification of characters, promotion of a standardized national language, and creation of a phonetic alphabet.

2. RATIONALE OF THE REFORM PROGRAM

The most authoritative exposition of the whole reform program has been presented by Premier Chou En-lai. In a speech[4] delivered on January 10, 1959, he made the following opening remarks:

> 'Current tasks of reforming the Chinese written language involve the simplification of the Chinese (Han) characters, popularization of the common speech . . . and the drawing up and putting into practice of the Scheme for a Chinese Phonetic Alphabet.'

Chou gave no reasons for the priority and touched only lightly on why simplification should be undertaken at all. He noted that 'nowadays the mass of the people have begun to master the written language and urgently demand that the characters be reformed – a situation that never existed in any period of our history', that 'simplified characters are easier to learn and to write than the characters in their original form', that 'the general tendency in the evolution of characters is toward simplification', and that since the people had for centuries been creating popular forms for their own use all that needed to be done was 'to collect and arrange in order what had been created by the people and, after thorough discussion, popularize the results'. 'The second task', said Chou, 'is the popularization of the common speech . . . .' Alluding to the 'great diversity in dialects' which exists in China, Chou added the following comments regarding the second task:

> 'This diversity in dialects had an unfavourable effect on the political, economic and cultural life of our people. . . . Without a common speech, we shall, to a greater or lesser extent, meet with difficulties in our national construction . . .. It is, therefore, an important political task to popularize vigorously the common speech with the Peking pronunciation as the standard.'

As to the relationship between dialects and common speech, Chou had this to say:

> 'Popularization of the common speech has as its aim the removal of the barrier of the dialects, not of prohibiting or abolishing the dialects.

> The answer to the question whether popularization of the common speech means to prohibit or abolish the dialects is definitely "No!" Dialects will exist for a long time. They cannot be prohibited by administrative order, nor can they be abolished by artificial measures .... It is an immensely difficult task to unify the dialects of the six hundred million Han people. To make it a reality, long and tireless efforts are required.'

Particularly noteworthy in the preceding remarks is the equating of 'popularizing the common speech' with 'unifying the dialects'. The implications of a policy aimed at unifying the dialects, as against simply asking dialect speakers to add a mastery of the common language to the speech of their birth, are not raised in this talk, and they become apparent only in an examination of the actual implementation of the program as a whole.

As to the third task, that of drawing up and popularizing the Scheme for a Chinese Phonetic Alphabet, Chou took pains to emphasize that:

> 'It should be made clear at the outset that the scheme is to annotate the characters phonetically and to popularize the common speech. It is not to replace the Chinese characters. Its first function is to give the pronunciation of the characters.'

In justification of the primary function of the Chinese Phonetic Alphabet, Chou noted that 'the efficiency of teaching and learning characters can be raised by using a phonetic alphabet ....' The second function of the scheme, according to Chou, was 'to transcribe the common speech, serving as a useful means of teaching and learning the common speech'. Towards this end the phonetic symbols were to be used 'to compile phonetic reading materials and pronouncing dictionaries'.

Another function of the phonetic scheme was 'to serve as a common basis on which the various national minorities may create or reform their own written languages'. Other functions noted included helping to teach Chinese to foreigners, to transliterate foreign names and scientific terms, and to compile indexes. Finally Chou took up the relationship of the phonetic scheme to the future of the Chinese characters. On this he said:

> 'One remaining question with which we are all much concerned is the future of Chinese characters. We all agree that as a written record they have made immortal contributions to history. As to whether or not they will remain permanently unchanged, whether they will

> change on the basis of their original forms, or whether they will be replaced by a phonetic language – Latin letters or other phonetic scripts – we need not draw a hasty conclusion. Any language is, however, subject to change, as evidenced by the changes of the characters in the past. There will be changes in the future .... On the question of the future of the Chinese language, there may be various views. We can bring them out for discussion and debate. I shall not dwell upon it any further since it does not fall within the scope of the task of the language reform.'

It appears from the foregoing remarks that while the possibility was held out that various views on the future of the Chinese language might be brought out for discussion and debate, the whole question was considered as falling outside the scope of the task of language reform. Within the literature on language reform there has indeed been little mention of this and related questions, such as the future of Chinese dialects and characters.

Despite the lack of full-scale discussion, there is no lack of comments which, while echoing the official views as sketched above by Chou En-lai, also indicate the existence of some dissatisfaction with the weight, timing, and precise implementation of various aspects of the reform. For example, in a pamphlet written at the beginning of 1956, one writer[5] noted:

> 'Some people say, since phoneticized writing certainly has many advantages, why is it that it has not long since been decided upon? Why did the All-China Writing Reform Conference of last year simply decide to give priority to simplifying Chinese characters, and why only recently has the State Council promulgated the plan for simplification of characters, rather than immediately and universally carrying out phoneticized writing?'

The writer answered these questions as follows:

> 'Our reply is that phoneticized writing certainly must be brought into being, but this is not something that can be done right away. The reason is that Chinese characters have a history of several thousand years, they are not phoneticized writing, and people in general are not familiar with the spelling out of sounds. Our dialects are also too complex, and there is not yet a generally used common language. There is also another problem with respect to Chinese characters, namely that in their lexicon there are many homonyms which are understandable if written in Chinese characters but unintelligible if

> spoken. These factors make plain that if Chinese characters are to be transformed into a phoneticized writing, there are a great many complicated problems which it will take time to investigate and weigh carefully. One cannot go at them impetuously in the hope of reforming the original Chinese characters out of existence in one fell swoop and replacing them completely with something else. Hence, the reform of Chinese characters must come about step by step. It will be necessary to complete a great deal of preparatory work so as to lay the foundations for the phoneticization of Chinese characters.
>
> Then also there is the problem of normalization of the Chinese language. Normalization simply means establishing a standard. Normalizing the Chinese language means fixing standards in phonology, vocabulary, grammar, and all aspects of the unified national common language, so that our language can have a single standard both in respect to speech and writing. Of course, the normalization of the Chinese language also cannot be carried out all at once. It can only come about after a great deal of work has been done.'

Among the numerous expressions of agreement with the official policy there is another worth citing as indicating something less than wholehearted enthusiasm:[6]

> 'Some people insist: "Reform of Chinese writing can only be along the lines of a phonetic writing. Since Chinese characters must be eliminated in the end, what is the point in giving consideration to simplified characters?" We know, as Chairman Mao has already stated, that the written language must be reformed under certain conditions; that is entirely correct. In view, of the evolution of Chinese characters and the political, economic, and cultural developments in modern times, it is quite incontestable that reform of Chinese writing must ultimately be along the lines of a phonetic writing. Such a tremendous reform cannot be achieved in a short period of time. For the time being we continue to use Chinese characters. Since Chinese characters are to be used, improving them a bit will have a certain value in studying them and really cannot be objected to. From the point of view of writing reform, simplified characters don't have many advantages but they don't have many disadvantages either. They cannot solve the basic problem, and can only make Chinese characters a tiny bit easier to write. It is only this very small contribution that simplified characters have to offer.'

3. SIMPLIFICATION OF CHARACTERS

The decision to go in for simplification of characters was in effect the fundamental decision of the whole reform program. On the one hand it marked the greatest departure from the mainstream of previous efforts at reform. On the other hand it had far-reaching effects on the other parts of the program. Published materials do not provide a clear picture of just how the step came to be taken. Some writers make it out to be the natural outcome of evolutionary changes in the Chinese system of writing. Thus Wei Chien-kung places the present simplification within the context of historical changes which included the creation of the Lesser Seal script in the third century B.C., the subsequent development of the even simpler Clerk Script, and the gradual extension since T'ang and Sung times of simplified characters similar to those now in use.[7]

According to I Hsi-wu,[8] however, the term *chien-t'i-tzu* 'simplified characters' is new. In his view the modern history of these characters goes back to the end of the Ch'ing dynasty, when several scholars advocated the use of simplified forms. With the beginning of the May Fourth Movement in 1919 more voices were raised in support of the idea. Among these were the veteran language reformer, Ch'ien Hsüan-t'ung, who from 1920 to 1934 advanced several proposals for the use of simplified characters.[9] According to I Hsi-wu and Tu Tzu-ching, in 1935 the Nationalist Ministry of Education from a list of 2,400-odd simplified characters submitted by Ch'ien selected 354 as the First List of Simplified Characters, which was sent out to provincial and city departments of education with orders for their adoption.[10] Subsequently the Ministry issued an order stating that it was not necessary to put the List into effect.[11]

From 1936 to 1948 there was apparently no activity worth chronicling in the area of simplified characters. During this period the language reform movement was dominated by the emergence of the Latinized New Writing and by the debate between its supporters and those of the National Language Romanization.

The resurgence of language reform activity which accompanied the establishment of the new government on October 1, 1949, was marked by the new weight given to simplification of characters. The unofficial Chinese Writing Reform Association, a widely based organization headed by Wu Yü-chang, a veteran of the New Writing movement, in its inaugural meeting of October 10 was charged by the chairman with a number of tasks, foremost among which was finding a system for Latinization of

Chinese and simplification of characters.[12] Ten days later Wu Yü-chang reported to a directorate of forty members on plans to form a number of special committees 'to study the formulation of a system of phonetic writing, to study methods of putting order into and simplifying characters, to study and survey the dialects, to study the languages of racial minorities and create writing systems for them, and to compile publications and dictionaries, etc., etc.'[13]

While the Writing Reform Association was busying itself along a number of different lines, it appears that the government had already decided to give top priority to work on simplification of characters. According to Wu Yü-chang, 'The government began research on simplifying Chinese characters immediately after liberation.'[14] Tu Tzu-ching, a veteran chronicler of events related to language and script reform, in the minutely detailed chronology referred to above (see note 10) has a number of entries indicating that the first acts of the new government in the language area were the following:

(1) On July 31, 1950, the Ministry of Education convened a conference of the Committee for Research on Chinese Writing Reform.

(2) A little over a week later, on August 9, the Ministry of Education convened a conference on Simplification of Characters.

(3) In the same month the Social Education Office of the Ministry of Education issued a two-volume list of 1500-odd commonly used simplified characters.[15]

During this initial year and in the years immediately following, government activity was concentrated almost entirely on matters relating to simplification. Such activity as took place on other aspects of language reform was largely confined to private individuals and organizations. Thus several New Writing groups were reactivated in a number of cities, and several journals and other publications having to do with the New Writing were put out.[16] The revival of Latinization activity was short-lived.[17] Y. R. Chao asserts that several members of the executive committee of the Chinese Writing Reform Association fell into 'disgrace or worse' in the years after 1949.[18] The same fate befell others, identified as 'rightists', who alleged that the simplification of characters was a failure and was opposed by the masses. They were accused of using their attack on reform of the written language as a pretext to attack the Party and government.[19]

Government success in winning support for its policy of concentrating on simplification of characters is evidenced by the fact that the first recorded accomplishment of the unofficial Writing Reform Association was the production in August 1951 of a two-volume dictionary of 3300-odd commonly used simplified characters.[20] A few months later, in December, the government approved a resolution to establish an official committee for Research on Chinese Writing Reform, which was formally set up the following February with a membership of fourteen persons, including Wu Yü-chang as Vice-Chairman. Its assignment was first of all to do research on Chinese characters and to draw up a plan for their simplification, and secondly to work out a new phonetic system.[21] In the following year the research undertaken by the Committee led to a tentative plan for reduction in the number of characters and simplification of the strokes. After considerable discussion and revision, this was completed at the end of 1954 as a Draft Plan for Simplification of Characters. In January of 1955 the Committee jointly with the Ministry of Education published the Plan, a total of 300,000 copies being distributed widely with the aim of eliciting comments.[22]

After nationwide discussion of the Plan, a major conference on Chinese Writing Reform was called in October of 1955. An amended plan was approved, passed on to the State Council, and finally promulgated on January 28, 1956.[23] With this the official stamp of approval was put on simplification of characters as the first step in the reform of written Chinese. The simplifications which have been adopted are by and large those which have been customarily used by Chinese in hasty and informal writing. Primarily they involve a reduction in number of strokes by such devices as letting part of a character stand for the whole, replacing a complicated character by a simpler homophone, condensing several strokes into one or two, and so on. The number of abbreviated characters is expected to total about 3,000, representing roughly half of the 7,000-8,000 characters occurring in ordinary modern Chinese.[24]

A good deal of confusion has attended the choice and use of simplified characters. At times some people coined abbreviated forms which nobody except themselves could make out. Some simplified forms were first officially presented for use and then withdrawn when it was discovered that they were objectionable for one reason or another. The Committee for Reforming the Chinese Written language was chided by Chou En-lai for not putting the confusion in the use of simplified characters under control.[25]

A certain confusion still exists in that the use of the simplified forms is not consistent. Elements which are supposed to be abbreviated only when used as components of other characters sometimes occur independently. Even within the same publication one frequently finds both the regular and simplified forms in use. Much of this confusion appears to be due to the inadequate availability of type faces for the abbreviated forms. It is likely that these difficulties are temporary and that they will be ironed out eventually. The first phase of the writing reform movement seems to be well on its way toward success.

4. PROMOTION OF A STANDARD LANGUAGE

The idea of promoting a standard language played a prominent role in earlier stages of the reform movement, though there were significant differences of opinion as to the precise role it was to play in relation to the Chinese dialects. For many reformers, including some of the supporters of the National Romanization, it was envisaged as an exclusive standard which would do away with dialects as soon as possible. On the other hand, supporters of Latinized New Writing advocated developing separate written languages for the various dialects in addition to adopting a standard language for purposes of communication among speakers of different dialects.

The position adopted by the Communist government was essentially a repudiation of the stand taken by supporters of Latinization and an acceptance of the views of their opponents. It has not been possible to determine just how this decision was reached. On the basis of what may be an inadequate search of the literature, it appears that no conferences were called to discuss the matter, and no supporters of the former Latinization position came forward to argue their case.

Such discussion as took place centered on problems of defining the standard language and promoting its development. The Chinese Writing Reform Association devoted attention to these questions from its inception in October of 1949. Official interest is indicated by the creation within the Ministry of Education of a Bureau for the Promotion of the Standard Language. Most important are the views expressed in a collection of documents that were published as the aftermath of a week-long meeting held in October, 1955, by the Technical Conference on the Problem of the Standardization of Modern Chinese under the auspices of the Chinese Academy of Sciences. The meeting was attended by linguistic experts, including several from the Soviet Union, Poland, and Rumania, by responsible government and party officials, and by numerous persons active in cultural and educational work.

Although it appears that at no point in the conference was any consideration given to the earlier stand of Latinization supporters vis-à-vis the dialects, a number of speakers and writers of articles represented in the above-mentioned collection of documents went well beyond the general expressions of support for a standard language by denouncing the underlying basis for the Latinization point of view, namely the emphasis on the disparities among the Chinese dialects. The denunciations were made on political as well as linguistic grounds.

The political aspects were raised in an attack on 'Western linguists' in the first paper[26] read at the Conference, by A. Graur, a Rumanian. Underlying his remarks were some well-known ideas of I. V. Stalin:[27]

> 'A nation is a historically evolved stable community of language, territory, economic life, and psychological make-up manifested in a community of culture.
>
> There is no nation which at one and the same time speaks several languages . . .
>
> Marx . . . admitted the need for a single national language as the superior form to which dialects, as lower forms, were subordinate.'

Basing himself on these ideas, Graur asserted:

> 'There are some Western linguists who think there are several Chinese languages, because the differences among the various Chinese dialects are rather large, to the point where the people who use these dialects cannot understand each other. This mistaken suggestion is from a political point of view very dangerous. Whoever says that there are several languages says in principle that there are several nations. To contend that there are several Chinese languages is to argue for the division of China into several states.'

Although Graur's comments are aimed specifically against Western scholars, they could with equal justice have been directed at the supporters of Latinization, who, while still in general referring to the various mutually unintelligible speech forms as dialects, nevertheless treated them in effect as separate languages by proposing that they be provided with separate orthographies.[28] In the thirties such suggestions were attacked in terms almost identical with those of Graur's, but at that time they came from the other end of the political spectrum.[29]

Views similar to those of Graur were expressed by Wang Li, one of China's foremost linguists, in an article originally published in *People's Daily* and reprinted in the *Collection of Documents.*[30] Wang stated:

> 'Chinese is the language of the Chinese people. As everyone knows, a common language is one of the characteristics of a nation. Hence the common language of the Chinese nation is one of the fundamental marks of the Chinese nation. Bourgeois linguists on the one hand cannot but acknowledge that the number of people who use Chinese ranks first in the world, and on the other hand they vilify our nation by insisting that the term "Chinese language" refers to a language family made of a great many varieties of mutually unintelligible languages. [At this point Wang has a footnote citing Bloomfield, *Language*, 44, and identifying him as "one of the most reactionary American linguists".] Their denial that we have a common language is equivalent to denying that we belong to a common nation. This obviously is nonsense. As a matter of fact, we have a written language which has been used in common for several thousand years and which attests to the unshakeable unity of the Chinese people. Moreover, for such a nation as the Chinese with its more than 550,000,000 people, it is natural that the dialects are numerous and the divergences great. These are facts. But if one compares the Chinese dialects, the grammar is basically the same, lexical differences are not great, and the phonology has rules of correspondence. In view of the fact that lexical differences are not great and that there are rules of sound correspondence, it is certainly not possible to say that there are a great many varieties of mutually unintelligible languages.
>
> While recognizing the iron fact that the Chinese people have a common language, we must still point out that the common language of the Chinese nation has not yet reached the ultimate stage of maturity – the stage of a completely unified standard. We must, still on the foundation of the unified written language, establish a unified spoken language.'

Wang Li called on all Chinese to contribute to the work toward unification of the national language. Graur particularly urged linguists to undertake this task, adding: 'This is not only a professional task, but also a patriotic duty.'

In view of the foregoing exhortations and denunciations with their emphasis on using political rather than linguistic criteria for defining a language, it is not surprising that the views expressed were allowed to remain unchallenged. No one pointed out that neither Bloomfield nor, with one possible exception,[31] the supporters of Latinization, who included such Communist stalwarts as Ch'ü Ch'iu-pai, ever suggested that the Chinese should be divided into a number of linguistically determined states. Nor was it pointed out that the alleged contradiction inherent in the concept of a single nation speaking a diversity of languages is a contradiction only on the basis of a particular definition of nation, and hence that Stalin's definition of a nation might possibly require modification when applied to the Chinese situation.

Although these basic questions were not raised there were some faint indications of dissent from the general line. Ni Hai-shu, a strong supporter of Latinization who was quoted above as earlier entertaining high hopes for a basic reform, referred to the fears of some dialect speakers that their dialects would soon be abolished, and expressed his own fears that there might be too narrow a definition of 'common language'.[32] The most explicit suggestion of dissent was made by a Polish participant at the conference, Witold Jablonski, in the following comments regarding the status of dialects:[33]

> 'At the present conference everyone has discussed the present status of dialects, but there has been rather little consideration given to their future. In some countries, for example in Poland, the status of local dialects in the national culture is rather high. This causes no harm to national unity. Not only is folklore respected by all, there are even some dialects which have their own independent literature. Those who engage in such literary activity are not confined to a few local writers of dialect. There are in addition a number of professional literary men who live in the big cities. This of course refers to a rather small country with a population of only 25,000,000 people. But what must be emphasized is that dialects far removed from the Polish literary language all have their own very flourishing literature.'

Jablonski's comments elicited no response. Most speakers simply elaborated on the prevailing line on standardization and, befitting their participation in a Technical Conference on the Problem of the Standardization of Modern Chinese, confined their remaining remarks to technical problems.

The main paper presented at the Conference was a joint report by Lo

Ch'ang-p'ei and Lü Shu-hsiang, two outstanding linguists, on the subject 'Problems of the Standardization of Modern Chinese'.[34] The authors summarized in familiar terms the arguments for having a single national standardized language. They listed the Chinese dialects and the number of speakers in the following table:

Northern	387,000,000
Kiangsu-Chekiang	46,000,000
Hunan	26,000,000
Kiangsi	13,000,000
Hakka	20,000,000
Northern Min	7,000,000
Southern Min	15,000,000
Cantonese	27,000,000

The authors pointed out that these dialects differed most in phonology, less in vocabulary, and least in syntax. With respect to phonological differences, they reiterated the view widely held by Chinese linguists that 'rules can be found for by far the greatest number' of these differences, thus simplifying the problem of teaching the standard language to dialect speakers.[35] A number of tasks were outlined. High on the agenda of things that needed to be done was the intensified study of dialects, especially along the line of contrastive analysis, in order to help dialect speakers learn the standard language.

In the discussions which followed the report by Lo Ch'ang-p'ei and Lü Shu-hsiang, as well as in those which both preceded and followed the conference, it is apparent that there has been a good deal of disagreement about many points involved in the problem of a standardized language. Opposition has been expressed, sometimes forthrightly, sometimes in guarded tones, to an imposed standard language. Reports have been frequent that in the classroom the use of the standard language, contrary to official urgings, is often confined to the language courses, with the local dialect remaining the medium of communication between teachers and students in other courses such as history, science, and so on. There has been much uncertainty as to just what a standard language is, as evidenced by the use of such terms as *piao-chun yü* 'standard language', *kuei-fan-hua* normalization', *kuo-yü* 'national language', *p'u-t'ung hua* 'common speech', and still others. The precise nature of the standard language in relation to the dialects, especially to the Peking dialect, has been much discussed, as evidenced by debates such as those on the status of Pekingese terminal *r* and other phonological features, on questions of standard versus dialect lexicon, and on how much flexibility should be permitted in syntactical structures, including innovations absorbed from Western languages.

Many of the topics raised in the discussion concerning the standard language have been admirably treated in several recent studies, notably those by Paul L-M Serruys and Miss Li Chi. The reader interested in further details is referred to these studies.[36]

A final word is in order regarding the general status of the standardization problem in China. Despite all the uncertainties and disagreements about many points, it appears that the effort to promote a standardized language is proceeding apace. The guide lines for the promotion of the common language were laid down in a twelve-point directive of February 6, 1956, from the State Council.[37] There has been a great deal of practically motivated linguistic research, some of it amateurish, some on a fairly sophisticated level. Although there is evidence of some resentment among dialect speakers at the imposition of a standardized national language, particularly when accompanied by denigration of the dialects, it is likely that there is overwhelming recognition even in dialect areas of the need for a lingua franca and acceptance as such of 'common national language which has the Northern Chinese dialects as its basis and the Peking pronunciation as its normative sound system'.[38] Actually teaching 154,000,000 people to master a form of speech which in some cases differs from their own as much, according to Y. R. Chao,[39] as does Dutch from English or Italian from Spanish is a task of colossal proportions. Accomplishments are bound to be uneven – greatest among those with educational opportunities and obvious need for a common language (teachers, actors, transportation and communication personnel, government officials, and so on), least among adult peasants and others whose need and opportunities are most restricted. Despite all the shortcomings of the program and the difficulties stemming from the present state of education, economy, and other aspects of Chinese life, there seems little question but that knowledge of the standard language will spread ever more widely in China.

5. CREATION OF A PHONETIC ALPHABET

Work on creating an alphabet was initiated in October, 1949, by the unofficial Writing Reform Association and was taken up shortly thereafter by the government, but at a much slower tempo than in the case of other reform activities. The public was invited to submit suggestions for an alphabet; it presented over 1,200 schemes up to 1957. Initially the government seems to have leaned toward the idea of devising a purely Chinese set of symbols as being more acceptable to the national sentiments of the people. Since none of the schemes along these lines proved to be very satisfactory, it was decided to drop this approach. The Cyrillic alphabet was also given consideration, but then discarded. It was finally decided to base the script on the Latin alphabet. The task of making the final choice was turned over to a committee of experts who included representatives of various schools, such as Latinization (Ni Hai-shu and Wu Yü-chang) and National Language Romanization (Lo Ch'ang-p'ei and Li Chin-hsi).

The first draft scheme was published in February, 1956, and was submitted to the people for their reactions. After extensive consideration a revised scheme was adopted toward the end of 1957, submitted to the National People's Congress for its approval, and then adopted officially following approval by the Congress in February, 1958.[40] The scheme was called *Han-yü p'in-yin fang-an*, translated variously as 'Chinese Phonetics Plan' or 'Chinese Phonetic Alphabet' or 'Chinese Phonetic Scheme', among others. In its own orthography it is generally written as *pīnyīn* or, without tone marks, as *pinyin*.

The scheme can be summarized as follows:

I. Consonants

	unaspirated stops	aspirated stops	nasals	fricatives	voiced continuants
labials	b	p	m	f	
dental stops, nasal, and lateral	d	t	n		l
dental sibilants	z	c	s		
retroflexes	zh	ch		sh	r
palatals	j	q		x	
gutturals	g	k		h	

II. Vowels

a, e, i, o, u, ü

III. Semivowels

y, w (as initials)

IV. Tones

1. ā(mā); 2. á(má); 3. ǎ(mǎ); 4. à(mà)

V. Juncture

(pí'ǎo)

The following points may be noted:

(1) The symbol *u* represents a high back vowel except after *y* and the palatal initials *j*, *q*, *x*, when it represents a high front vowel. This is a fairly ingenious solution to the problem of the symbol *ü*, the use of which can be confined to combinations with *l* and *n*: *lü* versus *lu*, *nü* versus *nu*.

(2) The system abandons the earlier attempt to follow the distinction made in some dialects between 'sharp' and 'round' sounds. Instead, the Peking pronunciation, which does not make the distinction, has been adopted as the basis for the transcription, e.g. *xi* for both 'west' (< si) and 'sparse' (< hi).

(3) The symbols have been so chosen that there is but rare occasion to use the juncture symbol. The need is illustrated in one official publication by the expressions *pi'ao* 'fur coat' and *piao* 'to float'. Actually, correct use of tone symbols would obviate the need in this case: *píâo* 'fur coat' versus *piāo* 'float'. A better example is *fáng'ài* 'to hinder' versus *fāngài* 'to rebuild'.

(4) The symbol *i* represents a high front unrounded vowel except after retroflexes and dental sibilants, when it represents the two distinctive vocalizations of these two sets of initials, e.g. *si* 'silk': *shi* 'wet'.

(5) Full tones are represented by one of the four tone symbols. The neutral tone is indicated by the absence of a symbol.

Although there are minor points of detail where exception might be taken to some of the solutions adopted, by and large the result is a compromise scheme eminently suited to its primary purpose of representing the sounds of the Peking dialect. It is with some justice that Wu Yü-chang says the scheme 'is developed on the basis of those of the past and embodies all their merits'.[41] Most noteworthy is the fact that while the National Language Romanization system of tonal spelling was rejected, the insistence of its supporters that tones be represented was adopted, thereby removing the most serious defect of the old Latinization scheme.

6. USES OF THE PHONETIC ALPHABET

Again and again in the literature on the reform movement the point is emphasized that the Phonetic Alphabet is not intended to replace characters – certainly not now, though perhaps sometime in the future, and then only after much preparatory 'study' and 'experimentation'. It appears that little official encouragement has been given to specific preparatory work. Insofar as they are not actually discouraged from working in this area, the reformers have been left much to their own devices.

Government interest has centered largely on current applications of the phonetic scheme. Chief among these is the annotation of characters to give the pronunciation so as to improve the efficiency in learning and teaching characters. Other uses, some mere extensions of the annotation function, are to aid the teaching and learning of the common speech, to serve as a basis on which the various national minorities might create their own written language, to help in translating foreign names and terms, to assist foreigners in their study of Chinese, to help solve the problem of compiling indexes, and so on.

The actual application of the phonetic alphabet has proceeded on an uneven course. There is considerable variety in the implementation of the program, with particular individuals and institutions going ahead along certain lines while others make their own improvisations. A study of some concrete applications of *pinyin* will be helpful in providing a fragmentary but still illuminating picture of how this phase of the writing reform program is actually progressing in China.

A good place to begin is with the first few grades of school. Chinese children start first grade at age seven. First they learn the alphabet, and then they proceed quickly to learn characters, using the alphabet to read and write the pronunciation of the characters. In one beginning character text the first lesson consists simply of three characters for *k'ai hsüeh le* 'Starting School', and by mid-year each lesson has not progressed beyond three to five short sentences.[42] Some second grade texts use the alphabet to give the sounds only of new characters,[43] in contrast to the frequent textbook practice of placing the transcription above each character. (Most often the transcription is written in separate syllables, generally but not always with indication of tones.) Beginning in the third grade, and especially in the fifth and sixth grades, even the new characters are in some cases not provided with phonetic annotation. In many cases teachers beyond the first or second grade do not even know the phonetic alphabet.[44]

Under these conditions it is not surprising to find many children experiencing a loss of control over *pinyin* in their preoccupation with learning new characters while trying not to forget those already learned. There is widespread lament over the phenomenon of *hui-sheng*, literally 'return to unfamiliarity'.[45] The term refers to loss of control over what has been studied, whether characters or alphabet, and can be translated as 'defamiliarization' or, in the not infrequent case of complete loss of literacy, as 'deliteralization'.

Of great interest in this connection is the account given by one writer, Jo Wen, of some observations in a first year class which he visited in Harbin on November 19, 1962. He made a close examination of the diaries of a number of children, noting that the first entries were entirely in *pinyin*, that the first characters, five in number, appeared on October 18 intermixed with *pinyin*, and that thereafter there was a gradual increase in the number of characters relative to *pinyin*. He divided the diaries into three groups according to the number of errors made by the pupils. Those in the first two groups had few errors. Reproduced below, with the original errors of the young author left in, is a sample of the writing done by one of the weakest students:

> **11 月 19 日 míng 天 yòu kăo shì 了 我 要· zhēng quĕ dă yì băn fēn 老 师 zhŏng 説 我 写 的 字 不 hăo 我 yí dìng yào huéi dào 家 lĭng liàn hăo 字 wán.**[46]
>
> 11 month 19 day tomorrow having another test I must trie to get a hundred the teacher allways says the characters I write are no good I have to go back hom and practice the characters until I have learned them the end.

The errors made by the young diarist are the following: *zhēng quĕ* should be *zhēng qŭ*; *yì băn* should be *yì băi*; *zhong* should be *zŏng*; *huéi dào* should be *huí dào*; and *lĭng* should be *lĭ*. It is worth remarking that there are no errors in the tones, but only in the segmental phonemes, and that the errors are not serious enough to impair intelligibility.

For a child who has been in school for less than three months, the ability to pen an intelligible communication is no mean achievement, one well beyond the capability of a comparable first grader in the United States. In less than three months Chinese children, even those toward the bottom of the class, are on the verge of achieving literacy in the alphabetic writing.

Many voices have been raised against an educational policy which, instead of consolidating what the child is able to accomplish in a few months in *pinyin*, goes on rather to neglect this writing by concentrating on characters. The well-known writer, Mao Tun, noted that this granddaughter after finishing first grade had mastered *pinyin* to the point where she could write letters to her mother when the latter went to work in the countryside. But in the second grade she was given so little practice in alphabetic writing that she lost the skill, without, of course, achieving literacy in the characters. Incensed at this situation, Mao Tun called for continued use of *pinyin* after the first grade so that children could retain mastery of such writing while acquiring a command of the characters – a policy which he described as 'walking on two legs'.

Similar views were expressed by many other writers. Jo Wen, cited above in connection with his examination of children's diaries, urged that in the first semester of first grade only *pinyin* should be taught, since this would enable children to write anything that they were able to say. He, too, urged a policy of 'walking on two legs'. Chou Yu-kuang, who has written extensively and often most informatively on matters of alphabetic writing, called for dividing the language courses into two parts, one concentrating on using *pinyin* and the other on using characters. The relative amount of time on each was to change from initial concentration on *pinyin* to the point where in the upper elementary grades (fourth to sixth), the ratio between characters and *pinyin* would be five to one. He called for such a program for adults as well as for children.[47]

Support along these lines came also from the linguist Lü Shu-hsiang. In an article published toward the end of 1962, Lü remarked that the work of the past few years was largely limited to the one aspect of using the alphabet as a tool for helping character recognition. He criticized the present readers with their emphasis on reading single characters, adding that it differed little from the old-fashioned method of declaiming the classics. He called for the creation of *pinyin* textbooks for teaching the common language. Apart from being written in the alphabetic script, the texts should indicate such things as stress, intonation, tempo, and juncture. He called for the use of such texts, and such texts alone, in the first semester of primary school, with the teaching of characters to be postponed until the second semester. But from beginning to end the textbooks in the elementary grades should, he felt, be provided with several sections of material entirely in *pinyin*, though in general without indication of stress, intonation, and so on. He emphasized the need for such materials in view of the fact that there were still no teaching materials based entirely on *pinyin* without characters.[48]

As a matter of fact, in contrast to the considerable outpouring of publications entirely in Latinization in the earlier period, it appears that since the adoption of the new alphabet not a single item of any kind, textbook or otherwise, has appeared entirely in *pinyin*. The expectation, voiced in 1954 in an English-language publication by the Vice-Chairman of the Committee for Research on the Reform of the Chinese Written Language, of some time 'translating into the new phonetic language all important works, treaties, and documents on politics, economics, literature, and science originally written in the old Chinese characters'[49] has as yet shown no signs of even beginning to be fulfilled.

In requesting the publication of materials entirely in the phonetic script some writers point out that such materials are much better adapted than those in characters to teaching the standard language to Mandarin speakers and especially to dialect speakers.[50] There have even been some suggestions from other than Latinization supporters as well that all-phonetic materials be published in the various dialects. Prior to the decision to emphasize a single standard language one writer suggested the creation of a General Table of Phonetic Symbols for the Dialects of the Whole Country. This was to form a fund from which the various dialects would draw according to their need in order to set up dialect phonetic schemes. These schemes then would in turn be used for publishing reading materials of a local character.[51]

In view of the official emphasis on promoting the standard language one would not expect these last suggestions to be carried out. Yet it is puzzling to find that draft phoneticization plans were drawn up for four Kwantung dialects (Cantonese, Hakka, Chaochow, Hainan) and published in the Canton *Nan-fang Jih-pao* for June 9, 1960.[52] As I have not come across any further information about these plans, it is not clear to me why they were created and what function they are supposed to perform. If they have gone beyond the 'draft' status it is likely that, unless there is a drastic change in policy, their use will be confined to character annotation for dialect speakers and contrastive phonological work to help such speakers learn the standard language. The fact that the draft phoneticization plans were published in a South China newspaper may be an illustration of the point made earlier that there is considerable unevenness in carrying out the writing reform program.

Another good example of this unevenness is seen in the use of *pinyin* in railroad telegraphy. Such use is most advanced in Manchuria, where the railroads had even earlier used other phonetic systems. Indeed, a history of railway telegraphy in Manchuria reads almost like a political history of the area: 1925, initiated use of the old National Phonetic

Symbols; 1941, changed to Japanese; 1946, changed back to National Phonetic Symbols; 1949, changed to Latinization; 1958, changed to *pinyin.*

In Harbin 95 percent of all messages sent or received are in *pinyin*; in Peking, 30 percent; in Shanghai, 8 percent. All railways are prepared to receive *pinyin* messages, but only those in the north use it to any extent in despatching messages.

The language used in the telegrams is by no means limited to form messages, which actually comprise only a small proportion of the total. All sorts of terms are used, as in listing the contents of a wayward trunk. Problems arise mainly from messages submitted to railway telegraph offices. The classical literary style, which often appears in such messages, is troublesome, but the greatest difficulties arise with messages the style of which is semiclassical-semivernacular or neither classical nor vernacular. Railway personnel seek permission from the senders to revise such wires into a more easily transmittable form. The railways have decreed: 'Telegrams should be based on the spoken style.'[53]

Apart from its use in railways, *pinyin* also serves as the basis of communication in the Chinese navy and in the fishing fleet.[54]

In 1961 the library of National People's University, of which Wu Yü-chang is president, began to use *pinyin* in its card catalogue. It was reported that after one year of use there was a reduction of 70-80 percent in errors of filing and a better than three-fold speed-up in filing cards and looking up entries.[55]

While the use of *pinyin* has been gradualy expanding in areas such as those mentioned above, it is worth noting that there is one area into which it has NOT spread, namely that of publications (other than for language-teaching purposes) aimed at a foreign readership. Journals such as *China Pictorial* and *People's China* and indeed apparently all English-language publications use the Wade romanization, in its minimal form, ignoring many of the distinctions made by that system. The name Ch'ü Ch'iu-pai, for example, appears as Chu Chiu-pai.

The inconsistencies and inadequacies in the use of *pinyin* reflect the somewhat ambiguous position of the government in respect to this phase of writing reform. Faced with what must be overwhelming preference for the traditional system of writing, by illiterates as well as by those already literate, by those inside as well as outside the government, the latter instead of embarking on a vigorous program to convince the people of the need for a basic reform, has chosen to emphasize simplified characters and a single standard language while permitting but minimizing *pinyin*.

It has thus chosen a course which can lead in various directions. Depending on the ability of the government to provide the people with the concrete requirements for learning (facilities, leisure, and so on), the course can lead to a gradual expansion in knowledge of the standard language and increase in literacy in a script which involves the least possible change. On the other hand, if the literacy program lags and *pinyin* loses its aura of strangeness, the emotional basis may be laid for giving ear to the not completely stilled voices of those who want a more basic reform in the Chinese writing system.

EPILOGUE: SPRING 1973

The preceding account of language and script reform in China was written in the early stages of the Cultural Revolution. During this long drawn-out upheaval, normal academic activities, including publication of scholarly journals such as *Chung-kuo yü-wen* [Chinese Language and Literature], were suspended, and there appears to have been little consideration – or at least little reported consideration – of matters relating to language and script reform. Recently there have been signs of a slow resumption, in altered form, of academic activities, but as yet no new information is available which would warrant any significant change in or addition to the account presented here.

NOTES

1. The material up to this point is summarized from my book *Nationalism and Language Reform in China* (Princeton: Princeton University Press, 1950).
2. Ni Hai-shu, *Chung-kuo yü-wen-te hsin-sheng*, 570.
3. H. Mills, 'Language Reform in China', *The Far Eastern Quarterly* 15, *passim.*
4. Chou En-lai, 'Current Tasks of Reforming the Written Language', in *Reform of the Chinese Written Language*, 7-29.
5. Wang K'ang, *Tsen-yang shih-hsing wen-tzu kai-ko* [How to Carry Out Writing Reform], 18-19.
6. I Hsi-wu, 'Chien-t'i-tzu-te chi-ko wen-t'i' [Some Problems Concerning Simplified Characters], in Cheng Lin-hsi, et al., *Chung-kuo wen-tzu kai-ko wen-t'i* [Problems of Chinese Writing Reform], 38.
7. Wei Chien-kung, 'Ts'ung Han-tzu fa-chan te ch'ing-k'uang k'an kai-ko-te t'iao-chien' [Conditions for Reform as Seen from the Development of Chinese characters], in Cheng Lin-hsi, et al., *Chung-kuo wen-tzu kai-ko wen-t'i*, 14.

8. I Hsi-wu, 'Chien-t'i-tzu-te chi-ko wen-t'i', 30-31.
9. Actually, Ch'ien Hsüan-t'ung took all sorts of positions, including abandoning Chinese in favor of Esperanto. (See DeFrancis, *Nationalism and Language Reform in China*, 68-69, 72-77.)
10. I Hsi-wu, 'Chien-t'i-tzu-te chi-ko wen-t'i', 31. Tu Tzu-ching, 'Chung-kuo wen-tzu kai-ko yun-tung nien-piao' [Chronological Table of the Movement for Chinese Writing Reform], in Cheng Lin-shi, *Chung-kuo wen-tzu kai-ko wen-t'i*, 147.
11. I Hsi-wu, 'Chien-t'i-tzu-te chi-ko wen-t'i', 31.
12. Mills, 'Language Reform in China', 521.
13. Chao Yuen Ren, 'Review of *Zhshfenz Yng de Beifang Xua Sin Wenzi Koben*', 388. The quoted excerpt is from a Hsinhua News Agency despatch of October 20, 1949.
14. Wu Yü-chang, 'Report on the Current Tasks of Reforming the Written Language and the Draft Scheme for a Chinese Phonetic Alphabet', in *Reform of the Chinese Written Language*, 31. Paul L. M. Serruys (*Survey of the Chinese Language Reform and the Anti-Illiteracy Movement in Communist China*, 47 and 167) notes some evidence of Communist interest in simplified characters before 1949.
15. Tu Tzu-ching, 'Chung-kuo wen-tzu kai-ko yun-tung nien-piao', 151.
16. Tu Tzu-ching, 'Chung-kuo wen-tzu kai-ko yun-tung nien-piao', 150-153.
17. The last *Latinxua* publication to which I have seen reference is a pamphlet entitled *Wo Kandao de Solian* [The Soviet Union I Saw], published in 1953. Wei Chueh, 'The Problem of Reforming the Chinese Written Language', 25.
18. Chao, 'Review of . . .', 340.
19. Chou En-lai, 'Current Tasks of Reforming the Written Language', 10-11; Wu Yü-chang, 'Report on the Current Tasks', 34.
20. Tu Tzu-ching, 'Chung-kuo wen-tzu kai-ko yun-tung nien-piao', 152.
21. Mills, 'Language Reform in China', 152.
22. Yeh Kung-ch'ao, 'Kuan-yü Han-tzu chien-hua kung-tso ti pao-kao' [Report on Work on Simplification of Chinese Characters], in Ch'üan-kuo wen-tzu kai-ko hui-i mi-shu-ch'u [Secretariat of the National Conference on Writing Reform], *Ti-i-tz'u ch'üan-kuo wen-tzu kai-ko hui-i wen-chien hui-pien* [Collection of Documents on the First National Conference on Writing Reform], 21.
23. Mills, 'Language Reform in China', 522-524. Also Tao-tai Hsia, *China's Language Reforms*, 1-2.
24. Mills, 'Language Reform in China', 524. This work and that by Hsia (see note 23) provide additional detail on the kinds of abbreviations used and the actual simplified characters adopted. The lists are incomplete.
25. Chou En-lai, 'Current Tasks of Reforming the Written Language', 12.
26. A. Graur, 'Kuan-yü tan-i-te min-tsu yü-yen' [On a Single National Language], in Hsien-tai Han-yü kuei-fan wen-t'i hsüeh-shu hui-i mi-shu-ch'u [Secretariat of the Technical Conference on Problems of the Standardization of Modern Chinese], *Hsien-tai Han-yü kuei-fan wen-t'i hsüeh-shu hui-i wen-chien hui-pien* [Collection of Documents of the Technical Conference on Problems of Standardization of Modern Chinese], 115-120.
27. Graur quotes the third sentence from Stalin's *Marxism and Linguistics*. (See *The Soviet Linguistic Controversy*, 72.) The first two sentences, though not quoted by Grauer, clearly underlie his use of the term 'nation'. They come from Stalin's

well-known work *Marksizm i national'nyi vopros*, 5-8. Russian *natsiya* is rendered into Chinese as *min-tzu*. Standing in opposition to these terms for 'nation' are the words *gosudarstvo* and *kuo-chia* for the concept 'state'. Elsewhere (p. 20) Stalin says a nation has a right to secede and form its own state. This means that for those who accept Stalin's ideas it follows that different languages mean different nations and hence possibly different states. Stalin's views were, of course, well known in China. His article of June 20, 1950, *Marxism and Linguistics* was promptly translated into Chinese and published in the next month. Tu Tzu-ching, 'Chung-kuo wen-tzu kai-ko yun-tung nien-piao', 151.

28. A rare instance of a Latinization supporter referring to the Chinese dialects as different languages is E. Siao, 'Latinization of the Chinese Script', 147.
29. DeFrancis, *Nationalism and Language Reform in China*, especially 238-240.
30. Wang Li, 'Lun Han-yü kuei-fan-hua' [On Standardization of Chinese], in Hsien-tai Han-yü kuei-fan wen-t'i hsüeh-shu hui-i mi-shu-ch'u, *Hsien-tai Han-yü kuei-fan wen-t'i...*, 287-290.
31. Siac ('Latinization', 147) expresses a point of view which is extreme even among Latinizers when he says: 'Out of the 400 million population of China not only the Mongols, Tibetans, Manchus, and a number of smaller nationalities, Liao, Lolo, etc., speak different languages, but even in the various provinces of China Proper there exist different cultures, customs, and languages'. Siao thus implies but does not flatly state that the Chinese do not form a single nation. Among other supporters of Latinization the idea that the Chinese DO form a single nation is not even questioned. All Latinizers, Siao included, take pains to refute the charge quoted by Siao that 'Latinization of the Chinese script means the breaking up of China into several states....' Thus Ni Hai-shu, in answer to a questionnaire in which I raised the question whether the creation of separate scripts for Cantonese and other dialects might eventually lead to the demand for the creation of a separate Cantonese State, stated flatly: 'Impossible... In addition to the regional alphabetized scripts there is an alphabetized script for the common language of the whole country. Moreover, the Cantonese are a hundred per cent consanguineous with the Chinese nation [Han tsu]; they have no reason or need to be independent' (Ni Hai-shu, 'Ta-fu mei-kuo John DeFrancis chün kuan-yü chung-kuo wen-tzu kai-ko-ti wen-t'i' [Answers to the Questionnaire of the American Mr. John De Francis Regarding the Problem of the Reform of the Chinese Script], *Wen hui pao* [Shanghai, March 5-6, 1947]).
32. Ni Hai-shu, 'Yung-hu Han-yü kuei-fan-hua kung-tso' [In Support of Chinese Standardization Work], in Hsien-tai Han-yü kuei-fan wen-t'i hsüeh-shu hui-i mu-shu-ch'u, *Hsien-tai Han-yü kuei-fan wen-t'i...*, 177-179.
33. Witold Jablonski, 'Kuan-yü Han-yü kuei-fan wen-t'e ti i-hsieh k'an-fa' [Some Views on the Problem of the Standardization of Chinese], in Hsien-tai Han-yü kuei-fan wen-t'i hsüeh-shu hui-i, *Hsien-tai Han-yü kuei-fan wen-t'i...*, 121-124.
34. In Hsien-tai Han-yü Kuei-fan wen-t'i hsüeh-shu hui, *Hsien-tai Han-yü kuei-fan wen-t'i...*, 4-22.
35. A dissent from this viewpoint has been expressed by a Western scholar in the following terms: 'Students of the dialects are unduly impressed by the idea of the laws of sound correspondence... It is doubtful how much the ordinary person who wants to learn the standard language can derive from these rules since they

presume that he is acquainted with Chinese historical philology and its specific terminology. Moreover, all these rules are subject to innumerable objections .... For the ordinary reader the rules are all very confusing and complicated' (Paul Serruys, *Survey of the Chinese Language Reform and the Anti-Illiteracy Movement in Communist China*, 58). Some Chinese share these views. Serruys (p. 159) quotes a participant in a course of standard language study as saying: 'The tragedy of the students of ancient phonology is that they have been deceived by the fascination of the regularities of these sound correspondences'.

36. For Serruys, see note 35. Miss Li's works, which like those of Serruys form part of the Studies in Chinese Communist Terminology put out by the Center for Chinese Studies at the University of California, include the following especially useful items: No. 1, *General Trends of Chinese Linguistic Changes under Communist Rule*; No. 4, *Part I: The Communist Term 'The Common Language' and Related Terms; Part II: Dialectical Terms in Common Usage; Part III: Literary and Colloquial Terms in New Usage*; No. 6, *A Provisional Grammar for Teaching Chinese with Introduction and Commentary*; and No. 9, *New Features in Chinese Grammatical Usage*. Also useful is H. H. Tung, 'Recent Studies in Phonetics and Phonology in China'.
37. Summarized in Mills, 'Language Reform in China', 528-530.
38. Serruys, *Survey of the Chinese Language Reform* ..., 51.
39. See references in DeFrancis, *Nationalism and Language Reform in China*, 192.
40. Chou En-lai, *Reform of the Chinese Written Language, passim.*
41. Wu Yü-chang, 'Report on the Current Tasks ...', 49.
42. Chou Yu-kuang, 'Fa-hui Han-yü p'in-yin tsai yü-wen chiao-yü shang te kung-tso' [Developing the Use of the Chinese Phonetic Alphabet in Language Education], 3.
43. Mao Tun, 'Kuan-yü hsiao-hsüeh-sheng hsüeh-hui p'in-yin tzu-mu yü hui-sheng te wen-t'i' [Concerning the Problem of Elementary School Children Losing their Mastery of the Phonetic Alphabet], 2.
44. Yin Tso-yen and Sung Shou-ch'o, 'Kuan-yü Han-tzu p'in-yin tzu-mu hui-sheng wen-t'i te i-ko tiao-ch'ao' [A Study of the Problem of Losing Mastery of the Phonetic Alphabet], 4.
45. Mao Tun, 'Kuan-yü hsiao-hsüeh-sheng ...', 2; Cheng Lin-hsi, *Chung-kuo wen-tzu kai-ko wen-t'i*, 40; Chang Hung-hsi, 'Tui chieh-chüeh p'in-yin tzu-mu hui-sheng wen-t'i te i-chien' [Views on Solving the Problem of Loss of Mastery of the Phonetic Alphabet], 5-6.
46. Jo Wen, 'I-nien-chi hsüeh-sheng hsieh jih-chi' [First Graders Write Diaries], 7.
47. Chou Yu-kuang, 'Fa-hui Han-yü p'in-yin ...', 4.
48. Lü Shu-hsiang, 'Tsai lun p'in-yin tzu-mu ho yü-yen chiao-hsüeh' [More on the Phonetic Alphabet and Language Teaching], 1-2; 'Ts'ung Han-yü p'in-yin fang-an hsiang-tao yü-yen chiao-hsüeh' [The Teaching of Language Considered from the Chinese Phonetic Plan], 7.
49. Wei Chueh, 'The Problem of Reforming the Chinese Written Language', 26.
50. Lü Shu-hsiang, 'A Further Discussion', 2; Cheng Lin-hsi, *Chung-kuo wen-tzu kai-ko* ..., 48-49.
51. Chou Ting-i, 'Han-yü fang-yen ho p'in-yin wen-tzu' [Chinese Dialects and Alphabetized Writing], in Cheng Lin-hsi, et al., *Chung-kuo wen-tzu kai-ko* ..., 137-138.
52. U. S. Consulate, Hongkong, *Current Background* 629 (July 25, 1960). The pho-

neticization plans are based on the Latin alphabet. Arabic numerals written at the top right of the syllable are used to indicate tones.

53. Chou Yu-kuang and Wang Yin-sheng, 'T'ieh-lu tien-pao ying-yung Han-yü p'in-yin te shih-ti tiac ch'a' [An On-the-Spot Study of the Use of the Chinese Phonetic Alphabet in Railway Telegraphy], *passim*.
54. Wu Yü-chang, 'Han-yü p'in yin fang-an zai ko fang-mien te ying-yung' [Various Uses of the Chinese Phonetics Scheme], 3.
55. National People's University Library, 'Li-yung Han-yü p'in-yin tzu-mu tsu-chih t'u-shu mu-lu te ching-yen' [Experience in Using the Chinese Phonetic Alphabet in Library Cataloguing], 2-3. The use of *pinyin* for cataloguing purposes at People's University is another illustration of the disagreement in China on implementing the reform program. An essential aspect of setting up an alphabetic file is of course to determine whether to file by letters, by syllables independent of the character, or by syllables taking into account the character represented, and so on. Chou Yu-kuang discussed this subject in a book (which I have not seen) published in 1961. A review in China's leading linguistic journal took Chou to task for discussing the subject on the grounds that it was 'too early' to raise it now. (Chang Cheng-li, 'Tui *Han-tzu kai-ko lun-chi* te chi-tien i-chien' [Some Views Regarding *Survey of Chinese Writing Reform*]', 509. Undeterred, Chou returned to the subject in an article published in the same journal: 'Han-yü p'in-yin tsai k'o-hsüeh shu-mu shang te ying-yung' [The application of the Chinese Phonetic Alphabet to Scientific Terminology], 95-96.

BIBLIOGRAPHY

Full references can be found under the following numbers in the bibliography to Wang, wm. S-Y, 'Bibliography of Chinese Linguistics' in Sebeok, T. (ed.), *Current Trends in Linguistics* 1967, 2, 188-499:

307	1910	2544
372	2009	2704
1444	2203	2787
1446	2315	2824
1488	2361	2904
1536	2362	2950
1600	2374	2951
1601	2377	2952

CHAIM RABIN 8

Spelling Reform - Israel 1968*

LINGUISTIC BACKGROUND

Spelling of Consonants

The Hebrew script is essentially consonantal, that is, the basic transliterated values of its twenty-two characters are: ' (glottal stop), *b*, *g*, *d*, *h*, *v*, *z*, *ḥ*, *ṭ*, *y*, *k*, *l*, *m*, *n*, *s*, ᶜ (pharyngal), *p*, *tz*, *q*, *r*, *sh*, and *t*. These values are historical, and in actual speech some of these are pronounced the same, varying according to the various traditional reading dialects still preserved by Jewish communities, especially in prayer, and in the two principal pronunciations now current in Israel: that of Jews originating in Asia and Africa (Sephardim) versus that of those whose forefathers came from Europe and America (Ashkenazim), to simplify the division somewhat.

Some of the above characters also have more than one sound: *b*, *k*, and *p* are in both Israeli dialects under certain conditions also pronounced [v], [x], and [f]; *sh* is in a number of words pronounced [s]; and ' and, in Ashkenazi dialect, ᶜ are often silent.

As far as the consonants are concerned, the spelling is thus strictly historical and requires considerable skill both in reading and writing.

Spelling of Vowels

Originally, long vowels were indicated within the consonantal spelling as follows: *v* stands sometimes for /o/, sometimes for /u/; *y* stands for /i/

* From Joan Rubin and Bjorn Jernudd (eds.), *Can Language be Planned?* (Honolulu: University Press of Hawaii), 95-121. Reprinted with permission.

and, on comparatively rare occasions, for /e/. At the end of a word, *h* indicates the presence of a vowel, mostly /a/, but sometimes /e/, rarely /o/. However, for over a thousand years vowel quantity has not been distinguished in pronunciation, and the short vowels /a, o, u, i, e/ sound just the same as the former long vowels. This means that the vowel indication is in fact simply part of the historical spelling, just as is the knowledge when to pronounce *v* and *y* as consonants and when as vowels.

In Bibles, prayer books, poetry, and dictionaries and grammar books for young children and language learners, full vowel indication is achieved by a system of symbols placed above, below, and inside the letters, as it is in so many Asian scripts. In Hebrew this system is called POINTING. There is no difficulty in reading a pointed passage, except for one symbol that indicates both /a/ and /o/; but it is difficult to learn how to point words correctly because, although there are fourteen vowel symbols representing original long, lengthened, short, and reduced vowels, today only five, or in some pronunciations six, different vowels are sounded. The original quantity of the vowels was regulated by syllable structure and other features; thus, in order to place them correctly, one has to know Hebrew grammar well: in fact, grammar teaching in schools today is largely concerned with inculcating correct pointing. In spite of this, few people are able to point any word or form at sight. The preparation and proofreading of texts with full vocalization is done by specialists, and they are well paid. Besides, there are no fixed rules for pointing the many foreign words in present-day Hebrew, even though their pronunciation is quite clear.

Vowel Indication as a Language Problem

The main problem about this system of vowel indication is its cost. While the setting of an average sixteen-page text of straight nonvocalized print cost $ 75 in 1969, the same text would cost over $ 150 if fully pointed. The symbols above and below the letters are set as separate lines and require justifying. A system for linotyping a much simplified pointing by having the vowel symbols cast on the same body requires approximately 250 keys and is used only for immigrant newspapers, which, as a result, are heavily subsidized. The pointing cannot be typed. Although a typewriter enabling the vowels to be typed in a separate operation (that is, each line being typed twice) has been designed, not enough orders were received to justify having the letters cast.

Long before the pointing was invented, it had become common practice to help the reader by inserting *v* and *y* not only where they are grammatically justified but also in places where /u, o, i/ were originally short vowels. This is called full (plene) spelling, as opposed to the grammatical (defective) spelling described above. The effect of this procedure can be gauged by stating that /i/ constitutes 6 percent of the sounds in a running text; /o/, 5.7 percent; and /u/, 2.3 percent; while the unrepresented vowels are /a/, 17.1 percent; and /e/, 13.5 percent. Moreover, the method does not help to distinguish between /u/ and /o/. A further help is provided by writing *vv* for consonantal /v/ and *yy* for consonantal /y/. In spite of its comparatively small statistical incidence, the full spelling does help a great deal in distinguishing, for instance, the active and passive modes in many verbs or in identifying the correct form of nouns, since Hebrew, like Arabic, extensively employs vowel patterns for grammatical purposes (for instance, *spr* can be read /safar/ 'he counted', /siper/ 'he told', /supar/ 'it was told', /sapar/ 'barber', /sefer/ 'book', and /sfar/ 'frontier'; full spelling will differentiate the verbal forms as *spr*, *sypr*, and *swpr*, but it still leaves the nominal forms undifferentiated).

Full spelling has never been employed consistently to indicate all cases of /u, o, i/. In practice it has always been used with extreme irregularity, the same forms being sometimes spelled in full and sometimes grammatically, the general tendency being to insert the helping letters when the writer becomes aware of the possibility of an alternative reading. Since the majority of words in a text can be read in alternative ways (sometimes in quite a number of different ways) but since only in a limited percentage of cases the alternative reading makes sense, it is rather a matter of chance whether the writer becomes aware of the alternative and takes precautions. The full spelling thus becomes a source of irregularity in spelling by introducing an arbitrary personal and momentary factor of choice. A survey of Israeli newspapers in 1966 showed that they differed somewhat in degrees of fullness but that none of them had anything like a consistent system of its own. The same word might appear with different spellings within a few lines. This applied both to Hebrew and borrowed words and to non-Hebrew proper names. In the telephone book, a name may appear in different places, according to how its owner chooses to spell it.

In principle, full spelling should never be used when a text is pointed, as the distinction between the different vowel symbols involves also the *v* and *y* of the grammatical spelling; therefore, any extra *v* or *y* leads to a grammatical mistake. In practice, however, already in the middle ages, pointing was quite frequently inserted in a fully spelled text. On the other hand, in letters and the like, educated writers will often insert one or two vowel symbols to make the meaning clear; and such 'partial pointing' is often used in the more expensive type of book. In theory, words thus treated should be grammatically spelled, but in informal writing this rule is often ignored.

Indeed, it is doubtful whether the average adult accustomed to full spelling is at all able to use grammatical spelling, except with a great deal of cogitation and frequent faults. Children and young people, on the other hand, employ grammatical spelling even when they do not point what they write. This is because of the insistence of the schools, where grammatical spelling is considered an indispensable prerequisite to correct grammar.

The young child nowadays learns to read and write by a syllable technique of consonant plus vowel symbol, reads for one to three years only pointed texts, and then gradually passes to unvocalized texts, still spelled in such a way that they could be pointed, that is, in grammatical spelling. This is also the way many books intended for children's private reading are printed. As the child goes on to reading newspapers and books printed for adults, he acquires the ability to read full spelling but continues to write grammatical spelling. Young typists and university students in most cases still adhere strictly (at least in theory) to this type of spelling. In his early twenties a person gradually abandons the school spelling and adapts to the irregular full-spelling habits of the adult world.

Summary of Spelling Problems

The problems offered by the situation here described can be set out as follows:

1. The existence of two spellings and the resulting need for relearning spelling at some time in every person's life.
2. The lack of regularity in the spelling most commonly used.
3. The insufficient indication of vowels in either system of spelling that leads to:

   (*a*) false identification of words, which has to be rectified in the light of the context in the sentence (on the other hand, it is rather rare that a sentence remains completely ambiguous to the end)

   (*b*) mispronunciations of correctly identified words and forms; it is claimed by educators that this is the source of the widespread use of nongrammatical speech forms, even in the language of educated people, as they have no visual corrective for the forms used in everyday language

(*c*) children are virtually cut off from reading anything not specially printed for them; this includes public notices, newspapers, and even private letters

(*d*) the transition from vocalized (pointed) texts to nonvocalized ones creates an additional difficulty for the child in a system of writing which in any case presents the common difficulties of historical spelling. It is claimed that this transition problem is partly responsible for the low reading achievements of part of the school population (other causes are no doubt the great difference in vocabulary and sentence structure between spoken and written Hebrew and the paucity of reading material couched in simple popular style)

(*e*) the situation much increases the difficulties experienced by the immigrant, the casual visitor, and the interested person abroad in learning Hebrew. The transition from pointed to normal spelling is much harder for the foreign learner than it is for the Israeli child who is familiar with the language. Observation proves that quite a proportion of new immigrants continue, for many years, to cling to the special newspapers printed for immigrants (supplementing the meager content of these by newspapers in their own language or in English), and few get as far as reading Hebrew literature. Some claims have been made that the spelling difficulties frighten off potential settlers; it is of course impossible to check such an assertion.

Proposals for Reform

During the past few decades, there have been dozens of proposals for reforming the Hebrew writing system by creating an adequate representation of vowels that can be written or printed within the line, or at least that can be printed more cheaply and easily than full pointing. There have been several proposals to rationalize partial pointing by restricting it to one or two vowel symbols only, which would be inserted whenever the vowel appears. It is claimed by the authors of these proposals that the consistent indication of this one vowel (or of the absence of a vowel) will enable the reader to supply the remaining vowels unequivocally. These proposals involve doubling (or trebling) the number of keys for printing or typing.

Another type of proposal consists in designing additional letters to represent the vowels, instead of placing them above and below the line. This would make it possible to set, print, and type fully vocalized texts by machines designed in the ordinary way and would involve fewer additional letters than partial pointing. Suggestions range from sets of symbols representing all items of the traditional pointing to restricted sets for the five or six vowels actually heard (this means supplying letters for /a, e, i/ [and perhaps /é/], as /o/ and /u/ can be indicated by the traditional dot accompanying *v* in pointing).

Some have proposed using the letters ', *h*, *v*, *y*, ᶜ, systematically to indicate vowels, as is done in Yiddish and was done in another Semitic language, Mandaean.

There have also been several suggestions for adopting a roman script. In the late twenties and thirties, even a short-lived newspaper, a book, and a book for teaching Hebrew were published in different systems of romanized Hebrew by well-known public figures. One scientist proposed romanization for scientific publications in order to avoid the difficulty of recognizing international scientific terms in unvocalized Hebrew transliteration. These proposals fall into two classes: those that transliterate the traditional spelling and, therefore, necessitate the addition of new letters, diacritic points, or digraphs; and those that represent a present-day Israeli pronunciation. It should be noted that the Hebrew Language Academy (see below) created an official system of roman transliteration for names and the like that has extra letters to be indicated by underlining (I am not aware of any proposal to introduce this particular system for printing continuous texts), and that various methods of romanization are currently employed in scientific linguistic texts and in beginners' teaching.

Difficulties of Implementing Spelling Reform

Two research projects in which I was involved have shown that the experienced reader who speaks Hebrew as his native or everyday language has no particular trouble with the process of reading by elimination, which the unvocalized Hebrew script demands. Tests have shown that fourteen-year-olds read unvocalized texts at the same speed and with the same degree of comprehension as they do pointed texts. It is true that when reading aloud at sight, almost every reader will misread words and have to correct himself when the continuation of the sentence shows him that he erred, but in silent reading this constant self-correction is apparently not noticed by the reader.

The average educated person is thus quite unaware of the problems of reading Hebrew, but if he thinks about the matter, he would see the advantages of the system: a Hebrew text is approximately 25 percent shorter than its translation into a European language; because of the absence of capitals and italics, Hebrew books can be produced much more cheaply than equivalent works in European languages (and this in spite of the comparatively tiny number of Hebrew speakers, 2.25 million); the absence of vowels is even felt to speed up comprehension by throwing into relief the consonantal root of words; an educated reader can understand, with little effort, texts written as much as two thousand years ago in their original spelling (not to speak of the Bible, which he always reads with pointing). The spelling difficulties I have enumerated earlier affect marginal and largely inarticulate groups: children, the uneducated, and new immigrants. The educated reader tends to feel that these people should make the same effort that he made himself in order to learn to read fluently, rather than causing him difficulties by changing his ingrained reading habits. Some even resent the very idea that others should have things made easier than they had themselves.

To this natural educated conservatism are added two specific features connected with the state of Hebrew as a language revived only ninety years ago from books – a language that is held by many to be still in the process of revival. The average person fully identifies himself with the ideology (1) that present-day Hebrew should be kept as close as humanly possible to the language of the 'Sources'; that is, the classical works written between 1200 B.C. and 500 A.D.; and (2) that linguistic continuity must not be broken by allowing changes in structure to penetrate into correct usage. It is only natural that the system of writing is viewed as part of this continuity and that its abandonment, or changes that affect the appearance of the text, are seen as betrayal of the Language Revival, if not of the National Revival. In a cultural atmosphere where books written about 200 A.D. or in 1100-1500 A.D. are currently read by nonspecialists, the problem of having to reprint a large number of books in case of a change in spelling has quite a different relevance than it does in a Western society where the average reader mainly reads contemporary works.

As stated above, Hebrew is spoken in Israel according to two pronunciation norms, both well-established and standardized. The young Israeli betrays in his accent nothing of the language his parents spoke, which in many cases he himself still can speak to some extent. His speech marks him in Israeli society as a member of the Ashkenazi or the Sephardi group, whether or not his parents' Hebrew pronunciation belonged to the type that sounded the pharyngals (Sephardi of today). But the two dialects show no signs of coalescing, and Israeli Hebrew is impartially represented by both of them. Both correspond in a sense to the present historical spelling. A more perfect spelling would have to represent particularly either the one or the other of the two dialects and thus lend the dialect an authority it does not have today. Moreover, many, if not most, of the users of the nonpharyngal (Ashkenazi) pronunciation theoretically admit that the pharyngal pronunciation is 'better' because it is closer to the spelling and that, in fact, they 'ought' to pronounce not only the pharyngals *ḥ* and ^{c} but also the *ṭ*, the doubled consonants, and the neutral vowel [ə]. This so-called Semitic pronunciation, which goes far beyond the Sephardi dialect in the matter of spelling pronunciation, is used by radio announcers and taught in many schools, though only a few individuals use it in daily life. At present it is possible to pay lip service to this ideal without bothering to adhere to it in practice (just as it is possible to admit that one should speak grammatically, without adhering to all grammar rules in one's speech); but a spelling reform might force a choice between the pronunciation as it is and the theoretical 'Semitic' form of pronunciation.

INSTITUTIONAL BACKGROUND

The revival of spoken Hebrew in Palestine began in 1881. Already in 1890, a 'Language Committee' was formed for the purpose of planning vocabulary extension and other matters. Although short-lived, it was reestablished in 1904 under the same name and has been functioning uninterruptedly since, but with a change in its status in 1953 to an official organ of the new state of Israel, under the name of 'Academy for the Hebrew Language'.

The Academy was established by a Law promulgated in 1953 as 'Supreme Institution for the Science of the Hebrew Language' for the purpose of 'directing the development of the Hebrew language on the basis of research into the language in all its periods and branches' (paragraph 2). 'Decisions of the Institution in matters of grammar, spelling, terminology, or transcription that have been published in the *Official*

Gazette by the Minister of Education and Culture are binding upon educational and scientific institutions, upon the government, its departments and institutions, and upon organs of local government' (paragraph 10). This is interpreted to mean that such publications in the *Official Gazette* must bear the signature of the said Minister. 'The participation of the State in the budget of the Institution shall form part of the budget of the Ministry of Education and Culture' (paragraph 11), and the 'Minister of Education and Culture is responsible for the carrying out of this Law' (paragraph 13). The members of the Academy number between fifteen and twenty-three (paragraph 4a), but the maximum number of twenty-three does not include members that have reached the age of seventy-five years, although such members continue to take part and to vote (amendment, 1969). In addition, there are up to twenty-three advisory members who can vote on all linguistic matters, but not in the election of new members or in changes of the Constitution. Members receive no pay. As constituted at present, the membership (including advisory members) comprises ten teachers of linguistics at universities, fifteen other university teachers, eleven writers, and eight from other professions (teachers, style correctors, etc.). The Academy employs a number of so-called Scientific Secretaries who are highly trained and experienced Hebrew linguists and who participate in committees and in the plenary meeting with voting rights.

The language-planning work of the Academy is carried on through committees. The majority of these are terminology committees, appointed ad hoc for the purpose of dealing with a specific subject and dissolved when the requisite dictionary has been completed. If, after a number of years, it is decided that the same subject be dealt with once more, a new committee is formed. These terminology committees usually have a majority of nonacademicians, people who are experts in the subject discussed and who have a leaning towards Hebrew terminology; the Academy is represented by one or more of its members and by one of the secretaries (who also keeps the protocol), its chairman always being an Academy member. A smaller number of committees deals with general language matters: grammar, day-to-day grammatical problems, grammatical terminology, style and usage, transcription, and the like. These consist of Academy members and scientific secretaries only who are usually appointed for two years at a time. A completely separate staff is engaged in the preparation of the Historical Dictionary, under the direction of the Vice-President (Acting President) of the Academy, Professor Z. Ben-Ḥayyim.

All decisions of committees require confirmation by the plenary meeting, which takes place five times a year. Such decisions are first circularized (sometimes at several stages of the work) to all members of the Academy, and may, if any member so desires, be discussed in the plenum. In practice, terminology is largely confirmed *en bloc*, with only some doubtful points being raised in the plenum, while decisions on general questions are rediscussed in detail by the plenum. All decisions are voted on. The gist of every speaker's remarks and the proportions of votes for and against are published in the Academy's *Memoirs*. Protocols are kept of the discussions in the nonterminological committees but are not published in print. Committees and the plenum are the only forums the Academy offers for discussion on matters of language planning. The Institution also publishes two periodicals, *Our Language* and *Our Language for the People*. At first both publications carried articles by members and nonmembers on principles and details of language planning, but since the Academy took over from the Language Committee both periodicals carry only scientific articles concerned with research into the language (in the past and in the present).

The question of spelling was treated as a matter for the direct attention of the plenum, and at the time of writing this no permanent committee has yet been set up for this branch of the Academy's activities, which, as we have seen above, had been specifically included in its tasks by the Constitutive Law.

THE EVENTS

The 1948 Rules

The earliest record of a discussion about spelling in the Language Committee is in the Memoirs (Zikhronot) of 1913, when a lecture on the subject was delivered by David Yellin (1864-1941). In 1920-1921 the same Yellin opened a discussion on the subject, advocating a strict grammatical spelling. The Language Council never officially decided on this, but Yellin's immense influence with the teachers led to the adoption of the grammatical spelling by all schools. This settled the matter temporarily but had little influence on the practice outside schools, and pressure grew for the Language Council to take up the challenge of regulating the adult unpointed spelling. 'At the request of various interested parties', the

Council appointed towards the end of 1938 a special committee to make proposals for 'full' spelling and for a system of transliteration of foreign words into Hebrew. The consultations opened with a major lecture, which was published in the Council's quarterly journal, and were remarkable for a new departure in the field of communications and public relations: Professor N. H. Torczyner (Tur-Sinai), who until his death in 1973, became president of the Council (and the Academy), delivered a series of lectures on the spelling problem on the newly established Palestine Radio. In summer 1940, the spelling proposal was sent out for consideration to all members of the Language Council and met with violent opposition, especially from the members in Tel Aviv. Finally, the Council decided to set up another special committee in Tel Aviv 'to examine the proposal', but this second committee turned out to be more sharply divided into extremist factions of innovators and conservatives, and some even demanded changes in Hebrew grammar before deciding on a spelling. After the Tel Aviv committee had returned its mandate without arriving at any agreed proposals, the plenary meeting of the Council discussed the original Jerusalem proposals and made some additions to them, but resolved that no final decision could be made and that the proposals should be placed before the general public for discussion: 'It was incumbent upon the Language Council to give an opportunity to all those circles in the community who were interested in spelling reform to study the proposals in detail and to express their opinion about them before the Council could adopt any binding decision whatever.'

In spring 1942, the proposals were published in the Council's quarterly journal, *Leshonenu* (11, 232-241). They were preceded by a preamble setting out the principles on which all members of the original Jerusalem committee were in full agreement. These are: to leave in force the coexistence of two spellings, 'grammatical' when pointed and 'full' when unpointed; the spelling must be based upon 'the Sources' of the language (the Bible and early Rabbinic literature) and its recognized grammar; to be adapted to present-day educational and practical needs; and, above all, to be acceptable to the public. It must therefore not be revolutionary in any way, and especially not add new letters or introduce new principles in the use of the existing letters. In fact, it should only regulate existing usage and hence cannot be expected to be consistent; rules could only give general guidance and would have to be complemented by a spelling dictionary to be worked out by the Language Council.

In view of these principles, we need not wonder that the proposed spelling was curiously asymmetrical. It rules that /u/ would be written throughout with a *v*, but /o/ would be indicated by *v* only when it corresponded to one of the three symbols sounded [o] in the pointing and not already marked by an added *v* (the so-called *ḥolam*), but not when it corresponded to one of the other two. While in this matter there was still a direct connection with the pointing, the regulation of the spelling of /i/ by *y* was further made dependent on whether the vowel stood in a closed syllable (in which case it was not to be marked) or in a syllable preceding a consonant doubled in the pointing orthography (but now no more pronounced double). As for consonants /v/ and /y/, these were to be indicated by a single *v* and *y* in the beginning of a word, but a double *vv* and *yy* when not in the beginning of a word.

The additions made by the plenary meeting required the distinction of /b/ from /v/, /k/ from /kh/, and /p/ from /f/ by inserting a dot into *b*, *k*, and *p*; of /sh/ from /s/ by placing a dot over the latter; and of /u/ from /o/ by placing a dot into the *v* when indicating /u/ – all these being taken over from the pointing system.

The proposed spelling made a large number of common words clearer but still allowed for much uncertainty in reading, since it indicated neither /a/ nor /e/ nor absence of vowel and since it left the majority of the occurrences of /i/ unmarked. Its use also required a command of grammar hardly to be expected from the general public.

After the publication of these proposals, the Council convened two public scientific conferences to discuss them. Since those from outside the Council who participated in these meetings appeared to agree to the general principles, though differing on matters of detail, the Council resolved in spring 1944 to set up a new 'Committee for Formulating the Spelling Rules', which included, apart from members of the original committee of 1938-1940, some of the most outstanding opponents of the proposals. The new body took a much longer time over its consultations, from January 1945 to the summer of 1947. Its members also took part in consultations with bodies such as the editorial boards of encyclopedias to investigate some of the practical aspects of their problem. In the autumn of 1947, they presented their proposals to the Central Committee of the Language Council. This body authorized the publication of the proposals after detailed discussion. They were published in *Leshonenu* (16, 82-87) in the spring of 1948 and reissued with a preface by the Council's President as a small booklet in the spring of 1949, this still being the principal official form in which these rules are circulated. As a sign of the times, the popular edition not only illustrates the rules by an excerpt from a well-known article on the evils of Jewish cultural assimilation in the diaspora but also adds a transcription of the Proclamation of Independence. The establishment of the independent State of Israel on May 14, 1948, gave these rules a new aspect. Whereas so far the Language Council had legislated for a voluntary school system of the Jewish population of Mandatory Palestine, it was now called upon to regulate an important aspect of the cultural activities and the communication needs of the sovereign state.

The new rules only slightly modified those of 1942, and all observations on the latter also apply to the new rules. The preamble once more stressed that the rules only regulate and standardize spelling habits already current and admitted that in some matters the individual user will have to decide between alternatives permitted by the rules. The compilation of a complete spelling dictionary is envisaged as a desirable but somewhat remote possibility. On the other hand, it is stated, for the first time, that 'the Language Council hopes that, if only teachers, authors, and the educated public will conscientiously observe these rules, much experience will be gathered in a few years, and will enable us to re-examine the rules and to improve them.' In another passage, the aim of the rules is referred to as 'progress towards complete vowel indication'. It thus appears that at least some of those active on the Council envisaged a continuous process of spelling reform by easy stages.

The wording of the two pages of introduction to the rules of 1948, from which relevant passages have been quoted, seems to indicate quite clearly that it was intended to be binding upon the public ('teachers, authors, and the educated public') in the same way as other decisions of the Language Council had generally been accepted as binding, in spite of the absence of any sanctions. The phrase used for the authorized 'publication' (*pirsum ba-rabbim*, literally, 'making them known to the general public') is one used for promulgations of legal decisions also.

The Council indeed made an attempt to get the rules adopted by the Hebrew school system, but this was prevented by the personal opposition of the director-general of the educational network, and the schools have since then continued to cling to the grammatical spelling for all grades. It is not clear whether any real effort was made to persuade the editorial boards of newspapers to adopt the Council's spelling rules. In practice, no newspaper follows these rules to any marked extent. The majority of educated Israelis are quite unaware that a body of rules for full spelling exists at all. It is thus true that apart from the publications of the Council and later of the Academy, the above spelling rules are applied consistently by the country's most prestigious publishing firm *Mosad Bialik* (supported by the Jewish Agency for Palestine), yet while that firm's publications are found on the shelves of all educated people and have been a model for other publishers, their spelling seems to have failed to arouse a desire for imitation.

There can be little doubt that one of the reasons for the lack of attention in the country to the 1948 rules was their timing. Their publication took place in the middle of the War of Independence, and this was followed by years of economic and political difficulties, while the country was in the throes of absorbing a massive immigration. Few people had their minds on such a minor matter as spelling rules. By the time people could apply themselves again to such matters, the rules had lost their novelty, and the very fact that they had not gained public acceptance made people suspicious of them. The main reason, however, was the lack of any legal authority for the Language Council's decisions, which had been responsible for the failure of imposing the rules upon the schools. It was to remedy this flaw that the leaders of the Language Council applied themselves vigorously to persuading the government to set up the Language Academy and to give it authority by law.

The 1962 Committee

When the Academy was established in 1953, it took over the Council's spelling rules for its own publications but did not immediately proceed to submitting those rules for official ratification by the Minister of Education and Culture. It was felt that the opportunity should be used for improving the rules before having them made law. Until the end of 1956, the Academy was busy with making rules for transcribing Hebrew names and the like into roman script for public notices and for many other needs of the State. Only after the rules for romanized transliteration had been passed did the Academy set up a committee for spelling, which besides the members of the Academy's grammar committee also included three appointees of the Ministry of Education and Culture (one of these was also a member of the Academy). One of the Ministry representatives withdrew after the first meeting. The spelling committee sat for two years in a body and in subcommittees and presented its proposals to the plenum of the Academy on April 8, 1962.

Owing to pressure of work in the plenum and the need to have the proposals styled by the Academy's scientific secretariate, about six months passed between the completion of the committee's work and their presentation. In the meantime, rumors had begun to circulate among members of the Academy and among the public about the revolutionary character of the proposals. Some six weeks before the date of the plenary meeting in which the proposals were to be presented, one of the larger newspapers published a preview based on information said to come from people in the know and implying that there already was adverse criticism. In order to prevent further leakage of information before the official release, the meeting of the plenum was arranged for a Sunday afternoon, and the letter containing the proposals delivered to the houses of the Academy members on Friday afternoon – Saturday being the weekly holiday on which no newspapers appear and no business is transacted. Nevertheless, the same newspaper carried an article on Sunday morning with all the more sensational details of the proposals. This rather weakened the effect of the unprecedented step – unprecedented for the Academy – that the press had been invited to attend both the meeting at which the proposals were to be announced and the meeting set for the following morning at which they were to be discussed. The papers, on the whole, reported briefly on the proposals and collected views, mostly adverse, from the academicians. One paper announced that 90 percent of the members would vote against the proposals.

The proposals were in two parts, one unanimous and the other put forward by one-half of the committee only. Even the unanimous proposal went quite a way beyond the 1948 spelling rules in marking the vowels: every /u/ was to be marked by a *v* with a dot in it; every /o/ by a *v* with a dot over it; every /i/ by a *y* with a dot or line over it; while the letters *v* and *y* without diacritics denote the consonants. Only a few, well-defined exceptions were admitted. Also the other diacritic symbols in the consonants of the 1948 spelling were to be used.

The other, nonunanimous proposal advocated the introduction of two new symbols to mark the vowels /a/ and /e/. It was left open whether these would appear above the line (though between the letters) or would be of the size of ordinary letters. The exact form was to be determined by a competition among graphic artists. For the purpose of presenting the proposal, /a/ was provisionally indicated by a raised ˇ and /e/ by a raised ˆ. (The choice of these symbols proved unfortunate, as the newspapers identified the a-symbol as 'roman v' and claimed that the proposal introduced roman letters into the Hebrew alphabet). If accepted, this would have provided – in combination with the unanimous proposals– an unambiguous representation of all vowels according to present-day Israeli pronunciation, since absence of vowel would now have been clearly distinguished, and the vowel [ə] is nonphonemic and conditioned by the phonetic context.

In the introductory lecture by Professor Z. Ben-Ḥayyim, chairman of the committee, it was made clear that the proposals involved the retention of the pointing, including its different, grammatical spelling, but only for 'passive' use, especially in religious books, as the new spelling would remove the need for the use of the pointing in schoolbooks and poetry. This was indeed the most complete solution for the spelling problem that was ever placed before the Academy by one of its appointed committees. It would have made the reading of all words unambiguous (except, of course, for true homonyms); since it left the consonants unchanged, however, it still perpetuated the difficulties experienced in writing Hebrew correctly.

While many of the speakers in the three meetings devoted to the discussion of the committee's proposals agreed to the first part, on which the whole committee had agreed, only one or two advocated acceptance of the principle of new symbols for the /a/ and the /e/. A number of speakers proposed solutions of their own, generally in the direction of some systematized partial pointing. One famous novelist among the members expressed the view that 'this generation was not yet prepared', that the time had not yet come for reforming the spelling. In the end, the chairman posed the question 'whether the Academy sees any necessity for dealing with the problem of reforming the spelling'. A vote was taken, and the reply was a unanimous 'yes'. As a result of this vote, a new special committee was appointed, including two of the members of the former committee, and four new members, among them two of those who had spoken most vigorously against the full spelling as such. According to the practice of the Academy, this meant that the proposals of the 1962 committee were still before the assembly. This was on January 8, 1963.

The 1964 Committee

Already on February 12, 1964, the new committee reported to the plenum. Its six members proposed six different solutions to the spelling problem. One was the proposals of the 1962 committee; the other five were not fully worked-out systems but general directives for working out proposals. The only one that had any novelty in it was to design an easier, 'popular' system of pointing, to be used concurrently with the established and inherited pointing system. In the discussion, the chairman of the committee declared that they were in fact seeking the guidance of the plenum before proceeding to the elaboration of any of the proposals that were put forward.

Several members now proposed that the Academy should for the present put off the discussion of the spelling reform *sine die*, seeing that there was so little common ground. A vote taken on this, however, revealed that only two were for it and fifteen against. Another proposal, to put off discussion *sine die* but to declare the 1948 spelling rules of the Language Council to be binding until further notice, was also rejected by a slightly smaller majority. A similar majority rejected the proposal, put forward by one of the linguist members, that a new committee should first institute a program of research before embarking on new proposals.

The 1967 Committee

In order to give some directive to the new committee, which was now to be appointed, a vote was passed on the question whether the solution should be on the lines of perfecting the unpointed spelling while retaining the pointed spelling ('two spellings'). This was decided by a large majority (eleven to four). Finally a new committee of five was elected, ironically under the chairmanship of the member who had proposed that a new committee should proceed only after a period of research. Only one of the 1964 committee members was included, and he had not been on the 1962 committee.

On February 28, 1967, three years later, the new committee reported with a proposal agreed by three of its five members but with far-reaching reservations (but no positive proposals) from the remaining two. The new proposals were basically identical with those agreed by the whole of the 1962 committee: to indicate throughout /u, o, i/ (with some exceptions for /i/), but to retain the double writing of the consonantal /*v*/ and /y/.

This proposal was discussed at two meetings, but as the discussion proceeded it became increasingly clear that an important body of members objected to the basic principle contained in the directive to the committee when it was elected – that its task was to develop and elaborate the unpointed spelling. These members again and again proclaimed that the only feasible solution lay in the direction of partial pointing. In the end it was decided to close the discussion and to hold, after some time, a meeting only for the purpose of voting for whichever of the systems so far proposed would be able to command the necessary majority. The advocates of partial pointing were asked to place detailed proposals before the Academy secretariate and, if possible, to get together on a joint system of partial pointing.

Already before the end of 1966, some educators who were not members of the Academy had placed before the Pedagogical Council of the Ministry of Education and Culture a plan to teach children to read by a system that would relieve them of the necessity of learning the full spelling after having read for a number of years nothing but the grammatical spelling. This was to combine the pointing with the full spelling, except that this would be accompanied by the pointing symbols as a kind of phonetic help. This, in fact, was the very system that had been used for some years already in the newspaper for new immigrants, which was widely used in courses for the latter. Since the whole pointing system is linked with the grammatical spelling, the proposal meant the violation of many grammatical rules that were currently taught in schools. One of its authors announced his intention of writing a new Hebrew grammar based on the combined spelling. Since there were no binding rules for full spelling, it was also proposed at one point that the Ministry's Pedagogical Council should decide on rules as applied to the combined spelling for schools. The plan was discussed for a number of months, and while some educators were inclined to accept it, members of the Academy were opposed to it. At no point in the discussions was the Academy officially approached, although several of its leading members were individually invited to participate in the discussions.

THE REFORM

The Academy members who had advocated partial pointing announced after some time their inability to arrive at an agreed proposal. On the other hand, a number of members, despairing of getting any agreement on one of various spelling proposals of the past six years, decided to ask the assembly to confirm the 1948 spelling of the Language Council. A proposal for a resolution was signed by ten members. It is quoted here in full:

'For many generations, two systems of spelling have been current in Hebrew, namely, pointed and unpointed. Though in each of the two systems we can discern in our literature various shades of usage, the pointed spelling is today employed in school teaching according to one well defined system of rules. This system, which in its time was regulated by the Language Council, has evident advantages for learning the language, and is rightly called Grammatical Spelling. However, side by side with the pointed spelling, there is in use an unpointed spelling system, which has never been displaced by the use of pointing. Its use, in fact, is wider than that of pointed script. However much the Language Council and the Academy were concerned – as is their task and as they were authorized – to arrive at a decision, they did not see their way to establishing one of the two systems as the exclusive one for writing Hebrew. The various systems for unification made by the Council and the Academy were unsuccessful. Today, too, the Academy does not consider the time ripe to do away with one of the two systems.

The use of the pointed spelling is absolutely necessary today, for instance, in teaching and children's education, in prayerbooks and poetry, as well as in various kinds of popular publications. Its use should be enlarged to include all written documents addressed to the general public, because through it the reading of Hebrew words becomes clear beyond doubt, and the language is guarded from the corruptions in speaking which have their cause in the spelling. In all cases where the pointing system is used, it must be according to the spelling rules established for the last few generations, and every deviation from these rules will be considered a mistake.

For generations now the unpointed system has been employed in a number of varieties, each of which seeks to compensate for the absence of vowel indication by using added *v* and *y* to various extents. After many discussions and experiments over a number of years, the Language Council established rules for unpointed spelling, which were designed to systematize it.

The Academy resolves to reaffirm and to recommend for adoption the system of the Academy in its final formulation, because it facilitates the reading of written Hebrew, restricts the possibilities of error in word identification, and brings order into the variety of attempts to make the reading of Hebrew easier.

The system of the Language Council, which already has a marked influence upon the usage of the general public (in periodicals and in the daily press), should also guide teachers in the schools. Practical experience in their use will show within a reasonable period of time whether these rules require improvements, and in which respects, and it will be the task of a special committee to take care of this.'

This resolution, cautiously phrased in order to be acceptable to academicians who saw in the pointed spelling the ideal solution for the problem, yet stated quite unambiguously three points that formed the focus of recent discussion:

1. The consonant spelling underlying the pointing system must remain the grammatical spelling; hence, the suggestion of a 'combined' pointed-full spelling is unacceptable.

2. The alternative to fully pointed spelling is not some system of partial pointing, but full spelling.

3. The insertion of the additional *v* and *y* in full spelling cannot be left to the discretion of the individual user (as had been advocated in the discussions) but must be regulated, and the rules taught in schools.

On April 4, 1968, a double meeting of the plenum was held to carry out the decision announced in spring 1967 to try to decide the spelling question by voting on the various proposals. Although the two new systems were proposed by individual members and although the assembly was asked to take into consideration the proposal of the 1967 committee, it was clear throughout the discussion that the issue was between those who agreed to an established full spelling and those who opposed it. At this point, there also developed an opposition between those who believed that a regulation of the unpointed spelling was an immediate necessity and members who advocated waiting for the development of alternative suggestions or for perfection and revision of the full spelling. The final vote was taken in two stages: (1) whether a full spelling should be recognized side by side with the pointed grammatical spelling ('two spellings'); and (2) on the resolution to establish the 1948 spelling as the binding set of rules. In each case, thirteen voted favorably and five against, without abstentions. By this vote, the 1948 spelling became the official policy of the Academy. In a subsequent meeting the proposal to establish a special committee for observing the working of these rules in practice and for suggesting improvements in due course was separately voted on and confirmed.[1]

[1] No such committee was ever appointed (1975).

The Directorate of the Academy appointed a committee of members to determine the exact manner in which the decision should be communicated to the Minister of Education and Culture and to determine what means should be adopted to make it known to the public. The work of this committee was later completed by the Directorate. On July 9, 1968, the full text of the resolution was communicated to the Minister with a request for his signature and for publication in the *Official Gazette*. The Acting President and one of the principal scientific secretaries went to see the Minister in order to explain the implications of the Academy's decision. Other meetings were held with leading officials of the Ministry in order to discuss the introduction of the new rules into school teaching. The official speaker of the Academy made contacts with journalists, and a number of newspapers carried articles that explained the decision. It was also planned to issue a booklet with the rules, phrased in a more popular way than in the booklet issued by the Language Council in 1949, but this was put off until after the official confirmation of the decision by the Minister. In subsequent publicity work, reprints of the 1949 booklet, with its type worn by frequent reprinting, were used.

There is no doubt that many of the members who voted for the resolution were moved by concern for the good name and continued influence of the institution to which they had devoted so much of their time and energy. This concern was stated by several participants in the discussion. It was felt that the image of the Academy was becoming established as being a body unable to guide the nation on the very issues for the sake of which it had been created, and that even a set of rules that did not satisfy them was better than not having any rules at all. The opposition to all solutions suggested hitherto had convinced them that any consistent proposal would be doomed to fail. In any event it was proved that the existing spelling – simply by the fact that it existed, even if its use was restricted – was able to rally a clear majority.

Some, however, were also guided by the belief that at the root of the Academy's inability to arrive at agreement was the lack of a common basis of discussion and that, once the issue were decided, basically in favor of the adoption of a regulated unpointed full spelling, it would become easier to introduce agreed improvements on this spelling.

NEW DEVELOPMENTS

Without any connection with the Academy's deliberations, a new development had taken place. A group of people in Jerusalem and Tel Aviv formed a 'Movement for an Unambiguous Hebrew Spelling'. They were headed by an official from the Foreign Office and included several leading journalists and some writers. Their first written proclamation was handed to the Language Academy, with a request to pass it on to its members, on April 3, 1968. In it a demand was put forward that either the Academy should proceed forthwith to a complete solution of the spelling difficulties, or, if it did not, the government should appoint another body to do so. The present spelling, the proclamation stated, 'causes perpetual insecurity in linguistic matters, endangers our psychological balance, and constitutes an obstacle to cultural, social, and economic progress. It also is a stumbling-block in the absorption of immigrants and in our ties with the Jewish people in other parts of the world. There exists a danger to the very existence and cultural level of the Hebrew language, in that it might in future not be fitted to serve as an exact tool for thought and artistic creativeness.' The government, it demanded, should expend the necessary sums for getting an army of experts to work: 'the people of Israel are worth 100 million pounds to teach them to read and write'. The result must be a law enforcing a spelling that could be easily read. Only for religious books and, perhaps, for poetry, the pointing and the grammatical spelling might be retained.

As requested by its authors, this proclamation was on April 4 placed in front of every member of the Academy who had turned up for the meeting. The discussion took place under the impression of thinly veiled threats and attacks against the Academy. It is doubtful whether any member was moved by this event to change his opinion, but the incident produced a heavy atmosphere of having failed in the Academy's purpose. The Academy's endeavors to get its decision fairly reported in the press coincided with a well-run publicity campaign of the Movement for an Unambiguous Spelling, in which the Academy was berated for having done nothing, after twenty years of deliberations, except 'to reconfirm the present position, in other words, to do nothing, and to give its blessing to a situation in which the two spelling systems, grammatical-pointed and unpointed-full spelling, continued to compete, neither of which answers the needs of our time.' The government was asked not to confirm the Academy's decision but to pass a law that, within a certain time, an adequate spelling must be introduced. The Academy was to be given a limited time for deliberations, in full collaboration with a body of 'sociologists, psychologists, graphic artists, printing technicians, journalists, publishers, and theatre people'. If it failed to come up with a perfect proposal, the government was to entrust the task to a specially convened body of experts. In some of its pronouncements, the Movement raised the specter of romanized Hebrew, which would surely come if the Hebrew script were not reformed in time.

At the same time, one of Israel's linguists began a press campaign for a romanized spelling. Meetings and discussions as well as radio programs tended to become debates between advocates of a vague but extreme movement for spelling reform and the partisans of the more extreme step of romanization. Between these two extremes, the voice of the Academy's representatives was much too moderate to be audible. A certain turn for the better came, when, after a rather unsuccessful congress, the Movement began to seek contacts with the Academy in late September and its leaders allowed themselves to be convinced that the Academy had taken a step forward in establishing binding rules for spelling, thereby creating a basis from which by gradual further changes an unambiguous spelling system might be reached. In October a delegation of the Movement actually appeared before the Minister of Education and Culture and urged him to make the Academy's decision law. On some occasions after that, members of the Academy appeared in public debates with members of the Movement, in which both sides agreed in urging the acceptance of the Academy's rules by the public, with the Movement only differing in insisting on a more rapid rate of change in the future.

At the time of writing this, February 1969, it is too early to say whether the intensive public discussion and the large amount of space given to the matter in the daily press have produced a change of public climate, in which the Academy's rules will be greeted as at least a partial solution and in which there will be a pressure for proceeding with further reforms in the direction of developing the full spelling. So far, the Movement has not grown beyond its original circle of members, nor has there been a tendency for writers independent either of the Academy or the Movement for an Unambiguous Spelling to enter into serious public discussion of the problems. The Minister of Education and Culture has not yet countersigned the Academy's resolution to make it law. A question asked in the Israeli parliament concerning the 'illegal' use of combined spelling (pointed full spelling) in the immigrant's weekly, financed by the Ministry of Education and Culture, did not elicit a statement on the government's intentions with regard to the spelling reform. The matter is thus still under deliberation.

As for the hope that newspapers would take up the new spelling voluntarily, there are no signs of this as yet. Nor has the Academy embarked so far on an intensive campaign to obtain such voluntary adherence. Thus no facts are available to show what response could be obtained.

DISCUSSION

Two factors contribute to the success of vocabulary planning. First, such planning meets a real need and serves the immediate purposes of well-defined groups in the country. Since these groups need a standardized technical vocabulary, they are generally willing to take the normative side of the activity into the bargain. Only few among the professional customers have strong views on language matters: most of them are apt to view the members of the terminology committees with the respect of one expert for another expert and to accept their judgment in linguistic questions. Second, vocabulary comes in small units, and its digestion by the social organisms that it affects takes place with only minor upheavals. Objections are always to specific terms only, and the unwillingness to accept one or two terms out of what is generally a list of hundreds is possible without visibly upsetting the process as a whole.

As against this, a spelling reform affects all at once the entire web of communication. It cannot be introduced gradually but requires an immediate willingness to change habits. In many cases, it also requires an outlay of money in new type or in the adaptation of typewriters, and especially in reprinting school books and, in the case of far-reaching reforms, reprinting large numbers of books in common use. The class that has to bear the brunt of the reform is not that of technical experts, indifferent to linguistic niceties, but educators, writers, journalists, proof-readers, and printing-room supervisors, people who are most closely tied with the working of the previous spelling system and probably emotionally attached to it through the long process of having acquired skill in handling it. One might almost surmise that the more complicated the spelling, the greater the unwillingness of its successful operators to abandon what cost them so much trouble to acquire and, in some cultures, what contributed so much to their status. It is also these people who are best qualified, and most inclined, to see the unavoidable flaws in the new spelling. On the other hand, they will often be temperamentally disinclined to visualize the need for compromise that is responsible for some of those flaws. Discussions on the Hebrew spelling reform have often amazed me by instances of writers and scholars, with deep attachment to linguistic tradition, insisting on absurdly far-reaching and over-logical reforms involving a recasting of the grammar.

The difference between the planning of vocabulary and of spelling exists in a similar form within the planning body itself. The requirements of vocabulary planning and the need to have a body with authority led to a policy of staffing the planning body with leading scholars, writers, poets, and outstanding educators, generally with people above the age of forty, who have made a success of their occupations. Such people have proved on occasion to be allergic even to vocabulary innovations and over-sensitive to literary and esthetic associations of words. They are, of course, all highly skilled in the use of the existing spelling, strongly aware of its historical roots, and personally unaffected by its difficulties. They may even have learned to turn these difficulties to their advantage, such as playing intentionally on the vagueness, or exploiting spurious graphic similarities. They can see all the flaws, and their whole training has conditioned them to insist on truth and consistency and to reject compromise, to the extent of unwillingness even to bow to the outcome of votes. This leads to a form of discussion in which, instead of having a growing consent, there is an increasing sharpening of positions. Unused to the give-and-take of policy making, many of those present react as if they took part in a scientific discussion in which the facts emerging in the argument serve mainly to provide further refinement and solidity to their own theory.

Another result of the social characteristics of Academy members is the low rate of attendance at plenary meetings. Members have many other calls on their time, some spend sabbaticals abroad or attend conferences, and the high average age means that a percentage is always unable to attend because of illness. The need to have vocabulary committees in different towns and the wish to associate all universities mean that many members have to travel to attend the meetings that take place at bimonthly intervals. The average attendance is eighteen to twenty-five, but with strong variations in individual composition. Thus any progress towards compromise at one plenary meeting is often nullified by the different personal composition of the next. The consistent and fruitful work of the committees is in strong contrast to the climate in which their proposals are subsequently debated in the plenary sessions.

The committee members have on various occasions given expression to their feelings of frustration because of this difference (though it needed such experiences to bring it home to them).

In the case of the Hebrew Language Academy, we have something in the nature of a control experiment. During the same year that the spelling was debated, the Academy has also been engaged in a large-scale program of laying down rules for the inflection of nouns. The cause for this is that, with regard to many nouns, the original sources of the language provide alternative formations and inflections and that the intensive creation of new nouns has set many new problems of this kind. The Permanent Committee for Grammar of the Academy (the same body that constituted the 1962 committee for spelling) has been working since before 1953 on a complete regulation of all possible forms of nouns, and its proposals were presented chapter by chapter to the plenum. The decisions often involved giving up linguistic habits cherished by the educated, historical connections and the like and dealt, like the spelling, with matters of direct concern to every speaker. The discussions were often drawn out, and members were inclined to insist tenaciously on their own opinion so that others felt these discussions to be unbearably dull. However, as the subject matter was divided into small sections and as there was no need at any point to insist on the bearing of any decision on the structure of Hebrew as a whole (which only the professional linguists among the members were trained to do anyway), it was possible to finish point after point, chapter after chapter, and, today, a large part of the work has been done. The new rules are now being taught in the schools, and there has been no marked opposition - on the contrary, the general attitude is one of relief that an official decision exists on these knotty points.

It can thus be argued that the feature that makes spelling reform so much more arduous to agree on than other areas of language planning is its systematic character. Instances can be produced of successful and easy spelling reforms that concerned only details, as, for instance, the German abolition of *th* for /t/ about 1900, or the short-interval spelling revisions of Holland and Norway. This consideration was, as we pointed out, in the minds of some of the members responsible for the decisions that were finally taken. There is something attractive about the idea of accomplishing a large-scale spelling reform in easy stages at, say, five- or ten-year intervals so that each step does not have a systematic character and does not change too much the accustomed look of the printed page.

Since, in such a procedure, texts written in the last-stage spelling would still be fully intelligible to those taught the spelling in its new stage, this would obviate mass reprinting of books. It may be assumed that widely read books would in any event be reprinted during a ten-year period and that books which no one saw any need to reprint during twenty years were likely to be read only by specialists who would be trained to understand older spellings. Those responsible for the reform would be able to take full advantage of experience and scientific follow-up studies, as well as advances in printing techniques and linguistics. There are at least two snags, however small. A change in spelling costs organizational effort and money, and the gradual change is likely to be considerably more costly to the national economy than would one large change. Carrying out a revolution over a number of decades presupposes a sense of planning and continuity of purpose such as can scarcely be expected from a body composed mainly of middle-aged and elderly scholars and literary men.

The Hebrew Language Academy did a great deal to improve its communications with the general public over the last few years. It employs a speaker whose task it is to seek out opportunities for publicizing the Academy's decisions in the press, the radio, and elsewhere and who reacts to the appearance of terms in the press that conflict with those established by the Academy. A well-printed regular newssheet, made specially to be exhibited on walls of schools, offices, and factories, discusses groups of terms and gives grammatical information. It appears, however, that these devices are not suitable for winning the public for a large systematic change such as a new spelling. In this, the Academy is so far dependent on government approval and the hope that the Ministry will be quick and efficient in enforcing the change upon the schools; and, for the rest, it has been relying upon the daily press. The latter, of course, will carry this item only as long as it has news value, and that is just not long enough to make any impression on the public. In fact, without the fortuitous appearance of the 'Movement for an Unambiguous Hebrew Spelling', the reform decision might have passed almost unnoticed.

In the discussions following immediately after the meeting in which the reform was voted, it became clear to the members of the Directorate that no one really knew how such a spelling reform was to be put into practice. There is great uncertainty regarding such questions as: how much time should be allowed before the date on which the new spelling would become obligatory?; what should be done about school children (should they be made to change suddenly, or should they be allowed to finish elementary school with the spelling they had already learnt)?; who should be made to pay for the extra letters printers would need?

It would be most important for countries envisaging spelling reform that some research should be undertaken by an international body to review the procedures by which recent spelling reforms were effected in a number of countries, both developed and developing, if possible with some critical evaluation and legal and sociological comment. Such guidance would save psychological errors, omissions, and unnecessary expense.

POSTSCRIPT 1976

Page 171 end: The Spelling Reform was published by the Minister of Education and Culture in the *Official Gazette* of May 27, 1969, thus making it law. Only the Preamble (p. 167) was reprinted, and those interested referred to the Academy's publications.

P. 175-176: After long deliberations by a special committee, the Ministry of Education and Culture decided that from 1973 onwards, schools would teach the official full spelling to all children as soon as they were ready to do without pointing.

When the 1968 decision confirmed and ratified the 1948 spelling, it was overlooked that in the original 1948 rules the dots distinguishing various values of certain consonant signs and the readings /o/ and /u/ of the letter *v* (see p. 160) were described as an 'optional rule' depending on typographical facilities. The Directorate (cf. p. 169 top) interpreted the will of the plenum as wishing to make this an obligatory rule, and published the spelling rules in this form. One Academy member queried the legality of this decision, and in 1974 an ad hoc committee confirmed that the decision was illegal, and the formulation of this rule had to be referred to the plenum. At the time of writing, this point has not yet been discussed. In June 1975, however, the plenum finally confirmed a system of spelling foreign names in Hebrew characters which takes all these diacritic points into accounts, and adds a sign for the vowel [e], namely, ׳ with the pointing sign for short /e/ under it (a device which had been used by newspapers for many years).

Section Four

The Revision of Modern Writing Systems associated with National Political Establishments

G. GEERTS / J. VAN DEN BROECK / A. VERDOODT 9

Successes and Failures in Dutch Spelling Reform

INTRODUCTION

In England, Germany, and France the history of spelling runs to a large degree parallel with orthographic evolution in the Dutch language area. These surrounding countries regularly went through intense discussions on the necessity of spelling changes. Over and over again, the arguments of protagonists and antagonists parallel those of people who in other issues are inclined to reform, or who prefer to maintain traditional values. In none of these countries have the problems ever been examined in their complete scope. As far as Dutch spelling is concerned, however, the proposed solutions have from time to time led to effective spelling reforms, which in our neighboring countries has been much less the case.

The difference most certainly is not due to the fact that Dutch experts have been able to answer various important questions better than did their foreign colleagues. Cohen and Kraak (1972) have extensively demonstrated that in spelling matters much more is claimed than proved. Moreover, they are probably the first to have made an inventory of the many problems involved in a scientific approach to spelling. In this 'scientification' of the discussion, attention is paid essentially to exact facts with respect to the connection between reading, learning to read, writing, learning to write, spelling prescriptions, psycholinguistic insights, and, supporting Fishman (1971: 354 ff.) we add, sociolinguistic research. One of the results of this is that emotional feelings about spelling are pushed somewhat into the background. Furthermore, it may be expected that henceforth scientifically trained persons will demand more scientific justification of the proposed reforms than has hitherto been the case. Also, because the growth of linguistic insight has undone absolutist views of spelling and because sociolinguistic examinations have denounced the punitive use of spelling rules (cf. van der Velde 1969; Kohnstamm 1972: 5), a greater tolerance has arisen towards spelling mistakes and individual spelling peculiarities. Hence, the frequency of spelling reforms will probably decrease rather than increase during the following decades.

Factors such as an international spreading of a language, great respect for tradition, a generally acknowledged central authority (the *Académie Française*), a rather early acknowledged standardization (especially in England and France), an authoritative dictionary (Samuel Johnson's in 1755), and political unity (in England and France quite different and much earlier than in Germany and in the Netherlands)[1] may have stopped spelling reforms elsewhere. Since the Dutch language area lacked these factors, the path to change was open. The history of these changes teaches us that the first reform calls up the second, and subsequent reforms follow.

It is possible that a completely scientifically justified spelling reform can be so satisfying in all respects that the chain of reactions that has taken place in The Netherlands does not occur. Such a complete solution would, however, also have to provide for an adequate adaptation of loan words, and, as a result of the principle of the *vernederlandsing*[2] of the spelling of such words, the necessity of new spelling reforms would nevertheless be implied because of continued borrowings and the gradual integration of borrowings. There is also the question of how long the phonetic evolution of autochtonous words can be ignored. As is quite clear from the English, German, and French situations, continual postponement of recognition leads to greater problems than we have in our present spelling (cf. Pée 1946: 445-451; Robertson and Cassidy 1954: 340-342; Sciarone 1963: 934 ff.; Meijers 1967: 144-163; Debus 1972; Vos 1972).

If, in other words, there is one spelling reform – made possible and subsequently imposed by a central authority (as has been the case in The Netherlands) – its success carries the seed of new changes and, as a result, its own failure. The question is whether such an evolution is more favorable than little or no change at all – a question for which no scientifically justified answer can as yet be given. An overview of the evolution of Dutch spelling will contribute to the clarification of our insights in this respect.

1. DIACHRONIC OVERVIEW OF PROBLEMS AND CHANGES IN THE ORTHOGRAPHY OF MODERN DUTCH

1.1. Mediaeval Dutch Spelling

The preservation of numerous texts gives us a good picture of the way in which mediaeval Dutch was written. Since we know how great the differences were between the Middle Dutch regional dialects, both geographically and chronologically, it is not at all surprising that there was no unity of spelling. On the contrary, each region, period, and author had its or his own 'system'. In addition, these systems were often inconsistent with themselves. Moreover, it was difficult for the writers to escape from the influence of the 'civilized' language of their time, i.e. Latin. Although they had at their disposal the grapheme *k* to designate [K], repeatedly they used the Latin *c*; [KS] could easily be written as *ks*, but under Latin influence this cluster was nearly always designated by *x* and for the same reason the phoneme combination *kw* was often spelled *qu*.

On the other hand, the five Latin vowel representations were insufficient for reflecting the much larger number of Dutch vowels, so that Dutchmen of the Middle Ages faced many difficulties in this respect. Furthermore, the regional diversity yielded different solutions to these problems.

A third source of confusion lay in the uncertainty concerning the stability of a word. The problem here is whether or not it is desirable to adapt the word image to the various usages of the word. For instance, must a word, which presumedly begins with a voiced consonant but as a result of assimilation due to a preceding voiceless consonant now begins with a voiceless *anlaut*, be spelled differently in the latter case than in the former? Is it desirable for a word whose stem in the plural appears to have a voiced consonant before the plural morpheme (—ən], to be written with a voiceless *auslaut*, paralleling the pronunciation in the singular where only the stem is used?

These three factors – the influence of a foreign language, the lack of sufficient vowel representations, and the question of congruency – have dominated the Dutch spelling controversies throughout the centuries.

Explicit rules that can be applied to solve spelling problems have not come to us from the Middle Ages. However, from the Middle Ages' practice of aiming at a one-to-one correlation of sound and sign, we have derived the practice of doubling and combining vowel symbols and doubling consonants following certain vowels to make up for the lack of vowel representation, as well as the idea that consistency of word images has many supporters. These issues are consistently recurring elements in the Dutch spelling evolution.

1.2. The Sixteenth and Seventeenth Centuries

As printers began to show interest in a widely acceptable spelling, the concern for effective regulation gradually increased. The influence of French grammar also led in this direction. In England, where by the end of the fifteenth century the first printers like Caxton also begin to show interest in spelling matters, attempts to regulate the spelling proved to be successful after a few decades, and one can assume that the standardization was effective by the middle of the seventeenth century. Such a general regulation, however, was not achieved in The Netherlands. Joos Lambrecht, Antonius Sexagius, Pontus de Heuiter (cf. Dibbets 1968), and others devised spelling regulations which often showed much ingenuity and insight but did not gain general acceptance. This failure must first be accounted for by the regional character of their proposals: without a standardized language, spelling unity is impossible. Second, the opposition between those who claim that spelling and pronunciation must be seen in direct relation to each other, and those who, inspired by humanism, state that historical and etymological insights must provide the leading principles for spelling regulators, caused numerous disputes.

The spelling regulators knew each other's work, opposed each other's proposals, and often vindicated their own standpoints. Generally, it can be stated that the diversity did not become less than it was in the Middle Ages, and that due to a greater eagerness for education the inclination to advance all sets of mostly superfluous innovations increased. Even with regard to such simple problems as the representation of a vowel in open syllables, there was no agreement: an [a] is written sometimes as *ae*, other times as *aa*, and equally often as *a*, etc. They even argued about the representation of the final consonant: the principle of congruency was contested by De Heuiter (Dibbets 1968: 58), Coornhert, Van Heule, Aldegonde and others, and defended by De Hubert, Ampzing, Van der Schuere and others (Caron 1972: 52). De Hubert wanted to push the process so far that words like [wil], [vat] and [laf] would be written as *will, vatt, and laff* in order to correspond to the forms *willen, vatten, and laffe*. Following the Latin example, De Heuiter prefered to write *x* to reflect [ks]: rox [roks].

Under such circumstances it can be no surprise to us that the influence of the regulators remained limited. Their proposals obtained neither authoritative support nor widespread practical application. Moreover, in their writings, deviations from their own rules occurred quite often.

By the end of the seventeenth century the Amsterdam literary association *Nil Volentibus Arduum* made a serious attempt to foster drastic spelling reform. The changes proposed were indeed important simplifications: many superfluous letters were to be deleted and foreign elements as *c*, *q* and *x* were to be excluded. But the time was not ripe for such proposals. They were considered to be too radically different from tradition, and were ridiculed and ignored.

1.3. The Eighteenth Century

In the eighteenth century the spelling disputes were elevated to language questions, about which Alewijn calmly noticed: 'Many can palaver about one sole letter as though the well-being of Europe depended on it.'[3] The well-known need for order and regularity in classicism and the Enlightnement extended to spelling matters as well. Like their predecessors, those of the Enlightenment failed to set up a united front and were unable to cope with the disorder.

For the further developments, it is important to notice that the influence of diachronic linguistics became greater. Whereas in a closed syllable [a] was more and more represented by the double sign *aa* and in open syllables by a single *a* – the same applied to [y] – etymology was increasingly taken into account for the words with [e] and [o]. By virtue of the origin of [e] from *ai*, the plural *kleeden* was written to correspond to the singular *kleed*, and *boomen* to match *boom* ([o] from *au*). Coornhert, followed by Vondel (one of the greatest Dutch authors of his time), was perhaps the first to make this distinction (Kollewijn 1916: 33), and the work of Lambert ten Kate (1723) gave a large degree of certainty in this matter. Up to 1947 this historical basis, to which nothing in the modern standard language corresponds, dominated the spelling of such words.

Also in the eighteenth century, A. Moonen (1706) was one of the founders of the spelling of the verb forms which, though contested, is still in force today (cf. Van der Velde 1956).

Discussions in the *Maatschappij der Nederlandsche Letterkunde* [Society of Dutch Literature] led to the formulation of rules which preserved their influence for many years. This *Maatschappij* thought it necessary to occupy itself with spelling in view of the preparation of an extensive dictionary of the Dutch language. Parallel with the spirit of the time, one of the principles of these spelling rules was that each word must be spelled according to its origin. Moreover, it was stipulated that the rule of analogy must be applied (except in relation to *v* and *z* [*slaven* and *huizen*] which are not retained in *auslaut*, but replaced by *f* and *s* [*slaaf* and *huis*]), that if necessary double vowel signs must be used, and that the etymologically justified difference between *ei* and *ij* (both phonetically [ei]), *e* and *ee* (both phonetically [e]) and *o* and *oo* (both phonetically [o]) must strictly be maintained.

Because the authority of an important society stood behind these rules, they were more widely accepted than any previous regulations. The fact that these prescriptions were also followed by P. Weiland in his *Nederduitsch Taalkundig Woordenboek* [Dutch Linguistic Dictionary], eleven volumes appearing from 1799 on, gave them even more authority (cf. Royen 1949: 337).[4] At the time of later regulations, these were taken into account as well.

1.4. The First Official Spelling Prescriptions

1.4.1. Siegenbeek

During the governing of Louis Napoleon, the Batavian Republic devised the first 'government spelling', which, as Kruisinga has written (Royen 1949: 337), was 'a consequence of the equalization system of the French revolution'.[5] In the name of *égalité*, *liberté* was tied up! This spelling regulation was by order of J. H. van der Palm, Minister of National Education in the Republic, and was devised by M. Siegenbeek, professor in Leiden. His *Verhandeling over de Nederduitsche spelling, ter bevordering van eenparigheid in dezelve* [Treatise on Dutch Spelling, for the Promotion of the Uniformity in the Latter] appeared in 1804 and his *Woordenboek voor de Nederduitsche spelling* [Dictionary for the Dutch Spelling] in 1805. The proposals of Siegenbeek were evaluated and approved by the government, and subsequently published by the Bataafsche Maatschappij voor Taal en Dichtkunde [Batavian Society for Language and Poetry] and recommended for educational and governmental use by Van der Palm (for additional details on Siegenbeek cf. Damsteegt 1967).

The maxim of the regulation was that spelling must reflect pronunciation. But, as before and after, its application was limited by congruency, derivation, and analogy. The classicist theories of the previous century preserved their omnipresence. Yet, Siegenbeek seems to have had some success, though certainly not everybody considered his regulations to be definitive. The support of the official authority could not prevent others, such as the important writers W. Bilderdijk and J. A. Alberdingk Thijm, from using alternative regulations.

After 1814 opponents of the regulation obtained more support from Belgium when the Siegenbeek Spelling was introduced there. In Belgium the spelling proposed by Jan des Roches (1761) was held in high esteem and was considered to be more in agreement with the local language than was the imported *Hollandse*[6] Siegenbeek spelling. Once more, a uniform spelling proved to be impossible since there was no generally acknowledged standard language. More than ever, political and nationalist motives entered into the spelling discussions. Both clericals and liberals opposed the 'foreign' spelling (cf. Elias 1964: 180 ff.). In 1830 a petition against the use of the *Hollandse* language was circulated and signed by thousands of Flemish farmers with a small 'x', because they could not read nor write. These political emotions continued to accompany and influence the evolution of the spelling. When Belgium became politically independent in 1830, independence in relation to spelling was a self-evident demand. And although linguists and literary men of Belgium and The Netherlands resumed contact after the political break, arriving at regulations for the whole Dutch language area remained difficult for a long time.

1.4.2. The Second Half of the Nineteenth Century

The second half of the nineteenth century was marked by lively spelling discussions. In Belgium, the supporters of Des Roches fought hard against a spelling reform which was thought by some to be necessary for education. The *Maetschappy tot Bevordering der Nederduytsche Taal- en Letterkunde* [Society for the Promotion of Dutch Philology and Literature], with the agreement of the government, offered a prize for the solution of the spelling problem. None of the proposed solutions was accepted by the *Maetschappy*, but in 1841 it introduced its own spelling regulation which was adopted by the Belgian government in 1844.

In the Netherlands the government initially did not want to repeat the Siegenbeek case: an official, governmentally imposed and prescribed spelling did not fit in with the new, antirevolutionary political thinking in which the equalization system of the French Batavian Republic was completely overthrown. All of this did not prevent the Siegenbeek spelling from being generally used; supporters of the authors, Bilderdijk and Alberdingk Thijm, and other individualists, as usual, kept spelling as they pleased.

Both Belgians and Dutchmen meanwhile searched for renovation and for unity. Congresses of philologists and literary men were mainly devoted to these themes. The agreement in 1851, in Brussels, on setting up a great *Woordenboek der Nederlandsche Taal* [Dictionary of the Dutch Language] was linked to the prior elaboration of a uniform spelling. This spelling was to be used in the *Woordenboek* and to this day the *Woordenboek* is still written in the spelling then devised. The latter was founded on the new insights brought about by historical-comparative philology, was based on clearly formulated and elucidated principles, and was (hopefully) to be acceptable for the whole Dutch language area. The historical foundations, introduced by Ten Kate and elaborated by Siegenbeek, were now to be supported by the pillars of Indo-European philology.

1.4.3. Te Winkel

Entrusted with the task of incorporating the findings of philology into the spelling problem, in 1859 Te Winkel published his first proposal; in 1863 he produced the *Ontwerp der Spelling* [Spelling Project], which in 1864, after some modifications introduced in agreement with Te Winkel, was accepted and prescribed by the Belgian Government. In 1865 there followed *De Grondbeginselen der Nederlandse Spelling* [The Principles of Dutch Spelling] with a preface by M. de Vries. In this way the De Vries and Te Winkel spelling came into being. The authors together compiled *De Woordenlijst voor de spelling der Nederlandsche taal* [The List of Words for the Spelling of the Dutch Language] (De Vries and Te Winkel 1866), on behalf of education, since they were of the opinion that their spelling was not only intended for the *Woordenboek*, but, as De Vries wrote in 1862, it was the solution which could reconcile the conflicting parties once and for all.

The key concepts in the *Grondbeginselen* were civilized pronunciation, congruency, derivation and analogy, and, in relation to loan words, 'good taste' (Te Winkel 1865: 234, 235).

The rule of civilized pronunciation ('Reflect in your writing the civilized pronunciation') 'is the first and most important rule' (Te Winkel 1865: § 41).[7] It does not imply a phonetic spelling, for 'the goal of the writing is already achieved, if the reader can *recognize* the word that is meant'

(Te Winkel 1865: § 44 – our italics).[8] Easy recognition derives from another important prescription: the rule of congruency. This rule provides a permanent, constant word image. It stipulates that a morpheme as a word, i.e. not as an inflected form, must be written 'with the same letters' (Te Winkel 1865: § 56)[9] in a derivation or in a composition. So, one should write [h*o*.vdel] as *hoofddeel* 'from *hoofd* and *deel*' and not as '*hoofdeel*, since exact understanding might be hindered by the latter way of writing'.[10] Such an example also shows that listening to the exact pronunciation should not be taken in the strict sense in which we would take it nowadays. *Hoofd* is not spelt according to pronunciation, but with a *d* on account of congruency with the plural form *hoofden*. The same applies with regard to [x] in words as *weg* [wɛχ], plural *wegen* [weɣən] and [p] in words such as *schub* [sχʌp], plural *schubben* [sχʌbən], but not in relation to [s] in words such as *huis* [hœys], plural *huizen* [hœyzən], nor in relation to [f] in words as *dief* [dif], plural *dieven* [divən]. Verb forms as (*hij*) *houdt* and (*hij*) *wordt*, pronounced as [hɔut] and [wɔrt] base their *d* on their connection with *houden* and *worden*, their *t* on the analogy with (*hij*) *speelt* [spe.lt].

The derivation rule implies the acknowledgment of 'the older form'.[11] It prescribes that in those cases where on account of pronunciation and congruency no choice can be made between different 'equally sounding letter signs',[12] that spelling must be chosen that harmonizes with the form 'out of the time, when the now equalized sounds still could clearly be discerned'.[13] On account of this rule a distinction is made between *lijden* [lɛidən] (middle Dutch lîden – to suffer) and *leiden* [lɛidən] (*leiden*, [lêden] – to guide), *koude* [kɔud] and *saus* [sɔus); between *kolen* [ko.lən] ('coals') and *koolen* [ko̱.lən] ('vegetables'), *delen* [de.lən] ('planks') and *deelen* [de.lən] ('parts'), between *visch* [vɪs] and *mis* [mɪs] etc. Neither are the suffixes *-lijk* [lək] and *-isch* [-ɪs] simplified, again on account of etymological considerations. The warning to be read (Te Winkel 1865: § 65), viz. that this principle most certainly may not be applied in opposition with the rule of civilized pronunciation, 'because it interferes with the spelling for all non-philologists',[14] does not seem to have been taken too seriously!

For the words whose spelling cannot be settled in the light of the three prescriptions mentioned, the analogy rule applies. The latter stipulates that such words must be compared with words of which the spelling 'is known for sure and which are apparently formed in a similar way' (Te Winkel 1865: § 65).[15]

The De Vries and Te Winkel regulation also deals with questions such as the use of the hyphen (Te Winkel 1965: §§ 154-158), the connecting sounds (§§ 161-213), the distribution of words in syllables (§§ 257-270), and the use of capitals. Moreover, attention is paid to the writing of loan words (§ 214-256).[16] Loan words are words which have been borrowed from foreign languages, but which are not completely *vernederlandst*[17] and yet not considered to be foreign anymore. Because of the hybrid character of these words the Dutch spelling rules cannot simply be applied to them, but neither is it desirable to leave them unchanged (§ 217). Their pronunciation has indeed been (partly) adapted – according to De Vries and Te Winkel they can be considered predominantly foreign if they are not inflected according to Dutch derivation rules – and consequently the foreign spelling does not reflect the exact pronunciation anymore. Hence a spelling adaptation is necessary, in so far as 'the original spelling could lead to unusual pronunciation' (Te Winkel 1865: § 241).[18] Two other elements, however, often appear to have restrained De Vries and Te Winkel from the application of this maxim: first, etymological recognizability where an unchanged spelling can occur, second, *Aesthetica*, which does not hold 'bastard spelling' in high esteem since 'all things considered' there is 'something coarse' in such spellings as *koncert* or *konsert* instead of *concert* (yet read [kɔnsɛrt] and *filozoof* instead of *philosoof* (yet read [filoz*o*.f]), 'which shocks the civilized and the literary man, as long as his eye has not got accustomed to such tasteless ways of writing' (§ 234).[19]

De Vries and Te Winkel neither expected nor hoped that 'men of letters' would soon get used to what was, according to their principles, the best spelling possible. On the contrary, since 'men of letters' were acquainted with foreign languages and hence knew what these words looked like in these foreign languages, they must be able to continue to make use of this knowledge, the more so since they are the ones that most employ foreign words and loan words (§ 228). If one would start writing the word *compascuum* as *kompaskuüm*, the 'Latinist' 'would have to think a few moments' (§ 230)[20] before he understood what was meant, and this had to be prevented.

That the 'ignorant' have difficulties in having to write the *f* sound heard in the *anlaut* of [filoz*o*.f], differently from the same f sound in *fijn*, and *z* of [filoz*o*.f], differently from the *z* of *zon*, was not for one moment taken into account. 'Some knowledge of foreign language (remains) necessary. The ignorant will always have to know that *artikel*, *titel*, *visit* and *machine* have been taken over from abroad; that in Greek *thermometer* is written with θ . . ., *synode* with υ and *citer* with *i* if he does not want to run the risk of writing *artiekel, tietel, viziete, masjiene, termometer, sinode, siter* (Te Winkel 1965: § 232).[21]

An as thorough as possible *vernederlandste* spelling of loan words is rejected by De Vries and Te Winkel because the unlettered would 'not at all be helped' (§ 233)[22] by it, but even more because such a spelling would shock the 'men of letters'. 'Consequently, that is one of the most important reasons' for its rejection (§ 234).[23]

In this attitude we find the root of the problems which in 1973 have not yet been solved.

Finally, we must refer to the fact that De Vries and Te Winkel also concerned themselves with the regulation of the nominal classification and the nominal and attributive inflection and pronominalization allied to this. It is impossible to discuss within the framework of this contribution the reason for this concern and the proposals made: principally this question has nothing to do with the history of the spelling. As, however, the coupling of gender and spelling regulation has for 100 years been the cause of so many heated discussions, which has made a sober approach of the pending spelling issues impossible, this fact must be touched upon here (cf. Royen 1949; 1953: 24-253).

1.4.4. The Roots of the Present Reform Movements

1.4.4.1. De Vries and Te Winkel. Contrary to the hope of De Vries and Te Winkel, the conflicting parties were not reconciled. According to a declaration of minister Thorbecke in 1866 the Dutch government 'cannot lend assistance to the recently glorified spelling of De Vries and Te Winkel', which according to another politician led to great confusion (Royen 1949: 270).[24] Hence there was no question of official recognition, nor of official introduction into the administration or schools. Some remained loyal to Siegenbeek, others tried to learn De Vries and Te Winkel spelling – including the twenty-six rules needed for the spelling of [e] and [o]! In Belgium, on the other hand, the spelling of De Vries and Te Winkel was – with a few minor modifications – officially accepted by Royal Decree November 21, 1864 (cf. *Spelling* 1864: 111-113).

The general public, Vosmaer wrote in 1869, 'does not yet feel like bowing its pen to the new spelling'. And he adds that he can only explain this 'as a sign of conservatism' (Royen 1949: 270).[25]

Meanwhile authoritative philologists like De Jager and Van Vloten continued to resist. Famous literary men such as Busken Huet and Multatuli, as well as many other writers, kept using their own individual spelling. The educational circles followed their own bent, which, as can be guessed from a report of an inspector in 1873, brought about great confusion.

According to a governmental report of 1912, the spelling issue was officially given a free run; the new spelling was not arrested, but stimulated (Royen 1949: 339). In 1883 the government showed its colors by writing the King's speech in the new spelling. Even then the new spelling did not become officially operative. Educational circles, however, gradually shifted from the old to the new spelling. De Vries and Te Winkel gained more and more support from the younger generations. The older ones continued to follow Siegenbeek. Hence a generation gap was introduced into Dutch spelling – a phenomenon which would recur in later evolution as well.

1.4.4.2. Kollewijn. Under the influence of new pedagogical insights, however, the scholarliness of the De Vries and Te Winkel spelling was experienced as a setback by teachers. The renovators especially devoted themselves to a SIMPLIFICATION. They thought less about 'men of letters' than about the man in the street and hence they drew the ire of the former upon themselves: this democratizational aspect was new and remained with the spelling conflict later on as well.

The new ideas were first uttered by R. A. Kollewijn in an article about 'Our Difficult Spelling. A Suggestion for Simplification' (Kollewijn 1891). Kollewijn stated that the system devised by De Vries and Te Winkel was so complicated that for many words it was impossible to predict which rule must be applied. He admitted that a simple, consistent spelling was impossible (Kollewijn 1916: 10), 'But where one cannot or may not be consistent, one should try to be practical'.[26] There should be no distinctions *introduced* in the written language which did not occur in the spoken language; there should be no distinctions maintained which had disappeared from the spoken language. Furthermore, Kollewijn made it clear that a living language changes constantly and that hence the spelling must be adapted from time to time. No longer were Grimm, the great German (historical) linguist, and his followers the foremost linguistic guides. They had been replaced by H. Paul. Spelling regulators were not inspired anymore by the romanticism of the past, but rather by the realism of the present and future. Kollewijn especially emphasized the first rule – pronunciation. He diverted the main guidelines of the spelling prescriptions from the hardly accessible etymologies to the aspects of pronunciation and congruency which are understandable for most people. Indeed, a spelling which exclusively reflects pronunciation is considered by Kollewijn to be utopian and certainly not practical (Kollewijn 1916: 15).

In 1893 there followed the founding of the *Vereniging tot vereenvoudiging van onze spelling en verbuiging* [Association for the Simplification of our Spelling and Inflection] (further referred to as *Vereniging*), which in 1895 brought about a number of concrete proposals for the simplification of the spelling De Vries and Te Winkel. In 1902 these proposals were slightly altered and formulated in the shape of nine *Regels van de vereenvoudigde spelling* [Rules of the Simplified Spelling] (further referred to as *Regels*).

As regards the spelling of Dutch words the *Regels* rejected etymological *ee*, *oo*, and *ch* (in *-sch*): no longer *deelen*, but *delen* ('parts' as well as 'planks') (rule 1); no longer *koolen*, but *kolen* ('coals' as well as 'vegetables') (rule 2); no longer *visch* but *vis* as well as *mis* (rule 5). At the end of a syllable [i] is spelled as *ie* (rule 3). The schwa is designated by *i* in *-lijk*, *gewoonlijk* (as in the already usual *-ig* words: *gelukkig*, *nodig*) (rule 4). Furthermore, the connecting sound is only written if it is heard: hence no longer *sterrenkunde*, but *sterrekunde*, no longer *oorlogsschip* but *oorlogschip*, etc. (rule 6).

In loan words [i] is represented as *i* in open syllables, and as *ie* in the *auslaut;* [e] no longer as *ae* (in words such as *pedagogie* and *preparaat*); [k] no longer as *c* (*lokomotief*, *kontributie*); [f] not as *ph* (*alfabet*, *fotograferen*); [r] not as *rh* (*retorica*). Moreover, the complete *vernederlandsing* of a number of loan words was insisted upon. For the rest, many double forms were allowed: [byro.] may be written both as *bureau* and as *buro*, [sɛnt] both as *cent* and *sent*, [ɛksamən] both as *examen* and *eksamen*, and [siste.m] both as *systeem* and *sisteem* (rule 7).

The ninth rule deals with the inflection which must be settled according to the 'civilized pronunciation' (Kollewijn 1916: 204-205).

1.4.4.3. Kollewijn's Proposals Rejected. These proposals are certainly not revolutionary: they are 'rather a continuation of successive measures in order to improve the spelling practically, on behalf of the entire population, without too great shocks' (De Vooys 1940).[27] They are mainly 'a necessary correction for the excess emphasis on etymology' (Stuiveling 1972: 178)[28] which characterizes the spelling of De Vries and Te Winkel. 'For the practical reformer one thing is indisputable: the spelling does not necessarily reflect the *origin* and the *history* of the words (Daman 1929: 7).[29] Yet, Kollewijn's proposals were strongly disputed. In 1908 the government even stipulated that the spelling of Kollewijn was not to be used in education.

It should be noticed that besides being influenced by the gender quarrels, this conflict was affected by sympathy and antipathy towards modern linguistics and modern pedagogy. One of the most important motives of the simplifiers is that they expect a simple spelling to save considerable time, which can be used for the necessary review of language instruction proper. This is why support is so great among those who are concerned with popular education. Whether this also has led to differences between young and old, or between conservative and progressive, left wing and right wing, or any other soecial opposition can hardly be demonstrated because of a lack of research data, but this possibility must certainly not be excluded, the more so since such opposition occasionally did occur later (cf. section 2).

Furthermore, it is important – this too recurs – that the opponents of De Vries and Te Winkel do not always agree on the points which need simplification and on the way in which it should be accomplished. As early as 1913, Kollewijn (1916: 198) stated that the spelling of De Vries and Te Winkel could no longer be defended, but also that the moderate proposals of the simplifiers were 'abundantly contested' (Kollewijn 1916: 119).[30]

1.4.4.4. The Continuing Conflict. At the top of the list of adversaries of spelling reform we find the literary men. They continually confused language and spelling, and often wrote as they pleased (cf. Daman 1929: 29, 31), but in an address to the Dutch minister in charge in 1910 they called the Simplified Spelling 'a disaster' for the population. The same ideas were taken over in 1917 in a motion of thousands of opponents of the Simplified Spelling. Prominent philologists, such as professors J. ten Brink and J. Kalff, the grammarian C. H. den Hertog and school directors and inspectors associated themselves with the protest. Some devised their own spelling systems: between 1894 and 1934 at least eleven were published (Daman 1941: 19). In 1909, 1916, 1919, and 1927 the Dutch Government officially interfered with the spelling. The report of the first official commission was devastating for the Simplified Spelling, but this could hardly be otherwise for the sole task of this commission was to examine how much was written in the new – i.e. in the forbidden – spelling. The commission demonstrated no interest in the motives of the simplifiers and it was convinced that love of ease was the real incentive of the teachers. The second commission presented a compromise arrangement but the latter was not accepted by the minister in charge. The same goes for the proposals of the commissions of 1919 and 1927.

It is striking that the opponents of the Simplified Spelling set down little in writing: the bibliography of Daman (1941: 91-106) mentions 150 items, only ten of which are by its adversaries. The large newspapers carried on their firm rejection of changes.

In Belgium the proposals of the Simplifiers are disputed as well, by M. Rooses, P. Fredericq, and A. Prayon van Zuylen, among others. In 1897 and 1903 the *Koninklijke Vlaamse Akademie voor Taal- en Letterkunde* [Royal Flemish Academy for Philology and Literature][31] expressed its dissatisfaction with the simplification on the basis that spelling reform would be dangerous for the future of Dutch in Belgium. This argument was also employed by others. They thought that the supremacy of French would be confirmed by it. The famous authors S. Streuvels and A. Vermeylen also put in a word with terms such as 'castration, murder, raping and mutilating' (Daman 1941: 70).[32] In 1920 and 1926 the *Academie* again showed itself opposed to spelling changes. However, not all members of the *Academie* shared its official point of view, as can be inferred from the attitudes of linguist members such as Vercoullie, De Vreese, and others (cf. infra 1.5.1.).

1.5. The Last Half of a Century

1.5.1. Modernization in Progress

The advocates of modernization formed a more united front, but as some could not agree with all rules of the Kollewijn spelling, they were not all members of the *Vereniging*. In addition, it should be stated that among them too there were often striking discrepancies between theory and practice: those who actually used the new spelling were much less numerous than those who advocated a spelling simplification. None of this alters the fact that the protest of the *Vereniging* was impressive, obstinate, and persevering. In 1894 the *Vereniging* had 309 members, in 1931, 4989; if this does not seem to be impressive, one should remember that some twenty educational organizations always were represented by single members and together these organizations comprised many thousands of teachers.

As opposed to many leading people, the teachers themselves have always been predominantly in favor of a simplification. In 1928 an inquiry among the teachers of Dutch showed that a solid 86 percent of them were advocates of the new spelling. Also in 1928 the Inspector of the Primary Education in Belgium wrote that it was desirable that the simplified spelling be introduced officially. At several examinations the Kollewijn spelling was allowed. Students from Utrecht, Leiden, Delft, and Amsterdam created branches of the *Vereniging*. Professors like Moltzer, Symons, Van Helten, and Logeman in the Netherlands, and Vercoullie, De Vreese, Scharpé, and Lecoutere in Belgium stood behind the simplifiers. In 1897 the first doctoral thesis was published in the new spelling; in 1929 Daman noticed that since 1897 fully ninety others had done the same, and the number mounted to 142 in 1933. The *Koninklijke Akademie van Wetenschappen* (Amsterdam) [Royal Academy of Sciences] and the *Maatschappij der Nederlandsche Letterkunde* [Society of Dutch Literature] (Leyden) did not mind accepting contributions in the new spelling. Many educational periodicals appeared completely or partly in the new spelling.

Moreover, some literary men are proponents of simplification. This can be found in the attitudes and writings of P. de Mont, J. Vermeersch, E. de Bock, A. M. de Jong whose bestseller *Merijntje Gijzen's Jeugd* [The Youth of Marijntje Gijzen] proved that the general public did not consider the new spelling to be childish, M. Emants, A. Verwey, J. Van Looy, P. N. van Eyck, and others.

Nearly all Dutch periodicals accepted contributions in the new spelling thus helping to spread its use. Some papers did not allow for any change (e.g. *De Nieuwe Rotterdamsche Courant* and *De Telegraaf* [Amsterdam] which after 1927, even fired a prominent contributor because of his modern spelling). In others (like *De Maasbode* [Rotterdam], only 'acknowledged philologists' were permitted to use the simplified spelling. *Het Volk*, on the other hand, permitted a few of its regular contributors to use the simplified spelling.

In 1897 the *Vereniging* was for the first time able to publish its own organ. From September 1, 1897, until May 1947, altogether fifty-one volumes appeared with 271 issues. In 1930 sales numbered 6000 copies.

In 1905 J. W. Engelkes published *De spelling-Kollewijn*, a brochure for educational purposes, which in 1930 went through its sixteenth printing.

However, the above mentioned official commissions which, as mediators, adopted some of Kollewijn's proposals repeatedly met with reaction.

It is also striking that Daman (1929: 36) was forced to notice that, with one exception, all commercial circles adhered to the old spelling; in 1941 their attitude was reported to be less conservative (Daman 1941: 44).

Finally, it is interesting to mention that in 1929 Daman (1929: 38) drew the attention of the Flemish to the fact that those individuals whose pronunciation of the standard language must rely on the written word for lack of spoken contact will be considerably helped by the new spelling because it more closely parallels the sound. In addition, he argued that the French speaking Belgians will learn Dutch more easily because they will no longer 'be discouraged by unnecessary difficulties' (Daman 1929: 39).[33]

1.5.2. Kollewijn's Partial Success

In the beginning of the 1930's agitation for spelling reform became exceptionally great. The supporters of Kollewijn seemed to be achieving their goal. In 1933 their adversaries set up a *Comité voor eenheid in de schrijfwijzev an het Nederlandsch* [Committee for Unity in the Writing of Dutch] but could not prevent Minister Marchant from setting up (in the same year) a commission of five philologists upon whose advice he prescribed (in 1934) six of the nine rules proposed by Kollewijn for the schools (omitting rules 4, 6, and 7). The endings *-eelen* and *-eeren* and the suffix *-isch* still remained unchanged (see supra, p. 191).

It should be no surprise that such a compromise did not satisfy everyone immediately, especially since at this time the gender question again resurfaced. Men of letters maintained their conservative standpoint and continued to utter their stereotyped cries, at times in the name of 'ten thousands of respectable citizens' (Daman 1947: 41),[34] at times for the defence of the inheritance of the ancestors, at times out of respect for the word of God. The famous poet P. C. Boutens spoke of 'the laziness spelling' (Daman 1941: 42).[35] The Amsterdam professor J. Wille considered the new spelling 'to be incompatible in its maxims and aims with Christian theology' (Daman 1941: 46).[36]

Most Dutch newspapers did not explicitly reject the compromise arrangement, but only a few shifted to the new spelling. Yet, they appeared to adapt their children's columns to the spelling used in education. Many other publications, including the periodicals of the broadcasting companies which had high circulations, soon appeared in the new spelling. In 1936 no less than twenty municipalities started using the simplified spelling. Many literary men, and among them some famous and popular authors like Theun de Vries, Jan Mens, Martinus Nijhoff, Bertus Aafjes, and Jan de Hartog, did likewise.

The Belgian Minister of Education, Lippens, wanted to follow Marchant. The newspapers, however, were firmly opposed and the *K.V.A.T.L.* refused to accept the new spelling. Minister Lippens resigned in 1934, but a commission set up by his successor also advised the adoption ofthe Dutch compromise regulation as soon as the Dutch government would introduce the new spelling on a nation-wide basis.

Soon thereafter a Belgian-Dutch commission, the Van Haeringen Commission, was created in order to propose a list of words in accord with the 1934 spelling. The latter commission was discharged from its task in 1936 by the successor of Marchant, minister Slotemaker de Bruïne, contrary to the desire of the Belgian government. In the person of J. Hoste another minister came to power in Belgium who, like his Dutch colleague, wanted to go back to the De Vries and Te Winkel spelling. This endeavor was supported by the *Nationale vereniging voor orde en eenheid in de schrijftaal* [National Association for Order and Unity in the Written Language] in the Netherlands, by the most important Belgian newspapers, and by influential philologists like Van Mierlo.

The *Vereniging* (of Kollewijn) then devoted itself to the maintenance and propagation of the Marchant spelling. In 1937 it distributed 50,000 copies of a manifest 'to the Dutch Population'. On behalf of the struggle in Belgium a Flanders issue was published (volume 41: 1 [May 1938]) in which the leading Belgian proponents F. van Dijck, J. Leenen, J. L. Pauwels, E. Franssen, and R. Verdeyen supplied abundant and well-reasoned information about the simplified spelling.

The publishing companies finally became impatient with the squabbles and insisted on the general introduction of the Marchant spelling, which in the meantime had been taught for three years.

Confusion was general. The Dutch *Tweede Kamer* (comparable to the English 'House of Commons') pronounced itself as being against the formation of a new spelling commission and in favor of official adoption of the 1934 (Marchant) spelling. The *Eerste Kamer* (comparable to the English 'House of Lords') did not sanction a national-socialist motion which proposed to withdraw the 1934 regulation from the schools. On July 4, 1938, the Minister of Education appointed the Fockema Andreae Commission, which was almost exclusively composed of nonphilologists. In Belgium, too, a commission was created, viz. the Teirlinck Commission which was charged with a similar task. Two members of this Belgian commission joined the Dutch one as well. On July 12, 1939, the Dutch minister published four Royal Decrees dated July 8, 1939, but on August

10 his successor, an ex-member of the *Vereniging*, suspended the implementation of these Decrees. The whole conflict focused much more on the gender question than on spelling per se. The situation remained unchanged; in the schools, rules 1, 2, 5, and 8 of Kollewijn were still maintained, with one exception: the suffix *-isch* [-is] was not to be written *-ies*. Rule 4 (*-lik* and *-liks*) had been dropped. In relation to rules 3, 6, and 7 no decision had yet been taken.

The outbreak of World War II marked the end of official squabbling. The polemics continued for a while; in the camp of Kollewijn's opponents the vehemence of few national-socialist publicists was striking. They fulminated against 'the ill winds of the nihilistic democratic and marxist gentlemen who in The Netherlands have smashed down everything that was the property of the whole population' (Daman 1941: 10).[37] Terms such as 'denationalization, Germanic blood family, cultural Bolshevists, red language corrupters'[38] proved that 'spelling' issues could be put to use for a variety of purposes!

Kollewijn died in 1942 but his advocates remained active. Daman stated that the general public was continually becoming more accustomed to the 'look' of the new word orthography and that, therefore, after the end of the war the press increasingly applied the new spelling.

1.5.3. The 1946 and 1954 Prescriptions

The Belgian and the Dutch governments in exile agreed in London that after the war they would try to adopt a joint regulation. This accounts for the fact that as early as March 20, 1944, a Belgian-Dutch commission was announced which would attempt to form 'a uniform orthography for the Dutch language, on the basis of the spelling of De Vries and Te Winkel, to be valid in The Netherlands and in Belgium'.[39] In October 1945 the commission was formed; it consisted of eight Dutch and eight Belgian members, among whom, according to Daman (1947: 19) were six Dutch and four Belgian advocates of simplification and three Dutch and three Belgian opponents thereof.

Soon, in February 1946, a proposal was forthcoming and as early as March 9 it was followed in Belgium by a Decree of the Prince-Regent 'arranging the spelling of the Dutch language . . . according to De Vries and Te Winkel, observing the following . . .',[40] after which came five rules and three transitional stipulations. This decree was more or less similar to what Marchant had stipulated for the Dutch schools. One of its most important simplifications, most certainly, was the optional dropping of the inflectional *-n* (cf. Pauwels 1934: 21 ff.).

In the Netherlands however, the Minister of Education first had to introduce a bill. This was done on June 29, 1946. Immediately the quarrels blazed up again. The secretary of the Dutch National Association for Order and Unity in the Written Language claimed in Dutch and Belgian newspapers that the Belgian representatives on the joint commission, with the help of the highest public servant of the Belgian ministry of education, had imposed their opinion on the majority of the official commission. He demanded that the 'spelling squabbles behind the scenes' (Daman 1947: 23)[41] come to an end.

In Belgium the newspapers and the *Vlaamsche Uitgeverijbond* [Flemish Association of Publishers] rejected the new compromise spelling and the authoritative Catholic philologist Van Mierlo again rushed into print to fulminate against the 'barbaric work' (Daman 1947: 21)[42] of the commission. Here, too, it was often suggested that the simplifiers had committed a coup. The Belgian minister Vos, however, noticed that it was not the extremists, but the 'moderates'[43] who had put their stamp on the new arrangement.

The Dutch *Tweede Kamer* accepted the so-called Gielen Bill on September 25, 1946. In this way the new spelling was protected by law in order to prevent future reforms from being carried through by means of a general set of government (i.e. by the minister without consulting the parliament). A few spelling instances were not included in the new legal arrangement: the orthography of Dutch geographic names,[44] loan words, historical names, and the question of medial letters[45] in compounds. However, all this still did not settle the matter yet: the *Eerste Kamer* still had to discuss the proposals and the adversaries of simplification used this opportunity for obtaining a few more concessions. On February 12, 1947, the bill was accepted in the *Eerste Kamer*. Both in The Netherlands and in Belgium the stipulations of the new arrangement took effect on May 1, 1947; its application was prescribed both for official and educational use. A *Vaste Commissie van Advies inzake de Schrijfwijze van de Nederlandse Taal* [Permanent Consultative Commission for the Orthography of the Dutch Language] was set up in the two countries in order to assist the ministers in the execution and application and eventually also in the reformulation of the reforms.

The above mentioned texts were more closely examined by a commission composed of six Dutchmen and six Belgians. It had to settle the remaining spelling issues, as well as to map out a list of words in which the exact spelling was to be determined, and which, moreover, was to designate the gender of the nouns (this part of the task had already been assigned to a similar commission in 1934, viz. the Van Haeringen commission, but it had never formulated its conclusions).

The list of words appeared in 1954 (*Woordenlijst* 1954, hereafter *Woordenlijst*), ninety years after the one of De Vries and Te Winkel. In the interval a lot of arguments had occurred but as to orthography there had hardly been any changes: the [e] and the [o] were now always represented by one sign in open syllables, and the [s], except for in *-isch*, was never written as *-sch*. As to loan words, on the other hand, several important simplifications were introduced: *ph* and *th* always became, respectively, *f* and *t*; *y* and *ae* usually became *i* and *e*, and *th* usually could be written as *t* (cf. Pauwels 1954). Furthermore, the use of hyphens, diaereses, and apostrophes was somewhat more orderly. The gender arrangement, which is left out of consideration here, received little public attention and appeared to have little influence on writing practices. The solution with respect to medial letters was ingenious, but not very appealing and not conducive to application. Moreover, the regulation of the spelling of loan words was actually no regulation at all, but an 'arbitrary system which is scientifically untenable and societally useless' (Stuiveling 1972: 179).[46] Some words had been completely *vernederlandst* and were written according to Dutch spelling rules (e.g. *sigaret*); others received two forms: either a Dutch 'preferable' spelling (*voorkeurspelling*) and an 'allowed' spelling (*toegelaten spelling*) in foreign orthography (e.g. *publikatie* vs. *publicatie*) or a foreign 'preferable' form and a Dutch 'allowed' form (e.g. *colporteren* vs. *kolporteren*); another set of loan words maintained foreign spelling alone (e.g. *colporteur*). It was a compromise between the progress desired by Dutch and especially Belgian educational circles, on the one hand, and Dutch Public opinion, which rejected radical adaptation on the other hand (van Haeringen 1954; see section 2. below). However teachers, pupils, and officials were forced to use the 'preferable' spellings,[47] which caused so much dissatisfaction that once more we can state that one arrangement necessarily called for another. *L'histoire se répète.*

1.5.4. 1969: Eindvoorstellen [Final Proposals]

The Belgian and the Dutch governments were aware of this dissatisfaction and asked the experts for advice. On December 1, 1956, the joint commission De Vos and Damsteegt presented a report for which the Dutch

Permanent Consultative Commission expressed its appreciation on March 20, 1957; the Woordenlijst commission also formulated its ideas (July 1, 1958). The majority of the experts held that the difficulties caused in the schools by the spelling of loan words had to decrease and that a system of rules had to be elaborated which offered useful guidance to those who needed it.

In 1963 a new Belgian-Dutch commission was appointed – the *Bastaardwoordencommissie* [Loan Words Commission], also called the De Vos-Wesselings Commission (see infra 207). After the death of De Vos, Pée replaced him and hence the Commission's name was changed to Pée-Wesselings.

Its report appeared in 1967 (*Rapport* 1967) and caused the usual emotional excitement. Passions blazed up again . . . to such an extent that the governments asked the Commission to reconsider its proposals; in 1969 a 'Final Report' appeared (*Eindvoorstellen* 1969). But the latter could not reconcile the parties. Once more the 'men of letters' took up positions against the educational circles. Whereas the arguments of the former could hardly be called original, the teachers more firmly than ever favored a radical simplification. Moreover, they did not limit themselves to the loan words: the spelling of Dutch words (notably the phonetically irrelevant difference between *ei* and *ij* [ɛi] and *ou* and *au* [ɔu]) and the writing of the verb forms entered into the discussions as well. The same went for the congruency principle: the radical simplifiers wanted to extend the phonological principle and hence they favored *hont* and *paart* (read: [hɔnt] and [pa.rt]) instead of *hond* and *paard*, so written because of the plurals *honden* and *paarden*.

2. THE REACTIONS OF THE MAIN TARGET GROUPS TO THE 1947-1954 SPELLING REFORM AND TO THE 1967-1969 PROPOSALS

2.1. Introduction

2.1.0. We will now take a closer look at the most recent effective spelling reform, and at the present proposals for a new one. The first is designated as the 1947-1954 reform, because its most important dates are 1947 (introduction in the Netherlands and in Belgium on May 1) and 1954 (publication of the *Woordenlijst*). The second is labeled 1967-1969 since 1967 is the year in which the Pée-Wesselings Commission published its first report (*Rapport* 1967), and 1969 is the year in which the *Eindvoorstellen* [Final Proposals] appeared. Both reports have provoked so much reaction that at this moment (March 1973) the spelling question is still far from settled. Hence we can only speak of proposals.

For each period we will concentrate on the various authorities and agencies rejecting or accepting the proposed reforms, paying particular attention to between-group differences. Purely practical reasons have imposed the limitation to these two periods. Data on previous reforms is indeed too scarce to give a systematic overview of the between-group differences that obtained formerly; it has turned out to be impossible, for instance, to trace in a detailed way the reaction of public opinion or even that of educational circles to the Siegenbeek spelling (1804).

Section 1. presented a fairly general overview of the spelling reforms throughout the history of the modern Dutch language, as well as of the various agencies and authorities rejecting and/or accepting them. However, this section aims at a more systematic discussion of the between-group differences for the periods 1947-1954 and 1967-1969. In this way we hope to reveal the different reactions which spelling reforms provoke. Moreover, this discussion is probably also rather relevant for previous reactions and attitudes to Dutch spelling reforms. The present proposals (1967-1969) are especially interesting because for the first time in the history of the two countries, the governments have submitted their plans to public opinion. By 1967 the overall insistence upon *inspraak* [participation] pervaded decisions about spelling as well. Hence the amount of data for 1967-1969 is much greater than for 1947-1954.[48]

Before starting our examination of the two periods, two preliminary remarks must be made. The first concerns the arguments which the various groups have made use of (2.1.1.) and the second outlines the different target groups (2.1.2.).

2.1.1. The Arguments Used in the Dutch Spelling Discussions

We have already suggested above that the arguments put forward are not sound. In evaluating them we largely follow Cohen and Kraak (1972). They clearly point out that the scientific research that ought to be carried out before any spelling problem can be seriously tackled has hardly begun (cf. also Meijers 1967: 120). There have been no intensive studies, for example, on the actual language mastery of children about to begin school (Cohen and Kraak 1972: 3). Neither is the relation clear between the two central principles which, according to Cohen and Kraak (1972:

1 ff., 41 *et passim*), need to guide every spelling question, viz. the utility (Dutch *bruikbaarheid*) of a spelling and the ease with which it is learned (Dutch *leerbaarheid*). The arguments used so far have no objective character and give no evidence of either exact experimentation or argument.

Cohen and Kraak (1972: 39) come to the conclusion that 'the problem of so-called spelling simplification can hardly be called simple'.[49] In their view the whole spelling issue is foremost a matter of spelling instruction, and 'this specific instruction will have to be devised in another way and will have to receive another place in the teaching of the vernacular' (1972: 41).[50]

Bearing all this in mind we shall now present the great majority of the arguments used in the Dutch spelling controversies from 1946 onwards. Similar lists have been made by Pée (1946: 440-444), Meijers (1967: 131-140), Paardekooper (1967: 21-27), and especially Bijlsma (1972: *passim*). Unlike these scholars, we have made a distinction between (1) arguments used both in Belgium and in The Netherlands and (2) arguments typical for the Belgian situation. Moreover, we have tried to distinguish (a) more 'emotional' arguments from (b) more 'objective' arguments.[51] Arguments in favor of reform (which is always viewed as a simplification) are preceded by a P(ro) and arguments against by a C(ontra).

If an argument is mainly negative, we first give the contra reform argumentation, followed then by the refutation of it by the advocates of spelling reform, and vice versa for pro arguments. Arguments that are interpreted in both ways are simply put next to each other and are preceded by the notation 'both ways argument'.

(1) *Arguments used in Belgium and in The Netherlands*

(a) *More Emotional Arguments*

1.C. Against any change whatsoever. Paardekooper (1967: 20) has called this the *wendier* reaction. In his view many people have a *wendier* in themselves, i.e. an opposition to reform (i.e. *wen*) animal (i.e. *dier*). One could also speak of the 'habituation' argument: one is accustomed to a certain spelling and, however inconsequent this may be, it will always take some time to get used to a reform and hence one would rather stick to the status quo (HABITUATION argument)

P. It simply is a matter of time. After a while one gets used to the new spelling and soon forgets the old (cf. Meijers 1967: 26).

2.C. Closely related to this is the ESTHETIC argument, which argues that a proposed change makes the spelling ugly.

P. It is no use arguing about tastes. But according to Paardekooper (1967: 20-21) this is one of the pretexts behind which the *wendier* prefers to hide (cf. also Pée 1946: 442; Meijers 1967: 110).

3.C. Spelling reforms make for corruption and impoverishment of the Dutch language (CORRUPTION argument).[52]

4.C. Changing the spelling is an expression of current permissive thinking. Following Boutens (cf. supra, p. 195) we call this the LAZINESS argument.

P. At this argument those in favor of simplification usually simply accuse their opponents of being too conservative or reactionary.

5. (Both ways argument)

C. This is the hundredth change in a relatively short time. Can't we finally stop making fools of ourselves (FREQUENT CHANGE argument).

P. If we change our spelling radically now, there will be peace for at least a century (cf. Paardekooper 1967: 28).

(b) *More Objective Arguments*

6.C. The new spelling breaks the links with surrounding cultures (i.e. English, French, and German). By making our spelling more Dutch and hence more different from the spelling of these three languages, we increase the probability of losing contact with these three cultures (SURROUNDING CULTURES argument).

P. These difficulties occur especially in connection with the teaching of French but most children, especially in the Netherlands, never learn French.[53] Moreover, initially difficult foreign spellings are easier to learn at an older age.

7.C. A new spelling breaks the links with our own culture of the past. We will not be able to read our own literature anymore. And even if older books remain accessible, they will still be considered old-fashioned because of their old spelling (cf. Henkemans 1963: 549 ff.; among others) (OLDER CULTURE argument).

P. The spelling change hardly makes the written culture more inaccessible. If books become unreadable, this must be accounted for by a different syntax or vocabulary, or by lack of familiarity with the period in which the book was written.

8.C. A spelling reform increases the number of homographs and hence the possibility of misunderstandings (HOMOGRAPH argument).

P. There are already many homographs which do not present problems and any future ones will not be problematic in the spoken language.

9.C. Each spelling reform requires respelling and reprinting of many books and this is too expensive (FINANCIAL argument).

P. Only the school books need respelling and because the present spelling is so difficult to learn, it costs even more time and trouble, and, despite all these costs, at least 40 or 50 percent of the Dutch speaking population cannot spell correctly (cf. Kohnstamm 1972: 5, 53). According to Paardekooper (1967: 28) a simplified spelling would also reduce printing costs.

10.C. The present spelling makes the history of the words clear (ETYMOLOGICAL argument).

P. There are already many words whose etymology cannot be recognized and this causes no troubles at all.

11. (Both-ways argument)

P. Language is something quite different from spelling. Spelling is only a code to represent sounds (WORD IMAGE argument).

C. A word image (*woordbeeld*), i.e. spelling, replaces content, i.e. language. If the image changes, the content changes rather radically. (This argument can be linked to the habituation argument.)

12.P. Spelling demands too much time in schools. Kohnstamm (1972: 5, 33-34) states that 80 percent of all school time in primary schools is devoted to spelling instruction. If the spelling would be simplified, teachers would be able to devote more time to real language teaching: critical reading, verbality (in the sense in which Labov 1969 uses the term), command of language (cf. also supra, p. 190; Meijers 1967: 131 ff.) (INSTRUCTION argument).

C. A difficult spelling is educationally and pedagogically justified: spelling should not be made too easy for children. Difficult spelling strengthens analytical thinking.

13.P. Spelling simplification is a social necessity. It is especially important that people of lower status be able to spell correctly because spelling is used as a means of social discrimination (in letters of application, for example). Hence, spelling ought to be arranged in such a way that not only the *élite*, but also the child from a linguistically deprived milieu can easily learn the correct spelling (cf. also Pée 1946: 444; Meijers 1967: 167; Kohnstamm 1972: 45-47) (SOCIAL argument).

C. Perhaps it is justifiable that people be discriminated or selected on the basis of their spelling. But, even if not, it is by no means sure that spelling simplification would lead to less social discrimination: first, it has not yet been proven that simplification would make spelling much easier to learn (cf. Cohen and Kraak 1972: 5 ff.) and, second, discrimination will always exist on one basis or another.

14.C. (Argument of [extreme] leftists.) If one wants to eliminate intolerance and discrimination, one must change our society completely and not limit oneself to what the Germans call *Kurieren am Symptom* ('curing the symptom') (REVOLUTION argument).

P. A social revolution may not come at all as for a long time but by changing the spelling now one would at least take away one weapon of discrimination (cf. Kohnstamm 1972: 48-50).

15.C. A simplified spelling, which is sometimes paraphrased as 'written as spoken', would favor people who speak standard Dutch as opposed to people who speak dialect (DIALECT argument).

P. Formerly, every dialect speaker first had to learn standard Dutch. Then he had to learn its illogical and complicated spelling. With the simplified spelling a dialect speaker still has to learn the standard variety, but its spelling will be a lot easier for him to learn.

(2) *More specifically Belgian Arguments*

(All can be said to be rather objective).

16. (Both-ways argument)

C. Recently, Dutch has been accepted not only theoretically but also practically as the equal of French in Belgium, yet some French speaking Belgians still regard our language as deficient or inferior. Changing our spelling all the time would strengthen the latter people in their ideas (this argument is also used in the Netherlands, but it is much more applicable to the Belgian situation) (PRESTIGE argument).

P. Simplification of Dutch spelling would rather increase the prestige of Dutch in Belgium because it would make standard Dutch more easily accessible to the Flemish population (cf. Pée 1946: 444).

17. (Both-ways argument)

C. A change in spelling would discourage those French-speaking Belgians who try to learn our language (DISCOURAGEMENT argument).

P. A simplified spelling is easier to learn and thus would encourage French-speaking Belgians to learn our language (ENCOURAGEMENT argument).

2.1.2. Seven Target Groups

Seven target groups have been distinguished (inspired by Fellman 1972: 11-16):

I. the government agencies involved (education, culture, and science)
II. educational associations (teachers unions, primary school teachers organizations, etc.)
III. writers and journalists and their associations
IV. authoritative academies
V. mass media (written press, television, and radio)
VI. other specific groups: industry, commerce, librarians, publishers, etc.
VII. public opinion in general

The last target population has been added because a few polls of public opinion were taken during the 1967-1969 period. For the earlier period the public opinion was reflected via target group IV.

If relevant we will make a distinction between Belgium and the Netherlands.

2.2. The 1947-1954 Period

As we have noted, the new reform took effect both in Belgium and in the Netherlands on May 1, 1947, and on August 24, 1954, the new *Woordenlijst* (1954) was presented to the press both in Brussels and in The Hague. This new list contained some 63,000 words in their exact orthography. The remaining questions raised in 1947 had been settled in the meantime and their solutions were included in the *Woordenlijst*. Two of these deserve some special attention because they often occur in the discussion about this *Woordenlijst*, viz. loan words and the gender of the nouns. As to these two moot points, the following compromise has apparently been worked out (cf. *Haagsche Courant* [August 25, 1954]): since most of the Belgian members of the commission were in favor of a progressive spelling of loan words and since most of the Dutch members wanted to adapt the gender of the nouns to its actual pronominal usage in the Netherlands, the Belgians gave in on matters of gender and the Dutch gave in on spelling of the loan words.[54] However, as they did not want to go as far as to impose their wishes upon each other and as they definitely wanted to retain unity of spelling between Belgium and the Netherlands, the commission arrived at a kind of Salomonian judgment: it allowed in many cases a double form. Hence one could write *vacant* but also *vakant*. The first form (*vacant*) has been called *voorkeurspelling* 'preferable spelling', the second (*vakant*) *toegelaten* 'allowed' or *progressieve* 'progressive' spelling (cf. supra, p. 199). In this way about 12,000 words received a double gender and double forms were allowed for many loan words (only 3 percent of the words in the *Woordenlijst*, but most of them of widespread use). Thus the commission legalized a practice which had been going on for centuries (cf. Couvreur 1972: 288). Yet, it was on this possibility of choice that many negative reactions subsequently focused (cf. infra).

At any rate, both in Belgium and in the Netherlands the *Woordenlijst* became law by means of Royal Decrees, since ratification by the Dutch Parliament was not necessary (cf. supra, p. 199). (In Belgium any spelling change could be legalized by a Royal Decree.) After a year, however, both governments proclaimed that 'preferable' spellings were obligatory in official use. The Belgian Minister of Education Collard even went further. On October 18, 1955, he declared that they would be prescribed for the schools as well. In the Netherlands, on the other hand, education was given relative freedom (cf. Couvreur 1972: 288). Consequently, although some words had two spellings, public service in Belgium and in the Netherlands and the educational system in Belgium only permitted one.

Before outlining the reaction of the various target groups, we must apologize for the incompleteness of our data for the period 1947-1954. We could not examine the minutes of the commission since they are still classified as secret. We have mainly gathered our data from newspaper clippings furnished by Couvreur, and from two interviews, one with P. Berckx, the Belgian secretary of the Pée-Wesselings commission and one with W. Couvreur, one of the Belgian members of the *Woordenlijst* commission and of the Pée-Wesselings commission.[55] From the Belgian governmental side, no clippings dossier is available for the 1947-1954 reform; therefore, our data cannot but be incomplete. Because of lack of time, it was impossible for us to locate everything published in that period. Yet even though our data is quite sparse, it can be considered to be rather representative because, as Berckx and Couvreur have indicated, little was published on the subject. The reason for this can be traced to both the impossibility of participation in the decision making process and to the generally positive reaction to the prospect of simplification, especially in Belgium.[56]

All this may become clearer during the following survey.

I. *The governmental educational agencies.* There is not much to be said here. The ministers of education appointed the Commission and when it had finished its work, the governments simply adopted the decisions of the Commission. The ministers seem to have been mainly concerned with maintaining the unity between Belgium and The Netherlands, as had been agreed upon in London in 1944. According to the Belgian newspaper *De Standaard* of August 8, 1954, the *Woordenlijst* Commission had first proposed separable arrangements for Belgian and for Dutch education, but the Belgian Minister Collard turned down this proposal and insisted on new negotiations which should lead to spelling unity (cf. also *De Standaard* [August 17, 1955]). The Permanent Consultative Commission also expressed itself in favor of the unity found in the 'double option' (cf. *De Standaard* [June 29, 1955]).

In no other respect did the ministers express any opinion diverging from the Commission's. Most probably they were convinced that given the naturally diverging wishes of Belgians and Dutchmen, the compromise achieved was the best solution possible.

II. *Educational circles.* All schools had to use the new spelling as soon as it became effective. Hence, any protest was in vain and the educational associations were not inclined to disagree anyway. On the contrary, several levels of authority in Belgium as well as in The Netherlands suggested that the new regulation was welcomed, at least as long as the 'preferable' spelling was not yet imposed.

1. The Netherlands. On December 29, 1954, the Dutch section of the authoritative *Vereniging van Leraren in Levende Talen* [Association of Teachers of Modern Languages] agreed with an overwhelming majority that they would faithfully apply the new regulation.

In a series of three articles by W. H. Staverman (September 7, 15, and 24, 1954) the educational periodical, *De Vacature- Nieuws- en Advertentieblad voor het Onderwijs*, expressed its satisfaction with the reform: Staverman was in favor of the possibility of choice, not because of the principle of choice itself, but because writing practice would ultimately determine which form would survive. Staverman was convinced that this would be the 'progressive' form (with *k* instead of *c*, for example); he only deplored the fact that the reform had not gone further in simplifying the orthography. Since every reform provokes a lot of resistance one should have adopted all of Kollewijn's rules so that one would eliminate all troubles at once (frequent change argument).[57] The (unexpressed) premise behind Staverman's view was undoubtedly the instruction argument (argument 11).

In another pedagogical periodical, viz. *Ons Eigen Blad* (published in Tilburg) S. Rombouts propagated the straight-forward application of the 'progressive' spelling (cf. *De Standaard* [January 31, 1956]). This view also resolved itself into the instruction argument and especially the social argument (cf. also Rombouts 1967).

The Dutch *Vereniging voor Hoofden van Scholen* [Association of School Directors] called the new spelling "too inconsequential' and it suggested going a bit further than the progressive spelling (notably to designate [s] written *c*, as *s*) (cf. *De Standaard* [July 5, 1956]).

All in all, it is possible to conclude that Dutch educational circles favored the new reform, especially because it was considered a step towards a more simplified spelling (cf. also *De Gazet van Limburg* [February 9, 1954]).

2. Belgium. Here, too, the new reform was welcomed by educators. But when it became clear by the end of 1955 that the 'preferable' spelling was going to be prescribed, negative reactions became strong, especially in the Catholic schools.[58] An important reason for this was that in the latter the *Modern Woordenboek* [Modern Dictionary] of J. Verschueren S.J. was widely used. Verschueren was a radical ('written as spoken') advocate. He had not waited for the *Woordenlijst*: around 1951 (the book is undated), he had published the fifth edition of his *Woordenboek* in the 'modern' spelling, i.e. more simplified and especially more practical than the 'progressive' spelling of the *Woordenlijst*.[59]

By 1959 students at teachers' colleges and students of Dutch at the university level also generally advocated a 'modern' spelling in the above mentioned sense (cf. *De Standaard* [March 3, 1959]). The situation in the schools was not improved by the fact that governmental writings gave evidence of orthographic inconsistency as some were in the 'preferable' spelling, some in the 'progressive', and most were partly in the former and partly in the latter. The private sector clearly advanced towards the progressive or even modern spelling (*De Standaard* [March 3, 1959]). The newspapers of the important *Standaard* group (*De Standaard*, *Het Nieuwsblad*), *De Nieuwe Gids*, and *Het Volk* had shifted to the 'progressive' spelling. All these newspapers happen to be Catholic. The non-Catholic newspapers gave evidence of a more conservative spelling. Hence, some concluded that the 'progressive' spelling and *a fortiori* the 'modern' spelling, 'propagated by father Verschueren ... in Flanders bears a right wing stamp' (Couvreur 1972: 272).[60]

III. *Writers.* There does not seem to have been any organized reaction of writers and/or journalists. We found only one article by the poet G. Gossaert, alias Prof. Gerretson, in the *Telegraaf* (March 12, 1955). Gerretson warmly defends the new reform since it would preserve and confirm the unity between the two countries. One should beware, however, of jumping to conclusions from this one instance. The conservative attitude of most writers in other periods are all too evident (cf. supra, pp. 190, 192, 195, and infra, pp. 219-222).

IV. *Academies.*

1. The Netherlands. The *Koninklijke Nederlandse Akademie van Wetenschappen, Klasse der Letteren* [Royal Dutch Academy of Sciences, Class of Literature] had been consulted by the Dutch minister involved before 1954 and did not express any critique of the new reform.

2. Belgium. Although the *Koninklijke Vlaamse Academie voor Nederlandse Taal- en Letterkunde* [Royal Flemish Academy for Dutch Philology and Literature] (hereafter *KVATL* – see fn. 31) had often given evidence of a conservative opinion in spelling matters,[61] there was no negative reaction to the 1947-1954 reform. The fact that the Belgian half of the *Woordenlijst* Commission consisted of a majority of *KVATL* members (cf. Couvreur 1972: 260, 288) probably accounted for this, the more so since the *KVATL* again appeared to be conservative in 1967-1969, when there was no one from *KVATL* among the Commission members.

V. *Newspapers and periodicals.* Taking into account that spelling reforms have usually provoked a storm of indignant reaction (cf. Couvreur 1972: 289-292), criticism from the newspapers was relatively calm in 1947-1954.[62] Nevertheless, the Belgian *Handelsblad* of June 6, 1946, indicated that 'many were pro and many against' the new reform.

The following general tendencies appear to have been present.

First, whereas most Belgian papers (and Belgian public opinion) seem to have taken a positive stand towards the new spelling reforms, at least in 1954, the Dutch press appears to have been mostly negative. In their opinion, the reform went too far. Moreover, many Belgian papers which advocated the new spelling still considered it a pity that the reform did not go further. Indeed, the 'radical spelling reformers constitute a not unimportant group in Belgium' (*De Standaard* [August 24, 1954]). However, few articles appeared against the reform as such, especially in 1954. Most negative reactions concentrated on the possibility of choice (and – in The Netherlands – on the gender question). The controversy about progressive versus conservative spelling was not an important issue. More attention was paid to the fact that, in relation to loan words, the Belgian members of the Commission were more progressive than were their Dutch colleagues. Generally, the compromise achieved was agreed upon. In connection with this, several Dutch papers stated that the Flemish wanted to hide the French origin of many loan words.[63]

Furthermore, much attention was paid to maintaining unity between the two countries.[64] Some papers also raised the idea of a powerful Belgian-Dutch 'Institute for the Dutch Language', comparable to the *Académie Française*.[65] All Dutch papers and periodicals are divided into two main clusters: those that are more right wing oriented and those that are more left wing oriented. As for religion, a further distinction has been made among the right wing papers between Catholic and non-Catholic.

1. Netherlands. Since only three clippings are available for the period 1946-1949 (all from the *Maasbode*) and none of them expressed an opinion about the reform, we have to devote all our attention to the reactions to the *Woordenlijst* which were expressed between August 1954 and the end of 1956. According to our clippings from this period, the following papers and periodicals clearly expressed themselves against the *Woordenlijst:*

(1) more right wing orientated: *Elsevier* (September 4, 1954), *The Haagsche Courant* (September 3), *De Gelderlander* (August 28), *De Stem* (August 27; September 4), *Trouw* (August 28), *De Maasbode* (August 26), *Burgerrecht* (September 11), *NRC* (February 14), *Het Vaderland* (September 11), and most (viz. nine) of the regional papers.[66]

(2) more left wing orientated: *De Volkskrant* (August 21). These cons range from extreme opposition (*De Gelderlander*, *De Stem*, *Burgerrecht*, *Trouw*, *Het Vaderland*, and a few regionals), over moderate opposition

(*De Volkskrant*, *NRC*, *Friesch Dagblad*, *Elsevier*), to a very mild negative position (*Haagsche Courant* and the regional *Provinciale Overijsselsche en Zwolsche Courant* [August 21]). Our data is too negligible to determine relations between the kind of argument and the political orientation of the papers. The extreme cons nearly always use emotional arguments: (1) the habituation argument (e.g. *Dagblad van Noord-Limburg*, *Maasbode*); (2) the esthetic argument (e.g. *Trouw*, *De Stem*); (3) the corruption argument (e.g. *De Gelderlander*, *Maasbode*); (4) the laziness argument (e.g. *Het Vaderland*, *De Stem*). The other cons make use of more rational argumentation.

The more objective arguments utilized are the older culture argument (*Haagsche Courant*), the surrounding culture argument (*Provinciale Overijsselsche en Zwolsche Courant*, and *Elsevier*),[67] and the word image argument (the regional *Dagblad van het Oosten* [August 27]). A peculiar point of view is found in the *Volkskrant* of June 3, 1955, where the new spelling is judged to be too Belgian. The Belgian paper *De Standaard* (August 30, 1954) writes in this respect that Dutchmen are a bit angry because for the first time in their history they have lost their hegemony in spelling matters. The other papers, like the *NRC*, are only opposed to the possibility of choice.

According to the *Telegraaf* of August 28, 1954 (right wing) the new spelling is 'ugly' (esthetic argument) but 'the children will have less difficulties now' (instruction argument). Thus, it can be said to hold a middle position between pro and contra. The same goes for the right wing periodical *Koningin en Vaderland* (September 3, 1954).

Clippings from only five papers and periodicals have been found in favor of the new spelling, viz. three leftist periodicals (*De Groene Amsterdammer* [September 4, 1954]; *De Nieuwe Linie* [September 4, 1954], and *Vrij Nederland* [September 4, 1954]) and two newspapers (*De Waarheid* [Communist] [September 4, 1954] and *De Tijd* [left wing] [August 31, 1954, and March 16, 1955]). The latter, however, might as well be argued to hold a middle position. Its issue of August 31, 1954, contains a mild criticism on the *Woordenlijst* by the philologist Weijnen, which is fairly favorable towards the new reform, and the March 15 and 16, 1955 issues contain two 'pro' articles by L. C. Michels who was a member of the *Woordenlijst* Commission. The article in *De Waarheid* also is written by an 'insider', viz. J. Knuttel, who only regrets that another of Kollewijn's suggestions (viz. the ending *-ies* instead of *-isch*) had not been included.

Of the three leftist periodicals, *Vrij Nederland* is the only one to give any arguments. The arguments are the social argument and the fact that the Dutch have to aid the Flemish in their struggle against French (by maintaining the unity and by not isolating Belgian Dutch between French and Northern Dutch). Furthermore, many Dutch newspapers protested against the fact that the *Woordenlijst* was planned to become operational as soon as it was published.[68] Due to their criticism, the Dutch Government delayed putting the *Woordenlijst* into operation until September 1, 1955. The Belgian government had agreed beforehand upon a transitional period.

It is clear from the above that the left wing press was more favorable towards the new reform than the right wing press.

2. Belgium. All our clippings from 1946-1954 are from the right wing press.

We have twelve clippings for the period 1946-1949, ten of which come from the Catholic *Handelsblad*, one from the liberal *De Nieuwe Gazet*, and one from the Flemish nationalist periodical *'t Pallieterke*. Five of the twelve articles contain only neutral information; of the remaining seven only one article (*Handelsblad* [May 14, 1946]) expresses a positive attitude towards the introduction of the Marchant spelling in Belgium. The other six reject the new reform, one in a moderate way (*Handelsblad* [May 19, 1946]) and two rather firmly (*De Nieuwe Gazet* [April 10, 1946] and the *Handelsblad* [x]).[69] One may assume that the liberals had always been strongly opposed to the 1947-1954 reform and the one article from a newspaper of theirs (*De Nieuwe Gazet*) confirms this.[70] It fulminates against the new reform both with more emotional arguments (notably the corruption argument) and with some more objective arguments (homograph and older culture arguments). In addition, it states that the new spelling is too *Hollands*. One of the arguments in the *Handelsblad* also narrows down to the anti-*Hollands* reflex and a cartoon in the same *Handelsblad* shows that the paper was afraid of new homographs. Two other arguments, the etymological and the dialect arguments, are taken over from Van Mierlo.

The one positive clipping (*Handelsblad* [May 14, 1946]) reflects the opinion of two 'competent persons', viz. J. van Mulders and F. Closset. The former makes use of, among others, the social and the prestige argument, and the latter refutes the financial and the older culture argument.

So, the positive reaction of Belgian newspapers and of Belgian public opinion only dates from 1954 and can mainly be found among Catholic papers. We have thirty-eight clippings, seventeen of which express an opinion. All seventeen are from Catholic papers. At the top of the advocates we find the authoritative *Standaard:* whereas in August 1954 it only expressed a mild pro,[71] it soon started propagating the 'progressive' or even 'modern' spelling of Verschueren. On September 1, 1954, it took up an article of Verschueren himself, who argued 'against the *intrusive* (our italics) French'[72] and for the Flemish need of one stable spelling like the French. And in 1955-1956,[73] eight clippings are found in which one way or another a 'progressive' standpoint was taken.[74] The main argument of *De Standaard* appeared to be the instruction argument[75] but occasionally the social argument occurred as well.[76]

The *Nieuwsblad* (March 6, 1955) and the *Handelsblad* (August 26, 1954) both belong to the *Standaard* group and naturally hold the same opinion; the same is true of *De Nieuwe Gids* which, on August 25, 1954, also advocated the 'modern' spelling, again because of the instruction argument. The issue of August 29, 1954, contained an article of J. L. Pauwels, one of the Belgian members of the Commission. In the Jesuit periodical *De Linie* (September 27, 1954), Verschueren once more defends his 'modern' spelling.

The French Belgian press seems to have felt a malicious pleasure in the Dutch spelling troubles. We have found no such articles, but according to the *Volkskrant* (August 27, 1954) and the *Stem* (September 4, 1954) the Flemish felt embarrassed due to the attitude of their French-speaking compatriots.

VI. *Others.* The only other target group for which there is any evidence in the 1947-1954 period consists of the publishers. According to Daman (1947: 21) the *Vlaamsche Uitgeversbond* [Flemish Association of Publishers] opposed the new reform. Later, however, the publishers seemed to have accepted the government's decision without much comment.

2.3. The 1967-1969 Proposals[77]

The 1954 reform had not given complete satisfaction, particularly with regard to loan words. This led to the De Vos-Damsteegt Commission (cf. p. 199) and in 1963 to a new Woordenlijst Commission, viz. the Pée-Wesselings Commission alias the *Bastaardwoordencommissie* [Loan Words Commission], because originally it was to deal with loan words only. Its official task was 'to advise both governments in which way, departing from the *Woordenlijst*, a spelling of loan words can be achieved without any possibility of choice. This spelling should aim at being as phonological as possible as well as at being as *vernederlandst* as possible' (*Eindvoorstellen* 1969: 7).[78] In its first report (*Rapport* 1967) the Commission stated however that since 'the present spelling regulation also offers difficulties which are of another kind than those raised by the loan words . . . the Commission has taken the liberty to make proposals on these issues and on a few others of less importance[79] as well' (*Rapport* 1967: 16).[80]

The negative reaction to the *Rapport* (1967) was so strong that the governments have so far postponed any decision about these proposals. Also, due to cabinet crises in both countries, the whole issue at this moment (March 1973) has receded into the background, but the present calm is certainly not more than a breathing space, and at the earliest possible opportunity the spelling contenders will cross swords again.

The whole controversy resolves itself into three clusters of issues.

First, there is the conservative standpoint of those who want to remain within the framework of the 1954 *Woordenlijst* and who suggest dropping simply one of the two spellings. Usually the 'progressive' spelling is proposed as the one to retain, but sometimes the more conservative 'preferable' spelling is advocated.

Second, there are the progressive proposals of the Pée-Wesselings Commission which comprise (1) a *vernederlandsing* of the loan words, hence, for example, *kompleks* (instead of *complex*), *sel* (instead of *cel*) and *kampanje* (instead of *campagne*); for a full list cf. *Eindvoorstellen* (1969: 41-50); (2) some less important new rules for the spelling of medial letters, use of hyphens, apostrophes, the division of words in syllables, and capitalization (cf. *Eindvoorstellen* 1969: 50-58); and (3) some 'proposals which in The Netherlands require a reform of the spelling law' (*Eindvoorstellen* 1969: 58).[81] Among these are two more of Kollewijn's rules, viz. *-ies* instead of *-isch* and *-lik* instead of *-lijk* (*Eindvoorstellen* 1969: 58). Proposal 5 suggests simplifying the verb system (*hij word* instead of *hij wordt*, *hij antwoorde* instead of *hij antwoordde*, and *jullie praten* instead of *jullie praatten*. For a complete survey, cf. *Eindvoorstellen* (1969: 58-59).

Third, there is the radical standpoint as reflected in the 'minimum program' of the *Aksiegroep Spellingvereenvoudiging 1972*. This *Aksiegroep* was set up in the fall of 1971 and combined four Dutch educational organizations, who together count some hundred thousand members, viz. the *ANOF* (*Algemene Nederlandse Onderwijzers Federatie*), the *VON*

(*Vereniging Onderwijs in het Nederlands*), the Dutch section of the *Vereniging van Leraren in Levende Talen*, and the *VWS* (*Vereniging voor Wetenschappelijke Spelling*). The latter has some Belgian members as well. These four organizations agreed upon a joint 'minimum program', which comprises the proposals of the *Eindvoorstellen* (1969) plus four important amendments. According to the *Hantlijding* (1972) the latter consist of (1) the replacement of final *d* by *t* where *t* is heard (*wort* instead of *word* and *wordt*, *hont* instead of *hond*); (2) the replacement of *ei* by *ij*, and (3) of *ou* by *au*, and (4) the rule concerning the spelling of *i* in open syllables (*giter* instead of *gieter*). Amendment (1) is especially radical since it implies the dropping of the congruency principle.[82]

Before outlining the reactions of the various target groups, an important change in the legal situation must be noted. On October 17, 1972, the *Vlaamse Cultuurraad* [Flemish Culture Council][83] unanimously agreed that in the future 'spelling will be established by Royal Decree, afterwards to be confirmed by Decree (of the Flemish Culture Council)'. For 'loan words and foreign words', however, 'a Royal Decree would suffice'.[84] The legal situation thus is exactly the same now in both countries.

The following general tendencies have emerged out of our survey of the target groups.

The most striking conclusion to be derived from all reactions is that moderation does not pay. For the radicals the Commission did not go far enough and for the conservatives it went too far. And, unfortunately for the Commission, there were few people who hold a middle position. The only point everybody seemed to agree upon is that the 1954 arrangement was no good either. All stated that the possibility of choice must be dropped (cf. Van Mechelen 1971: 3; Craeybeckx 1972: 44-45). The general reaction was much stronger in The Netherlands than in Flanders, 'where the "silent majority", in spite of the official conservative pressure, has for years chosen the progressive spelling of the loan words' (Couvreur 1972: 267).[85] All in all the Belgians may be argued to be slightly more conservative than the Dutchmen.[86]

What has been stated above as to the limitations of our data partly holds here as well. Though many clippings, letters, brochures, articles, etc. (altogether about 700 items) have been put at our disposal, our dossier is again incomplete since our own search has only partly made up for the lack in the dossier of the Belgian Ministry of Culture.[87]

I. *The ministries involved*[88]

1. The Netherlands. As early as 1964, the Minister of Education submitted a provisional report of the Pée-Wesselings Commission for the opinion of several agencies and associations, viz. some twenty educational agencies (one of them the Dutch Academy), the written press, and the publishing companies. Since most reactions were negative, in 1967 the minister asked the Commission to revise its work and this procedure repeated itself with the other reports until the publication of *Eindvoorstellen* (1969). On November 20, 1970, the Dutch cabinet principally agreed with a change in the spelling law (and hence with the *Eindvoorstellen*).[89]

The viewpoint of the educational circles has also been taken into account. In the fall of 1971 the minister promised the four associations constituting the *Aksiegroep* that their amendments to the Commission's proposals would be submitted to the Dutch Parliament together with the latter (cf. *Het Katholiek Schoolblad* [December 11, 1971]; Couvreur 1972: 269).

However, the whole matter was supposed to be first agreed upon by all ministers involved (Dutch and Belgian) at a meeting in The Hague on March 26, 1972. Since the latter did not result in anything positive, another meeting was held in Steenokkerzeel (near Brussels) on May 23, 1972. (Both meetings were also attended by several members of the Pée-Wesselings Commission.) Again in May, however, no decision was taken and the whole issue was delegated to a small 'work group' which once more had to weigh the pros and cons. According to several Dutch papers[90] the conservative Belgian ministers were the cause of the difficulties (cf. below 2. Belgium). That there is some truth in this can be derived from two instances in which Dutch ministers have expressed a personal point of view.

In August 1972, a Dutch Minister of Parliament, Mr Wilbers, asked the ministers Van Veen (Education) and Engels (Culture) several questions, the last of which was whether the ministers agreed with the statement that spelling simplification and democracy have something to do with each other. The answer of the ministers ran as follows:

> 'If a spelling simplification frees more time in primary schools for the teaching of command of language [instruction argument] and if, as a result of such a simplification, larger groups of our population will be able to write Dutch without mistakes, this would undoubtedly contribute to a situation in which educational services would become

accessible to more persons than has hitherto been the case [social argument]. Consequently, this could certainly serve democracy.'[91]

And the then Prime Minister De Jong declared that in his view the main advantage of simplification would be that more time would be freed for more important language instruction (again the instruction argument) (*Parool* [November 21, 1970]).

Since the Dutch ministers defended the Commission's work, it may be appropriate here to point out that the Commission let itself be guided by the instruction argument as well (cf. *Eindvoorstellen* 1969: 11, 15, 20, 31, 34).

The Permanent Consultative Commission expressed its adherence to the *Eindvoorstellen* in a confidential report in 1969. In a reaction to the *Aksiegroep*'s proposals in 1972, it confirmed this viewpoint.

2. Belgium. From the Belgian governmental side, nothing much happened until the end of 1970 when the acceptance of the Commission's proposals by the Dutch cabinet forced the Belgian government to make a decision. It transmitted the *Eindvoorstellen* for study to a limited committee of ministers, in which, as Couvreur (1972: 270) states, 'the conservatives with the gentlemen Fayat, Vermeylen, and Lefèvre constituted the majority'.[92] On March 25, 1971, this committee mapped out a resolution consisting of three points:

(1) uniformity of spelling without further possibility of choice
(2) unity of spelling between Belgium and The Netherlands
(3) necessity of spelling pact

On the matter of judging the *Eindvoorstellen*, the Commission declared itself to be incompetent (cf. Couvreur 1972: 270). F. Van Mechelen, Belgian Minister of Dutch Culture, has repeated these three points in *De Standaard* of May 2, 1972, and in the *Cultureel Supplement* of the *NRC-Handelsblad* of May 19, 1972. On both occasions he added two other points, the first of which concerns the establishment of a Belgian-Dutch Institute for the Dutch language, and probably also reflects the opinion of the government.[93]

These four principles were also defended by the Belgian delegation at the summit meeting in Steenokkerzeel (May 3, 1972). The delegation argued that without subtracting from the scientific value of the *Eindvoorstellen*, a quick solution must be found in order to resolve the present situation. Hence it suggested deciding upon the 'progressive' spelling of the 1954 *Woordenlijst*, after which the whole issue should be delegated to the future Greater Dutch Academy (cf. Couvreur 1972: 293 and *De Tijd* [May 24, 1972]). So, the Belgians had indeed taken a more conservative standpoint. This probably emerged out of fear for the conservative section of public opinion in Flanders, which in the person of Craeybeckx (1972) had found a decided leader (cf. infra p. 222). Formerly, however, the Minister of Culture Van Mechelen had pronounced a different opinion. A comparison of Van Mechelen's utterances in relation to the summit meeting in The Hague (March 16, 1972) with Van Mechelen (1971) illustrates this.

Van Mechelen (1971: 7-10), he informed the Belgian parliament of his own attitude towards the spelling issue. After a long presentation in which he makes use of, among others, the social argument, the instruction argument, and the (positive side of the) prestige argument, he concludes that the proposals of the Pée-Wesselings Commission 'until closer inquiry, deserve "a favorable prejudice"'.[94] According to the *Binnenhof* of March 17, 1972, Van Mechelen said different things than he did in The Hague. There he had argued that since the proposals of the Pée-Wesselings Commission still are too radical for Belgium and since in The Netherlands there is a radical movement (Van Mechelen refers of course to the *Aksiegroep*), a quick decision in favor of the 'progressive' spelling of 1954 should be made in order to prevent a gap between the two countries. Van Mechelen also said he was shocked by the proposals of the *Aksiegroep*.

Another more probable explanation for Van Mechelen's shift is that he found no support for his progressive ideas among his Belgian colleagues. Indeed, from no other minister has any progressive utterance been noted. On the contrary, the utterances of Lefèvre, Secretary of State for Science, give evidence of an emotionally negative attitude.[95] Lefèvre also has claimed that 'democracy has not got anything to do with spelling reforms'.[96] The minister of Education Claes seems to be of the same opinion (*Accent* [August 26, 1972]).

It remains to be said that in both 1966 and in 1967 the Belgian Permanent Consultative Commission expressed a favorable attitude towards the Commission's proposals (cf. Couvreur 1972: 261).[97] The diverging viewpoints of the governments must also be accounted for by the differing attitudes of educational circles in the two countries.

II. *Educational circles.* Our data has revealed a strong difference between Belgian and Dutch teachers. Whereas the latter are in favor of the radical *Aksiegroep* proposals, the former advocate the 1954 progressive 'spelling', but both want to get rid of the possibility of choice.[98]

1. The Netherlands. The existence of the above mentioned *Aksiegroep* in itself is naturally a plain indication of the orthographic radicalism of Dutch educational circles. The reports of the Pée-Wesselings Commission were welcomed but most commentators regretted that the Commission had not gone further in the direction of simplification. Of our fifty-six clippings from sixteen different educational periodicals (plus several 'motions'), only two clippings[99] expressed a conservative standpoint and these two were both 'letters to the editor'. On the other hand, only one comment[100] favored radical simplification to such a degree that it showed no appreciation at all for the Commission's work.[101] The remaining clippings confirmed the radicalism of the various educational associations and agencies, as well as their response to the work of the Pée-Wesselings Commission.[102]

The arguments used can nearly always be narrowed down to the instruction argument: only four clippings have been found that do not mention it explicitly and only one in which the argument was refuted.[103] The verb forms were most frequently discussed. Indeed, it was argued that more time is lost in teaching of the verb forms than in teaching loan words.[104] Moreover, 41 percent of the children of the sixth grade of primary school still make mistakes in the verb forms. The social argument also often recurred (nine times).[105] Van der Velde (1969) clearly showed that the higher the level of continued education, the lower the number of spelling mistakes.[106] Here again it was argued that verb forms deserve more attention than other spelling problems.

Next to these two main arguments, several of the negative arguments frequently used by the conservatives, especially by the writers, were refuted in the ways we have outlined above in our list of arguments. They combined the financial argument (*Onderwijs en Opvoeding* [November 1967]), the surrounding cultures argument (*De Katholieke Kweekschool* [December 10, 1969]), the frequent change argument (*Schoolblad* [May 18, 1967]; *Onderwijs en Opvoeding* [October 1967]),[107] the older culture argument (*Schoolblad* [June 1, 1967], the homograph argument (*Resonans* [January 1969]), and the etymological argument (*Onderwijs en Opvoeding* [October 1967; January 1968]). The other side of the latter argument, however, was also used.

Anyway, in the fall of 1971, the *Aksiegroep* was founded. Its most important spokesman was G. A. Kohnstamm, an educational psychologist. As he put it[108] the aims of the *Aksiegroep* were (1) to promote parliamentary discussion of their proposals, (2) to persuade as many individuals and organizations as possible to use their spelling, and (3) to publish lists of the institutions and organizations which implement the spelling of the *Aksiegroep*. The group has succeeded in its first aim, but has more or less failed in its two other aims. The beginning was promising. The *Aksiegroep* started with a propaganda campaign in the Dutch press, which, as Couvreur (1972: 269) puts it, found much response in The Netherlands.[109] On December 11, 1971, there was a fifty minute television broadcast which was completely devoted to the educational and social necessity of a quick simplification of the Dutch spelling. In this broadcast a dictation was presented, which the schools were asked to give to ten to twelve year old children, first in the old spelling, then in the spelling of the *Aksiegroep*. The dictation concentrated on the verb form. In the *VARA Na-kijk Krant*, published in connection with this broadcast, the results of the two different dictations were recorded. Out of a total of 1711 children, the percentage of correct dictations rose from 12 percent (in the old spelling) to 78 percent in the new.[110]

So, in the beginning, the *Aksiegroep* was convinced that nearly all the members of its four integral organizations stood behind their action. But after a year, this turned out not to be so. Hence, the *Aksiegroep*, initially formed for one year, was recently dissolved (*Gazet van Antwerpen* [January 20, 1973]). In an interview with *Trouw* (February 3, 1973), Kohnstamm stated that the turning point was the government's prohibition of the use of the *Aksiegroep*'s spelling in the Ned. Economische Hogeschool [Dutch Economic University], Rotterdam. If this important institution would have used their spelling from January 1, 1972, onwards, everything could have developed much more favorably for the *Aksiegroep*. However, Kohnstamm also admitted that only half of the teachers agreed with the *Aksiegroep*'s simplification of verb forms and even less with their other simplifications, and that in connection with the instruction argument much more scientific research needs to be done. Yet, he still held that their proposals would be useful, especially for children who still must learn to spell.

2. Belgium. In Belgium there has been no such action as the Dutch *Aksiegroep*. Belgian educational circles appeared to advocate the most conservative of all three proposals, viz. the 'progressive' spelling of 1954. In 1972 the important *Vereniging van Vlaamse Leerkrachten* [Association of Flemish Teachers] announced a clear motion in this connection (*Gazet van Antwerpen* [June 8, 1972]). As a matter of fact, only one explicit case

has been found of an educational institution welcoming the work of the Pée-Wesselings Commission. This concerns a letter from a secondary school,[111] dated June 10, 1966, to Mr. Berckx, the Belgian secretary of the Commission. The argument used in this letter was once again the instruction argument.

On the other hand, only one teacher of the Louvain Minimen-instituut was in favor of reform (cf. Craeybeckx 1972: 113), while, much more revealingly, no less than sixteen general inspectors of primary and secondary school networks have spoken out against the *Eindvoorstellen* (see Craeybeckx 1972: 150-158). In Craeybeckx (1972: 150-157) three of them put forward their views. The first, L. Pollentier, proposed to drop the 'preferable' spelling of 1954 and to make the 'progressive' one obligatory. He much doubted the validity of the instruction argument. The second, G. Vannes, warned against too many homographs (also in the verb forms), and defended the present spelling with the instruction argument (argument 11 C). The same was done by J. Vercammen, who, in the light of the etymological argument, even made a plea for the 'preferable' spelling of the *Woordenlijst*.

Another negative voice came from Mr. Kestermans, in *Neerlandia* (July-August 1967), who reacted against the radical ideas of Paardekooper (1967). Kestermans argued with the word image, instruction (like Vannes), older culture, surrounding cultures, and etymological arguments. He also considered the new regulation too *Hollands*, especially the proposed rules of the medial letters.

Finally, the 'Sector Education' of the *Algemene Centrale der Openbare Diensten* [General Union of the Public Services] wanted a revision of the *Woordenlijst* in order to make a 'justified choice' (Craeybeckx 1972: 159)[112] between either the 'preferable' or the 'progressive' spelling.[113]

III. *Writers and journalists*

1. Writers. Both in Belgium and in The Netherlands most writers have maintained an extremely conservative standpoint[114] and hence a separate presentation of each country is superfluous. They considered any spelling change as an undesirable interference with their instrument of work. The Belgian author G. Walschap even spoke of 'profanation' of the language (*De Standaard* [May 2, 1972]).[115]

The champion of the Belgian adversaries of the *Eindvoorstellen*, viz. Craeybeckx (1972), found the most support among the writers. About seventy authors, including some who are famous, adhered to Craeybeckx's protest.[116]

Two authoritative Dutch associations of writers – the *Vereniging van Letterkundigen* [Association of Literary Men] and the Dutch P. E. N. Centre[117] – also expressed opposition to the Commission's proposals. They seemed to be opposed to any change whatsoever of the present arrangement. Indeed they did not even mention dropping the possibility of choice. The Belgian *Vereniging van Vlaamse Letterkundigen* [Association of Flemish Literary Men], which comprises nearly all Flemish writers, also disagreed with the *Eindvoorstellen.*[118]

All kinds of arguments have been quoted, but an emotional undertone was nearly always present. As to the more emotional arguments, the following statement of M. van der Plas may suffice to reflect the attitude of the more reactionary authors: 'I am against a world of least resistance. I am against a world which only considers the current moment important. Against a world in which roots are eradicated, origins made unrecognizable, traditions thrown away as useless rubbish. I am against the spelling reform proposals of the Pée-Wesselings Commission' (Craeybeckx 1972: 88).[119] The leftist writers, like Mulisch (1972) (cf. also Craeybeckx 1972: 84-85), used the revolution argument. Thus, nearly all authors,[120] however different their political ideas, were united in their disapproval of spelling simplification which to them meant language pollution (cf. Kohnstamm 1972: 55).

As to other arguments we must limit ourselves to the most important, i.e. most frequent, ones. The social argument was ridiculed by W. van Dieren (Craeybeckx 1972: 57-58) and refuted by M. van Paemel (Craeybeckx 1972: 86) and A. Koolhaas (Craeybeckx 1972: 76). The latter also rejected the instruction argument. Many Belgian authors also mentioned the prestige and the discouragement arguments.[121] Finally, the older culture argument occurred as well (Craeybeckx 1972: 68). The Dutch P.E.N. Centre mentioned the social, surrounding cultures, etymological, word image, financial, and corruption arguments. The Dutch *Vereniging van Letterkundigen* argued that each spelling reform implies long and chaotic discussions which distract attention from the main issue: 'the justified handling of the language as means of communication'.[122]

2. Journalists. In a publication by Craeybeckx (1972: 142-149), a few Belgian journalists vindicated their rejection of the proposals of the Pée-Wesselings Commission. These five journalists represent the three main political tendencies in the Belgian press: two work for a socialist paper or periodical, two for a Catholic one, and one for a liberal publication. Three of them wanted to get rid of one of the two spellings of 1954: Geudens

advocated the 'preferable' spelling, Staes the 'progressive', and Marynissen expressed no favorite. The arguments used were the corruption argument (mentioned three times), the prestige argument (twice), the discouragement, the older culture, and the etymological arguments (each employed once).

IV. *Academies.* The Dutch academy took a positive position, and the Belgian a negative position towards the work of the Pée-Wesselings Commission.

1. The Netherlands. As before[123] the Dutch academy was consulted by the minister involved and expressed a relatively positive opinion (cf. Couvreur 1972: 259; *De Standaard* [May 2, 1972]).

2. Belgium. According to Couvreur (1972: 290), the then Minister of Dutch Culture, R. van Elslande, made an 'unforgivable blunder'[124] in 1963 by not appointing one or more members of the *Koninklijke Vlaamse Academie voor Taal- en Letterkunde* (hereafter KVATL) to the Pée-Wesselings Commission.[125] Contrary to 1947-1954, when the *Woordenlijst* Commission included several academy members (cf. supra. p. 210), the KVATL rejected the proposals of the Commission. A complete survey of the polemic between the KVATL and the Pée-Wesselings Commission has been recorded in Couvreur (1972: 264-265, 269-274, 287-288) and need not be repeated here. On June 21, 1967, the KVATL expressed itself in favor of *vernederlandsing* of loan words but only within the framework of (the 'progressive' spelling of) 1954 (Couvreur 1972: 264). The arguments of the KVATL, as they are explained in *Motie* (1972), resolve themselves into the habituation argument linked with the word image argument, the prestige argument, and the surrounding cultures argument.

Besides the KVATL there is another Flemish academy, viz. the *Vlaamse Academie voor Wetenschappen, Letteren en Schone Kunsten van Belgie.*[126] It, too, sent a negative motion to the Minister of Dutch culture in 1967 and reminded the minister of this in 1972 (cf. Craeybeckx 1972: 124-125, 134; *Het Volk* [April 24, 1967]).

V. *Mass media*

1. Newspapers and periodicals. We have read 596 clippings whose origins are shown in the following table:

Origins of Clippings Pertaining to the 1967-1969 Proposals[127]

	1967	1968	1969	1970	1971	1972	Total
Dutch papers	147	13	39	13	57	134	403
Dutch periodicals	17	2	8	1	9	17	54
Belgian papers	77	4	14	2	3	30	130
Belgian periodicals	6	—	—	—	—	3	9
Total	247	19	61	16	69	184	596

The publication of the 1967 *Rapport* and the two summit meetings in 1972 have clearly provoked the most reactions. Of these 596 clippings some 275 (i.e. 46.3 percent) contain more than press agency information, which does not mean that they would all be 'editorial' articles. Of course, the approximately forty-five strictly editorial articles have received most of our attention. The latter reveal that in the beginning (1967-1970), the Belgian (Catholic) papers reacted more positively than did the Dutch, but in 1972 Belgian enthusiasm lessened considerably.

Because of lack of space and in order not to overburden our text with footnotes, we shall not give a detailed survey of all papers and periodicals for and against the proposals. Neither shall we give an elaborate list of all arguments used by the various papers. However, all the material still is accessible to anyone who is interested. We will limit ourselves to our conclusions based upon our analysis of the clippings mentioned.

a. The Netherlands. As had previously been the case in 1947-1954, the most important Dutch papers generally rejected the new spelling proposals, but there were a few exceptions, notably the more left wing orientated papers and periodicals. Moreover, all papers gave information about all points of view. The *Aksiegroep* was given much attention, though there was only one article which explicitly defended the *Aksiegroep*'s proposals, viz. *De Nieuwe Linie* of November 7, 1971. Moreover, this was not an editorial article.

Three groups can be distinguished: (1) those against the proposals comprised five right wing papers and one left wing (*Het Vrije Volk*); (2) several papers (three right wing and two left wing) held a neutral or middle position; (3) finally, quite a few dailies and weeklies expressed a mildly positive point of view (three right wing and four left wing).

The most frequent argument from both sides was the instruction argument, but all other arguments occurred as well, notably – for the cons – the emotional ones. Furthermore, several papers accused the Flemish of having transferred the Belgian language struggle to The Netherlands, since they insisted on a thorough *vernederlandsing* of French origin words (e.g. *k* instead of *c*). The same view was repeated in the accusation of, for example, the *Haagsche Courant* (May 20, 1967), that the commission had especially *vernederlandst* the French loan words but not the English. On the other hand, according to Couvreur, Dutchmen would be averse to German *k*.

Also striking is the fact that many Dutch newspapers tried to ridicule the new spelling by concentrating on some peculiar results of the *vernederlandsing*. Hence the spelling was stigmatized as the '*odeklonje* spelling' (instead of *Eau de Cologne*). Another illustration of this was the often recurring sentence *bebie eet keek* (instead of *baby eet cake* 'baby eats cake').

b. Belgium. With respect to the 1967-1969 proposals there appeared to be a clear correlation between the political tenor of newspapers and their attitudes towards the reports of the Pée-Wesselings Commission, at least along the Catholic versus non-Catholic dimension. As in 1954, the proposed changes met only positive response in the Catholic press. The non-Catholic dailies and weeklies – either left wing 'socialist' or right wing 'liberal' (cf. fn. 70) – all reacted negatively. According to Couvreur, the influence of Father Verschueren (cf. supra) still made the 'simplified' spelling too 'Catholic' for the socialists. Moreover, the fact that a Catholic minister (Van Mechelen) was in charge of spelling matters must not be neglected either.

The French newspapers reacted negatively as well. They also accused the Flemish of unmotivated and exaggerated anti-French feelings. This accusation, which was also expressed by some Dutch papers, was firmly and extensively refuted by the Flemish press. The Flemish nationalist *'t Pallieterke* (March 23, 1967) even stated that the Dutchmen seemed to be inclined to break up the cultural unity between the two parts of the Dutch language area. This unity was a topic which received more attention than the arguments for defending or rejecting the Pée-Wesselings proposals per se. Of the thirty-two spelling clippings that were found in the *Gazet van Antwerpen*, for example, nearly every article stressed the importance of this unity.

In relation to the other arguments, it is striking that they were seldom used, though nearly all of them occurred. However, it should be noticed that the emotional arguments constituted a small minority.

2. Television.[128] Both Belgian and Dutch national broadcasting companies paid attention to the spelling controversy.

The Belgian television (*B.R.T.*) broadcasted a controversial debate about the spelling matters (*Trefpunt* [March 18, 1972]). The discussion participants were J. van In (publisher), Mrs. van Straelen-van Rintel (inspector *Stedelijk Onderwijs* [Urban Education], Brussels), J. L. Pauwels (member of the Flemish Academy [*KVATL*]), and Minister van Mechelen. Unfortunately, Belgian television has no written transcript of this program.[129]

On the Dutch television there were (at least) three broadcasts. There was a controversial debate between opponents and advocates of the Pée-Wesselings proposals on the April 5, 1967, broadcast by the socialist *VARA*. A few weeks earlier, on March 13, 1967, both Mulish (contra) and Berits (pro) had been interviewed by M. Bouwman in her program *Mies-en-Scene* (*VARA*). Finally, there was the fifty-minute program which propagated the ideas of the *Aksiegroep*, once more by the *VARA* (on November 11, 1971).

VI. *Other target groups*. The following target groups also have been found to express a viewpoint: the publishers (VI 1), the academics (VI 2), the translators (VI 3), and the librarians (VI 4).

1. Publishers. According to our data some publishers in both countries agreed with the proposals of the Pée-Wesselings Commission and some did not, but all expressed their dissatisfaction with the recent spelling unrest.

a. The Netherlands. As early as 1964 the Dutch publishing companies had been consulted and had given negative advice (Couvreur 1972: note 9). However, we found only one instance of a Dutch publishing company expressing an opinion in public. This was a statement of the important firm *N.V. Wolters-Noordhoff*, which publishes at least one third of the Dutch school books (cf. *Het Nieuwsblad van het Noorden* [May 31, 1969]). One of its directors stated that the present unrest caused much trouble.

b. Belgium. In a letter of March 6, 1967, to Mr. Berckx, the director of the *Uitgaven De Procure*, a Catholic publishing company, advocated the proposals of the Commission. His main argument was the instruction argument. On the other hand, in *De Standaard* of May 2, 1972, another publisher, Mr. Pelckmans, argued that many small publishing companies would go bankrupt if the proposals of the Commission were to be accepted.[130] He advocated an immediate choice between one of the two present spellings, and suggested relegating the remaining problems to the wisdom of a new, greater Dutch language Academy.

The publishing company *Heideland-Orbis N.V.*, which by Belgian standards is no small company, mentioned an estimated loss of about $ 1,000,000. It claimed that already published volumes of encyclopaedias, whose other volumes were still to follow, would not be saleable anymore and that copies already sold would have to be replaced (cf. *Knack* [March 29, 1972]; *Spellingkwestie* 1972: 17).

Van In, one of the leading (Catholic) publishers in Belgium (notably of school books), appeared to be an advocate of either no spelling reform at all, or a radical reform so that there would be a lasting spelling pact (frequent change argument) (cf. Couvreur 1972: 270; *Knack* [March 29, 1972]). The present uncertainty, however, was viewed as detrimental.

The only conclusion to be inferred from these four instances is that the publishers themselves did not have a unanimous standpoint. Anyway, each spelling reform has a double effect on them: part of their books would not be saleable anymore, and part would need early reprinting in the new spelling.

2. Academics. Both in Belgium and in The Netherlands several scholars turned down the proposals of the Commission as being too radical.

a. The Netherlands. After the publication of the 1967 *Rapport*, Kruyskamp started a campaign against it (cf. infra). For his 'committee of action' he gained the support of 128 professors (among whom were sixteen linguists) and 825 research fellows at Dutch universities and other institutes of higher education (cf. *Het Parool* [June 8, 1967]; *Het Algemeen Dagblad* [June 9, 1967]). Their motivation boils down to the homograph and especially the word image arguments, particularly with respect to scientific terminology. In their view changing the spelling of scientific terms might be dangerous. It should be noted that the Commission explicitly allowed academics to use the older spelling of scientific terms (*Eindvoorstellen* 1969: 10). Another argument was that Dutch scholars might become afraid of publishing in their mother tongue because of the frequent spelling changes which it has undergone.

b. Belgium. In Belgium many scholars have supported the campaign of Craeybeckx. Craeybeckx (1972: 122-137) lists 201, forty-five of whom explained their views (Craeybeckx 1972: 112-134). According to Couvreur the scholars provided a typical example of what Paardekooper (1967) called the *wendier* reaction (habituation argument). There is probably much truth in this but, naturally, the forty-five scholars did not mention this argument. Moreover, people are mostly unconscious of the *wendier* in them. Anyway, the testimonies of these academics may be summarized as follows.

Only one scholar wanted to maintain the present spelling as it is, with its possibility of choice (Craeybeckx 1972: 129). Ten wanted to drop this choice (Craeybeckx 1972: 112, 114-117, 119, 126, 129, 133). Of the latter only one advocated maintenance of the 'progressive' spelling, three the 'preferable' spelling, and one asked for something new. The arguments have been listed in order of frequency:

– emotional arguments (Craeybeckx 1972: 112, 113, 120, 122, 124, 126, 127, 128, 178)

– etymological argument: the special pertinence of this argument in scientific nomenclature was stressed (Craeybeckx 1972: 116, 122, 126). A somewhat deviating opinion was expressed by Vandewiele (Craeybeckx 1972: 132), who was not averse to introducing 'Dutchlike' (*Nederlandsklinkend*) words in scientific nomenclature because of their greater 'suggestive power'

– word image argument (Craeybeckx 1972: 114, 133)

– prestige argument (Craeybeckx 1972: 120, 125)

– five arguments were only mentioned once, viz. the financial (1972: 126), older cultures (1972: 121), surrounding cultures (1972: 115), dialect (1972: 130), and discouragement (1972: 123) arguments.

An interesting standpoint was taken by Hacquaert, president of the *Nationale Raad voor Wetenschapsbeleid* [National Council for Scientific Policy]. In his view, the new spelling would discourage those who still had the courage to publish scientific work in their own language, since it would make their text less comprehensible for foreigners who do not know Dutch, but know German or another Germanic language (Craeybeckx 1972: 121).

3. Translators. The Dutch translators turned down the Pée-Wesselings proposals.[131] Like the Dutch 'Association of Literary Men' (cf. supra p. 223) they argued that 'good communication' was the most important thing in the teaching of the vernacular and regretted that it was neglected under the pretext of spelling difficulties.

4. Librarians. A few instances have been found in which Belgian librarians rejected a new spelling reform. E. Willekens, director of the *Stedelijke Bibliotheken Antwerpen* [Urban Libraries Antwerp] referred to the Norwegian example (cf. Craeybeckx 1972: 103-106),[132] which he thinks has resulted in 'chaos'. The 1947-1954 spelling reform was an effective improvement in his view, among others because of the suppression of the no longer functional inflection. (This is the only case in both periods in which this argument is mentioned.) The possibility of choice, however,

was criticized. The same was said in a motion of the *Vlaamse Vereniging van Bibliotheek- en Archiefpersoneel* [Flemish Association of the Personnel of Libraries and Archives] (cf. Couvreur 1972: 282). Willekens' specific arguments against any spelling change concentrated on the libraries for children: whereas adults certainly would 'survive' the existence of books in two spellings, this would be intolerable for children. As a result of spelling change, children's books would all need respelling and reprinting. A minor argument of his was that the catalogues of all libraries also would have to be reclassified. The latter argument was also brought forward by P. Gorissen, director of the University Library of Kortrijk (Couvreur 1972: 120). H. Lampo, inspector-in-chief of the public libraries in Flanders, especially mentioned the financial argument. According to him the costs of the reform would amount to about 300 million francs ($ 750,000).

As to The Netherlands, the 'Directors of the Royal Library and of Other Libraries' signed the petition of Kruyskamp against the proposals of the Commission (*Algemeen Dagblad* [June 9, 1967]).

VII. *Public opinion.* In our research we found the results of two Dutch polls. Furthermore, we will pay special attention to those who are self-appointed spokesmen of conservative public opinion, viz. Kruyskamp in The Netherlands and especially Craeybeckx in Belgium, as well as to the attitude of the most authoritative cultural foundations in Belgium.

1. The Netherlands. The conclusions of the two polls are more or less similar. The first was carried out by the *Nederlands Instituut voor de Publieke Opinie* [Dutch Institute for Public Opinion]. According to this reliable institute, 63 percent of the Dutch adult population (age eighteen or older) held that the spelling should not be changed. Advocates of a reform were more numerous among the younger generations (younger than thirty-five: 42 percent) than among the older (older than sixty-five: 18 percent). As to their political leanings, the supporters of a renovation are more left wing oriented (D 66: 42 percent; PvdA: 38 percent) and the adversaries more right wing (KVP and ARP: 72 percent against change and CHU 69 percent). However, both pros and cons were found among all age groups and among all political groups (cf. *Het Binnenhof* [August 16, 1972], *Trouw* [August 19, 1972], and *Gazet van Antwerpen* [July 26, 1972]).

The other poll (by the *Inter/View N.V.* in Amsterdam), carried out a few months earlier (viz. April 1972), asked more precise questions. It presented everyone with four rather radical spelling reforms more or less similar to the *Aksiegroep*'s proposals.[133] Twenty-three percent were in favor of all four changes and 47 percent only wanted one, two, or three of these reforms to be introduced. The remaining 30 percent wanted no change whatsoever. Again, older people usually rejected the changes (cf. *Het Binnenhof* [April 15, 1972]).

The most fervent Dutch anti-reform fighter was undoubtedly C. Kruyskamp, Doctor in Dutch Philology and main editor of the Dutch 'Webster', viz. *Van Dale's Great Dictionary of the Dutch Language*. It would lead us too far to go into details here. Suffice it to say that according to our data he has written no less than nineteen articles (not letters to the editor) in Dutch and (one) Belgian papers.[134] Sometimes his arguments have been emotional (*Parool* [March 7, 1967], and a letter, dated January 19, 1972, to his Belgian 'colleague' Craeybeckx), but mostly they seem to be of a more objective kind.[135]

Paardekooper, in *Neerlandia* 71 (1967), 85, suggested that there might be a connection between the fact that Kruyskamp was a member of the Commission in 1954 and that he was not appointed to the Pée-Wesselings Commission. According to Pauwels (personal communication) who was also a member of the *Woordenlijst* Commission, this was not so. Kruyskamp had always been conservative. At any rate, the following quotation of Meijers (1967: 131) probably applies well to persons like Kruyskamp and Craeybeckx:

> 'Spelling conservatism is a very natural thing: its adherents fight for the maintenance of "their" spelling, i.e. a spelling which they have learned, which they "master", of which they "have a perfect command" ... One may assume that the possession-instinct plays an important part in this spelling conservatism.'[136]

2. Belgium. Lode Craeybeckx (1972: 26), lawyer and socialist mayor of the city of Antwerp, undertook a major action against the 'monstrosities'[137] of the Pée-Wesselings Commission and *a fortiori* of the *Aksiegroep*. In order to preserve our language from such abortions, and in the name of the 'good thinking' citizens, he entered into battle with the Commission. Couvreur (1972: *passim*) abundantly revealed the strategy of the mayor and his many supporters. Craeybeckx used all kinds of arguments, but most of them were rather emotional and the corruption argument was his favorite.[138] His inexpertise or rather pseudo-expertise was convincingly demonstrated by Couvreur (1972: *passim*). The latter also shows that, to put it euphemistically, there was considerable opportunism among

the supporters of Craeybeckx.

The following statement may conclude the 'Craeybeckx' chapter for the time being (for more information see Craeybeckx 1972; *Spellingkwestie* 1972):

> He [Craeybeckx] refuses any discussion but seeks as many authoritative persons as possible who are simply opposed to any reform. The changing of the spelling itself is the problem for him (*De Nieuwe* [March 31, 1972]).[139]

Finally, the three main Belgian cultural foundations, viz. the *Davidsfonds* (Catholic), the *Vermeylenfonds* (Socialist), and the *Willemsfonds* (Liberal), expressed their opinions.

The *Willemsfonds* wanted to replace the alternative forms of the 1954 *Woordenlijst* by a 'justified' uniform spelling (cf. Couvreur 1972: 282).

The same opinion was held by A. Gerlo, president of the *Vermeylenfonds.*

The *Davidsfonds*, on the other hand, was in favor of rather radical changes more or less similar to those of the Pée-Wesselings Commission. Its president,[140] R. Derine, defended his view by the word image and the frequent change arguments (cf. Couvreur 1972: 292-293).

2.4. Conclusions

Our discussion of the seven target groups in relation to the 1947-1954 reform and the 1967-1969 proposals may be summarized as follows.

All groups, but especially the Belgians, wanted to maintain the unity between the spelling of Dutch in The Netherlands and in Belgium. The group most in favor of reforms, which were considered to be simplifications, was constituted of educational circles. Their main motivation was the instruction argument. In 1947-1954 the more radical among them were to be found in Belgium; in 1967-1969 the more radical among them were in The Netherlands. The most recent events, however, suggest a weakening in their front because of lack of support at the base.[141] Their major opponents (in 1967-1969) were the writers and some authoritative figures (such as Craeybeckx, Kruyskamp) who pretended to be experts in spelling matters but whose arguments were mainly 'emotional', though other arguments, such as the etymological, the older cultures and the surrounding cultures arguments, occurred as well.

Political or social points of view also influenced the spelling controversy. In The Netherlands the supporters of spelling reform appeared to be more numerous on the left wing, though advocates and opponents were found among all political leanings. In Belgium, on the other hand, the Catholics obviously were more progressive in spelling matters, notably in 1947-1954, but this was probably due to the great influence of the radical reformer, Father Verschueren. Socialists and Liberals were opposed to spelling reform in Belgium as were some important Catholic politicians.[142] Hence, it is not surprising that in relation to the 1967-1969 proposals, the Belgian government took a conservative standpoint.

In our view the obvious conclusion is that all the arguments used (pro as well as con) are much too shaky, and that therefore the whole controversy is quite superficial (Cohen and Kraak 1972: *passim*); for some combatants it seems to be just an occasion to settle personal grudges (Couvreur 1972: *passim*).

3. FACTORS EXPLAINING ACCEPTANCE AND REJECTION

It is difficult to isolate the most important factors of success or failure. Moreover, the scientific literature about the revision of orthographies in general is still in its infancy and lacks the concepts, the technical data collection methods, and the analysis skills needed to inquire into the intensity, extensity, or continuity of either the change forces and processes or the counterchange factors (Fishman 1971: 363).

Nevertheless, from the data patiently assembled about past and pending Dutch spelling reforms, it seems that fundamentally a phonological orthography is aimed at. But 'what such a spelling of Dutch would precisely look like and if it would be easily learned and diffused, these are questions without unambiguous answers. There is, indeed, very little phonological research already done in relation to Netherlandic and even less study has been undertaken about the relationship between phonological structure and the structure of the orthography. Moreover, from different sides voices are risen which allude to the important sociological aspect of the spelling problem. Many have pleaded the cause of the children of the lower classes. Now they prefer to call it the sake of the (linguistically) deprived children. But in both cases their advocates are in favor of a simpler spelling' (Cohen and Kraak 1972: 5, 6).[143]

It is here that linguists, who still have to start their fundamental research on the relationship between phonological structure and the orthographic structure, but who are certainly aware of a lot of INTRA-CODE INCONSISTENCIES, discover the great importance of EXTRA-CODE PHENOMENA. These societal preferences or antipathies for writing conventions are generally associated with some other language or languages. They have recently been listed and catalogued (Nida 1954; Smalley 1964).

Among the 'practical limitations to a phonemic orthography' (Nida 1954) we could also mention several principles which were encountered at the beginning of Dutch spelling, such as 'the congruency rule, the derivation rule, and the analogy rule' (see supra, p. 186 ff.). We will concentrate on two more sociological limitations: the desire for similarity and the desire for dissimilarity.

The DESIRE OF SIMILARITY was already present in relation to Latin (p. 181). It is still present in the 'argument of the surrounding cultures' (Belgium and the Netherlands) and in the 'discouragement and prestige arguments' (Belgium) (cf. supra, pp. 202-203, 205-206). This desire is similar to that reported by the *Institut Français d'Afrique Noire* in its conclusion that speakers of African vernaculars in Francophone countries want their orthographies to look as French as possible (Smalley [1964] and Fishman [1971: 335-356] list several similar cases in other parts of the world).

The opposite case has been less fully documented, namely, that in which communities have desired a more distinctive writing system, one that would more effectively differentiate their language from others with respect to which they sought not similarity but dissimilarity. That seems to be the case with the proposals about the spelling of loan words in Dutch. This important parameter in Dutch spelling reforms has created in the past and could create again in the future strong centrifugal tendencies with respect to the languages from which different groups desire to be different (cf. supra, pp. 199, 211, 226). We underline here only the desire of many Dutch speaking Belgians to write *k* and not *c* in words such as *kultuur* because *c* is too similar to French, and in Holland where, on the contrary, many prefer the *c* instead of the *k* in *cultuur* because *k* is too reminiscent of German spelling.

All in all, the influence of nonlinguistic factors, namely political ones, seems to be strong (cf. Van Raalte in *Resonans* [February 1970]). But these sociological factors are generally not taken into account by spelling reformers (Burns 1953).

It is our hope that this linguistically and sociolinguistically oriented description of attempts at modernizing Dutch spelling will be of some help for the micro- and macroanalysis of responses to orthographic reform processes more generally.[144]

NOTES

1. In the sixteenth century The Netherlands included all the provinces of the Low Countries, i.e. a territory containing the present Kingdom of The Netherlands, the Kingdom of Belgium, the Grand Duchy of Luxemburg, and northern France. These provinces were subsequently separated by wars, again and again, except for the short period between 1815 and 1830. Since 1830 'The Netherlands' means only the present-day Kingdom of The Netherlands. The Netherlandic, or, as we prefer to say, the Dutch language, is now the official tongue of most of the present Netherlands and of northern Belgium, where the Flemings live. Belgium also has two other official languages: French in the south and German in the east (see also Lissens 1962).
2. Literally 'Dutchification', i.e. essentially adaptation to Dutch spelling rules.
3. Dutch text: 'Velen kunnen over een enkele letter redekavelen alsof er het welzijn van gantsch Euroop aan hinge.'
4. Weiland also wrote the official *Nederduitsche Spraakkunst* [Dutch Grammar].
5. Dutch text: 'een uitvloeisel van 't gelijkmakingssysteem van de Franse revolutie'.
6. This term has a specific negative connotation in Belgium compared to the neutral *Nederlandse* ('Dutch').
7. Dutch text: 'Stel in Uw schrift de beschaafde uitspraak voor'; 'de hoofd- en grondregel'.
8. 'Het doel van het schrift wordt reeds bereikt, wanneer de lezer het bedoelde woord herkennen kan.'
9. '. . . met dezelfde letters'.
10. '. . . *hoofddeel*, omdat de juiste opvatting door de laatste schrijfwijze zou belemmerd worden'.
11. '. . . de oudere vorm'.
12. '. . . gelijk luidende lettertekens'.
13. '. . . uit den tijd toen de nu gelijk geworden klinkers nog duidelijk onderscheiden konden worden'.
14. '. . . omdat het de spelling voor alle niet-taalkundigen moeilijk maakt'.
15. '. . . met zekerheid bekend is en die oogenschijnlijk op overeenkomstige wijze gevormd zijn'.
16. The Dutch term is *bastaardwoorden*, literally 'bastard words'.
17. Literally 'dutchified', adapted to Dutch.
18. '. . . de oorspronkelijke spelling tot eene ongewone uitspraak aanleiding zou geven'.
19. 'bastaardspelling'; 'wel beschouwd'; 'iets plomps'; 'hetwelk den beschaafde en geletterde ergert, zolang zijn oog niet aan het zien van zulke smakelooze schrijfwijze gewend is'.

20. '. . . zich wel enige ogenblikken moeten bezinnen'.
21. 'Eenige kennis van vreemde talen (blijft) noodzakelijk. De minkundige zal altijd moeten weten, dat *artikel, titel, visite en machine* uit den vreemde zijn overgenomen; dat in het Grieksch *thermometer met θ, . . ., synode* met *v* en *citer* met i geschreven wordt, wil hij geen gevaar lopen *artiekel, tietel, visiete, masjiene, thermometer, hipothenusa, sinode, sieter* te spellen.'
22. 'volstrekt niet door geholpen'.
23. 'dat is dan ook wel een der voornaamste redenen voor de afwijzing'.
24. Dutch text: '(haar medewerking) niet verleenen aan de nu zo verheerlijkte spelling De Vries en Te Winkel'.
25. 'heeft nog geen lust onder de nieuwe spelling de pen te buigen'; 'als een verschijnsel van conservatisme'.
26. 'Maar waar men niet konsekwent wezen kan of wil, trachte men prakties te zijn'.
27. 'veeleer een voortzetting van herhaalde maatregelen om de spelling, ten dienste van het *gehele* volk, praktisch te verbeteren, zonder te grote schokken'.
28. 'een noodzakelijke correctie op de overmaat aan etymologie'.
29. 'Voor de praktiese hervormer staat evenwel één ding vast: de spelling moet geen middel zijn om de *afkomst* en dus de *historie* der woorden aan te geven.'
30. 'ruimschoots bestrijding (vinden)'.
31. Hereafter referred to as KVATL. This academy is not comparable to the *Académie Française* in one important aspect: its decisions are not binding for the Dutch language in Belgium. They are only of an advisory nature. Recently its name has been changed to *Koninklijke Academie voor Nederlandse Taal- en Letterkunde*; i.e. *Vlaams* (Flemish) has been replaced by *Nederlands* (Dutch).
32. 'castratie, moord; verkrachten en verminken'.
33. '(door) onnodige moeilijkheden worden afgeschrikt'.
34. 'tienduizenden ordelijke burgers'.
35. 'luiheidspelling'.
36. 'strijdig in haar beginselen en bedoelingen met de christelijke wereldbeschouwing'.
37. 'de verziekte geesten der alles neerhalende democratische en marxistische heeren, die in Nederland alles hebben kapot gemaakt wat het eigendom was van heel het volk'.
38. 'denationalizatie, Germaansche Bloedfamilie, cultuurbolsjevieken, roode taalverpesters'.
39. *Belgisch Staatsblad* 3208 (April 5, 1946), 2nd column: 'op grond van de spelling – De Vries en Te Winkel, een eenvormige schrijfwijze van de Nederlandsche taal, geldig in Nederland en in België tot stand te brengen'.
40. 'houdende regeling van de spelling der Nederlandse taal . . . volgens De Vries en Te Winkel, met in achtneming van het volgende . . .'
41. 'spelling geknoei achter de schermen'.
42. 'vandalenwerk'.
43. 'middelmatisten'.
44. A commission which was charged in 1948 with the spelling regulation of these names has not yet finished its activities (*NRC-Handelsblad* 22: 5 [1971]). According to Damsteegt (personal communication), who is the president of this commission, the Dutch delegation is now completing its work on the spelling of geographic names in The Netherlands.

45. The letter connecting the two parts of a composition, e.g. *station-s-chef.*
46. 'een arbitrair systeem dat wetenschappelijk onhoudbaar en maatschappelijk onbruikbaar is'.
47. In a circular of the Dutch Minister of education (dated August 26, 1955) it is stated that: 'the consistent use of the one [i.e. permissible] spelling, however, is not considered to be a mistake'. (Dutch text: 'Het gelijkmatig gebruik van de andere spelling wordt echter niet als fout aangemerkt.')
48. For the latter period we have gathered 181 newspaper clippings, whereas for 1967-1969 this number amounts to no less than 596. On the relevance of these data, cf. infra.
49. 'In wat . . . is besproken, komt duidelijk naar voren dat het probleem van de z.g. spellingvereenvoudiging . . . nauwelijks eenvoudig kan worden genoemd.'
50. 'dat specifieke onderwijs zal op een andere wijze . . . moeten ingericht worden en zal een andere plaats moeten krijgen in het moedertaalonderwijs'.
51. The qualifier 'more' suggests that the boundary between the two is not always clear. Sometimes even the most objective arguments appear to be pervaded by deeply rooted emotions.
52. For the refutation of this argument we refer to argument 11P.
53. Paardekooper (1967: 22) mentions the figure of 98 percent.
54. The gender must once more be left out of consideration. It should be noticed, however, that both parts of the compromise are not of equal importance (cf. van Haeringen 1954 and Geerts 1965).
55. Both interviews were conducted by J. Van den Broeck, the one with Mr. Berckx on January 25, 1973, the one with Mr. Couvreur on February 23, 1973.
56. The data have placed some further constraint on our work. Since we have only obtained fifteen clippings from the years 1946 to 1949, opposed to 141 in 1954, it is clear that we have devoted most of our attention to the reactions to the *Woordenlijst*. The 1954 clippings all come out of the *Knipselkrant* [clipping paper] published by the Dutch Ministry of Education, Arts, and Sciences (*Onderwijs, Kunsten en Wetenschappen*), notably the numbers 133A, 140A, 144A, and 149.
57. In this way Dutch educational circles remain faithful to their previous attitudes (cf. supra, p. 194) and a similar view is also expressed in 1967-1969.
58. In Belgium there are two educational systems: a public one and a Catholic one. The latter has a slightly higher enrollment than the former.
59. Verschueren called his spelling the '*Konsekwente Progressieve Spelling* (*K.P.S.*)'. A complete survey of this *K.P.S.* can be found in Table III of the 1965 edition (published by Brepols Turnhout in Brussels). In the introduction to the 1965 edition, Verschueren still fulminated against the spelling of the *Woordenlijst*, although from the seventh printing (1962) onwards he has used the 'preferable' spelling. In 1963 Verschueren was appointed a member of the Pée-Wesselings Commission, but after a few meetings he stopped attending because his radical ideas were not supported by his colleagues (cf. Couvreur 1972: 290).
60. 'Gepropageerd door pater Verschueren . . . heeft de progressieve spelling in Vlaanderen een "rechts" stempel.'
61. Viz. in 1897, 1902, 1920, 1926, and 1934 (cf. supra).
62. That is, if our relatively scarce data do not provide us with a false impression, especially for the period 1946-1949. As we have already said (cf. fn. 56), Couvreur,

who gave us his clippings for the 1947-1954 period, did not intend to create a complete dossier. 141 out of 181 clippings (i.e. 77.9 percent) date from the period August 23-September 11, 1954 (the *Woordenlijst* was presented to the press on August 24, 1954).

63. Cf. *Provinciale Drentsche en Asser Courant* (August 28, 1954), *Elsevier* (May/June 1954), *Vrij Nederland* (September 4, 1954), and *De Standaard* (September 1, 1954).
64. Cf. for Belgium *De Standaard* (August 24, 26, 28, 1955) and *De Linie* (June 17, 1955); and for the Netherlands *De Telegraaf* (March 12, 1955) and *Vrij Nederland* (September 4, 1954).
65. Cf. for Belgium *De Standaard* (August 26, 1954); and for The Netherlands *Het Algemeen Handelsblad* (September 2, 1954).
66. For example, *Dagblad van het Oosten* (August 28), *Friesch Dagblad* (September 7), *Het Gooi- en Ommeland* (August 26), *Delftische Courant* (August 31), *Dagblad van Noord-Limburg* (August 27), altogether eighteen papers, but in seven of them no opinion is expressed. (They only contain press agency information.)
67. *Elsevier* attacks the new spelling for its overly anti-French orientation.
68. Cf. *De Waarheid* (September 11, 1954), *De Volkskrant* (August 26, 1954), *De Tijd* (August 26, 1954), *Het Parool* (August 31, 1954).
69. x refers to papers whose exact origin we could not trace. Such deficiencies in our data did occur occasionally. In 1967 forty-three clippings (i.e. 7.3 percent) found in the dossier of the Belgian Ministry of Dutch Culture had incomplete references.
70. Unfortunately, we do not have any clippings from a socialist paper for this period. The Socialists, together with the Catholics and the Liberals, constitute the three main political factions in Belgium.
71. *De Standaard* (August 25, 1954); cf. also the issues of August 26 and 30.
72. 'Tegen het opdringerige Frans.'
73. The progressive tendency of *De Standaard* must have lasted beyond 1959 (cf. *De Standaard* [March 3, 1959]).
74. 1955: February 3, 10, 19, March 2, August 28; 1956: January 31, February 2, July 5.
75. *De Standaard* of February 3, 10, 19, 1955, and March 3, 1959.
76. *De Standaard* of February 10, 1955.
77. A complete and detailed history of the 1967-1969 proposals can be found in Couvreur 1972.
78. 'adviseren, op welke wijze, in afwijking van de woordenlijst, een spelling van bastaardwoorden zonder keuzemogelijkheid kan worden bereikt, waarbij een zo consequent mogelijke opzet in fonologische zin en een zover mogelijk gaande vernederlandsing wordt nagestreefd'.
79. For a list of the issues involved, cf. supra, p. 200, and infra.
80. 'de huidige spellingregeling ook moeilijkheden biedt, die op ander terrein liggen ... heeft de commissie de vrijheid genomen op deze punten en op enkele andere van minder gewicht eveneens voorstellen te doen'.
81. 'Voorstellen die in Nederland wijziging van de spellingwet vereisen.'
82. An extensive comparable word list of the three kinds of proposals (further labeled *Woordenlijst*, Pée-Wesselings, and *Aksiegroep*) is given by Rombouts (1972: 35-232).

83. In the framework of the bicameral Parliament, Belgium has since December 1970 two 'Culture Councils': a Flemish one, consisting of all Dutch-speaking members of parliament, and a French one, consisting of all French-speaking members of parliament. A German one will be created later.
84. *Gazet van Antwerpen* (October 18, 1972), also quoted by Couvreur 1972: 293: 'de spelling van oorspronkelijke Nederlandse woorden wordt geregeld bij koninklijk besluit, achteraf te bekrachtigen bij dekreet (van de Cultuurraad)', while 'voor bastaard- en vreemde woorden een koninklijk besluit zou volstaan'.
85. 'waar de "zwijgende meerderheid" in weerwil van officiële konservatieve dwang sinds jaren voor een progressieve spelling van de bastaardwoorden heeft gekozen'.
86. Several early reactions to the 1967 report by the Dutch press suggested, on the other hand, that as in 1947-1954, there would have been a difference between the more progressive Belgian and the more conservative Dutch members of the Pée-Wesselings Commission, but this is firmly rejected by the Commission itself (cf. *Rapport* 1967: 39; *Eindvoorstellen* 1969: 61; *Persbulletin* 1967: 4). Among the Dutch papers concerned are *Het Vrije Volk* (March 7, 1967), *Het Parool* (March 3, 1967), *De Telegraaf* (March 1, 1967), and *Het Algemeen Handelsblad* (April 6, 1967).
87. According to Berckx it especially contains negative reactions since the Commission was more interested in them.
88. The Ministers or Secretaries of State of Culture and Science have also been concerned with spelling matters. These departments did not yet exist separately in 1947-1954. The exact names are for Belgium: *Ministerie van Nederlandse Cultuur*, *Ministerie van Nationale Opvoeding* and *Staatssecretariaat van Wetenschapsbeleid;* for the Netherlands: *Ministerie van Cultuur, Recreatie en Maatschappelijk Werk*, *Ministerie van Onderwijs* en *Ministerie van Wetenschapsbeleid.*
89. Cf. a letter dated December 14, 1970, of the Belgian ambassador in The Hague to the Belgian Minister of Foreign Affairs; cf. also Couvreur 1972: 269.
90. Cf. *Haagsche Courant* (March 18, 1972); *De Telegraaf* (May 14, 1972); *NRC Handelsblad* (March 17 and May 5, 1972).
91. *Verslag van de Handelingen der Tweede Kamer, zitting 1971-1972*, 3765: 'Indien door een spellingvereenvoudiging meer tijd op de lagere scholen zou kunnen worden vrijgemaakt voor het onderwijs in een juist taalgebruik, en als door een dergelijke spellingvereenvoudiging grotere groepen van de bevolking in staat zullen zijn het Nederlands zonder fouten te schrijven, dan zou dit er ongetwijfeld toe bijdragen, dat de onderwijsvoorzieningen voor meer personen dan tot nu het geval is geweest gemakkelijker toegankelijk worden. De democratie zou hiermede aldus zeker gediend kunnen zijn.'
92. 'waarin de behoudsgezinden met de heren Fayat, Vermeylen en Lefévre de meerderheid vormden'.
93. The last of Van Mechelen's five principles has a different shape in the *Standaard* than in the *NRC*. In the former Van Mechelen states that this institute should be set up as soon as possible and in the latter he makes a plea for using Dutch words instead of loan words.
94. 'tot nader onderzoek "gunstig vooroordeel" genieten'; cf. also *Het Vaderland* (March 29, 1972).

95. Cf. e.g. *NRC* (March 17, 1972), *Binnenhof* (March 17, 1972), and *Vaderland* (March 17, 1972).
96. *Volkskrant* (March 17, 1972): 'Democratie heeft niets met spellinghervorming te maken' (cf. also *Leeuwarder Courant* [March 20, 1972]).
97. In 1966 it was on a preliminary report.
98. For the Netherlands, cf. the following educational periodicals: *Het Schoolblad* (April 6, 1967), *Ons Onderwijs* (December 1967), and *Onderwijs en Opvoeding* (October 1967); for Belgium, cf. Craeybeckx 1972: 150-159.
99. *Het Schoolblad* (May 11, 1967) and *Onderwijs en Opvoeding* (June 1967).
100. B. W. Schippers in *De Kweekschool* 4: 7-8 (July-August 1969), 160-161.
101. Except for the six that contain only information without comment.
102. Cf. e.g. *Het Schoolblad* (April 6, 20, and May 25, 1967); *Schoolkrant voor Ouders van nu* (January 5, 1972); *Onderwijs en Opvoeding* (December 1967); *P.C.B.O. Blad* (January 5, 1972); *Het Katholiek Schoolblad* (April 26, 1967); cf. also a letter dated May 11, 1967 of the *ANOF* to the Minister of Education.
103. K. Buringa in *Ons Onderwijs* (December 1967); he argues that the deficient command of language is not due to the spelling but to carelessness towards language use.
104. Cf., for example, F. Overmans in *Het Katholiek Schoolblad* (April 26, 1967).
105. Cf. e.g. *Het Schoolblad* (May 18, 1967); *Het Katholiek Schoolblad* (February 20, 1971); *Resonans* (May-June 1969); *P.C.B.O. Blad* (January 5, 1972).
106. Cf. also *Schoolkrant voor Ouders van nu* (January 5, 1972).
107. Cf. also a letter of the *Vereniging voor Wetenschappelijke Spelling*, dated February 1, 1967, to the Dutch Minister of Education and the Belgian Minister of Dutch Culture.
108. For more information cf. *P.C.B.O. Blad* (January 5, 1972) and *Het Katholieke Schoolblad* (December 11, 1972).
109. Cf. also *Het Katholieke Schoolblad* (December 11, 1971).
110. In a confidential note, the Permanent Consultative Commission rightly raises the point that the results might have been equally good with the spelling according to the *Eindvoorstellen*, but the *Aksiegroep* neglected to acknowledge or investigate this.
111. I.e. a Catholic school in Wervik in the province of West-Flanders.
112. 'gefundeerde keuze'.
113. That this is nearly an impossible task is illustrated by Couvreur (1972: 288).
114. Cf. also Meijers 1967: 138-139; *Het Schoolblad* (May 11, June 1 and 5, 1967) and others.
115. 'Heiligschennis'.
116. The full list can be found in Craeybeckx 1972: 47-109. Among the most important are, from the Belgian side, L. P. Boon, H. Claus, A. Demedts, J. Geeraerts, M. Gijsen, K. Jonckheere, H. Lampo, I. Michiels, and W. Ruyslinck. Some of the most famous Dutch supporters of Craeybeckx are S. Carmiggelt, J. Cremer, J. de Hartog, W. F. Hermans, A. Koolhaas, H. Mulish, V. van Vriesland, and S. Vinkenoog. Mulish and Van Vriesland also defended the conservative standpoint in a Dutch television debate broadcast on April 5, 1967.
117. The former in a letter dated April 27, 1972, to the Ministers of Education and of Culture, and the latter in a letter dated December 5, 1967, to the Minister of Education.

118. The *NRC-Handelsblad* (April 17, 1972) states that 83 percent of all members expressed a negative opinion.
119. 'Ik ben tegen een wereld van de minste weerstand. Ben tegen een wereld die alleen het eigen actuele bestaansmoment van belang acht. Tegen een wereld waarin wortels uitgeroeid worden, oorsprongen onherkenbaar gemaakt, overleveringen en tradities als nutteloze ballast afgeworpen worden. Ik ben tegen de voorstellen tot spellingshervorming van de Commissie Pée-Wesselings.' Cf. also W. F. Hermans (Craeybeckx 1972: 69), as well as P. G. Buckinx (Craeybeckx 1972: 50), and others.
120. Indeed, not all members are against. As in the 1930's (cf. supra, p. 194) there are some exceptions who could be said to confirm the rule. They are Buddingh, Hellinga, Lucebert, Polet, Vogelaar, and Wolkers (cf. Kohnstamm 1972: 56).
121. Jonckheere (Craeybeckx 1972: 75) and Gijsen (Craeybeckx 1972: 59) mention both; cf. also Decorte and Demedts (Craeybeckx 1972: 55).
122. Letter of the *Vereniging*, dated April 27, 1972, to the Dutch Ministers of Culture and Education: 'de verantwoorde omgang met de taal als communicatiemiddel'. For some individual testimonies of authors in newspapers cf. *De Standaard* (March 1, 1972) (Mulish); *Volkskrant* (March 18, 1967) (G. Bomans); *Het Parool* (March 31, 1967) (E. van Altena).
123. In the 1930's (cf supra, p. 194) and in 1946-1954 (cf. supra, p. 210).
124. 'Een onvergeeflijk blunder' (his quotation marks).
125. Another mistake was that, unlike in the Netherlands, no authorities or agencies whatsoever were consulted (cf. supra, p. 217).
126. Recently its name has been changed into *Nederlandse Academie voor Wetenschappen, Letteren en Schone Kunsten van België*.
127. These articles whose references were incomplete (i.e. 7.3 percent) have not been taken into account (cf. fn. 69).
128. In Belgium and in The Netherlands broadcasting (radio and television) is nationalized but open for all points of view ('pluralistic').
129. Cf. a letter received, dated January 19, 1973, from L. van Uytven, *Directeur Aktualiteit van de B.R.T.*
130. Pelckmans does not support this statement but, judging from the context, it is probably because they will no longer be able to sell their books in the old spelling.
131. A motion of the *Nederlandse Genootschap van Vertalers* [Dutch Association of Translaters] to the Dutch Minister of Education has been added to the letter dated April 27, 1972, of the Dutch Association of Literary Men to the same minister.
132. The same is done by Bolckmans (Craeybeckx 1972: 114); cf. Haugen 1959.
133. (1) *hij antwoort* (instead of *antwoordt*); (2) *huit* (*huid*); (3) *sjofeur* (*chauffeur*); (4) *ij* instead of *ei*.
134. Cf. e.g. *Het Parool* (March 7, 1967), *Haagsche Courant* (May 24, 1967), *NRC Handelsblad* (March 12, 1971), *Het Vaderland* (July 16, 1971), *Accent* (January 29, 1973), and *Het Laatste Nieuws* (February 27, 1968).
135. Cf., for example, homograph argument (*Accent* [January 29, 1973]), etymological argument (*Schoolblad* [October 12, 1967]), word image argument (*Het Laatste Nieuws* [February 27, 1968]), instruction argument (*Parool* [March 7, 1967] and *Schoolblad* [October 12, 1967]).
136. 'Spellingconservatisme [is] een zeer natuurlijke zaak: de aanhangers daarvan

strijden voor het behoud van "hun" spelling, dat wil zeggen een spelling die zij geleerd hebben, die ze "beheersen", die ze "onder de knie hebben"... men (mag) aannemen dat in het spellingconservatisme een bezits- en beheerinstinct een belangrijk aandeel hebben.'

137. 'misbaksels'.

138. Cf. e.g. the four articles of Craeybeckx in *De Volksgazet* (January 8, February 2, April 7, and April 15, 1972).

139. 'Hij weigert diskussie, maar zoekt zoveel mogelijk mensen die zonder meer tegen wijziging zijn. Het wijzigen van de spelling is voor hem het probleem.'

140. At this moment there is no president.

141. Cf. the interview of Kohnstamm in *Trouw* (February 3, 1973).

142. Cf. the utterances of Lefèvre in The Hague (supra, p. 219).

143. 'Waar zo'n spelling voor het Nederlands precies op neer zou komen en of hij gemakkelijk geleerd en toegepast zou kunnen worden, zijn echter alles behalve vragen met een voor de hand liggend antwoord. Er is met betrekking tot het Nederlands weinig fonologisch onderzoek verricht, en nog minder is er onderzoek gedaan naar de relatie tussen de fonologische struktuur en de struktuur van de ortografie... Van verschillende kanten is opgemerkt dat de spellingsproblematiek ook een belangrijk sociologisch aspekt heeft... Ten behoeve van wat in vroegere spellingdiskussies het volkskind heette en nu het taalkundig gedepriveerde kind... wordt gepleit voor vereenvoudiging van de spelling.'

144. It remains for us to acknowledge our indebtedness to the following persons and institutions. Our special thanks go to P. Berckx and especially W. Couvreur, without whose information this paper would not have been possible. Furthermore, we would like to thank the Belgian Ministry of Dutch Culture and the Dutch Embassy in Brussels for their help. Finally we are grateful to W. Couvreur, B. C. Damsteegt, J. L. Pauwels, W. Pée, and F. van Mechelen for their most valuable comment and advice.

BIBLIOGRAPHY

Bijlsma, W.

1972 'En de boom wort hoe langer hoe dikker', *De Groene Amsterdammer* (February 2). Also in D. Kohnstamm (ed.), *Ik hoop dat de spelling verandert wort* (1972), 57-62.

Burns, D.

1953 'Social and Political Implications in the Choice of an Orthography', *Fundamental and Adult Education* 5, 80-85.

Caron, W. J. H.

1972 *Klank en Teken. Verzamelde taalkundige studies* (Groningen: Wolters-Noordhoff).

Cohen, A., and A. Kraak

1972 *Spellen is spellen is spellen. Een verkenning van de spellingsproblematiek* (The Hague: Nijhoff).

Couvreur, W.

1972 'Sluipmoord op de spelling', *Wetenschappelijke Tijdingen* 31: 5, 257-294.

Craeybeckx, L.
1972 *Sluipmoord op de spelling* (Amsterdam and Brussels: Elsevier).
Daman, J. A.
1929 *De vereenvoudigde spelling en de spellingsbeweging. 1891-1929* (Middelburg).
1941 *Vijftig jaren van strijd 1891-1941*, gedenkschrift (Purmerend: Muusses).
1947 *De laatste jaren van de spellingstrijd. Een blik terug* (s.l. Vereniging tot vereenvoudiging van onze spelling).
Damsteegt, B. C.
1967 'Momenten uit de geschiedenis van de spelling van de bastaardwoorden in Noord-Nederland', *Handelingen van de Koninklijke Zuidnederlandse Maatschappij voor Taal en Letterkunde en Geschiedenis* 21, 259-268.
Debus, F.
1972 'Spelling en spellingproblemen in het Duits', *De Gids* 135, 225-229.
Dibbets, G. R. W.
1968 *Nederduitse Orthographie van Pontus de Heiuter- (1581). Een inleiding* (Assen).
Eindvoorstellen
1969 *Eindvoorstellen van de Nederlands-Belgische commissie voor de spelling van de bastaardwoorden* (The Hague: Staatsuitgeverij).
Elias, H. J.
1964 *Geschiedenis van de Vlaamse gedachte*. Volume III: *Verwezenlijkingen en ontgoochelingen. De scheiding der wegen, 1860-1883* (Antwerpen: De Nederlandse Boekhandel).
Fellman, J.
1972 *What do Members of the Academy of the Hebrew Language Know and Think about its Operation?* (Jerusalem: Language-Behavior Section). Mimeographed
Fishman, J. A.
1971 'The Sociology of Language, an Interdisciplinary Social Science Approach to Language in Society', in J. A. Fishman (ed.), *Advances in the Sociology of Language* (The Hague: Mouton), 217-404. (1976, 2nd ed.)
Geerts, G.
1965 *Genus en geslacht in de Gouden Eeuw* (Brussel: Belgisch Interuniversitair Centrum voor Neerlandistiek).
Haeringen, C. B. van
1954 *Genus en geslacht. Het voornaamwoordelijk gebruik in gesproken taal* (Amsterdam: Meulenhoff).
Hantlijding
1972 *Hantlijding. Minimumprogramma Spelling 1972* (Amsterdam: Aksiegroep spellingvereenvoudiging).
Haugen, E.
1959 'Language Planning in Modern Norway', *Anthropological Linguistics*, 1: 3 (1954), 6-21. Also in J. A. Fishman (ed.), *Readings in the Sociology of Language* (The Hague: Mouton, 1968), 673-687.
Henkemans, H.
1963 'Een leek over allergie', *Maatstaf* 11, 547-550.
Kate, L. ten
1723 *Aenleiding tot de kennisse van het verhevene deel der Nederduitsche Sprake* (Amsterdam).

Kohnstamm, D. (ed.)

1972 *Ik hoop dat de spelling verandert wort*, publication of the Aksiegroep Spellingsvereenvaudiging (Purmerend: J. Muusses).

Kollewijn, R. A.

1891 'Onze lastige spelling. Een voorstel tot vereenvoudiging', in Kollewijn, *Opstellen over spelling en verbuiging* (Groningen: Wolters, 1916), 1-18.

1916 *Opstellen over spelling en verbuiging* (Groningen: Wolters).

Labov, W.

1969 'The Logic of Nonstandard English', *Georgetown Monographs on Language and Linguistics* 22 (Washington: Georgetown University Press), 1-22, 26-31.

Lissens, R. F.

1962 *Benamingen van onze letterkunde in encyclopedien en literaire lexicons* (Gent: Koninklijke Vlaamse Akademie voor Taal en Letterkunde).

Mechelen, F. van

1971 'Antwoord op de interpellatie van senator J. van In over de voorgenomen wijziging van de spelling van de Nederlandse Taal', stenciled (Brussels: Ministry of Dutch Culture).

Meijers, J. A.

1967 *Het Nederlandse spellingdrama. Een poging tot relativering* (Amsterdam: De Bussy).

Moonen, A.

1706 *Nederduitsche Spraekkunst, ten dienste van in- en uitheemschen uit verscheidene schrijveren en aentekeningen opgemaekt en uitgegeven* (Amsterdam).

Motie

1971 *Motie van de Koninklijke Vlaamse Academie voor Taal- en Letterkunde m.b.t. de spelling* (Gent).

Mulisch, H.

1972 *Soeplepelen met een vork* (Amsterdam: De Bezige Bij).

Nida, E.

1954 'Practical Limitations to a Phonemic Orthography', *Bible Translator* 5, 58-62.

Paardekooper, P. C.

1967 *Wendier tegen wetenschap. Een voor-spelling van de toekomst* (Den Bosch: Malmberg).

Pauwels, J. L.

1934 *De Spellingkwestie: het standpunt van een Zuidnederlandse vereenvoudiger. Met een aanhangsel: De regels van de Nieuwe spelling* (Antwerpen: De Sikkel).

1954 *Toelichting bij de Nieuwe woordenlijst van de Nederlandse Taal* (Leuven: Vlaamse Drukkerij).

Pée, W.

1946 'Spellingvereenvoudiging', *Nieuw Vlaamsch Tijdschrift* 14, 438-451.

Persbulletin

1967 *Persbulletin samengesteld door de Voorlichtingsdienst van het Ministerie van Onderwijs en Wetenschappen* (=*Persbericht* 1753).

Rapport

1967 *Rapport van de Belgisch-Nederlandse Commissie voor de spelling van de bastaardwoorden* (Brussel: Ministerie van Nationale Opvoeding en Cultuur).

Robertson, S., and P. Cassidy
1954 *The Development of Modern English* (New York: Prentice-Hall).
Rombouts, S.
1967 '*Naar een betere spelling*' (= *Opvoedkundige brochurereeks 185*) (Tilburg).
1972 *Kun je nog spellen . . .* (Utrecht and Antwerpen: Het Spectrum).
Royen, G.
1949 *Romantiek uit het Spellingtournooi* (Utrecht and Nijmegen: Dekker and Van de Vegt).
1953 *Taalrapsodie. Taalkundige en didaktische varia van her en der* (Bussum: Brand).
Sciarone, B.
1963 'Een geneesmiddel tegen spellingsallergie', *Maatstaf* 11, 933-940.
Siegenbeek, M.
1804 *Verhandeling over de Nederduitsche Spelling ter bevordering van eenparigheid in dezelve* (Dordrecht).
1805 *Woordenboek voor de Nederduitsche Spelling.*
Smalley, W.
1964 *Orthography Studies: Articles on New Writing Systems* (London: United Bible Societies).
Spelling
1864 *Spelling der Nederduitsche taal. Koninklijke Besluiten genomen ter regeling dier spelling en verslag der commissie, die gelast is geweest met de middelen om tot de eenparigheid te geraken* (Gent: Drukkerij C. Annoot-Braeckman).
Spellingskwestie
1972 *Spellingskwestie* (Antwerp: Cabinet of the Mayor of Antwerp).
Stuiveling, G.
1972 'Het spel van de spelling', *De Gids* 135, 169-190.
Velde, I. van der
1956 *De tragedie der werkwoordsvormen* (Groningen: Wolters).
1969 *Spellingvereenvoudiging. Onderwijskundige en sociale noodzakelijkheid* (Amsterdam and The Hague: A.N.O.F.).
Vooys, C. G. N. de
1940 'Uit de geschiedenis van de Nederlandse spelling', *De Nieuwe Taalgids* 34, 337-349.
Vos, A. L.
1972 'Het Engels en de spelling', *De Gids* 135, 220-224.
Vries, M. de, and Winkel, L. te
1866 *Woordenlijst voor de spelling der Nederlandse taal* (The Hague and Leiden: Nijhoff-Sijthoff).
Winkel, L. Te
1863 *De Grondbeginselen der Nederlandsche spelling. Ontwerp der spelling voor het aanstaande Nederlandsch Woordenboek* (Leiden: Noothoven Van Goor).
1865 *De grondbeginselen der Nederlandsche Spelling. Regeling der Spelling voor het Woordenboek der Nederlandsche taal* (Leiden: Noothoven Van Goor).
Woordenlijst
1954 *Woordenlijst van de Nederlandse Taal. Samengesteld in opdracht van de Nederlandse en de Belgische regering* (The Hague: Staatsdrukkerij).

DAG GUNDERSEN

10

Successes and Failures in the Reformation of Norwegian Orthography

Any advanced student of the modern Norwegian language and its history will at least understand, and quite possibly agree to, the often-heard opinion among Norwegians that nowhere on earth can a comparable amount of time, energy, brain power, and money possibly have been spent on language questions. Throughout the last 150 years, the effort of planning, normalizing, and regulating the national written language and its use in education and administration defies quantification. One aspect has been the publication of printed matter ranging from one-page pamphlets to large books on 'the language question'. A bibliography of such writings from the last one hundred years and mostly from the present century, lists about 950 items, not including school books, most government papers, and newspaper and periodical articles (Haugen 1968; bibliography complete through 1967). This figure reflects a long-lasting free-for-all which has by no means been restricted to an officially recognized expertise. Private publication by individuals and nonofficial bodies has been the rule rather than the exception, in accordance with a tradition since early in the nineteenth century of 'writing to one's newspaper', and the even older tradition of publishing one's opinions in matters of public interest.

This has given us a wild-growing flora of Norwegian language writings. The one trait most of them have in common is that they set out with an explanation and evaluation of history and the present situation. Usually it is intended to be objective, but as it goes along it becomes partisan and often polemic. Neutral and exhaustive periodical surveys are few and far between. Of definitive books on the development of the language normalization in Norway (which is not synonymous with the development of the Norwegian language) only two may be said to exist: Burgun (1919-1921), dealing with the nineteenth century, and Haugen (1966a; 1968), dealing with the twentieth century. Both were written by non-Norwegians.

What has kept native scholars from tackling this job? Some factors may be suggested, such as

(a) their awareness of the daunting complexity of the task.

(b) uncomfortable feelings aroused by the controversial aspects of it. More often than 'the language question' or 'the language normalization' the central term has been 'the language struggle' (N: *språkstriden*).

(c) most native scholars have had a personal engagement in the matter which has given a partisan or sectorial bent to their interest; moreover it is probably impossible for a native writer to be completely unbiased on the language question.

(d) To a large extent the same arguments have been used over and over again, partly with the same slogan-like formulations,[1] as new protagonists take over (a headline from one of the livelier periods of 'struggle' ran: 'A new berserk takes the field', O. Dalgard, *Arbeiderbladet* [November 12, 1964]; cf. Haugen 1968: 353, fn. 44). In time one realizes that the last word is never said. 'The Norwegian language question does not boil down' (Indrebø 1937: 47). With growing disillusionment, the question arises whether it is indeed worth the effort to try to analyze or even describe this process which is never finished – I feel this acutely.

Unfinished as it is and chaotic though it may appear, not only to non-Norwegians, the process of reaching a written norm of modern Norwegian nevertheless provides a case material of value to the student of language planning and of sociolinguistics. Most important in this respect is the work done in both fields by Einar Haugen, who from his vantage position of knowing Norwegian without being Norwegian has been able to give an unbiased presentation of this difficult material and make it meaningful in comparative study.[2]

As for successes and failures most people would probably agree to one or both of two statements: language planning in Norway has not been a total success, and it has not been a total failure.

Common terms in the field of language normalization[3] have been 'the language question', 'the language problem', and 'the language struggle'. But it has also been referred to by compounds of *rettskrivnings-*, e.g. *-debatt* 'debate', *-forslag* 'proposal', *-reform* (Knudsen, et al. 1937-1957). *Rettskrivning* (German *Rechtschreibung*) corresponds to 'orthography', and thus has a wider denotation than 'spelling'.

The reforms initiated by official authorities have focused on spelling and inflection. They have largely neglected syntax, style, vocabulary, and meaning. At the present time, however, one may point to a certain change in this. The heavy influx of English loan words has led to a greater awareness of structural problems connected with vocabulary.

Nonofficial normalization through spelling lists and other guidelines for those who find themselves more or less in agreement has always had in it a strong element of opposition to the official rules, and to the same extent has had to concentrate on the themes of disagreement provided by the official planners. This again means spelling and inflection. But in their general concern and criticism of the official norm, the nonofficial planners[4] have, at least at times, been active in a wider field, for example, they have pointed out how some of the official rules, in their opinion, generate errors of style by mixing traditional word forms with constructs that are without foundation in the spoken language.

THE AIMS

Linguistic Independence from Denmark[5]

The influence of Danish through more than 400 years of political union ended when the union broke up in 1814. The constitution of that year (revised version of November 4, §§ 33 and 47) makes a point of mentioning 'the Norwegian language'.[6] But the written language to which the constitution refers continued to be Danish in spelling and inflection throughout the entire nineteenth century, except for a few details of no great importance. Among linguists it was regularly called *dansk-norsk* (Danish-Norwegian, Dano-Norwegian), implying that spelling and inflection was common to both languages, but not vocabulary to the same degree.

While this situation existed, it presented a special dilemma. A certain distance, and perhaps quite a wide one, between spoken and written language is normal in any nation. It is still the same language. But in Norway's case the difference was between a foreign written language and spoken varieties developed from Old Norwegian. This not only made the gap a particularly wide one, but to the average dialect speaker the national written language was hardly comprehensible, just as were the dialects to the average official bred in the Danish tradition. Ivar Aasen, the foremost observer of Norwegian dialects and the creator of *landsmål*, describes the situation in words that vibrate with the frustration in the *vox populi* (Aasen 1864, reprint 1965: Preface, X):

> 'Whereas basic learning [*børnelærdom*] and all other necessary knowledge ought to be imparted in a form that follows the people's speech fairly closely, learning was here presented in a foreign form, so that it was often misunderstood and usually only halfway or little understood. Moreover, it was difficult to remember and still more difficult to pass on to children and relations in everyday conversation. And the immediate consequence of this had to be that common folk did not learn more than they had to, and for the rest left this learning business (*alt dette Kundskabsvæsen*) to the sundry good heads that were bright enough to pick up anything one might wish.
>
> Thus it will be clear enough that it is hurtful to a people having to receive learning in a language that belongs to an other people and not to itself.'

The nationalistic feeling and need of self-assertion through a language of one's own has perhaps been overemphasized by writers of the history of the Norwegian language in the nineteenth century. If so, the reason is that this feeling came much to the front with many of the authors of this period, and even more so in part of the debate of the present century. Certainly the feeling was a real one. But it should not be allowed to lead us away from the everyday reality of Aasen's description, which is that a non-Danish, Norwegian written language was needed because it was the only one that most Norwegians could thoroughly understand and use.[7]

The transition from a Danish to a Norwegian written language has largely taken place in the present century, starting with the official reform of 1907 and going further step by step with the reforms of 1917 and 1938. The 1938 orthography, with the modifications of 1959, is still used. Central points in all these reforms have been

(1) the introduction of 'hard consonants' (unvoiced stops *p*, *t*, *k* instead of Danish *b*, *d*, *g* in noninitial position) as obligatory in many words and optional in many others

(2) gemination of consonant in final position after short vowel, e.g. *gikk* instead of Danish *gik* 'went'

(3) shortened forms of some nouns and verbs, e.g. *fader*/*far* 'father', *have*/*ha* 'have'

(4) the inflection of certain categories of nouns[8]

From 1917 on must be added

(5) the introduction of diphthongs in many words where Danish has monophthong, e.g. *stein* instead of *sten* 'stone'.

How these reforms have been introduced and how they have worked will be discussed at more length later. The outcome has certainly been that written Dano-Norwegian today is distinct from Danish, although a person who can read the one language can easily read the other. On this point the spelling reforms have therefore been successful, even though each step of the transition has been accompanied by increasing controversy.

Today one of the activities of official language planning in the Scandinavian countries is to cooperate. Parallel work is being done by the national language commissions to choose joint technical terms in various fields, and several lists have been published. As a practical concession to Swedish and Danish, the Norwegian Language Commission, when planning the 1959 modification of the 1938 reform, chose 'separate spelling' (i.e. in two words) of several phrases that had till then been written as one word, e.g. *om bord* 'on board', *over bord* 'overboard' (Kirke- og undervisningsdepartementet 1957: 116: col. 1).

An official form of written Dano-Norwegian (later called *riksmål* 'national language' and *bokmål* 'book language') may be traced through printed and written sources back to ca. 1520. It is a fact that the basis of modern *bokmål* is sixteenth century Danish with an element of Norvagisms. Modernizing it step by step has been one method. Launching a new standard has been an other. This was what Ivar Aasen did in the middle of the nineteenth century. To say that he 'created' or 'constructed' it may give a wrong impression, even though nobody spoke (or speaks) it as their mother tongue from infancy. It was a common denominator of the rural dialects, with the structure of standard Old Norwegian as a guideline in the choice between alternative forms. Since this structure was best preserved in the western and midland dialects, Aasen built his standard, called *landsmål* 'country language', later *nynorsk* 'New Norwegian', mainly on these (Haugen 1966b).

Since 1885 *landsmål/nynorsk* has been considered an official standard, on a par with *riksmål/bokmål*. Thus from that year on Norwegian has had two official written standards.[9]

Unification

A reform of the *landsmål* orthography was carried out in 1901, with the effect of making it somewhat less etymological. With the reform of 1907 *riksmål* took the main step from Danish towards Norwegian. The reforms of 1917, 1938, and 1959 have dealt with both standards. Their main objective, or one of them, has been to bring both standards closer together. After 1901 and 1907 this was perfectly possible, as they were no longer different languages, but varieties of the same language.[10]

There has been general agreement about the possibility of gradually reducing the gap between the two standards. There has even been a general feeling that the ultimate outcome would be the assimilation of both into one 'common Norwegian' (*samnorsk*) standard. But nothing has caused such controversy as the question of tempo and extent, and nowhere has the difference between official and nonofficial planning appeared more clearly. Up to 1972 the official policy was planned unification in the course of a foreseeable future, while the nonofficial one was 'natural development', however long it would take to reach one standard.

Today the situation is diffuse, to put it mildly. The Norwegian Language Council, which in 1972 replaced the Norwegian Language Commission as the official language-planning body, does not have planned unification among its objectives. At the same time it is bound by law 'to further cooperation in the cultivation and normalization of our two language forms and to support those tendencies in the development that in the long run will bring the two language forms closer together'. What happens, then, in the short run? For one thing Norwegian in both of its written standards is the recipient of an ever-flowing stream of loan words. They are mostly introduced in *bokmål*, because they often appear as technical terms in literature where that standard is the usual one. But when needed they pass on to *nynorsk* easily enough, and nearly always in the same spelling, since they are as strange to the one as to the other, e.g. *design*, or fall into a well-known pattern common to both, e.g. *bidireksjonal*. It seems somewhat ironic that while the problem of unification is being put off to an uncertain future in order to ensure 'language peace' for the present time, it is automatically being furthered in a field where nobody is too happy to find it, since the result, rather than common Norwegian, is common un-Norwegian.

Adaptation to the Spoken Language

The *riksmål* reform of 1907 justifies the change to 'hard consonants' with its being 'in accordance with the common, cultured spoken language, i.e., with the pronunciation that in the greater part of the country is usual in the careful, but unstilted everyday speech of persons of culture (*i dannede folks omhyggelige, men ukunstlede dagligtale*).'[11] The officially appointed committee which prepared the 1917 reform uses expressions such as 'the living spoken language on both sides', 'the committee must always keep in mind that it should clear the way to a development towards a national unification based on the true spoken language of the people' (*national samling paa grundlag av folkets virkelige talesprog*) (Indstilling 1917: 1-2). The instruction by *Stortinget* (the Norwegian parliament) to the committee which prepared the 1938 reform had as its point 1 'to bring the two languages closer together with respect to orthography, word forms, and inflections, based on Norwegian folk speech' (*på norsk folkemåls grunn*).[12] The latter phrase has been most central, and controversial, from then on. As a term it lacks in clarity, but the progress from 'persons of culture' to 'the Norwegian folk' clearly indicates the democratization of the policy in official language planning. Since *landsmål/nynorsk* from the beginning was built on rural dialects and therefore a democratic effort in itself, the words quoted have mainly applied to *riksmål/bokmål*. On the *nynorsk* side the problem has been that of adapting the western and midland basis to the increasing mobility towards the eastern districts and their cities. This adaptation, though much challenged by adherents of traditional *landsmål*, was carried out especially in 1938 and 1959, at the same time bringing *nynorsk* closer to *bokmål* and thus fulfilling a double aim.

A quite different point has been determining the optimal distance between spelling and pronunciation, and in this field it is difficult to find a clear line in the planning activities, official or nonofficial. Certain elementary errors, such as confusing the infinitive marker *å* with the conjunction *og* 'and' because both are pronounced [ɔ], are a constant headache to school children and their teachers, and one that will probably be with them, since little systematic planning is being done here. Word histories and etymological relationships are still important guidelines in Norwegian as in most other standard languages, and often are allowed to outweigh simplicity and rationality.[13]

Simplification

After what has just been said it may seem unnecessary to discuss this point at all. Nevertheless, considerable effort has been made to simplify the official spelling of both standards for the benefit of education and in order to bring them at least somewhat closer to pronunciation. Of the two standards, *landsmål/nynorsk* has had the furthest to go because of the alignment to Old Norwegian given it by Ivar Aasen.

Whether the result so far is satisfactory is debatable. To try for total consistency is out of the question. But it seems rather futile to change certain members of a word family in order to make them consistent with certain others, but not with all. For example:

Before 1959:	trafi*kk*	'traffic'
	å trafi*k*ere	'to traffic'
	trafi*k*ant	'traveler'
	fabri*kk*	'factory'
	å fabri*k*ere	'to manufacture'
	fabri*k*ant	'manufacturer'
	fabri*k*at	'manufacture'

1959: *Verbs* derived from nouns with a geminate in final position are to have the same geminate, thus *trafi*kk*ere*, *fabri*kk*ere*; other derivates are unchanged.

All the official reforms have allowed a wide variety of alternate orthographical forms and inflections of many words and of certain subcategories, especially of nouns and verbs. In some cases this has been done as part of the unification process, launching one form common to both standards, but allowing a more traditional alternative which is known to be widely used within one of them. Other alternate forms may be said to make up a waiting list, being considered on the way either out or in. In the first case they may be stricken out in the next reform, in the second case they may in time be made compulsory.

This principle has been inescapable in Norway's language situation, and it is fairly easy to apply. But the planner who applies it can never be quite certain what the outcome will be, i.e. whether his choice will prove acceptable to the opinion makers of practical life. The results have not been altogether fortunate. Some of the common forms have had little or no basis in one of the standards and have therefore proved unable to replace a more traditional form. Thus *trøtt* 'tired' in *bokmål* can compete with the older form *trett*, but the derivate *utrøttelig* 'untired(ly)' feels unfamiliar to most users and cannot replace *utrettelig*. Several of these older forms have refused to die, and among these some words of high frequency, such as *bokmål syv* 'seven' for *sju*, *tyve* 'twenty' for *tjue*, and *tredve* 'thirty' for *tretti*.

Outside of schools and official administration there is no power to promote a spelling form that users do not want. It is hardly an exaggeration to say that the planners of the 1917, 1938, and 1959 reforms did not give enough importance to the question of acceptability, and they have therefore added more fuel than necessary to 'the language struggle'.

For the individual user it is nearly impossible to make a wholly consistent selection among doublet forms. The official spelling lists cannot give him much help in this. Besides, nobody consults a spelling list unless he is in doubt, and the user may not be in doubt at all when choosing a familiar, but wrong or nonofficial spelling form. It is perhaps the only one he knows or thinks of.

The result is that however strict one would like to make demands for consistency in theory, they cannot be carried too far in practice or the average user would be bogged down in errors with little chance of improving his spelling anyway.

The committee which prepared the 1938 reform was instructed 'to reduce the number of doublets (obligatory – optional) which now exist in both languages' (Haugen's translation in Haugen 1966a: 117-118). It was unable to do so because it was also instructed to further unification. However, all the orthography reforms that have had optionality as a principle have been followed by a stratagem intended to restore a degree of simplicity. It is called a textbook norm (*læreboknormal*). It consists of a selection of spelling forms and inflections that are made compulsory in textbooks for certain types of schools and for government offices, whereas pupils, students, and others may choose freely among all permissible forms.

The present textbook norm was adopted in 1959, and the discussion both before and after its introduction formed one of the peaks of 'the language struggle'. The main point of discord has been what forms to include and which to exclude. The question has also been raised whether users not bound by it really have a free choice. It has been argued that the forms one sees in most of one's textbooks are given a force of penetration that will soon exclude all others. Defenders of the textbook norm have argued that a narrower standard is of value in schools and administration, where it will also serve as a national standard (*riksnormal*). The wider choice is meant to help the school children in particular (Norsk språknemnd 1966: 12).

The question whether the principles of optionality and restrictivity in language planning can really coexist peacefully seems relevant in this connection, but it has not been important in the Norwegian language debate.[14] In Norway they do coexist, though with a good deal of friction. Their results have often been attacked from various quarters and can hardly be called an unqualified success.

Norwegianization

Norwegian has always been a borrowing language. Among the foreign elements assimilated into its structure the largest come from Middle Low German and Danish. A common distinction in Norwegian is between *lånord*, used of any loan word, and *fremmedord* 'foreign word', used of a loan word that has not yet been assimilated and therefore feels foreign to the user. This is a somewhat diffuse criterion, and the fact is that *fremmedord* has mostly been used of words of classical origin such as *atmosfære* and *oksygen*. Many such words have been with us for centuries, and when they are still considered foreign, it is because they are opaque.[15] There is nothing in their spelling and inflection to mark them as foreign. To the language planner they present no problem at all when he demands of them (translated from Vinje 1973: 15):

(1) conformity to current patterns of formation and inflection
(2) conformity to our graphonomic system
(3) conformity to our phonological system

A solid pattern for spelling them in Norwegian has been created through reform, so that *x* automatically becomes *ks*, *-ction* becomes *-ksjon*, etc. A great number of recent loan words are of this type, and they are easily accessible.

That they do after all present a grave problem is not apparent till they are shifted from specialist language to the general language, where they contribute greatly to the opacity and ambiguity of the everyday language that the average newspaper reader and television viewer has to cope with. Being mostly technical terms they are also part of the technological development that widens the generation gap because the old understand less and less of the work of the young (cf. Widmark 1970).

Finding loanshifts and other substitutions for such words used to be a lively activity, culminating in K. Knudsen's mighty volume *Unorsk og norsk* [Un-Norwegian and Norwegian] in 1881. Today little is being done in this field. In its advisory capacity, the Norwegian Language Council may be asked if *extrinsic* and *intrinsic* may be given a Norwegian equivalent; the answer will be 'yes, *ekstrinsik* and *intrinsik*', with an added list of Norwegian words that may be adequate (Norsk språknemnd 1970: 8). But it is a common experience that a number of suggestions of fairly equal status have little chance of replacing a foreign word once it has been brought in, unless one of them is singled out and promoted actively.

The great majority of new loan words in Norwegian are Anglicisms. We have dealt with one main type, the international scientific vocabulary. The other main type consists of words with English spelling and mostly with English pronunciation when used in Norwegian. That this type constitutes a problem is of course much more easily apparent, and efforts to regulate their spelling and use are proportionally active. Rather surprisingly a certain amount of nonofficial purism has been noticeable in recent years. Thus in football terminology we now hear of *hjørnespark* instead of 'corner', *midtbane* instead of 'center', and *målvakt* or *målvokter* instead of 'keeper'.

The Norwegian Language Council regulates orthography, in between major reforms, through the spelling lists for school use which it does not edit itself, but approves or rejects in its capacity of advisory organ to the Ministry of Church and Education, which has the final say. As examples we may take *røff* and *tøff* for 'rough' and 'tough', and *teip* as doublet form beside *tape*. The Council also publishes annual reports with their most recent decisions.

But the regulating activities always lag behind the import. This is inevitable, but it creates a good deal of confusion among users. Should they write *crash* as in English, *krasj* in order to conform to our graphemic system, or *kræsj* to reproduce pronunciation? By the time the planners get around to the word, the 'Sprachschaden' (language damage) (Weisgerber 1968: 208) may be irreparable. The first spelling given a word, whether desirable or undesirable, has a way of becoming permanent. In conclusion, therefore, we must admit that whatever efforts are being made in this field, in the case of Norwegian they will not be sufficient.

THE PLANNERS AND THEIR OPPONENTS

Official language planning in Norway is the responsibility of the *Storting* (Parliament), where the main lines are mapped out. This is policy making as well as politics, and the Norwegian word *politikk* aptly enough has both meanings. To put the parliamentary language policy/politics into effect has been the business of The Ministry of Church and Education. In the case of the spelling reforms the Ministry appointed expert committees to prepare a recommendation.

After further adjustment and further treatment in the *Storting* (in its Church and Education Committee, or in a general debate), if that body so wishes, the Ministry puts a proposal before the Cabinet, which passes it by Royal Decree (Cabinet decision signed by the King and countersigned by the Prime Minister). The decree usually contains a clause instructing the Ministry to put the decision into effect in the schools, e.g. Royal Decree of January 7, 1938, § 5: 'The Ministry of Church and Education is authorized to give appropriate rules concerning the time and the means of carrying this reform out in the schools.' All in all this has given the Ministry a great deal of influence in the planning procedure, such as being responsible for the textbook norms mentioned above. These have not been subject to higher approval, except for the textbook norm of 1959, now in use, which went by that name but was also an extensive revision of the 1938 orthography. It was therefore passed by Royal Decree of April 3, 1959. An arrangement with permanent advisors to the Ministry was replaced when the Norwegian Language Commission was established by a *Storting* decision, in operation from January 1, 1952, to February 1, 1972. Apart from preparing the textbook norm of 1959, the greater part of its advisory activities was to prepare a report concerning the language in each book for school use that needs Ministry approval. In its last year, 1971, the Commission secretariat (two secretaries plus external consultants attached to the Commission) examined 209 books (Norsk språknemnd 1971: 6). To the publishers of school books, this service was and still is compulsory, but gratis, and in spite of the criticism that some of them have leveled against the Commission, no one has denied that a by-product of enforcing the required orthography has been to raise the general level of textbook prose.

A pioneer planner in Norway, K. Knudsen, once formulated the problem of acceptability thus (Knudsen 1887; cf. Gundersen 1967: 25-26):

> 'One would expect people gladly to give up old and backward habits for new and better ones. But no! Ingratitude, ridicule and other persecution are the certain wages of the language reformers [*mål-bøterne*], and the more certain the more urgently needed their work is. What people once have had hammered into their heads they stick to, however clearly you prove to them that it is untrue, impractical or otherwise inadequate.'

Many later planners have had occasion to subscribe to Knudsen's words. They have all had opponents at their heels, individual ones in the nineteenth century, pressure groups in the twentieth. These groups have been organized from the turn of the century onwards – AGAINST the introduction of *landsmål/nynorsk* as official standard on a par with *riksmål/bokmål*, AGAINST the unification program, FOR the furthering of a common Norwegian (*samnorsk*) standard, FOR the furthering of *landsmål/nynorsk* in one of its possible variants, and AGAINST others. It is probably true that the language struggle has provided 'abundant evidence of the ways in which democracy works' (Haugen 1966a: 276), and 'released forces that might not otherwise have been released or had the chance to develop' (Kirke- og undervisningsdepartementet 1966: 9, col. 1). But in retrospect one sees how these forces could on several occasions have been redirected just a little to work in the same direction instead of against each other.

In 1964 the then Minister of Church and Education, Mr. Helge Sivertsen, took an initiative to moderate the language struggle by appointing a committee which was representative of the main language organizations and several political parties. It was headed by Professor Hans Vogt, then rector of the University of Oslo and a linguist of international standing. Its mandate was

> 'to evaluate the entire language situation of the country and propose measures which the committee feels may further the conservation and development of our Norwegian linguistic heritage.'

The committee was expressly asked to assess whether the Norwegian Language Commission might be developed into a body with a wider representation, or whether it should rather be replaced by a new body. It was also asked to determine if new rules were needed for the language use in schools, administration, and broadcasting, and if so to propose laws or rules (Kirke- og undervisningsdepartementet 1966: 3).

The Vogt Committee filled the order, which was indeed a tall one. Some of its proposals have not yet been acted upon. Others are under consideration, for example, rules for the national broadcasting and a new law regulating the use of both standards in official administration.[16] The most important effect so far has been the establishment of the Norwegian Language Council, which replaced the Norwegian Language Commission from February 1, 1972, carrying on where the Commission left off – as advisor to the Ministry and to the public in general, and working together with the other Scandinavian commissions, and others, in questions of terminology, etc.

The Council is larger than the Commission (forty-four members compared to thirty), and those major language organizations which refused to cooperate with the Commission are represented in the Council. The Ministry had the right to appoint a number of the representatives to the Commission, but not to the Council. On the other hand *Stortinget* as a new arrangement appoints a certain number of the representatives to the Council, though not necessarily among its own members.

It cannot be said that *Stortinget* has wished 'to take the language question out of politics', which was a slogan in the conservative *riksmål* camp. But the Council can exercise a freer initiative towards the Ministry than the Commission could, and on the whole has greater authority.

The first steps have recently been taken by the Council to initiate a new orthography reform. This has been demanded for years by conservatives both in the *nynorsk* and the *bokmål* camp, who have felt that many traditional words and orthographic forms still widely used have been improperly kept out of the official standards. The reform was their condition for participating in the work of the Council. It is yet too early to predict how well the new direction in planning will turn out, what areas it will try to cover, how long it will take to produce results, whether they will be more widely accepted by society, and indeed whether the whole cooperation will continue in the future or break up into the old reluctance to compromise.

SUCCESS OR FAILURE?

Einar Haugen (1966a: 1) sums up a hundred years of language planning in these words: 'When the movement began, Norway had a stable language of writing that was virtually identical with Danish. Today it has two competing languages, neither of which is stable.' A Norwegian who learned to spell before 1907 has now seen four different orthographies. This does not include a couple of minor reforms plus that of 1959, which might as well have been called a new orthography as a modification of that of 1938. Important language habits are acquired early in life and are not easily changed. To K. Knudsen's reasons why people will not change their old habits, one ought also to add that they do not wish to change something well-known for something less known, or a finished product for an unfinished. Also they wish to devote their attention to the content rather than the external form of what they write.

Should not the reformation of Norwegian orthography by now have led to two standards, or preferably one, that the average user would be able to write easily and correctly? It has not. The user is much in need of a spelling list – official or nonofficial. Such lists are a great article for publishers and booksellers.[17] Outside schools and government offices many write the official orthography, but many others do not. It is already being discussed whether the new Language Council, after its first years in operation, is proving to be a success or a failure.[18] Although the Council has seen a substantial increase in its budget, it can hardly hope to cover adequately or rapidly enough all important areas of planning. During the post World War II era the *nynorsk* standard has had a weakening position in schools, and has been constantly under attack from the *riksmål* side, however much lip service has been paid to its qualities as a literary language and to Ivar Aasen's genius as its creator. The dialects, from where its main strength has come, may face a precarious future under the pressure of industrialization, mass media, and a rapidly increasing mobility in the nation.

To stop here, however, would be to paint the picture too gloomily. If we compare the nineteenth-century orthography of each standard to that of today, we find steady progress in democratization and in conformity to the spoken language by which everybody, and especially the young generation, has benefited. It is open to debate how much of this would have come anyway by 'natural development', but it would certainly have come later rather than sooner.

We must also consider what is 'the spoken language'. If beside the dialects we think of a spoken standard, Norwegian does not have one that is generally acceptable apart from the reading pronunciation of the written standards. It is therefore particularly important that these have been regulated through repeated reforms so as not to be too incongruent with everyday speech. Viewed from this angle some important things become clearer. We cannot expect 'language peace' where three generations of speakers have to leave their mark on the written standards. And we cannot expect, nor do we want, these standards ever to become finished products.

NOTES

1. Such as: 'Language is a living organism', which I have first come across in a *Storting* (parliament) debate from 1885, and of which Vinje (1970: 249) says that it 'is still alive, and this not only in vulgar propaganda'.
2. Many other of Haugen's works than those cited here are of interest in this connection. For a complete bibliography see either Naess and Skard (1971: 374-386), or Firchow, et al. (1972: 11-23).
3. When using terms such as 'language normalization' and 'language planning', I do not add 'in Norway' or 'of Norwegian' where this is reasonably clear from the context.
4. I use the term 'planners' deliberately, though it is controversial, with reference to the various language organizations of Norway, and especially those on the *riksmål* side. They have not seen themselves as planners, but only as givers of good advice to be taken or not taken by the individual user. Without discussing in further detail the various factors that may influence the user's choice, e.g. if he holds a subordinate position in the business world, I wish to point to the fact that since 1952 one of them, *Riksmålsforbundet* [The Riksmål League], has published its own spelling list, *Riksmålsforbundets ordliste*, which is widely used in business, by some of the major newspapers, and by many others. It is a blend of 1938 and 1917 forms, and in my opinion is an important effort in language planning.
5. I have taken this phrase from Hellevik (1971). I am grateful to Mr. Hellevik for allowing me to make use of his paper. Haugen (1966 a: 27) calls it 'The liberation of Norwegian'.
6. This expression was not in the original version of May 17, given during the brief period of independence before the new union with Sweden. The revision of November 4 was necessitated by the new union, and the references to 'the Norwegian language' clearly aimed at barring Swedish as a possible rival. However, the influence from Swedish was negligible during the time of the union, which broke up in 1905. On the other hand, Norwegian has acquired a noticeable element of recent Swedish loan words, mostly after 1945. Vinje (1972) lists about 370 of them. As one influencing factor he mentions that 25 percent of Norwegian owners of television sets take in Swedish programs.
7. Thus I consider this statement by Einar Haugen (1969: 946) too one-sided: 'The only motivations that have been strong enough to promote major spelling reform have been nationalistic in nature, as in Norway; the result has also been a more rational and democratic spelling, but this is incidental. Norwegians could be persuaded that Danish spelling was bad and irrational for them only because it

was hammered into their ears early and late that it was "foreign" and unworthy of a free nation.' In Haugen (1966a: 282) the account is more balanced: 'Although patriotism was the primary motivation of the language movement, class cleavage was a strong secondary one.'

8. Summary of the 1907 revision in Kirke- og undervisningsdepartementet (1938).
9. After the second World War the use of *nynorsk* as a primary language in elementary schools has shown a downward trend, and is now well below 20 percent. In recent years the Norwegian Broadcasting Corporation has tried to reach 25 percent *nynorsk* in verbal programs, but has so far fallen short of this aim. The main reason offered is difficulties in recruiting *nynorsk* users as staff and program contributors.
10. This view, like most others in the Norwegian language debate, has been opposed in some quarters where *nynorsk* is held to be a minority language. See Holmestad and Lade (1969: 52): R. O. Hanoa, 'The nynorsk (New Norwegian) minority in Norway', whereas in the same book (p. 23) M. Oftedal holds that 'The real situation as I see it is that we have only one Norwegian language with two official variants and a multitude of dialects.'
11. Royal Decree of February 19, 1907, quoted from Gundersen (1967: 73).
12. Einar Haugen's translation in Haugen (1966 a: 117), with discussion of the phrase 'Norwegian folk speech' (p. 118).
13. A committee to evaluate the 1935 reform proposal (which became the 1938 reform), appointed by an otherwise conservative *riksmål* body, even today appears quite utopian when it attacks the proposal for not going into the 'undemocratic' distance between spelling and pronunciation, and as examples cites a number of ordinary words that were and still are spelled etymologically, and probably will be for a long time. 'Our orthography therefore suffers from the same defects as do the spellings of the great cultural languages' (Riksmålsvernet 1936: 3-4).
14. The Ministry of Church and Education, which approved and introduced both the orthography of 1938 and the textbook norm of 1959, had this to say in 1968: 'Since the orthography has been arranged with both main forms and optional forms so that both types are valid, caution should be exercised in introducing restrictions in the free choice already given' (Kirke- og undervisningsdepartementet 1968: 62, col. 1). This, however, referred to whether or not broadcasting staff should *speak* on the air according to the textbook norm or the entire orthography.
15. S. Ullman's well-known term, as the opposite of *transparent* (cf. Nielsen 1966: 37).
16. The old law of June 6, 1930, makes it obligatory for holders of office, where certain types of higher education are required, to be able to write both standards. A special 'grandfather clause' exempts persons born before January 1, 1905.
17. The Ministry of Church and Education says: 'One can hardly expect the average student to be able to remember and keep apart all the different forms, obligatory, doublets, permitted and not permitted (but often traditional); even editors of spelling lists use spelling lists '(Kyrkje- og undervisningsdepartementet 1968: 49, col. 1).
18. For example, an interview with L. R. Langslet, conservative *Storting* member, in *Aftenposten* (February 14, 1973).

BIBLIOGRAPHY

Aasen, I.

1864 *Norsk Grammatik*. Quoted here from the 1965 reprint (Oslo: Universitetsforlaget).

Burgun, A.

1919-1921 *Le développement linguistique en Norvège depuis 1814* 1-2 (Kristiania).

Firchow, E. S., K. Grimstad, N. Hasselmo, and W. A. O'Neil (eds.)

1972 *Studies by Einar Haugen. Presented on the Occasion of His Sixty-fifth Birthday – April 19, 1971* (The Hague: Mouton).

Gundersen, D.

1967 *Fra Wergeland til Vogt-komiteen* (Oslo: Universitetsforlaget).

Haugen, Einar

1966a *Language Conflict and Language Planning. The Case of Modern Norwegian* (Cambridge, Mass.: Harvard University Press).

1966b 'Construction and Reconstruction in Language Planning: Ivar Aasen's Grammar', *Word* 21, 188-207. Reprinted with author's comments in Firchow, et al. (eds.), *Studies by Einar Haugen Presented on the Occasion of His Sixty-fifth Birthday – April 19, 1971* (The Hague: Mouton, 1972), 461-478.

1968 *Rikssprák og folkemål* (Oslo: Universitetsforlaget). (A translation from Haugen 1966 by D. Gundersen, with additions by the author, and an enlarged Norwegian bibliography.)

1969 'Review of V. Tauli: *Introduction to a Theory of Language Planning*', *Language* 45, 939-949.

Hellevik, Alf

1971 'Aims and Limits in Norwegian Language Planning', unprinted paper read at The University of Edinburgh (May 25).

Holmestad, E., and A. J. Lade (eds.)

1969 *Lingual Minorities in Europe. A Selection of Papers from the European Conference of Lingual Minorities in Oslo* (Oslo: Det Norske Samlaget).

Indrebø, G.

1937 *God norsk* (Bergen: Lunde).

Indstilling

1917 *Indstilling fra Retskrivningskomiteen* (Kristiania).

Kirke- (Kyrkje-) og undervisningsdepartementet

1938 *Ny rettskrivning 1938. Kirke- og undervisningsdepartementets foredrag og innstilling om rettskrivningsreformen.*

1957 *Framlegg till læreboknormal 1957.*

1966 *Innstilling om språksaken fra Komitéen til å vurdere språksituasjonen m.v. oppnevnt ved kgl.res. 31. jan. 1964.*

1968 *St.meld. nr. 15 (1968-1969). Om språksaka.*

Knudsen, K.

1887 *Kortfattet redegjørelse for det dansknorske målstræv* (Kristiania).

Knudsen, T., H. Noreng, and A. Sommerfelt (eds.)

1937-1957 *Norsk riksmålsordbok* (Oslo: Riksmålsvernet/H. Aschehoug).

Naess, H. S., and S. Skard
1971 *Scandinavian American Interrelations. Americana Norvegica* 3 (Oslo: Universitetsforlaget).
Nielsen, N. Å.
1966 'Dansk sprogrensning. Træk af udviklingen efter 1750', in: Norsk språknemnd, *Årsmelding* (1966), 36-45.
Norsk språknemnd
1966 *Årsmelding* [annual report from The Norwegian Language Commission].
1970 *Årsmelding.*
1971 *Årsmelding.*
Riksmålsvernet
1936 *Rettskrivningen. Utgitt av Riksmålsvernet* (Oslo: H. Aschehoug).
Vinje, F.-E.
1970 'Review of V. Tauli: *Introduction to a Theory of Language Planning*', in *Indogermanische Forschungen* 75.
1972 *Svecismer i moderne norsk* (Oslo: Cappelen).
1973 *Språkplanlegging. Mål og metoder* (Trondheim: Tapir).
Weisgerber, L.
1968 'Wissenschaft und Sprachpflege', in *Sprachnorm, Sprachpflege, Sprachkritik. Sprache der Gegenwart* 2 (Düsseldorf: Pädagogischer Verlag Schwann).
Widmark, G.
1970 'Generationsskillnaderna i språket', in *Språkvård* 2, 3-10.

MÁIRTÍN Ó MURCHÚ

11

Successes and Failures in the Modernization of Irish Spelling

1. THE ORTHOGRAPHY OF OLD IRISH

The development of a writing system for Irish using the letters of the Latin alphabet must have been completed at the latest by the end of the sixth century A.D., though the earliest extant contemporary records date from more than a century later. The more distinctive and, to newcomers, more bewildering features of Irish orthography can be traced back to these early records.

1.1. In adapting the Latin alphabet to the requirements of Irish, eighteen primary letters were employed: *a b c d e f g h i l m n o p r s t u*. In addition, *œ k y z* were used as infrequent variants of *e c i s; q* was sometimes used as another variant of *c*, and *x* as an equivalent of *chs*. Vowel letters were marked with an acute accent to indicate long quantity as, for example, in *bán* 'white' /ba:n/ in contrast with *ban* 'of women' /ban/.

1.2. The phonological value which these letters were to have in writing Irish was determined by the relationship between the spoken British Latin, with which the Irish were acquainted, and traditional Latin orthography. In British Latin (see Jackson 1953), for example, intervocalic voiced stops, represented in spelling by *b, d, g*, had become voiced fricatives [v ð γ] and voiceless intervocalic stops, represented by *p, t, c*, had become voiced [b d g]. Thus, for the British and Irish the spellings *scribo modus lego dæmon populus pater ecclesia* represented pronunciations something like [skri:v(o) moð (us) le:γ(o) dẽvon pobul(us) pader egleš(a)]. A comparison of the spellings with the corresponding phonological forms shows that *m* and *p*, for example, have different values according to their position in a word: in word-initial position *m* and *p* represent [m, p] while medially they represent [ṽ b]. These and further examples allow a generalization that *p t c b d g m* had different values according to whether they occurred in word-initial position or in other positions in the word (i.e. /p t k b d g m/ and /b d g v ð γ ṽ/).

The Irish faithfully transferred the anomalies of this system into Old Irish spelling. For example, all the words just quoted were introduced into Irish during the British missionary period of the fifth and sixth centuries and in Old Irish documents are spelled *scríb-*, *mod*, *lég-*, *demon*, *popul*, *pater*, *eclais* (for pronunciation see 2.2. infra). The weakness of this system of orthography was that the contrast of voiced/voiceless in stops was not expressed in word-medial and word-final positions, and the contrast of voiced stop/voiced fricative was not expressed in word initially. Thus, *at* represents /at/ 'swelling', but *gat* represents /gad/ 'withe'; *a bó* represents either /a vo:/ 'his cow' or /a bo:/ 'her cow', and so on.[1]

1.3. The example *a bó* introduces a morphosyntactic feature, common to Celtic languages, called INITIAL MUTATION. This particular form involves the occurrence or nonoccurrence of the mutation generally termed LENITION. This mutation is expressed in the substitution of congeneric fricatives for stops and, of the other consonants relevant to this discussion, in the substitution of /h/ for /s/ and the elision of /f/ (i.e. L + f → ø). In fact, apart from *f* and *s*,[2] fricatives occurred in morpheme-initial position only in the context of lenition, but, since the spelling system was unable adequately to indicate voiced fricatives, it was unable to show all expressions of this important mutation. The lenition of /p t k/ → /f θ x/ was represented by the use of digraphs available from Latin orthography, i.e. by *p t c* → *ph th ch*, as in *popul*: *mo phopul*, *teg*: *mo theg*, *cat*: *mo chat*.[3] There was no corresponding method available of unambiguously indicating the lenition of /b m d g/ → /v ṽ ð γ/. Thus, the spelling *a bó* is ambiguous as is, for example, *a máthir* which represents both /a v ã: θ ir'/ 'his mother' and /a ma: θir'/ 'her mother'.

The mutation of /f/ → ø and of /s/ → /h/ came to be indicated by a clever extension of the use of the *punctum delens* of Latin manuscripts, e.g. *sétig* /se:d'iγ'/: *a ṡétig* /a he: d'iγ'/, or *fáilte* /fa:l't'e/: *ind ḟáilte* /ind a:l't'e/.[4]

In summary, then, the mutation of voiceless stops to voiceless fricatives was indicated by writing *h* after the initial consonant letter; the mutation of /f s/ → /ø h/ was shown by writing the *punctum* over the consonant letter; the mutation of voiced stops to voiced fricatives, because of a limitation inherent in the spelling system, was not expressed.

The other significant initial mutation, termed NASALIZATION or ECLIPSIS, involves the prenasalization of morpheme-initial stops. In the Old Irish period when the orthography was established, prenasalized voiced stops were still a feature of the language,[5] but prenasalized voiceless stops had, following a sound change which had occurred in Proto-Old Irish (e.g. /nk → g/), already become simple voiced stops. These were written according to the orthographical convention for representing voiced stops intervocalically, i.e. by the letters *p*, *t*, *c*. Thus, *a gabur* 'her goat' is distinguished from *a ngabur* 'their goat', but *a cat* represents either /a kat/ 'her cat' or /a gat/ 'their cat'. Again, then, an adequate expression of this mutation is lacking because of a fundamental limitation in the orthography.

1.4. The most exotic feature of Old Irish phonology which was required to be expressed by the new orthography was the contrast of palatalized/neutral/velarized consonants which by the Old Irish period had developed in word-medial and word-final positions (see Thurneysen 1946: 55).[6] These contrasts were indicated by writing *i* after *u o a* (*e*) to indicate palatalization of a following consonant, and by writing *u* after (*o*) *a e i* similarly to indicate velarization. This usage is illustrated by the singular paradigm of *ball* 'limb': *ball* /bal:/ nom.; *baill* /bal:'/ gen.; *baull* /bal:^{w}/ dat. Again, though, there are defects in the system: the neutral/velarized contrast cannot be marked if the nuclear vowel of the syllable is *u* or *ú* and equally the neutral/palatalized contrast cannot be marked if the nuclear vowel of the syllable is *i* or *í*, e.g. *dún* could represent /du:n/ or /du:n^w/, *min* could represent /min/ or /min'/.

2. THE CLASSICAL MODERN ORTHOGRAPHY

2.1. Over the centuries methods of rectifying these defects gradually emerged:

(i) *b d g m* came to be used in word-medial and word-final positions to represent /b d g m/ rather than /v ð γ ṽ/. This was made possible by the analogous extension of *h* – often now written as a suprascript and in free variation with the *punctum* – from use in combination with *p t c* to represent voiceless fricatives to use in combination with *b d g m* (i.e. *bh dh gh mh*) to represent voiced fricatives.

(ii) The nasalization mutation of voiceless consonants came to be indicated by writing the initial consonant double or by prefixing the relevant voiced consonant letter, e.g. Old Irish *a cat* 'their cat' was written *a ccat* or a *gcat*.

(iii) In the consonantal system the distinctive feature of velarization merged with neutral leaving a simple binary contrast of nonpalatalized-palatalized. This was more adequately expressed in the later spelling by a more complete system of glide letters: *o* was employed as a glide letter to mark nonpalatalized quality after *i*, *í*, e.g. /min/ is now written *mion* and /min'/ is written *min*. *a* similarly marked nonpalatalized quality after *e*, *é*, e.g. /fer/ 'man' is now written *fear*.[7]

2.2. The following sets of words illustrate the relationship between the Old Irish system and the later, or Classical Modern, system:[8]

Old Irish, from c. seventh century			*Classical Modern*, from c. fourteenth century	
a. The representation of voiced-voiceless stops:				
popul	'people'	/pobul^{w}/	*pobal*	/pobəl/
pater	'prayer'	/pad'er/	*paidear*	/pad'ər/
a cat	'their cat'	/a gat/	*a gcat*	/ə gat/
gat	'withe'	/gad/	*gad*	/gad/
eclais	'church'	/eglas'/	*eaglais*	/egləs'/
b. The representation of voiced fricatives:				
scríb	'write'	/skri:v/	*sgríobh*	/skri:v/
in bó	'the cow'	/in vo:/	*an bhó*	/ən vo:/
mod	'manner'	/moð/	*modh*	/moγ/
lég	'read'	/le:γ/	*léagh*	/le:γ/
demon	'demon'	/dẽvon/	*deamhan*	/dẽvən/
c. The elaboration of glides:				
toíb	'side (nom.)'	/təiv/	*taobh*	/tə:v/
toíb	'side (gen.)'	/təiv'/	*taoibh*	/tə:v'/
síl	'seed (nom.)'	/si:l/	*síol*	/si:l/
síl	'seed (gen.)'	/si:l'/	*síl*	/si:l'/
fér	'grass'	/fe:r/	*féar*	/fe:r/

2.3. While all of these orthographical developments had made their appearance by the end of the fourteenth century, they were not consistently applied in manuscripts by the majority of scribes until after they had been exemplified in the first printed books and thereby stabilized. Although a standard literary language was carefully maintained by the schools and a revised standard orthography was in principle available, the confusion of the Middle Irish period (c. tenth-thirteenth centuries) was continued into the classical modern period insofar as spelling was concerned.[9] The following entry for 1502 taken at random from the *Annals of Connacht* (Freeman 1944) illustrates the kind of fluctuation which was common (this entry would seem to be early sixteenth century):

> *Da ab do bi a n-imbresainn fa abdhaine Essa Ruaid i. Art h. Gallchobair 7 Eoin h. Loisde dfagbail pais fo cenn aonlai co n-oidhqi 7 aderaid gurob bass do luthghair fuair in fer deighenach dib.*

This can be normalized to classical modern spelling as follows:

> *Dá ab do bhí i n-immreasainn fa abdhaine Easa Ruaidh .i. Art ua Gallchobhair 7 Eoin ua Lóisde d'fhaghbháil bháis fo cheann aonlaoi go n-oidhche 7 adearaid gurab bás do lúthgháir fuair an fear déidheanach díobh.*[10]

By comparison with the normalized version the following features may be noted in the original passage:

(i) The accent marking long quantity in vowels is omitted throughout the passage.

(ii) The *a* glide indicating nonpalatalized quality in a consonant following *e* does not occur, e.g. *cenn, fer*; in polysyllables, however, the consonant quality is marked by a following glide, e.g. *imbresainn, aderaid*, or is indicated by the vowel letter of the following syllable, e.g. *Essa, deighenach*. The *o* glide does not occur in *dib*/di:v/.

(iii) The voiced labial stop is written *b* in *ab, abdhaine, bass*. The voiced labial fricative is also written *b* in *bi, dfagbail, dib;* in *pais* it is written *p* – a not uncommon type of confusion from the older system in which /b/ can be written *p* and, therefore, so can /v/ since in the present state of instability fricatives are not consistently marked (see iv below). The older dental fricative, now a velar, is written *dh* in *abdhaine, oidhqi*, but *d* in *Ruaid*; the sound change of dental fricative to velar fricative is reflected in the unhistoric spelling *deigenach*. The voiced velar fricative is written *g* in *dfagbail* but *gh* in *luthghair*.

(iv) The voiceless velar fricative is written *c* in *fo cenn* and *q* in *oidhqi*, rather than *ch*, etc.; this is the result of a negligence in writing the *punctum* or *h* arising from the fluctuation in marking voiced fricatives, e.g. *b* or *bh*, *d* or *dh*, etc.

2.4. Despite this kind of confusion a clear conception of the principles of the later system had obviously emerged by the sixteenth century, since they were fairly systematically followed and consequently firmly established by the first books to be printed in the language. The first was John Carswell's *Foirm na n-Urrnaidheadh*,[11] followed by Seán Ó Kearnaigh's *Aibidil Gaoidheilge & Caiticiosma*,[12] William Daniel's *Tiomna Nuadh*,[13] and the various publications of the Franciscans in Louvain beginning with Giollabrighde Ó hEodhasa's *An Teagasg Criosdaidhe*.[14]

All of the books printed in Irish during this period were motivated by the religious controversies of the time and were doctrinal or devotional in character. Yet their normative influence on the writing of the language generally was extensive as is clear from the fact that later Irish manuscripts of the seventeenth and eighteenth centuries have completely adopted the principles of the classical modern orthography. As a result, this automatically became the orthography which was adopted when Irish secular literature began to appear in print towards the end of the eighteenth century, beginning with the publication in 1789 of Charlotte Brooke's *Reliques of Irish Poetry*,[15] and gradually growing in volume as the nineteenth century progressed until the Irish revival activity[16] of the late nineteenth and early twentieth centuries brought about a vast increase of publications. Adherence to the classical modern norm by the Irish revival movement ensured that this was the orthography codified in Fr. Patrick Dinneen's immensely influential dictionary,[17] which was first published in 1904 and again in 1927, with the assistance of a subvention from the Irish government, in revised and enlarged form.

2.5. Even now this orthography exhibited some fluctuation and this was seized upon by Professor R. Atkinson in his submission to the Commission on Intermediate Education in 1899 when he argued that Irish did not merit inclusion in the intermediate curriculum because, *inter alia*, Irish speech and spelling lacked fixed form. At this time, though, variation was slight and Dr. Douglas Hyde, in his reply to the Commission, claimed with some justification that, if usage in regard to the spelling of unstressed syllables such as *-aigh/-uigh*, *-as/-us*, and of stop consonants after *s* (e.g., *sp-* or *sb-*) could be determined upon, then the greatest source of instability would have been removed (see De híde 1937).

3. THE DECLINE OF THE CLASSICAL MODERN NORM

3.1. In any event, the first decades of the present century saw a decline rather than an increase in the stability of Irish orthography. By the time Douglas Hyde came to write his autobiographical *Mise agus an Connradh* in 1931 he was moved to remark that 'Irish spelling is far more uncertain and far more irregular now than it used to be' (De híde 1937: 65). This was due to the fact that, following a period of controversy in which the position of Fr. P. Ó Laoghaire and his followers prevailed, the 'speech of the people' was adopted as the base for the modern literary language and the classical models were abandoned.[18] The objective now became 'the preservation of the existing spoken tongue and its elevation to the dignity of a literary language' (see Ó hIarfhlatha 1905). The result was an increased concern with the forms of the spoken language and a growing demand that the writer 'give us the language exactly as he speaks it himself, and as he hears it from the best native speakers' (see Ó hIarfhlatha 1905). Since the spoken language consisted of regionally diversified dialects, writers who felt that a faithful adherence to a particular variety ought to be reflected in spelling, as well as in grammar and lexicon, began variously to devise modifications of the classical spelling, which as a representation of any variety of the spoken language was in any case by now extremely cumbersome.[19] The following table gives some indication of the relationship between classical modern spelling and the principal variants of the spoken language:

Classical			Modern Variants		
Spelling		Phonology	(omitting stress differences)		
oidhche	'night'	/oγ'x'ə/	/i:x'i	i:hi	i:/
geimhreadh	'winter'	/gẽv'r'əγ/	/g'ĩv'r'əv	g'i:r'i	g'i:v'r'i/
samhradh	'summer'	/sãvrəγ/	/sãvrəv	saurə/	
adhbhar	'matter'	/aγvər/	/a:vər	aur/	
faobhar	'edge'	/fə:vər/	/fi:vər	fe:r/	
saoghal	'life'	/sə:γəl/	/si:l	se:l/	
bunadhas	'basis'	/bunəγəs/	/bonu:s/		

3.2. Predictably in this situation, disorganized attempts to modify the traditional spelling gave rise to a great deal of variation; and, apart from the lack of overall uniformity, most writers failed to achieve internal consistency. Initially, this state of affairs did not perturb the majority of those involved in the revival movement since it was argued that 'the exact representation of the words as they are uttered, as far as this is attainable with the material at our command, will neither increase nor lessen the dialectal varieties existing, it will merely enable the reader to pronounce with certainty where he may now be in doubt, while sparing the writer a considerable amount of worse than useless labour' (see Ó hIarfhlatha 1905).

3.3. One of the more extreme developments during this period was the *Letiriú Shímplí*[20] which was devised around 1910 by Osborn Bergin and Shán Ó Cuív in consultation with Fr. Richard O'Daly. This simplified spelling was based on a nonstructural analysis of the phonetics of West Cork Irish and derived many of its features from the spelling of English. For example, /i:/ was spelled *y* after nonpalatalized consonants in open syllable, e.g. *by* /bi:/ 'yellow', *dy* /di:/ 'blackness', *ly* /li:/ 'lying', *cry* /kri:/ 'heart', and *í* after palatalized consonants, e.g. *trí* /t'r'i:/ 'three', lí /l'i:/ 'complexion', tí /t'i:/ 'house (gen.)'; after nonpalatalized /s/, however, /i:/ is spelled *í* presumably because the English digraph *sh* is available to express /s'/, thus /si:/ 'sitting' is *sí*, /s'i:/ 'fairy' is *shí*. As even these few examples suggest, the *Letiriú Shímplí* was, in fact, an awkward spelling system and anything but simple, though, when one knows how to interpret it, it does fairly accurately express the dialect forms.

While the *Letiriú Shímplí* itself was too extreme a departure from traditional Irish orthography as well as too closely associated with a single variety of the language to have been widely adopted, it no doubt helped to encourage a more widespread abandonment of the classical modern norm and a more deliberate effort to reflect dialect in spelling.[21]

3.4. At the same time there were, of course, the conservatives who held that, in the light of the diversity of the modern dialects, the traditional classical spelling was the best solution to the problem of a standard orthography, and were concerned only that spellings be as historically accurate as possible, e.g. that /li:/ 'lying' be spelled *luighe* rather than *luidhe*, or that /bi:/ 'yellow' be spelled *buidhe* rather than *buighe*, and so on. This was the position of Fr. Dinneen whose Irish-English dictionary had an immense normative influence: 'It is believed that the interests of simplicity as well as uniformity, a uniformity that affords a working basis even for dialectic variations, are best served by retaining the traditional orthography' (Dinneen 1927: ix). This was also the position maintained by L. Mac Cionnaith S.J. who edited the government-sponsored English-Irish dictionary published in 1935.It prevailed up to the 1940's.

3.5. Middle ground was held by those who maintained that the more redundant features of the classical modern norm could be eliminated without weakening its effectiveness as an equitable orthographic expression for all modern varieties of the language. This seems, for example, to have been the position of Professor T. F. O'Rahilly.[22] In a contribution to a symposium on the standardization of Irish (see Lehmacher 1923) in a reference to the classical modern spelling he wrote: 'Such cumbrous spellings as *beirbhiughadh* (for *beiriú*), *imthighthe* (for *imithe*), *faghbháil* (for *fáil*), *urradhas* (for *urrús*) and *filidheacht* (for *filíocht*) would be a severe handicap on any language, and are simply impossible in the case of Irish if we really mean to give it a fair chance of life.' Since it was in fact possible to apply simplifications of the order proposed by O'Rahilly to a large part of the lexicon of the written language without loss of the level of universality of representation possessed by the classical norm, support for this degree of modification grew and eventually prevailed.

3.6. A diversity of approach and a great deal of instability was probably not a serious handicap while the cultivation of Irish depended entirely on voluntary enthusiasts. With the establishment of the Irish Free State in 1922, however, and the consequent promotion of the language in Public Administration and its establishment as an obligatory subject in all primary schools and subsequently secondary schools, the necessity for some degree of standardization began to be felt. In this situation, Irish academics, whose contribution could have been immense, remained aloof from, or even hostile to, the problems of redeveloping Irish as a national language. For example, Professor Osborn Bergin, the doyen of Irish scholars at the time, took the regionalist position and held that 'in a living language the spelling must be the servant not the master' (see Lehmacher 1923).[23] In this, as in so many other things, he had many disciples, and scholarly publications in Irish on the whole tended to be dialectal and maximally diversified in regard to spelling. For the moment, therefore, since expert assistance was not available, official and state-sponsored publications had little option but to remain conservative and continue to use the unwieldy traditional orthography.

The first attempt to break out of this mould was made when Mr. de Valera was preparing his new constitution which was enacted in 1937. He wanted the Irish language version, which was to be the first official version, to appear in what might be a universally acceptable and reasonably permanent form. To this end, he set up a committee, chaired by Professor

T. F. O'Rahilly, to work out a standard orthography.[24] It seems that the conservative and innovating factions on this committee were quite unable to agree and it broke up without having produced a set of definitive recommendations. In any event, with the exception of two modifications,[25] the Irish version of the first draft of the constitution, published in 1937, is in the classical spelling as codified in Dinneen's dictionary. O'Rahilly, however, submitted his own recommendations, presumably on the lines indicated in 1923, and these formed the basis for work on a new spelling norm which was then undertaken by members of the translation section of the Oireachtas staff.[26] Their recommendations, *Litriú na Gœilge*, were eventually published in 1945 and in a revised version in 1947.

4. THE NEW STANDARD SPELLING

4.1. The norm set out in *Litriú na Gœilge* was basically quite conservative. All the traditional features of Irish orthography were preserved.[27] The specifications made in it were of two kinds:

(a) In cases where usage had never been stabilized one particular variant was recommended, e.g. that *a* rather than *o* or *u* be written for the nucleus of unstressed syllables as in the second syllables of *easpag*/ aspəg/ 'bishop', *ioncam* /uŋkəm/ 'income', *solas* /soləs/ 'light'; or that *p t c*, rather than *b d g* be written for the second element of *s* clusters as in *speal* 'scythe', *stair* 'history', *scéal* 'story'.

(b) It recommends many of the simplifications in word structure of the type which had originally been proposed by O'Rahilly.[28] These involved the recognition of: (i) the development of single long syllables from older sequences of two syllables separated by a fricative interlude; (ii) the loss of fricatives from the initial or final position of consonant clusters with compensatory lengthening of the preceding or following vowel; (iii) the reduction of certain consonant clusters, the substitution of stops for fricatives, etc.

These changes in phonological shape and the corresponding changes of spelling recommended by the new norm are illustrated by the following tables:

Classical Spelling	Phonology[29]	Gloss	New Spelling	Phonology[30]
a. Reduction of earlier bisyllables:				
cuibhdhe	/kuv′γ′ə/	'more appropriate'	*cuí*	/ki:/
suidhe	/suγ′ə/	'sitting'	*suí*	/si:/
buidhean	/buγ′ən/	'troop'	*buíon*	/bi:n/
fighe	/fiγ′ə/	'weaving'	*fí*	/f′i:/
feadha	/feγə/	'wood'	*feá*	/f′a:/
meadhán	/meγa:n/	'middle'	*meán*	/m′a:n/
b. Reduction of sequences of unstressed syllables				
duilleabhar	/dul:′əvər/	'foliage'	*duilliúr*	/dil:′u:r/
bunadhas	/bunəγəs/	'basis'	*bunús*	/bonu:s/
ardughadh	/ar:dəγəγ/	'raising'	*ardú*	/a:rdu:/
ceanamhail	/kenəvəl′/	'affectionate'	*ceanúil*	/k′anu:l/
sgéalaighe	/ske:liγ′ə/	'storyteller'	*scéalaí*	/sk′e:li:/
filidheacht	/fil′iγ′əxt/	'poetry'	*filíocht*	/f′il′i:xt/
c. Loss of fricatives and compensatory lengthening:				
adhbhar	/aγvər/	'matter'	*ábhar*	/a:vər/
foghnamh	/foγnəv/	'functioning'	*fónamh*	/fo:nəv/
inghean	/in′γ′ən/	'daughter'	*iníon*	/in′i:n/
bradghail	/bradγəl′/	'thieving'	*bradaíl*	/bradi:l′/
d. Simplification of consonant clusters, substitution of consonants, etc.:				
líomhtha	/lĩ:vhə/	'polished'	*líofa*	/l′i:fə/
dearbhtha	/dervhə/	'definite'	*dearfa*	/d′arəfə/
ceardcha	/ker:dxə/	'forge'	*ceárta*	/k′a:rtə/
cródha	/kro:γə/	'brave'	*cróga*	/kro:gə/

4.2. When similar kinds of phonological change resulted in substantial divergences between the modern varieties, the decision normally was to retain the spelling of the classical modern norm. Change of the type outlined in a and c (above) in some phonological contexts, produces complex nuclei rather than simple long nuclei in many important varieties of the language. The classical spelling is then left unaltered as in the following words:

Classical and Modern Spelling	Gloss	Classical Phonology	Modern Variants
gabhar	'goat'	/gavər/	/gaur go:r/
domhan	'world'	/dõvən/	/daun do:n/
bodhar	'deaf'	/boγər/	/baur bo:r/
foghlaim	'learning'	/foγləm′/	/faulim′ fo:lim′/

rogha	'choice'	/roγə/	/rau rə:/
aghaidh	'face'	/aγiγ'/	/aig' ai a:γ'/
leigheas	'cure'	/leγ'əs/	/l'ais l'ε:s/
adhmad	'timber'	/aγməd/	/aiməd a:məd/

Of these, the diphthongal forms are generally the more common, but traditional Irish orthography has no more parsimonious way of representing them since diphthongs of this kind did not exist in the classical modern language. This deficiency is by far the most awkward feature of the modern Irish spelling system, as is illustrated by the cumbrous spelling of the relatively recent English loan words *price* and *size* as *praghas* and *saghas.*[31] In general, the principle of retaining the traditional spellings in cases of diversification is not a satisfactory one and is mainly due to conservatism. Thus, there seems to be no other reason why the nucleus of *gabhar domhan bodhar*, for example, could not be represented by a single grapheme, e.g. *ou* or *ow*, instead of by the diverse historical forms. Or to take another example, the retention of the historic spelling *-adh* for a verbal inflection which is variously pronounced [–əx –əg –əv] has been severely criticized on the grounds that, although the modern forms may be irreconcilable, the spelling *-adh* is not supported by any of them (see Ó Cadhain 1962).

4.3. On the other hand, when no changes to the graphemic repertoire of the traditional orthography were required, modifications of spelling were recommended, even though these are not warranted by a systematic collation of the variants of the spoken language. In this case the overriding principle was the achievement of simplicity of structure. Thus, the forms *cruaidhe* 'harder', *páighe* 'pay', *truaighe* 'pity' have been simplified to *crua*, *pá*, *trua* which represent a monosyllable pronunciation, /kruə pa: truə/,[32] despite the fact that significant varieties of the modern language have bisyllabic forms for these words, e.g. /kruəγ'ə pa:γ'ə truəγ'ə/. Yet the bisyllabic forms are in no way derivable from the new spelling, whereas the monosyllabic forms are derivable by a simple rule from spellings such as *cruaidhe* or better **cruaighe*, etc. The choice as norm in these cases would suggest that in the development of the new spelling, the principle of equity of dialect representation gave precedence to the search for simplicity of form when the latter was supported by a majority of the people consulted[33] and could be expressed within the graphemic limits of the traditional orthography, e.g. without the introduction of new diphthongal graphemes. Clearly, the new spelling norm represents a compromise between conservatism, on the one hand, and different approaches to reform, on the other, and, as with all compromises, it is not entirely consistent and few were completely satisfied with it.

4.4. The new norm has remained largely unchanged since it was published in final form in 1947. Its use spread rapidly. It was adopted immediately for official publications, then for school texts, grammars, etc. It was confirmed by Professor T. de Bhaldraithe's state-sponsored English-Irish dictionary published in 1959 and it will also be the norm for a new official Irish-English dictionary which is nearing completion. Nowadays, even when it is not adopted in detail by an individual writer, it forms his frame of reference, i.e. he modifies the modern rather than the classical modern spelling.

It was, of course, opposed both by regionalists and conservatives as well as by reformers who felt that the reform ought to have been more radical. The conservatives were, perhaps, the most bitter. An ultraconservative position is exemplified by Sceilig, pseudonym of Seán S. Ó Ceallaigh,[34] who in 1949 wrote: 'We got . . . some unnamed group to mutilate the traditional orthography which we should regard as a sacred heritage, an edifice of the intellect into which had been put the thought and judgement and progressive skill of our sages and evangelists for twelve hundred years.' He also argued, as conservatives had been doing for more than a generation, that the traditional spelling expressed paradigmatic relationships which simplification obscured and, for this reason, it expedited rather than impeded the progress of school children and others. Take, for example, the following table:

	1. Classical, 'explain'	2. Classical and Modern, 'praise'	3. Modern, 'explain'
2 sg. impv.	*mínigh*	*mol*	*mínigh*
verbal noun	*míniughadh*	*moladh*	*míniú*

The argument was that there is a clear similarity between the paradigms *mínigh-míniughadh* and *mol-moladh* and that this is obscured when the classical modern *míniughadh* is modified to *míniú*, as in column 3. The only flaw in this argument was that most users and learners of the language were, because of the great divergence between traditional spelling and pronunciation, scarcely aware of such nice paradigmatic parallels and, in the event, were more than willing to accept the modified forms.

4.5. One of the areas in which the new norm has been slowest in taking effect has been in the more scholarly activity of editing modern manuscript material of the seventeenth, eighteenth, and nineteenth centuries. This constitutes a vast corpus of modern Irish writing which, however, has been receiving rather less attention during the last twenty-five years than during the first half of the century. Both prereform approaches to the problems of modern Irish spelling are represented in editions of texts from this corpus. The more common and earlier practice was to emend manuscript spellings with reference to the classical modern norm. Thus, for example, Professor Tadhg Ó Donnchadha in his edition of Seán Ó Murchû's verse (Ua Donnchadha 1954)[35] from an autograph manuscript emended some of the latter's 'modern'[36] spellings as follows:

Ó Murchú's Spelling	Emended Spelling[37]	Gloss	Ó Murchú's Phonology	New Spelling
a ttíos	*i dtígheas*	'in householdry'	/i d'i:s/	*i dtíos*
tíocht	*tidheacht*	'coming'	/t'i:xt/	*tíocht*
chóir	*chomhair*	'proximity'	/xo:r'/	*chóir*
ríoga	*ríoghdha*	'royal'	/ri:gə/	*ríoga*

Ó Murchû's own spelling in these cases was much more in harmony with his own pronunciation and, accordingly, with the modern norm.

The other main approach was to edit texts in a spelling which reflected the speech of their author or place of origin as revealed by metrical correspondences, unhistoric forms occurring in the manuscript, etc. Apart from producing spellings which were uninterpretable except by the expert, this approach resulted in a great deal of internal inconsistency, even in the work of highly professional editors. For example, in an anthology of seventeenth century verse edited by Professor Cecile O'Rahilly (1952) /kri:/ 'heart' is spelled *cruí* and *croí* (classical *croidhe*, new spelling *croí*), /n:-n/ 'infant' is spelled *naoíon* (classical *naoidhean*, new spelling *naíon*), but the derived adjective is spelled *nuíanta*, and so on.[38]

Both approaches made such publications increasingly confusing to ordinary readers and students who more and more were being exposed only to the new norm. This has now at last begun to be appreciated and there is a consequent greater willingness on the part of editors of this material to take cognisance of the new standard spelling in their work. Not that their position is an easy one. They are constrained by the fear of censure by their more conservative colleagues, who are out of sympathy with the new norm, for breaking a basic principle of their discipline if they produce texts which are unwarranted by the manuscript tradition itself. Then, as well, because of the inconsistencies which remain in the new standard vis-à-vis the classical modern norm and the variants in the spoken language, and because since 1958 it has been closely associated with a new official grammatical norm, it has seemed to many editors too rigid in scope and too inflexible to express adequately the formal and stylistic range and distancing[39] which may characterise modern manuscript texts.

A recent attempt to harmonise the requirements of the new norm with hose of a manuscript text has been Professor de Bhaldraithe's edition (1970) of portions of the nineteenth-century diary of Amhlaoibh Ó Sûilleabháin. In this edition the principle of normalization was 'to adopt present-day spelling except when it was felt that the author's own spelling was a better representation of his speech'. This, however, is a prose text which escapes the added difficulties inherent in catering for the metrical structure of verse with its greater degree of phonological markedness and archaicism, but the same scholar has more recently formulated proposals for editing verse from modern manuscripts (de Bhaldraithe 1972). At any rate, it seems certain that the tide has now turned among textual scholars in favour of giving recognition to the new standard and that it will in future be their main frame of reference in regard to spelling. This application of the standard will undoubtedly increase its instability initially, but in the long term, since the need for a modern standard has now been accepted, the result should be the emergence of a more flexible and universally respected norm. Not that future changes will be radical; they will be merely the elimination of inconsistencies and an improvement of flexibility and range; for the foreseeable future it seems likely that the new standard spelling as outlined will continue to be the most acceptable compromise between the different possible approaches to the spelling of Modern Irish.

5. IRISH AND ROMAN CHARACTERS

No discussion of recent changes in Irish orthography could well omit some account of the question of script and type, especially, perhaps, since the man in the street is far more aware of changes which have taken place in this regard than in spelling per se.

5.1. The characters which were used in writing Irish in the manuscript tradition were an Irish development of the Roman characters which were used universally in Latin manuscripts in the early Middle Ages. The Irish variants of these characters, however, evolved divergently and were little influenced by later styles in Europe. Anglo-Norman influence, for instance, began to appear in the *Annals of Inisfallen* in 1197, less than thirty years after the Norman invasion, in the form of gothic characters for *f* and *s*.[40] In some later periods in the same Annals (e.g. 1253-1273), Irish was written completely in a fine gothic script. This proved to be an ephemeral fashion and Irish came again to be written in Irish characters, but the conflict between the two scripts seems to have resolved itself in a feeling that there was a distinctive script to be used exclusively for writing Irish. Thus, in sections of the *Annals of Inisfallen*, written in the fifteenth century, the convention of using Irish script for Irish and the gothic script for Latin emerged. This is in clear contrast with the earlier parts of the Annals[41] in which the same basically Irish script is used both for Latin and Irish. By the seventeenth century this was the established practice: Irish script was used for Irish and Roman script was used for quotations and names in Latin, English, and other languages.

5.2. The first appearance of the language in print was with the publication in Edinburgh in 1567 of John Carswell's translation of the Liturgy of John Knox. It was printed in the normal Roman type of the time. The first book printed in Ireland, Seán Ó Kearnaigh's *Aibidil Gaoidheilge & Caiticiosma*, was, like all books published in the language during that period, also religious in character. It was printed in Dublin in 1571 from a fount specially cut in London at the behest of Elizabeth I. For this type, letters resembling those of Irish manuscript writing were cut for *d e f g i p r s t* (Lynam 1924) which, apart from *p*, were the most divergent in the Irish script. For the rest, italic and Roman characters were used, but the overall visual effect is certainly of Irish manuscript writing and the concept of a distinctive Irish script was accordingly carried into print. William Daniel's *Tiomna Nuadh* was also printed from this type.

The use of Roman type would presumably have had associations with English and Elizabethan domination for Irish speakers and, whereas this was probably more acceptable in Scotland where it was in accordance with the teachings of John Knox that Protestant peoples should draw together and minimise their differences, in Ireland it would have been an impediment to the dissemination of the literature of the Reformed Church. On the other hand, the affective power and symbolism of the appearance of such literature in a distinctively Irish type would undoubtedly have been great, and it was presumably for this reason that the Elizabethan authorities incurred the trouble and expense of having it done – and for the same reason that the Franciscans had to hasten to emulate them. This situation presages what happened again in the early nineteenth century when the Irish Society found that hostile suspicions were overcome and interest in Bible-reading classes vastly increased when it had its Bible reprinted in an Irish type cut in London in 1818 by R. Watts (Lynam 1924).

After the type which was made for Elizabeth I, the next Irish fount was cut by the Irish Franciscans in Louvain for the printing of Counter-Reformation material. Their first publication was Giollabrighde Ó hEodhasa's *An Teagasg Criosdaidhe* which appeared in 1611. The Franciscans' type was a more exact replica of Irish manuscript writing and was undoubtedly influential in reinforcing the concept of a distinctive Irish type. At any rate, the Franciscan example of replicating manuscript letters was closely followed in the few founts which were cut for Irish between 1611 and the end of the eighteenth century: the fount of the Sacra Congregatio de Propaganda Fide (Rome, 1676); Moxon's fount (London, 1680); the fount of the Irish College (Paris, 1732); and the fount cut for Charlotte Brooke (1789).[42] Charlotte Brooke's *Reliques of Irish Poetry* was the first anthology of Irish secular literature to be printed. It marked the beginning of an involvement of the new upper classes with the indigenous literature and language of Ireland which, in the first instance, was inspired by the Romantic movement (see Breatnach 1965), and later grew into a permanent academic interest in Irish literature which, in turn, produced a gradual burgeoning of publications. There thus began a period of experimentation with types for Irish – five new founts appeared during the first twenty-five years of the nineteenth century (see Lynam 1924) – which continued throughout the century and produced some aesthetically fine types such as Petrie's (1841) and Thom's (1862). In the present century another attractive Irish type was designed by Colm Ó Lochlainn.

5.3. The *punctum* (*delens*), which initially was used as a marker of lenition of *f* and *s* and later was used in free variation with *h* as a marker of all fricative consonants, began increasingly in the printed texts of the nineteenth century to replace *h* altogether. By the end of the century when the Irish revival was under way, the *punctum* had completely ousted *h* and had come to be regarded as an integral feature of the Irish script. On the other hand, the use of *h*, as in the publication of John Carswell and James Gallagher, was regarded as the equivalent of the *punctum* in Roman script. This was perhaps an unfortunate development for Irish type as it entailed its having nine special letters[43] and so increased its vulnerability to the charge of impracticality. The only attempts made to break away from this distribution of the *punctum* and *h* were unhappily in the wrong direction: in his 1877 edition of Gallagher's sermons, Canon Burke used the *punctum* with Roman type and some years ago Liam Miller designed a new type in which the *punctum* was also used with Roman letters, except for *t* and *f* which were cut in the Irish style in order to combine more neatly with the *punctum*.[44] Since these attempts served neither the cause of practicality nor that of maintaining a distinctive Irish type, they found little support.

5.4. Roman script seems to have been unacceptable to Irish readers at the end of the sixteenth century. It was still so at the beginning of the nineteenth century when the Irish Society was at work. The same attitude continued to prevail after the revival movement had begun. Dáithí Ó hIarfhlatha (1905), for example, states that 'the Roman alphabet is to the great majority of readers inseparably connected with English sounds'; and E. W. Lynam held that 'Any one who is familiar with Irish in the Irish character will find not only difficulty but annoyance in reading it in Roman type. The language loses much of its individuality, just as Greek does in Roman Type.' Despite such sentimental attachment to the Irish type, the revival effort generated an inevitable pressure to adopt Roman type: it was more universally available, a fact which gained significance as writing in the language increased, and, after the foundation of the State, it greatly facilitated the printing of bilingual forms and other official documents. In addition to such pragmatic considerations, there was to be encountered the more emotive argument that Roman type gave written Irish a 'modern', 'progressive' appearance suited to its new status as a national language.

5.5. Roman type began, therefore, to be used extensively in the Irish publications of the new State. There was, of course, some vacillation. It would appear, for example, that, when L. Mac Cionnaith was preparing his English-Irish dictionary, his first instructions were that it be edited in Roman type, but these were subsequently reversed and it was eventually produced in Irish type. Similarly, the Irish version of the draft constitution of 1937 was in Irish type. However, the new spelling norm, published in 1945 and 1947, was in Roman type and, thereafter, the complete abandonment of Irish type was but a matter of time. Among state agencies one of the more dilatory in this regard was the Department of Education. For many years school texts had one chapter printed in Roman type to familiarize students with its use, but more than one generation of pupils had passed through school before the next logical step was taken. Eventually, though, the decision was made to adopt Roman type only; it had been introduced to all classes in primary schools by 1963-1964 and to all classes in secondary schools by 1970.

The situation, therefore, is that students now coming up to University find the classical modern spelling difficult, the Irish type perplexing, and a combination of both a substantial impediment to reading fluency. The task now, as yet scarcely begun, is to reproduce in modern familiar form for students and general readers alike what was worthwhile in the large corpus of Modern Irish writing which was published during the first half of this century.

NOTES

1. The orthographical representation of the Old Irish consonantal system can be summarized as follows (consonantal quality contrasts are omitted):

p	t	k		*p*	*t*	*c*	
b	d	g		*b—p*	*d—t*	*g—c*	
f	θ	x	h	*f ph*	*th*	*ch*	*ṡ*
	s				*s*		
v	ð	γ		*b*	*d*	*g*	
m(ṽ)	[n: n			*m*(*m*)	[*nn n*		
	l: l				*ll l*		
	r: r]				*rr r*]		

The letter *h* was used, somewhat haphazardly, as a morpheme-boundary marker in the case of morphemes with vowel initial, and not as the representation of /h/. When the latter represented lenition + /s/ it was written *ṡ* (see 1.3.), otherwise it was not expressed in Old Irish spelling, e.g. ***a hathir*** represents either /a haθir′/ 'her father' or /a aθir′/ 'his father'; these would at a later period be written ***a hathair*** and ***a athair***. In the case of the bracketed correspondences the spellings have remained unchanged to the present day and will concern us no further.

2. /h/, when not the expression of L + /s/, was itself a mutation of an initial vowel which was not indicated in the Old Irish spelling (see fn. 1).
3. The meanings are: 'community': 'my community', 'house', etc., 'cat', etc.
4. Meanings are: 'wife': 'his wife'; 'joy': 'the joy'.

5. They were later to become simple nasals, though the spelling has remained unchanged to the present day.
6. In the later language, neutral/velarized merged.
7. As stated, these innovations emerged gradually; the new system of glides came considerably later than the extension of *h* to combine with *b d g m*.
8. The orthographical representation of stops and fricatives in the Classical Modern system was (again omitting quality) as follows:

p	t	k		p	t	c				
b	d	g		*b* (*bp*)	*d*(*dt*)	*g*(*gc*)				
f		x	h	*f* *ph*		*ch*		*th*	*sh*	*h*
	s				*s*					
v		γ		*bh*		*gh*	*dh*			
m(ṽ)				*m* *mh*						

In these correspondences recognition is given to the later sound changes of /$\theta \rightarrow$ h/ and /ð → γ/ which must have characterized the colloquial standard of the Classical Modern period, though strict poetic diction may have been archaicizing in regard to these features.
9. This is all the more noteworthy since the majority of scribes of the period would have belonged to hereditary literary families and so were thoroughly acquainted with the grammatical norm.
10. *.i.* is the equivalent of *i.e.*, and 7 represents *agus* 'and'; both are still in use. *h* is an abbreviation of (*h*)*ua* 'descendant' which is common in patronymic surnames; its modern form is *ó*. The passage translates: 'Two abbots who were in contention for the abbacy of Eas Ruadh [*anglice* 'Assaroe'], i.e. Art Ó Gallchobhair and Eóin Ó Lóisde, died within a single day and night [twenty-four hours] of one another, and they say that it was of joy that the second one died.'
11. A translation of the Liturgy of John Knox, it was published in Edinburgh in 1567. Linguistically, it is in the standard classical literary language and, therefore, for our purposes not especially Scottish in character.
12. 'Irish Alphabet and Catechism', published in Dublin in 1571.
13. 'New Testament', published in Dublin in 1602.
14. 'The Christian Teaching', published in Louvain in 1611.
15. Though this, like any other publication before or after, had its share of unhistoric spellings.
16. The number of Irish speakers had declined from being perhaps 75 percent of the population at the beginning of the century to no more than 15 percent at the end.
17. A dictionary which a prominent writer and man of letters, Máirtín Ó Cadhain, suggested should be a bedside book for every dedicated writer of Irish (see Ó Cadhain 1969).
18. In fact a great deal of writing in a much more modern variety of the language existed in manuscripts from the eighteenth and nineteenth centuries, but the early revivalists were unacquainted with most of it. Séathrún Céitinn who died c. 1644 would have been regarded as the last representative of the classical period in prose.
19. The redundancies of the classical spelling were mockingly illustrated by M. Healy in the *Freeman*, October 1893, with a transliteration of the English *Our Father* which began: *Adhbhar feadar thughadh eart in theithbhean, thealóghad bí daghaidh naogham* . . . (quoted from de hÍde 1937: 64).

20. 'Simple Spelling'; this phrase in classical spelling would be *Litriughadh Simplidhe*; in the modern norm *Litriú Simplí*. On Bergin's involvement in this work see Bergin (1940).
21. Fairly consistent systems of representing local varieties without departing too radically from the graphemics of Irish orthography were developed for the publication of folklore material by, for example, K. H. Jackson, S. Ó Duilearga, and É. Ó Tuathail.
22. One cannot be completely sure, as in his editions of eighteenth and nineteenth century verse his practice was to normalize towards a regional spelling without maintaining a high level of internal consistency either (see de Bhaldraithe 1972).
23. Bergin's view was the common one that a scholar's responsibility was to maintain an 'objective' detachment and not get involved in planning, 'manipulation', etc.
24. And also, perhaps, morphology. I have seen no account in print of this committee or of its work; the information which is here recounted I received in conversation from Professor B. Ó Cuív, to whom I am indebted.
25. Namely, the plural morph *-eadha* and the verbal ending *-ughadh* are simplified to *-í* and *-ú* respectively (see 4.1. infra).
26. Oireachtas = Congress, i.e. both houses of Parliament.
27. *v* was introduced, however, to express /v/ and /v′/ when these occur in nonlenited word-initial position (i.e. in the base forms) in relatively recent loan words from English, e.g. *véarsa* 'verse', *vásta* 'waste', *vóta* 'vote'; *z* which went out of use after the Old Irish period is now being introduced again in the spelling of technical words, e.g. *ózón* 'ozone'.
28. Most of them are consistent with the simplifications he suggested in Lehmacher (1923).
29. The pronunciation indicated in this column is classical modern (colloquial) which had diverged from that represented by the spelling; thus, /suɣ′ə/ rather than /suð′ə/, etc., and /$\theta \rightarrow$ h/ (see fn. 8).
30. The phonological representation given here omits word stress which accounts for divergencies among modern variants, e.g. /dîl:′u:r/ or /dil′û:r/, etc.
31. The Irish *saghas* means 'sort, kind'; see Buck, *A Dictionary of Selected Synonyms in the Principal Indo-European Languages*, § 2.242, where not surprisingly the etymology is not discerned.
32. cf. 4.1 (a).
33. These included teachers of Irish in English-speaking areas (see Ó Cadhain 1962), who would naturally favour the adoption of the most simple and regular forms in all cases of divergence (cf. Ó Glaisne 1965).
34. In the *Capuchin Annual* (1949). S. S. Ó Ceallaigh had been Minister for Education and a prominent figure in the first Dáil (Parliament) and in the subsequent Anglo-Irish war.
35. Though this work did not appear until 1954, it almost certainly had been in the press with the notoriously slow Government Publications Office before the new spelling norm was published; Tadhg Ua Donnchadha retired in 1944 and died in 1949.
36. Seán Ó Murchú, sobriquet 'na Ráithíneach', died in 1762.
37. The emended forms are not always strictly classical: the accent in *tígheas* is unhistoric, for example; *chomhair* is a hypercorrection due to confusion with a

different word; this word *chóir* was always monosyllabic. And so on.

38. De Bhaldraithe (1972) has a complete account of editorially introduced fluctuation in these texts.
39. For example, some editors have not distinguished between an application of the spelling rules of the new norm and the 'simplification' of inflection. The distinction is not always easy to draw, of course, but the editor needs to be sensitive to matters of chronological distancing, etc.
40. *Annals of Inisfallen* (1933) and Mac Airt (1951). For illustrations of Irish script see Jensen (1970: Figures 518, 519).
41. *The Annals of Inisfallen* were begun in the eleventh century with compilations from earlier sources; the periods 1092-1214 and 1258-1285 consist of a series of contemporary entries. Altogether thirty-nine main hands have been distinguished in these Annals (see Mac Airt 1951), and they are, therefore, of great value for the study of Irish calligraphy and writing.
42. During this period a few Irish books were printed in Roman type, e.g. Fr. Theobald Stapleton's *Catechismus* (Brussels, 1639) and Bishop Gallagher's *Sixteen Irish Sermons* (Dublin, 1736). Fr. Stapleton not only used Roman type but a spelling system not dissimilar to *An Letiriú Shímplí* (see 3.3.).
43. For *p t c b d g m f s* with suprascript punctum.
44. The third edition of Myles na gCopaleen *An Béal Bocht* (1964) was printed in this type.

BIBLIOGRAPHY

Annals of Inisfallen, The
1933 Reproduced in facsimile, with a descriptive introduction by R. I. Best and Eóin Mac Neill (Dublin: Royal Irish Academy).

Bergin, O.
1940 'Obituary on Shán Ó Cuív', *Éigse* 2.

Breatnach, R. A.
1965 'Two Eighteenth-Century Irish Scholars: J. G. Walker and Charlotte Brooke', *Studia Hibernica* 5.

De Bhaldraithe, T.
1972 'An Litriú i bhFilíocht Aiceanta na NuaGhaeilge', *Ériú* 33.

De Bhaldraithe, T. (ed.)
1970 *Cín Lae Amhlaoibh* (Dublin).

De hÍde, D.
1937 *Mise agus an Connradh* (Dublin).

Dinneen, P.
1927 *Irish-English Dictionary* (Dublin: Irish Texts Society).

Freeman, A. Martin (ed.)
1944 *Annála Connacht* (Dublin).

Jackson, K. H.
1953 *Language and History in Early Britain* (Cambridge: Harvard University Press).

Jensen, H.
1970 *Sign, Symbol and Script*, translated from German by G. Unwin (London).
Lehmacher, G.
1923 'Some Thoughts on an Irish Literary Language', with comments by (i) Most Rev. Dr. Sheehan; (ii) Osborn Bergin; (iii) F. W. O'Connell; (iv) T. F. O'Rahilly; (v) Tomás Ó Máille, in *Studies.*
Lynam, E. W.
1924 *The Irish Character in Print* (Oxford). Reprinted with an introduction by Alf MacLochLainn (I.U.P., 1968).
Mac Airt, S. (ed.)
1951 *The Annals of Inisfallen* (Dublin).
Ó Cadhain, M.
1962 'Letter', in *An tUltach.*
1969 *Páipéir Bhána agus Páipéir Bhreaca* (Dublin).
Ó Glaisne, R.
1965 'Leasuithe ar Chaighdeán na Gaeilge', *Studia Hibernica* 5.
Ó hIarfhlatha, D.
1905 Various Notes, *Gaelic Journal* 15-16.
O'Rahilly, Cecile (ed.)
1952 *Five Seventeenth-Century Political Poems* (Dublin).
Thurneysen, R.
1946 *A Grammar of Old Irish*, English edition by D. A. Binchy and O. Bergin (Dublin).
Ua Donnchadha, T. i.e. Torna (ed.)
1954 *Seán na Ráithíneach* (Dublin).

Section Five

The Revision of Modern Writing Systems not associated with National Political Establishments

JOSHUA A. FISHMAN 12

The Phenomenological and Linguistic Pilgrimage of Yiddish: Some Examples of Functional and Structural Pidginization and Depidginization*

INTRODUCTION

This paper is the second (see also Fishman and Luders-Salmon 1972) in what I hope will ultimately be a series of case studies of the *normative* (i.e. preferred and institutionalized) EDUCATIONAL USE OF NONSTATUS VARIETIES OR LANGUAGES in speech communities with language repertoires in which more statusful varieties are also definitely present. The purpose of this series is to provide examples of educational-linguistic contexts that many teachers know to exist, but which so rarely seem to get written up that when they are they appear to be reversals or departures from the purportedly invariant allocation of the status language/variety and it alone to formal educational functions. Thus, it is my hope to combat a myth which claims that good schools are necessarily monolingual and acrolectal institutions.

This myth is erroneous and injurious. It harms educational planning not only in those parts of the world in which education has long been bilingual or bidialectal but also in those areas where bilingual/bidialectal education could greatly facilitate the educational process and foster its influence among segments of society that otherwise (and quite rightfully)

* From *Kansas Journal of Sociology* 10: 2 (Fall, 1973). Reprinted with permission. Dr. Fishman was on leave, 1970-1972, as Co-Director, International Research Project on Language Planning Processes, Coordinator of the Israeli Section thereof, and, 1970-1973, as Visiting Professor, Hebrew University, Jerusalem, when this paper was originally prepared for a conference on Creole Languages and Education, organized by the University of the West Indies, July 24-28, 1972. The author is deeply indebted to M. Schaechter and D. L. Gold for critical reactions to an earlier draft of this paper.

consider modern, formal education to be foreign, artificial, or devisive, if not all three at once.

The myth that I would like to counteract is not merely countereducational in the 'developing' and 'disadvantaged' nations and regions of the world, but it is also injurious to the relatively 'wealthy' and 'advantaged' of the world, among whom it fosters both insensitivity and intolerance toward the genuine repertoire of language varieties and societal functions that all complex communities reveal. Both language and society are ever so much more multifaceted than many schools seem to admit, and, as a result, the mutual and deleterious estrangement of schools from the parents and students whom they serve is furthered.

Like most myths the one that I would like to counteract through papers such as this stems from a confusion between what is self-serving and what is true. Thus, it is claimed that with the onset of modern mass education in nineteenth century Western and West-Central Europe only a single H-like variety of the official national language was admissible as target-and-process language of national school systems. This myth further claims (and, to an extent, legitimizes itself accordingly) that the monolingual/acrolectal situation sketched above was merely a continuation of an earlier classical or traditional educational pattern. In that prior period, too, this myth maintains, only an H variety, often a classical language not the mother tongue of either students or teachers, was normatively admissible as target-and-process language. Thus, modern burgeoise/mass education and earlier aristocratic/elite education are purportedly alike in their linguistic policies which proscribed their respective L-like varieties for such functions as writing, reading, and serious advanced study. While the myth grants that a variety of the L of one period often became the preferred H of the next, as a result of major social change and upheaval, the monolingual/acrolectal exclusivity of the school purportedly remained unchanged in principal.

Upon closer examination, this view appears to be more a superposed normative wish than an accurate statement of the normative facts in either period of history. Indeed, the documentable incidence of normative educational acceptability for other-than-H-like varieties (i.e. of varieties/languages not at all most-statusful, not at all most closely related to the central integrative symbols/processes, and not at all most closely related to the most powerful roles of society) is not at all negligible.

My concern here is not only that valid recognition be given to the informal language of students to each other, or to the language of teachers to elementary students, although such concerns too must not be deprecated. My concern is also that we recognize the large number of cases in which an H variety remained (and remains) the target language without thereby ever becoming the normal language of instruction or school discourse. It would be salutory, indeed, for all teachers of speakers of Black English, teachers of speakers of White English, and teachers of speakers of various kinds of Creole and Pidgin English, to know that the world-wide number of schools in which H-written texts are constantly read and discussed in an L-variety much more familiar to students and teachers, is truly legion. Indeed, education in much of Norway, England, Spain, Greece, much of the Arab world, and the United States to boot would be impossible were not the monolingual/acrolectal myth more honored in the breach than in the observance. Certainly, the myth as such was fully rejected in the Eastern European Ashkenazic case to which I will now turn. Here we find that a 'phenomenological pidgin' (see below) was normatively established in the company of a sanctified classical language, and so firmly was this the case that not even the coming of the Messiah was expected to alter its functional co-allocation to the domain of education.[1]

THE CASE OF YIDDISH

If we hold to Hymes' three-factor theory of pidginization (reduction, admixture, and intergroup use [Hymes 1971] it is not at all evident that Yiddish ever fully merited the designation of a pidgin. It is primarily the absence of any evidence of a crystalized (i.e. of a set or stabilized) reduction stage which leads me to question the appropriateness of this designation for Yiddish, but the fact that its intergroup function was also marginal deepens the doubts concerning its status as a pidgin. Thus the primary characterization remaining is that of admixture and this, indeed, is a characterization of which the Yiddish speech community itself has always been aware, to such an extent that segments of it themselves viewed the language as a pidgin. Indeed, from the end of the eighteenth century to the beginning of this century, it was not uncommon among Eastern European Jews to refer to Yiddish as *zhargon* and this designation is still encountered (though much more rarely) to this very day (Fishman 1975).

Although this was not always a pejorative designation (e.g. Sholem Aleichem often referred to Yiddish by this name, as did religious and other writers who were well-disposed toward its written use for important purposes), it did show widespread cognizance of the fusion nature of the language. Not uncommonly this fusion nature, related as it was not only to the recorded and remembered history of dispersions and expulsions suffered by the speech community, but also to awareness of the etymological components from Hebrew-Aramic, co-territorial and contiguous languages, led to a more or less negatively tinged view of the language on the part of many of its speakers. This negative view in reference to admixtures is relatable to Stewart's dimensions of historicity (Stewart 1968) in the sense that where historicity is viewed as crucial, admixtures – because of their greater recency – are likely to be more sensitively and negatively discriminated.

Thus whether or not Yiddish was a pidgin, it has always been widely evaluated as such, both within the speech community and without. In the history of Yiddish this phenomenological pidginization has been more important by far than whatever the linguistic facts of the case may be.

CONTRAST LANGUAGES

If it is the phenomenology of the speech community – rather than the typological expertise of linguists – which is crucial in determining the functional allocation of varieties, and this phenomenology in turn is frequently contrastively influenced by comparisons with the other varieties within the community's repertoire, at least two such contrast languages have always influenced the phenomenological (attitudinal, affective) and the functional position of Yiddish.

1. Hebrew. This classical and sanctified tongue has usually been viewed as a source language for all eternal Jewish pursuits. Thus, even when it was viewed as classical in Stewart's sense (i.e. when it was regarded as possessing historicity, standardization and autonomy, but lacking vitality), it was considered no less crucial as an object of study. Up until the latter part of the nineteenth century, Hebrew (and its sister-variety Aramic) was virtually the only target language for study of the Bible, the Talmud (Mishnah and Gemorah), the Commentaries, and the Prayer Book, i.e. of those texts which simultaneously defined the purpose and curriculum of the Jewish community's far-flung elementary, secondary, and tertiary schools. It was only the emergence of varieties of Jewish education, that devised curricula other than the traditional ones, that permitted Yiddish to be viewed in a school context other than contrastively vis-à-vis Hebrew. In this contrast Yiddish was not merely viewed as a dialect (or, at best, as vernacular) relative to a classical, but it was, as will be seen, often considered to be a pidgin relative to a classical. Nevertheless, every shred of evidence we have about the earliest stages of Yiddish (Weinreich dates Earliest Yiddish as roughly from circa 1000 to 1250; Mark does not use that designation and dates Old Yiddish from circa 1000 to 1348) indicates that it was quickly admitted to the function of language of instruction, i.e. of the language to be used in order to make the holy texts understandable to students whose mother tongue it was.

Interestingly enough, this instructional use for Yiddish provided it with a name or label in the community that may even predate the name 'Yiddish' itself. Among the earliest extant references to Yiddish are those utilizing the designation *loshn-ashkenaz* ('the language of Ashkenaz', i.e. of the land across the Rhine, or of the Jews dwelling therein) and *taytsh*. The latter is derived from some form of *tiutsch* (later *deutsch*), i.e. the local name for the local language in those parts. Among gentiles this noun was related to a verb which meant to render meaningful by translating into the vernacular. In Yiddish it came to mean 'meaning' or 'translation into Yiddish'. The Yiddish translation of traditional texts is referred to as *ivre-taytsh* (even today, in traditionally oriented Yiddish publications), although by now this designation generally stands for an archaic variety of Yiddish. The version of the Bible for women is known to this very day as the *taytsh-khumesh*, since women usually knew no Hebrew and, therefore, could not read the *khumesh* (Pentateuch) in the original. The designation *yidish* did not come to be the most common designation, at least not in print, until quite late (eighteenth century).[2] Certainly the role of Yiddish as the language of traditional instruction, of oral and written translation of sanctified texts, of scholarly disputation and, at times, of responsa and commentaries, had become firmly established centuries before.

The purpose of the above sketch is to counteract the view that where a firm diglossia relationship exists the L variety cannot be willingly and normatively admitted for formal and advanced educational purposes. Indeed, it can, provided the H variety is also given the deference which it is felt to deserve in the domains appropriate to it.

In the nineteenth century Yiddish was often viewed and referred to as the 'handmaiden' or 'servant' of Hebrew among carriers of 'enlightenment' seeking to reach the masses. Traditional circles used other but similarly L-implying designations, not so different from those formerly applied to Aramic or other post-exilic Jewish languages (Weinreich 1973) reviews the evidence with respect to several such in detail). Thus the deference distinction made it possible to accomplish two desirable goals simultaneously:

(a) to preserve the H status of Hebrew (a status which ultimately preserved it for twentieth century revival as a spoken language) and, yet,

(b) to enable members of the community to pursue studies in their mother tongue (this being no small matter in a community that prized universal male education)

Thus, one spoke Yiddish even for the most statusful functions, while one read and wrote Hebrew, even for obviously secular purposes. Traditionally, writers of Yiddish were almost as few and far between as speakers of Hebrew, although many males knew more than enough to do both in both languages.

2. *The Co-Territorial Vernacular(s).* The very fact that Yiddish came into being is itself testimony that there was an initial period of close contact with the non-Jewish co-territorial population. Although that contact was sufficient to lead to the well nigh complete displacement of Loez (Laaz), the Jewish language spoken immediately before settlement in the general area of Lorraine (Loter), it was not sufficient to make the inter-group communicative norms that *loshn-ashkenaz* originally followed (or shadowed) predominant also for intra-group purposes. Strong intra-group norms (particularly in conjunction with the infinite array of traditional practices requiring an extensive nomenclature not available in co-territorial languages) rendered any non-Jewish variety contrastively undesirable and nonfunctional for such purposes. This view long made non-Jewish varieties unacceptable for any educational purposes since education was long completely Jewish by definition. The process was not necessarily a conscious one at all, and the distinction between 'German' and 'Yiddish' (designations that became common only centuries later) need not have been in the minds of many (if any) speakers. Nevertheless, the structural and functional differences between inter-group and intra-group varieties of *loshn-ashkenaz* must have come into being quite early.

After the development of Yiddish from German-stock-upon-a-substratum-of-Hebrew-Aramic-and-Loez (Laaz) no further post-exilic language developed among Ashkenazic Jews. Why that is need not concern us here, although it represents a fascinating problem for between-group as well as within-group sociolinguistic analysis. What might well concern us here, however, is the fact that German, too, became a conscious model for part of the Yiddish speaking community. Even among German Jews, German was not admissible into the synagogue as the language of worship or into the schools as the language of instruction until far into the nineteenth century, by which time the majority of Ashkenazim had left Germany behind them for more than four centuries and had no more need of German than we do. Yet, unwelcome as it was 'for Jewish purposes', German remained a model which intruded upon Yiddish in the written language specifically and in the view that Yiddish was a pidgin more generally. For us to understand this development we must realize that German, in most of central and in much of eastern Europe, from the mid-sixteenth century and into the twentieth century, was the world language, the practical language of wider communication, the language of science, technology, and modernity; in short it was not only in contrast with Hebrew but also in contrast with German that Yiddish was viewed as being merely pidgin. Whereas German could not compete with Yiddish in so far as being the handmaiden of Hebrew, Yiddish could not compete with German in so far as nonsanctified respectability was concerned. Thus, two contradictory contrastive processes entered into the relationship between Yiddish and the languages with which its users most frequently compared it. On the one hand Yiddish was energetically de-Germanized (lexically) for contact-with-sanctity purposes. On the other hand it often seemed that in writing, particularly for more secular purposes ('secular literature'), it was just as energetically Germanized. At the same time Yiddish was both propelled toward and away from Hebrew with which it also had a 'double approach-avoidance' relationship. All of these processes can be most easily illustrated via orthographic examples, although lexical and phraseological examples abound and are more than amply cited by Weinreich (1953; 1973).

TOWARD-HEBREW DEVELOPMENTS

Yiddish, like all other post-exilic Jewish languages, seems to have been written in Hebrew characters from the outset.[3] As a result, perhaps, it generally adopted several Hebrew orthographic conventions: use of final letters, use of silent aleph before words beginning with vocalic *vov*/u/or *yud*/i/, the almost complete retention of traditional Hebrew spelling for words or forms of Hebrew origin, etc. Indeed, even words of non-Hebrew origin were long spelled in ways as to stress similarity with various Hebrew orthographic conventions, e.g. minimally representing vowels, the practice of writing Yiddish with Hebrew vowel points (even though this was, generally speaking, superfluous, one Yiddish orthography developed its own vowel indicators via letters and letter combinations), and, finally, writing the indefinite article as part of the noun to which it pertained, a visual pattern prompted by the absence of separate indefinite articles in Hebrew. In general, writing Yiddish developed in a community with a definite body of spelling conventions derived from another language (Hebrew) and these were only slowly and partially adapted to the genetically unrelated and less prestigious language.

AWAY-FROM-HEBREW DEVELOPMENTS

Wherever Germanic-origin grammatical morphs were added to Hebrew origin roots, there was long the convention of separating the two by parentheses, different typeface or apostrophes – a separation between the holy and the profane. In addition, since the Yiddish reader (particularly if female) could not always be expected to know Hebrew well, the practice of 'full spelling' became rather widespread for Hebrew words in Yiddish, since such spelling helped the reader pronounce words correctly that he might otherwise have mispronounced if the more traditional 'defective spelling' of Hebrew were utilized. The entire practice of established letter indications for vowels in Yiddish is a development away from Hebrew. When carried to its extreme, as it was by Soviet Yiddish publications, this led to a 'naturalized spelling' of words of Hebrew origin so that these were spelled like any other Yiddish words, i.e. with complete vowel representation much beyond what was called for by the 'full spelling' in Hebrew. The Soviets also discontinued use of final letters, thus making a major visual break with the tradition of Hebrew writing. The Yivo's reintroduction of a largely abandoned and originally Hebrew visual differentiation between /p/-/f/ (as well as between /s/-/t/ and /b/-/v/ and /kh/-/k/ in Hebrew-origin words), in a fashion no longer followed by modern Hebrew, may also be seen as an away-from-Hebrew attempt.[4]

TOWARD-GERMAN DEVELOPMENTS

For the longest time – indeed to this very day in some circles – Yiddish was (has been) spelled with attention paid to German orthographic conventions. As a result, the Yiddish syllabic /n/ and /l/, both of which are grammatical indicators, were long (and often still are) spelled according to German conventions that call for a vowel before either. Under nineteenth century 'enlightenment' pressure, Yiddish spelling became replete with silent *h*'s and unneeded *e*'s in order to mirror German usage. Yiddish /v/ has been written *f*, /i/ has been written *ie*, and various other similar practices might be noted, not always necessarily because of original modeling on German, but such modeling certainly helped retain these conventions when the original dialectal reasons no longer obtained. Basically, the entire phonological principle in Yiddish spelling (as opposed to the etymological principle which dominated Hebrew spelling) may be viewed as a de-Semitization or Westernization, if not only a Germanization, of older Jewish writing conventions. A more definitely German influence has been that which led Yiddish writing to recognize word boundaries in print on a German model, particularly as conjunctions and the definite article are concerned. To this list may be added a few lexical items that, though derived from Hebrew, have generally been 'naturalized' by most Yiddish writers, e.g. *balebos*, *shmuesn*, *klezmer*, *shekhtn*.

AWAY-FROM-GERMAN DEVELOPMENTS

Modern (twentieth century) pro-Yiddish movements and their linguistic guardians adopted the slogan 'further from German'. The past half-century of Yiddish linguistic effort is marked by a strong *ausbau* effort (to use Kloss's [1967] concept) vis-à-vis German. This is particularly true in lexical matters, but, of necessity, has had its orthographic counterparts as well. Thus the dropping of the several German spelling conventions just enumerated, above, has been a prime goal of almost all modern Yiddish orthographic schools (Schaechter 1972).

BIPOLAR, DOUBLE APPROACH-AVOIDANCE

Lest it seem that 'further from German' necessarily meant 'toward Hebrew' or vice versa, in the sociocultural development of Yiddish orthography, it should be stressed that this was not the case. All four possible positions came into being, as indicated by Figure 1, below, although the modern period tends to be one of 'away' movement on both dimensions, just as the earliest period was one of toward modeling on both.

German \ *Hebrew*	*Toward*	*Away from*
Toward	1. 'Traditional' Yiddish spelling, well into the middle of the nineteenth century. Found today in reprints of 'old favorites'.	3. 'Enlightenment' publications (of the middle and latter nineteenth century) seeking to simplify Hebrew constructions (e.g. via 'full spelling') and to stress secularity via similarity to German.
Away From	2. Modern 'religious' literature, e.g. texts of the *Bnoys Yerusholayim* schools in Israel and the revised spelling of the religious schools in pre-World War II Poland.	4. A less extreme form is that of the Yivo's 'standardized Yiddish spelling'. A more extreme form is that of the Soviets, particularly 1920's to 1940's. Even more extreme recommendations have received scanter attention.

Figure 1. Four Systems of Yiddish Orthography

AWAY-FROM-PIDGIN MENTALITY

Yiddish has classically had a double inferiority complex. Vis-à-vis Hebrew it was but a companion, accessory, or handmaiden; vis-à-vis German it was a fusion language without historicity, autonomy, or standardization. Its centrality to the entire Jewish educational experience for nearly a thousand years of Ashkenazic history did not save it from being viewed as a pidgin. Only certain modern Jewish cultural movements, arising during the first quarter of the twentieth century, have dared view it as worthy in its own right. As such, it was declared to be 'a Jewish national language' at a language conference in 1908 attended by most major Yiddish writers and language activists. As such, it became not only the medium of instruction but also the object of instruction in modern Jewish schools (usually with a socialist or nonpartisan ideology, but sometimes with a Zionist or Communist ideology). As a result, the traditional Hebrew-Yiddish diglossia was disturbed by such schools as well as by other modern Jewish movements.

Jewish education in the twentieth century has been increasingly monolingual: either in Hebrew, in Yiddish, or in the co-territorial vernacular. In many 'Yiddishist' schools, Hebrew sources were initially not studied at all, later studied only in Yiddish translation and abbreviation, and, more recently, have been reintroduced in abbreviated and simplified Hebrew versions. These are the very schools in which the orthographic and the more general linguistic independence of Yiddish has been most stressed. Thus functional changes in Yiddish (vis-à-vis education) and structural changes in Yiddish (vis-à-vis models and antimodels) have tended to go hand in hand (Fishman i.p.,a.).[5]

SUMMARY AND CONCLUSIONS RE YIDDISH

The case of Yiddish reveals that a phenomenological pidgin may be treated similarly to a pidgin/creole defined in accord with linguistic criteria. Like the latter, it may be held in lower repute by its own users, relative to other varieties in the community's repertoire that seem to be more homogeneous because their historicity is unknown or sanctified.

Like many phenomenological and/or linguistically defined pidgins/creoles, Yiddish came into more diversified educational and symbolic high cultural use only as a result of far-going social-cultural-political changes in its speech community. This change invariably required both disruption of the classical diglossia pattern (Hebrew = *H*; Yiddish = *L*) which previously existed, as well as the structural modification of the language to render it more fit for the new functions assigned to it. In this respect Yiddish illustrates that phenomenological pidgins must experience processes similar to those experienced by all modern vernaculars before and when they are assigned wider functions.

Nevertheless, unlike most phenomenologically and/or linguistically defined pidgins/creoles, Yiddish was admitted into important educational functions of a traditional sort from the very outset. However, this did not keep it from being viewed as of lesser worth than either of the contrast languages with which the community commonly compared it vis-à-vis the domain-appropriate functions of those languages. Only with movements striving for education-for-modernization did some portion of the Yiddish speech community abandon the phenomenological pidginization that had hitherto generally marked user's views of this language and which had restricted the functions for which it was presumably fitted.

GENERAL SUMMARY AND CONCLUSIONS

Before bringing this presentation to a close I would like to tentatively raise the question not only of when a co-occurrence like the one presented above is likely to obtain (since the co-occurrence of *L* and *H* in school is really so frequent as to be the disguised rule rather than the exception that it is often made out to be), but also of when it is likely to be the preferred, avowed, and institutionalized *practice*. It seems to me that a more vernacular-like process language and a more vernacular-distant target language are likely to normatively co-occur when two other desiderata are met: (1) When the admission of the *L*-like variety as the process language of the school does not threaten the functions of the *H*-like variety as target language and as language of even more statusful role relations than those controlled by the school per se. Thus, the *H*-like variety continues to be normatively much needed and wanted, both in school and out of the school, and the *L*-like variety is viewed not as a threat, but rather, as an avenue for attaining the target, even, as sometimes happens, when the *L* variety, too, is elevated to writing. (2) When 'mastery of *H* by all students' (idyllic though that would be) and 'good education for all students' (idyllic though that would be) are not considered to be identical goals, even if they do tend to be viewed as increasingly overlapping as higher education is approached and reached. Indeed, when put to the acid test, such communities opt for 'good education for as many as possible' rather than for elitist education for the few, i.e. for *H* as a subtarget in a hierarchy of targets rather than for *H* as the prime and only target.

Finally, let me admit that a relatively delicate balance of forces is involved. As long as teachers and students are from the same speech community, share the same behavioral (including language behavior) norms and values, role access is high, role compartmentalization is low, and disturbing outside influences are kept to a minimum, the balance can maintain itself without great difficulty. If it is upset and the well-known cycle of *L*-displacing-*H*-so-as-to-become-*H*-itself is established, then the former *L* will inevitably also change rapidly in structure, rather than merely in function. Such change, in accord with whatever models and anti-models are in socio-cultural (and therefore in linguistic) vogue, will repeatedly reveal the extent to which particular networks of users have or have not rejected the earlier allocation of societal roles and language functions that formerly obtained in the speech community as a whole, when *L* was not yet widely written and not yet widely viewed as a target in the educational system.

NOTES

1. Not only was it believed that Jews would continue speaking Yiddish on weekdays (but the Holy Tongue on Sabbaths) when the Messiah came, but that one of the means by which the good Lord had compensated Moses for not permitting him to enter the Promised Land was to let him see into the future and thereby to witness little boys studying the Pentateuch in the original accompanied by an oral Yiddish translation. Thus, Yiddish and Hebrew were viewed as symbiotic not only in the present, but in the past and future as well. Accordingly, some orthodox Jews spoke (and some still speak) Hebrew on Sabbaths and Jewish holidays, both in order to intensify the holiness of such days as well as to maintain oneself in readiness for the Messianic Age.
2. The earliest extant printed reference to *yidish* is in *kine af gzeyres-ukraine* [Lament on the Evil Events in the Ukraine] (Amsterdam, c. 1649).
3. Italic ('Judeo-Italian') written in Latin letters dates only from the nineteenth century, and so, it seems, does Dzhudezmo when written in Latin characters.
4. Yivo orthography calls for, respectively: בֿ - בּ ; כֿ - כּ ; תֿ - תּ ; פֿ - פּ
5. The following four spelling of *Kibed av ve-em* (honoring one's mother and father) illustrate the four major present-day orthographic approaches in Yiddish with respect to Hebraisms:

Traditional:	כבּוד אב ואם
Simplified ('full'):	כּיבּוד אב ואם
Soviet (naturalized):	קיבּעד אַוו וועיים
Yivo (standardized):	כּיבּוד־אַבֿ־ואם

BIBLIOGRAPHY

Fishman, Joshua A.
1975 'The Sociolinguistic Normalization of the Jewish People', in *A. Hill Festschrift*. (E. C. Polome, ed.) Austin, Univ. of Texas Press.
i.p.a. *Readings in the Sociology of Yiddish.*

Fishman, Joshua A., and Erica Luders-Salmon
1972 'What has the Sociology of Language to say to the Teacher? (On Teaching the Standard Variety to Speakers of Dialectal or Sociolectal Varieties)', in Cazden, Courtney, Vera P. John, and Dell Hymes (eds.), *Functions of Language in the Classroom* (New York: Teachers College Press), 67-83.

Hymes, Dell
1971 'Introduction', in Dell Hymes (ed.), *Pidginization and Creolization* (Cambridge: Cambridge University Press), 65-90.

Kloss, Heinz
1967 '"Abstand Languages" and "Ausbau Languages"', *Anthropological Linguistics* 9: 7, 29-41.

Schaechter, Mordkhe
1972 *Yidishe ortografye: Konspekt fun a kurs* (New York: Benyumen Shekhter Foundation for the Advancement of Standard Yiddish).

Stewart, William A.
1968 'A Sociolinguistic Typology Describing National Multilingualism', in J. A. Fishman (ed.), *Readings in the Sociology of Language* (The Hague: Mouton), 531-545.
Weinreich, Max
1953 'Yidishkayt and Yiddish: On the Impact of Religion on Language in Ashkenazic Jewry', in *Mordecai M. Kaplan Jubilee Volume* (New York: Jewish Theological Seminary of America). Also in J. A. Fishman (ed.), *Readings in the Sociology of Language* (The Hague: Mouton, 1968), 382-413.
1973 *Geshikhte fun der yidisher sphprakn* (New York: Yivo Institute for Jewish Research). An English translation is in preparation.

DAVID L. GOLD

Successes and Failures in the Standardization and Implementation of Yiddish Spelling and Romanization

I. INTRODUCTION[1]

A. Background

In a nutshell, the history of Yiddish spelling is that of adapting the alphabet of a Semitic language (Hebrew-Aramic) and the orthographic traditions of one Semitic and two Romance languages (Western and Southern Laaz) to the phonology of a Germanic one.[2] Although the oldest dated extant running text is from the thirteenth century, it can be assumed that writing in Yiddish began as soon as Jews settled in appreciable numbers on Germanic-speaking territory, i.e. some two or three hundred years earlier.[3] Especially for the earlier stages of Yiddish, it must also be assumed that most writers of Yiddish (letter writers, copyists, scribes, literati) were also proficient in Hebrew-Aramic and, during the period of Laaz/Yiddish bilingualism, in one of the Laaz languages, too. Early Yiddish spelling, indeed, does show the influence of Hebrew-Aramic and Laaz norms, several of which are still followed today.[4]

Some of the problems encountered in adapting the Hebrew alphabet to Yiddish were

(1) how to represent new phonemes such as /č/, /ž/, and /ǰ/, the correlation of palatalization acquired under Slavic influence, and front rounded vowels (all of which were not found in Hebrew-Aramic);

(2) how to ensure phonemic representation in a language with more phonemes than graphemes;

(3) how to utilize graphemes with identical phonological values.[5]

B. Periodization

In terms of approaches to the problems of Yiddish spelling, four periods can be distinguished:

(1) the era of individual experimentation without express formulation of rules;

(2) the era of appending spelling rules to books (not necessarily grammars);

(3) the era of articles and debates in print, with proposals for codification or reform;

(4) the era of national or international conferences with publication of detailed codexes and orthographical dictionaries.[6]

In terms of actual spelling conventions, three main periods stand out:

(1) that of traditional spelling (with various subperiods of purely linguistic interest);

(2) that of Germanized spelling; and

(3) that of neotraditional spelling (with several offshoots).

The second, and especially the third, periods will be discussed in some detail in this paper.

C. Orthographic Principles

The various systems that arose in each of these periods can be compared with one another by reference to several principles of orthography which have at one time or another been suggested or actually implemented by various writers or spelling codexes:

(1) PHONEMIC principle: all phonemic oppositions must be represented graphically;[7]

(2) MORPHOPHONEMIC principle: if the phonemic principle obscures visual identity between phonologically conditioned allomorphs of the same morpheme, all such allomorphs must be spelled identically;[8]

(3) ETYMOLOGICAL principle: words must be spelled as in the source language;[9]

(4) INTERDIALECTAL principle: orthography must not be based on any one regional variety, but constructed in such a way that all speakers can read and write it with a minimum of difficulty (i.e. the graphemes must represent diaphones and diamorphs);[10]

(5) HISTORICAL principle: deeply rooted traditions must be maintained;[11]

(6) principle of DIFFERENTIATION OF HOMOPHONES;[12]

(7) principle of FREEDOM OF CHOICE: each member of the community may spell as he chooses.[13]

Most of these principles conflict with one another and the differences between one codex and the next lie mostly in how the conflicts were resolved, i.e. in the various possible hierarchical orderings of the principles.

The main feature of Germanized spelling (which arose in the nineteenth century) was its emphasis on the etymological principle. Since 'Yiddish is corrupt German', so the 'argument' ran, 'the norms of the pure and correct language should be extended to the bastard variety too'. That Yiddish and German employed different alphabets was no barrier to German orthographic influence since many graphemes in Yiddish were by convention identified with German counterparts, e.g. *ayen* /e/ = German *e*, *hey* /h/ = German *h*, etc. The more or less morphophonemic spelling of the late traditional period was thus largely abandoned in favor of a foreign norm: Yiddish spelling was 'spruced up' with silent letters, superfluous doubling of consonantal graphemes, and other slavish imitations of German orthography.

With the rise of a healthier attitude towards Yiddish at the end of the nineteenth century, there came a return to the traditional norms (see, for example, Sholem-Aleykhem 1888).[14]

In essence this meant a return to the (morpho)phonemic, interdialectal, and historical principles, employed until the germanicizing period. With respect to the etymological principle, however, the new systems diverged: although all of the neotraditional codexes largely abandoned it with regard to the Germanic, Slavic, and international components, opinion was divided with respect to words of Hebrew-Aramic origin, which in the traditional system had almost invariably been spelled as in the source language, e.g. ⟨mʔkl⟩ 'dish' /majxl/, not ⟨myy^{a}kl⟩: The Soviet system, developed in the 1920's, abandoned the etymological principle entirely (cf., however, section II. B. below), whereas the other two neotraditional systems preserved it.

With the abandonment of Germanized spelling, the principle of differentiation of homophones could not be followed, since its implementation depended almost entirely on the availability of 'silent' letters used in imitation of German orthography, e.g. /štejn/: ⟨styyn⟩ 'stone' ≠ ⟨stδhδn⟩ 'to stand' (cf. German *Stein* vs. *stehen*).[15] And in all systems, principle (7) applies only to personal names, i.e. an individual may write his given and family names as he wishes.

II. THE INTERBELLUM PERIOD

The years from 1918 to 1939 saw one of the most creative periods in Jewish culture, with the mushroom growth of new types of Jewish schools from the primary to the university levels, the flowering of Yiddish literature, journalism, and theater, the founding of Jewish research and cultural institutions, the development of sophisticated language planning, and the emergence of a sense of language loyalty among ever growing segments of the Yiddish-speaking community.

Interest in spelling reform and codification was a natural concomitant of these developments. Debate in newspapers and magazines continued, but work now also proceeded in a more orderly fashion: through teachers' commissions in Warsaw (see Kahn 1972), Vilna, Bialystok, Riga, Kiev, Minsk, and Kharkov, and through the newly established research institutions (the Yiddish Scientific Institute – now the YIVO Institute for Jewish Research – and the Jewish divisions of the Belorussian and Ukrainian Academies of Science). Three major codexes were the result of these labors:

(1) the Standardized Yiddish Orthography (SYO), elaborated by the YIVO and the TSISHO (Central Yiddish School Organization in Poland) in the 1930's, which traces its roots largely to Max Weinreich's proposals of 1930 (M. Weinreich 1930) and ultimately to Zalmen Reyzen's of 1920 (Reyzen 1920);

(2) the Soviet system, largely the work of A. Zaretski, stemming ultimately from Veynger's 1913 proposals (Veynger 1913a; 1913b);

(3) the Orthodox system, elaborated (entirely?) by S. A. Birnbaum (1924; 1929; 1930; 1931; 1938; 1944; Szajkowski 1966: 29-30).[16]

The degree of success which each of these codexes enjoyed before the Holocaust depended largely on the means of implementation each had at its disposal. Where codification and implementation could proceed by governmental decree (as in the Soviet Union), the relevant codex became almost universal, at least in print (cf. Kupershmid 1930); the fate of the other two, which lacked government support, was correspondingly less bright. The Orthodox system was implemented in the *Beys-Yankev* schools, with 20,000 pupils (cf. Birnbaum 1960) and in several Orthodox publications. The SYO was of course obligatory in all YIVO and TSISHO publications and 'had won other positions' too (Schaechter and Weinreich 1961: 6).

The murder of six million Jews, about five million of whom were

Yiddish-speakers, at the hands of the Nazis and their collaborators all but wiped out the central and eastern European Yiddish-speaking communities. Spelling usage among the small Yiddish-speaking groups that did survive in Poland and Rumania will be discussed together with Soviet spelling (section II.B. below).

Since the most hotly and most widely debated point in the 1920's and 1930's was the etymological principle as applied to the Hebrew-Aramic component, a fuller discussion of this principle and of Soviet spelling in general is in order.

A. The Spelling of the Hebrew-Aramic Component

As Yiddish spelling moved farther away from Hebrew-Aramic norms (cf. fn. 4), a dual-track spelling emerged whereby most Hebrew-Aramic words continued to be spelled more or less etymologically, but most other words eventually came to be spelled (morpho)phonemically. Endowed, so to speak, with a degree of sanctity (cf. *loshn-koydesh* 'language of holiness' = Hebrew-Aramic), their traditional spelling remained largely unaltered (cf., however, Gold i.p.a.).

The morphophonemic spelling of this component (hereafter RESPELLING) was first proposed, it seems, in the twentieth century.[17] According to Halpern (1926), the Warsaw newspaper *Der Veg* had printed fictitious letters-to-the-editor with respellings c. 1906-1907; intended as a joke, these 'letters' caught Halpern's eye, who then submitted an article on the need for respelling. In refusing the article, the editor of *Der Veg* claimed that respelling was a sign of 'ignorance', that it would represent too sharp a break with tradition, and that the newspaper, which received real letters with respellings anyway, did not want to legitimize such 'errors'.

Nathan Birnbaum proposed respelling at the Czernowitz Yiddish Language Conference of 1908 – a gathering of Yiddish-speaking literati, journalists, and community leaders interested in promoting the use and rights of the Yiddish language – as did Zhitomirski three years later (M. Weinreich 1930: 36; 225), but it was Veynger (1913a; 1913b) who first used respelling as a matter of principle. A more conservative suggestion was made by Borokhov (1913) at the same time, viz. that respellings be permitted for those words whose Yiddish pronunciation differed considerably from their Hebrew-Aramic pronunciation, e.g., *bal*(*e*)*bós* 'boss' (Ashkenazic Whole Hebrew /baálhabáyis/).[18]

Momentum for respelling gathered after the First World War, especially in secularist circles. At the 1921 School Conference in Warsaw, for example, a resolution calling for respelling got only one vote, but at the Yiddish Press Conference in Vilna six years later, a similar resolution got thirteen out of twenty-nine votes. Quite surprisingly, the Rabbi (!) of Irkutsk suggested in 1926 that respelling be permitted as an alternative to the traditional orthography, and that vowel points (*nekudes*) be used if the latter were preserved (Beylin 1926). Orthodox circles, however, were opposed to any 'tampering' with the etymological spellings.

Max Weinreich's *Shturemvint* (1927) respells less frequent Hebrew-Aramic-origin words in footnotes (the body of the text retaining the traditional spelling), either as a pedagogical aid or as a cautious sounding out of public opinion.[19]

As early as 1920, a group of Yiddish poets who had settled in the United States came out in favor of respelling, mainly for esthetic and rationalist reasons.[20] That pressure for abandonment of the etymological principle became so great in the following decade can be seen from the fact that two of the three spelling conferences organized under YIVO auspices in 1931 approved resolutions calling for respelling (those held in Vilna and in Buenos Aires [*Barikht* . . . 1931; Szajkowski 1966: 33]), with only the London conference voting it down (Szajkowski 1966: 34).

Since these meetings had only advisory powers, the Philological Section of the YIVO, which was charged with the definitive redaction of the rules, was not bound by their decisions. In effect, the Standardized Yiddish Orthography, as embodied in the Rules of 1937, did not provide for respelling, not even as an alternative. We may surmise that this was due to fear of alienating religious, Hebraist, and Zionist circles, a desire to avoid too radical reforms,[21] and, especially, a desire to avoid identification with communist circles.[22] According to Zosa Szajkowski, the YIVO also wished to avoid displeasing the then anticommunist regime in Poland (oral communication).

B. Soviet Reforms

Taking postrevolutionary Russian orthographic reforms as their model, Soviet Yiddish linguists began reforming and codifying Yiddish orthography during the 1920's and arrived at a definitive codex by the early 1930's. Unlike Yiddish language engineering in other countries, Soviet Yiddish linguistics ('linguotechnics') did not have to reckon with possible opposition from religious, Zionist, Hebraist, or other conservative circles;

language reform, moreover, could proceed by governmental decree, a distinct advantage which other orthographists did not enjoy.

The major reform, decreed in 1920, was the respelling of Hebrew-Aramic-origin words, motivated on these grounds:

(1) the traditional spelling was a religious/bourgeois vestige incompatible with the new declericalizing/socializing ideology;

(2) one etymological component of the language should not be spelled differently from the others;

(3) respelling was a step towards the total 'rationalization' of the language;[23]

(4) with the virtual disappearance of traditional education in the Soviet Union (*kheyder*, *talme-toyre*, *yeshive*), even fewer Yiddish users than before were acquainted with Hebrew-Aramic (cf. fn. 4) – this was true to a large extent in other countries too;

(5) it was therefore hoped that Yiddish users both within and without the Soviet Union who had previously found it hard to read their own language would now be attracted to the Soviet Yiddish press and literature;[24]

(6) respelling would, it was expected, eliminate mispronunciations.

The second, even more radical break with tradition and with spelling reform/codification in other countries was the elimination of the word-final allographs of five graphemes. Unlike spelling, which affected thousands of words and was motivated on reasonable grounds, elimination of the allographs was quantitatively minor (the seventeen remaining graphemes having only one realization), and Soviet Yiddish linguists were therefore hard put to explain why such a minor improvement was worth the high price of a radical break with tradition. Most of the Soviet articles on Yiddish spelling are indeed silent on the question of the allographs, though here and there an appeal is made to 'ease in reading, writing and typesetting, and lowering of printing costs'.[25]

The allographs were eliminated in 1928, the new rules promulgated in 1932 (Lekht 1932), a spelling dictionary published in the same year (see Reyzen 1933) and all further discussion then ceased.

The subsequent history of the Soviet codex within the USSR is eloquent testimony to the subservience of 'linguotechnics' itself to political considerations: Mark (1952: 29) reports that 'during the second World War, when [Soviet Jewish leadership] tried for a time to effect a rapprochement with Jews outside the Soviet Union, it was willing to forego respelling and reinstate word-final allographs in publications earmarked for foreign consumption'.[26] All Yiddish publishing was suppressed, however, in 1949, and when it was resumed on a modest scale in 1959, the Soviets were again willing to modify the codex in order to make their publications more palatable to non-Soviet readers. Although the three books issued in 1959 (all apparently for internal use) do adhere to the codex in its entirety, the bimonthly (and since 1965, monthly) *Sovetish Heymland* has reinstated the allographs (but not etymological spelling of the Hebrew-Aramic component), presumably because the journal is widely distributed outside the USSR.[27]

The *Birobidzhaner Shtern*, on the other hand, a small newspaper now issued five times a week in the Jewish Autonomous Oblast on the Sino-Soviet border, is almost exclusively intended for home consumption and has therefore not tampered with the codex of 1932.[28]

Outside the USSR, Soviet orthography was given a mixed reception. It was generally not followed by communist publications, e.g. in Poland or the United States, probably for fear of losing long-time readers. On the other hand, the *Yugnt-Veker*, published in Warsaw by younger members of the (anticommunist) Jewish Labor Bund between 1922 and 1939, did institute respellings in November 1932. The *Folkstsaytung*, however, issued by the adult members of this organization, preserved the traditional orthography.[29]

Postwar Yiddish publications in communist Poland and Rumania, on the other hand, have adopted neither of these reforms, again probably because they represent too radical a break with tradition.

All of these examples point to the conclusion that the bond between political ideology and spelling is often quite tenuous (cf. Gold 1971b: 225).[30]

III. THE POSTWAR PERIOD

A. The Spelling Debate in the United States

With the bulk of pre-World-War-II Yiddish speakers and cultural/research activities in Eastern Europe, it was natural for most of the debate and codification to take place in the Old World. A few articles on the subject did appear, however, in the United States, written by European-born linguists who either had settled in this country (e.g. Harkary 1888; Joffe 1909) or had sent contributions from Europe (e.g. Prilutski 1921; Weinreich 1931), though an 'indigenous' spelling commission was active in New York City from 1917 to about 1919 (Levin 1952). It issued a codex which was however never implemented.[31]

With the destruction of Eastern European Jewry during the Holocaust, the transfer of the YIVO to New York City in 1940[32] and the suppression of Jewish cultural life in the Soviet Union after 1948, interest in spelling shifted largely to the United States.

Although the proclamation of the Rules of 1937 (SYO) had closed the spelling debate in YIVO and TSISHO circles, pressure was exerted by Judah Joffe and Yudel Mark for a reopening of the question (cf. fn. 31). Debate was therefore invited in the columns of *Yidishe Shprakh*, the YIVO's periodical 'devoted to the problems of Standard Yiddish', but unlike the prewar issue of respelling, which was of major linguistic and sociolinguistic import, the chief questions in the postwar discussions were the rather minor issues of spacing, hyphenation, and use of the silent *alef*.[33]

The most ardent champion of the SYO was Max Weinreich, the YIVO's Research Director, whose first defense of the Rules came in 1949 (Weinreich 1949):

> Why has so much energy been expended on regulating [Yiddish] spelling since Lifshits and the *Kol-Mevaser* [a lexicographer and periodical, respectively] eighty years ago? . . . Why did people in different countries toil with so much zeal? . . . The answer lies in the specific sociopsychological situation of Yiddish: since the mid-nineteenth century, the language has been fighting for recognition in a society where it had been disparaged and where unstandardized spelling had been one of the arguments against it[s recognition]. That use of the Rules is not more widespread is only a gauge of our organizational situation [*gezelshaftlekher maymed*], not evidence for defects in the Rules . . . . And if you should ever hear the sweet little question, "What's the difference *how* it's spelled – people don't buy Yiddish books *anyway*!", you have to realize that this person is wittingly or unwittingly a downgrader [*bagreber*] of Yiddish. This chaos [*tsekhrastetkeyt*] is largely responsible for the present situation. Without a norm, without the realization that a norm exists and the feeling that a norm is needed, our cultural development is inconceivable . . . . I must confess that I see no urgency for change. Every change reduces the present relative stability and is therefore a step backwards.

If reform is needed, Weinreich goes on to say, then those who want changes must first recognize the validity of the SYO and the status of the YIVO as the only competent authority able to modify them, as well as agree to abide by any changes made in the Rules.

In his reply (1959), Mark, then editor of the YIVO's *Yidishe Shprakh* and coeditor of the unabridged Yiddish dictionary then in preparation at the YIVO, openly admitted that he did not follow all of the Rules in private correspondence and in articles and books published by other organizations, thus foreshadowing his open break with the SYO a few years later ('Revision of the Rules is on the agenda.').

Weinreich's rejoinder (1959) again stresses the broader, sociocultural implications of the question:

> 'Why do we need a standardized orthography at all? For three reasons: (1) for the sake of comprehension [which, he admits, can largely be satisfied even with a nonstandardized orthography since variant spellings hardly ever constitute a serious obstacle for the skilled reader], (2) for the sake of orderliness [*tsikhtikeyt*], a notion which has been with us since about 1850, and (3) for the sake of *shprakhikeyt* [status of a "full-fledged language"], a twentieth-century idea. Yiddish has been fighting for recognition as a "language" both internally (within the Jewish community) and externally (among non-Jews); since invidious comparisons are made between Yiddish and various co-territorial languages (which *do* have standardized orthographies), people tend to look on Yiddish as something less than a "language".'[34]

These three factors, he concludes, are at the root of 'our yearning for a standardized Yiddish spelling'.

In this paper, Weinreich also developed the notion of the *takones-kolektiv* 'rules-collective' (roughly, 'rule-abiding citizenry'), membership in which is a necessary, but not a sufficient, requirement for participation in any possible reform of the orthography.[35]

Mark's surrejoinder (1959b) dealt with two problems:

(1) Is a uniform orthography achieved by implementing the present Rules and then reforming them if necessary, or should the present codex be reformed before universal implementation is attempted or possible?

(2) Who is empowered to change the Rules?

He first summarized Weinreich's position, viz. that implementing the SYO should not be confused with a desire by some people to reform it

('With a few changes, everybody will accept the Rules', argue the latter); there can be no talk of change at the present time – if we want to put an end to the spelling chaos, the answer is not to tamper with the present orthography, but to adopt it pure and simple. Mark, on the other hand, felt that the Rules were too hard for most Yiddish users and therefore unimplementable.[36]

The second question is, of course, especially important in cases like that of Yiddish, where the language does not enjoy state recognition and there is no government body concerned with its development. The YIVO has held that as the sole research institution devoted to the Yiddish language and other aspects of Ashkenazic life, only it is competent in this field (e.g. Kalmanovitsh 1930; M. Weinreich (ed.) 1930: v; *Barikht* . . . 1931: 5; M. Weinreich 1959: 52; Weinreich and Borenstein 1965).

The YIVO has nevertheless also recognized that language-oriented laymen must be heard, too, though they need not necessarily have the final word, and therefore invited teachers, editors, publishers, and printers to its spelling conferences during the 1930's.[37] The final redaction of the Rules, however, was solely in the hands of the Philological Section of the YIVO.

Yudel Mark, on the other hand, believed that all participants in reforming and codifying should be on an equal footing: 'a great poet, a respected writer, the author of a Yiddish textbook, the administrator of a Yiddish school system, teachers, publishers, editors, typesetters, printers, essayists, short-story writers, *kultur-tuers* "community leaders"' as well as philologists/linguists should, in his opinion, have equal votes (Mark 1959b: *passim*).

With this article, the spelling debate in print came largely to a close.[38]

Mark had in the meantime bolted from the *takones-kolektiv* by printing a 'Questionnaire on Orthography' in *Yidishe Shprakh* (Mark 1958b), stating that 'the editors of the unabridged Yiddish dictionary [then being compiled at the YIVO under Mark and Joffe's editorship] have asked us to publish the following questionnaire . . .' – i.e. 'Yudel Mark has asked Yudel Mark . . .' In both capacities, as editor of two YIVO publications, Mark was clearly acting on his own, whereas to the innocent reader it seemed that the questionnaire had been formally approved by the YIVO and that reform was actually being contemplated by that body.

Details of the survey were released by Mark a short while later (Mark 1959a); of the 262 writers, linguists, teachers, editors, publishers, typesetters, and leaders of community organizations who received it, 177 (67 percent) replied.[39]

Mark's reformed spelling was used in the unabridged dictionary, as a result of which the YIVO withdrew support from the project (cf. M. Weinreich 1961). Needless to say, the addition of yet another faction has not brought the orthographic unity many still yearn for.

B. The Committee for the Implementation of the Standardized Yiddish Orthography (*CISYO*)

The Standardized Yiddish Orthography, as embodied in the Rules of 1937, was of course not intended for use only in the YIVO'S or TSISHO's publications. Like all codifying bodies (or individual codifiers), these organizations sought the widest possible acceptance for their codex. In addition, however, to the usual obstacles faced by language engineers working in languages without government recognition or support, the YIVO was in this respect confronted by another problem: by tradition the YIVO has conducted only pure research and has not engaged in polemics of any kind, even when implementation of the Rules of 1937 was concerned.[40]

In order, therefore, to provide an organizational structure for efforts to implement the SYO, the CISYO was founded as an independent body of linguists and language-oriented laymen in 1958 at the initiative of Mordkhe Schaechter. Whereas in the 1940's and especially the 1950's, Max Weinreich stood 'like an oak in a storm' in defense of the SYO,[41] the CISYO served to bring out a few latent supporters of the SYO among Yiddish writers, journalists, teachers, and community leaders who had previously remained on the sidelines of the spelling debate.

With Max Weinreich as chairman and Mordkhe Schaechter as vice chairman, the CISYO coopted linguists, teachers, editors, or community leaders who, it was hoped, would introduce the SYO in their own publications and exert influence on others to do so.[42]

The first project of the CISYO was the compilation of a spelling dictionary (Schaechter and Weinreich 1961); the relative ease with which funds for publication were raised within the Yiddish-speaking community and the moderate sales of the book showed that there was more latent interest in the SYO than its rather limited use in print might otherwise imply.[43]

The second project, exertion of pressure on the largest Yiddish non-daily periodical outside Israel, *Di Tsukunft*, followed in 1963 and 1964. Two hundred and twenty readers' signatures were obtained for a petition calling on the magazine to adopt the SYO, but it was ignored.[44]

The CISYO then organized a spelling course, given at the YIVO from October 1965 to January 1966.[45] A detailed course outline was published, of which a second revised edition of 300 copies was soon sold out (Schaechter 1972). During the period the course was given, the YIVO held a 182-item exhibit on the history of Yiddish orthography (Szajkowski 1966). It is noteworthy that all mention of the spelling debate of the 1940's and 1950's as well as Yudel Mark's own survey and system was hushed up at the exhibit, yet nine items on the Soviet codex and seven on the Orthodox one were included. It was evidently felt that they no longer constituted a challenge to the SYO, the former being limited to the few Soviet publications, the latter to all intents and purposes being a private system, used only by S. A. Birnbaum after the Holocaust. Mark's system, on the other hand, *was* felt to threaten the SYO.

The latest move by the CISYO has been the picketing in April 1970 of the two largest New York dailies, the *Forverts* and the (now defunct) *Tog-Morgn-Zhurnal*, whose spelling deviated considerably from the SYO. Officially organized by Yugntruf – Youth for Yiddish, a group of high-school and college students, but actually under the leadership of Mordkhe Schaechter, the demonstration drew about twenty-five people. Curiously, most other members of the CISYO did not actively support the move, which was unsuccessful (Gold 1972a; 1972b; Schaechter 1970a; 1970b; 1970c).

Since 1971 the CISYO has been trying to establish a streamlined method whereby printers can readily obtain type with the necessary diacritics for implementing the SYO and individuals or institutions can have their Yiddish typewriters converted to the SYO.[46]

C. *Problems of Implementation*

Although there is hardly any outright opposition to the SYO at this time (since the 1960's), there is still widespread indifference or, at best, mere lip service being paid to the SYO. The efforts of the CISYO have therefore been largely aimed at remolding people's attitudes towards the need for an orthographic norm.[47] And although it is true that many Yiddish users DO have a sense of *Sprachpflege*, it is usually directed towards Hebrew-Aramic or to the local non-Jewish prestige language, but not to their native tongue as such.[48]

Another problem is the general absence of any sanctions – rewards or punishments – for spelling behavior.[49] And although it is true that a sizeable number of Yiddish users apparently do want to follow the Rules (cf. the sales of the spelling dictionary and course outline, the number of signatures collected on petitions, and attendance at the spelling course), most are simply beyond the learning stage.[50]

The entire problem of spelling loyalty, furthermore, is overshadowed by the even more ominous one of language loyalty. As the community grows older and smaller, with no appreciable numbers of younger Yiddish users joining (or remaining within) the linguistic community, agitation in favor of the SYO becomes a tempest in an ever smaller teapot.[51] For instance, in the same year (1973) the SYO was introduced in the *Kinder-Zhurnal* (a small, low-circulation monthly read mostly by people over fifty, but actually intended for children), a major Yiddish daily (in Argentina) had to close for lack of readers. The SYO may therefore be 'gaining' ground, but the number of publications is actually shrinking.

D. Degree of Implementation of the Various Codexes

An examination of all Yiddish publications in the United States and Canada made in 1961 (Schaechter 1961) in respect of forty-six rules of the SYO showed that, aside from four publications which adhered to the SYO, no two publications agreed on all forty-six points ('as if each had created a personal national anthem' [Schaechter 1961: 360]). Six years later, a survey of fourteen publications in the United States, France, Israel, Argentina, the Soviet Union, and Mexico revealed that in respect to seven words only five publications, again only those following the SYO, were in agreement; the others achieved only an approximation (from two of four SYO spellings), but no two agreed with each other on the spelling of all seven words (Kshenski 1967). The SYO is fully adhered to in several periodicals and books and by a few individual Yiddish users.

The Soviet codex is now limited to use in USSR publications (but most have reinstated the word-final allographs); the Orthodox codex is now used only by its originator in private correspondence and wherever he can have his own articles printed in it.[52]

Yudel Mark's codex is used in the unabridged Yiddish-Yiddish *Groyser Verterbukh Fun Der Yidisher Shprakh* and in school textbooks written or edited by Mark (published by the Congress for Jewish Culture or the Jewish Education Committee of New York). Approximations of

Mark's codex or of the SYO were also used in some educational materials published by the Workmen's Circle before it fully adopted the SYO.

Jewish schools have in fact potentially been the most powerful force in implementing a given codex and therefore deserve special treatment.

Traditional Jewish education (mostly for males) stressed study of the Bible and Talmud in the original Hebrew(-Aramic). Although Yiddish was the sole means of oral communication in the *kheyder* 'traditional elementary school for males' and the *yeshive* 'traditional school of higher studies for males', Yiddish per se was not taught.[53]

Beginning in the twentieth century, and especially after World War I, new types of Jewish schools were established by various ideological groups. Yiddish continued to be the medium of instruction for most subjects (in other schools Hebrew or a non-Jewish language, such as Polish or Russian, was the medium), but more emphasis was given to Yiddish language and literature, i.e. in addition to being a medium of instruction, it became a subject. These schools generally adopted one of the neotraditional orthographies, in the elaboration of which teachers had in fact always participated (cf. sections II, III).

Whatever influence these schools might have had in respect of orthography was, however, circumscribed and short-lived: students of the 1920's and 1930's were, of course, too young to assume positions of leadership in the Yiddish media and the Holocaust itself snuffed out their lives in the 1940's. A few did survive and many of them made their way to other countries, but their influence has largely not been felt.

What of the majority of Yiddish speakers in centers of immigration outside Eastern Europe? Most of them left the Old Country before the flowering of the Yiddish schools in the 1920's and 1930's. They therefore usually lack formal education in their mother tongue, disciplined study of its standardized variety (cf. fn. 47), and even awareness of the existence of a standardized orthography.

Yiddish schools outside Eastern Europe (in the United States, Canada, Argentina, Mexico, France, Australia, South Africa, etc.) have for other reasons had little influence as well. From the 1920's to the 1940's it was probably true that most of the pupils in Yiddish schools outside Eastern Europe were native Yiddish speakers. When they reached maturity, however, most of them left the Yiddish-speaking community; the few who remained have, with rare exceptions, played no role in the Yiddish media. Most students in the 1950's, 1960's, and 1970's, on the other hand, have not been native speakers (or even primary Yiddish speakers), and it is even rarer to find them remaining in the Yiddish-speaking community. Among those who do remain, the ones who assume positions of leadership and responsibility are rara avises indeed. In sum, although the SYO or close approximations thereof are taught in almost all Yiddish schools, their long-range influence has been practically nil.[54]

E. Spelling and Ideology

There seems to be no correlation between spelling usage and ideology (cf. section II. B.), except in the matter of respellings. On one hand, the socialist *Forverts* and the orthodox *Dos Yidishe Vort* use approximately the same spelling, viz. they deviate furthest from the SYO than all other publications and are closest to the Germanized spelling. On the other hand, two ideologically similar groups such as the Jewish Labor Bund (publisher of *Undzer Tsayt*) and the Workmen's Circle do not agree on spelling matters, viz. the former approximates the SYO to some degree but is deviant in terms of many diacritics, spacing, and hyphenation, whereas all of the latter's publications now follow the SYO in its entirety. This must often be considered a fortuitous situation, however, since spelling usage often depends simply on who happens to be in charge of such matters in any given organization or publication.[55]

Much more significant is the degree to which language loyalty in general and language cultivation in particular have developed in each of the Jewish subcommunities. Thus, Khsidim and socialist groups, like the Jewish Labor Bund and the Workmen's Circle, have developed notions of language loyalty (the Khsidim tacitly, the latter explicitly but often on paper only), yet the Bundist periodical is much closer to the SYO than many Khsidic publications because socialist groups have proceeded to the second stage, viz. an approximation of *Sprachpflege*, largely under the influence of the Central Yiddish School Organization in Poland (TSISHO).[56] Khsidic groups, on the other hand, have by and large not developed any special notion of linguistic purity or correctness.[57]

Within the language-cultivating subgroups themselves there is a continuum of approximation to the SYO: the highly regarded literary quarterly *Di Goldene Keyt*, edited by the poet Avrom Sutskever, has adopted the SYO *in toto*, whereas *Di Letste Nayes*, a Tel Aviv daily enjoying wide prestige, follows most but not all of the Rules of 1937. It is interesting to note that the editors of both periodicals are members of the CISYO.

Efforts at implementing the SYO in the English-speaking Jewish community and in the non-Jewish community have, on the other hand, met with little opposition, though of course the extent to which these sectors employ Yiddish is trifling. An occasional leaflet, brochure, or circular, campaign literature before elections [probably limited to New York City], and an occasional flyer or pamphlet issued by governmental bodies practically exhaust the range of Yiddish publications outside the Yiddish-speaking community itself. Since these organizations 'couldn't care less', the CISYO has had no trouble in persuading the New York City Department of Hospitals to follow the SYO in a brochure aimed at Yiddish-speaking New Yorkers, and I easily convinced the U.S. Department of Agriculture to do likewise when preparing its Yiddish flyer on food stamps.

IV. FURTHER REFORM AND CODIFICATION

A. Further Reform

Most members of the *takones-kolektiv* 'rules collective' feel that further reform, while it might correct some of the few imperfections in the present codex, would actually do more harm than good. It was early realized that too much tampering 'would lose the reader' (Slutski 1928), not only on sentimental grounds if time-honored traditions were abandoned, but on purely objective grounds as well since he might experience difficulty in adjusting to radical changes.[58]

It has also been feared that reforms might create new camps (cf. Yudel Mark's survey) in a community which already has 'a million presidents'. Further considerations have been the fact that so few people now have the necessary theoretical and practical knowledge to reform the SYO that any changes might be for the worse; the fact that since Yiddish is generally declining, reform would be too expensive a luxury at this point; and the fact that there is a large measure of sentimental attachment to the Rules of 1937 – viewed by many as one of the last and lasting achievements of the millenial Ashkenazic subculture of Judaism, attained on the very eve of its destruction by the Nazis and their collaborators (cf. the many statements to this effect by Max Weinreich).[59]

Max Weinreich and others, in fact, tried to cut off debate on spelling reform simply by stating that the time for discussion was over and that it was now time for implementation.[60] In view of the splintered nature of the Yiddish-speaking community, this seems to be the wisest approach to the question of further reform.

Since no other spelling system now enjoys the wide prestige and partial implementation that the Standardized Yiddish Orthography does, it would seem that, with the exception of Soviet publications and perhaps some others, some Yiddish users will continue to move closer and closer towards the SYO, but that a number of periodicals will eventually simply cease publication without having made any appreciable move towards the SYO.

B. Further Codification

In several areas where the Rules of 1937 took no stance, codification is still possible. In some instances, preparatory work in the form of articles and suggested codexes has already been done.

(1) *The Spelling of the Hebrew-Aramic Component.* Even though the SYO requires Yiddish words of Hebrew-Aramic origin to be spelled 'etymologically', there is variation within the traditional Hebrew-Aramic orthography itself: plene vs. defective spelling (Yiddish prefers the former in most cases), use of hyphens in multiword lexemes (e.g. *bifney kol am veeyde* vs. *bifney-kol-am-veeyde* – the trend in the *takones-kolektiv* is towards use of hyphens), etc. A detailed study of the spelling of the Hebrew-Aramic component since earliest times would of course be a necessary prerequisite for further codification in this area.

(2) *The Spelling of Toponyms.* Although much work has been done in recording toponyms from informants and from written sources, little has been done to standardize their form (this problem embraces both morphology and orthography). There is universal agreement that Eastern European toponyms should be transcribed as traditionally pronounced in Yiddish (e.g. *varshe* 'Warsaw' rather than, for example, **varshava*, cf. Polish *Warszawa*), but the rule is often broken in respect of certain 'traditional' spellings that do not reflect traditional pronunciations: 'lemberg' (for *lemberik*), 'tshernovits' (for *tshernęvits*), 'mlave' (*melave*), 'kiev' (*kiv*), 'bratslav' (*broslev*), 'l(y)ubavitsh' (*lębavitsh;* cf. fn. 75), 'yas' (*yos*), 'nalevkes' (*nalefkes*), 'kasrilevke' (*kasrilefke*), and all other Slavic-origin toponyms in *-efke*.

With regard to toponyms outside Eastern Europe, there is much hesitation. In many cases, there is an unfortunate tendency to transcribe or transliterate such toponyms in terms of the local non-Jewish language rather than as pronounced in Yiddish: 'buenos-ayres' (for *boynes-ayres*), 'toronto' (*teronte*), 'boston' (*bostn*), 'shikago' (*tshekage*), 'berkli' (*boykle*), 'di bronks' (*di broneks*), etc. Many of these spellings have become so rooted in written Yiddish that they have all but eliminated the traditional, 'folksy' pronunciations from spoken Yiddish as well: older *nev-york* or *nay-york* now sounds quaint and often evokes a smile from more 'sophisticated' speakers, who use *nyu-york*.

In other cases, several variant forms have arisen. Some toponyms have been transliterated, partially transcribed and partially transliterated, or have entered Yiddish through more than one channel. The various written Yiddish equivalents for 'Los Angeles' illustrate this point: *los-angeles* (transliteration), *los-ankheles* (transcription of the Spanish pronunciation of the toponym, mostly found in Yiddish publications from Latin America), *los-andzheles* (partially transcribed as pronounced in Yiddish coterritorial with English and partially transliterated), *los-endzheles* (transcription of the normal Yiddish pronunciation). An especially interesting case is the two variants for 'Quebec': the traditional pronunciation and spelling is *kvebek* (based on the traditional English pronunciation), but *kebek* is sometimes seen nowadays, either as a transcription based on the French pronunciation or on a recent 'trendy' rendition of the toponym among English-speaking Canadians sympathetic with the French nationalist movement in that province. In any case, the normal pronunciation (and most frequent spelling) is still *kvebek*. Similar problems also exist for *palm-bitsh/pam-bitsh*, *keymbridzh/kambridzh/kembridzh*, *vankuver/venkuver*, etc.

The few statements on place-names have been ambiguous and self-contradictory. Thus, the list of Yiddish names of the states, as published by the YIVO in 1942 (Anon. 1942), is a jumble of transliteration, transcription of English pronunciation, and transcription of normal Yiddish pronunciation. A comparison of the 'official' list with various YIVO publications shows, moreover, that the former is not followed nor is there any consistency of usage in the latter (Gold i.p.c.).

In some cases, one suspects that the early attempts at codification of new place-names were aimed specifically at avoiding so-called 'mispronunciations', i.e. phonologically integrated pronunciations of competent native speakers not under the prescriptive influence of English,

Spanish, or other norms. Thus, Reyzen (1933) calls for close adherence to the *Schriftbild* of toponyms rather than to their actual Yiddish pronunciation, e.g. 'klivland' (for *klivlend*), and 'shikago' (for *shikage* or – even more authentically – *tshekage*). At the same time, however, he takes the opposite viewpoint respecting certain Slavic-origin words and criticizes Soviet spelling for often having been under the strong influence of Russian pronunciation in determining the spelling of Slavic-origin words and of words of 'international' origin that entered Yiddish through one of the Slavic tongues, i.e. for having maintained a mild form of the etymological principle with regard to the Slavic component.

(3) *Personal Names.* A similar problem arises with respect to names of famous foreign personages. Some suggest they be transcribed as closely to the original pronunciation as possible (see Lehrer 1941; Mark 1947), while others feel that the Yiddish spelling should reflect the normal pronunciation of the uninhibited Yiddish speaker (see Glassman 1941). In some cases, transliterated names have given rise to specifically Yiddish pronunciations, e.g. *linkoln* /linkoln/.

(4) *Syllabification.* There are occasional statements on this question (e.g. Mark 1971), but no full-scale discussion is as yet available.

(5) *Punctuation.* Most of the work in standardizing Yiddish punctuation was done by Zaretski (1928a; 1930), Falkovitsh (Zaretski and Falkovitsh 1931), and Mark (1930; 1953; see also Anon. 1930; Levin 1954). Although there are many universal conventions, e.g. commas in enumerations, there is also a high degree of free variation, e.g. comma vs. zero after *verba dicendi.*

Punctuation has understandably never inflamed the passions of Yiddish linguists and language-oriented laymen, and there is at present little interest in achieving a norm.

(6) *Hebrew-Letter Phonetic Alphabets.* Philological/linguistic works where phonetic/phonemic citation is necessary usually employ the I.P.A. system or some other recognized notation, but it early became clear that a Hebrew-letter scheme was also needed for technical reasons, viz. the difficulties of typesetting material in both scripts – which read, moreover, in different directions – and the consequently higher printing costs.

Works by Noyekh Prilutski (1917-) used such a Hebrew-letter phonetic alphabet, and other devices can be found in various articles by Max Weinreich and Uriel Weinreich. S. A. Birnbaum's orthography is itself in many respects broadly phonetic, but its originator wants it of course to be adopted as THE Yiddish orthography. Another system, for philological purposes, was proposed by Yudel Mark in 1946 (Mark 1946c).

V. PRIMARY AND SECONDARY ROMANIZATIONS[61]

One of the earliest and certainly the most ardent champion of Romanization was Yankev Sotek (c. 1860-?), who published articles in and about Romanization in various Rumanian Jewish periodicals (e.g. Sotek 1903) as well as a romanized collection of poems by Velvl Zbarzher (Sotek [ed.] 1902).[62] At the Czernowitz Yiddish Language Conference of 1908 (see section II.A.), Romanization was advocated by Sotek and the Yiddish writers Sholem Ash and Y.-L. Perets, apparently in an effort to have Yiddish 'recognized' outside the Jewish world.[63]

Joffe, who came out squarely for primary Romanization in 1909, claimed that Yiddish was written in Hebrew characters because its speakers hated *treyf-posl* 'secular or heretical books' and also so that non-Jews would not be able to read Yiddish; 'however, because Jews are now participating in western culture, an alphabet is needed that will represent sounds in such a way that even non-Jews will understand Yiddish and that will be modeled on those of the civilized peoples (Joffe 1909: 30)'.[64]

Debate continued through the 1910's and 1920's, with articles pro and contra as well as a handful of short-lived Romanized publications.

Ben-Adir (1912) countered Joffe's arguments by warning that the *latin-yidishistn*, as he called the advocates of Romanization, would split the Yiddish readership into two camps. M. Mieses (1909-1910) argued as follows:

(1) the claim that since Yiddish is a Germanic language it must not be written in the Semitic alphabet is spurious; Yiddish is genetically Germanic, but socioculturally a Jewish language (cf. fn. 64);

(2) the argument that through Latinization 'Europe would understand us' is trivial; only a few non-Jews are curious about Yiddish and Latinization is therefore not worth the effort;

(3) Latinization is a sign of assimilation.[65]

The first attempt at a Romanized publication was apparently *Ynser*

Śrift (Kaplan and Botwinik 1912), a literary journal of which only one issue appeared.[66]

Another Romanized periodical was the likewise ephemeral *Unhoib* (Ziemand 1923), whose single issue appeared on June 20, 1923. The editorial (p. 1) states that the magazine is aimed at Jewish youth in western Europe who understand Yiddish but who never had the opportunity of learning to read it, i.e. the Romanization was intended for secondary purposes. In this issue Tirski (1923) pleads the cause of Romanization, adoption of which will permit Jews to 'scotch once and for all the charge that Yiddish is a "jargon"' [?] and thereby induce non-Jews to have more respect for Yiddish [?].

A brief defense of primary Romanization was made by Shpilreyn in his 1926 Yiddish course at the Second State University of Moscow (Shpilreyn 1926) as did Kenig in the same year (Kenig 1926); the former viewed Yiddish as an instrument, the latter as a sentiment.[67] Two articles against (primary) Romanization also appeared in that year: Litvak (1926) argued that the interdialectal principle would have to be abandoned ('Which Yiddish dialect would be taken as the basis for the Romanization?'), that the Latin letters did not have universal values, and that universal implementation would not be assured ('We have no government.'). Vevyorka (1926) states succinctly: 'Our written language is from both the phonological and rational standpoints [*fonetishkeyt*, *ratsyonalishkeyt*] by far not among the worse written languages. On the contrary Yiddish is one of those languages in which the distance between the spoken and written languages is relatively slight.'

Whereas discussion of Romanization was a purely 'internal matter' in most Yiddish-speaking communities, in the Soviet Union it was part of a much broader debate with obvious political overtones. The debate concerned the Romanization of ALL Soviet minority languages and perhaps of Russian too (cf. Weinreich 1953). Shpilreyn and Vevyorka's exchange was but a foretaste of the full-scale discussion of the question which followed six years later.

Although Zaretski (1928d: 25) had flatly stated that the question of primary Romanization was 'not timely' (*nit aktuel*) – at a time when the Romanization of other Soviet languages was in full swing (cf. Weinreich 1953: 48) – by 1930 it was a major item on the agenda of the Central [Yiddish] Orthographical Commission (Anon. 1930).[68] The major Soviet statement on the Romanization of Yiddish appeared in 1932 (Shtif and Spivak 1932). Shtif and Spivak saw primary Romanization as a token of 'internationalism' and the Hebrew script as a symbol of 'bourgeois nationalism'. They repeated many of the old arguments for Romanization and presented some new ones too.[69]

In 1934 there appeared a major Romanized Yiddish publication in the Soviet Union, Beregovski's collection (1934) of Yiddish folksongs, intended evidently for scholars outside the Yiddish-speaking community with some knowledge of the language. The preface (p. 4) indicates the reasons why the Hebrew script was not used: (1) musical notation is easier when the script reads from left to right, and (2) the Central Orthographical Commission has decided that scholarly works should be gradually printed more and more in Romanized Yiddish. Another collection of songs followed (Jampolski 1935), then came a rebirth of Russian nationalism, the scrapping of Romanization, and the introduction of Cyrillicization (cf. U. Weinreich 1953: 48 ff.). Meanwhile, the number of Yiddish publications was declining yearly, reaching zero in 1949, and Cyrillicization/Romanization was once again 'not timely'.[70]

Outside the Soviet Union, interest in Romanization was at this time apparently waning. At least three issues of a Romanized periodical appeared in Warsaw (Shtif and Spivak 1932; *Progres* c. 1931), and an anthology of Yiddish poetry appeared in Czernowitz in 1934 (Gininger, et al. 1934; M. Weinreich 1934), intended for 'assimilated Jews' and the 'backward masses' (*opgeshtanene masn* [!]), in whom the compilers hoped to 'awaken an interest in and understanding of Yiddish literature' (Gininger, et al. 1934: 87). What they intended was therefore merely a secondary Romanization.[71]

The last major Romanized publications were several books and periodicals published by and for displaced persons after the Holocaust (cf. Feldschuh 1949; Kosowski 1950). It is not clear, however, whether Romanization was motivated by the fact that most Hebrew type had been destroyed by the Nazis or that the intended readers did not know the Hebrew script (many Hebrew-script publications did appear in the DP camps during the same period, i.e. 1945-c. 1950).

The last proponent of primary Romanization was Y. Berenfeld. His alternate use of Romanized and non-Romanized paragraphs in a 1964 article (Bernfeld 1968) has been called 'sheer exhibitionism' by a friend of his.[72]

The elaboration of a codex for secondary Romanization has been of interest to the YIVO Institute for Jewish Research since its founding in 1925. A draft codex was brought before the 1931 Spelling Conference in

Vilna by Cemach Szabad (M. Weinreich 1930: 32, 191) and discussion continued in *Yidishe Shprakh* from 1941 to 1949 (Birnbaum 1944; 1947; 1948; ['Discussion . . .'] 1947; Kheyfets 1941; Mark 1946c; 1947; Roback 1946; 1949). Since debate concerned secondary Romanization and was therefore of marginal interest to most language-oriented laymen, it occupied relatively few pages of the journal and did not at all inflame passions as the spelling debates had.[73] That Romanization has been of even less interest to the English-speaking world, where it would find its most frequent users, is shown by the fact that no discussion of it is known in English except my short article (Gold 1974).

Sometime in the late 1940's or early 1950's the YIVO arrived at a standardized secondary Romanization for international use. Adopted in YIVO publications, by the Library of Congress (with a few deviations), and by many individual writers and researchers, the codex has not however gained wide acceptance because it has not been published or made known in any other way to the general public.[74] The resulting present chaos is therefore expectable.

VI. CYRILLICIZATION

Aside from secondary Cyrillicizations of book and periodical titles (or title pages) for the convenience of non-Yiddish-reading librarians, news-dealers, etc. (cf. Birnbaum 1929), only two fully Cyrillicized publications are known, a nineteenth-century edition of the Bible for use by Jewish soldiers in the Russian Army and a translation of some of Krilov's fables.[75]

With the rebirth of Russian nationalism in the 1930's (cf. U. Weinreich 1953: 48-51), Romanization of Soviet minority languages was scrapped in favor of Cyrillicization, which, like Romanization, was seen as a move away from outmoded 'tradition' towards 'Europeanization' and 'westernization' (cf. Fischer 1936: 134). It certainly would have been more successful in attracting new Soviet readers to Yiddish than Romanization would have been, but neither was implemented.

No printed discussions of primary or secondary Cyrillicization for Yiddish are known, publishing in the language itself having declined from 668 titles in 1932 to zero in 1949 (Levenberg 1968: 180).[76] A study of the Cyrillicized Bible and translations and of the secondary Cyrillicizations on title pages, etc., would be useful.

VII. SCRIPT REFORM

Script reform, to be distinguished from spelling reform or the development of ornamental scripts for artistic purposes, has evoked little interest. The first proposals in this regard were apparently made by Goldberg (1922), with replies from Yashunski (1923), Rubin (1923), and Glas (1923).

Adumbrating the distinctive-feature theory as applied to graphemics, Goldberg (1922) suggested the abandonment of old scribal decorations and the retention of only the 'root-lines' (*shoyresh-linyes*) of each grapheme. He proposed the conventional, ornamental type for titles and the new, simplified type for ordinary texts (to give the printed page more variety) as well as the modification of graphemes hard to distinguish in print, e.g. *giml/nun*, *mem/tes* (cf. Martinet's security margin). Goldberg pointed out the difficulties of stylizing the alphabet for ornamental purposes (because it was already heavily stylized), and called for straight lines of the same thickness for all graphemes as well as the abandonment of all curves. He gave samples of three new scripts and suggested that they and the 'ornamental' script be assigned various functions (e.g. 'italicization').[77]

Yashunski (1923) argued against Goldberg's proposals, but Rubin and Glas were largely receptive to them, mainly on pedagogical grounds. Rubin (1923) called for the replacement of the digraphs for /ž/ and /č/ by unigraphs – a proposal that has been made by others as well – and Glas (1923) advocated a script which permitted letters to be joined – a convenience for the writer.[78] None of these reforms – Goldberg's, Yashunski's, Rubin's, and Glas' – has been adopted.

A further suggestion, limited only to the digraphs for /v/, /ej/ and /aj/, was made by Max Weinreich (1930).[79] He proposed that the digraphs for these phonemes, which consist of double *vov* in the first case and double *yud* in the second and third (with a diacritic for /aj/,) be made in one stroke, i.e. that the *vovs* and *yuds* be joined in handwriting as well as in printing. The suggested unigraph for /v/ was included as an alternative in the Rules of 1937 for handwriting only, and has enjoyed some measure of success.[80] The other variants were not approved and Weinreich himself desisted from using them.[81]

Except for esthetic purposes, only two scripts are now employed: the thick, 'ornamental' letters for ordinary purposes and thin letters for emphasis.[82]

VIII. SUMMARY AND CONCLUSIONS

The strategy in language planning at any linguistic level (orthographic, syntactic, lexical, etc.) is at least twofold: the first step is to create a model for imitation and the second is to promote it over rival models.

By 1937, Yiddish users as a whole had several models at their disposal: variants of the traditional orthography, variants of the Germanized orthography, mixed traditional-Germanized variants, variants of the *moderne ortografye*, the Soviet codex, the Orthodox codex, and the Standardized Yiddish Orthography. Although all were potentially available to every member of the community, their actual status as models depended on several factors:

(1) *Age*. Orthographies, like any linguistic form, can spread from one regional variety of a language to another, from one social variety to another. All things being equal, the more time a form has a chance to spread, the greater its area of use. It is therefore not surprising that the SYO, the youngest of the models, was in pre-1939 Eastern Europe less widespread than variants of the *moderne ortografye* (dating from the early 1920's) and even less widespread (at least in private use) than the traditional-Germanized variants (dating from the nineteenth century).

(2) *Source*. Diffusion along the social plane is usually quicker than along the purely geographical one. A codex proclaimed in Vilna, for example, was more readily available to Yiddish literati in Warsaw and Paris than to Vilna butchers and bakers. Since the spelling codexes emanated, of course, from the intelligentsia, they needed time to diffuse downwards.

(3) *Availability*. Proclaiming a codex, issuing a booklet of rules, a sample text, or a spelling dictionary is not enough-though some members of the community with a high degree of language or spelling loyalty need nothing more. A model must be taught at school or be easily imitable from the printed materials.

Although the three major codices of the 1930's could count on respective school systems (all Soviet schools for the Soviet codex, the *Beys-Yankev* schools in Poland for the Orthodox codex, and the TSISHO schools for the SYO), the schools did not have a long-range effect, except perhaps in the Soviet Union where many school-age Yiddish-speakers of the 1930's did reach maturity.

These codices did have some publications at their disposal, but they were generally pedagogical or learned periodicals aimed at a restricted audience. Again, only in the Soviet Union, where spelling reform and codification had the backing of a government, were the periodicals made INSTRUMENTS rather than *targets* of change in a short time.

(4) *Ideology*. The relationship between ideology and spelling has not always been hard-and-fast in Yiddish. Active proponents of germanized spelling, to be sure, looked on Yiddish as 'bastardized German', but many Yiddish-users who did not take this view (or who had no opinion at all) wrote according to germanizing norms (to varying degrees) simply out of habit, because they were taught that way. In another respect one and the same spelling principle may be endowed with different ideological import: respelling was seen as 'anti-bourgeois' and 'anti-religious' in the Soviet Union, but as 'logical' and 'rational' by many noncommunists elsewhere. And we have already pointed out other cases of nonparallelism between spelling and ideology such as (a) the failure of communist publications outside the USSR to adopt the Soviet Codex; (b) the willingness of the Soviets themselves to deviate from their codex beginning in the 1940's, and (c) the greater similarity between the *Forverts* and *Dos Yidishe Vort* than between the former and *Undzer Tsayt*.

Despite these anomalies, ideology HAS had some influence in determining the diffusion of the various codexes: although the proponents of the SYO, for example, have, just as those of any of the other codexes, wanted to see their rules adopted universally, they have felt it only natural to put their own house in order before turning to their neighbors'. The CISYO, for instance, has concentrated all of its efforts on the non-orthodox, noncommunist sectors of the Yiddish-speaking community; only recently has Mordkhe Schaechter made overtures to some communist publications in the United States (*Yidishe Kultur*, *Morgn-Frayheyt*), but orthodox publications have not been approached.

Efforts to promote one codex or another were of course cut short by the tragic catastrophes that befell almost the entire community: the murder of five million speakers, the liquidation of Jewish cultural life in the Soviet Union, and the massive shift to other languages in countries of immigration. Yiddish is a declining language, which by the 1970's is spoken largely by sixty- and seventy-year-olds in ever decreasing numbers. Although language planning has thus not made much progress, the limited Yiddish experience may still allow us to make some recommendations for other transnational groups speaking nonofficial languages.

(1) Orthographists should be drawn from all ideological movements and be willing to compromise on ideologically significant aspects of spelling (e.g. respelling of the Hebrew-Aramic component in the case of Yiddish).

(2) Innovations should be kept to a minimum – codify rather than reform.

(3) Sanctions should be established for spelling habits.

(4) Where the printed media have little interest in reform or uniformity, it is often easier to 'infiltrate' the media themselves by placing the right people in key positions. It may also be easier to found rival institutions (periodicals and publishing houses).

(5) The 'model' that should be eliminated FIRST is chaos. Where a codex is rivaled not only by another system or systems, but by (near) chaos itself, it is better to work at eliminating the latter. Two or three codices, after all, among which there is usually a high degree of mutual legibility (as in English), signify a high degree of spelling uniformity; absolute unity may not be worth the effort.

Einar Haugen has suggested that language planning is concerned with eight chief problems:

(1) promotion or prevention of change,
(2) promotion of uniformity or diversity,
(3) resistance to or encouragement of borrowing,
(4) purification or hybridization,
(5) expansion or restriction of the code's resources,
(6) pursuance of beauty or efficiency,
(7) achievement of accuracy or expressiveness,
(8) maintenance or replacement of the code (channel, in this case).

Although applicable especially to the lexical level, these concerns are also pertinent to the present paper:

(1) All orthographists have aimed at a degree of change, from the radical reforms proposed by Veynger in 1913, through the less radical Soviet reforms (respelling, abolition of word-final allographs), to the moderate proposals of the other neotraditionalists. Yet the very term NEOTRADITIONALIST implies a resistance to change, and the term is in fact not a misnomer: what the neotraditionalists of the 1920's and 1930's were essentially aiming at was a return to the indigenous orthographic traditions of the pre-Germanizing aberration of the nineteenth and early twentieth centuries.

(2) Uniformity vs. diversity can be understood in three ways: (a) all orthographists wanted their codex to be universally implemented; (b) all wanted it to consist of only one set of rules (except for some early proposals that each of the major regional varieties be given a separate set); and (c) the number of principles should be reduced as much as possible (all codexes have in fact largely abandoned the Germanizing principle, but only the Soviet Codex has also [largely] discarded the etymological principle).

(3) All neotraditionalists have in principle been against the borrowing of German orthographic conventions, although only the Orthodox codex has fully abandoned them. BORROWING cannot, incidentally, apply to Hebrew-Aramic and Laaz conventions, which have been inherited.

(4) This point is encompassed under (2) and (3).

(5) Suggestions for the creation of new typefaces have not been followed.

(6) If efficiency is taken to mean full (morpho)phonemicization and beauty interpreted as the elimination of diacritics which 'clutter' the line, all systems try to strike a balance between too many and too few of the latter. The pre-World-War-I system of full pointing was in this respect overefficient and too unesthetic.

(7) Accuracy and efficiency are more or less synonymous in the present context: the phonemic principle calls for all phonemes to be represented unambiguously and the morphophonemic principle ensures that all phonologically conditioned allomorphs of the same morpheme have one graphemic shape.

(8) Romanization, seen as foreign artificiality replacing indigenous authenticity, did not strike a responsive chord.

Three salient features in the external history of Yiddish are pertinent to this study: the transnational and minority status of its speakers, the greater attention traditionally paid to another Jewish language, and, except for the brief Soviet interlude, the nonofficial and unprotected status of Yiddish.

In the absence of agencies of implementation, of status as a prestigious language, and of sanctions for linguistic behavior, one is at once surprised and not surprised at the development of the language: on one hand, a relatively uniform written variety has arisen in a language community which at its spatial maximum stretched from Alsace to the Baltic and from Holland to the Black Sea; on the other, widespread indifference – sometimes even open hostility – to language cultivation in general and to orthographic uniformity in particular.

Yes, we are not surprised, but we are certainly disappointed. Yet perhaps our disappointment stems from concern (overconcern?) for precision, orderliness, uniformity, standardization – concerns of the Industrial Era.[83] It is, in fact, not surprising that the era of codification (arbitrarily set as beginning in 1863) coincides almost perfectly with several profound changes in traditional Ashkenazic life: the gradual emptying out of the *shtetl* and concomitant hyperurbanization, industrialization, secularization, and westernization. It is therefore not unexpected that the subsector of Ashkenazic Jewry which has best resisted these new winds – Orthodox Jewry (both Khsidic and non-Khsidic) – remains indifferent to these concerns. Elucidation of the relationships between Yiddish language cultivation and these profound changes in central and eastern European Jewish life is still on the agenda of Yiddish sociolinguistics.

NOTES

1. Yiddish forms are cited in the Standardized Transcription, essentially a (morpho)-phonemic rendition of Standard Yiddish; when reference is made to spelling per se, forms are given in angled brackets according to the transliteration system devised by Uriel Weinreich (1954). All translations are the author's.

   The boundary between Eastern and Western Yiddish is roughly the pre-1939 German-Polish border and its southward extension; Eastern Yiddish consists of Northeastern Yiddish and Southern Yiddish, the latter being divided into Central Yiddish and Southeastern Yiddish.

   It is my pleasant duty to thank Mordkhe Schaechter for detailed comments on an earlier version of this paper.
2. In contemporary Yiddish linguistics it is customary to speak of the *Hebrew-Aramaic* (etymological) component. In accordance with S. A. Birnbaum's suggestion (1970) that the Jewish varieties of *Aramaic* be called *Aramic*, *Hebrew-Aramic* is herein used.

   Jews settling on Germanic territory around the turn of the millenium spoke Western and Southern Laaz (also known as Zarfatic and Italkian, respectively), the Jewish correlates of medieval French and medieval Italian (cf. M. Weinreich 1956.)

   When Yiddish-speaking Jews began moving onto Slavic territory, new problems arose; could the solution to the problem of representing /č/, /ž/ and /ǰ/ (cf. note 5), which are largely found in Yiddish words of Slavic origin, be explained by reference to Knaanic orthography?
3. The text is an eleven-word sentence from 1272-1273 (cf. M. Weinreich 1968). The closeness of spelling conventions used in this text and those found in later Yiddish documents shows that Yiddish was being widely written at this time. Had

this text been a one-shot affair, which happened to have occurred to a single individual, one would not expect to find spellings that fit in so harmoniously with the entire Yiddish tradition. Since the text is found in an otherwise all-Hebrew (sacred) prayerbook, it is no wonder it has survived to this day.

4. Hebrew-Aramic traditions: (1) rendition of the consonants but not all of the vowels by unit graphemes; (2) silent *alef* before word-initial vocalic *yud* or *vov*; (3) /v/ rendered by *tsvey vovn*, /ej/ by *tsvey yudn* (Birnbaum 1931; 1953). Laaz traditions: (1) frequent use of word-final silent *alef;* (2) /č/ represented by *tsadik* with a *haček*. The Laaz traditions are found only in early texts. Some researchers have seen Hebrew influence in the older Yiddish convention (which is sometimes found even today) of fusing the indefinite article and the following noun (e.g. *atish* 'a table' rather than *a tish*); but in Hebrew there is no indefinite article and though the definite article *is* fused with the following noun in Hebrew (e.g. *hashulchan* 'the table'), this practice has never been followed in Yiddish (*der tish* 'the table', **dertish*). The SYO and Soviet Codexes decided on *a tish* rather than *atish* probably as a result of European influence.

As literacy in Yiddish spread, the percentage of those with a knowledge of Hebrew (-Aramic) steadily decreased; nowadays it can be said that most Yiddish literates do not know Hebrew (-Aramic).

5. The eventual solutions were: representation of the new phonemes by digraphs (for /č/ and /ž/) and a trigraph (for /ǰ/); representation of palatalization by *yud* in some words; use of digraphs and trigraphs for diphthongs and front rounded vowels; use of diacritics to make up for the lack of graphemes; use of only one grapheme if two or more had identical values (in words of non-Hebrew-Aramic origin).

By the sixteenth century there was no longer any hesitation in representing vocalic phonemes and by the middle of the eighteenth century all phonemes came to be represented more or less unambiguously, except for palatalized consonants in some positions and for most words of Hebrew-Aramic origin in general. The entire period until the last quarter of the eighteenth century can be called the TRADITIONAL PERIOD in Yiddish spelling.

The development of Standard Yiddish has been divided into two major periods by Max Weinreich: the First Literary Standard was based on varieties of Yiddish spoken on Germanic territory and declined after the beginning of the nineteenth century, when Western Yiddish itself began declining as a spoken language; the Second Literary Standard is based on varieties of Eastern Yiddish and began emerging towards the end of the eighteenth century, when the bulk of Yiddish-speakers were by then concentrated on Slavic territory and the First Literary Standard proved inadequate for their needs. Western Yiddish spelling was generally uniform for any given period, but beginning in the 1820's, when Western Yiddish was in evident decline, spelling norms broke down and individual writers' idiolectal or dialectal features become more and more discernible. This situation can be likened to a similar one in Dzhudezmo (see note 72): Dzhudezmo spelling in the traditional Hebrew script is fairly uniform for any one period, but with the almost complete shift to roman characters, at a time when the linguistic, cultural, and social cohesiveness of the Dzhudezmo-speaking community was breaking down, there came much more heterogeneity in spelling practice. Much of it was of course due to the absence of traditional models and the consequent necessity to turn to foreign orthographies (French, Italian, and later, Turkish and Spanish) for guidance.

6. These 'periods' have not followed one another in a neat and clear-cut fashion. The first Yiddish spelling rules are found in a Latin grammar of Hebrew dated 1514 (i.e. they are intended for non-Jews) and the first rules in a Jewish book are from 1542 (Szajkowski 1966). The debating period probably began in 1863 (Tsederboym 1863), reaching a peak in the interbellum years, continuing somewhat abatedly in the 1940's and 1950's and subsiding in the 1960's and 1970's. The period of conferences started in 1908, culminating in several meetings during the 1920's and 1930's. The era of individual experimentation ended more or less on the eve of the first World War, although one or two full-fledged 'private' systems still exist and some Yiddish users still have a few 'pet' spellings.
7. Before the formulation of the phonemic principle, or at least before it reached the attention of the Yiddish world, there was much talk about 'phonetic' spelling (*shrayb vi du redst* 'write as you speak' or *shrayb vi du herst* 'write as you hear'), though most codifiers/reformers soon realized that 'phonetic' spelling was not practical (Reyzen 1920; Kalmanovitsh 1930; Birnbaum 1930). The first use of the word *fonem* 'phoneme' in a discussion of Yiddish spelling is found in Gininger (1951), though many had of course become acquainted with the term earlier.

   Failure to recognize the phonemic principle among the more knowledgeable orthographists has been rare: (1) Joffe (1909), for example, faults the Hebrew script for not distinguishing [n] and [ŋ] (allophones of /n/) and (2) the 'silent' *alef* has been defended on grounds that it DOES stand for some phonetic substance =*fester aynzats* 'rough glide' [Kalmanovitsh 1930: 13-14]; spiritus lenis [Prilutski 1921]), but Max Weinreich (1959: 39) has correctly pointed out that even if this is really so (acoustic analysis is lacking), the phone in question is not a phoneme.

   Since there are not enough graphemes to represent all the phonemes, all systems make use of certain diacritics: suggestions for the creation of new graphemes have not struck a responsive chord.
8. Sometimes called the ETYMOLOGICAL principle (Birnbaum 1930: 135), the ETYMOLOGICAL/MORPHOLOGICAL principle (Reyzen 1920), or the MORPHOLOGICAL principle (Schaechter 1972). Some writers have suggested it be partially abandoned (Birnbaum 1930) or did not take it into account (e.g. Shteynboym 1956: 102). The principle is generally abandoned in all systems when speakers no longer feel that two morphs are allomorphs of the same morpheme, though native intuitions do not always coincide (cf. Dwight Bolinger's work in this area). The Soviet system has gone farthest in abandoning this principle even when most speakers would probably agree that various morphs are allomorphs of the same morphemes.
9. Sometimes called the HISTORICAL principle (Reyzen 1920; Roback 1946; Birnbaum 1930); the first to distinguish historical and etymological principles was apparently M. Schaechter (1972).
10. Also called the DIALECTAL/LITERARY principle (Reyzen 1920) or the UTRAQUISTIC principle (Reyzen 1933: 386; Gininger 1951). The first to call for its maintenance was apparently Zamenhof (1910: 97-104), whose paper was actually written about 1880. His call was echoed by Zhitomirski (1911), although early Russian codifiers abandoned it entirely: Lifshits' spelling (c. 1870), for example, largely reflected his

native Berdichev Yiddish (cf. Szajkowski 1966: 10-13); Vorobeytshik proposed three or four orthographies, one for each of the major regional varieties (termed a 'reactionary democratic idea' by Zaretski [1926: 123]); Veynger (1913a; 1913b) based his orthography on what he felt should be standard Yiddish pronunciation, rather than on all the major regional varieties.

At the other extreme is S. A. Birnbaum's suggestion that orthography indicate the REALIZATION of each diaphone in each of the major varieties of Eastern Yiddish, a proposal that Prilutski (1921) had also made.

The traditional systems, the Soviet system, and the Standardized Yiddish Orthography steer a middle course between these extremes, aiming at an orthography that reflects the largest number of regional and standard phonemic oppositions possible without becoming overly burdensome for the largest number of speakers possible.

Failure to realize that Yiddish orthography has traditionally been more or less interdialectal led to much needless discussion as to what dialect the spelling was supposedly 'based' on or should be based on (e.g. Borokhov 1913: 18; Kalmanovitsh 1936: 284-285).

11. For example, word-final allographs of five graphemes; silent *alef* before word-initial vocalic *yud* or *vov*.
12. Although it has been proposed in the past that this principle be extended to a great number of homophones (e.g. Sholem-Aleykhem 1888: 475; Zamenhof 1910), it has generally not been accepted by orthographists because (1) there is no limit to the number of semantic distinctions that could be represented graphically (cf. the question of polysemy vs. homonymy), (2) not distinguished in the spoken language, homophones need not be differentiated in the written language either, since situational and syntactic contexts disambiguate possible misunderstanding; and (3) recourse would have to be had to 'superfluous' letters, all too reminiscent of Germanized spelling. In rare cases, homophones may be distinguished in the SYO only if one of them is of Hebrew-Aramic origin: *tsar* = ⟨cδr⟩ 'sorrow' or ⟨cʔ^{a}r⟩ 'czar'.
13. First formulated by M. Schaechter (1972), but probably tacitly recognized by other orthographists, too. This principle applies only to given names and surnames, e.g. such names of Hebrew-Aramic origin may be written (morpho) phonemically. Any name may be 'spruced up' up with superfluous letters to give it a 'distinctive cachet' (usually by adding silent *heys* or *ayens* or by doubling a consonant – all in imitation of German orthography), etc.
14. The few remnants of Germanized spelling in the SYO are given in Schaechter (1969: 290-293) (to which we can add the spelling ⟨byy^{a}⟩ 'near', which the Soviet Codex represents more accurately as ⟨bʔ⟩; when the SYO (unfortunately) decided to represent *shva* by *ayen* (cf. German *e*) instead of by traditional *yud*, the codifiers left some forms in their pre-German spelling (e.g., *litayn* 'Latin', *kipitl* 'chapter', *libavitsh* [toponym in Belorussia], rather than **letayn*, **kepitl*, **lebavitsh*).
15. In English, on the other hand, the differentiation of homophones has always been lauded as one of the advantages of traditional spelling (e.g. Vachek 1973: 191).
16. S. A. Birnbaum (1933) gives the various systems somewhat tendentious labels: his Old Maskilic is herein called the Germanized system; his New Maskilic is what was

eventually to become the Standardized Yiddish Orthography (itself not a neutral term by any stretch of the imagination!); his Neo-Traditional corresponds to what is now generally called the Orthodox System; his Quasi-Traditional is a cover term for many uncodified spelling practices found in publications that adhere to no codex; and his Bolshevistic System is now usually called the Soviet System (cf. note 22).

17. Respelled Hebrew-Aramic-origin words are sporadically found in earlier texts too: (1) the anti-Khsidic writer Yoysef Perl (early nineteenth century) often used respellings in parodying Khsidim, who apparently did not know the 'correct' spelling of (many? some?) Hebrew-Aramic-origin words (Kalmanovitsh 1936); (2) Max Weinreich reports (1930: 36) that nineteenth-century writers like Perl, Ayzik-Meyer Dik, and Mendele Moykher-Sforim knew their Hebrew-Aramic well enough, but were nonetheless simply 'careless' in their spelling; (3) Reyzen writes (1920: 154 ff.) that *folksbikhelekh* 'popular works' used respellings in exceptional cases so that Yiddish readers less proficient in Hebrew-Aramic would understand them, but that a misspelled Hebrew-Aramic-origin word was so stigmatized that an author would often avoid an Hebrew-Aramic-origin word whose spelling he was unsure of and use a lexeme from another component or a borrowing from New High German rather than risk misspelling it. That misspelling an Hebrew-Aramic-origin word is generally considered more serious than that of any other words is borne out by the anecdotal evidence in note 48: (4) Teltse-Rifke Gold, b. 1912 in Łagów (near Opatów, Kielce Province, Poland), reports that as late as the 1920's girls in their hometown were normally taught only the respellings. Respellings were probably also taught in many cases where the child was expected to receive only a rudimentary Jewish education, i.e., it was probably not limited to girls (T.-R. Gold also reports that her brother, b. 1914, was also taught respellings). Whether there exists, therefore, a Yiddish analog of 'une orthographe des dames' (cf. Charles Bruneau, *Petite Histoire de la Langue Française* [Paris, 1955], 275) remains to be investigated.

18. On the distinction between Merged and Whole Hebrew see M. Weinreich (1954: 85-86). Many such respelled Hebrew-Aramic-origin words are now considered acceptable, at least in the SYO (cf. Schaechter and Weinreich; U. Weinreich 1968). A fuller list can be found in Gold (i.p.a.). For more information on respelling in the 1910's see Reyzen (1920: 155-156).

    On the other hand, Yiddish words derived from other Jewish languages are always spelled morphophonemically, regardless of their spelling in the lending language (e.g. the Yiddish terms for 'Ladino' and 'Dzhudezmo').

19. On Max Weinreich's attitude towards respelling see note 21.

20. 'But the full enjoyment of the fruits of fusion in rime [i.e. of riming Yiddish words derived from various stock languages] has been impeded by the retention of the traditional spelling of Hebrew-origin words in Yiddish. Although this is justified, culturally, by the special status which that stock language has preserved for users of Yiddish, linguistically it is an anomaly which already troubled such a nineteenth-century master of Yiddish and Hebrew prose as Mendele Moykher-Sforim, and was found to irritate much more seriously the modern Yiddish poets .... The modern poets, who have been concerned precisely with the total integration of the language, could not help but find that the disparate spelling systems for words

of different components only aggravate the unhealthy analytic attitude. Nowhere has the orthographic dualism been as vexing as in riming position. There it obscures intended paralellisms by differing spellings of rime words . . . and occasionally yields unwanted "eye rimes" . . . . The special spelling of Hebraisms was proclaimed outmoded in 1920 by the particularly self-conscious and advanced group of poets, *In Zikh.* "All Yiddish words are equal," they wrote in their manifesto. "As poets – not as propagandists – we shall spell all Yiddish words alike, regardless of their pedigree." Their example was followed widely even by poets outside the group. As B.-J. Bialostotzky put it, "Why should the visual obstruct our free riming of words and our finding of additional word and image relations?'" (U. Weinreich 1959: 426-427). One of these non-In-Zikhist poets is Wolf Younin; a copy of his *Lider* (Yunin 1936) in my possession bears a holograph dedication in which the poet started to write *khaverte* 'Mrs.' in the traditional orthography and then inked over the 'mistake', spelling it as in the Soviet Codex. The book has respellings but preserves the word-final allographs.

21. Max Weinreich (1931) felt that although respelling was theoretically, logically, and linguistically justified, it was psychologically unwarranted since the reader was accustomed to the etymological spellings. He did recognize the need to respell the Hebrew-Aramic component in children's books, however.
22. 'The iron logic of spelling unification might well have prevailed were it not for the fact that a similar reform, undertaken in the Soviet Union in absolute rejection of the Jewish past, had become a symbol of vulgar antitraditionalism which was unpalatable to the majority of Yiddish users. Until 1939, the poets in and about the In Zikh group held out; but the political events of that year, and the discontinuance of the journal *Inzikh*, apparently made it impossible for them to continue publishing in a unified spelling. Now Yiddish writing – in any orthography – has been suppressed in the USSR since 1949; but not until the association between Soviet Communism and Yiddish spelling reform is forgotten is the unification of the orthography likely to be considered again. However such uniquely Yiddish riming possibilities as . . . might never have been discovered or accepted if not for the episode of a unified orthography' (U. Weinreich 1959: 427). Scorn for the Soviet system is often expressed by respelling of the Yiddish equivalents of 'truth [orthography]' (= 'Soviet orthography'), e.g. as in Mark (1952: 29), 'true [orthography]' (e.g. Litvak 1936: 638) or 'comrade'. The neutral term is *sovetishe ortografye* and the ameliorative term is *oktyaber-ortografye* 'orthography of the October Revolution'. Another neutral term is *farbandishe ortografye* 'union orthography', found, for instance, in Alter Katsizne ['Should Yiddish Orthography Be Changed?'], *Literarishe Bleter* 105 (1926), 302. Katsizne was also in favor of respellings. See also note 16.
23. Zaretski (1926) considered that the first step in rationalizing Yiddish spelling was to distinguish all phonemic oppositions graphically.
24. Max Weinreich (1930: 31) doubted that respelling had or would attract substantial numbers of new readers; no statistics are available.
25. Mark (1952: 29) claims that respelling and elimination of word-final allographs were 'intended as a break with Jews in other countries'. It would seem, however, that the break was more with Jewish tradition than with any contemporary Jewish community abroad. Soviet Jewish leaders and writers have always been eager to

see their publications read abroad.

In searching for more or less rational motivations for various reforms, the reader of Soviet scholarly literature must often wade through a morass of ideological jargon and pure and simple name calling. Zaretski (1926: 121), for instance, calls for the elimination of word-final allographs on the grounds that they are 'idlers and exploiters' (*leydik-geyers un eksploatatorn*). A slightly more serious, but hardly weighty, argument was that the Latin alphabet had no such allographs, so why should Yiddish?

26. I have been unable to find proof, however, that they actually did set aside these reforms; a spot check of several wartime publications (notably *Eynikeyt*, the newspaper issued largely for foreign readers) showed that respelling and mono-allographic graphemes had not been abandoned.
27. Levenberg (1968: 182) quotes the editor of *Sovetish Heymland* as having stated that seven of the twenty-five thousand copies are distributed in thirty foreign countries. For a linguistic analysis of the spelling in this journal see Schaechter (1969-1970).
28. The statement that 'Soviet efforts to declericalize Yiddish spelling by abandoning the four end-of-word letters of the traditional Hebrew alphabet have... been abandoned' (Fishman 1972: 12) is only partially true: though respelling is now universal in the Soviet Union, the word-final allographs have been restored in most (but not all) publications.
29. The *Yugnt-Veker* did preserve, however, the word-final allographs. Respelling has always received a more sympathetic response outside the USSR than the elimination of the allographs; many non-Soviet linguists and language-oriented laymen have called for the former (cf. section II.A.), but only Goldberg (1922) is known to have favored the second reform. Cf. also Uriel Weinreich's wistful afterthought cited in note 22 ('... not until the association ...').
30. Controversy has in fact not centered around which regional orthographic variants to standardize, but which ideological ones (e.g. respelling vs. etymological spelling for the Hebrew-Aramic component) and historical ones (e.g. /a/ by *alef* with or without a diacritic) should be standardized.
31. Y. Shteynboym (1956: 98), a member of the commission, reports that 'even though [the spelling commission] was made up of journalists, editors, teachers, and people with a good knowledge of Yiddish, not all could get themselves to abide by the regulations they [themselves] had set up'. The climate in New York Yiddish circles was at that time hardly conducive to spelling codification. Z. Szajkowski reports that the Yiddish humorous magazine *Der Kundes* printed derisive caricatures on the commission's work (oral communication) and Shteynboym himself describes the negative attitude of the then editor of the *Forverts*, Abraham Cahan, to spelling codification. I have not been able to determine when the commission became defunct, though from a stray remark by Joffe (*Pinkes*, New York, 1927-1928, p. 138) it can be inferred that it was still meeting in the fall of 1919.
32. When its cofounder and guiding spirit, Max Weinreich, was able to escape to the United States in 1940, the YIVO reconstituted itself in New York, absorbing its American office, the *Amopteyl* (= *Amerikaner Opteyl* 'American Section'). The latter consisted of a library and archives, and had published a half dozen books, but its importance was probably far smaller than its name suggested. Weinreich's

presence in New York overshadowed the linguists and other researchers associated with the Amopteyl; the linguists, furthermore, felt that the Vilna headquarters had not sufficiently reckoned with their opinions in drafting the Rules of 1937 (e.g. Mark, Joffe) and the YIVO's Executive Committee was therefore finally prevailed upon to approve a new discussion of the SYO. Joffe (1950: 49) claims that writers like Leivick and Opatoshu, the literary critic Niger, the historian Shatzki, and several prominent community leaders, such as Shteynboym and Shtarkman, were against the Rules, but M. Schaechter has informed me that in the hundreds of newspaper and magazine articles by Niger, Leivick, and Opatoshu there is not one word against the Rules of 1937 (written communication).

33. Spacing and hyphenation were of some linguistic importance, however, since the discussion turned in essence on the definition of the Yiddish word; they were also of some sociolinguistic interest because they involved the question of whether German norms should be followed in this respect.

The debate lasted until the end of the 1950's, the main participants being Max Weinreich and Yudel Mark. Joffe's, Levin's and Shteynboym's articles in *Yidishe Shprakh* are not of sociolinguistic importance and the interested reader can find the pertinent references in the bibliography. The thrust of several articles by S. A. Birnbaum, who rejects the Standardized Yiddish Orthography and standard Yiddish pronunciation entirely, is that his orthography, which enjoyed a brief period of use in interbellum Poland (cf. Birnbaum 1960), but which by the 1940's was being used only by the originator himself, should replace the SYO. His main criticisms of the SYO are that certain vestiges of Germanized spelling have not been eliminated (this is largely correct; cf. Schaechter 1969: 290-293) and that the SYO does not indicate the realization of every diaphone in each of the major varieties of Eastern Yiddish ('When I come across a new word, say with . . ., I have to stop because I don't know whether it should be pronounced . . .' (Birnbaum 1944: 105). The SYO is fully (morpho)phonemic for Standard Yiddish (U. Weinreich 1949: 26; 1951) and partially so for each of the regional varieties, though subphonemic for each of the latter in different respects. Since Birnbaum does not recognize standard pronunciation, his criticism of the SYO is from this standpoint justified; however, to achieve a fully phonemic orthography for all of the major Eastern Yiddish varieties, Birnbaum must resort to a wealth of diacritics, thus burdening an orthography already overloaded with diacritics with even more of them.

In summarizing each of the major articles in the spelling debate, I will try to emphasize the arguments of purely sociolinguistic interest. If most of the quotations are from Max Weinreich's papers, it is simply because he was the only one to see the deeper sociocultural implications of the decades of efforts to standardize Yiddish spelling and implement the resultant codex.

34. Comparison with other languages has been turned to advantage by all parties: (1) Mitlyanski (1918) reported that Soviet Yiddish reformers took their cue from the postrevolutionary changes effected in the Russian orthography; (2) Reyzen (1920: 128) went even further and claimed that neotraditional Yiddish spelling as a whole (*naye ortografye* 'new orthography') was gaining ground partially because the revised Russian codex served as a model for Yiddish users (i.e. interest in reforming Russian orthography sensitized Yiddish users to similar problems in

their own language); (3) Yiddish linguists became wary of too much reform partially because they realized that the four revisions in Polish orthography between 1918 and 1939 had made many Polish-users lose interest in keeping up with the latest 'reforms'; (4) the obligatory use of diacritics in other languages is often used as an argument for their mandatoriness in Yiddish too (e.g. Schaechter 1972: 6); (5) the vagaries of English spelling are sometimes adduced as proof that a standardized Yiddish orthography is unnecessary – the counterargument being that, while the fit between grapheme and phoneme may be poor in English, the 'chaos' is nonetheless more or less 'standardized'.

35. Only *ortografn* 'orthographers' (not necessarily linguists) can have a hand in spelling reform and codification.

As an example of the complications involved in standardizing Yiddish spelling, we can cite the following: laymen often ask why the SYO is not 'uniform' in the use of diacritics in *beys/veys*, *kof/khof*, *pey/fey*, *shin/sin*, and *tof/sof*. The principle followed by the SYO codifiers was, I surmise, that (a) if only one member of any of these pairs is used only in words of Hebrew-Aramic origin (and therefore of less frequent occurrence than its partner), it should be the marked form (*veys* is therefore written with *rofe*, *kof* with a *dogesh*, and *sin* with a dot) and its more frequent partner (*veys*, *khof*, and *shin*) should be unmarked (there thus being only one distinctive feature distinguishing the partners); (b) if both partners are used only in words of Hebrew-Aramic origin (and therefore both are relatively infrequent), they should be distinguished by only one feature (this is the case only for *tof/sof*) and it is a toss-up which partner to mark (either *tof* with a *dogesh* – as the SYO requires – or *sof* with *rofe*); (c) if both partners are used in all components (and thus of high frequency), they should be distinguished by *two* distinctive features (as is the case for *pey* and *fey*, the former being written with a *dogesh* and the latter with *rofe*). The underlying idea, of course, was to use as few diacritics as possible (cf. Ray's remarks in note 53) and, if they *had* to be used, to require them generally in the less frequent partners only. Could the notions of functional load and of markedness (as they were then being elaborated by the Prague School of linguists) have been known to the codifiers of the SYO (who applied them to graphemics) or did they stumble on them independently, intuitively? See also the second paragraph of section VII.

36. A comparison of the SYO, Mark's 'reforms', and actual usage does not bear this out: the SYO calls for spacing between elements of an adverbial phrase (e.g. *in gantsn* 'entirely') and most publications (except Soviet ones) do follow this rule (cf. Kshenski 1967), yet Mark's system requires *ingantsn*. Conversely, elements of the SYO which have not met with too much success (the 'hard' rules), such as the use of diacritics, are retained in Mark's system.

37. The spelling conference convened under YIVO auspices in Buenos Aires in 1931, acting in a purely advisory capacity, consisted solely of nonlinguists (fifty-two representatives of newspapers, school systems, teachers' unions, writers' clubs, actors, publishers, printers, and teachers) simply because no Yiddish linguists were at that time residing in Argentina or Uruguay. The various conferences sponsored by the YIVO in Poland in the 1930's also included language-oriented laymen, but only in an advisory capacity.

It is important to note that although there has been widespread antagonism and even open hostility towards Yiddish linguists/philologists/ language engineers on the part of much of the Yiddish-speaking leadership (*kultur-tuers, klal-tuers* literally 'culture doers', 'community doers'), that most Yiddish linguists, etc., have been active members of the Yiddish-speaking community in such positions as journalists, authors, leaders of community institutions, teachers, etc. The situation is not analogous to that of a missionary, government official, or other 'outsider' trying to impose an orthography on a group he does not belong to.

38. After refuting Weinreich's arguments, Mark returns to the favorite question of the postwar debate – spacing and hyphenation. It is unfortunate that so much ink was wasted on this subject.
39. In my opinion, only one of the 177 respondents, Salomo Birnbaum, has enough theoretical and practical knowledge to participate in such a reform in more than an advisory capacity. Yet since he rejects the SYO outright (and therefore Mark's offshoot), his participation would really be beside the point. Mordkhe Schaechter has informed me that two of the pollees were not habitual Yiddish readers, two innocently thought that they were merely being asked for an opinion and had no idea the survey was being used for ulterior motives (one later calling it a fraud [*ganeyves-daas*]) and that those who realized this refused to participate. Almost all of the pollees could not spell according to the SYO, were unacquainted with the spelling debates and reforms of the preceding seventy-five years, and had no special interest or competence in language engineering. A few of their comments on the survey are eloquent (quoted in Mark 1959a): one called on the YIVO's Philological Section to undertake a new codification (the Philological Section had been dissolved in 1946); another called spelling a 'practical' and not a 'theoretical' problem; and a third was happy to see that the survey was 'not concerned with rules but with individual words'.
40. The TSISHO did not survive the Holocaust.
41. The simile is Mordkhe Schaechter's (1964: 17). Weinreich of course had many supporters (notably Uriel Weinreich and Chaim Gininger – linguists and teachers – and Szymon Dawidowicz – YIVO editor and proofreader), but he was far and away the most ardent supporter of the SYO and the only one to defend it (at length, moreover) in the columns of *Yidishe Shprakh*.
42. Although several members have introduced the SYO in the publications they edit, a major newspaper like the Tel Aviv daily *Di Letste Nayes* and publications of the Argentine office of the YIVO, the heads of which are committee members, have still failed to introduce all of the diacritics and do not follow all of the rules for spacing and hyphenation.

Even more disappointing have been public statements by some members on their intentional deviations from the Rules: in replying to Mark's 'Spelling Survey', Michael Astour, Shloyme Suskovitsh, and Avrom Sutskever stated that they 'try to follow the SYO, but deviate from them in the following cases . . .' (Mark 1959a: 78, 79, 81). Mordkhe Tsanin (Mark 1959a: 82) wrote that when his Hebrew-Yiddish dictionary was being set, he decided to make the dictionary 'more accessible [?] to the reader by not following . . .'. Shmuel Rollanski (Mark 1959a: 82-83), though claiming to be a 'follower of the Rules by principle' (*printsipyeler onhenger*), has shown otherwise by his responses to the survey and in the publications he edits.

43. From Max Weinreich's foreword (Schaechter and Weinreich 1961): 'This handbook is intended not only for professional writers, teachers, and staff-members of community institutions, but also for everyone who writes Yiddish and wants Yiddish. We cannot overemphasize how important writing Yiddish correctly and uniformly in both public and private is for our cultural development.... It was extraordinarily difficult to set up spelling norms for Yiddish because the norms had to be created on a voluntary basis – without the discipline achieved by a long-standing educational tradition and without state constraint. The war shook our entire cultural edifice to its very foundations.... The differences in spelling are glaring even in print; each publication has its own spelling and different contributors to the same publication sometimes differ from one another. Even the same writer may not always be consistent in his spelling. Such disorganization is damaging not only to those who use Yiddish, to those who want to learn Yiddish, but to our entire cultural collective [*kultur-kolektiv*] as well. The very fact that Yiddish is spoken and written on every continent gives special importance to the efforts made to standardize our spelling.... The Rules symbolize our growth potential.... The dignity of Yiddish – both within and without the Yiddish-speaking community – requires that it have one orthographic form throughout the world' (pp. 5-6). The reference to the absence of an educational tradition refers to the little or no attention paid to Yiddish as a subject of instruction in traditional Jewish schools (cf. section III.D.).
44. Small in 'non-Jewish' terms, 220 signatures probably represents about two percent of the monthly's average printing. Nine signatories later canceled their subscriptions.

    Before the CISYO was established, Mordkhe Schaechter had organized a letter-writing campaign directed at the two major New York dailies, the *Tog-Morgn-Zhurnal* (now defunct) and the *Forverts;* despite firm promises of reform, none was forthcoming. The Committee had also conducted a low-keyed campaign in 1958 and 1959 aimed at all Yiddish periodicals, yet despite 'willingness to accept the SYO' expressed by forty-seven of them (M. Weinreich 1959: 56), not more than a handful have actually done so. Many community leaders were apparently indifferent to efforts at implementing the SYO: at a gathering honoring the appearance of a Yiddish textbook on October 16, 1959, for example, Hyman Bass, executive secretary of the World Congress for Jewish Culture, said (evidently with some pride) that he 'didn't care whether [the textbook] was with dots or without dots, with bars or without bars' (see letter of M. Schaechter to H. Bass, October 18, 1959, in the CISYO files at the YIVO Archives).
45. 'Every man of letters, every teacher, every typesetter, every secretary – in a word, everyone who uses his language professionally – must be able to spell correctly and not just according to his own discretion. But even people who do not write Yiddish for publication must be able to spell properly. Formerly there was no standardized orthographic system and no authoritative institution which could formulate and proclaim the [standardized] spelling. But times have changesd....' (Weinreich and Borenstein 1965).

    Taught by Mordkhe Schaechter, the course consisted of ten lectures and was attended by eighty-one people aged seventeen to seventy-seven, a far larger number than the organizers had expected (cf. Schaechter 1972: 4 ff.).

46. Individual persuasion through personal contact and private letter has not been neglected. Since 1951, Mordkhe Schaechter has written several hundred letters to editors, publishers, journalists, and writers in all Yiddish-speaking communities, and, since 1957, has tried to exert influence publicly through his column in *Afn Shvel* (Schaechter 1957-) as well as by articles in other journals and collective volumes. His contributions to the entire struggle to create a sense of language cultivation and language loyalty cannot be overemphasized.

The strategy employed in these efforts includes: (a) refusal to contribute to any publication in which the SYO was not followed; in this way, Mordkhe Schaechter was successful in having the *Seyfer Leavrom* (Shtarkman 1969-1970) and, with the help of Isaiah Trunk and Chaim Gininger, the *Almanakh Yidish* (Pat 1961) published according to the SYO. I contributed two articles to *Der Veker* (Gold 1970b; 1970c) on condition that the magazine adopt the SYO; however, when only my own work appeared in the SYO, I refused to participate further. In some cases, however, this strategy has not worked: Max Weinreich and Mordkhe Schaechter withdrew as consultants to the unabridged Yiddish dictionary (Mark and Joffe 1961-) when sample pages of it were issued in 1954 in another spelling, but the editors were unmoved (Mark 1959b: 95). (b) requiring that one's own publications, from books to New Year's Cards, adhere to the SYO (as in the case of Mordkhe Schaechter's, Lifshe Widman's, and Bella Gottesman's publications); (c) satirical articles written under pseudonyms or anonomously (e.g. Gold 1971a; Shlayfshteyn 1970); (f) express mention of nonstandardized spelling in book reviews (e.g. Anon. 1972; Roskies 1970); and (g) 'gentle reminders' (e.g. Anon. 1971) that contributors to periodicals should follow the SYO – but no publication, not even the YIVO's, has ever refused an article because it does not follow the SYO.

47. Cf. notes 44, 45, 46. 'The Rules were the result of many years of work in the standardization and codification [of Yiddish spelling] and they therefore symbolize the continuity of Standard Yiddish after the Holocaust' (M. Weinreich 1961). 'The Standardized Yiddish Orthography is . . . symbolic of a certain period of Jewish creativity and of its achievements and aspirations . . . . [It] is important not only instrumentally, but also sentimentally. Only those who are entirely lacking in that community sentiment and discipline with which the spelling system was created can now afford to deviate from the SYO' (Joshua A. Fishman, in Preface to Schaechter 1972: 2).

The idea that one has to learn to spell or learn Yiddish 'evokes latent antagonism in most Yiddish writers, the majority of whom have not even attended an elementary school conducted in Yiddish' (Schaechter 1964: 4). 'It is better to follow a rule even when it results in a *Schriftbild* that looks odd at first sight than to follow the momentary notions of an individual' (Max Weinreich in Schaechter 1964: 5). 'Not everyone who can write a good poem is capable of deciding questions of spelling' (Schaechter 1964: 5). 'With a few exceptions we are simply not used to such a thing as orthographic discipline and even less so to orthographic loyalty' (Schaechter 1964: 17). 'With the transfer of the YIVO to the United States, its accomplishments in standardizing Yiddish spelling became seriously endangered. On one hand [we were faced by] a community lacking the notion of *Sprachkultur* [cf. section III.D.] and, on the other hand, [had to contend with] 'connoisseurs' [*deye-zogers*] of every stripe' (Schaechter 1964: 17).

48. Anecdotal evidence: (a) 'Any little change or mistake [in the spelling of a Hebrew-Aramic-origin word] makes [the word] incomprehensible and ridiculous in the eyes of the expert' (Golomb 1910: 7); (b) Mordkhe Schaechter, who taught Yiddish in an afternoon school from 1956 to 1962, recalls that a school director once visited his classroom and, noticing a misspelled Hebrew-Aramic-origin word on the blackboard, discreetly pointed it out to him in a tone of shock and shame; an error in a non-Hebrew-Aramic-origin word was not noticed, nor does the director himself know the SYO (which was being taught at his school); (c) this writer planted errors in several letters to a Yiddish teacher of long standing, but only those in Hebrew-Aramic-origin words were noticed.
49. Explicit mention of spelling and Romanization in book reviews (cf. note 46) is apparently a recent and ephemeral phenomenon, being limited to two reviews in *Yugntruf*, where it was introduced at my suggestion. Six 'language-columns' are known from the postwar period: M. Zakin and M. Volanski, 'Undzer Shprakh', *Ikuf* (Buenos Aires, 1945-1953): A.-A. Roback, 'Shprakh Un Folklor', *Dafke* (Buenos Aires); 'Shprakhvinkl', *Heymish* (Tel Aviv); Wolf Younin, 'Shprakhvinkl', *Tog-Morgn-Zhurnal* (now in the *Forverts*); Rakhmil Tsukerman, 'Undzer Shprakh-vinkl', *Yugntruf* (New York, 1965-1966); and Mordhke Schaechter, 'Laytish Mame-Loshn', *Afn Shvel* (New York City and Mexico City, 1957-). Literary prizes do exist, but spelling is never a consideration.
50. Anecdotal evidence: (a) petitions to the *Tog* and *Forverts* in 1970 had to be checked to make sure that signatures contained all the necessary diacritics; most did not; (b) a reviewer in the *Tog* warmly applauded the appearance of Schaechter (1972), but did not use the SYO himself (e.g. in private correspondence); (c) 'there is definitely a greater desire to achieve a standardized Yiddish orthography [in Argentina than in the United States], but this has by no means been achieved. Not only in the newspapers but also in the books published by the large community publishing houses is there confusion about spacing and hyphenation . . . . People think they are following the Rules when they [violate such and such a Rule], but they still say with conviction, 'We abide by the SYO''' (Mark 1963: 35).

Further obstacles to the emergence of a sense of *Sprachpflege* are the general absence of any sanctions – rewards or punishments – for linguistic behavior and the absence of an 'aristocracy' (in the conventional sense), a prestigious capital city which could set a norm, or of a territory with a compact Yiddish-speaking majority where 'prestigious' forms could diffuse at a relatively quick rate. The destruction of the Yiddish heartland during the Holocaust and the earlier mass migrations (since 1880) have fragmented the Yiddish-speaking community even more than before.

Yet though it is probably true that indifference to language is the norm for the majority of human beings and the absence of *Sprachpflege* in this case is therefore only natural, it is nonetheless astounding that even in such unfavorable circumstances, a relatively uniform Standard Yiddish (phonologically, morphologically, syntactically, and lexically speaking) has emerged and is recognized – though not necessarily always adhered to – by Yiddish users in almost every community.

The statement that absence of *Sprachpflege* is probably the norm does not apply to some Amerindian languages; for Chitimacha see Morris Swadesh, 'Sociological Notes on Obsolescent Languages', *IJAL* 14 (1948): 226-235; for

Navaho see Gladys A. Reichard, 'Linguistic Diversity Among the Navaho Indians', *IJAL* 11 (1945): 156-158; and for Menomina see several statements by Bloomfield.

It is curious that *Sprachpflege* vis-á-vis Whole Hebrew Aramic was probably limited mostly to the levels of orthography, phonology, and morphology, but less so to those of syntax, lexicon, and semantics, where the influence of other Jewish languages is evident to varying degrees.

51. Yiddish has never had to contend seriously with the question of alphabet loyalty (cf. section V).

52. His contribution to M. Weinreich ([ed.] 1930) was of course printed in the Orthodox Codex because there was as yet no SYO (Birnbaum 1930). In deference to the *doyen d'âge* and *doyen d'ancienneté* of Yiddish linguistics, his contribution to Dawidowicz, et al. (1964) was also left unchanged orthographically (Birnbaum 1964); Birnbaum (1953) is in the SYO, except for five words and a paragraph cited from one of his previous articles; Birnbaum (1960) is also in the orthodox spelling, but only as regards graphemes, spacing, and hyphenation (not however the diacritics; cf. the editor's comment: 'as an exception we print [Dr. Birnbaum's] letter in his orthography'), as are his comments on Mark's survey (1959a: 79). When S. A. Birnbaum gave a course at the YIVO's Max Weinreich Center for Advanced Jewish Studies in the spring of 1972, his mimeographed course outline also appeared in the orthodox spelling, which the YIVO permitted as a gesture of goodwill. Birnbaum (1968) is also printed according to this system, though not in respect of the diacritics.

An eloquent defense of the Orthodox Codex can be found in S. Birnbaum (1930a).

53. There seem to be tacitly recognized degrees of seriousness of deviation from the norm: most serious (for *all* Yiddish-users) is the misuse of graphemes in the Hebrew-Aramic component (addition/omission/substitution of graphemes); less serious is their misuse in other etymological components; and least serious is the misuse of diacritics (in any component).

In private correspondence, though sometimes in print too, one also finds errors due to phonological difficulties: (a) hypercorrections (e.g. ⟨glvybn⟩ 'to believe' for ⟨glyybn⟩); (b) misspelling of recent loans that are not fully integrated into the dynamics of Yiddish phonology (e.g. ⟨zʔp⟩ 'soup' for ⟨zvp⟩); and (c) failure to observe the morphophonemic principle (e.g. ⟨bryf⟩ 'letter' for ⟨bryvv⟩).

Given the widespread omission (and sometimes overuse) of diacritics, it has often been suggested that they be partially done away with; yet unless new graphemes were introduced (which is unpalatable to most Yiddish-users), the alphabet would not reflect all phonemic oppositions. All of the diacritics, incidentally, have historical validity, i.e. they are 'vintage'.

The writer asked eight native-speakers (age range: ±45-±65) and one non-native who had taken a summer course in Yiddish to *copy* three lines of running text (nineteen words) printed in the SYO. Three had a perfect score (one was the non-native), none made any mistakes in copying the graphemes, but five received less than a perfect score with respect to the diacritics (deviations ranged from omission of two or three of a total of fourteen to *all* of them). The same persons were then asked to copy a string of fifteen graphemes, five of which had diacritics;

every subject got a perfect score since in this case the graphemes with diacritics were in four out of the five instances placed next to the corresponding diacriticless graphemes, the contrast thus being obvious. The omitter of all the diacritics had received an intensive Hebrew education and the others had had varying degrees of formal training in Hebrew and Yiddish.

In Hebrew, the diacritics are normally used only in prayerbooks, printed editions of the Bible, and in teaching materials. Other texts are normally unpointed, though difficult, unfamiliar, or new words may also be found with the appropriate diacritics even in an otherwise unpointed text. An alternative to pointing is the use of full spelling (*scriptio plena, ketiv male*), i.e. the indication of certain vowels by means of graphemes. Both pointing and full spelling are sometimes found in Hebrew dictionaries. The SYO requires a diacritic in only nine cases; thus, though Yiddish and Hebrew both use diacritics, their emic status is different: in Yiddish they are mandatory, but in Hebrew they are not.

Max Weinreich reports (1959: 46-47) that full pointing was used in Yiddish for about sixty years in the nineteenth and early twentieth centuries. With the rise of modern Yiddish literature and the Yiddish press, there arose new generations of Yiddish-readers for whom reading had to be made as easy as possible; at first vowel points were placed under the consonantal graphemes (as in Hebrew) and, at a later stage, under the corresponding vocalic grapheme (as all codexes now require); although it was perhaps pedagogically sound to indicate vowels in this double fashion (grapheme + diacritic), the effect on the eye was bad: a page cluttered with superfluous and distracting marks. It has sometimes been said that the writers, printers, typesetters, etc., hit on the idea of using full pointing in Yiddish to ease the burden of Hebrew-readers just learning to read Yiddish; but it seems that in traditional Ashkenazic society, every Hebrew-reader was sure to be a Yiddish-reader – the 'new' readers Weinreich refers to are probably illiterates who were learning to read and write Yiddish and who were, in fact, swelling the ranks of the Yiddish-reading public and making the rise of modern literature and press possible. On the existence of pre-nineteenth-century pointed Yiddish manuscripts see S. Birnbaum (1930a).

The neo-traditional systems did away with most of the diacritics. Zaretski (1928c) cautioned against the use of too many of them because they were 'logically unnecessary' and caused difficulty in reading and writing (see also Kupershmid 1928).

In some Yiddish circles there exists, however, a *digraphia* analogous to the Hebrew case: at the Congress for Jewish Culture and the Sholem-Aleykhem Folk Institute (New York), for example, materials intended for students of Yiddish appear in a close approximation of the SYO (i.e. with most of the mandatory diacritics), whereas publications intended for the adult reader generally do not. A similar situation existed at the Workmen's Circle until the digraphia was almost completely eliminated by Joseph Mlotek (in favor of the SYO); at YIVO there still exist some digraphia, but only in respect of handwritten and typewritten documents – all printed documents appear in the SYO. Supporters of the SYO would of course like to see such digraphia eliminated at all of these organizations.

Several points made in this note seem to bear out Punya Sloka Ray's hypotheses concerning orthographic reform (1963: 97): (a) 'a new sign is the most expensive to acquire' (cf. the total failure at script reform in Yiddish); (b) 'a diacritic is cheap to introduce . . ., [but people] tend to leave it out'; (c) 'a digraph is the cheapest to introduce . . . [and] cheaper to maintain than a diacritic, though not as cheap as a new letter or a new value for an old letter' (the Yiddish digraphs for /č/, /ž/, /v/, /ej/, /aj/, /oj/, and /au/ and the trigraph for /ǰ/ are universally employed). Note, however, that Palestinian/Israeli Hebrew has apparently experienced no trouble in shifting from the (Yiddish-origin) representation of /č/, /ž/, and /ɟ/ by polygraphs to a (probably Dzhudezmo-origin) representation consisting of grapheme + diacritic [čadi, žayen, ǰimel].

54. It is perhaps significant, however, that the only non-YIVO publication founded after 1937 to have adopted the SYO from the outset is *Yugntruf*, written and edited exclusively by non-eastern-European-born high-school and college students, most of whom, however, are not native primary speakers of Yiddish. Much of the credit for this accomplishment goes to M. Schaechter, the publication's mentor.
55. An even more obvious instance of discrepancy between spelling and ideology is the case of communist publications outside the USSR, which do not now use the Soviet system (see Gold 1971b: 225).
56. Thus, the Workmen's Circle's publications adopted the SYO as soon as Joseph Mlotek became its educational director and *Afn Shevl* did so when M. Schaechter became editor in 1957. Rather than expend time and energy on pressuring publications and organizations to adopt the SYO, it might be much more effective to try to place the 'right person in the right position at the right time'.
57. It is unfortunate that where Yiddish has the best chances of survival, in the Khsidic and some other ultra-orthodox communities, interest in language engineering has not developed; and where it has, viz. in secularist groups, the language is steadily declining. For an opinion on the future of Yiddish among a certain group of Khsidim see Jochnowitz (1968).

    The debates of the 1940's, 1950's, and 1960's took place exclusively in the nonreligious, noncommunist sectors of the Yiddish-speaking community. On the one hand, it was felt that religious groups (Khsidic and non-Khsidic) would want to have little or no intercourse with secularists, and, on the other hand, communist circles were tabu to those associated with the YIVO and the CISYO. Communist publications such as the *Morgn-Frayheyt* and *Yidishe Kultur* have mistakenly interpreted such 'nonintervention' as meaning their Yiddish is above reproach.
58. All codifiers (except perhaps Veynger; see Shlosberg 1930) have therefore been guided by the dictum that the written word should be made as accessible to the reader as possible with the smallest number of changes possible (cf. Vevyorka 1926); many prefer to speak, therefore, of codification rather than reform, thereby stressing their conservative attitude towards spelling changes. How each orthographist (to use a neutral term) interpreted the word 'accessible' and just how many changes were absolutely necessary varies of course from case to case.

    Most of Veynger's extreme reforms (e.g. abandonment of the interdialectal principle, representation of /f/ in any position by the word-final allograph of the grapheme ⟨f⟩, a single *vov* for /v/, etc.) were not accepted; others are now largely abandoned even within the Soviet Union (e.g. not using the word-final allographs), while still others have generally not spread beyond the boundaries of the USSR (e.g. respelling).

There is a high degree of mutual legibility between the codices, i.e. a person trained to read any one of them can easily accustom himself to any of the others. Interference may occur in the following cases: (1) when a reader of the Soviet system tries to read Hebrew-Aramic origin words as spelled traditionally; (2) when a reader of one of the neotraditional systems tries to read texts with full pointing (cf. note 53) or texts in the Germanized spelling (in either case, the visual effect is one of too much 'cluttering' – of vowel points in the first case and of graphemes in the second); and (3) when a reader of a non-Soviet codex tries to read texts without word-final allographs or with respellings (here the interference is probably much less than in the first two cases). The lowest degree of mutual legibility is found between Veynger's system and all of the others; I could not, for instance, read a line of Veynger (1913a) and (1913b) without severe eye strain. It is eloquent that the only real innovation in the SYO, (the optional) unigraph for /v/, has not taken hold to any great extent.

Some community leaders, indifferent or hostile to the SYO, claim that the Rules of 1937 call for too much innovation and that their introduction would 'confuse' the reader, thus leading to a drop in circulation (this fear was expressed as early as 1918 with respect to the codex of the New York Spelling Commission; see Levin 1952: 49). In the case of Yiddish, however, failure to adopt the SYO has sometimes led to a small drop in circulation, i.e. some extremely loyal members of the *takones-kolektiv* will not subscribe to (or write for) a publication that has not introduced it, and, conversely, will read a publication that has done so, even if its contents are not particularly interesting.

Suggestions that the SYO be introduced gradually (say one Rule a month) have not been followed.

59. Joshua A. Fishman, on the other hand, sees further reform as a sign of vitality: the SYO 'is not the last one; there will be another rebirth, another spiritual awakening in Yiddish. New sentiments and new symbols will then be created and linked to a [new] consensus on an even more perfect, an even more systematic, orthography. Till that time comes, let us learn the present Standardized Yiddish Orthography' (in Schaechter 1972: 3).

60. First expressed by him, it appears, in U. Weinreich (1930: 3). Cf. M. Schaechter (1972: 4-9): 'With a people of "a million presidents", the teacher must avoid situations where he can unwittingly encourage further innovation, new "schemists" [*bal-amtsoes*], new "Divine Creators" [*mayse-breyshesnikes*]. No, they would constitute no real danger in the 1970's; there is not a magazine, publisher, or school system that would be impressed today by a new, potential "reformer" – but even a cat can spoil everything. The teacher must refute such disunifying [*umgezelshaftlekh*] arguments like "My father in Toronto doesn't use a *komets*, so why should I?" or "*Sovetish Heymland* writes . . ., so why should I have to . . .?" The teacher should be indefatigable in pointing out that just like French, German, Polish, Hungarian, Czech, Rumanian, Portuguese, etc., require certain diacritics, so too does Yiddish . . . . "And what if I don't? Will you shoot me?" No, there will be no shooting or exile to Siberia, but a Yiddish-speaker with an uncultural [*umkulturel*] attitude towards his language cannot be a cultivated person [*kulturmentsh*] . . . . Just as in other languages, the Rules might have been different – but learning to spell means learning the Rules as they are, not as they might have been in theory.

The growth of a cultivated language [*kulturshprakh*] and a cultural community [*kultur-tsiber*] is inconceivable otherwise.'

61. Primary Romanizations are intended as permanent and universal replacements of a non-roman script (e.g. Albanian, 1908, and Turkish, 1926); secondary Romanizations are employed only when members of the language community would otherwise not be able to read their own language, for persons outside the language community, or where the normal script cannot be used (e.g. for lack of type). It is not always clear whether the proponents of Yiddish Romanization were aiming at primary or secondary replacements of the Hebrew script; wherever possible, I have tried to infer their intentions from often hazy statements. 'Latinization' and 'Romanization' are herein used synonymously.

    Romanized Yiddish in philological works is found as early as the seventeenth century (e.g. Wagenseil, Buxtorf). Although S. A. Birnbaum doubts that such Romanizations can be useful in reconstructing older stages of Yiddish phonology (since Romanizers usually 'respelled' Yiddish in terms of Germanic, Hebrew-Aramic, Slavic, etc., cognates; cf. Gold i.p. b), a study of these Romanizations might nonetheless be useful.

62. Nathan Birnbaum had called for the Romanization of Yiddish and Hebrew as early as 1902 (Birnbaum 1902). He apparently abandoned this proposal at a later date. Litvak (1926) states that A. Vayter (1905) had come out in favor of Romanization at about the same time, but that he later regretted making this suggestion. Another early proponent was Ludwig Zamenhof (1910). According to Reyzen (1920: 127), primary Romanization was favored by N. Birnbaum, Sotek, and Zamenhof, but that the plan was 'doomed to failure from the outset'. See also Himowich (1904) and Shtarkman (1929).

63. Sotek: 'Yiddish can be raised to the level of a European language only when it is Latinized' (Reyzen n.d.: s.v. Sotek); Perets: 'If our Yiddish is to have the same rights as other world languages, it must be accessible to the world. We therefore want our best cultural treasures to be transcribed into Latin letters' (Gininger, et al. 1934). Sotek called for the dissemination of Romanized texts 'in certain semi-assimilated [Jewish] circles', i.e. among linguistically assimilated members of the Jewish intelligentsia. He in fact claimed that as a result of his efforts three thousand readers had been gained for Yiddish literature in Rumania alone (M. Weinreich [ed.] 1931: 93-94).

    Perets was evidently advocating secondary Romanization for the benefit of non-Jews. Sotek, too, would seem to have been in favor of secondary Romanization for Jews who did not read Yiddish, yet his initial statement ('Yiddish can be raised . . .') implies primary Romanization (cf. Reyzen in note 62). Max Weinreich (1930: 31, 32) doubted that Romanization had attracted or would attract substantial numbers of new readers, yet he did favor Romanized texts for non-Jews who wanted to learn Yiddish.

64. Actually, all Jewish languages have been traditionally written in Hebrew characters because (1) it is the alphabet Jews have best been acquainted with; (2) it is endowed with a degree of sanctity; and (3) there has usually been no special reason to employ any other alphabet.

    Although the Hebrew alphabet can always be learned by any non-Jew just as easily as any Jew, it has probably nonetheless been a deterrent to the less ambitious or curious. And though there is further evidence that Jews have often realized the 'exclusivist' functions of this script (e.g. the writer recalls seeing a sign in Montreal, c. 1963, with 'Room For Rent' written in Hebrew letters according to their Yiddish values, or a Hebrew-script advertisement that appears in the English-language *The Jewish Observer*, '*Ruft Hatsole EV 7-1750 Far Fraye Emoydzhensi Oksidzhen*' 'Call Rescue, EV 7-1750, For Free Emergency Oxygen', a message obviously intended only for Jews), this was probably not one of the major reasons why the Hebrew script has been traditional for all Jewish languages. Some writers unfortunately see the Latin alphabet as 'normal' and any 'deviation' from it as requiring 'justification' or 'explanation'. Thus, though it is true that zeal for separateness is often manifested by graphic distinctiveness, it is probably an exaggeration to claim that the 'use of the Hebrew alphabet represents a sort of graphic declaration of separation, if not of independence' (Carr 1958: 210). This would be true only if Jews switched from some other script to the Hebrew one.

Joffe also gives several reasons why the Hebrew alphabet is unsuited for Yiddish: (1) there are more phonemes than graphemes (especially since some graphemes are homophonous); (2) two phomemes are represented by digraphs; (3) *yud* can stand for consonantal /j/, vocalic /i/, and palatalization; (4) *tsvey yudn* can represent /aj/, /ej/, or /ji/; (5) palatalization is often not indicated; (6) [ə] is not consistently represented by one and the same grapheme; (7) [n] and [ŋ] are not distinguished. These deficiencies have either been remedied in the SYO or are trivial: (1) diacritics now permit the phonemic principle to be observed; (2) digraphs for /č/ and /ž/ (and a trigraph for /ǰ/) are not considered burdensome; (3) context determines whether *yud* is vocalic or consonantal (although consonant plus /y/ is not always distinguishable from the same consonant when palatalized); (4) diacritics now permit these three sequences to be distinguished graphically; (5) this problem has still not been solved; (6) *shva* is not a phoneme; (7) a phonemic orthography need not distinguish subphonemic variation.

Joffe proposed a Latin alphabet consisting of twenty-four letters plus three of these letters with a diacritic, thus permitting each speaker to write 'as he speaks'; as will be pointed out below, Romanization requires abandonment of the interdialectal principle and thereby does permit, to some extent, idiolectal writing – a doubtful advantage.

Perhaps the chief reason why Judah A. Joffe (1873-1966) championed Romanization was that he himself had trouble writing Yiddish in the Hebrew script; many remember how at lectures and meetings he would take notes in Romanized script because he could not write the Hebrew letters fast enough.

65. One could also add: (1) Latinization would create digraphia since Yiddish speakers would still have to learn the Hebrew script for Hebrew; (2) Romanized Yiddish is no easier to learn than Yiddish in the traditional script; (3) 'recognition' would not necessarily be ensured after Romanization; and (4) most Yiddish users, moreover, are hardly eager to obtain such 'recognition'.

66. The Romanized title shows that the values of the Latin letters were those of Polish and that the variety of Yiddish transcribed was Southern Yiddish (probably Central Yiddish).

67. Shpilreyn finds that the Hebrew alphabet cannot distinguish *j* from *i* ([1] from [i]) and palatal /l/ from the nonpalatal variety, and has no grapheme for [ə]; but

these are hardly weighty reasons for Romanization: in many varieties of Yiddish (including Standard Yiddish), [1] and [i] are allophones of one phoneme, and *shva* is not phonemic in any variety. If the Hebrew script is deficient with respect to palatalization, it is much easier to remedy the deficiency within the existing framework than to abandon it entirely.

Kenig brooks no 'sentimentalism' or 'estheticism' ('Some say, "The Hebrew letters are pretty."') and calls on the Yiddish community to recognize that Yiddish is a 'European', not an 'Asiatic', language that is used in Europe and the New World. His principal argument is that Yiddish in the usual script is dying faster than the Yiddish language itself, i.e. the numbers of those who can speak and understand it but not read or write it are constantly growing. Kenig also claims that children can learn to read romanized Yiddish faster than in the normal script.

68. The arguments in favor were: (1) Latinization is part of the 'cultural revolution'; (2) Yiddish is not a Semitic language [but socioculturally it is a *Jewish language* and like all Jewish languages has traditionally been written in Hebrew characters – D.L.G.]; (3) Latinized Yiddish is more convenient for mathematical formulas, musical notation, and interlinear translations; (4) the Latin letters are more legible and easier to join; (5) Latinized Yiddish is more accessible to non-Jews; and (6) it represents a break with Hebrew, 'which has no place in our cultural life'. The arguments against Latinization were: (1) it would require reeducation of the Yiddish readership and reprinting of books; (2) it would mean a break with Yiddish-users in other countries; and (3) a standardized orthography would be unattainable because the interdialectal principle could no longer be observed (but primary Romanization could conceivably have maintained the interdialectal principle: if it chose, for example, to represent 'to come' by *Kumen*, speakers of Southern Yiddish, where this word is rendered /kimen/, would simply learn to pronounce the *u* as /i/]. The consensus of the commission's members was evidently for Romanization because the anonymous author of this report goes on to counter every one of the arguments against Latinization.

69. (1) The influx of International Standard Vocabulary makes the language more understandable; Latinization will thus help to make Yiddish even more international and more accessible to non-Jews; (2) the most 'progressive' of alphabets is the Latin one; (3) workers in other countries who know the Latin alphabet and understand Yiddish will then have access to the language [what of the millions who do already know the Hebrew script or the Yiddish-users in countries using the Cyrillic alphabet? – D.L.G.].

70. Levenberg gives the following publication figures: 668 (1932), 391 (1933), 348 (1934), 437 (1935), 431 (1936), 356 (1937), 348 (1938), 339 (1939), 359 (1940), 202 (1941), 2 (1942), 24 (1943), 18 (1944), 14 (1945), 19 (1946), 52 (1947), 60 (1948), 0 (1949). Five Romanized poems appeared in 1962 (Kompaneyets 1962). In songbooks, Romanization also appears, either both in the texts and under the musical notes (e.g. Moyshe Beregovski, comp., *Evrejskie Narodnie Pesni* [Moscow, 1962]) or just under the notes (e.g. Z. Kompaneyets, comp., *Naye Yidishe Lider* [Moscow, 1970]).

71. Intended as the first volume in a series, it was the only one issued.

72. Boris Chubinsky (oral communication).

According to Reyzen (1920: 127), N. Birnbaum also favored the primary Romanization of Hebrew. A comparative study of Romanization of various Jewish languages, its motivations, successes, and failures, would be useful. Note the following: (a) interest in the primary Romanization of Hebrew began at about the same time as the Yiddish Romanization movement: Weinberg (1971-1972: 15) lists eight proposals, one from 1898, the others from 1927 to 1962, and reports that 'the idea of Romanizing the Hebrew script goes back to the beginnings of Hebrew as a modern language and it has by no means been abandoned at the time of the present writing'. 'Ittamar Ben-Avi writes in the preface to *Avi* (Jerusalem, 1927) that his father, Eliezer Ben-Yehuda [the reviver of spoken Hebrew] did not want to propose Romanization himself, but that he encouraged his son to do so' (Weinberg 1971-1972: 18); *Avi* is entirely Romanized. (b) In Turkey, Romanized Dzhudezmo was forced on the Jewish community in 1926 when all languages used in the country were Romanized by government decree. Some members of the Dzhudezmo-speaking community, moreover, were probably quite happy at this decision since they saw it as a sign of westernization (cf. the Yiddish Romanizers). Romanized Dzhudezmo, often called *frankuspanyól*, had in fact been in use even earlier in Turkey and other Balkan countries as well; Mieses (1909-1910) refers to Romanized Dzhudezmo as a sign of cultural decay. A few Romanized works from an earlier period, obviously intended for Marranos returning to Judaism, are also known. Nowadays, few speakers can read the language in the Hebrew script and the last remaining newspapers (one each in Israel and Turkey) are entirely Romanized. That a Jewish-language publication issued in Israel should have to be Romanized is not surprising since it is largely aimed at a foreign-born readership that has by and large not had the benefit of an Israeli education – nor would training in Hebrew necessarily equip Dzhudezmo speakers to read their language in the Hebrew script. Herbert Paper reports the following case for an Israeli-educated bilingual speaker of Parsic (Farsic) and Hebrew: the young man had always admired a (Hebrew-script) Parsic manuscript his parents had brought from Iran, but lamented that though he understood it when read aloud by his father, he could not read it himself (oral communication). The writer can cite the similar case of a young lady fluent in spoken Polish and written/spoken English who 'cannot read' the former. (c) Italkian started to appear in Romanized script in the 1700's and to the extent the language has been used at all in print in recent years, Romanization is always employed. (d) Tatic (Dzhuhuric), formerly written in Hebrew characters, was Romanized in the Soviet Union in the 1920's (S. Birnbaum 1951). (e) There is some Romanized poetry in the Karaitic (native name: *Karay*) of Northern Karaites (Poland, Lithuania) and Karaitic is also known to have been written in Arabic characters (ibid.). (f) There are some Parsic writings in Persian characters.

It is worthwhile to contrast the Yiddish and Turkish situations vis-à-vis primary Romanization: (a) both movements were led by new élites eager to break with 'the past' (the traditional Jewish élite has consisted of rabbis and other rabbinical scholars); (b) both of the new élites were eager to identify with the same new tradition, viz. Western Europe; (c) Turkey's successful adoption of Romanization was of course due to official sanction, but also to the fact that the high rate of Turkish illiteracy made it a concern to only a small minority of Turkish-speakers, whereas the traditionally high literacy rate among Yiddish-speakers meant that many more people would have had to be won over to Romanization.

73. Brief summary: S. A. Birnbaum's Romanization, like his spelling codex, reflects the phonology of the chief varieties of Eastern Yiddish. If such a polyphonetic system is unfeasible, he says, then the regional variety spoken by the majority of Yiddish speakers should be the basis for any Romanization (viz. Southern Yiddish); Birnbaum does not recognize Standard Yiddish Orthoepy. Some discussants spoke of 'transcription in English' (i.e. a national Romanization for English-speaking countries or perhaps only for the United States), but A. A. Roback wanted the Romanization to be international if possible. He also pointed out the danger of using diacritics because experience with spelling has shown that they are hardest to implement. He also raised the question of 'Jewish' vs. 'English' names of the same individual (see Gold 1971b; 1973). Joshua A. Fishman pointed out that even a national Romanization for English-speaking countries would be hard to achieve because there were no set correspondences between grapheme and phoneme in English. For other languages, national Romanizations might prove less difficult (e.g. for Spanish), but new problems would arise in each case.
74. The Standardized Transcription is now being prepared for publication (Gold and Schaechter i.p.d.). Since 1968, I have undertaken a modest letter-writing campaign aimed at publishers, editors, and writers, with some success; like spelling, Romanization is rarely mentioned in book reviews (cf., however, Orenstein 1971).

    The American National Standards Institute has now appointed a committee to codify the Standardized Transcription (as developed by the YIVO Institute for Jewish Research). It will be adopted as the United States standard and then submitted to an international body, which has also received some (unfortunately amateurish) proposals from France, Belgium, Holland, and Denmark. Some Yiddish-users who are extremely loyal to the Standardized Transcription have changed the spelling of their given names in conformity therewith: *Leybl* Kahn, *Mordkhe* [properly *Mortkhe*] Schaechter; curiously, surnames have not been altered (**Kan*, **Shekhter*). If there *are* surnames that *do* conform to the Standardized Transcription, this is purely coincidental (e.g. *Gold*, *Fishman*, *Silkes*).
75. The Bible was published in Yekaterinoslav (now Krasnograd); a copy has been seen by Reb Khayem Liberman, librarian of the Lebavitsher Rebe, Brooklyn, New York; further details are unavailable. The fables appeared in Aleksandriya, Kherson, in 1902; the title page and one page of text of the Cyrillicized version are reproduced in the Hebrew-script edition (Kleyf 1921).

    S. A. Birnbaum reports (1951) that Tatic may have been Cyrillicized after the Romanization of the 1920's (on Cyrillicization replacing Romanization in the Soviet Union see U. Weinreich 1953) and that a book in Cyrillicized Northern Karaitic (Karay) appeared in 1904.
76. See note 70.
77. Goldberg erroneously claimed that the usual script did not provide for emphasis, but spacing of letters, as in German, was certainly in use by the 1920's, as may have been the use of thin letters, too. Both are now used for 'italicization'.
78. It has always been possible to join many of the letters in the present script too. If Glas was suggesting this be extended to printed texts as well, there would be no apparent gain either esthetically or in terms of typesetters' convenience. Reyzen (1920: 138) also proposed the creation of unigraphs.

79. In words of non-Hebrew-Aramic origin, /v/ is represented only by this digraph and many Hebrew-Aramic-origin words require it too (others are spelled with *veys*). Zamenhof and Veynger had earlier proposed only one *vov* (Zamenhof 1910; Veynger 1913a; 1913b), and Soviet orthographists decided in 1928 to 'make *tsvey vovn* "two vovs" into one letter if technically possible' (Slutski 1928b); it is not clear whether this meant one *vov*, as in Veynger's system, or running two of them together, as Weinreich proposed.

In preparing the work, M. Weinreich ([ed.] 1930) had a Vilna printing firm cast the necessary type for the /v/ unigraph (which actually does look like a *v*) and asked the contributors to this volume whether they would consent to its use in their papers. Mark and Kalmanovitsh did, and theirs and Weinreich's contributions so appear; Mark later abandoned use of the unigraph when he saw how it looked in print (Mark 1963: 35-36). No other printed work is known with this unigraph.

80. It is used by many graduates of the Vilna Jewish Teachers' Seminary (where Max Weinreich had taught) and graduates of the TSISHO schools in Poland, in most Yiddish schools in Argentina (Mark 1963: 35), and by several people close to the YIVO. This unigraph was adopted in the YIVO's logogram and has also acquired somewhat of a symbolic value, viz. it is a means of expressing loyalty to the ideals of the YIVO or to the SYO. Curiously, although Max Weinreich always used it in writing, his ex libris and signature consistently show the digraph (e.g. Dawidowicz, et al. 1964: ii).

81. Such deference to the rule of the majority and absolute loyalty to the Rules were typical of Max Weinreich: 'with a few exceptions we are simply not used to such a thing as orthographic discipline and to loyalty even less so' (Schaechter 1964: 17). Of the 236 suggestions made by Weinreich (1930), 116 were fully incorporated into the SYO, sixteen partially accepted, and 104 rejected entirely – but Weinreich subsequently never deviated from the SYO even in 'minor' details. An interesting sidelight on his attitude is cast by his former secretary: 'when dictating a letter he would often stop to translate, to explain – he wanted me to understand every word I was writing. Accuracy in writing and in spelling was paramount. At first I could not understand why every word and letter had to be correct, and why he attached so much importance to the little bars and dots – at a time when he was so busy with more important research projects and administrative tasks. He reread every letter to make sure it was perfect before being mailed; he wanted Yiddish to be respected and he wanted the YIVO to be respected, but knew that respect would not be forthcoming from others if he himself did not have enough respect' (Mlotek 1969: 3).

82. Several typefaces were used in the past (see M. Weinreich 1939), depending on the intended reader, the subject matter, and, in some cases, on the etymological origin of individual words (e.g. the Hebrew-Aramic component was often set off in some way from the 'non holy' components). A study of who wrote what for whom in what script, at what time, and a comparison with efforts to modify the Hebrew script, which are largely contemporaneous with those made in Yiddish, would be useful (see Weinberg 1971-1972). Highly desirable, incidentally, would be a detailed descriptive study of Yiddish handwriting practice and, for pedagogical purposes, a set of handwriting guidelines.

83. Cf. the term 'language engineering', which sounds ominously Orwellian to the

layman. 'Language planning' is probably only slightly less frightening.

Notice also Mordkhe Schaechter's preoccupation (note 60) with *kultur*, which is, interestingly, a nineteenth century loan from German.

I have not been able to sketch the history of Yiddish stenography and stenotyping in this study for lack of competence; the following bibliography will be useful to someone able to undertake such a study: P. [F.?] Shargaradskaya, *Idishe stenografye: a lernbukh far yedn (in finf lektsyes)* (Berlin, 1925); M. L. Elik [= Ellick], *Lernt idishe stenografye: a praktishe metode far shnelshrift: sistematish oysgearbet far der praktik: klas-oysgabe fun 1937* (New York, 1949); N. Shatski, *Stenotipye (kurtsshrift far der shraybmashinke un pen)* (Minsk, 1935); N. Shatski, *Yidishe stenografye far zelbstbilding* (Minsk, 1929); *Idishe stenografye* (New York, 1930 or later [the title page of the YIVO's copy, = 13/24860, is missing]). Private lessons in Yiddish stenography were given in New York City by Ada Lieberson (according to Lyuba Condell and Hannah Fryshdorf, two of her former students) and Manya Goldberg gave private lessons in New York City and a course in Yiddish and Hebrew typewriting and stenography at the Jewish Teachers' Seminary of New York City – the course is still listed in the school's catalog but has not been given for a number of years.

BIBLIOGRAPHY

Unseen items, for some of which full bibliographical information is missing, are asterisked. The English translation of titles in Yiddish and Russian is given in brackets.

Anon.

1918 ['Spelling Rules'], *Kultur Un Bildung* 13-14, 5-7.

1920 ['The Reform of Yiddish Spelling'], *Komunistishe Velt* (Jan./Feb.), 30.

1926 ['Language Commission: Program for 1926-1927 . . . Writing System'], *Byuleten* [of the Jewish Division, Institute for Belorussian Culture], 2: 8.

1928a ['Table of Proposals on Orthography'], in M. Litvankov (ed.), *Yidishe Ortografye: Proyektn Un Materyaln Tsum Tsveytn Alfarbandishn Yidishn Kultur-Tsuzamenfor*. (Kiev).

1928b ['On the New Yiddish Orthography'], *Di Yidishe Shprakh* 13, 49-50.

1929a ['Definitive Ratification of the New Yiddish Orthography'], *Ratn-Bildung* 9, 78-80.

1929b ['Decisions of the Central Orthographical Commission, January 21, 1929'], *Di Yidishe Shprakh* 14, 57-60.

1929c ['From the Central Orthographical Commission'], *Di Yidishe Shprakh* 17-18, 55-58.

1930 ['From the Central Orthographical Commission'], *Di Yidishe Shprakh* 21-22, 85-90.

1930 ['Resolutions Adopted at the First All-Union Yiddish Language Conference, Kiev, February 8-13, 1921'], *Di Yidishe Shprakh* 25, 15-24.

1932 ['The Work of the Philological Section from October 15, 1931 to May 1, 1932'], *Di Yidishe Shprakh* 29-30, 117-118.

1936 ['The Alphabet'], *Algemeyne Entsiklopedye* 3, 261-269.

1942 ['The Names of the States in Yiddish'], *Yidishe Shprakh* 2, 129-130.
1943 ['Spelling'], *YIVO-Biblyografye 1925-1941* (New York).
1946 ['Discussion of Spelling Problems'], *Yidishe Shprakh* 6, 140.
1971 ['Note to Contributors'], *Yugntruf* 23, 24.
1972 ['New Books from New Settlers in Israel'], *Yugntruf* 26, 11.

Barikht Fun Ortografishn Kongres
1931 (Buenos Aires).

Bastomski, Sh., and M. Khayemson
1939 *Lebedike Klangen* (Vilna).
1940 *Shrayb Rikhtik – Arbetbukh Af Yidish Loyt Di Takones Fun YIVO Un TSISHO* (Vilna).

Bekler, Pesl
1952 (letter to the editor), *Forverts* (January 16).

Ben-Adir (= Avrom Rozin)
1912 ['A Harmful Fantasy – An Open Letter to the Latin-Yiddishists'], *Dos Naye Lebn* 4, 244-247.

Beregovski, M.
1934 *Jidišer Muzik-Folklor* (Moscow).

Bernfeld, Y.
1968 ['Stutshkov's Yiddish Dictionary'], in Moyshe Levoni (ed.), *Yidishe Dyalogn: Asifes Fun Yidishn Veltkongres* (Paris), 197-212.

Beylin, Sholem
1926 ['Towards the Spelling of Hebrew Words in Yiddish'], *Filologishe Shriftn* 1, 289-290.

Birnbaum, Nathan
1902 'Hebraeisch und Juedisch', *Ost und West* 2, 457-464.
1906 *(?), *Di Naye Tsaytung* (Warsaw).

Birnbaum, Salomo A.
1924 ['The Sounds and Spelling of Yiddish'], *Yidishe Filologye* 2, 176-180.
1929 ['Transcriptions of Yiddish'], *Filologishe Shriftn* 3, 485-496.
1930a *Yidishkeyt Un Loshn* (Warsaw).
1930b ['The Principles of Yiddish Spelling'], in Max Weinreich (ed.), *Der Eynheytlekher Yidisher Oysleyg: Materyaln Un Proyektn Tsu Der Ortografisher Konferents Fun YIVO* (Vilna), 18-19, 86-87.
1931 ['Two *vovn* like the Gentiles'], *Beys-Yankev*, 32-33.
1933 'Die Umschrift des Jiddischen', *Teuthonista* 9, 90-105.
1938 ['A Universal Written Language and a Universal Pronunciation'], *Yidish Far Ale* 9, 245-246.
1944 ['Interdialectal Spelling and Transcription'], *Yidishe Shprakh* 4, 104-109.
1947 ['A Reply to the Critics of My Suggestions for a Transcription System'], *Yidishe Shprakh* 7, 29-36.
1948 ['Five Comments'], *Yidishe Shprakh* 8, 12-14.
1951 'The Jewries of Eastern Europe', *The Slavonic and East European Review* 29, 420-443.
1953 ['From Germanisms to the Cave in the Judean Desert'], *Yidishe Shprakh* 13, 109-120.
1960 (letter to the editor), *Yidishe Shprakh* 20, 31.

1968 ['How Old Is Yiddish?'], in Moyshe Levoni (ed.), *Yidishe Dyalogn: Asifes Fun Yidishn Veltkongres* (Paris), 245-250.
1964 ['Yiddish Translations of the Psalms Over the Past Six Hundred Years'], in Lucy Dawidowicz, et al. (eds.), *For Max Weinreich On His Seventieth Birthday: Studies in Jewish Languages, Literature, and Society* (The Hague), 526-600.
1965 'Specimens of Yiddish from Eight Centuries', in Uriel Weinreich (ed.), *The Field of Yiddish: Second Collection* (The Hague), 1-23. Reviewed by Eli Katz, *Language* 44 (1968), 139.
1971 'Jewish Languages', *Encyclopaedia Judaica* (Jerusalem).

Borokhov, Ber
1913 ['The Tasks of Yiddish Philology'], in Shmuel Niger (ed.), *Der Pinkes* (Vilna), 1-22.

Braude, Gershon Zev, and Berl Segal
1961 ['Old Roots of Jewish Names and of Yiddish Orthography'], *Yidishe Shprakh* 21, 21-24.

Carr, Denzel
1958 'Some Problems Arising from Linguistic Eleutheromania', *The Journal of Asian Studies* 17, 207-214.

Dawidowicz, Lucy, et al. (eds.)
1964 *For Max Weinreich On His Seventieth Birthday: Studies in Jewish Languages, Literature, and Society* (The Hague).

Devenishki, Y.-M.: see A. Vayter entry.

['Discussion of the English Transcription of Yiddish Book Titles and Authors' Names']
1947 *Yidishe Shprakh* 7, 36-46.

Feldschuh, B.
1948 *Sheyres-Hapleyte-Biblyografye* 1 (Stuttgart).
1949 *Sheyres-Hapleyte-Biblyografye* 2 (Stuttgart).

Fischer, Jehiel
1936 *Das Jiddische und sein Verhältnis zu den deutschen Mundarten* (Leipsic).

Fishman, Joshua A.
1972 *Language in Sociocultural Change* [Stanford).

Gelenberg, M.
1930 ['Yiddish on the Streets of Warsaw'], *Literarishe Bleter* 314, 346-347, 392-394.

Gininger, Chaim
1951 ['Towards the Axiomatics of Yiddish Spelling'], *Yidishe Shprakh* 11, 30-38.

Gininger, Chaim, Note Helfer, Hersch Segal, Itzik Schwarz (comps).
1934 *Naje Jidiśe Dichtung: Klejne Antologie* (Czernowitz).

Glas, Y.-Y.
1923 (Reply to Kh. Golberg, ['On Reforming the Yiddish Alphabet']), *Bikhervelt* 2, 35-38.

Glassman, B.
1941 ['On the Yiddish Spelling of *Shakespeare*'], *Yidishe Shprakh* 1, 151-154.

Gold, David L.
1968 ['The Yiddish World and the Jewish Student'], *Yugntruf* 15-16, 4-5, 29.
1969 (letter to the editor), *Dorem-Afrike* 187, 27.
1970a (letter to the editor), *Yugntruf* 19, 21-23.
1970b ['Salvation Hasn't Come Yet'], *Der Veker* 1122, 8-10.

1970c ['A Trip to Poland, June 1967'], *Der Veker* 1124, 9-11.
1971a ['Linguistic Curiosities'], *Yugntruf* 23, 12.
1971b 'R. M. R. and Beatrice L. Hall's "Some Apparent Orthographic Inconsistencies in American Family Names of Yiddish Origin"', *Names* 19, 223-228.
1972a 'Now Defunct Yiddish Daily Had Been Picketed by Yiddish Youth Organization', Jewish Student Press-Service News Release (March).
1972b 'Yiddish Youth Group Has Its Second and Third Confrontations With the Yiddish Establishment', Jewish Student Press-Service News Release (March).
1972c ['Spelling-Shmelling, Why Are The Linguists Pestering Us?'], *Forverts* (October 23).
1973 'Review of J. R. Rayfield, *The Languages of a Bilingual Community*', *Language Sciences* 24, 21-28.
1974 'Yorsayt, jahrzeit, yahrzeit: oy yiddish', *Sh'ma* 4, 143.
i.p.a. ['Orthographic Bi-uniqueness in Yiddish Words of Hebrew-Aramic Origin'], *Yidishe Shprakh*.
i.p.b. ['The Yiddish Names of the States Revisited'], manuscript.

Gold, David L., and Mordkhe Schaechter
i.p.c. 'The Standardized Transcription and Transliteration of Yiddish', manuscript.

Goldberg, Kh.
1922 ['On Reforming the Yiddish Alphabet'], *Bikhervelt* 1, 379-384.

Golomb, Tsvi-Nisn
1910 *Milim Bilshoni-Hebreish-Yidishes Verterbukh* (Vilna).

Halpern, Falk
1926 ['On Hebrew Spelling in Yiddish'], *Literarishe Bleter* 107, 333.

Harkavy, Alexander
1930 ['Some Remarks on Spelling'], in Max Weinreich (ed.), *Der Eynheytlekher Yidisher Oysleyg: Materyaln Un Proyektn Tsu Der Ortografisher Konferents Fun YIVO* (Vilna), 85.
1888 ['A Letter About Our Language: A Criticism of the Orthography in the *Nyu-Yorker Yidishe Ilustrirte Tsaytung*'], *Nyu-Yorker Ilustrirte Tsaytung* (January 27), 10.

Himowich, A. A.
1904 'Shall Yiddish Be Written in Latin Characters?', *The American Hebrew* (July 29), 281-282.

Hofshteyn, D.
1928 ['On an Important Detail'], *Di Yidishe Shprakh* 8-9, 59-60.

* Itkovitsh, M.
1934 ['For a Scientifically Correct Spelling'], *Der Emes* 103, 3.

* Jampolski, L. (ed.)
1935 *Idiše Kinder-Lider* (Minsk).

Jochnowitz, George
1968 'Bilingualism and Dialect Mixture Among Lubavitcher Hasidic Children', *American Speech* 43, 182-200.

Joffe, Judah A.
1909 ['The Sounds of Yiddish and the Alphabet'], *Dos Naye Lebn* 1, 529-532, 701-703.
1950 ['Let Us Analyze, Not Merely Debate: Towards the Analysis of Some Spell-

ing Rules'], *Yidishe Shprakh* 10, 49-59.
Kahn, Leybl
1972 ['A Survey of Yiddish Terminological Commissions'], *Yidishe Shprakh* 31, 35-42.
Kalmanovitsh, Zelig
1930 ['Is A Phonetic Spelling of Literary Yiddish Possible?'], in Max Weinreich (ed.), *Der Eynheytlekher Yidisher Oysleyg: Materyaln Un Proyektn Tsu Der Orthografisher Konferents Fun YIVO* (Vilna), 3-17.
1936 ['Yoysef Perl's Yiddish Writings'], *Yivo-bleter* 10, 266-302.
Kaplan, Michel, and B. Botwinik (eds.)
1912 *Ynser Ṡrift* (New York).
Kats, Yoysef
1937 *Vi Azoy Darf Men Shraybn* (*Klolim Fun Yidishn Oysleyg*) (Warsaw).
Kazakevitsh, H.
1927 ['*av-* or *au-*'], *Di Yidishe Shprakh* 1, 48.
Kenig, Leo
1926 ['Sentiments and Logic – A Word on the Question of Reforming Yiddish Spelling'], *Literarishe Bleter* 133, 765-767.
Kheyfets, B. J.
1941 ['Problems of Transcription'], *Yidishe Shprakh* 1, 125.
Kleyf, Moris
1921 *Mesholim*, 2nd edition (Berlin).
* Kompaneyets, Zinovi
1962 *Finf Lider Fun Yidishe Sovetishe Dikhters* (Moscow).
Kosowski, B.
1950 *Biblyografye Fun Di Yidishe Oysgabes In Der Britisher Zone Fun Daytshland, 1945-1950* (Bergen-Belsen).
* Krinski, Magnus
1908 ['On Yiddish Orthography'], *Roman-tsaytung*.
Krupin, Nokhem
1957 *Hantbukh Fun Hebreizmen In Der Yidisher Shprakh* (Buenos Aires).
Kshenski, Meyer
1967 ['Correct and Incorrect Spelling in the Yiddish Press'], *Yugntruf* 8, 9.
Kupershmid, Sh.
1928 ['Diacritics in the New Spelling'], *Di Yidishe Shprakh* 11-12, 35-36.
1930 ['The New Spelling in the *Shtern*'], *Di Yidishe Shprakh* 23-24, 93-96.
Lehrer, Leybush
1941 ['*shekspir* or *sheykspir*?'], *Yidishe Shprakh* 1, 86-89.
Lekht, M. (ed.)
1932 *Di Sovetishe Yidishe Ortografye: Klolim Funem Nayem Yidishn Oysleyg* (Kharkov-Kiev).
Levenberg, Sh.
1968 ['Yiddish in the Soviet Union'], in Moyshe Levoni (ed.), *Yidishe Dyalogn: Asifes Fun Yidishn Veltkongres* (Paris), 179-183.
Levin, Yankev
1930 ['Orthographic Notes'], in Max Weinreich (ed.), *Der Eynheytlekher Yidisher Oysleyg: Materyaln Un Proyektn Tsu Der Ortografisher Konferents Fun YIVO* (Vilna), 66-72.

1942 ['On the Pronunciation of Some Words'], *Yidishe Shprakh* 2, 182-183.
1952 ['Towards the History of the Attempts to Regulate Yiddish Spelling in the United States'], *Yidishe Shprakh* 12, 48-50.
1954 ['A Suggestion for the Use of the Comma in Yiddish'], *Yidishe Shprakh* 14, 18-20. With a reply by Yudel Mark.
1958 *Verterbikhl Fun Hebreish-Yidishe Verter* (New York).

Levoni, Moyshe (ed.)
1968 *Yidishe Dyalogn: Asifes Fun Yidishn Veltkongres* (Paris).

Litvak, A.
1926 ['*Alef-beys* or *Alfabet*'], *Di Tsukunft* 31, 636-638.

Litvankov, M. (ed.)
1928 *Yidishe Ortografye: Proyektn Un Materyaln Tsum Tsveytn Alfarbandishn Yidishn Kultur-Tsuzamenfor* (Kiev).

Lokshteyn, A.
1957 (letter to the editor), *Yidishe Shprakh* 17, 28.

Loytski, Kh.
1932 ['The All-Union Orthographic Conference in Kiev, November 21-24, 1931'], *Afn Shprakhfront* 28, 45-50. Issue misnumbered as issue 26.

Makagon, A.
1927 ['Spelling – A Few Suggestions'], *Di Yidishe Shprakh* 2, 43-46.

Mark, Yudel
1921 *Shul-gramatik* (Kovno).
1930 ['On a Punctuation System'], in Max Weinreich (ed.), *Der Eynheytlekher Yidisher Oysleyg: Materyaln Un Proyektn Tsu Der Ortografisher Konferents Fun YIVO* (Vilna), 88-117.
1946a (Reply to Zakin 1946), *Yidishe Shprakh* 6, 40-43.
1946b (Reply to Max Weinreich, 1946), *Yidishe Shprakh* 6, 44-45.
1946c ['Two Systems'], *Yidishe Shprakh* 6, 118-123.
1947 ['Footnotes to the Rules of Yiddish Spelling'], *Yidishe Shprakh*, 7, 1-20.
1947 ['On the Proposed English Transcription of Yiddish Names and Book Titles'], *Yidishe Shprakh* 7, 36-46.
1948 ['A Few Brief Footnotes to Salomo Birnbaum's Comments'], *Yidishe Shprakh* 8, 15-16.
1951 ['On A Standardized Pronunciation'], *Yidishe Shprakh* 11, 1-25.
1952 ['Bird's-Eye View of the History of Yiddish Spelling'], *Yidishe Shprakh* 12, 23-29.
1953 ['Rules for the Comma in Yiddish'], *Yidishe Shprakh* 13, 1-5.
1958a ['Problems in the Standardization of Yiddish'], *Yidishe Shprakh* 18, 33-50.
1958b ['Questionnaire on Orthography'], *Yidishe Shprakh* 18, 89-91.
1959a ['Results of a Spelling Survey'], *Yidishe Shprakh* 19, 73-83.
1959b ['Where Do We Now Stand With Respect to the Standardized Orthography'], *Yidishe Shprakh* 18, 83-96.
1959c ['In Defense of the Silent *alef*'], *Yidishe Shprakh* 19, 1-16.
1963 ['Impressions of a Journey'], *Yidishe Shprakh* 23, 33-39.
1971 (note on syllabification), *Yidishe Shprakh* 30, 94-95.

See also T. R-S entry.

Mark, Yudel, and Judah A. Joffe (eds.)
1961 *Groyser Verterbukh Fun Der Yidisher Shprakh* (New York). See 'Our Spelling', pp. *khof-beyz, khof-giml.*
[Mendele Moykher-Sforim]
1927 ['Mendele's Letters to Sholem-Aleykhem'], *Di Yidishe Shprakh* 11-12, 1-2. On Mendele's attitude towards spelling.
Mieses, M.
1909- ['In What Alphabet Should We Write Yiddish?'], in Moyshe Frostik, (ed.),
1910 *Yudisher Kalendar* 3, 59-64.
Mitlyanski, Y.
1918 ['A Revolution in Yiddish Orthography'], *Kultur Un Bildung* 7, 8-10.
Mlotek, Chane
1969 ['The Late Dr. Max Weinreich'], *Yugntruf* 17, 3-7.
Orenstein, Eugene
1971 'Review of Milton Doroshkin, *Yiddish in America*', *Yugntruf* 22, 19-20.
Oyerbakh, Efroyem, et al. (eds.)
1956 *Der Nayer Leksikon Fun Der Yidisher Literatur* (New York).
Pat, Yankev, et al., (eds.)
1961 *Almanakh Yidish* (New York).
Prilutski, Noyekh
1921 ['Our Orthographical Commission'], *Naye Himlen* (Warsaw and New York), 88-93.
* *Progres*
c. 1931 (Warsaw).
Ray, Punya Sloka
1963 *Language Standardization/Studies in Prescriptive Linguistics* (The Hague).
Reyzen, Zalmen
1920 *Gramatik Fun Der Yidisher Shprakh* (Vilna).
1921 ['Yiddish Orthography'], *Di Naye Shul* 5, 50-52.
1933 ['Nokhem Shtif's Last Piece of Work'], *Yivo-bleter* 5, 382-400. Review of the *Ortografisher Verterbukh* (Moscow, 1932).
1937 ['Orthography'], *Algemeyne Entsiklopedye* 4, 397-401.
n.d. *Leksikon Fun Der Yidisher Literatur Un Prese.*
Roback, A. A.
1946 ['On Dr. Birnbaum's Transcriptions'], *Yidishe Shprakh* 6, 113-118.
1948 ['Various Notes'], *Yidishe Shprakh* 8, 70-72.
1949 ['A Few Words on Transcription and Dialects'], *Yidishe Shprakh* 9, 52-55.
1959a (Reply to A. Lokshteyn's letter to the editor), *Yidishe Shprakh* 17, 60-61.
1959b ['Footnotes to the Dictionary's Survey'], *Yidishe Shprakh* 19, 16-21.
Roskies, David
1970 ['New Books'], *Yugntruf* 21, 10-14.
R-S, T. ('Yudel Mark)
1957 [= On the Proper Pronunciation of Several Hebraisms'], *Yidishe Shprakh* 17, 25-26.
Rubin, Y.
1923 (Comments on Kh. Goldberg, ['On Reforming the Yiddish Alphabet']), *Bikhervelt* 2, 33-35.

Schaechter, Mordkhe
1957 ['Correct Yiddish'], *Afn Shvel.*
1961 ['We're Not Standing Still'], in Y. Pat, et al. (eds.), *Almanakh Yidish* (New York), 351-362.
1964 ['Max Weinreich's Contribution to the Growth of Yiddish'], *Di Goldene Keyt* 50, 17 pp.
1969 'The "Hidden Standard": A Study of Competing Influences in Standardization', in Marvin I. Herzog, Wita Ravid, and Uriel Weinreich (eds.), *The Field of Yiddish, Third Collection* (The Hague), 284-304.
1969- ['The Language of *Sovetish* Heymland'] Part 1, *Yidishe Shprakh* 29, 10-42. ('Orthography', 26-29).
1970a ['A Call to Arms'], *Yugntruf* 19, 1.
1970b ['A Time to Be Still and a Time to Speak Up'], *Yugntruf* 19, 1-7.
1970c ['For the Dignity of Yiddish'], *Yugntruf* 20, 1-3, 12-16.
1971a ['The Language of *Sovetish Heymland*'] Part 2, *Yidishe Shprakh* 30, 32-65.
1971b ['*beklal* "in general"'], *Yidishe Shprakh* 31, 31.
1971c (letter to the editor), *Yugntruf* 22, 22-23.
1972 *Yiddish Orthography: An Outline for A Course*, 2nd edition (New York). With a preface by Joshua A. Fishman.
See also Yud-Ben-Fey and Y. Shlayfshteyn entries.
Schaechter, Mordkhe, and Max Weinreich
1961 *Guide to the Standardized Yiddish Orthography* (New York).
Shafir, M.-M.
1942 ['Some Common Spelling Mistakes'], *Yidishe Shprakh* 2, 187.
Shlayfshteyn, Yitskhok (= M. Schaechter)
1970 ['About Words and Other Nonsense'], *Yugntruf* 21, 8-10.
Shlosberg, B.
1930 ['Yiddish Spelling in the Soviet Union'], in Max Weinreich (ed.), *Der Eynheytlekher Yidisher Oysleyg: Materyaln Un Proyektn Tsu Der Ortografisher Konferents Fun YIVO* (Vilna), 72-84.
Sholem-Aleykhem
1888 ['On Yiddish Spelling'], in Sholem-Aleykhem, *Di Yidishe Folksbiblyotek* (Kiev), 474-476.
Shpilreyn, A.-M.
1926 *Yidish: A Konspekt Fun A Kurs In Dem Tsveytn Moskver Melukhishn Universitet* (Moscow).
Shtarkman, Moyshe
1929 ['On the Latinization of Yiddish'], *Pinkes* 2, 89. Summary of A. A. Himowich, 'Shall Yiddish Be Written in Latin Characters?'.
Shtarkman, Moyshe (ed.)
1969- *Seyfer Leavrom* (Los Angeles).
1970
Shteynberg, Y.
1949 *Hebreizmen In Der Yidisher Shprakh* (Wrocław).
Shteynboym, Yisroel
1956 ['The Rules of Yiddish Orthography Reconsidered'], *Yidishe Shprakh* 16, 97-107.

Shtif, Nokhem
1928 ['Towards the History of Yiddish Spelling'], *Di Yidishe Shprakh* 8-9, 33-60.
Shtif, Nokhem, and E. Spivak
1932 ['On Latinization'], *Afn Shprakhfront* 29-30, 93-100.
Slutski, B.
1928a ['The Second All-Union Cultural Convention in Kharkov and Language Standardization: April 9-14, 1928'], *Di Yidishe Shprakh* 10, 49-60.
1928b ['On the Spelling Question'], *Di Yidishe Shprakh* 8-9, 27-32.
1932 ['Comrade Kamenshteyn Creates His Own Orthography'], *Afn Shprakhfront* 32-33, 105-108.
* Sotek, Yankev
1902 *Velvl Zbarzher: Makel No'am* (Brǎila). Ed. by Y. Sotek.
1903 'Uenser Lauschen', *Cronika Israelita.*
Spivak, E.
1928 ['A Few Remarks on the Spelling Reform'], *Di Yidishe Shprakh* 8-9, 25-28.
[Szajkowski, Zosa]
1966 *Catalogue of the Exhibition – The History of Yiddish Orthography from the Spelling Rules of the Early Sixteenth Century to the Standardized Orthography of 1936* (New York).
Tirski, J.
1923 ['Yiddish in the Latin Script'], in B. Ziemand (ed.), *Unhoib* (Vienna), 2-5.
* Tsederboym, Aleksander
1863 (remarks on spelling), *Kol-mevaser* (Summer).
Vachek, Josef
1973 'Review of W. Haas (ed.), *Alphabets for English*, and W. Haas, *Phonographic Translation*', *Language* 49, 190-194.
Vaysman, B.
1932 ['In the Book Laboratory'], *Afn Shprakhfront* 28, 35 ff. Issue misnumbered as issue 26.
* Vayter, A. (= Y.-M. Devenishki)
1905 (Brochure on Latinization.)
Vevyorka, Avrom
1926 *Der Oysleyg Fun Yidish* (Moscow).
Veynger, Mortkhe
1913a *Mayn Alef-Beys* (Warsaw).
1913b *Mayn Oysleygung* (Warsaw).
1927a ['*lerern*'], *Di Yidishe Shprakh* 1, 47.
1927b ['*eng* or *eyng*, *enk* or *eynk*?'], *Di Yidishe Shprakh* 5-6, 81-84.
1928a ['Linguistics and Spelling'], in M. Litvankov (ed.), *Yidishe Ortografye: Proyektn Un Materyaln Tsum Tsveytn Alfarbandishn Yidishn Kultur-Tsuzamenfor* (Kiev), 27-33.
1928b ['On the Yiddish Alphabet and Spelling'], in M. Litvankov (ed.), *Yidishe Ortografye: Proyektn Un Materyaln Tsum Tsveytn Alfarbandishn Yidishn Kultur-Tsuzamenfor* (Kiev), 34-35.
Weinberg, Werner
1971-1972 'A Bibliography of Proposals to Reform the Hebrew Script', *Studies in Bibliography and Booklore* 10, 1-18.

Weinreich, Max
1926 *Shrayb On Grayzn* (Vilna).
1927 *Shturemvint* (Vilna).
1930 ['Draft of a Standardized Spelling'], in Max Weinreich (ed.), *Der Eynheytlekher Yidisher Oysleyg: Materyaln Un Proyektn Tsu Der Ortografisher Konferents Fun YIVO* (Vilna), 20-65.
1931 ['Should we write < ʔmθ > or < δmδσ >? (On the YIVO Spelling Conference in Vilna)'], *Forverts*, June 7.
1934 'Review of C. Gininger, et al. (comps.), *Naje Jidiše Dichtung: Klejne Antologie*', *Yivo-bleter* 7, 268-271.
1939 *Di Shvartse Pintelekh* (Vilna).
1946 (Reply to M. Zakin, ['Some Questions from Argentina']), *Yidishe Shprakh* 6, 43-44.
1949 ['What's the Matter with Yiddish Spelling?'], *Yidishe Shprakh* 9, 1-21 (with a reply by Yudel Mark, pp. 21-22).
1954 'Prehistory and Early History of Yiddish: Facts and Conceptual Framework', in Uriel Weinreich (ed.), *The Field of Yiddish* (New York), 73-101.
1956 'The Jewish Languages of Romance Stock and Their Relation to Earliest Yiddish', *Romance Philology* 9, 403-428.
1959 ['The Standard Yiddish Orthography – History and Significance'], *Yidishe Shprakh* 19, 33-64.
1961 ['A Clarification from the YIVO'], in Y. Mark and J. A. Joffe (eds.), *Groyser Verterbukh Fun Der Yidisher Shprakh* 1 (New York), (p.) *Zayen*.
1968 ['A Seven-Hundred-Year-Old Yiddish Sentence (Analysis of a Highly Significant Linguistic Find)'], *Yidishe Shprakh* 23, 87-93; 24, 61-62.
Weinreich, Max (ed.)
1930 *Der Eynheytlekher Yidisher Oysleyg: Materyaln Un Proyektn Tsu Der Ortografisher Konferents Fun YIVO* (Vilna).
1931 *Di Ershte Yidishe Shprakh-Konferents* (Vilna).
Weinreich, Max, and Yudel Borenstein
1965 ['A Course in Yiddish Orthography'], *Yugntruf* 4, 9-10.
Weinreich, Uriel
1949 *College Yiddish* (New York).
Fifth revised edition (1971). [Second printing, with some changes (1974)].
1951 ['On the Standard Pronunciation of Yiddish'], *Yidishe Shprakh* 11, 26-29.
1953 'The Russification of Soviet Minority Languages', *Problems of Communism* 6, 46-57.
1954 'Notes on Transcription, Transliteration and Citation of Titles', in Uriel Weinreich (ed.), *The Field of Yiddish* (New York), vi-viii.
1959 'On the Cultural History of Yiddish Rime', in *Essays in Jewish Life and Thought: Presented in Honor of Salo Wittmayer Baron* (New York), 423-442.
1968 *Modern English-Yiddish Yiddish-English Dictionary* (New York).
Weinreich, Uriel (ed.)
1954 The Field of Yiddish (New York).
1965 The Field of Yiddish: Second Collection (The Hague).
Yashunski, Y.
1923 (Comments on Kh. Golberg, ['On Reforming the Yiddish Alphabet']), *Bikhervelt* 2, 29-32.

Yehoyesh, and Kh. Spivak
1911 *Yidish Verterbukh; Anthalt Ale Hebreishe (Un Khaldeishe) Verter* . . . (New York).
Yud-Ben-Fey (= M. Schaechter)
1969 ['Yugntruf Revolution in New York (A Story of A Thousand and Two Nights)'], *Yugntruf* 18, 7-10.
Yunin, Volf (Younin, Wolf)
1936 *Lider* (New York).
Zakin, M.
1946 ['Some Questions from Argentina'], *Yidishe Shprakh* 6, 38-39.
1948 ['Remarks and Suggestions About Spelling'], *Yidishe Shprakh* 8, 23-25.
Zamenhof, Ludwig
1910 ['Samples from a Yiddish Grammar'], *Lebn Un Visnshaft* 7, 89-106.
Zaretski, A.
1926 ['The Movement for the Reform of Our Spelling'], *Di Royte Velt* 1, 116-124.
1927 ['On the New Yiddish Spelling'], *Der Hamer* 2, 53-56.
1928a ['On Yiddish Punctuation'], *Di Yidishe Shprakh* 11-12, 23-32; 13, 15-20.
1928b ['Questions About Yiddish Spelling'], *Di Yidishe Shprakh* 8-9, 1-24.
1928c ['A Serious Defect in the New Orthography'], *Di Yidishe Shprakh* 10, 19-22.
1928d ['The Proposed Spelling Reform'], in M. Litvankov (ed.), *Yidishe Ortografye: Proyektn Un Materyaln Tsum Tsveytn Alfarbandishn* Yidishn *Kultur-Tsuzamenfor* (Kiev), 3-26.
1928e ['About an Orthographical Commission'], in M. Litvankov (ed.), *Yidishe Ortografye: Proyektn Un Materyaln Tsum Tsveytn Alfarbandishn Yidishn Kultur-Tsuzamenfor* (Kiev), 56-57.
1928f ['Yiddish Orthography in Poland'], in M. Litvankov (ed.), *Yidishe Ortografye: Proyektn Un Materyaln Tsum Tsveytn Alfarbandishn* Yidishn *Kultur-Tsuzamenfor* (Kiev), 58-66.
1928g ['A Bibliography for the Orthography Discussion, 1921-1928'], in M. Litvankov (ed.), *Yidishe Ortografye: Proyektn Un Materyaln Tsum Tsveytn Alfarbandishn Yidishn Kultur-Tsuzamenfor* (Kiev), 65-70.
1930 ['The New Yiddish Punctuation'], *Di Yidishe Shprakh* 25, 29-36.
Zaretski, A., and E. Falkovitsh
1931 *Yidishe Punktuatsye: Proyekt* (Moscow, Kharkov and Minsk).
* Zhitlofski, Khayem
1926? (Article on Romanization), *Di Tsukunft* (sometime before May).
Zhitomirski, K.
1911 ['Yiddish: Its Essence and Meaning'], *Vyestnik Obščestva Rasprostranyenya Prosvyeščenia Myeždu Yevreyami v Rossiyy* 3, 3-20; 4, 3-21.
Ziemand, B. (ed.)
1923 *Unhoib* (Vienna).
Zinger, Y.-Y.
1926 ['An Important Question'], *Literarishe Bleter* 103, 260-261.

PAUL B. HENZE

14

Politics and Alphabets in Inner Asia

I. BACKGROUND

Central Asia has a rich history. As far back as written record and archaeological evidence go, the area has been swept by a bewildering succession of cultural, political, and religious influences.[2] Toynbee has compared the steppelands of Inner Asia with the sea and has found that historical forces have operated in these areas in much the same fashion as in maritime regions. Like the sea, the steppes have served as a highway between peoples. They have facilitated trade, conquest, and the spread of cultural influences.[3]

In conjunction with other forces of culture and civilization, many forms of writing have spread across Central Asia through the centuries. No alphabets seem to have been indigenous to Central Asia. Most of them originated on the fringes of Asia and spread inward. Until modern times the primary pattern of alphabetic diffusion through Central Asia was from west and south toward the northeast. A good example is the Mongolian alphabet. Its ultimate origins have been traced to the Syriac (Aramaic) script used by early Christians in the Eastern Roman Empire. The Syriac script was adapted for their own use by the Sogdians, an Iranian people, from Nestorian Christians.[4] The Sogdian alphabet was in turn taken over by the Turkic Uigurs. The Uigurs made some adjustments to suit the peculiarities of their language and changed the style of writing from horizontal to vertical. The Naiman Turks, close neighbors of the Uigurs, adopted their method of writing and transmitted it to the Mongols at the beginning of the thirteenth century.[5] This alphabet, with relatively little basic change, remained in use among Mongols until World War II. The Arabic alphabet spread across Central Asia in somewhat similar fashion, arriving with Islam in the ninth and tenth centuries, but it underwent little independent development when it was used for indigenous languages.[6]

The most dynamic period of Central Asian history was from the thirteenth to the sixteenth centuries. The Mongols and then the Turks experienced a great burst of military and political energy. Their conquests carried them into China, India, and Persia, to Russia, and into the heart of Europe. The political effect of their conquests was far greater than the cultural. The vast quantities of energy which these peoples had to spend to bring most of Eurasia under their power left them both politically and culturally weakened in their home territories. The sixteenth century marked a turning point in Central Asian history. After 1600 a period of relative cultural and religious stability set in. Stability soon degenerated into stagnation. Cultural and religious stagnation was closely bound up with political stagnation. Inner Asia ceased to be an active force in world history and gradually became instead a region where outside forces, converging from different directions, began to compete for the opportunity to influence the future development of the area in accordance with their own special interests. The nineteenth century saw the beginning of a new era in Central Asian history. Power rivalries became more clear-cut and the heart of Central Asia came under the control of Russia. New cultural influences began to make themselves felt. The period of change which began in the nineteenth century has not yet come to an end, though the pace of change has accelerated tremendously during the last few decades.[7]

The question of alphabets is directly relevant to a study of the political, social, and cultural changes that have taken place in the interior regions of Asia during the last half-century. An examination of the problem of alphabets and linguistic transformation also sheds some light on the possible course of future developments in these regions.

Coincident with the onset of the period of stagnation in Central Asian history that began about 1600, the alphabetic picture crystallized and remained stable until the twentieth century. If we take the term 'Inner Asia' to include all the territory east of the Caspian, north of the Hindu Kush and the Himalayas, south of Siberia, and west of the parts of China that are actually settled by Chinese, we find that three principal alphabets survived in this region into modern times: the Arabic, the Mongolian, and the Tibetan. The Arabic alphabet has been almost exclusively associated with Islam, and the Mongolian and the Tibetan with Buddhism.

The Uigur alphabet remained in use for official court purposes among the Turkic peoples until the time of Tamerlane, but in this field, too, Arabic script eventually gained the upper hand.[8] All Turkic and Iranian peoples who professed Islam entered the twentieth century firmly attached to the Arabic alphabet.[9] This was also true of all native inhabitants of Chinese Turkestan. Arabic script has also been used to a limited extent by the Chinese Moslems (Dungans) of Kansu and neighboring areas for ritualistic and decorative purposes.[10]

The Arabic alphabet is not entirely suitable for accurate transcription of Turkic languages because of its limited possibilities for accurate representation of vowels. This deficiency was nevertheless in one sense a virtue, for it meant that some dialect differences were obscured in the written language. Use of the Arabic alphabet for the Central Asian Turkic languages facilitated the introduction of Persian and Arabic words and the diffusion of Persian and Arabic cultural influence throughout Central Asia. Until the Bolshevik Revolution, the Moslems of Central Asia were an integral part of the Islamic world. The Arabic alphabet had both symbolic and practical significance for the maintenance of religious and cultural ties – potentially political ties as well – with the countries of the Middle East and with other more advanced Moslem peoples in the Russian Empire, particularly the Kazan and Crimean Tatars.[11]

The antecedents of the Mongolian alphabet have already been mentioned. The Tibetan alphabet has its origins in the Sanskrit. Though originally derived from outside sources, both the Mongolian and Tibetan alphabets went through a long period of independent development in Central Asia. These two alphabets are quite unrelated and involve rather different representation principles, but they have one interesting characteristic in common: both were originally fitted to an archaic form of their languages. Both Mongolian and Tibetan writing, therefore, involves the use of more letters than are actually pronounced; there are silent consonants, and vowels are not necessarily spoken as they are written. This feature is present to a greater degree in Tibetan than in Mongolian, but in both languages it tends to minimize the influence of local dialects on the written language. In a different way the same effect was produced as when Arabic script was used for the Turkic languages.

The Mongolian alphabet continued in use into the twentieth century, in all areas where Mongols live: Inner Mongolia and parts of Manchuria, Outer Mongolia (now called the Mongolian People's Republic), Jungaria, the regions inhabited by Buryats around Lake Baikal, and among the mixed Mongol tribe who migrated to the lower Volga in the seventeenth century. The latter were deported by the Soviet authorities during World War II and restored to their territory in 1957-1958.[12]

The Tibetan alphabet was used throughout Tibet and in the regions bordering Tibet inhabited by Buddhist peoples closely related to the Tibetans. Until recently, educated Mongols usually learned Tibetan as well as their own language, for it was regarded as the sacred language of Lamaist Buddhism.

To a limited extent some of the Turkic tribes of the Altai region made use of the Mongolian alphabet for writing their Turkic dialects.[13] There is also at least one instance of a Turkic group, the Sari Yugor of Kansu, adopting the Tibetan script for their language. This occurred at the beginning of the eighteenth century.[14] When the Russians penetrated into the Altai in the nineteenth century, Russian missionaries devised Cyrillic alphabets for some of the Turkic groups in the area. These alphabets were little used, but they are interesting as historical curiosities and indirect antecedents of the Cyrillic alphabets which the Russians imposed upon these and all other Central Asian Turkic languages during the late 1930's.

Russian as the language of officialdom, and to some extent of trade, spread rapidly in Russian Central Asia following the conquests of the nineteenth century. Russian was not widely learned by the native peoples, however, and its influence on the native languages was slight. No attempt at Cyrillicization of the major Turkic or Iranian languages was made or contemplated.[15]

Occasional use of the Chinese system of writing in Inner Asia has occurred from earliest times, for there appear to have been colonies of Chinese traders in these regions as far back as historical records go. There were also periodic Chinese military expeditions into the far interior. In areas which have been traditionally regarded as part of the Chinese Empire in modern times – Tibet, Sinkiang, Mongolia – there have been Chinese officials and merchants employing the classical Chinese ideographic method of writing. Chinese ideographs, however, are not well suited for representing the sounds of the structurally different Mongolian and Turkic languages. Therefore, while most of these languages – particularly those in direct contact with Chinese culture – have been represented in Chinese characters at one time or another,[16] no complete or lasting adaptation of the Chinese system to any of them has ever occurred. Chinese characters have continued in use in modern times in parts of Central Asia where there are Chinese; otherwise they have seldom been used.

The alphabetic picture of Central Asia which has been sketched out above prevailed until the Bolshevik Revolution in the territories conquered by Russia. Then a period of rapid change began. Some measure of the rapidity of the change can be gained by considering, for example, the position of a fifty-year-old Uzbek or Buryat now living in the U.S.S.R. If he had originally learned to read and write in the Arabic or Mongolian alphabet of his childhood, he has since had to readjust himself to two completely different alphabets in order to read anything that is now published in his native tongue. In addition to having learned two new alphabets, he has twice had to go through lengthy periods of uncertainty about the way his language is supposed to be spelled, which words are regarded as suitable for literary use and which ones are not, and whether many of the grammatical forms are appropriate. The process of adapting the Central Asian languages to new alphabets has involved much more than a shift in method of writing. There has been much vacillation and controversy over the particular local dialects chosen as the basis for the new written languages. The linguistic history of the period has been filled with discussion about such problems as from where to borrow new words, whether to revive old forms, and how to eliminate earlier foreign borrowings. Though the 1950's and 1960's were less unsettled than the two preceding decades, most of these problems are still far from settled.[17]

II. LATINIZATION

A modified and improved Arabic alphabet was adopted for Uzbek in 1923. Similarly improved Arabic alphabets were introduced for Kazakh and Kirghiz about the same time.[18] It was declared Communist policy to raise the level of literacy as rapidly as possible, but the Arabic alphabet was not considered a desirable medium for this purpose. Abandonment of the Arabic alphabet had the political advantage of cutting off the rising generation from earlier books and written materials as well as current periodical literature from the Moslem countries south of the Russian borders, and especially from Turkey which was undergoing its own nationalist revolution during this period. In spite of Lenin's pronouncements about the transformation of Russian Central Asia into a shining example of socialism in practice and a base from which the entire Colonial East could be liberated, actual Soviet policy from the beginning aimed at cutting Central Asia off from all contact with the outside world. Russian Central Asia eventually became even less accessible under the Soviets than it had been under the tsars and the native emirs. The first and most important step in the process of isolating the area was the elimination of the Arabic script. A decree of August 7, 1925, forbade importation into the U.S.S.R. of materials printed in the Arabic alphabet. Meanwhile, an officially encouraged movement for the substitution of the Latin alphabet for the Arabic had made great progress across the Caspian, in Soviet Azerbaijan.

The language of Azerbaijan is similar to the Turkish spoken in Turkey and is only slightly more distantly related to the principal Turkic languages of Central Asia. There had been talk of abandoning the Arabic script in Azerbaijan before the Revolution. Because there was some intellectual support for the idea of a new alphabet there, the shift to Latin letters came swiftly and without quite as much governmental pressure as was later required in some of the other Turkic-speaking areas. The Latin alphabet was introduced in 1924. On May 1, 1925, a decree of the Azerbaijan Supreme Soviet made it compulsory for newspapers and official use, though the Arabic alphabet continued in concurrent use until 1929.

In 1926 a Turcological Congress was convened in Baku and the Latinization of all the Turkic languages of the U.S.S.R. was proclaimed official policy. The following year a Unified Turkic Latin Alphabet was adopted and a permanent committee was established in Baku to propagate the new alphabet and aid in its adaptation to all Turkic dialects. The Unified Turkic Latin Alphabet was simply the normal Latin alphabet supplemented by a few extra letters and signs designed to meet the special phonetic requirements of all the Turkic languages. It was both phonetically sound and practical for everyday use. It was almost, but not quite, identical with the Latin alphabet which was adopted in Turkey in 1928.

The very concept of a unified Turkic alphabet meant that its proponents aimed at achieving the fullest possible degree of linguistic uniformity among speakers of Turkic languages in the U.S.S.R., with the intention of facilitating contact among them and creating a sense of unity and common purpose. Enver Pasha was still a live memory among Russian Communists in the mid-1920's, and manifestations of pan-Turkism were already condemned and forbidden as anti-Soviet and reactionary. Among the Turkic peoples of the Soviet Union there nevertheless remained a strong sense of common kinship, though such feelings could not be expressed except in linguistic and cultural terms. The Unified Turkic Latin

Alphabet was evidence of the strength of this feeling. For the time being, the Communists were willing to allow the Turkic peoples this much of a common bond. Later even this small concession would be withdrawn. Already the trend toward deliberate emphasis and magnification of the differences between the Turkic peoples was gaining strength. Central Asia, for example, was divided into elaborately delineated 'national' republics and autonomous regions during the 1920's and as little political recognition as possible was given to the age-old economic and cultural links in the area.[19]

Turkey adopted the Latin alphabet in November, 1928. Under the personal guidance of Ataturk, vigorous measures were taken to accomplish the shift from Arabic script as rapidly as possible. Less than a year later, use of the old alphabet for official purposes, for publishing, and in the schools was forbidden. As in the Soviet Union, alphabetic reform in Turkey involved far-reaching linguistic reform as well. Foreign words, idioms, and grammatical forms were eliminated and replaced by new words and forms taken from many Anatolian dialects, ancient Turkish texts, and other Turkic languages. In many instances new words and whole sets of terminology had to be invented to fit the needs of modern life. The process of linguistic reform in Turkey has taken many years and can hardly be said to be fully finished yet.[20] Latinization in Turkey probably helped to accelerate the pace of Latinization in the U.S.S.R., for intellectuals among the Turkic peoples of the U.S.S.R. – though officially discouraged from doing so and reluctant to display overt interest in Turkey for fear of being branded pan-Turkic nationalists – were keenly interested in developments there.[21]

From 1927 to 1930 the Unified Turkic Latin Alphabet was adapted to all the Turkic languages of Soviet Central Asia – Kazakh, Uzbek, Turkmen, Karakalpak, and Kirghiz. Uigurs living in Soviet Central Asia, numbering about 100,000, also had their language readjusted to the new alphabet in 1930.[22] Their cousins in Sinkiang, of course, continued to use the Arabic script. The Persian dialect of the Central Asian Tajiks was also given a Latinized literary form during the late 1920's. Up until that time, the written language of the Tajiks had been Classical Persian in Arabic script. The new Latinized Tajik language naturally emphasized local dialectical peculiarities and great efforts were made during the next two decades to prove that Tadzhik was really an ancient language akin to, but basically different from, Persian.[23]

Officially the changeover to the Unified Turkic Latin Alphabet was completed throughout Soviet Central Asia by 1930. In some places, local scholars had worked out Latin alphabets of their own, differing somewhat from the Unified Turkic Latin Alphabet. There were arguments in favor of the local versions, but everywhere, because of official pressure, the unified alphabet finally prevailed. From 1930 onwards, all publishing was done in the new alphabet and schools taught only Latin letters. Special classes were held for adults. It was at this same time that a cultural revolution on a large scale was initiated and a great campaign to wipe out illiteracy began. The rate of literacy among the masses of native Central Asians had never been high, though Uzbeks and Tajiks were as a rule somewhat more likely to know how to read and write than Kirghiz and Turkmen. By the end of the 1920's, each of these peoples had developed small groups of intellectuals who took a lively interest in the linguistic, cultural, and historical questions. The Uzbeks, obvious cultural leaders of Central Asia, were particularly fortunate in this respect.[24]

In spite of the limitations placed upon them by requirements of Communist dogma, these Central Asian intellectuals of the 1920's and early 1930's were still permitted considerable freedom of thought and expression. Soviet nationalities policy was still rather generous. One could be anti-Russian. One could condemn tsarist imperialism. Within the various national groups there were extended discussions and many-sided arguments on questions of interpretation of the national past, literary issues, and language reform. Turkmenistan experienced heated literary and linguistic controversies during the 1920's. One group apparently proposed that the new literary language be based on a revival of older Turkmen forms; another group wished to direct the development of the Turkmen language as much toward Antolian Turkish as possible.[25] There was much opportunism as well as much amateurishness among local intellectuals, and much meddling by Russian Communists who did not understand the issues clearly.

The dialect originally chosen as the phonetic basis for the Latinized version of the Uzbek language was that of the town of Turkestan (actually located in Kazakhstan), while the grammar and vocabulary followed rather closely the usage of the Uzbek capital, Tashkent. This language, which was officially approved until 1937, showed real promise of developing into a Central Asian Turkic lingua franca, because it could be read and for the most part understood by Kazakhs, Karakalpaks, and Turkmen.[26] In 1937 an extensive reform of the Uzbek literary language was carried out. The Latin alphabet was retained, but the phonetic pattern of Tashkent was introduced while more of the words and forms of the dialects of the Fergana Valley were accepted as standard. Literary Uzbek was in this way made more distinct from its Turkic neighbors. The political significance of this change is, of course, not hard to see. *Divide et impera* – Moscow was more eager than ever to make the Central Asian nationalities feel as separate from one another as possible.

Strife and changes such as those which have been mentioned briefly in Turkmenistan and Uzbekistan occurred in all the other Central Asian republics. Latin alphabets were also introduced among the smaller Turkic groups living in the Altai, the Shors, and the Oirots.[27] The then still nominally independent inhabitants of Tannu Tuva 'adopted' the Latin alphabet in 1930. Until this time the Tuvinians had used the Mongolian script. Their written language was practically identical with classical Mongolian in spite of the fact that their local dialects were basically Turkic. Mongolian had been the official language of the government and the Tuvinian People's Revolutionary (Communist) Party. The Russians apparently feared that Tuva was developing in too pro-Mongol a direction. The new Latinized Tuvinian language was based on an amalgam of local dialects with a generous admixture of Russian words. The standards of the new Tuvinian written language were established by a commission of Russian scholars. For nine months after the introduction of the new language was decreed, the Tuvinian-Mongolian script newspaper *Ünen* (*Truth*, i.e. *Pravda*) was published in both languages. It was then changed to completely Latin-alphabet Tuvinian. The methods which the Russians used in forcefully changing not only the alphabet but also the language of Tuva at this time – when the area was still allegedly an independent republic – are most revealing, for they foreshadow the harsher methods of linguistic transformation which were to be used throughout the Soviet Union a few years later.[28]

Buryat-Mongolia, which had become an autonomous Soviet republic (A.S.S.R.) in 1923, also experienced Latinization in the late 1920's. There had been an upsurge of pan-Mongol sentiment among the Buryats after the turn of the century. Buryat intellectuals were eager to forge closer ties with the Qalqa Mongols, the dominant group in Outer Mongolia. The Buryats emphasized similarities between their language and Qalqa when they Latinized it. This brought a crisis in 1932-1933 and Russian intervention. As a result, the Buryats were forced to adopt Russian words in considerable number for political and scientific terms and to avoid the use of classical Mongolian terms, or new words based on older Mongolian roots, still in use in Qalqa.[29]

With isolated nationalities, like the Tuvinians and the Buryats, the Russian Communists employed more direct methods of linguistic coercion than with the peoples of Soviet Central Asia. In the Mongolian People's Republic they were more cautious. Here the Russians were eager to maintain a greater illusion of independence so as not to offend Chinese sensitivities or challenge Japanese ambitions too directly. Though a Latin alphabet was devised for the Qalqa Mongolian language in 1931, it was never officially decreed as compulsory and the old Mongolian script continued in use. Russian words were not forced upon the Qalqa Mongols, and, unlike the non-Russian areas of the Soviet Union, the Mongolian People's Republic enjoyed comparative linguistic peace during the 1930's.

As Stalin tightened his grip on the Communist Party and the Party consolidated its control over the outlying areas of the Soviet Union during the 1930's, the freedom of cultural development which the non-Russian nationalities of the Soviet Union originally enjoyed became more and more circumscribed. The Soviet Government became more predominantly Russian in spirit and larger minorities became increasingly suspect of being susceptible to foreign influences. This trend reached its culmination in the Great Purges of the late 1930's. Among the prominent victims of the purges were the political and cultural leaders of the non-Russian nationalities. Khojaev, the Uzbek Prime Minister, and Ikramov, the Uzbek Communist Party Secretary, were condemned to death for treason in 1938. Large-scale arrests and executions occurred in the Central Asian republics.[30] With the native leadership thus swept from the scene, the way was now clear for the Communists to proceed swiftly with the subjugation of these areas to more complete exploitation, more direct pressure for Russification, and more decisive measures to make the break with the past complete. The most striking outward symbol of change was the introduction of the Cyrillic alphabet.

III. CYRILLICIZATION

The Soviet Union's second 'Alphabetic Revolution'[31] came in 1939-1940. The groundwork had been laid for it during 1937-1938. The relatively free debate and the controversies over fine points of phonetics and vocabulary which had made the Latinization campaign lively and interesting were largely absent from the Cyrillic Revolution. The Great Purges had barely ceased. The atmosphere was tense. The non-Russian nationalities, shorn of their native leadership, were confused and frightened. They knew they were faced with the prospect of inevitable submission to increased Russification. The Russians made no secret of the fact that the shift to Cyrillic was meant to make it easier for the minorities to learn Russian. It soon became evident that the shift was also intended to make it easier for the non-Russian languages to assimilate Russian words. One of the most eminent Soviet Turcologists, Professor N. A. Baskakov, described the change and justified it as follows:

> 'The Arabic alphabet used by some peoples and the Latin alphabet introduced later could not keep pace with the development of the national languages of the previously backward peoples of the U.S.S.R. The adoption of the Russian script by most of the languages has not only contributed to their development, but has been of notable assistance to the various nationalities of the Soviet Union in their successful mastery of the Russian language and in the assimilation of Russian culture. It has in fact provided them with a uniform basis on which to acquire literacy in their native tongues and in Russian. Alphabets and scripts on the basis of the Russian have been worked out by most of the national republics and regions with due regard to the mutual exchange of experience and advice by the local and central scientific research organizations. As a result, the modern alphabets based on the Russian script fully represent the phonetics of the languages, contribute to the rapid acquisition of native languages in the schools, and to a remarkable extent assist the nationalities of the Union in learning Russian. The exceptional importance of the Russian alphabet calls for special care in its use. The task of the simultaneous inculcation of literacy in both the native and Russian languages can only be successfully performed by achieving the maximum equality in the value of the letters. In the alphabets based on Russian devised for each language, there should be as little conflict as possible between the value of those symbols and letters common to both the native language and the Russian, which are only used for the phonemes of the national language, and other symbols and letters, also common to both, which are used only for loan words. This does not of course apply to special symbols not used in the Russian alphabet, which can only be used in root words of each language.[32]

There was no Unified Cyrillic Turkic Alphabet. This fact indicates the change of temper in the decade that had passed since Latinization took place. After the purges, the Communists were no longer willing to allow the Turkic peoples of the U.S.S.R. even the semblance of alphabetic unity. The Cyrillic alphabets devised for the Central Asian languages were deliberately made as different from each other as possible.[33] Likewise dialects that differed as much as possible from the related neighboring languages were chosen as norms for the Cyrillic written languages.

By 1941 the Central Asian Turkic languages, Tajik, and the Turkic languages of the Altai and Buryat-Mongolian had all been changed over to the Cyrillic alphabet. 'Independent' Tannu Tuva again made the change in step with the rest of the Soviet Union. The Mongolian People's Republic lagged. It was a little more difficult to find justification for the shift there, and the Russians were busy enough supervising the change in the U.S.S.R. itself. There was talk of changing to Cyrillic in Mongolia in 1941, but nothing happened, though a group of scholars was at work on a plan for Cyrillicization. Mongolia continued to use its own ancient alphabet until 1946 when Cyrillic was finally introduced.[34]

The shift to Cyrillic involved many practical problems, as had the shift to Latin ten years before. Printing establishments had to be provided with new sets of type, public signs changed, books reissued in the new type. On the whole, however, this aspect of the change appears to have been easier than it was the first time. Once again the Communists had armed themselves with a convenient method for combating a past with which they wished, in part, to break. Many of the native Central Asian poets, playwrights, novelists, and journalists who had been carefully nurtured by the Soviet regime during the late 1920's and early 1930's had been liquidated during the Great Purges. Their works were labeled treasonous and were proscribed.[35] In Orwellian fashion, a whole rewriting of history had to take place. Millions of volumes had to be destroyed. The alphabetic change facilitated this process. As time went on, the Communists could console themselves, all materials printed in the Latin alphabet would become less and less accessible to a newer generation reared on Cyrillic.

The outbreak of war in 1941, the preoccupation of the Soviet leaders with the German invasion, the easing of Communist pressures in most of the areas inhabited by non-Russians in order to reduce disaffection and disloyalty – all these things meant that the peoples who had just acquired new Cyrillic alphabets were to some extent left to do with them as they pleased until after the war was over.

Once the war was won, the Communists began to devote themselves to domestic problems again. The German invasion had provided ample justification of the Russians' worst fears about many of the minority peoples of the U.S.S.R. Thousands of Central Asians had thrown down their arms and defected to the Germans during the early phases of the invasion. Crimean Tatars and North Caucasian peoples into whose territories the German armies penetrated had seized what they considered an opportunity to rid themselves of both Communism and Russian domination and revolted. All this convinced Stalin that pre-war Soviet policy toward the minorities had been much too soft; tighter control and more rigid training were needed to make good Soviet citizens of them. The crackdown in Central Asia began early, but at first proceeded rather slowly. The assault on the native cultures increased rapidly in tempo in the late 1940's and the campaign reached its height during the last three years before Stalin's death.

Events on the 'linguistic front' during the postwar period reflect the spirit of these years as a whole. Russification of the Central Asian languages was accelerated. The Turkic languages continued to be kept as far apart as possible in spelling, grammar, and native vocabulary, but Russification affected them all in much the same way. Russian words were made mandatory for the majority of political, economic, scientific, and technical terms. Geographic terms were likewise thoroughly Russified. Decreeing that words be used is one thing; getting people to use them in everyday speech is, of course, quite another. Much of the Russian vocabulary forced upon the Central Asian languages was slow to take root.[36]

Another field where controversy developed was the question of spelling borrowed Russian words. The rule was soon established that all words taken from the Russian must be spelled exactly as in Russian even though the phonetic requirements of the local languages might normally demand that changes in spelling should be attempted to conform to native pronunciation. Some efforts were made to extend this principle to cover even the few Russian words which had been assimilated into the Central Asian languages in pre-Revolutionary times, but they were not too successful.[37]

The early post-World War II purging of Central Asian cultures involved much sharp criticism of contemporary literary and historical works, but few physical liquidations of authors. Epic poems such as the Kirghiz *Manas* cycle and the Mongol *Geser* legends, which at an earlier stage had been publicized throughout the Soviet Union as great examples of native epic literature, were attacked as reactionary. The great Persian and Turkic classic poets fared somewhat better. Nevai, Jami, Rumi, and Firdausi, Avicenna and Omar Khayyam were declared Uzbek and Tajik national heroes, just as Nizami was claimed for Soviet Azerbaijan. The works of all these poets are now considered part of the 'common cultural heritage of the Soviet people', though their writings are carefully selected and edited before publication in textbooks and mass editions.[38]

Central Asian history gave the Soviets more difficulty than literature. Local histories produced during the early 1930's could not meet the requirements of the postwar period. There was much rewriting of history during the late 1940's and early 1950's. No local history which did not demonstrate that the Kazakhs, the Uzbeks, the Mongols, and all the others were not predestined to associate themselves with the Russians – and therefore justified to a considerable extent the conquest and exploitation of these peoples by Tsarist Russia as a progressive step – had much chance of meeting approval in Moscow. Even when Central Asian historians drastically distorted the past of their peoples, few of them succeeded in getting approval for their works. Books published were subsequently harshly attacked and in some cases withdrawn from circulation. After Stalin's death, the pace of Russification in Central Asia slowed slightly.[39]

The eminent Soviet Turcologist, Baskakov, devoted the last portion of his long article, 'The Turkic Peoples of the U.S.S.R. – the Development of Their Languages and Writing', which appeared in 1952,[40] to the unsolved problems of the Turkic languages. Among them he mentioned the proper selection of dialects as bases for literary languages, the establishment of rules for handling new words, and the construction of proper grammatical terminology. He also outlined a number of measures necessary for the improvement of existing alphabets and standardization of spelling, and went so far as to suggest that the alphabets of the various Turkic languages be coordinated to bring them 'as close as possible to Russian and thus remove present inconsistencies'. He concluded his article with a statement typical of the times:

> 'Execution of all these tasks has been made possible by the programs and methodological instructions set forth in J. V. Stalin's works of genius.'

Soon it was no longer fashionable among Soviet linguists – or politicians!

– to cite Stalin's 'works of genius', but the problems of alphabets and dialect bases for the Soviet minority languages remained. From time to time a tendency to consider some of the problems from a common viewpoint could be detected, but Soviet Turcologists had to be careful not to go too far.[41] The problem of alphabet reform remained one of the most controversial issues as the shortcomings of the Cyrillic alphabets in use in Soviet Central Asia became increasingly clear.

The alphabetic problems of the Karakalpaks, one of the smallest of the Central Asian peoples, make an interesting case study. The Karakalpaks, who numbered somewhat under 200,000 in the 1950's, are more closely related to the Kazakhs than to the Uzbeks and before the Revolution formed part of the old Khanate of Khiva. In the Soviet era they have always formed part of the Uzbek Republic.[42] By the time Karakalpak underwent Cyrillicization in 1940, it had already undergone three alphabet reforms in the previous sixteen years: a reformed Arabic alphabet was in effect from 1924 to 1928, a Latin alphabet from 1928 to 1938, and a modified Latin alphabet from 1938 to 1940. Each Central Asian language had to receive a Cyrillic alphabet with different refinements. Karakalpak was given an awkward spelling system in which the exact pronunciation of the umlaut vowels was indicated not by the letters themselves but by the forms of adjoining consonants or an extra letter (the Cyrillic 'hard sign') added to the end of words or syllables. For the other Central Asian Turkic languages diacritical marks or slightly altered forms of the basic letters were used for these sounds, thus preserving a true phonetic system. The Cyrillic alphabet as applied to Karakalpak was obviously much less satisfactory than either the earlier reformed Arabic or Latin alphabets had been.[43]

This alphabet proved so impractical that the necessity for reform had to be recognized. A linguistic conference was held in the Karakalpak A.S.S.R. in September 1954.[44] The conference was attended by such notables as Baskakov and the archaeologist Tolstov. The inadequacy of the original Karakalpak Cyrillic alphabet was sharply condemned:

> 'The great shortcoming of current Karakalpak orthography, as many speakers mentioned, is the fact that it does not reflect the phonetic structure of the Karakalpak language . . . The question of modifying and making more precise current Karakalpak orthography is most urgent, as was noted unanimously by all speakers.'

A revised alphabet with separate letters for each vowel sound was proposed by K. U. Ubaidullaev, and all those present at the conference approved the revisions. It was agreed that the new alphabet would be presented for confirmation to the Council of Ministers of the Karakalpak A.S.S.R. after the reactions of the Academy of Science of the Uzbek S.S.R. and of the Institute of Linguistics of the Academy of Sciences of the U.S.S.R. had been obtained.

The report on the conference contained two other features worthy of note. K. U. Ubaidullaev, who proposed and explained the revised alphabet, adhered to the usual position in respect to Russian words. 'Russian-international words which have come into the Karakalpak language must be written as they are written in Russian.' There was some mention of a common approach to all of the Turkic languages:

> 'As for the question of the correct method of writing compound words, speakers during their discussion came out in favor of writing them separately in the overwhelming majority of cases. During the discussions the necessity of studying the question of joined and separate words on a common plane for the whole group of Turkic languages was mentioned by many speakers.'

The second Turkmen Linguistic Congress, held in October, 1954,[45] brought forth many proposals, which, although they seem not to have been accepted, testify to the relative instability of the alphabetic and linguistic situation in this Central Asian Republic. One of the participants proposed that three new letters be added to the Cyrillic alphabet as now used for the Turkmen language. His suggestion was turned down because 'this change in Turkmen spelling would not be justified in practice because the number of errors made by students in writing would probably increase to a marked degree'. On the other hand, another participant proposed that seven letters – all required to write Russian words but not necessary to represent Turkmen sounds – be dropped from the Turkmen alphabet. This proposal was rejected 'because increasing or decreasing the number of letters in the alphabet . . . would unavoidably lead to a significant change in Turkmen spelling'.

Although the participants in the congress seem to have diagnosed a wide variety of alphabetic and linguistic difficulties and suffered from no lack of suggestions for improvement, the Congress as a body was reluctant to make any changes for fear that these would cause still more complications. On the question of spelling of words taken from Russian, the Congress apparently had no alternative but to confirm the party-line position:

> 'Great attention was given to the principles of correct writing of words taken from the Russian language, and the opinion was expressed that they would be written as they are written in Russian and not as these words are pronounced in the Turkmen language. A difference in the way of writing them not only introduces confusion and encourages illiteracy in parallel study in schools of the Russian and Turkmen languages but also puts a brake on the cultural development of the Turkmen people.'

While words taken from Russian continued to be written as in Russian when used in Turkmen, they had to take Turkic morphological and grammatical endings. Lists of words cited by some of the speakers at this Congress provide interesting examples of the strange results that Turkmen-Russian mating had produced: *tekhnikalyk redaktor* 'technical editor'; *burzhuazlyk dovlet* 'bourgeois government'; *liberallyk*, *liberalchylyk*, or *liberalizmchilik* 'liberalism'; *opportunistlik*, *opportunistchilik*, or *opportunizmchilik* 'opportunism'.[46]

The second Turkmen Linguistic Congress cleared up little of the confusion confronting the Turkmen in writing their language. The Congress concluded that it was impossible to decide how certain words such as *dostluk/dostlyk* 'friendship' should be spelled. The Turkmen Stalin Prize winning author Kerbabaev suggested that one uniform way of spelling the names of towns be adopted so that there would not be different Russian and Turkmen spellings for many of them (Tashauz/Dashkhovuz, Kara-Kala/Garygala), but no decision seems to have been made on this question either.

Problems similar to those which have beset the Karakalpaks and the Turkmen troubled the other Central Asian peoples. Since not only their alphabets but to a considerable degree even their literary languages had been forced upon them, it was not surprising that these peoples found it awkward to adapt to them. The logical approach for both Russian scholars as well as the native peoples – to attempt to find a solution for some of these problems on a common plane – went against the Communist policy of emphasizing the separateness of each nationality and discouraging meaningful political and cultural contact between them.

Nevertheless the mere suggestion that a unified Turkic alphabet again be considered was in itself an exciting development when it appeared in the prestigious journal *Sovetskoe Vostokovedenie* in September 1956.[47] The author of the article, A. K. Borovkov, was little known at the time, though in subsequent years a steady stream of highly competent publications has revealed him to be a first-rate linguistic scholar. It has always been typical of Soviet technique to let a relatively junior figure launch a discussion of a controversial subject. If the 'discussion' does not go well, if a shift of line occurs, the author may even be disavowed or condemned for having raised the controversial issue in the first place.

Borovkov took no undue chances. His article was written in such cautious fashion that his thoughts often seem inconsistent and muddled. He devotes the first part of his article to praise of the Cyrillic alphabet. He points out that the Cyrillic alphabet, as used by Slavic languages other than Russian, has additional letters which might well be considered for use in non-Slavic languages, and mentions two additional letters used in Ukrainian, five used in Serbian, and one diacritical mark used in Belorussian as examples. One expects this line of thought to reappear later in the article, but he never returns to it. The main point which he seems to have intended to get across in his article is that unification of the alphabets of practically all the non-Slavic languages of the U.S.S.R. would be desirable. Toward the end of the article successful earlier experience with the unified Latin alphabet is mentioned in support of this point of view:

> 'The experience of the earlier Latin alphabet demonstrated convincingly that the unification of the Turkic, Mongolian, and several other alphabets is completely possible and appropriate. The "Yanalif" typewriter and the typographical machines were standardized to such an extent that they could be used at the same time by practically all the national republics and regions using the unified script. At the present time the situation has become so complicated that for relatively minor differences in alphabets it is in nearly all cases necessary to change the keyboards of typewriters and printing machines. Reading of literature in related languages has also been made difficult.'

Borovkov tried to justify proposed changes on practical grounds in terms of financial savings in the production of typewriters and the operation of printing machines. He was cautious about referring to the fact that divergent alphabets hamper communication between closely related Turkic peoples. Only at one other point is this problem directly mentioned:

> 'Different methods of applying the Russian alphabet could not help showing up in the results. For example, the phonetically extremely

> similar Karakalpak and Kazakh languages (practically only one sound, "h", distinguishes them, being present in Karakalpak and absent in Kazakh) are completely different in writing: The alphabets in both languages are different; the orthographic solution of identical features is accomplished in different ways.'

Borovkov gave a vivid picture of variations in the use of letters and application of spelling principles in the various Soviet Turkic languages. While in addition to the normal Cyrillic alphabet, the Kirghiz language employs three supplemental letters, Uzbek uses four, Kazakh nine, and Uigur as written in Kazakhstan eight; the revised Karakalpak alphabet required six additional letters.

Borovkov's conclusions were not clear. He proposed a revised system of six pairs of vowels for all the Turkic and Mongolian languages, but he shied away from proposing a complete system of consonants. He stated that diacritical marks should be avoided and cited a condemnation of them by the Russian Academy of Sciences in 1924 in support of his point of view, but he nevertheless concluded by recommending the use of diacritical marks for vowels and a system of hooks and other odd appendages for some Cyrillic consonants which seem far more objectionable (and awkward for typing and printing) than diacritical marks. He avoided taking a clear position on the spelling of Russian words adopted by the minority languages.

Concluding his article, Borovkov again mentioned the financial gains which a unified alphabet would bring, pointed to the disadvantages of private initiative in changing alphabets, and stated:

> 'It would be extraordinarily timely to request the Soviet of Nationalities of the Supreme Soviet of the U.S.S.R. to take upon itself the direction of this great and complicated task.'

In the light of the way the Soviet political system works, this was indeed a bizarre suggestion. It is not surprising that nothing came of it. What is surprising, however, is that so little has changed in the nearly two decades that have elapsed since. There has been continual controversy, much learned, and some popular discussion of the problems of Central Asian alphabets, languages, and literature, but no important 'reforms', no violent shifts in any direction. Before we carry the story up to the present, let us shift eastward and go back in time to have a look at how the Chinese Communists have dealt with the alphabetical and language problems of their minority peoples.

IV. CHINA[48]

Until the Chinese Communist conquest of 1949-1950, the Central Asian regions of China had been only loosely and sporadically controlled by Chinese central governments. Outer Mongolia was for all practical purposes lost before the outbreak of World War I. Tibet remained isolated and managed its own affairs. The Tibetan-Chinese borderlands were in a state of anarchy from the late 1920's onward. Sinkiang was largely under Russian control from 1930 until the early 1940's. The Chinese never relinquished their claim to any of these territories, but China proper was too unsettled for any Chinese government to be able to exercise consistent influence on the economic, political, or cultural development of the Central Asian border regions.

The Soviets had been mostly interested in gaining short-term strategic and economic advantages during the period of their dominance in Sinkiang. They made no serious efforts to reform the social habits of the people or to interfere with the native languages or the Arabic alphabet which was in common use among Uigurs, Kazakhs, and – to the extent that they were literate at all – the smaller groups of Uzbeks, Tajiks, and Kirghiz. Religion was not subjected to persecution. Both Turkic and Chinese Moslems practiced their faith without serious hindrance.

Parts of Inner Mongolia were occupied by the Japanese during the 1930's and early 1940's. The Japanese experimented with an 'Autonomous Mongol Government' and dabbled in pan-Mongolism. They made great efforts to ingratiate themselves with all Mongols. They did not attempt to reform the linguistic, religious, or social habits of the Mongols. They did encourage literacy among the Mongols and subsidized the publication of a great deal of literature – mostly political – in Mongolian.

As early as April 1947 the Chinese Communists proclaimed an 'autonomous' Inner Mongolia.[49] This marked the beginning of a concerted campaign to win the Mongols and other non-Chinese elements to the Communist side. As additional areas inhabited by Mongols were brought under control, they were added to the Inner Mongolian Autonomous Region. A great deal of political propaganda was printed in the traditional Mongolian alphabet. The Chinese Communists respected Mongol religious and cultural feelings and encouraged pan-Mongol nationalism. They appear to have had considerable success in winning Mongol confidence and support. The same approach was used as the Communists advanced farther into Northwest China. Chinese policy toward the Turkic peoples of Sinkiang was similar to that followed by the Russians toward their Moslem Turkic subjects during the early stages of the Bolshevik Revolution. The national sensitivities of all these peoples were ostentatiously catered to. As in Inner Mongolia, the Chinese printed and distributed a great deal of political literature among the peoples of Sinkiang, practically all of it in the Arabic script.

When the conquest of Tibet was completed in 1950, the Chinese Communists had succeeded in rounding out the traditional borders of the Chinese Empire with only one exception, Outer Mongolia, which remained firmly under Russian control.[50] Firmly entrenched in power, the Chinese Communists next proceeded to elaborate their policy for the non-Chinese inhabitants of the country along classic Soviet Russian lines. Though non-Chinese peoples form a far smaller proportion of the entire population of China than is the case with non-Russian (or even non-Slav) peoples of the Soviet Union,[51] the Chinese Communists adopted a system of graded 'autonomous' districts and regions on the Soviet pattern. But the Chinese showed no intention of extending their system of autonomy so far as to establish separate 'republics' for the major non-Chinese groups. In comparison with the Chinese, even the larger minority groups are so small in numbers that such an extreme manifestation of ostensible 'equality' would be impractical. Though the Inner Mongolian Autonomous Region was established in 1947 and enlarged in 1954 by the addition of the province of Sui-Yuan, the Uigurs of Sinkiang were not organized into an autonomous region until the summer of 1955. Preparations for a similar arrangement in Tibet went slowly. Many smaller autonomous units were set up in various parts of western China – for Mongols and Kazakhs in Sinkiang and for various Thai-related groups in Yünnan.

The Chinese stated their policy clearly and succinctly:

> 'Great importance is now attached to the development of the languages of the national minorities. The Committee on Cultural and Educational Affairs of the Government Administration Council has set up a special committee to study the spoken and written languages of the national minorities, to organize and guide research in that field. This committee will help create written languages for those nationalities having no written languages of their own and improve existing written languages of others. The creation of a written language for the Yi people of Sinkiang Province marks the beginning

> of such work. The People's Government is also using existing favorable conditions to full advantage for publications in the languages of the national minorities. The Commission of Nationalities Affairs has published over 700,000 volumes of books and magazines in the Mongolian, Tibetan, and Uigur languages. Definite progress has also been made in developing local newspapers and publications in minority languages. Broad sections of the Mongolian, Tibetan, Uigur, Kazakh, and Korean people can now read in their own language Marxist-Leninist classics and Mao Tse-Tung's works, documents of the Central People's Government, books on scientific and technological subjects, as well as literary works. In Sinkiang Province, the *Selected Works of Mao Tse-Tung* have appeared in Uigur and Kazakh.'[52]

Another source describes publications activity in Inner Mongolia alone:

> 'From 1947 through 1951, 200 titles of different works in the Mongolian language totalling 1,300,000 copies were published. The total number of books and newspapers published in the Mongolian language in 1953 reached 2,700,000 copies.... Separate brochures of the works of Mao Tse-Tung which form part of the first volume of his *Selected Works* have been published in Mongolian.'[53]

All these publications in minority languages were issued in traditional alphabets. In 1955 it was announced that the language of the Mongols of China would be reformed on the basis of the Cyrillic alphabet.[54] A September 19, 1955, dispatch of the New China News Agency stated that the new alphabet would be introduced into Inner Mongolia in two stages covering a period of six years. The first stage would last until 1958; during this period teachers and printers will be trained in use of the new letters, printing establishments equipped, and school books prepared. Newspapers and magazines would publicize and explain the use of the new alphabet. During the second stage, 1958-1961, the new alphabet would gradually replace the old in schools and newspapers, and for official use.

Early in 1956, it was decided that the plan for applying the Cyrillic alphabet in Inner Mongolia should be speeded up. Four, instead of the previous six, years were to be allotted for completion of the plan. A conference on implementation of the new plan took place in Hühehot, capital of the Inner Mongolian Autonomous Region. Soviet experts attended. It was announced in November 1956 that popularization of the new alphabet had actually got under way in Inner Mongolia in July. Seven thousand teachers were said to have been trained and a million textbooks prepared. It was calculated that an illiterate person could master the new alphabet and be able to read after six months' study. One hundred thousand persons were said to be proficient in the new alphabet by November, 1956.[55] By May 1959 it was claimed that 92 percent of all Mongols up to the 'prime of life' had mastered the new Mongolian Cyrillic written language in use in Inner Mongolia. Whether this figure was accurate was less important than the fact that Inner Mongolia had experienced a massive influx of Chinese settlers during the 1950's, and the administration of the area, in spite of its officially 'autonomous' status, was dominated by Chinese officials who had little interest in encouragement of the Mongolian language and often insisted that Mongols use Chinese in their dealings with the authorities.[56]

A conference on reform of all minority languages had been held in Peking from December 6-15, 1955. This conference directed that the work of providing alphabets for languages which had none must be completed before 1960. In languages where written scripts were defective, improvements or changes would be made. It was decided to send seven working teams to various parts of the country to supervise work on minority languages. A Soviet expert, Serdyuchenko, gave a report on Soviet experience in creating written languages for minority peoples.[57]

In south and southwest China the Communist authorities moved rapidly to devise new alphabets for the minority peoples of these regions. Practically all these languages are structurally akin to Chinese. The Latin alphabet was used for most of them. Since the Latin alphabet was at that time thought likely to be adopted eventually for Chinese itself, employment of it among minority groups of south and southwest China and the spread of literacy among them had the appeal of facilitating Sinicization.

It was announced in November 1956 that the revised Miao[58] script would be based on the Latin alphabet.[59] In Yünnan a linguistic committee was set up to supervise changes among the non-Chinese nationalities of the region, numbering over 2,000,000 people. The committee announced that it planned by the end of 1957 to achieve a 'uniform and systematic formulation' of the more than a dozen languages of the region and to devise appropriate phonetic alphabets for them, a rather ambitious undertaking.[60]

While the Latin alphabet was widely applied among minorities living along the southern and southwestern borders of China, the Cyrillic alphabet was favored not only in Inner Mongolia but initially also among most non-Chinese peoples living in northwestern China, the area which was officially designated the 'Sinkiang-Uigur Autonomous Region' in 1955. A conference on alphabet reform for this region was held in Urumchi in August 1956. It was decided that Cyrillic alphabets would be adopted for the Uigurs, Kazakhs, Kirghiz, and Sibos.[61] Whether these Cyrillic alphabets were to be different from those already in use among Uigurs,[62] Kazakhs, and Kirghiz of Soviet Central Asia was not announced, but it was implied by the fact that the official report of the conference specifically stated that Uzbeks and Tatars in Sinkiang would adopt the same Cyrillic alphabets used by their kinsmen in the U.S.S.R. The Uigurs, numbering more than 3,500,000, and the Kazakhs, numbering nearly 500,000, together with the nearly 500,000 Chinese who then lived there, formed the basic population of Sinkiang.[63] The Mongols of Sinkiang, it was decided, would use the same Cyrillic alphabet being introduced in Inner Mongolia. The conference did not decide on the alphabet to be adopted by the Tajiks of Sinkiang, and for some of the other smaller groups it was agreed that further research should be done before a final decision could be made. On the last day of the Urumchi conference, Saifuddin, Chairman of the Government of the Sinkiang-Uigur Autonomous Region, addressed the participants. He told the conference that all problems could not be solved immediately and that further efforts would have to be made to carry out more scientific research work after the conference:

> 'The current languages of the Sinkiang nationalities all have a long historical background. They have made important contributions to the development of their national cultures as well as to the enrichment of the culture of the Motherland. They have also contributed largely to the consolidation of national unity. But on the other hand, these languages in their present written forms have various defects: The forms of words are variable, there are complicated supplementary signs and they are generally inconvenient in handwriting, furthermore they cannot fully represent the entire spoken languages of the different nationalities and therefore in daily use as well as in publications, newspapers and books the users are confronted with many difficulties. They certainly cannot meet the requirements of Socialist cultural construction. When the new written languages based on the Slavic alphabet are popularized, all these handicaps will be removed. It will also facilitate the learning of the lan-

guages by the cadres of other nationalities, particularly the Han Chinese, and will enable the cadres of the different nationalities in the Autonomous Region to better help each other and learn about each other.'[64]

During the first ten years of Communist rule, it can be seen, from what has just been recounted, that Chinese language policies for minority peoples were relatively idealistic, generally imitative of Soviet experience, and rather diffusely applied. A great deal of loosely organized academic research was devoted to problems of alphabets and language development. Great successes were often claimed for work among small groups. The larger minorities – the Mongols, the peoples of Sinkiang, and the peoples of the southwest (including the Tibetans, who were an especially difficult problem) – were far more awkward to deal with.

Meanwhile, as the Peking Government consolidated its control over the entire country and became preoccupied with economic development as well as military bolstering of its borders, idealistic minority development policies clashed increasingly with hard economic and strategic requirements. Large numbers of Chinese were moved into all the border regions inhabited by minorities.[65] Neither the immigrant farmers and laborers nor the Chinese officials in these areas were inclined to pay much attention to minority sensitivities or aspirations. Their attitudes, often condemned from Peking but with little effect in the 'autonomous' regions themselves, were hard to distinguish from those held by the kinds of people Communist theoreticians condemn as colonial exploiters. A great deal of strain developed. Tensions were exacerbated by the rivalry with the Soviet Union which was already a real political fact by the late 1950's. In the southwest, where Soviet rivalries and border claims played no role, the expanding conflicts in Indo-China had a similar effect.

It is not surprising, therefore, that basic changes – which had already in fact taken place – were announced in Chinese Communist minority language policy in 1959. The purpose of creating and stabilizing minority written languages was now clearly stated to be to 'give the masses a more thorough course in Socialist and Communist education'.[66] The minorities were now expected to 'grasp the tendency for spoken and written languages to draw closer to the Chinese language. Any plea for the preservation of purity of the existing minority languages must be resolutely attacked.' When a minority language was similar to Chinese in structure, it was to be written in the same Latin letters adopted for phoneticization of Chinese, and attempts were to be made to encourage uniformity in spelling and alphabets of minority languages. Finally, minority peoples were to be made to understand that they were all expected to learn Chinese. Mastery of Chinese was seen as necessary for their full economic development and incorporation into the Chinese Communist political system.[67] This was the period of the 'Great Leap Forward'.

Meanwhile in Sinkiang, Cyrillic alphabets adopted only a short time before for the predominantly Turkic languages of this area were replaced with Latin alphabets. Even the small Mongol element in Sinkiang was said to be shifting to a Latin alphabet.[68] The Mongols of Inner Mongolia remained the only Chinese minority officially using a Cyrillic alphabet – an understandable exception in terms of Peking policy because of the special Chinese interest in the Mongolian People's Republic. Interesting evidence came to light here in the early 1960's, however, that the Cyrillic alphabet was far from firmly rooted. No less an authority than a secretary of the Central Committee of the Mongolian Communist Party complained in January 1963 that 'Some persons are obstructively minimizing the progressive significance of the new written language and advocating return to the old written language.'[69] Can it be that 'some persons' referred not only to Mongols, but also, perhaps, to certain Chinese?

As early as 1934, the Chinese Communists had proclaimed the rights of national minorities to self-determination, in imitation of Soviet contentions. The outline of the constitution of the Chinese Soviet Republic published that year specified:

> '. . . the right of self-determination of the national minorities within the territorial confines of China to the extent that these nationalities have the right to secede from China and to establish their own independent states.'[70]

By September 1949 the Common Program of the Chinese People's Political Consultative Conference listed five guiding principles of Communist minority policy – but self-determination was no longer among them:

1. Equality of each of the national minority groups with the Han majority group.
2. Freedom of each of the national minority groups to preserve its language, religion, and customs.
3. Indivisibility of the Chinese nation.

4. Right to regional autonomy of national minority groups.
5. Right of members of national minority groups to serve in the armed forces.[71]

The 1954 Constitution defines minority rights in a still more restricted fashion:

> 'The People's Republic of China is a unitary multinational state. All the nationalities are equal. Discrimination against or oppression of any nationality and acts which undermine the unity of the nationalities, are prohibited. All the nationalities have the freedom to use and develop their own customs and ways. Regional autonomy applies in areas where a minority nationality lives in a compact community. All the national autonomous areas are inseparable parts of the People's Republic of China.'[72]

During the 1960's the Chinese minorities continued to receive propaganda homage and claims of political and cultural progress as well as economic gains were lavish. Chairman Mao declared to Edgar Snow in early 1965 in commenting upon Indonesia's withdrawal from the United Nations:

> 'As for China, was it not in itself a United Nations? Any one of several of China's minority nationalities was larger in population and territory than some states in the UN whose votes had helped deprive China of her seat there.'[73]

The notion of China as a UN in miniature is rather far-fetched. The Chinese themselves never claimed a higher proportion of minority nationalities than 6 percent of their total population. The Chinese minorities were in an essentially different situation from those in the Soviet Union. The implication that Communist China was a happy family of free and equal peoples was even more specious than similar Soviet claims.

Thus while propaganda became more strident, reality became grimmer. *Nationalities Research*, the scholarly journal devoted to minority cultural and language problems, was merged in early 1961 with a much less scholarly sister journal, *Nationalities' Solidarity*. Industrialization of the border areas was now claimed to be necessary for complete development of the minorities. Colonization by Chinese settlers continued. Revolt flared in Tibet in 1959 and simmered for several years. It proved impossible to proclaim officially the establishment of the Tibetan Autonomous Region, last of the five major minority areas to be set up, until September 1965. There was an exodus of Thai-related peoples across the Yünnan border when communes were established in the region. In 1962 thousands of Kazakhs and Uigurs from Sinkiang fled to the Soviet Union amid recriminations and counterclaims from both Moscow and Peking. In subsequent years there were further flights from Sinkiang into the Soviet Union as the pressures of Communist ideology and Chinese national interests came to weigh more heavily on the local peoples. This was also, however, a highly active period for Communist Chinese foreign policy. The Peking government proclaimed itself the champion of all suppressed peoples in Africa, Asia, and Latin America. What was really happening among China's own minorities had to be masked by exaggerated propaganda claims.[74] Soon both propaganda and what had been reality were swept up in the whirlwind of the Cultural Revolution.

There was a great deal of confusion and unevenness in application of minority policies during the mid-1960's. Some minority leaders were undoubtedly able to take advantage of the situation for the benefit of their own peoples. The onslaught of the Red Guards brought hitherto undreamed of challenges both for minority leaders and for Chinese officials assigned to minority areas. Minority peoples displayed greatest attachment to religion and traditional cultural values and symbols. This made them especially attractive as targets for ideological zealots. Party leaders and local Chinese officials, on the other hand, were concerned about moving ahead with the economic development of the minority areas and strengthening them militarily. They resisted export of the Cultural Revolution to them. Some were able to hold out for some time because by this time each of the principal 'autonomous' regions was in charge of Communist leaders who had learned to maintain considerable freedom of action for themselves. Before the Cultural Revolution could take effect in these regions, therefore, the leaders themselves had to be directly attacked and pushed aside.

The fate of Ulanfu, a Mongol, Communist since the 1920's and principal figure in national minorities policy formulation, is typical. He was formally accused of opposing Mao's thought in November 1967. It was said that he had already led the 'small handful of those in power' who

> '. . . undermined the mass movement of various nationalities to study and apply Chairman Mao's works creatively under the pretext of "putting the question of nationalities to the fore." . . . They put reactionaries and counterrevolutionaries in important posts under the pretext of respecting local minorities in selecting cadres.'

Ulanfu was said to have worked against Chinese Communist policies since the late 1940's and accused of having resisted the influx of Chinese into Inner Mongolia.[75] These accusations were the culmination of a hectic period of nearly a year during which Ulanfu and the Inner Mongolian leadership had both politically and militarily defended themselves against Red Guard, and eventually People's Liberation Army, attacks. Ulanfu continued to resist until January 1968, but was declared defeated in a broadcast late that month:

> 'After a struggle of several days, notable victories have been scored and several serious political cases involving the agents of Ulanfu . . . were brought to light. Bad elements sabotaging the proletarian Cultural Revolution and socialist construction either openly or behind the scenes were exposed, while a handful of bad leaders who had wormed their way into the revolutionary ranks were purged. This dealt a telling blow to the special agents of the United States, Japan, the Chian gang, and Soviet and Mongolian revisionism, all ghosts and monsters of society, landlords, rich peasants, counter-revolutionaries, bad elements and rights who have not been reformed, and the handful of ruffians, bandits, blackmailers, swindlers and speculators disturbing the market. Ammunition, blueprints for manufacturing guns, radio stations, material collected and plans hatched by Ulanfu's remnant clique for attacking the new red power, badges, seals, name lists of the counterrevolutionary organization, incriminating funds, and goods obtained through illegal profiteering speculation were also seized.'[76]

Ulanfu was later reported to have been imprisoned in Peking.

The intemperate language of the Inner Mongolian radio was matched and at times exceeded in other minority areas, especially Sinkiang. The Soviets entered much more directly into the propaganda battle in this area. Radio Tashkent stepped up its Uigur-language broadcasts and alleged, among other things, that Uigur books had been burned and Uigur works of art destroyed. The flourishing cultural life enjoyed by the Soviet Union's own small Uigur minority was contrasted with conditions in China. The Chinese Communists counterattacked by claiming that Soviet revisionists were trying to 'lead the people astray'. The People's Liberation Army eventually had to be brought into Sinkiang, too, to restore order.[77]

It is hard to escape the conclusion that the Cultural Revolution undid much of what had been accomplished in China's minority areas during the previous two decades. Parallels with the Great Purge period in the Soviet Union are striking. The situation in China's minority regions was probably even more confused when the Cultural Revolution had subsided than it had been in the Soviet Union in 1939-1940. On the other hand, the seriousness of these problems was reduced somewhat for the Chinese themselves (though hardly for the minorities!) by the fact that numerically the minority peoples are so much weaker and vulnerable to the effects of Chinese colonization. Nevertheless the minorities occupy half of the area of the country and most of their territories are border regions. They are thus destined to play a role out of all proportion to their numbers in Sino-Soviet rivalries of the future.

In the post-Cultural Revolution period, the status of alphabets and language reform projects in Chinese minority areas has been unclear. Press announcements, as much from what they do not say as from the actual information they provide, indicate that language reform schemes must have been delayed years in implementation as a result of the confusion of the 1960's. Radio Urumchi announced in September 1972, for example, that new written forms of Kazakh and Uigur, using the Latin alphabet, were being enthusiastically promoted and popularized in Sinkiang. The 'new written language' was said to be now 'partly or fully accepted in various fields of communication, including television, newspapers, books and magazines, movie advertisements and trademarks'. 'Counterrevolutionary revisionist fallacies concerning the reformation of the written language pushed by swindlers like Liu Shao-Chi' were denounced.[78] It appears that what is being talked about here is the use of the same Latin alphabet (*pinyin*) accepted for auxiliary use for transcription of Chinese, though this alphabet has never acquired anything more than the status of an officially sanctioned transcription system and appears likely to continue in this status indefinitely. There is even some reason to believe that Chairman Mao himself remains opposed to adoption of any Latin alphabet and remains committed to the idea that alphabetization of Chinese, if it ever comes to pass, should involve creation of a unique alphabet derived from the character system.[79]

Fragmentary information from Tibet indicates that experiments with *pinyin* for teaching Tibetan in primary schools have been undertaken. Traditional Tibetan script continues in use, however, for newspapers. The *Tibet Daily* is published in both Chinese and Tibetan editions. Reports from Yünnan, Tibet, and the Northwest indicate that great emphasis is being put on teaching minorities elementary Chinese. Military recruits from southwestern minority areas are being given priority instruction in Chinese. In Inner Mongolia, however, there have been reports of Chinese being encouraged to learn Mongolian as well as Mongols learning Chinese. The Cyrillic script appears to continue in use only in Mongolia, but there is some reason to believe that the old Mongol script may also continue to be used.

The most unusual alphabetic development reported from China since the end of the Cultural Revolution is a report from Yünnan in 1971 to the effect that Chinese characters were being used for transcribing Chairman Mao's works into minority languages.[80] For Chinese-type languages, use of Chinese characters is conceivable. The system could not be used in any practical way for languages which are structurally completely different from Chinese, such as Mongolian and the Turkic languages. For the latter, as well as Tibetan, it seems logical that Latin alphabet based on the Chinese *pinyin* system should be accepted as the norm. This alphabet has the advantage of facilitating orientation toward Chinese itself and at the same time insulating peoples who use it from materials printed in the Cyrillic version of their languages in use in the Soviet Union.[81]

V. USSR – THIRTY YEARS OF CYRILLIC EXPERIENCE

It took three years for the reforms in the Karakalpak alphabet which had been discussed in 1954 to be put into effect. Other Cyrillic alphabets remained unchanged. Looking backward from the early 1970's, it is interesting to compare the past thirty years with the twenty years that preceded this recent period of stabilization. In the 1920's all of the Soviet Turkic languages which had used Arabic script experienced one or more reforms aimed at adapting Arabic script to more modern requirements. Then, at the end of the 1920's, came the hectic period of Latinization when the Unified Turkic Latin Alphabet was used as a basis for new alphabets for practically all these languages.[82] Barely ten years had passed (less than ten for some languages) when Cyrillicization occurred. The experience of the Turkic languages was repeated by Tadzhik and the Mongolian languages. All of these Soviet minority peoples thus underwent three major alphabetic reforms in less than twenty years.

The fact that there has been so little alphabetic change since the early 1940's is quite in keeping with the spirit of Soviet life and society as a whole during this period: the past thirty years, in contrast to the early period of innovation and radical reform, have been a time of consolidation, stabilization, and, in some respects, even stagnation. Soviet society has become increasingly conservative. Soviet social and cultural policies have become increasingly less innovative. Change for its own sake is not only no longer popular, it is frowned upon. A society that has continued to try to present itself to the world at large, and particularly to the less developed world, as revolutionary, dynamic, scornful of tradition and conventionality, has been extremely cautious in its domestic policies and programs. The excesses of the Stalinist period were gradually rectified following the old tyrant's death. Peoples who had been deported during and immediately after World War II were one by one permitted to return to their home territories, restored to Soviet history and geography books, and again considered subjects for legitimate scholarly research.[83]

In Central Asia pressure for economic rationalization caused some relaxation of the practical aspects of the earlier policy of keeping each nationality tightly fenced off from its neighbors. At the same time, however, evidence has accumulated that the Central Asian minorities have gradually developed a certain degree of separate national consciousness which Moscow has been pleased to encourage. Though the atmosphere in which Soviet minorities have lived and developed during the past two decades, since the death of Stalin, can hardly be called liberal in any real sense, and though there have been periods of tightening and relaxation in policies imposed from Moscow, the period as a whole has been characterized by a laissez-faire spirit, of leaving well enough alone, of muddling through. Confronted with a choice between continuity and change, the Soviet authorities have usually, consciously or otherwise, opted to let things go on as they are. Since we are dealing here with alphabets as an aspect of cultural and political history, we cannot go into detail on too many of the controversies which have occurred during this period on questions of history, religion, and survival of traditional customs and attitudes toward life. All these have been more interesting for what they reveal of what has NOT changed than of what has changed, more enlightening about Communist intentions and frustrations than about achievement of Communist goals. Let us mention a few of the trends and developments in this period that shed particular light on the situation that now exists in this part of the world in respect to linguistic development and alphabetic reform.

The comparative study of the Turkic languages – which had always gone on in the U.S.S.R. but had had to be done mostly in *samizdat* form from the mid-1930's to the mid-1950's – gradually became an overtly respectable area of scholarly activity again. The first volume of researches in the comparative grammar of the Turkic languages, which the Academy of Sciences of the U.S.S.R. published in 1955 under the editorship of N. K. Dmitriev,[84] was followed by three more in the next seven years.[85] The Kazakh Academy of Sciences meanwhile published a small collective volume on questions of grammar of the Turkic languages in 1958.[86] In 1960 N. A. Baskakov brought out a handbook dealing with Turkic languages on both a historical and contemporary basis which described languages spoken outside the U.S.S.R. as well as Soviet minority languages. He introduced it with the modest sounding declaration that

> '... the book ... represents a first attempt at a short description of the development and formation of all the Turkic languages within the framework of their mutual interconnections and relationships as a single group of related languages; it is essentially a collection of preliminary information or a brief introduction to Turcology, to the historical-comparative study of the Turkic languages.'[87]

Baskakov's book was much more comprehensive than he made it appear to be, but was remarkable only because the peculiar ideological prejudices of Soviet Communism had made this a prohibited subject for so long.

A facsimile edition of the great comparative Turco-Tatar dictionary of the Kazan Turcologist Budagov which had appeared in 1869 was reissued in 1961.[88] A veritable flood of works on Turkic studies continued through the 1960's into the 1970's.[89] The field of comparative linguistics expanded to include the Mongolian languages and relationships between the Mongolian and Turkic language groups,[90] as well as historical studies of Central Asian Turkic.[91] Even more significant, perhaps, was the fact that a multivolume edition of the collected works of the most prolific of all Russian Central Asian historians, V. V. Bartol'd (1869-1930), began to appear in the early 1960's. Bartol'd, 'the Gibbon of Turkestan',[92] whose competence as a scholar and whose breadth of historical vision were remarkable and whose spirit was alien to all the petty preoccupations of Soviet Communists with sociopolitical engineering, had been awkward for the Soviets to deal with. Too eminent to be condemned, he was for the most part ignored during the period of Stalinist orthodoxy. Now he can again be treated with the honor and esteem Russian Turcologists and historians have always felt for him.

The period of relative relaxation in Soviet minority policies which set in during the first years after Stalin's death continued until the end of the 1950's. Then, in the heyday of Khrushchev, whose approach to difficult problems was often characterized more by flair and bravado than by practicality, a new policy of accelerated movement toward merger of Russian-Slavic and minority cultures into a new Soviet culture was announced. What became known as the *Sblizhenie-sliyanie*[93] theory was defined in the 1961 Communist Party Program:

> 'Full-scale Communist construction signifies a new stage in the development of national relations in the U.S.S.R. in which the nations will draw still closer together and their complete unity will be achieved .... Economic and ideological unity will increase and the Communist traits common to their spiritual make-up will develop.... The effacement of national distinctions, especially of language distinctions, is a considerably longer process than the effacement of class distinctions.... In the conditions of the fraternal friendship and mutual trust of peoples, national languages are developing on the basis of equality and mutual enrichment.... The existing process of voluntary study of Russian in addition to the indigenous language has favorable significance.... The Russian language has, in effect, become the common medium of intercourse and cooperation among all the peoples of the U.S.S.R.'[94]

After Khrushchev's fall in 1964, the campaign for intensified Russification of the minorities eased, though concessions to minority sensitivities continued to be offset by assimilationist pressures. *Sblizhenie* continued to be held up as a practical aim, but less and less was heard of *sliyanie* – it was relegated to that misty period in the future when full communism will have been achieved and all the contradictions and antagonisms that seem to be a natural feature of all normal, living human societies, will somehow disappear.

By the early 1970's it had become apparent that some fundamental trends had become consolidated in Soviet Central Asia and in many of the other predominantly minority areas in the Soviet Union. Though there was a tremendous influx of Slavs into Central Asia during the period of development of the 'New Lands' in the 1950's and, to some degree, this influx continued during the decade of the 1960's,[95] the natural increase of the native population was so great that it completely offset the effect of Slavic immigration. The percentage of each Central Asian minority in its

Figures

Politics and Alphabets in Inner Asia
by Paul B. Henze

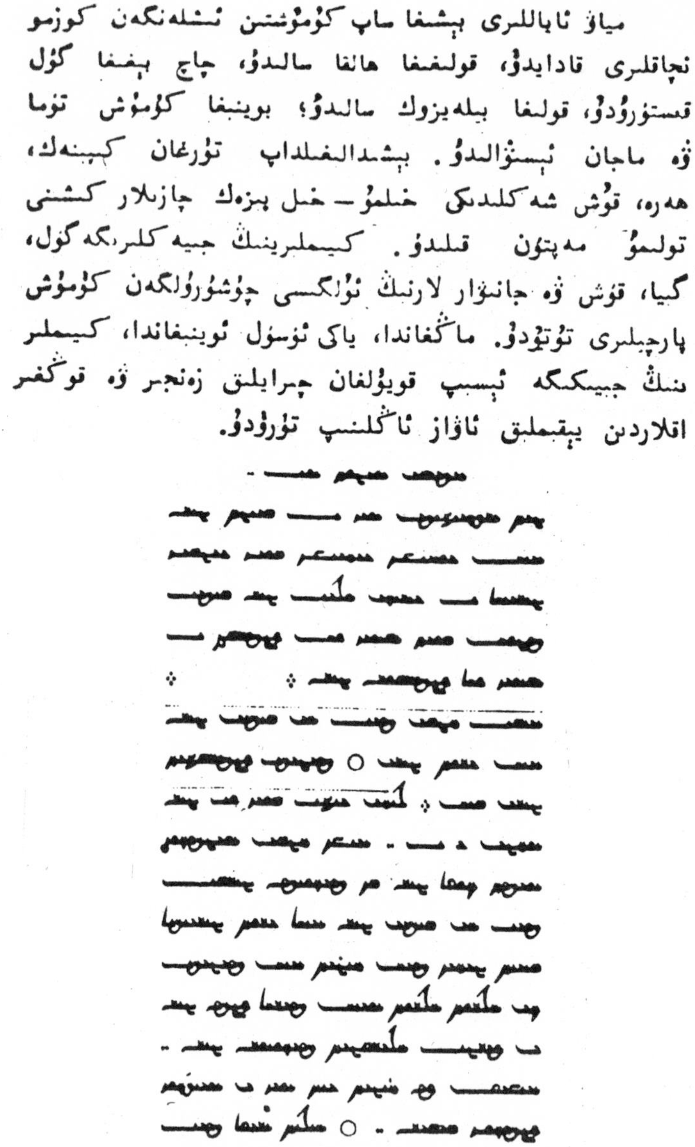

Fig. 1. Above, examples of Uigur scripts: Arabic and classical Uigur, almost identical with classical Mongolian. There are also Cyrillic and Latin alphabets for Uigur, the former used in the USSR, the latter in China. From *Opredelitel'yazykov mira po pis'mennostyam*, G. P. Serdyuchenko (ed.), Moscow, 1964.
Right, page from the Gospel of St. Matthew in classical Mongolian, published by the British and Foreign Bible Society in Shanghai, 1925.

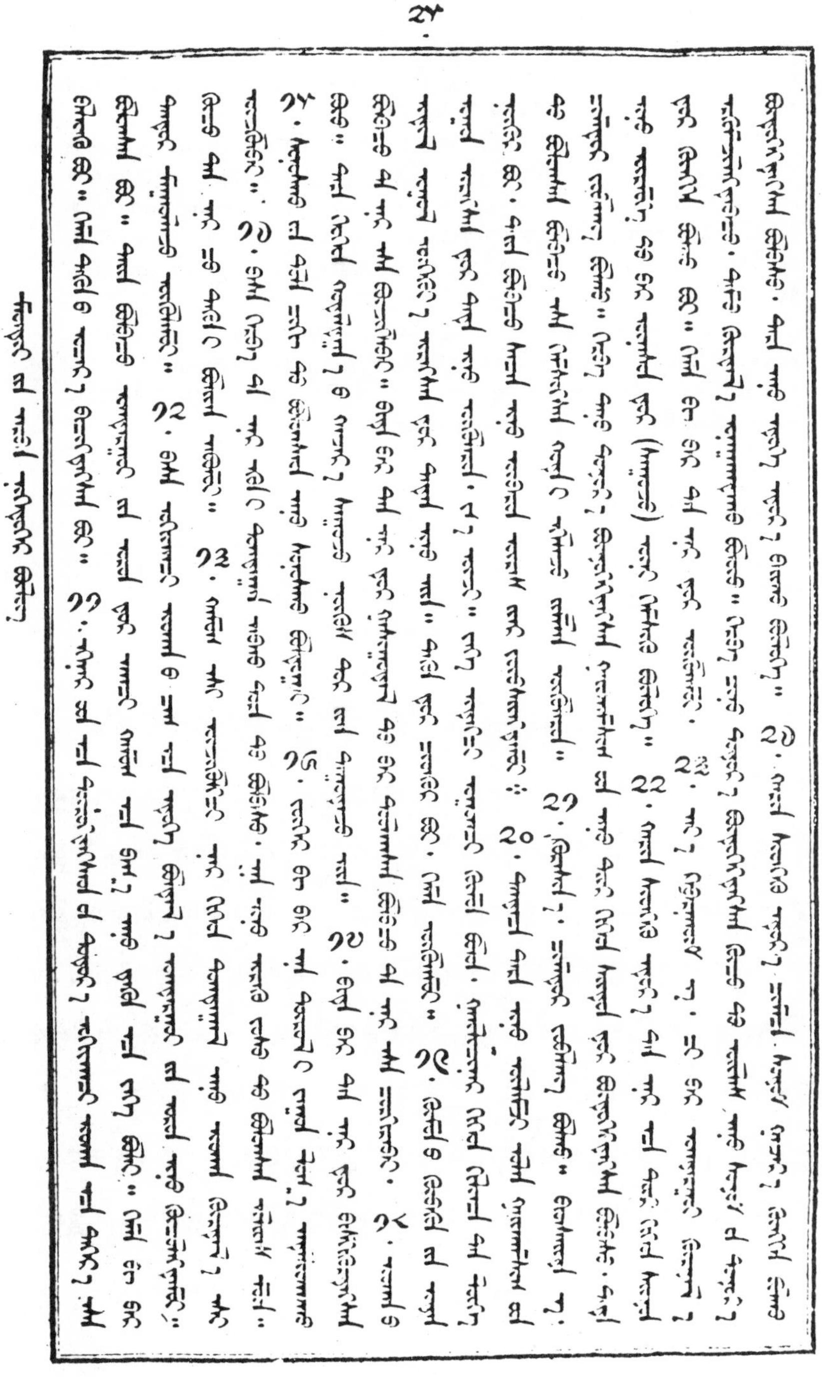

Giз vunƨ laз Ƃɯn rəuƨ, deŋƅbəiƨ cuŋз dɯg guƅ naƨ reiƅ, daз bəiƨneiч cuci yɯnmingunŋse liuч, guŋye, rəuƨ bauƅ bɯnз-dəuз, vunva, rəuƨ youƅ hag ƌəiз ƌei. Gyoŋз lɯgnyeƨ sou cəmƅ dəuз camgya lienƅ diet ba.

Vonƨ Liзyenƨ, de dɯg secay rəuƨ, cəmƅ dɯg bouч yɯnmin daibyau ƌəɯ yienƅ rəuƨ. Ƃouy vunƨ famiŋ sougogi həny, de yenƨobonƨ bei Ƃəƨgiŋƅ cangvan bəi lo. Goŋ vunƨlauy dəɯƨ dɯyy həny, de liз daiŋ dəuƨ deuз hag vunva ƌɯencieŋ, ən ciet neiy youŋ ən guek rəuƨ ma gaŋз dɯg ən ciet huŋ ƌe...

De soŋ boƅ lɯg cuŋз dɯg youŋ ƌəɯ guŋcaŋ guƅ hoŋ, bouyboƅ dɯg lauduŋ mofan, bouyɯg dɯg cigi fənsɯ.

Cəiƨgya doybaŋ dɯg gienƅ səiƅ ƌei. Bouybouy-cɯŋbo gvaŋ ƌəiз, ƌei dɯg giз lisieŋ rəuƨ.

(Fig. 2a)

འདི་ནི་ལི་ཉིན་གྱིས་བརྩམས་པའི་ "ཚོད་སྒྲུབ་རིག་པའི་སྐོར་གྱི་གནད་…
དོན་ "ཞེས་པ་དེའི་ནང་གསེས་ "དངོས་པོ་གཅིག་ཏུ་འདུས་པ་ཞིག་གཉིས་སུ་འབྱེད་
རྒྱུ་དང་། རང་རིས་དེའི་འགལ་བའི་ཕྱོགས་མཐའ་དག་ཤེས་པར་བྱེད་རྒྱུ་ནི་ཚོད་
སྒྲུབ་རིག་པའི་ངོ་བོ་ཡིན། "ཞེས་པར་གསལ་ཞིང་། ཡང་ལི་ཉིན་གྱིས་བརྩམས
པའི་ "ཧེ་གེར་གྱི་ 'གདན་ཚིགས་རིགས་པའི་ ' ནང་དོན་གནད་བསྡུས་ "ཞེས་པ་ …
དེའི་ནང་གསེས་ "ཚོད་སྒྲུབ་རིག་པ་དེ་འགལ་ཟླ་གཅིག་ཏུ་འདུ་བའི་སྐོར་གྱི་རིགས་
བཤད་ཅིག་ཡིན་ཞེས་མདོར་བསྡུས་ཀྱི་སྒོ་ནས་གདན་འཕེབས་བྱས་ཚོག། དེ་
ལྟར་བྱུང་ན་ཚོད་སྒྲུབ་རིག་པའི་སྙིང་པོ་ངེས་འཛིན་བྱེད་ཐུབ། ཡིན་ན་ཡང་དེ་
ནི་གསལ་འགྲེལ་བྱེད་དགོས་པ་དང་འཕེལ་རྒྱས་གཏོང་དགོས་པ་ཞིག་ཡིན། "ཞེས་

(Fig. 2b)

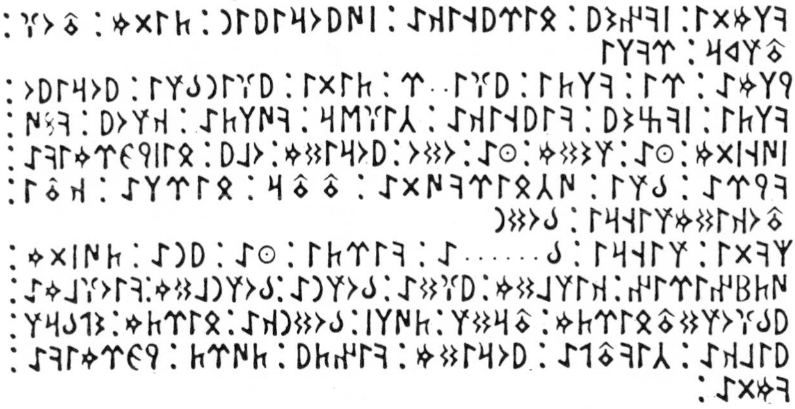

(Fig. 2c)

Fig. 2.

(a) Chuang – the language of a sizeable minority who live in southern China. The alphabet is basically Latin but has incorporated a number of Cyrillic and special characters. From *Opredelitel' yazykov mira po pis'mennostyam*, G. P. Serdyuchenko (ed.), Moscow, 1964.

(b) Classical Tibetan script – from *Opredelitel' Yazykov mira po pis'mennostyam*, G. P. Serdyuchenko (ed.), Moscow 1964.

(c) Turkish runic script – from S. E. Malov: *Pamyatniki drevnetyurkskoi pis'mennosti Mongolii i Kirgizii*, Moscow-Leningrad, 1959, pp. 32-33.

102-көнүгүү. Мурда илептүү сүйлөмдөрдү, андан кийин суроолуу сүйлөмдөрдү жазып алгыла.

Укчу, жолдош!
Мени менен жарышасыңбы?
Күчөтөлү жумушту!
Сен кандай кинолорду көрдүң?
Айда, шофёр!
Карма рулду!
Машинаңды зуулдат!

103-көнүгүү. Төмөнкү сүйлөмдөрдү көчүргүлө. Илептүү сүйлөмдүн аягына илеп белгисин койгула.

Балдар, ойногула, эркин өскүлө.
Билимдүү болгула.
Жаркыраган жаз келсин
Ура, жакында дем алыш
Баракелде, жигитсиң

104-көнүгүү. Төмөнкү сүрөткө карап, өзүңөр илептүү сүйлөм ойлоп жазгыла.

Fig. 3. Above and right, specimens of Kirgiz Cyrillic script from a second-grade textbook. K. Bakeev, *Kyrgyz tili*, Frunze, 1957, pp. 42-43.

Илептүү сүйлөм, көбүнчө, корккондо, сүйүнгөн-дө, чочуганда айтылат.

105-көнүгүү. Төмөнкү сүйлөмдөрдү көчүргүлө. Ар бир сүйлөмдүн аягына илеп белгисин коюп, андан кийинки сүйлөмдүн биринчи сөзүн баш тамга менен баштап жазгыла.

Үлгү: *Бах, ширин экен! Ох, өтө сонун экен!*

Бах, ширин экен ох, өтө сонун экен төх, жакшы гүл экен аттигинай эрте келсемчи ой, кайсы жакка кетти ий, муздак экен го.

Чакырыктар

Пионер, даяр бол!	*Дайым даярмын!*

Ынтымактуу иштөөгө үйрөнгүлө!

Окуудан отличник болгула!

Биздин Родинаны коргоочуларга салам!

Жашасын СССРдеги элдердин ынтымактуулугу!

2.

Миёни „а“ ва „р“ ҳарфҳои дигар
Бимонӣ, меҳурӣ ду меваи тар?

Машқи 127. Ин шеърро хонед, баъд ба дафтаратон бардоред. Ба зери калимаҳое, ки *ӣ* доранд, хат кашед.

Хонед!

Чӣ хуш вақтест овони ҷавонӣ,
Ки бо шодӣ ба мактабҳо бихонӣ!
Насиҳатҳои Ленинро, ки хондӣ,
Тамоми рӯи оламро ту донӣ!
Зи хубиҳои дониш ман чӣ гӯям,
Худат ҳам баҳра бурда метавонӣ.
Бувад аз таҷриба, аз хондан оид,
Тамоми корҳои паҳлавонӣ.
Агар мактаб бихонӣ, бахтъёрӣ,
Нахонӣ, дар пушаймонӣ бимонӣ.
Чу мактаб модари дуйӯмини туст.
Ба ту шафқат кунад ҳам меҳрубонӣ.
Бихон, эй ғунчаи боғи советӣ,
Агар хонӣ, ту доим шодмонӣ!

Луғат:

Овон—замон, давр. Оид—хосил, рӯидан. Шафқат—меҳрубонӣ.

Fig. 4. Above and right, specimens of Tadzhik script from a first-grade textbook, S. Arzumanov & V. Asrori, *Zaboni Tochiki*, Stalinabad, 1955, pp. 64-65.

§ 26. Ҳарфи *Й*.

Маймун. *Чайра.* *Майна.*

Машқи 128. Калимаҳои зеринро бо овози баланд хонед.

Чой, лой, най, ғумой, сарой, тайёр, байт, байрақ, майдон, ҳайкал, байн, кай, сой, той.

Ҳарфи й худаш танҳо ҳиҷо шуда наметавонад.

Машқи 129. Ҷумлаҳои поёниро хонед, баъд калимаҳои й-дорро аз ҷумла ҷудо карда, ба дафтаратон нависед.

Падарам чой ва чойник харида омад. Ман ҳар рӯз нону қаймоқ мехӯрам. Дар пахтазори колхози мо ғумой нест. Бачаҳо барои футболбозӣ майдонча сохтанд. Мактаби мо байрақ дорад. Ба муносибати иҷро шудани плани пахта дар колхози мо тӯй шуд.

Машқи 130. Калимаҳои зеринро ба дафтаратон бардоред. Дар вакти навиштан ба ҳиҷоҳо ҷудо кунед.

ТОН

КАЗИЙ
ТИ ВА
ОРГАНИ.

31-нчи
ЙИЛ ЧИҚИШИ

№ 126 (9161)

29
МАЙ
ЯКШАНБА
1955 ЙИЛ

БАҲОСИ
20 ТИЙИН

БУГУНГ

Узбекистон ССР Олий Совети Президиуми, У
кистон ССР Министрлар Совети ва Узбекистон
Марказий Комитетида (1-нчи бет).

Совет Узбекистонининг бир куни (1-нчи бет).

Ишлабчиқариш қувватидан тўла фойдаланай.
(2-нчи бет).

Т. Қамбаров. — Правление раиси—колхоз иш
чиқаришида ҳал қилувчи фигура (2-нчи бет).

Ғўза парвариши ишларини кенг равишда мех

Совет Ўзбекистонининг бир

☆

БЕШИНЧИ БЕШЙИЛЛИК ПЛАНИ БАЖАРИЛДИ

Чирчиқ шаҳридаги «Промкомбинат» артелининг ишчи ва мастер, инженер-техник ходимлари социалистик мусобақани кучайтириб, янги меҳнат ғалабаларига эришдилар. Артель коллективи бешинчи бешйиллик планни 20 майда муддатидан олдин бажарди.

«Промкомбинат» артелининг а'золари саноат корхоналари Бутуниттифоқ кенгаши қатнашчиларининг мурожаатига жавобан маҳсулот ишлаб чиқаришни янада кўпайтиришга қарор қилдилар. Улар 1955 йил охиригача меҳнаткашларга бешинчи бешйиллик пландан ташқари яна 4 миллион 600 минг сўмлик кенг исте'мол буюмлари ишлаб бериш мажбуриятини олдилар.

БИРИНЧИ ЎРИМДАН 30 ЦЕНТНЕР БЕДА

СИРДАР'Ё, («Қизил Узбекистон» мухбиридан). Тошкент область, Сирдар'ё районидаги Каганович номли колхоз чорва молларни ем-хашак блан етарли та'минлаш юзасидан бирқатор тадбирларни амалга оширди. 8 кишидан иборат тузилган ем-хашак тайёрлаш бригадаси (бошлиғи ўртоқ М. Бўтақўзиев) районда биринчи бўлиб бедани ўришга киришди. Бу ишга 2 та се-

☆

ЮЗЦЕНТНЕРЧИЛАР ДАЛ

☆

Пахтадан юқори ҳосил етиштириш учун курашнинг
бораётган юзцентнерчи бригада ва звеноларнинг пахтан
ғўзаларни сифатли парвариш қилиб, ўсимликнинг яхши р
пасига шоналашига эришмоқдалар. Юзцентнерчиларнинг
рисида республикамизнинг ҳамма томонларидан ҳар куни
хат-хабарлар келиб турибди. Қуйида биз ана шу хат-хаба

☆

Ғўзаларимиз шона

Бригадамиз ўтган йили колхозда биринчи бўлиб пахта етиштиришнинг янги усулини—ғўзаларни квадратлаб жойлаштириш ва қатор ораларини икки томонлама ишлаш усулини кенг миқ'ёсда қўлланди. Бу бизга механизациядан унумли фойдаланиб, қўл меҳнатини оз сарфлаш ва пахтадан юқори ҳосил етиштириш имкониятини берди. 62 гектар пахта майдонининг ҳар гектаридан давлатга 40 центнердан оқолтин топширдик.

Эндиликда бригадамиз а'золари янги прогрессив усуллар пахта ҳосилини муттасил ошира боришда ғоят катта аҳамиятга эга эканлигини яхши тушуниб олдилар. Шунинг учун улар бу йил колхозимизда юзцентнерчилик ҳаракатининг ташаббускори бўлиб чиқдилар. Биз ўзимизга

та'минлаш учун
га чириндитупр
рилган кўчатлар
Биринчи парв
озиқлантиришга
ернинг ярмидан
кунгача минерал
лашмаси блан оз
Биз 50 гектар
гектар ерга эса
бўйича экканмиз
килинаётган ғўза
да. 47 гектар ер
налади. Биз юқор
сра бўшаштирмай
ғўзаларни ҳам те
гулга, гулни тўқ
бирларини кўрмо

Fig. 5. A section of the front page of *Kizil Uzbekiston*, 29 May, 1955.

ПРОЛЕТАРИИ ВСЕХ СТРАН, СОЕДИНЯЙТЕСЬ! ПРОЛЕТАРІ ВСІХ КРАЇН
БАРЛЫҚ ЕЛДЕРДІҢ ПРОЛЕТАРЛАРЫ, БІРІГІҢДЕР! პროლეტარებო ყველა ქვეყნ
ПРОЛЕТАРЬ ДИН ТОАТЕ ЦЭРИЛЕ, УНИЦЬ-ВЭ! VISU ZEMJU PROLETARIEŠI,
ՊՐՈԼԵՏԱՐՆԵՐ ԲՈԼՈՐ ԵՐԿՐՆԵՐԻ, ՄԻԱՑԵ՛Ք! ӘХЛИ ЮРТЛАРЫҢ ПРОЛЕТАРЛ

СОВЕТТІК СОЦИАЛИС

ЖОҒАРҒ

ВЕДОМ

ССРО ЖОҒАРҒЫ СОВЕТІ І

Социалистік Еңбек Ерлерін—ССРО Совхоздар министрлігінің Эстон ССР-ндағы „Удева" совхозының қызметкерлерін— Ленин орденімен наградтау туралы

ССРО Жоғарғы Советі Президиумының 1949 жылғы 3 марттағы Указына лайық, 1949 ж ал шаруашылығынан мол өнім алып, Социалистік Еңбек Ері атағын алуға праволы ететін табыс еткендері үшін мыналар наградталсын:

ЛЕНИН ОРДЕНІМЕН

1. **Пальм** Мария Федоровна — Социалистік Еңбек і, сауыншы, жыл ішінде 8 сыйырдың әрқайсысы н орташа есеппен 6129 килограмнан сүт алған, тің майы 252 килограмнан болған.

2. **Паукку** Иван Иванович — Социалистік Ері, малшы, жыл ішінде 30 сыйырдың әрқайсі орташа есеппен 5636 килограмнан сүт алған, майы 230 килограмнан болған.

ССРО Жоғарғы Советі Президиумының Председателі Н. ШВЕРН

Москва, Кремль. 1950 жылғы 11 июльде.

ССРО Жоғарғы Советі Президиумының Секретары А. ГОРК

Смоленск облысының Сычевка ауданындағы „Вперед к социализ колхозының бұзаушысы Социалистік Еңбек Ері А. А. Рощинан Ленин орденімен наградтау туралы

ССРО Жоғарғы Советі Президиумының 1949 лғы 3 марттағы Указына лайық, 1949 жылы мал руашылығында Социалистік Еңбек Ері атағын уға праволы ететін жоғары көрсеткіштерге жет- і үшін жыл ішінде жасы төрт айға толмаған 35 бұзаудың әрқайсысының салмағын күн тәуліг таша есеппен 1229 грамнан өсірген Сычевка нындағы «Вперед к социализму» колхозын заушысы Социалистік Еңбек Ері Анна Анти Рощина Ленин орденімен наградталсын.

Fig. 6. Section from the front page of the Soviet Official Gazette in Kazakh, 28 July 1950.

own republic increased decisively during the period 1959-1970.[96] The 1970 census revealed that the native populations of the Soviet Central Asian republics had had one of the highest growth rates in the world during the previous eleven years – each nationality, including the Kazakhs, having increased between 46 and 53 percent during this time. In Central Asia as a whole Russians increased by 37 percent during the same period, a far higher percentage than Russian growth in the U.S.S.R. population as a whole – barely 10 percent. These figures demonstrate that even with a continued relatively high rate of Russian immigration into Central Asia the indigenous peoples have reversed a negative trend that had persisted from the 1920's through the 1950's.[97] With an increasingly youthful population still adhering to a well-established tradition of large families, a high rate of population increase among the Soviet Central Asian minorities can be expected at least during the next two or three decades.

The predominantly Muslim peoples of Soviet Central Asia have not only been reproducing at a rapid rate; they have been strengthening their position in many other ways. Though still predominantly rural, the Central Asian populations now include a large urbanized element, approximately 30 percent of the minority population of the region as a whole.[98] The urban element is almost entirely literate, the rural population largely so, at least in elementary fashion. Each Central Asian nationality has again developed a cultural and political elite which has a good deal of self-confidence. These peoples as a whole continue to be conscious of their distinct Muslim past, concerned about their own history, proud of their native languages. The 1970 census, for example, revealed that 98 percent of the Muslim minority nationalities resident in their own republics had retained their own language as the primary one; in fact, this percentage increased in comparison to the 1959 census.[99] Detailed examination of current Uzbek vocabulary as used in the daily press has revealed that a general trend toward de-Russification of vocabulary exists.[100] More striking still are statistics on circulation figures for the Uzbek press as compared with the Russian-language press. *Sovet Ozbekistani*, the Tashkent Uzbek-language daily, increased in circulation by 125 percent during the ten-year period 1956-1965; during the same period *Pravda Vostoka*, the Tashkent Russian-language daily, increased its circulation only 15 percent.[100] The Cyrillic alphabet which the Uzbeks now use, whatever difficulties it may have caused for them when it was first adopted, is clearly no longer an obstacle to the expansion of their cultural and political life.[101]

The well-established general tendency of the conservative Soviet ruling elite to take no drastic steps toward change in any sphere, to let matters take their course, especially in areas such as cultural policy, is reinforced by two more specific aspects of Soviet international policy to the benefit of the Central Asian minorities. The Soviet leadership is still eager to demonstrate that the U.S.S.R. is a true internationalist society, with equality for all peoples, free of racial prejudice and discrimination, and, therefore, a model for less developed multinational countries to emulate. Strongly oppressive measures could not be taken against the Soviet minorities in sustained fashion without serious consequences for Soviet prestige in Africa, Asia, the Middle East, and Latin America.

More important still is the Chinese problem. Borders are an issue of transcendental importance in the Sino-Soviet dispute. Turkic and Mongol peoples straddle these borders. Both the Soviets and the Chinese now openly claim that the other's minorities are disadvantaged compared to their own. If minorities are severely mistreated, they can flee to their kinsmen on the other side of the border, as occurred repeatedly from China in the 1960's. The minority peoples themselves, who are increasingly well-educated and politically more sophisticated, can listen to radio broadcasts in their own languages from both sides whether they can read each other's alphabets or not. They are inevitably going to be tempted to play off both masters against each other. Thus both the Soviets and the Chinese limit each other's freedom of action in dealing with their minorities. Under these circumstances, we must expect that the Central Asian peoples will continue to find increased room to maneuver for themselves and will develop their national life and culture in the framework of their own basic traditions. Sooner or later all this will have to have more political significance than it has now.

Against this background it is not surprising to find a new movement developing for basic reform of the alphabets of the Turkic languages of the U.S.S.R. The intellectual elites of these peoples and scholars concerned with their problems feel strong enough to raise and debate these issues again in a manner in which they have not dared discuss them in print since the 1920's. An extraordinary book appeared in 1972 dedicated to the problem of adjusting the alphabets of all the Turkic nationalities.[102] Edited by N. A. Baskakov, who has been active in this field for more than twenty years, it represents the work of scholars from all parts of the Soviet Union where work on the Turkic languages has been done. Most of these are non-Russians. In the book's introduction, Baskakov declares:

'The present collective volume is devoted to the history of the creation of alphabets for the hitherto unwritten Turkic languages and the carrying out of basic reforms in the writing of the older written Turkish languages and also to the problem of the completion of the unification of existing Turkic alphabets. All republican academies and institutes involved in research and practical work on the normalization of the Turkic literary languages took part in putting this collective volume together.

The problem of the unification of the alphabets of all the Turkic languages is extremely complicated because the alphabet of each separate language was worked out in isolation, almost without the participation of any kind of coordinating center. Nevertheless, the Russian alphabet served as the basis for all contemporary Turkic alphabets to which for the different languages were added the appropriate supplementary signs for specific sounds existing in that particular language. In this way there exists a single basis for contemporary Turkic alphabets and consequently a common theme for discussion of the completion and unification of this base and those supplementary signs which are used for specific sounds of the different Turkic languages . . .

The basic purposes of the collective volume are, in the first place, to set out the work that has been done on creation and elaboration of alphabets; second, to determine the basic shortcomings of particular alphabets; and third, to introduce proposals for eliminating these shortcomings in the framework of further discussion of them and clarification of the possibilities of bringing about appropriate corrections.'

Baskakov's introductory summary article is followed by twenty articles on separate Turkic languages, each of which provides a concise alphabetic history of the particular language. Obscure Turkic languages such as Gagauz, Nogay, and Shor are given equal treatment with major Turkic languages such as those of Central Asia and Azerbaijani. Dates of each reform of Arabic alphabets, introduction of Latin and Cyrillic alphabets, and subsequent adjustments in these are given. Separate sounds and letters are discussed in detail and comprehensive tables are provided for easy comparison of the way different alphabetic and phonetic problems were dealt with in the different Turkic languages. Baskakov's own summaries, in contrast to some of his earlier writings when he had to labor under the ideological restrictions of the Stalinist and Khrushchev eras, are remarkably frank and devoid of all obvious Communist politicizing. He sums up the Cyrillicization period as follows:

> '. . . the working out of alphabets on a Russian base took place in 1938-40 in isolated fashion by local scientific research institutions which, though they made use of previous experience of Latinization . . . made their decisions on the choice of symbols for each alphabet without any obligatory coordination of principles of how particular sounds should be used in relation to common sounds in all or separate groups of Turkic languages. It is natural therefore that current Turkic alphabets based on Cyrillic contain many inconsistencies. To represent the same sounds in different languages different symbols have been used. In some languages to represent two or more sounds or a combination of sounds a single symbol is used and to represent a single sound in others, two symbols. These and many other peculiarities not only differentiate closely related Turkic languages but also represent serious shortcomings in their alphabets which often do not correspond to the phonetic structure of a particular language . . . . The Unified Turkic Latin alphabet consisted of 39 sounds. The total number of signs on the basis of Cyrillic consists of 74 symbols in spite of the fact that the group of symbols actually necessary to represent the separate sounds of the Turkic languages has not changed and remains 39.'

Baskakov goes on to maintain that the complexity of the Turkic alphabets currently in use in the U.S.S.R. does not make it easier for speakers of Turkic languages to learn Russian, but makes it more difficult:

> 'We have already shown the impossibility of having the modern Turkic languages utilize along with the Russian alphabet all the features of Russian orthography which would supposedly help Turkic-speaking students learn Russian. The partial utilization of features of Russian orthography would only make learning Russian more difficult. Therefore it would be more rational in applying the Russian alphabet to differentiate rigidly between specific characteristics of Russian orthography and specific phonetic features of each separate Turkic language in order to permit the teachers of native languages and Russian to demonstrate the similarities and differences of the native language and of Russian on the basis of

> native and Russian orthography. This would to a great degree and with greater effectiveness enable the teacher to attain a higher degree of understanding of both the native and the Russian languages than is possible now.... In this way it would be completely possible to use in the alphabet of each separate Turkic language only those Russian letters which correspond to the actual sounds of the language without using those which are used only for representing specific features of the phonetic structure of the Russian language alone.'

These are persuasive arguments, though awkwardly worded, but it would seem unrealistic to expect changes in Cyrillic alphabets to come quickly. The Soviet minority peoples have now used their present writing systems for more than thirty years and, in spite of their shortcomings, are undoubtedly sufficiently accustomed to them that change will be difficult. Baskakov recognizes this fact in the concluding paragraphs of his discussion of Cyrillic alphabet reform:

> 'Having examined all aspects of the problem of improving and perfecting the alphabets of all the modern literary Turkic languages of the peoples of the U.S.S.R., we come to the general conclusion that the unification of all these alphabets is possible with significant reduction of the symbols of the combined alphabet... which, utilizing Cyrillic, could comprise 39-40 letters, i.e. the same number of letters as the unified Latin alphabet. However the practical realization and implementation of such a complicated reform and unification of all the alphabets of the Turkic languages is hardly possible in a short period of time.'

It is ironic to reflect that the kind of change Baskakov advocates – the creation and application of a Unified Cyrillic Turkic Alphabet – could only be accomplished as a result of directives from Moscow. It seems unlikely that these would be forthcoming under present Soviet conditions, Baskakov's argument about facilitating the learning of Russian notwithstanding.

VI. REFLECTIONS AND CONCLUSIONS[103]

There is much to be said in justification of alphabet reform in Soviet Central Asia and in adjoining areas of China populated by related minority nationalities. Traditional societies can be modernized more effectively if their internal communications systems function efficiently.[104] Language adjustments are important for economic and social development as well as cultural progress. A developing society which is beset by language problems is forced to expend a good deal of its energy in unproductive ways. It was logical, therefore, for linguistic and alphabetic reform to be on the action agenda in Central Asia and in other Soviet minority-populated areas, and natural for it to come up as an issue in China, too, when the new regime took power there thirty years after Communists had taken over in Russia. Interest in language and alphabet reform was not simply a Moscow-generated enthusiasm in the Soviet Union. There had been a substantial interest in this subject among the more advanced minority peoples in pre-Revolutionary times. The initiative which resulted in reform of Arabic alphabets in use by most Turkic minorities at the time of the Revolution was, primarily, artificially inspired from the outside. There was a great deal of minority enthusiasm for the creation of the Unified Turkic Latin Alphabet too.

Alphabet change, like all other aspects of language reform, is bound to entail complications. Excessive complications developed in the Soviet Union because the relatively simple problem of alphabetic change became intertwined with wide-ranging considerations of social and political reform and manipulation of national feelings. As the Soviet system became consolidated under Stalin, the major preoccupation of the central government became consolidation of its own power, both internally and in respect to real or imagined foreign enemies. Inevitably the Soviet system became more Russian-oriented and the Soviet government became, in effect, a camouflaged continuation of the Russian Empire. In spite of high-sounding declarations of the right to secede, the threat of minority separatism, was seen as a major danger. Memories of the Enver Pasha episode and exaggerated fears of the power of pan-Turkish and pan-Turanist ideas combined with the hard fact of Basmachi resistance in Central Asia to convince the Soviet leadership that strong measures had to be taken to prevent Central Asians from trying to go their own way in any fashion – politically, economically, or culturally. When the shift to the Cyrillic alphabet came, it was carried out in a paranoic atmosphere. Change was dictated from the center, or carried out locally by over-eager officials fearful of the consequences of not executing Moscow's orders faithfully enough. It is only in a totalitarian context – an inquisitorial atmosphere, in fact – that the incongruities that resulted during Cyrillicization could occur.

Encouragement of a single Turkic literary language in Central Asia would have been relatively easy in the 1920's or even in the 1930's, for the basis for it already existed. Modern literary languages have been formed in most countries by a process of emergence of a centrally positioned dialect which has the capacity to absorb words and syntax from other regions and mold them into a broader national language. Modern High German, deriving from the Saxon base, has been superimposed over a wide range of dialects which are still so different from each other (if you compare the German of Schleswig, for example, with that of Switzerland) that they are not mutually intelligible. Standard Italian or standard French form an umbrella over dialects of equally wide range. The most extreme examples of literary languages encompassing a tremendous variety of disparate but related dialect-languages are probably classical literary Arabic and Mandarin Chinese. In comparison to these, the Turkic languages are surprisingly uniform. Most of the common root words used on the streets of Istanbul will be understood all the way across Asia to Sinkiang. A Unified Central Asian Turkic language was, therefore, just as practical a venture as a Unified Turkic Latin Alphabet. Fear of Turkic nationalism prevented the Soviet leadership from encouraging or permitting its development.

Instead a quite opposite policy was followed. Each Turkic dialect was elevated to the status of a separate language and the special peculiarities of each dialect were highlighted. There are no parallels for this kind of handling of the language problem in nontotalitarian societies, for it requires a high degree of zealotry, an unusual commitment to dogmatic principles, and a good deal of sheer force to persist in setting up each identifiably distinct dialect or language grouping as a separate entity. Karakalpak compared to Kazakh is no more a separate language than the English of Lancashire compared to the English of London – much less so, in fact. Kazakh and Uzbek are no more divergent than Sicilian and Milanese. Turkmen differs from Azerbaijani and Anatolian Turkish less than the Spanish of Anadalusia from that of Galicia. The real interests of the Central Asian peoples would have been served by encouragement of not only alphabetic unity, but as much linguistic unity as possible. Within the Soviet Communist system, the real interests of these peoples had to be subordinated to the power-political requirements of the central government in Moscow.

In China the details have been different but the overall pattern and the results have been much the same. Alphabetic reforms have probably, on balance, been much more confusing and costly for the Chinese minorities than they were for those in the U.S.S.R. After an initial period of imitation of Soviet experience – adoption of the same alphabets in some cases – the Chinese shifted to the opposite extreme. Alphabets were chosen (except in the case of the Mongols) that differed from those in use in the Soviet Union. More recently we have seen the emergence of Chinese national interest as the predominant factor governing the choice of alphabets, for it appears that the same Latinization system adopted as an auxiliary system for the Chinese language itself – *pinyin* – is to be used for most, if eventually not all, of the languages of the minorities of China.

The minorities of China are in a much weaker position to assert themselves than those of the Soviet Union, but there is still no reason to assume that the Chinese will necessarily be any more successful in Sinicizing most of their minorities than the Soviets have been in Russifying theirs. Modern totalitarian systems with all their powers of persuasion and coercion have been notably unsuccessful in changing basic features of human nature or curbing nationalism. The most striking feature of Soviet experience during the three decades since Cyrillicization of minority languages was carried out has been the capacity of minorities to adjust to these alphabets, whatever their shortcomings, and use them as a vehicle for self-assertion.

What do the Soviet and Chinese experiences in alphabetic reform offer the rest of the world, and in particular developing countries who might face similar problems? They offer lessons of many kinds, but not many examples to be emulated. No people would choose, on their own, to submit themselves to the confusion the Uzbeks and Tajiks and Uigurs and Mongols have undergone in the area of alphabetic and linguistic reform. Peoples managing their own affairs independently would want to plan changes more carefully and carry them out, perhaps more gradually, with more attention to their own special requirements. Nevertheless the Soviet and Chinese experiences are worth studying in order to gain greater understanding of some of the complications that can arise as alphabetic reforms are undertaken. It is encouraging to find, at last, accurate accounts of the actual experiences of Soviet minority peoples with alphabetic reform such as those which are contained in the recent collective volume on Turkic alphabets discussed in section V above.[102]

As for the Turkic, Mongol, and other minorities of the Soviet Union and China, one can only hope that in the future they may have less dogmatism to contend with, less centralized pressure, and less tendentious political pressure as they go on living with and making the best of the alphabets they now have to work with. Though they are less than perfect, they can make good use of them to expand their cultural and political horizons and, in time perhaps, they can adjust and adapt them better to serve their own needs.

NOTES

1. Initial portions of this chapter are adapted from the author's two articles on the same subject which appeared in the *Journal of the Royal Central Asian Society* (London, January 1956 and April 1957).
2. V. V. Barthold, *Four Studies on The History of Central Asia* 1 (Leiden, 1956), provides an excellent summary of the history of what is now Soviet Central Asia and Kazakhstan. The same author's *Turkestan Down to the Mongol Invasion* (London, 1958) provides much more detailed treatment of the early period.
3. Arnold Toynbee, *A Study of History* (Abridgement of Volumes I-VI by D. C. Somervell) (London, 1946), 166-167; also the 'Note: Sea and Steppe as Language Conductors', pp. 185-186 of the same edition.
4. A somewhat different line of evolution led from the Sogdian script to the distinctive Turkish 'runic' alphabet which was in use in Central Asia and Siberia from the sixth to the tenth centuries. The Soviet scholar S. E. Malov published three basic works on this alphabet during the 1950's: *Pamyatniki Drevnetyurkskoi Pis'mennosti* (Moscow, 1951); *Yeneseiskaya Pis'mennost' Tyurkov* (Moscow, 1952); and *Pamyatniki Drevnetyurkskoi Pis'mennosti Mongolii i Kirgizii* (Moscow, 1959). An excellent synthesis of scholarly work on Turkic runic inscriptions, both Russian and foreign, has been provided byS. G. Klyashtorny, *Drevnetyurkskie runicheskie pamyatniki kak istochnik po istorii Srednei Azii* (Moscow, 1964). His bibliography, pp. 181-211, lists all works relating to the subject which had appeared up to that time.
5. B. Ya. Vladimirtsov, *Sravnitel'naya Grammatika Mongol'skovo Yazyka* (Leningrad, 1929), 19-33.
6. A. K. Borovkov, *Leksika Sredneaziatskovo Tefsira XII-XIII vv.* (Moscow, 1963).
7. Several excellent works deal with the more recent period of Central Asian history, e.g. Richard A. Pierce, *Russian Central Asia, 1867-1917* (Berkeley, Ca., 1960); Geoffrey Wheeler, *The Modern History of Soviet Central Asia* (London, 1964).
8. C. Brockelmann, *Osttürkische Grammatik der Islamischen Literatursprache Mittelasiens* (Leiden, 1954), provides a thorough study of this period of Central Asian linguistic and alphabetic history.
9. Iranian and related Indo-European peoples were in earlier periods much more important in Central Asia than they are today. Until the fifteenth century Iranian influence was greater than Turkic in the southern oases. The Tajiks and a few small Pamir tribes represent the only Iranians who have maintained their identity

in Central Asia into modern times, though there is still a significant Iranian substratum among the Uzbeks. The Iranians of Central Asia, like the Turks, were early converts to Islam and adopted the Arabic alphabet.

10. 'Chinese Moslems practically all speak the Chinese language as their mother tongue.... A considerable number learn more or less Arabic; the mullahs use it in conducting services and others repeat transliterations of Arabic sounds represented by Chinese characters. Believers who make the Pilgrimage often learn some Arabic, and the ordinary Moslem is proud to display his knowledge of even a few words of "the tongue of the Angels". In decorations and on utensils the Arabic script is found in abundance. Yet there is no linguistic difference between the Moslem and his neighbors of other faiths in the ordinary affairs of life' (Mason, *The Mohammedans of China* [London: The China Society, 1922], 7-8).
11. Alexandre Bennigsen and Chantal Lemercier-Quelquejay, *Islam in the Soviet Union* (London, 1967).
12. Robert Conquest, *The Nation Killers* (London, 1970).
13. Unlike most of the Turks of Central Asia, these Altai Turks, left behind in what appears to have been part of the original Turkic homeland, were never converted to Islam and consequently had no contact with the Arabic alphabet.
14. Wurm, *Turkic Peoples of the U.S.S.R.* (London: Central Asian Research Centre, 1954), 12.
15. Russian-native cultural relations in Central Asia before the Revolution are well summarized by Zenkovsky in '*Kulturkampf* in Pre-Revolutionary Central Asia', *American Slavic and East European Review* (February 1955), 15-41.
16. The famous *Secret History of the Mongols*, for example, though originally composed in Mongolian, has survived only in a Chinese 'phonetic' transcription. The original Mongolian text has had to be laboriously reconstructed from the Chinese characters by scholars so that this valuable chronicle can be read and understood. Cf. Haenisch, *Die Geheime Geschichte der Mongolen* (Leipzig 1948), iii-xvi. A complete Soviet edition of the Chinese text was issued by B. I. Pankratova (ed.), *Yuan'-chao Bi-shi* (*Sekretnaya Istoriya Mongolov*) (Moscow, 1962).
17. Edward Allworth, *Uzbek Literary Politics* (The Hague, 1964).
18. The Volga Tatars, culturally the most advanced of all the Moslem Turkic peoples of Russia, also adopted a reformed Arabic alphabet in the early 1920's. The practicality and popularity of this reformed alphabet made the introduction of the Latin alphabet among the Tatars difficult. Even Tatar Communists at first opposed it. Latinization was achieved among the Tatars by decree in 1929. See Kolarz, *Russia and her Colonies* (London, 1952), 36.
19. C. W. Hostler, *Turkism and the Soviets* (London, 1957); S. Zenkovsky, *Pan-Turkism and Islam in Russia* (Cambridge, Mass., 1960).
20. See Uriel Heyd, *Language Reform in Modern Turkey* (= *Studies of the Israel Oriental Society* 5) (Jerusalem, 1954). This very readable and highly informative study of the process of linguistic transformation in Turkey during the last twenty-five years gives a vivid impression of all the complications involved in such an undertaking. The alphabet shifts carried out in the Soviet Union have involved far more difficulties and confusion than in Turkey, for there has been more direct political interference, and political requirements have varied greatly at different periods. Furthermore, there was not one, but two Soviet alphabet shifts, and no

sooner had people become accustomed to the Latin alphabet than they had to change to Cyrillic. The Soviet Turkic languages have not only gone through a process of purification from foreign elements, like Turkish (Turks distinguish between their present language, *Turkish*, and the pre-reform language, *Ottoman*), but more recently they have also been subjected to the exact opposite – the necessity of assimilating a great number of Russian words and expressions. When one keeps all these things in mind, one sees how simple – with all its complications! – the Turkish linguistic reform has been compared to the ordeal which the Turkic (and most other non-Slavic) languages of the U.S.S.R. have had to undergo.

21. Sir Olaf Caroe has suggested that the success of Latinization in Turkey gave the Russians second thoughts about the long-range desirability of the Latin alphabet for the Turkic peoples of the U.S.S.R. and that Cyrillicization as the final goal was probably accepted by the Communist leadership in the early 1930's; see his *Soviet Empire* (London, 1953), 156.
22. Works which provide interesting details about the Latinization process include: W. K. Matthews, *Languages of the U.S.S.R.* (Cambridge, 1951), 70-71; Kolarz, *Russia and her Colonies*, 34-37; Wurm, *Turkic Peoples of the U.S.S.R.*, 12-13.
23. Teresa Rakowska-Harmstone, *Russia and Nationalism in Central Asia: The Case of Tadzhikistan* (Baltimore, 1970), 241-250.
24. Alexander Park, *Bolshevism in Turkestan, 1917-27* (New York, 1957), 353-376.
25. See Kolarz, *Russia and her Colonies*, 293-295.
26. Because of Iranian influence, the Uzbek dialect of the town of Turkestan preserved the principle of vowel harmony lost in the dialects of Tashkent and the Fergana Valley, but still adhered to in the neighboring Turkic languages; preservation of vowel harmony coupled with Tashkent vocabulary and idioms helped make the original Latinized literary Uzbek more readily intelligible to speakers of Kazakh, Karakalpak, and Turkmen; see Wurm, *Turkic Peoples of the U.S.S.R.*, 13-14. Also Allworth, *Uzbek Literary Politics*.
27. The Shors have since disappeared as a separate national entity as their territory has been engulfed by Russian colonists. The Oirots, numerically much stronger, still exist but under another name. Since 1948 they have been called *Altaitsy* ('People of the Altai') and the term Oirot is now never used in Soviet writings. Kolarz, in *Peoples of the Soviet Far East* (London, 1954), 169-176, gives a summary of the history of these two small peoples under Russian rule.
28. For an excellent summary of the history of Tannu Tuva since the mid-nineteenth century see Kolarz, *Peoples of the Soviet Far East*, 161-169. A two-volume collective history of Tuva (*Istoriya Tuvy*) was published in Moscow in 1964.
29. See Kolarz, *Peoples of the Soviet Far East*, 124-126.
30. The most definitive account of this period is Robert Conquest's *The Great Terror* (New York and London, 1968) which includes many references to minority nationality leaders.
31. Kolarz, *Russia and her Colonies*, 37-38.
32. N. A. Baskakov, 'The Turkic Peoples of the U.S.S.R. – the Development of their Languages and Writing', originally published in *Voprosy Yazykoznaniya* (Moscow, June 1952); an English translation with a commentary by Dr. Stefan Wurm was published by the Central Asian Research Centre (London, 1953); the above

quotation is from pp. 30-31 of this edition.

33. As had been the case when the Latin alphabet was adapted to the Turkic languages, extra letters and signs were necessary in the Cyrillic for sounds peculiar to Turkic such as the *ö* and *ü* sounds, the *ng*, the *gh*, and the *j*, to mention only the most common. The Cyrillic letters for sounds peculiar to Russian but not present in the Turkic languages are not generally used to represent other Turkic sounds, for this would conflict with the principle stressed by Baskakov in the passage quoted above that alphabets must be so devised as to facilitate the learning of Russian by speakers of native languages.
34. The leadership of the Mongolian People's Republic demonstrated their desire to conform to Soviet requirements in a Council of Ministers decision of March 25, 1941, in favor of change to the Cyrillic alphabet. The press shifted to Cyrillic as of January 1, 1946. The old alphabet continued in use for many purposes, however, until January 1950. A. R. Rinchine, *Uchebnik Mongol'skovo Yazyka* (Moscow, 1952).
35. 'The liquidation of the original nucleus of Uzbek cultural leaders was as complete as the elimination of the Uzbek political leaders who led the nation until 1937. Most of the prominent Uzbek poets and writers acclaimed in the first fifteen years of the Soviet regime must not be even mentioned today' (Kolarz, *Russia and her Colonies*, 279). See also Allworth, *Uzbek Literary Politics.*
36. It is interesting that many of the Russian words introduced into the Central Asiatic languages were originally borrowed from western European languages. Typical examples, whose meaning is readily recognized by Europeans include: *revolyutsia, proletariat, respublika, partia, kommunizm, sotsializm, demokratia, fabrika* ('factory'), *kombain* ('combine'), *traktor, filizofia, matematika, khimia* ('chemistry'), *biologia, atom, kultura, gazeta* ('newspaper'), *teatr, muzei* ('museum'), *sport, telefon, radio*, etc. (listed in Baskakov, 'The Turkic Peoples of the U.S.S.R. . . .' 19). The Central Asian languages have thus been partly' westernized' while being 'Russified'. Modern Russian itself is by no means a pure language and its political, economical, and scientific terminology includes a higher proportion of words borrowed from Western languages than is usually realized. (See Matthews, *The Structure and Development of Russian* [Cambridge, 1953], 158-173). It should be remembered, however, that the Central Asiatic languages were expected to accept these Western words in their Russian garb, to spell and pronounce these in the Russian way, in spite of the fact that it would be natural for them to be assimilated into the Turkic languages in somewhat different form as many of them have been in Turkish, for example.
37. Baskakov, 'The Turkic Peoples . . .', 33-35, 45-47.
38. Ponomareva and Chernykh, *Tadzhikskaya Literatura* (Moscow, 1961), a reference handbook, lists all prerevolutionary classic poets who are now generally accepted as contributors to Tadzhik literature. All the great Persian classic poets are included. It is as if Chaucer and Shakespeare were claimed as belonging to "Australian literature"!
39. All of the literary, historical, and linguistic controversies of the 1950's and 1960's are covered in numerous articles in the comprehensive and meticulously objective *Central Asian Review* which appeared in London four times per year during the period 1953-1968. This excellent journal also contains many articles dealing with

Chinese minorities and their problems.

40. See footnote 32 above.
41. The first volume of a comparative grammar of the Turkic languages appeared in late 1955: Academy of Sciences of the U.S.S.R., *Issledovaniya po sravnitel'noi grammatike tyurkskikh yazykov, I – Fonetika* (Moscow, 1955), 334. (See my review in the *Royal Central Asian Journal* [January 1957], 70-72.)
42. S. P. Tolstov, et al. (eds.), *Narody Srednei Azii i Kazakhstana* 1 (Moscow, 1962), 408-528.
43. N. A. Baskakov, *Karakalpakski Yazyk* 2 (Moscow, 1952), 127-132, gives a detailed description with extensive examples of the various Karakalpak alphabets.
44. Reported in *Voprosy Yazykoznaniya* 3 (1955), 146-148.
45. Reported in *Voprosy Yazykoznaniya* 2 (1956), 147-151.
46. Actually, of course, few of these 'Russian' words are of Slavic origin at all. They are common international terms, forced upon Turkmen and most other non-Slavic languages of the U.S.S.R. in Russian garb, a form which often makes it much more difficult for them to be phonetically and grammatically assimilated than if they had been acquired by more natural processes. Cf. footnote 26 in 'Politics and Alphabets in Inner Asia', *Royal Central Asian Journal* (January 1956).
47. A. K. Borovkov, '*K voprosu ob unifikatsii tyurkskikh alfavitovv S.S.S.R.*', *Sovetskoe Vostokovedenie* 4 (1956), 101-110. (Approved for printing September 8, 1956.)
48. Since it is being treated separately in this volume, this chapter will not discuss the large and fascinating problem of reform of the Chinese writing system itself.
49. Dylykov, *Demokraticheskoe Dvizhenie Mongol'skovo Naroda v Kitae* (Moscow, 1953).
50. The Outer Mongols declared their independence of China in 1911, but the Chinese never recognized it. All Chinese governments and parties during the 1920's and 1930's stubbornly insisted that Outer Mongolia belonged to China. This was also the position taken by most of the world powers. Even Mao Tse-Tung is quoted by one source (Edgar Snow, *Scorched Earth* [London, 1941], 289, as quoted by Friters) as saying that Outer Mongolia would naturally become part of the federated Chinese state the Communists would establish when they achieved power. At the end of World War II, as a result of a general readjustment of Chinese-Soviet relations, the Kuomintang government agreed to recognize the independent status of the Mongolian People's Republic. This occurred in early 1946. G. Friters, *Outer Mongolia and its International Position* (Baltimore, 1949), is a well documented study of the legal and political status of Outer Mongolia during the first half of the twentieth century. It is interesting to note that Outer Mongolia was lost to the Chinese more recently than Taiwan.
51. According to the 1953 census, the non-Chinese population of China totalled 35, 320, 360, or slightly more than 6 percent of the entire population. They are currently estimated to total ca. 45,000,000, which would indicate a small rate of natural increase in twenty years.
52. *Policy Towards Nationalities of the People's Republic of China* (Peking, 1953), 67-68.
53. Ovidenko, *Vnutrennyaya Mongoliya* (Moscow, 1954), 83-84.
54. N.C.N.A. dispatch (August 17, 1955).
55. *People's Daily* (Peking, November 25, 1956).

56. Henry G. Schwarz, 'Communist Language Policies for China's Ethnic Minorities: The First Decade', *China Quarterly* (Oct.-Dec. 1962).
57. N.C.N.A. Peking dispatch (December 15, 1955).
58. The Miao number nearly 3,000,000 and are the second most numerous nationality (after the Chuang themselves) of the Kwangsi Chuang Autonomous Region, which was formally proclaimed in 1958.
59. N.C.N.A. Kweiyang dispatch (November 8, 1956).
60. N.C.N.A. Kunming dispatch (November 24, 1956).
61. A small Manchu-related people, settled primarily in the Ili Valley, numbering approximately 10,000.
62. It is curious to note that a Russian-Uigur dictionary published by the Academy of Sciences of the Kazakh S.S.R. in July, 1955, used Arabic script. Since the language of the Uigurs living in Russian Central Asia was Cyrillicized in 1941 and all publishing in Uigur in the U.S.S.R. was then being done in Cyrillic, such a dictionary would appear to have been for the use of Uigurs in Sinkiang. A Soviet textbook of the Uigur language (Najip, *Uigurski Yazyk* [Moscow, 1954]) also employed the Arabic script and included a short dictionary of new words and terms, mostly words and phrases needed for translation of Communist political and economic writings.
63. According to statistics given by S. I. Bruk in his article 'Etnicheski sostav i razmeshchenie naseleniya v Sin-tszyanskom-Uigurskom Avtononomnom Rayone Kitaiskoi Narodnoi Respubliki', *Sovetskaya Etnografiya* 2 (1956), 89-94, these three groups together then formed 94.6 percent of the total population of the region. For further information on the composition of the population of Sinkiang, see the abridgement of the Bruk article in the *Central Asian Review* 4 (1956), 433-437, and the chapter 'The Peoples of Sinkiang', in O. Lattimore, *Pivot of Asia* (Boston, 1950), 103-151.
64. N.C.N.A. Urumchi dispatch (August 27, 1956).
65. Henry G. Schwarz, 'Chinese Migration to Northwest China and Inner Mongolia, 1949-59', *China Quarterly* (Oct.-Dec. 1963).
66. *Nationalities Research* (July 6, 1959), as cited by Schwarz.
67. Henry G. Schwarz, 'Communist Language Policies for China's Ethnic Minorities: The First Decade', *China Quarterly* (Oct.-Dec. 1962).
68. N.C.N.A., Urumchi (June 21, 1958), cited by Schwarz.
69. Robert A. Rupen, 'Mongolia in the Sino-Soviet Dispute', *China Quarterly* (Oct.-Dec. 1963).
70. Cited in C. T. Hu, *The Education of National Minorities in Communist China* (Washington, D.C.: U.S. Department of Health, Education and Welfare, 1970). An almost identical statement from 1931 is cited in Brandt, Schwartz, and Fairbank, *A Documentary History of Chinese Communism* (New York, 1966), 217.
71. C. T. Hu, *The Education of National Minorities . . . .*
72. C. T. Hu, *The Education of National Minorities . . . .*
73. Edgar Snow, 'Interview with Mao', *The New Republic* (February 27, 1965).
74. George Moseley, 'China's Fresh Approach to the National Minority Question', *China Quarterly* (Oct.-Dec. 1965).
75. June Dreyer, 'China's Minority Nationalities in the Cultural Revolution', *China Quarterly* (Jul.-Sept. 1968); Ann Sheehy, 'Soviet Views on Sinkiang', in *Mizan*

(London, Sept.-Oct. 1969).

76. Cited in Paul Hyer and William Heaton, 'The Cultural Revolution in Inner Mongolia', *China Quarterly* (Oct.-Dec. 1968).
77. Dreyer, 'China's Minority Nationalities . . .'.
78. Urumchi regional service in Mandarin (September 29, 1972).
79. Constantin Milsky, 'New Developments in Languages Reform', *China Quarterly* (Jan.-Mar. 1973).
80. *China News Analysis* 909 (Hong Kong, February 9, 1973).
81. A Soviet work completed in 1969 and published in 1970 provides interesting information on the state of alphabets and language in Sinkiang. It uses both the old Uigur Arabic alphabet and the Chinese *pinyin* version of the Latin alphabet. It states that though Chinese influence on Uigur had been modest until 1950, it has been overwhelming since, and notes that use of large numbers of Chinese words and phrases had been decreed by law. The influx of Chinese into Sinkiang is described in rather dramatic terms: 'If the number of Chinese in Sinkiang in 1949 amounted in all to no more than 300,000 persons, according to 1967 data it had grown to over 4,000,000. In actual fact, there are actually far more Chinese in Sinkiang.' A Soviet source on Sinkiang, writing at the end of the 1960's, can hardly be taken as unbiased. Nevertheless the picture provided has a certain credibility: local minority culture and language appear to have been largely subordinated to Chinese. T. R. Rakhimov, *Kitaiskie elementy v sovremennom uigurskom yazyke* (Moscow, 1970).
82. The Chuvash, a large Turkic group living in the Urals, are an interesting exception. They had adopted a Cyrillic alphabet in the late eighteenth century and have continued to use this same alphabet, with minor changes, into the Soviet period.
83. The Crimean Tatars, a small but highly advanced Turkic group, have never been reinstated as an 'autonomous' entity, but some have been allowed to return to their home territory, which became part of the Ukraine after World War II, and their language and culture now receive occasional scholarly attention.
84. See footnote 41 above.
85. *Issledovaniya po sravnitel'noi grammatike tyurkskikh yazykov*, II, *Morfologia* (Moscow, 1956); III, *Sintaksis*, (Moscow, 1961); IV, *Leksika* (Moscow, 1962).
86. *Voprosy grammatiki tyurkskikh yazykov* (Alma-Ata, 1958).
87. N. A. Baskakov, *Tyurkskie yazyki* (Moscow, 1906).
88. Lazar Budagov, *Sravnitel'ny slovar' turetsko-tatarskikh narechii* (Sanktpeterburg, 1869). Reissued by the Academy of Sciences of the U.S.S.R., 2 vols. (Moscow, 1961).
89. For example, *Istoricheskoe razvitie leksiki tyurkskikh yazykov* (Moscow, 1961); *Issledovaniya po sintaksisu tyurkskikh yazykov* (Moscow, 1962); *Yazyki narodov SSSR, Tom II, Tyurkskie yazyki* (Moscow, 1966); A. M. Shcherbak, *Sravnitel'naya fonetika tyurkskikh yazykov* (Moscow, 1970).
90. G. D. Sanzheev, *Sravnitel'naya grammatika mongol'skikh yazykov* (Moscow, 1964); *Tyurko-mongol'skoe yazykoznanie i fol'kloristika* (Moscow, 1960).
91. A. M. Shcherbak, *Grammatika starouzbekskovo yazyka* (Moscow, 1962).
92. Obituary notice in the London *Times* (August 26, 1930).
93. *Sblizhenie* means 'coming closer together'; *sliyanie* means 'blending'. The theory is really quite simple – the Russians and minorities come closer together until they

blend into one.

94. Cited in T. Rakowska-Harmstone, 'Recent Trends in Soviet Nationality Policy', *The Soviets in Asia* (Mechanicsville, Cremona Foundation, 1972).
95. 1.2 million people migrated into Central Asia during the period 1959-1970 (Rakowska-Harmstone, *Russia and Nationalism . . .*, 241-250).
96. 'Population Trends in Central Asia and Kazakhstan', *Mizan* (London, May-June 1969).
97. Roman Szporluk, 'The Nations of the U.S.S.R. in 1970', *Survey* (London, Autumn, 1971); Ann Sheehy, 'Soviet Central Asia and the 1970 Census', *Mizan* (London, August 1971).
98. Urban to rural ratios, according to the 1970 census, for Central Asia are as follows: Kazakhstan – 51-49; Uzbekistan – 36-64; Kirgizia – 37-63; Tadzhikistan – 37-63; Turkmenistan – 48-52. The urban population contains a larger proportion of Russians and other non-Central Asian nationalities. The statistics are Soviet official census figures as reproduced in the excellent symposium edited by Edward Allworth, *Soviet Nationality Problems* (New York and London, 1971).
99. James Critchlow, 'Signs of Emerging Nationalism in the Moslem Soviet Republics', *The Soviets in Asia*, as cited in footnote 94 above.
100. Critchlow, 'Signs of Emerging Nationalism . . .'.
101. Statistics from Azerbaijan, the major Turkic republic in the Caucasus, are even more astonishing. While the Azerbaijani-language literary journal increased its circulation during the period 1960-1968 from less than 7,000 to nearly 30,000, the Russian-language literary journal published in Azerbaijan declined in circulation during the same period from 3,125 to 2,500! As cited by Critchlow, 'Signs of Emerging Nationalism . . .'.
102. *Voprosy sovershenstvovaniya alfavitov tyurkskikh yazykov SSSR* (Moscow, 1972).
103. Many excellent works deal in depth with the issues discussed only briefly in this final section. Among the most informative are: E. Allworth (ed.), *Central Asia, a Century of Russian Rule* (New York, 1967); Elizabeth Bacon, *Central Asians under Russian Rule* (Ithaca, N.Y., 1966); H. Carrere d'Encausse, *Reforme et Revolution chez les Musulmans de l'Empire Russe* (Paris, 1966); L. Tillett, *The Great Friendship* (Chapel Hill, N.C., 1969); Allworth, et al., *Soviet Nationality Problems* (New York, 1971).
104. It is impossible to argue that a modern society MUST have a simple alphabetic system of writing, for Japan and China demonstrate that complex ideographic systems can be effectively utilized. Even in Japan and China, however, auxiliary alphabetic systems have been found to be desirable for coping with certain requirements of modern technology.

EDGAR A. GREGERSEN

Successes and Failures in the Modernization of Hausa Spelling*

Discussions of spelling are notorious for generating more heat than light. This paper is meant to be an exception, but even so I have not hesitated in making judgments left and right. I hope that whatever heat is produced will in turn produce at least an enlightening glow.

Hausa, a Chadic language of the Afro-Asiatic (or Hamito-Semitic) phylum of languages, is spoken widely throughout West Africa. Hausaland proper was divided in the nineteenth century by the English and the French into areas now under the jurisdiction of two separate and independent countries, Nigeria and Niger. In each country a different though similar orthography exists for Hausa, both using modified forms of the Latin alphabet. In addition, many people in the Hausa-speaking world write in Arabic script. Hausa itself is not the official language of any country although proposals to make it so have been made from time to time in Nigeria.

In this paper I shall consider the merits of these orthographies. It would perhaps be useful to begin by considering the kinds of relationships that obtain between competing writing systems. Structurally, these relationships fall into three main categories.

(1) Systems without mechanical equivalence. The prime example that

* Many people have helped me in the preparation of this paper and I am delighted to thank them here. F. W. Parsons, Neil Skinner, David Arnott, and Mallam E. R. Othman gave me important information about the situation in Nigeria (Professor Arnott included information about the UNESCO-sponsored meeting he attended as an advisor). Dr. Clifford Hill generously provided me with several publications from Niger. I am especially grateful to Dr. Russell G. Schuh for truly copious and enormously informative communications about the Niger situation.

comes to mind is Chinese, where the traditional logographic system cannot be converted by mechanical rules to any proposed Romanization, or vice versa. Apart from Ancient Egyptian written both with hieroglyphs (a combination of syllabic and logographic signs) and with Greek letters in its later (Coptic) stage, there seem to be no comparable examples in Africa, unless the still mysterious Nsibidi 'script' reported from southern Nigeria may have been logographic so that the modern alphabetic writings presently in use in that area would stand in such a relationship to it.

(2) Systems with reciprocal mechanical equivalence. Presumably the orthographies using Arabic script, recently proposed by the government of the Sudan Republic as part of their Arabization policy, are mechanically convertible with the Romanized forms already in use. For Southern Sotho, one spelling is used in Lesotho and another in South Africa (both use the Latin alphabet), with equivalences on the order of the following (the correspondence are taken from Tucker 1971):

Lesotho	ĕ	ŏ	tš	ch	psh	fsh	kh	ng̃
South Africa	y	w	tsh	tjh	pjh	fj	kg	nq

This category is not meant to be taken too rigorously since no systems in practical use display 100 percent equivalence.

(3) Systems with nonreciprocal mechanical equivalence. Modern Greek is a good example (see Pring 1964). In the 1920's the Soviet Union developed an official orthography for the use of its Greek-speaking communities. This orthography is essentially phonemic using the resources of the traditional Greek alphabet. Elsewhere in the Greek-speaking world a nonphonemic orthography, essentially etymological or at best morphophonemic, is the only one now used. As a rule it is possible to give conversion rules to go from the traditional spelling to the Soviet one – usually by collapsing the values of the symbols used; thus traditional ιη υ ει οι → Soviet ι. It is not possible to go the other way round. Indeed, if the orthographies of most Western languages were to be reformed, 'collapsing' of differences would be a prominent feature, largely because some of the phonemes of earlier periods of the language, which the orthography still represents, have merged with other phonemes. In English, for example, *meat* and *meet* would be written alike (according to the conventions of the Simplified Spelling Society as *meet*), as would *sight-site-cite* (as *siet*). Differentiation or expansion, on the other hand, would be relatively rare, although occasionally found (thus, present *wind* would become *wind* noun and *wiend* verb).[1]

The recently developed spelling of Hausa used in Niger stands in a relationship of nonreciprocal mechanical equivalence with that used in Nigeria. But although the former can be viewed as a reform of the latter, the reform was basically one of expansion rather than collapsing. The reason for this is quite simply that not enough distinctions were indicated by the creators of the Nigerian system. To understand the situation better, let us review the history of Hausa spelling.

Before the introduction of Arabic script, no indigenous writing system was developed by the Hausa, although several instances of indigenous writing of considerable antiquity have been alleged for other West African groups. The evidence now suggests that these are for the most part examples of stimulus diffusion from European conventions, sometimes Arabic writing, and in one instance possibly even the American Indian Cherokee syllabary (for a detailed discussion of the problem of indigenous scripts see Dalby 1967; 1970). Contact between the Hausa and Islamic groups certainly occurred long before the fifteenth century and some knowledge of writing in Arabic script was therefore quite early. The earliest extant examples of Hausa in Arabic script (which is usually referred to as *àjàmi*) date, however, probably from the late eighteenth century. The National Archives in Kaduna contain over 20,000 manuscripts in *àjàmi.*[2]

With the English takeover of Nigeria in the nineteenth century, the Latin alphabet was effectively introduced to the Hausa. (Writing in Latin letters is sometimes referred to as *bookòo* as opposed to *àjàmi.*) Some of the early developers of Romanization for Hausa included, as one might expect, missionaries such as Canon Charles Robinson, and administrative officers such as Alder Burdon – for the most part linguistically naive (see Kirk-Greene 1964; Taylor 1929). They tended to work within the tradition established by Sir William Jones in 1788 of writing 'vowels as in Italian, consonants as in English', although the few linguists on the scene such as Schön occasionally made use of such nontraditional symbols as /š/ for English /sh/ (IPA symbol [ʃ]).

In 1848, the Church Missionary Society (CMS) sanctioned the use of subscript dots to create letters without adequate representation in the Latin alphabet; for Hausa, this meant the adoption of /ḅ ḍ ḳ/ for what were later to be written as 'hooked' letters: /ɓ ɗ ƙ/. The CMS conventions were set forth in their publication *Rules for Reducing Unwritten Languages to Alphabetical Writing in Roman Characters, with Reference Especially to the Languages Spoken in Africa.* By 1910 an effort was made to establish an official orthography, and in 1912 an article entitled 'Rules for Hausa Spelling' was published under the aegis of Hanns Vischer, then Director of Education of Northern Nigeria. These rules authorized conventions that characterize the present official orthography used in Nigeria including the absence of tone markings of any kind and the ignoring of vowel length.

These rules were later to be modified somewhat in line with the proposals of the International African Institute, established in 1926. The Institute sponsored an augmented Latin alphabet (the 'Africa Alphabet') to be used in establishing 'a practical and uniform method of writing African languages'. As a matter of fact the first memorandum of the Institute was *Practical Orthography of African Languages*, in which the principles of orthography recommended as well as the Africa Alphabet itself were justified on psychological, pedagogical, and pragmatic grounds. For instance, diacritics were to be avoided because they were difficult to print and tended to blur the outlines of words, which should be as distinct as possible. In point of fact, with only a few exceptions these recommendations were borrowed from those developed by the International Phonetic Association. The Institute's proposals did not find universal favor and the eminent linguist Carl Meinhof withdrew from the Council of the Institute because of them (Tucker 1971). He himself believed that the practical orthographies of languages spoken in colonies should reflect the orthographies used by the metropolitan country. He apparently accepted the inevitable consequence of his position, viz. that a single language community divided up between two or more colonial powers should have two or more orthographies. Thus he argued that [ʃ] should be spelled *sh* in the English colonies, *ch* in the French, and *x* in the Portuguese (Meinhof 1931). It is perhaps ironic that Hausa spelling is now dichotomized along a colonial isogloss, although the dichotomy has little to do with the spellings used in the exmetropolitan countries. More recently, Meinhof's position has been defended by a number of scholars, notably Maurice Houis, who has labeled the 'English conventions' (presumably the Africa Alphabet) a failure (Houis 1957-1958). Few scholars take this view at present.

In the 1930's there were several spelling reforms in Hausa. They were prompted in large measure by the completion of a truly monumental dictionary of Hausa sponsored by the government of Northern Nigeria and compiled by Dr. G. P. Bargery. Bargery had adopted several of the Africa Alphabet conventions so that where the 1912 spelling rules required the symbols (ch ḅ ḍ ḳ/, Bargery used /c 'b 'd k'/, respectively. The dictionary appeared in 1934. Dr. R. M. East, the Superintendent of Education of Northern Nigeria who was also in charge of the Translation Bureau at Zaria, decided that his agency would follow Bargery's modifications. East modified Bargery's modifications in turn after consultation with Dietrich Westermann, then director of the International African Institute and – at least in my opinion – the foremost linguist concerned with African languages of his time. These modifications included the adoption of alternate representations for /'b 'd/ permitted by the Africa Alphabet, viz. /ɓ ɗ/, as well as an analogical creation of a new form: /ƙ/ for /k'/. Apart from these modifications, the Bargery spelling is the basis for the present official Nigerian orthography and as a matter of fact the modern spelling rules published by the North Regional Literature Agency (NORLA) begin by specifically stating that

> For the spelling of all single words Bargery's Dictionary is followed, except where otherwise stated in this pamphlet.

The exceptions include minor revisions in word division, the use of capitals, and the indication of sound alternations across word boundaries.

In Niger and in other Francophone areas, only French was written and taught in the schools until an adult literacy campaign was launched by UNESCO in the 1960's. The first international conference on the matter was the UNESCO Meeting of Experts on the Use of the Mother Tongue for Literacy, held at Ibadan in December 1964 (many of these developments are given in Armstrong n.d.). The meetings concerned with the creation of a practical spelling for Hausa in Niger and other Francophone areas were held in 1966. The first at Bamako produced an orthography for Hausa that differed from the Nigerian standard in a number of ways even though the Gaskiya Corporation, a publishing company in Zaria, had produced a mass of material in that standard. This same conference also produced revised orthographies for Fulani (Fula), Tuareg (Tamashek), Mande, and Kanuri. Several prominent Hausanists were present, including David Arnott of the School of Oriental and African Studies in London, and Claude Gouffé of the Ecole Nationale des Langues Orientales Vivantes. In September 1966, a number of problems for the Hausa orthography alone were considered in a meeting at Niamey. Although there was a Nigerian representative, the recommendations of these meetings have had no impact at all on official usage in Nigeria. In Niger, the recommendations are followed in the relatively few publications of the

Centre d'Alphabétisation at Niamey, the Centre Régional de Recherche et de Documentation pour la Tradition Orale, as well as in various local newsletters such as the Zinder literacy newspaper, *Muryar Damagaram*. These publications are relatively rare in the United States and hard to get copies of, so I am not completely informed as to their extent. However, to my knowledge, they are all produced from stenciled materials and there are no publications produced by letter press. In sheer bulk and elegance of production they cannot compare with the Gaskiya publications, particularly the newspaper *Gaskiya Ta Fi Kwabo*.

The original plans for the Nigerian spelling made provision for the indication of vowel length, tone, and the difference between /r/ and / /. The last point was eventually dropped altogether, and tone is shown mostly in aspectual forms of verb phrases, if at all:

ta baa shi ruwaa ya shaa	'she gives him water and he drinks (it)'
tà baa shi ruwaa yà shaa	'let her give him water that he might drink'
taa baa shi ruwaa yaa shaa	'she gave him water and he drank it'
taà baa shi ruwaa yaà shaa	'she will give him water and he will probably drink it'

These examples are taken from a publication of the Department de Maradi Alphabétisation Fonctionelle entitled *Initiation des cadres à la transcription haoussa*. In the Gaskiya orthography all of these sentences would be written identically:

ta ba shi ruwa ya sha

The major innovation of the UNESCO-sponsored spelling was the indication of vowel length. In addition there was a more consistent use of /w/ and /y/.

How shall we evaluate the successes and failures of these systems? Unfortunately, a great deal of relevant information is lacking. We have no accurate data on literacy, on the time required to learn the different systems, or on the relative ease in reading the two orthographies. Of course we might simply wait and see, applying a kind of linguistic Darwinism and labeling that system as successful as that which survives. In so doing we could perhaps further argue that good orthographies drive out the bad, with the operationally impeccable implication that what we are left with is the good.

But few scholars would long brook such foolishness, no matter how rigorous. In the nineteenth century, spelling reformers looked to 'phonetic' writing as the desideratum. Henry Sweet held that broad transcriptions (in modern jargon, essentially phonemic transcriptions) were the ideal basis for orthographies – even with the indication of dialect differences and contextual alternations. More recently linguists of the generative-transformational school have challenged this position and have declared that English spelling – long singled out as one of the worst writing systems, together with Chinese and Japanese – is really pretty good. It shows morphophonemic relationships and underlying phonology in a way that approaches the systematic phonological analyses of the generativists themselves. Moreover, since they deny any validity to the notion of the phoneme, the rubric that a good orthography must be essentially phonemic would imply – if only indirectly – that the phoneme plays a significant part in the competence of the native speaker – an embarrassing position.

For reasons that will be discussed below, Sweet's position must probably be modified. On the other hand, I must admit that I cannot accept the view that English has a good spelling no matter how close it comes to the latest fashion of analysis proposed by any particular school of linguistics. Something is wrong if it takes ten to fifteen years to learn how to spell one's own language if the same thing could be accomplished, in, say, only a few months using a different orthography. My view is unashamed utilitarianism. My criteria for excellence in spelling: efficiency and democracy. Any spelling that requires several years to master, perforce plays into whatever class struggle exists. Furthermore, the reality of the systematic phonology proposed by the generative grammarians is subject to how widely one spreads one's morphophonemic net. It has been suggested that, for example, because of alternations such as those found in *destroy-destruction* (where phonemic /ɔy/ varies with /*uk*/) the underlying form for *boy* is *buk*! (I have skipped a few steps in the analysis for want of space.) Even if one could establish this to everyone's satisfaction (and so far this has not been one; some even dare maintain that the underlying form for *boy* is *bɔy*!), the creation of a practical orthography would have to ignore such proposals because they are so clearly ephemeral. It should not be forgotten that underlying representations and etymologies and so on exist whether the official spelling represents them or not.

But from a purely utilitarian point of view a phonemic transcription would not be entirely desirable either, for reasons that Daniel Jones, Jack Berry, and others have cogently presented in a number of essays (see Jones 1942; 1948; 1962; n.d.; Berry 1958; Pike 1947; Gouffé 1965). For one thing a written language lacks too many of the contextual cues that spoken language readily employs: supplemental gestures, intonations difficult to represent, special voice qualities. And although elisions, reductions, and sandhi-forms present few problems in speech, they might prove to be difficult in reading. Invariable words in fixed spellings that can be interpreted readily by speakers of a number of dialects – surely these are criteria that make sense. Furthermore, a certain number of morphophonemic spellings would probably be useful. Consider the spelling in English of the possessive form, which never to my knowledge poses significant problems to learners. It is an invariant -'*s* although there are three major realizations phonemically: /-s/, /-z/, /-iz/. I suggest that the best solution for such an item is an invariant spelling just as it is in current English spelling, although in this particular instance -'*z* rather than -'*s* would be preferable: *kat'z, dog'z, hors'z* (the Simplified Spelling Society writes the first as *kat's*, however).

In Hausa spelling there is a limited amount of morphophonemic spelling; thus, in the Gaskiya form we find *baƙon* /bà:kʷ'ân/ 'the visitor' spelled with an *o* in the second syllable because the indefinite form ends in *-o*: *baƙo* /bà:kʷ'o:/. Perhaps more morphophonemic spellings could be introduced without impairing ease of learning. For one thing, because of the systematic relationship of what are now written as *s* and *sh*, *d* and *j*, *t* and *c* (the second of the pair occurs before high front vowels), *sh j c* might be interpreted as *sy dy ty* or the like.

An orthography should be usable by speakers of more than one dialect, if possible. In technical jargon, such an orthography would be diaphonic. For the most part, Hausa spelling in the Gaskiya norm has ignored dialect differences in favor in the Kano dialect, or a polished version of it. However, the Kano dialect has collapsed a number of oppositions found in other dialects. Thus, *sw tw* have been simplified to *s t* in Kano but retained elsewhere. The spellings with *w* might prove preferable.

A final general consideration is that a spelling system should be similar to other spellings. To this extent I agree with Meinhof, but his own view was provincial in the long run. Let me say at once that I am an advocate of World Orthography, and that I feel that the reference point for judging a new spelling is not how well it agrees with English or French, but how well if follows World Orthography recommendations. Proponents of this system (essentially the same as that proposed by the

International African Institute, but extended to all the languages of whatever continent) have occasionally favored inflexible practices. For example, long vowels are to be written as double vowels; diphthongs such as *aĭ* are to be written as *ai*, and hence indistinguishable from a non-diphthongal two-syllable sequence *ai*. Maasai is a case in point, where both *aĭ* and *ai* occur. They should have been differentiated as *ay* and *ai*, or the like.

World Orthography has been considered primarily for African and Indian languages and consequently problems in the representation of American Indian languages or even Arabic have not been fully examined. There are no truly successful letters devised for the affricates of Slavic (although the Slavicist's use of /ˇ/ to produce new forms such as *č ǰ ř*, where *c*, for example might have to be used for *ts*, is a practical proposal that merits adoption). Similarly, the Arabic 'emphatics' (pharyngeals) have not been considered in World Orthography; but the adoption of the IPA symbols [ᵵ ᵭ ᵴ] would be extravagant. Since no language is reported that contains contrasting pharyngeal and retroflex consonants, the same symbols may be used for both. Thus, the World Orthography symbols for retroflex consonants [ʈ ɖ ʂ] may be used for Hindi ट ड ष and Arabic ط ض ص.

In summary, I think a good writing system is: (1) easy to acquire, (2) easy to write (this refers to the design features of the symbols themselves), (3) easy to read, (4) essentially phonemic and at least able to indicate the basic repertoire of phonemes, (5) diaphonic as much as possible, (6) moderately morphophonemic, especially in the representation of affixes, (7) in as much agreement with international conventions such as those of World Orthography as internal consistency will permit.

Using these criteria, how do the Hausa writing systems stand up?

The UNESCO-Nigerien spelling meets these requirements best. Impressionistically it seems to me that the Gaskiya-Nigerian conventions are not even as good as those as associated with *àjàmi*, except for the use of Latin script.

There is general agreement about the inventory of phonemes in Hausa. The list given here presents the analysis of Greenberg (1941) and Ladefoged (1964). The orthographic equivalences are given for Gaskiya-Nigerian and UNESCO-Nigerien as well as *àjàmi;* the Classical Arabic values are indicated for these symbols as well.

Greenberg	Ladefoged	G	U	A	Classical Arabic Values
p[3]	f	f	f	ڢ	(f)[4]
b	b	b	b	ب	(b)
’b	ʔb	ɓ	ɓ	ب	
m	m	m	m	م	(m)
w	w	w	w	و	(w)
p^y[3]	fj	fy	fy	فير	(fiy)
t	t	t	t	ت	(t)
d	d	d	d	د	(d)
’d	ʔd	ɗ	ɗ	ط	(ṭ)
s	s	s	s	س	(s)
z	z	z	z	ذ	(ð)
ʒ’	s’	ts	ts	ظ	[not used]
n	n	n	n	ن	(n)
r	ɾ̱	r	r	ر	(r)
R	ɽ	r	r	ض or ر	(ḍ)
l	l	l	l	ل	(l)
č	t̠ʃ	c	c	ث	(θ)
j	d̠ʒ	j	j	ج	(j)
š	ʃ	sh	sh	ش	(ʃ)
y	j	y	y	ي	(y)
’y	ʔj	’y	ƴ	ي	
k	k	k	k	ك	(k)
g	g	g	g	غ	(γ)
g’	k’	ƙ	ƙ	ق	(q)
k^y	c	ky	ky	كير	(kiy)
g^y	ɟ	gy	gy	غير	(γiy)
g^{y}’	c’	ky	ky	قير	(qiy)
k^w	k^w	kw	kw	كو	(kuw)
g^w	g^w	gw	gw	غو	(γuw)
g^{w}’	k^{w}’	kw	kw	قو	(quw)
h	h	h	h	ح	(ḥ)
ʔ	ʔ	’	’	ع	(ʕ)
i	i	i	i	ـِ	(i)
i·	i:	i	ii	ـِى	(iy)
e	e	e	e	ا.	[not used]
e·	e:	e	ee	.اى	([not used] y)
a	a	a	a	ـَ	(a)
a·	a:	a	aa	اَ	(aʜ)
o	o	o	o	ـُ	(u)
o·	o:	o	oo	ـُو	(uw)
u	u	u	u	ـُ	(u)
u·	u:	u	uu	ـُو	(uw)

Neither Greenberg nor Ladefoged considers dialects with the additional phoneme /tʃ'/ (to use Ladefoged's system of notation). In UNESCO-Nigerien, this is represented for those dialects that use it as /c'/. Although the labialized and velarized consonants are treated as unit phonemes by both Greenberg and Ladefoged, they are analyzed as clusters in all three orthographic systems. Actually, a number of other comparable forms occur such as /by bw ny/, but these are not considered by either Greenberg or Ladefoged. The UNESCO-Nigerien orthography recognizes /hw/, which usually corresponds to /f/ in the Gaskiya-Nigerian norm. Before /i e/, /k^y g^y k^{y}'/ are written as the equivalent of /k g k'/ in all three orthographies. Before /u o/, /k^w g^w k^{w}'/ are similarly simplified in representation.

Both Gaskiya-Nigerian and UNESCO-Nigerien use the hooked letters /ɓ ɗ ƙ/. It is difficult to evaluate them although on the whole they seem to be successful. Interestingly enough, Wolff in his 1954 proposals for a comprehensive practical orthography for the languages of Northern Nigeria suggested that all implosive and glottalized consonants be written with an apostrophe following a consonant symbol (except in the case of /'y/ and /'w/); thus, /b' d' k'/. In a footnote, however, he notes that 'In printing the "hooked" letters will remain in use' (Wolff 1954: 16 ff.). Combinations of this sort have several advantages over the hooked letters. They are productive and would produce parallel representations of parallel phonetic facts, cutting down on ad hoc (though practical) devices, such as the present /ts/ for /s'/ in both Gaskiya-Nigerian and UNESCO-Nigerien. They are easy to print and type with the usual type available. Even *Gaskiya Ta Fi Kwabo*, the leading Hausa newspaper published in Nigeria which follows the policies of the Hausa Language Board, was for a time without hooked letters when it was taken over by new company, New Nigerian Newspapers Limited. Rather than use apostrophes, the company decided on the unwise course of merely omitting hooks. Rumor has it that the typewriters of the Hausa Language Board itself lack hooked letters; I have copies of technical terms proposed by the board in which the hooks are actually missing. But there are other considerations as well.

Tucker (1971: 632 ff.) points out that 'for a symbol to be orthographically satisfactory, it must have a viable upper case as well as lower case form – in roman and italic as well as in cursive form'. In connection with this he mentions that the translation of the Penal Code in Hausa failed to make use of hooked letters in italicized quotations simply because proper forms were not available. In printing however the appearance of the lower case hooked letters is good. The capitals are not as successful: / Ɓ Ɗ Ƙ /. The Africa Alphabet lists as a capital for /b/ the form /Б/, from the Russian alphabet, which was used in this way in Zulu until quite recently (where /Б/ is now written as /b/, and /b/ is written as /bh/.) The Bantu scholar C. M. Doke used /Ɗ/ as the capital of /ɗ/. There is no form suggested in the Africa Alphabet.

Apart from this profusion and lack of consistency in design, we must also note that in handwriting, the hooked letters are for the most part ignored. The cursive forms suggested in textbooks and even by the International African Institute (when it does suggest them) are simply not 'cursive' enough and tend to look like printed forms. I suggest the following forms for handwriting, mostly adopted from Gothic script:

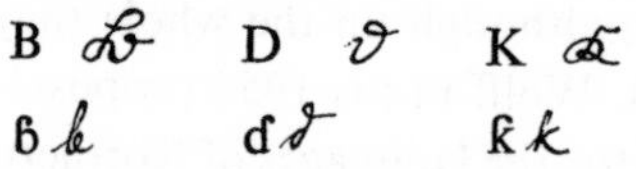

The /ƙ/-forms are perhaps least satisfactory. I cannot see why /ƙ/ was adopted at all, since /q/ was available and unambiguous. As a matter of fact, Abraham used /q/ in his two Hausa textbooks; furthermore, and most importantly, Arabic loan words transliterated with a /q/ in English are invariably Hausanized with a /ƙ/: *Qur'an* – Hausa *Alƙur'ani*, etc.

The adoption of a unique letter for /'y/ in UNESCO-Nigerien, viz. /ƴ/, is an unfortunate decision in an otherwise admirable scheme. It is to be hoped that the form will be abandoned for /'y/. However, morphophonemic and diaphonic considerations suggest the use of another form instead: /ɗy/. Nearly all forms with /'y/ have dialect variants with /ɗiy/, e.g. *'yancìi*, Sokkoto dialect ɗ*iyaucìi* 'state of being free'. The most common forms with /'y/ (which occurs in only a few items) are *'yaa* 'daughter' and *'yaa'yaa* 'children', which are related to ɗ*aa* 'son' (cf. Sokkoto ɗ*ìyaa* 'daughter', ɗ*iyaa* 'children'). Forms with /ɗy/ do not otherwise occur.

The only consonants not distinguished in both Gaskiya-Nigerian and UNESCO-Nigerien are /ɽ/ and /ɼ/, both written as /r/. An earlier plan to differentiate the two as /r/ and /r/ in UNESCO-Nigerian was abandoned. In native Hausa words, the two are in complementary distribution–generally /ɽ/ finally and before /n/, /ɼ/ elsewhere. In foreign words only /ɽ/ tends to occur, but there is considerable regional and stylistic variation (Gregersen i.p.). For these reasons the decision not to indicate a difference seems fairly well-motivated although in an ideal system the possibility of representing such a distinction at least should be available.

The use of /'/ for the glottal stop is satisfactory but not ideal. The IPA form is superior: /ʔ/ (I suggest /Γ/ as the corresponding capital). Its use would free /'/ for uses similar to those found in English: – to indicate contractions and various kinds of morpheme boundaries. Like other consonants, /ʔ/ can occur lengthened and should then be written doubled as other long consonants are. In actual practice, however, the length is often ignored. Apart from in *àjàmi*, initial glottal stops and final glottal stops after short vowels and /n/ are not indicated. But these are (apparantly always) predictable: their indication would be superfluous.

The combinations /aĭ/ and /aŭ/ are written as /ai/ and /au/ in Gaskiya-Nigerian except when followed by /y/ and /w/, respectively, within the same word. Thus, *kyau* 'beauty' but *yawwa* 'bravo' (the form *yauwa* is also found). In UNESCO-Nigerien, the superior spellings /ay/ and /aw/ are used consistently. They are superior if only because they indicate morphophonemic relations that are obvious, e.g. (using UNESCO-Nigerien spellings) *kyaw* 'beauty' is related to *kyaawaawaa* 'beautiful (plural)', which shows a general plural adjective reduplication pattern where the final stem consonant is repeated: /C_1aaC_1aa/ (cf. *daaɗii* 'pleasantness' – *daaɗaaɗaa* 'pleasant').

The main point of systematic divergence between Gaskiya-Nigerian and UNESCO-Nigerien (and also between Gaskiya-Nigerian and *àjàmi*) involves the representation of long vowels. Gaskiya-Nigerian normally does not indicate long vowels at all, and this is surely the main drawback of the system. Rarely is a macron used in cases of supposedly intolerable homonymy: *dā* /dâ:/ 'olden times' vs. *da* /dà/ 'with'. But usually both are indicated as *da*. In UNESCO-Nigerien, long vowels are always indicated and are doubled (e.g. *daa*/*da*). In *àjàmi*, long vowels are also indicated consistently, except in word final position. They are indicated as a short vowel plus a consonant; thus, /i:/ is indicated as though it were /iy/, /u:/ as /uw/, and /a:/ as /a/ plus a kind of dummy consonant we could indicate as /H/ (alif). Although the Africa Alphabet conventions have consistently recommended the use of double vowels to indicate long ones, there are a number of reasons that make me believe that a system approaching that found in *àjàmi* would be preferable. A long vowel in an ideal system might be indicated as short vowel plus /h/. This solution has not been seriously considered in the creation of a practical orthography for Hausa (although I have suggested the analysis in an earlier paper – Ames, et al. [1971: 27]). However, the convention adopted in UNESCO-

Nigerien is perfectly satisfactory and so I shall not pursue the matter of alternative solutions further.

The Gaskiya-Nigerian convention of indicating vowel length only when ambiguity could arise has led to the practice of never indicating it at all. A particularly striking and somewhat amusing incident associated with this practice is to be found in the Hausa translation of the Nigerian Penal code, already mentioned in another connection. The translator, the eminent Hausanist F. W. Parsons, took considerable pains to avoid ambiguities in the subject markers, particularly forms for 'he' (usually a variant of *ya* in the Kano standard). These markers indicate intense and aspect through vowel length and tone distinctions. In Gaskiya-Nigerian these distinctions are not indicated, of course, so that *ya tafi* could mean variously: (1) 'he has gone' (*yaa tàfi*), (2) 'and then he went' (*ya tàfi*), (3) 'may he go' (*yà tàfi*). For the subjunctive form *yà*, Parsons introduced the dialectal *shi*. But for the perfective *yaa*, Parsons says that it will be consistently written as *ya* with a macron (*yā*). However, a footnote given at the end of Parsons's introduction reads as follows (Northern Nigerian Penal Code of 1959: p. 18 f.):

> In this Edition for Technical Reasons it has been found impossible to print the Macron. It is hoped to do so in subsequent Editions.

It must be conceded, however, that vowel length is in a few instances predictable. For example, before a syllable-final consonant vowels are invariably short. Furthermore, since the short vowels /e/ and /o/ are rare and occur for the most part in recently borrowed foreign words, the Gaskiya-Nigerian spellings /e/ and /o/ nearly always have the value of /ee/, /oo/.

As for tones, only UNESCO-Nigerien has the symbol repertoire to represent them. In UNESCO-Nigerien, a low tone CAN be indicated by /ˋ/, though it seldom is. This convention goes along with the standard scholarly transcription and requires that what Greenberg (1941) has called the 'compound tone' be analyzed as high plus low tone, which seems to be the simplest treatment in any event. The only difficulty, if tone were consistently indicated, is an aesthetic one: words with a short vowel with a compound tone followed by a high consonant symbol such as /f/ would have to have a dangling tone mark: *kwaˋf* 'cup'. I think a transcription such as *kwâf* would be preferable, particularly in handwriting. Given the fact that UNESCO-Nigerien has been adopted in areas with relatively easy access to French type and typewriters, the use of a circumflex is not ruled out on technical grounds. But other factors have tended to reduce the writing of tones, most notably the fact that native speakers have shown remarkable resistance to their use. Perhaps the fairly low functional load of tones – in comparison, say, with that of tones in Yoruba – plays a role here. I hardly think so. Rather, it may be that the metaphors used in explaining tone (presumably 'high'-'low' spatial ones) may be misleading, or that something equally trivial is at fault. In my own experience, I was never able to teach my Hausa informants to indicate tone consistently, although vowel length was a different matter. I find this remarkable in light of the widespread use of Hausa 'drum language', which involves an essentially accurate analysis of tones.

Whatever the pedagogical difficulties experienced in the teaching of tone notation, I feel that it is a mistake not to indicate it. The precedent of not writing it in textbooks or in serious publications (such as translations of the Bible, the penal code, or the like) precludes the possibility that it will ever be adopted later. Wolff in his recommendations for practical orthographies for Nigerian languages discusses the problem of writing tones and hopes that it can one day be solved. He believes that the problem can more easily be dealt with when everyone is literate. On the contrary, I believe the problem will be considerably greater then because once entrenched, an orthography is apparently perpetuated by the vested interests of those who know it and are unwilling to learn another. Also, there are various cultural reasons for maintaining what has become part of a heritage.

A striking example of the difficulty of changing an orthography is the failure to Romanize Russian after the revolution, coupled with the compulsory de-Romanization of various writing systems established by the Soviet government for a number of non-Russian speaking groups throughout the Soviet Union – an action taken not as Trager (1972: 308) suggests because Romanization proved unsuccessful, but rather in the wake of the nationalistic retention of Cyrillic in Russian itself. Similarly, Venda spoken in southern Africa has retained its hyper-disjunctive spelling using symbols from the Lepsius alphabet despite (one might almost say, to spite) the conjunctive non-Lepsius conventions of neighboring Bantu languages. Yet another example, but this time an admirable one, is that reported for the American Indian language Tarascan spoken in Mexico, where decent phonetic symbols were introduced and retained despite enormous pressures from Hispanicizing government officials (Sjoberg 1966).

To return to the representation of tones in Hausa spelling. Gaskiya-Nigerian does not indicate tone at all. *Àjàmi* indicates it indirectly and only sporadically in word-final syllables: a final high-tone syllable ending on a vowel whether long or short is written with a long vowel symbol; similarly, a final low-tone vowel is written as short even if actually long. These conventions seem to have misled Bargery in his transcription of length, although it must be added that prosodic contrasts crumble or at least are obscured in some way in final syllables when words are pronounced in isolation.

The treatment of sandhi varies in the three orthographic systems. In Gaskiya-Nigerian, the treatment of such sound changes is inconsistent. For example, the words *an* 'one (perfective)', *zan* 'I (future)', *in* 'if', and a few others are written with a final /m/ rather than /n/ before a following word beginning with a labial consonant. But not *sun* 'they (perfective)', *mun* 'we (perfective)', or other similar forms. A final /r/ in causative verbs is changed to /d/ before the particle *da* (*zubar* 'pour', but *zubad da*), but feminine nouns ending on /r/ in the relative construction do not change the /r/ to /d/ before *da* although the pronunciation is identical with the verb form. There is a single exception: the noun *sa'a* 'hour, time' in the relative before *da* is written with /d/ when used as a conjunction (*sa'ad da* 'when'). In *àjàmi*, the underlying rather than the sandhi form is frequently written, and indeed even within words homorganic clusters such as /mb/ are often written as /nb/ without any clear morphophonemic motivation; thus, *tàmbayàa* 'question' is usually written with /n/ even though there are no obvious related forms in /n/. In UNESCO-Nigerien, sandhi seems to be ignored for the most part, although the relative perfective pronouns are written with a final consonant that is identical with the initial consonant of the following verb: *yat tambayee shi* 'he (rel. perfective) asked him', *yac cee* 'he said', etc. (this form does not occur in the Gaskiya-Nigerian norm because the Kano dialect taken as standard has no consonant: *ya tambaye shi*, *ya ce*, etc.). The word division that UNESCO-Nigerien uses in such instances varies in actual practice. On a single page written by the same person one might find three possibilities: *yac cee*, *yac-cee*, *yaccee*.

I believe that in accordance with the principle of invariant words mentioned as a desideratum above, sandhi forms should be avoided as much as possible – particularly if not indicated consistently. Once again the UNESCO-Nigerien conventions are better than those of Gaskiya-Nigerian. A related question of word boundaries will not be considered here in any detail. It may be of interest to other Africanists that the spelling of verb phrases in both Gaskiya-Nigerian and UNESCO-Nigerien conventions is generally disjunctive, i.e. in writing, verbs are separated from several items syntactically related that never occur as free forms – subject markers, object pronouns, negative particles, tense/aspect markers. Elsewhere on the African scene, most notably among Bantuists following Doke, disjunctivisim has become the orthographic equivalent of leprosy and the 'good guys' all swear by conjunctivism, which requires that bound forms for the most part be written solid with a verb. An inflexible conjunctivism may not be the most desirable solution if only because considerations of word length could play a counteracting role. But sure consistency of some kind should be attempted. It is not clear to me, for example, why in Gaskiya-Nigerian the subject markers are written solid with the continuous particle (*kana*, *yana*, etc.) but not with the relative continuous (*ka ke*, *ya ke*) or the habitual (*ka kan*, *ya kan*). Nor why possessive pronouns are written solid with a preceding appertentive (verbal) noun but not object pronouns with a preceding verb; e.g. *yana ganinsu* 'he sees them' [he-continuous seeing-of them] but *ya gan su* 'he saw them' [he-perfective see them]. In *àjàmi* such problems are largely decided by the convention that 'words' with only one consonant symbol are joined to an adjacent word. But by and large word division has proved to be one of the less controversial issues in Hausa spelling.

The final point I should like to consider briefly is that of the variety of Hausa itself that is represented in spelling. With *àjàmi*, writers apparently write their own dialect. The same thing is generally true of UNESCO-Nigerien. But in Gaskiya-Nigerian, the norm is taken as a form of the Kano dialect minus egregious Kanoisms when possible. But among Nigerian speakers of Hausa at any rate, choice of elegant language used for example in didactic poetry tends to follow the Sokkoto dialect. Furthermore, the Kano dialect has merged several contrasts still preserved elsewhere, including Sokkoto for the most part; thus, /t^w/ s^w/ /c'/ ɗiy/ have become /t/ /s/ /ts/ /'y/, respectively. The development of a 'Union Hausa' with compromise spellings not favoring any one dialect might be useful. As a point of departure we might take the present Gaskiya-Nigerian Kano standard modified by the introduction of the contrasts just mentioned. The use of the pronoun form *swâa* 'they' rather than the present *sa* (= *sâa*) in the potential is especially well motivated because of form with /w/ in the other persons: *mwa* 'we', *kwa* 'you plural'.

The discussion throughout this paper has appealed to criteria the reader may or may not agree with. But I think by any pertinent criteria – linguistic or pedagogical – UNESCO-Nigerien is the best available spelling for Hausa; however, it probably will not be able to supplant Gaskiya-Nigerian for some time, if at all. Consequently, UNESCO-Nigerien may be fairly short-lived. Mallam E. R. Othman of *Gaskiya Ta Fi Kwabo* has informed me that his publication considers the orthographic decisions of the Hausa Language Board in Nigeria to be binding and that the Board after much serious argument and consideration has rejected the introduction of changes in Gaskiya-Nigerian to bring it in line with UNESCO-Nigerien. Neil Skinner, in a personal communication, has pointed out to me that to his knowledge publications in UNESCO-Nigerien are for the most part not available in Nigeria or are rare and not in any demand. He adds by way of contrast that *Gaskiya Ta Fi Kwabo* itself is 'fairly happily read when it can be obtained, up in Niger'.

These facts do not indicate the superiority of Gaskiya-Nigerian for mysterious reasons not considered. Rather they serve to underline the stark reality that spelling reformers have been aware of for some time: to do battle against intrenched but inadequate orthographies, there is need of 'pull', a great deal of money, decent printing facilities, and enthusiasm bordering on fanaticism.

NOTES

1. The writing system suggested for English by the Simplified Spelling Society ('Nue Speling') introduces no new letters. Digraphs with /e/ are used to show 'long' values of vowels, where dictionaries usually use macrons; thus /ae/, /ee/, /ie/, /oe/, /ue/ represent the names of the vowel letters as they might be indicated in Nue Speling. See Ripman and Archer (1948) and Jones (1948 and n.d.).
2. As stated by Hamidu Alkali in the First Report concerning the proposed Centre for Hausa Studies at Abdullahi Bayero College, Kano (n.d.).
3. Kano Hausa speakers use either *p* or *f*; hence the apparent discrepancy here.
4. The Arabic forms used are a variety of Maghrebine alphabet. Hence ڢ (f), ڧ (q), rather than the usual printed forms ف (f), ق (q).

BIBLIOGRAPHY

Ames, David W., Edgar A. Gregersen, and Thomas Neugebauer
1971 'Taaken Sàmàarii: A Drum Language of Hausa Youth', *Africa* 41:1, 12-31.
Armstrong, Robert G.
n.d. 'Language Policy in West Africa', unpublished manuscript.

Bargery, G. P.
1934 *A Hausa-English Dictionary and English-Hausa Vocabulary* (London).
Berry, Jack
1958 'The Making of Alphabets', *Proceedings of the VIIIth International Congress of Linguists* (Oslo), 752-764.
Dalby, David
1967 'A Survey of the Indigenous Scripts of Liberia and Sierra Leone: Vai, Mende, Loma, Kpelle and Bassa', *African Language Studies* 8, 1-51.
1970 'The Historical Problem of the Indigenous Scripts of West Africa and Surinam', in David Dalby (ed.), *Language and History in Africa* (New York), 109-119.
Gouffé, Claude
1965 'La lexicographie du haoussa et le préalable phonologique', *Journal of African Languages* 4: 3, 191-210.
Greenberg, Joseph H.
1941 'Some Problems in Hausa Phonology', *Language* 17: 4, 316-323.
Gregersen, Edgar A.
i.p. 'The Social Status of Hausa r-Sounds', *Proceedings of the Hamito-Semitic Colloquium 1970* (London).
Houis, Maurice
1957-1958 'Comment écrire les langues africaines? Nécessité d'un humanisme africain', *Présence Africaine.*
Jones, Daniel
1942 *The Problem of a National Script for India* (Hertford).
1948 *Differences between Spoken and Written Language* (Association Phonétique Internationale).
1962 *The Phoneme, Its Nature and Use*, 2nd edition (Cambridge).
n.d. 'Dhe fonetik aspekt ov speling reform', *Simplified Spelling Society* (London).
Kirk-Greene, Anthony
1964 'The Hausa Language Board', *Afrika und Übersee* 47, 187-203.
Ladefoged, Peter
1964 *A Phonetic Study of West African Languages*, revised edition (Cambridge).
Meinhof, Carl
1931 'Principles of Practical Orthography for African Languages', *Africa* 1, 228-239.
North Regional Literature Agency
1958 *Hausa Spelling* (Zaria).
Northern Nigerian Penal Code of 1959 (Tsarin laifuffuka da hukuncinsu)
n.d. (no place).
Pike, Kenneth L.
1947 *Phonemics: A Technique for Reducing Languages to Writing* (Ann Arbor: University of Michigan Press).
Pring, Julian
1964 'Spelling Reform in Modern Greek', in David Abercrombie et al. (eds.), *In Honour of Daniel Jones* (London), 357-367.
Ripman, Walter, and W. Archer
1948 *New Spelling*, revised by D. Jones and H. Orton (London).

Sjoberg, Andrée F.

1966 'Socio-Cultural and Linguistic Factors in the Development of Writing Systems for Preliterate Peoples', in William Bright (ed.), *Sociolinguistics* (The Hague).

Taylor, F. W.

1929 'The Orthography of African Languages with Special Reference to Hausa and Fulani', *Journal of the African Society* 28, 241-252.

Trager, George L.

1972 *Language and Languages* (San Francisco).

Tucker, A. N.

1971 'Orthographic Systems and Conventions in Sub-Saharan Africa', in Thomas A. Sebeok (ed.), *Current Trends in Linguistics* 7: *Linguistics in Sub-Saharan Africa*, 618-653.

Vischer, Hanns

1911-1912 'Rules for Hausa Spelling', *Journal of the African Society* 11, 339-347.

Wolff, Hans

1954 *Nigerian Orthography* (Zaria).

STEPHEN A. WURM

16

The Spelling of New Guinea Pidgin (Neo-Melanesian)

1. NEW GUINEA PIDGIN

New Guinea Pidgin – or Neo-Melanesian as it had been suggested to be called, though that name never gained wide acceptance – is an English-based pidgin language used widely in Papua New Guinea, the eastern half of the New Guinea area. Its importance as a language goes far beyond that usually characteristic of pidgin languages in other parts of the world: it is spoken and understood by close to one million people – between one third and one half of the population of the area referred to – and is in several ways an important prestige language in the framework of the nationalistic awakening of the indigenous population and its rapid progress on the path to self-government and independence.

Knowledge of Pidgin has been spreading with enormous rapidity in Papua New Guinea, and it is quickly moving closer and closer towards universality, superseding, or at least overshadowing, other lingua francas in the area whose presence, like that of Pidgin itself, has been the direct result of the unparalleled multiplicity of languages in the New Guinea area (about seven hundred distinct local languages are found in Papua New Guinea alone). Pidgin is the obvious candidate for becoming the national language of an independent Papua New Guinea, with English used as the second official language for certain pursuits such as higher education and contacts with the outside world. Already it has been the usual debate language in the Papua New Guinea House of Assembly for several years, and its use on more and more advanced levels of expression is increasing. Local Pidgin literature is beginning to develop, and in some areas the language has become creolized or is in the process of creolization.

2. INTRODUCTORY REMARKS ON THE SPELLING OF NEW GUINEA PIDGIN

In the light of what has been said above, it is clear that the question of a standardized orthography and spelling for the language is a matter of great importance, in particular with a view to its ever increasing use in writing. Unfortunately, this question and its history are not happy topics, and the present situation is far from satisfactory.

Pidgin is an English-based pidgin in regard to the origin of the great majority of its vocabulary, but its phonology and grammar are basically Austronesian in their underlying principles: characteristic features of Western Melanesia in evidence in Pidgin, and Papuan traits are observable in some respects.

The English origin of much of the vocabulary of Pidgin has been a decisive factor in the spelling of Pidgin words from the beginning, and still is so today in several ways. Virtually every one of the spelling systems so far devised for the language, even those making allowances to the special nature of Pidgin phonology, has betrayed an inclination on the part of its designer to take into account the English origin of the words as manifested in features of their spelling, and to imitate – in extreme cases either completely involuntarily, or fully intentionally – characteristics of the English spelling system even though they may be at variance with Pidgin phonology. Cases of more or less involuntary imitation were attributable to pressure from English phonological and spelling principles and patterns, whereas cases of fully intentional imitation were guided by the philosophy that Anglicized features of Pidgin spelling might facilitate the subsequent learning and spelling of English by indigenous Pidgin speakers, and that the increased Anglicization of Pidgin might eventually turn it into English anyway and lead to the disappearance of an idiom upon which most English speakers had been looking with great disfavor and distaste.

Many cases which come under the heading of imitation of English spelling principles in contrast to Pidgin phonological facts have to be regarded as intermediate between these two extremes, i.e. constituting cases in which the designer of the spelling was undoubtedly aware of his imitating the English model without his doing it for the expressed purpose of bringing the written words nearer in form to their English etymological sources so as to facilitate the learning of the latter by the indigenous writers of Pidgin.

A good example of the perhaps rather involuntary imitation of English spelling principles is the tendency of several Pidgin spelling systems, including the two most widespread ones, to distinguish between voiced and voiceless stops, i.e. *b* and *p*, *d* and *t*, *g* and *k*, in many instances in accordance with the spelling of the English source words, even though, for instance, the pronunciation of a word-initial sound rendered by *d* in these spelling systems may be persistently *t*, e.g. in the Pidgin equivalent of 'this' which is spelled *dispela*, but pronounced with an initial unaspirated dental *t*. Significantly, it is spelled *tispela* in Murphy (1943) who uses one of the spelling systems which tend to make wide allowance for the actual pronunciation of Pidgin stops. At the same time, such spelling systems are full of glaring inconsistencies in this respect under the pressure of English spelling habits: for instance, 'dog' is spelled *dog* in Murphy (1943) though the final stop is always a voiceless unaspirated *k*, and the initial stop not infrequently voiceless. The spelling *dok* ~ *tok* would be consistent with the spelling *tispela* for 'this'.

Interesting evidence highlighting the appearance of letters representing voiced and voiceless stops in Pidgin spelling systems under pressure from English spelling habits is provided by one of the spelling systems used in Bichelamar (Pislama), a Pidgin language closely related to New Guinea Pidgin and widely used in the New Hebrides. In addition to its English-derived vocabulary content, it has numerous French-derived lexical elements. In the spelling system referred to (Camden 1969), devised by a speaker of English apparently not familiar with French, all English-based words appear with voiced and voiceless stops in accordance with the English spelling, whereas with the French-based words no one-to-one correspondence is observable between the appearance of letters denoting voiced or voiceless consonants in them and the presence of such consonants in the French source words, e.g. *gavman* 'government' (pronounced *kapman*), *gyaman* 'to lie' (pronounced *kyaman* and derived from *gammon*), but *pepet* 'small animal' (pronounced *mbembet* and derived from *bébête*).

Another typical example is the use of both *l* and *r* in all Pidgin spelling systems, with their appearance being determined by their use in the English source words. In many Pidgin dialects, the sound represented by both *l* and *r* in writing is only one sound, i.e. an alveolar, or sometimes retroflexed, flap. It must however be admitted that in the Tolai language in northern New Britain from where the ancestral form of present-day New Guinea Pidgin spread out close to a century ago, *l* and *r* are distinguished, and this manifests itself in the numerous Tolai words in Pidgin, e.g.

limlimbur 'to amuse oneself'. However, this distinction has not become a part of the phonemic structure of many present-day Pidgin dialects.

A good instance of obviously quite intentional approximation of the written form of a Pidgin word to the English form is the Pidgin word *plank* 'a board' in one of the major spelling systems which has now been declared obsolete (the 1955 standard orthography, see 3.2.1.): that word is invariably pronounced with a final *-ng* as in 'sing'.

Another case is the spelling of the Pidgin equivalent of 'hot' as *hot* (*pela*) in the same spelling system, though the pronunciation is invariably *hat*, with an open *a* sound (a short form of the pronunciation of *a* in 'father'). At the same time, the word *stap* < English 'stop' is always spelled with *a*, though its vowel sound is identical with that of *hot* (*pela*). The reason for this discrepancy has obviously been a conscious effort on the part of the designer of the spelling to make the Pidgin equivalent of 'hot' look like the English word in its written form, and also to distinguish it from its homophone *hat* (*pela*) 'hard' which belongs to a different morphological class of adjectives (Wurm 1971).

This point brings into focus some of those characteristics of the major spelling systems which have been devised to reduce the number of homographic forms, i.e. of forms with identical spelling and different meanings. For instance, the Pidgin equivalent of 'jeep' is spelled *jip*, and that of 'ship', *sip*, but both are pronounced with an initial *s*.

3. NOTES ON THE HISTORY OF PIDGIN SPELLING SYSTEMS

3.1. Developments until 1955

3.1.1. Spelling Systems

In early attempts at writing Pidgin, the words were spelled essentially according to the spelling of the English source words, or of what was believed to be the English source words (e.g. the predicative particle *i* was written *he* though it is in fact derived from a particle used in Austronesian languages of Melanesia), and this usage persisted in the English-speaking orbit for quite some time in isolated instances, often mixed with spelling principles of a different kind. For instance *this fellow boy he cranky him he bugger up him lamp belong him finish* for what would be in the 1969 revised standard spelling (see 3.3.1.) *dispela boi i kranki em i bagarapim lam bilongen pinis* 'this fellow is stupid, he has ruined his lamp'. Mixed forms such as *walkebaut* (today *wokabaut*) '*to walk*', *crossim* (today *krosim*) 'to scold' are frequently encountered in passages of writing employing such spellings.

However, an important part of the early attempts to write Pidgin and to produce written passages in it took place before World War I in what was then German New Guinea, by German speakers whose bias with regard to spelling habits and language orientation was different from those of English speakers, and who looked upon Pidgin essentially as a foreign language in its own right, though recognizing its close lexical affinity with English. Among these, missionaries excelled, and the Roman Catholic Society of the Divine Word (SVD) missionaries created a Pidgin orthography which was used quite widely in those days, both in their missionary activities, and also by the German administration (Hall 1966). It persisted for many years in some Catholic missionary agencies. It followed English with the usage governing the appearance of voiced and voiceless stops in the English source words, but with regard to the representation of vowel sounds in the spelling system, the five vowel symbols *a*, *e*, *i*, *o*, *u* indicated sounds in accordance with the German usage, and in this respect, and regarding the appearance of other consonant symbols, the spelling was entirely consistent. It was, at the same time, based upon the philosophy that Pidgin, being so largely English in its vocabulary, should reflect English in its spelling up to a point, and it attempted to approximate, in the spelling, the European (German) speakers' pronunciation in relation to the English-based words in Pidgin. While it was admitted that the indigenous speakers' pronunciation did not reflect the spelling of the words as decided upon, the opinion was held that he could, and should, be taught to pronounce Pidgin in conformity with the spelling, and that the European, not the indigenous speaker, was to decide how a word should be spelled.

This spelling system was referred to as the Alexishafen spelling, Alexishafen, near Madang, then being the headquarters of the SVD Mission. Though widely used, it was by no means generally adopted after its creation, or at a later date. Missionaries of other denominations and even Catholic missionaries in other parts of New Guinea created orthographies of their own which deviated from the Alexishafen spelling to a greater or lesser extent. The approach to the spelling problem by what might be described as the Rabaul School is of particular interest in this. The SVD missionaries in the Rabaul area, in agreement with the Administration education officials, took the stand that Pidgin was primarily and basically a language of the indigenes, and that the spelling of Pidgin should therefore follow, as closely as possible, Pidgin pronunciation as heard from indigenous speakers.

In the light of this philosophy, orthographies following it – most missionary orthographies and the majority of others – were characterized by the following two main features: consistency with regard to copying the English source words in the choice of letters representing voiced and voiceless stops was abandoned to a varying degree in an attempt to imitate the actual indigenous Pidgin phonetic values of stops in English-based words, and vowel symbol usages differed considerably. In addition, the Lutheran Mission in Madang adopted the symbol ŋ for *ng* in the light of the alphabets which they had devised for writing the indigenous lingua franca, Kâte, Yabêm, and Graged (Gedaged, Bel) utilized by them (Hall 1966).

The Methodist Mission in Rabaul followed a different approach in adapting a spelling system introduced for writing Austronesian languages of Melanesia, to writing Pidgin, and *g* and *k* sounds were both rendered by *k*, and the symbol *g* used for representing the sound of *ng* in 'sing' for which in the other Pidgin spelling systems the symbols *ng* or ŋ were found. Also, in common with the usage adopted for writing Austronesian languages, the sound symbolized by *y* in most other Pidgin spelling systems, as well as in English, was rendered by *i*. This spelling system resulted in forms such as *log* for *long*, *iu* for *yu*, etc. (Hall 1955b).

In the years extending until well after World War II, Pidgin spelling systems proliferated, and by the mid-fifties, nine different major, and a considerable number of additional minor, systems were in actual use by various missions, different news media such as the Rabaul News and the Wewak News, in Pidgin grammars such as Murphy (1943), and by different government departments. So, for instance, the Department of Health and the Department of Agriculture used spelling systems which were greatly at variance with each other.

Attempts at standardizing Pidgin orthography were undertaken by the Department of Education in the late forties and early fifties, but they had to be abandoned for lack of cooperation from the various parties concerned. The only common ground which began to emerge was the gradual recognition of the principle that spelling should be based on the pronunciation of indigenous, and not the European, speakers, but there were considerable differences in the interpretation of this principle and the pressure of English spelling habits continued to be strong.

3.1.2. Factors Influencing Spelling Systems until 1955

The guiding principle underlying Pidgin spelling systems until 1955 was the notion that the decision concerning the shape of individual orthographies rested with European speakers of Pidgin. Pidgin words were spelled either according to the manner in which European speakers of Pidgin pronounced them, with greatly varying acceptance of pressure from English spelling habits, or with varying allowances made for what Europeans regarded as the indigenous pronunciation of Pidgin words. Other factors such as pressure from spelling habits associated with the writing of indigenous languages entered the picture with regard to Pidgin orthographies used by several missions such as the Lutheran Mission in Madang and the Methodist Mission in Rabaul. Virtually no attempt at cooperation with a view to standardization of Pidgin spelling was made by different agencies using varying spelling systems, and moves aiming for standardization as initiated by the Department of Education of the Administration, as an outside agency, failed because of the unwillingness to compromise on the part of the parties concerned. Only in a minority of the cases was such a resistance based on the conscious pursuance of a clearly conceived philosophy relating to the specific nature and the merits of particular spelling systems. In other instances, it was a matter of inertia and unwillingness to change or simply lack of interest, with such attitudes deeply rooted in the conviction shared by many Europeans in New Guinea (and outside) that Pidgin was not really a language at all but only corrupt English for which some corrupt way of writing it was perfectly adequate, and attempts at giving it some well-designed orthography were an unnecessary waste of time and effort.

The spelling of recent loan words from English in the various spelling systems is of interest here. In the orthographies used by news media and government departments, a strong tendency was observable to spell such words as in English, without any attempt at indicating their actual Pidgin pronunciation in the spelling. Mission orthographies showed a much greater inclination to respell such loan words in terms of the principles underlying the given orthographies in their approximation of indigenous Pidgin pronunciation.

3.2. Developments from 1955 until 1969

3.2.1. Spelling Systems

In 1955, the Department of Education of the Administration of the then Territory of Papua and New Guinea took the stand that decisive official action directed towards the standardization of Pidgin orthography was earnestly called for R. A. Hall of Cornell University, who had for many years been concerned with the study of New Guinea Pidgin, had a little earlier made detailed orthographical suggestions (Hall 1955a) on the basis of his phonemic analysis of Pidgin, and his suggestions were used as the basis of studies directed towards a standard Pidgin orthography. On behalf of the Administration such studies were carried out by two linguists, T. Dietz and L. Luzbetak, and involved extensive consultations with mission bodies and school authorities. The two linguists received little support from the various missions which were using Pidgin extensively at the time, and sometimes met opposition and were subjected to strong social pressure, along with receiving a great number of suggestions for their task.

As a result of their studies, the two linguists devised a new orthography for Pidgin, which, though admittedly less than phonemic, was based on objective evidence gathered from indigenous speakers and reflected essentially the northern coastal dialect of Pidgin, with the Madang usage given the greatest weight. This orthography was approved by the Department of Education, the Administrator of Papua and New Guinea, and the Minister for Territories in Canberra, and was promulgated as the standard Pidgin orthography in an official publication issued by the Department of Education (Department of Education 1956). It was adopted, with a few minor additions, in Mihalic's Pidgin Grammar and Dictionary (Mihalic 1957).

Resistance to this new orthography was at first quite strong on the part of various mission bodies, but gradually most of the missions on the New Guinea mainland adopted the standard orthography once it was backed by the Administration.

For the short span of two years, Pidgin orthography and spelling appeared to be well on its way towards general standardization, though a number of agencies were continuing the use of spelling systems of their own, and some criticism was leveled against the standard orthography because of some of its features which constituted concessions to English spelling (e.g. *plank* 'board', pronounced with a final *ng* as in 'sing').

Unfortunately, the Administration itself brought about the downfall of the standardization which it had itself introduced. While there had been considerable reluctance to adapt to the standard orthography on the part of the various Administration departments and the European officials working in them, no attempt was made to insist on the indigenes hired to do the official translating and writing in Pidgin to adhere to the standard orthography. The excuse was that since Pidgin was their own language, they ought to know how to spell it. The result was chaos, with the multiplicity and diversity of spelling systems greater than before, at least outside the missionary orbit.

At the same time, some missions which had adapted to the standard orthography introduced some modifications into it largely with a view to cancel out the concessions to English spelling in it and to bring it closer to the actual pronunciation of Pidgin in the northern coastal, more specifically the Madang, dialect. The Lutheran Mission in particular acted in this manner and devised a modified standard Pidgin orthography. At the same time, there had been increasing pressure upon the Lutheran Church by indigenes literate in Pidgin that two phonemically relevant distinctions indicated in the standard orthography and in the modified version used by the Lutherans be omitted from the orthography. One of these was the distinction between *ng* (*ng* in 'sing' and *ngg* (*ng* in 'finger'). The indigenes suggested that these two phonemically distinct sounds both be rendered by *ng*. They also felt that there was no need to indicate the phonemic distinction between *ai* and *aii* as in *taim* 'time' and *traiim* (i.e. *trai-im*) 'to try' and wanted them both spelled as *ai* only. The Lutherans accepted these suggestions and incorporated them into the spelling used in the Pidgin translation of the New Testament which was published in 1969 and has become the largest and most circulated book ever published in Pidgin: 40,000 copies of this 861 page book were sold within nine months of its appearance. This wide circulation, almost exclusively in indigenous hands, has contributed to familiarizing in indigenous speakers of Pidgin with the particular modified standard orthography employed in it.

3.2.2. Factors Influencing Spelling Systems between 1955 and 1969

The period under discussion was, at its beginning, characterized by a serious attempt by the Administration, in particular the Department of Education, to bring order into the chaotic situation prevailing with regard to the spelling of Pidgin, and to establish a standard orthography, taking the necessary scientifically based action to carry out this aim. The driving motive behind this attitude was the official approval in 1955, of the use of Pidgin in the then Territory of Papua and New Guinea by the Minister for Territories in Canberra, with the following proviso: that the purpose of this approval is to further the aim of teaching all children in controlled areas to read and write English; that Pidgin is to be used only as a medium of instruction and then only in schools in areas where it is in general use; that the production of primers, readers, and textbooks in Pidgin is not to be allowed to prejudice or limit the production and distribution of similar material in English for use in all phases of school work.

The Minister also approved the following further action –

(1) the selection of a regional form of Pidgin to be adopted as the standard form for the Territory;

(2) the adoption of a linguistically sound standardized orthography;

(3) the preparation and publication of a Pidgin grammar and dictionary; and

(4) the preparation for publication of school primers, readers, and textbooks.

This procedure followed the recommendation of the use of Pidgin officially in the Territory by the Education Advisory Board and the Committee on Languages under the auspices of the Department of Education in March 1955. The Director of Education recommended to the Administrator of the Territory that these suggestions be adopted, and this was approved by the Minister. The first action was to prepare a standard orthography which was subsequently carried out, and a grammar and dictionary utilizing the new standard orthography was prepared and published (Mihalic 1957).

Resistance to the new orthography was quite strong, both on the part of missions and of agencies in the Administration and elsewhere. The reasons for the resistance by the missions were essentially based on traditionalism and intermission rivalry, and the fact that the author of the new Pidgin grammar and dictionary as well as one of the members of the two-man orthography team (L. Luzbetak) were members of the Catholic Mission undoubtedly contributed to some extent to these attitudes in the missionary sphere. Resistance in Administration agencies and elsewhere was largely motivated by attitudes of inertia and lack of interest, the fact that missions, i.e. the Catholic Mission, were known to have significantly contributed to the creation of the new standard orthography, and last but not least, the feeling on the part of many Europeans in the Territory that it seemed an awful waste of time to worry about how this contemptible corrupted jargon was spelled, seeing that it was not a real language anyway but only a bastardly corruption of English. The unrealistic and misinformed decision of the United Nations Trusteeship Council of 1953 urging Australia to immediately abolish and prohibit the use of Pidgin in the Territory may have given a boost to many of those who displayed the above-mentioned attitudes towards the new standard orthography of Pidgin.

Nevertheless, the official backing by the Administration of the new standard orthography brought about a gradual – albeit reluctant and grudging – adaption to it both by mission bodies and administration agencies.

However, the second characteristic feature of the period under discussion put an end to this development, and the retirement of the Director of Education, W. C. Groves, under whose tenure of office the new standard orthography had been introduced, may well have been of considerable significance for the nature of the further developments.

This second characteristic feature mentioned above was the decisive influence of indigenous attitudes towards Pidgin spelling and an almost total permissiveness towards them in Administration agencies and outside, and the strong notice taken of them in some mission circles. At the same time, the declared earlier official recognition of Pidgin became an ineffectual decision and was, in practice, annulled by a forceful insistence on the use of English in all possible situations. The attitude that Pidgin was only a passing phenomenon and destined to soon disappear into oblivion under the impact of English was encouraged.

Under these circumstances, the permissive and uncaring attitudes on the part of many towards the gradual discontinuation of the standard orthography in many agencies seems understandable.

It remains to look into the possible reasons motivating indigenes, employed by the Administration and other agencies to carry out translation and written work in Pidgin, not to adhere to the standard orthography and to spell Pidgin in many different ways as has been mentioned above in 3.2.1. These reasons were essentially threefold:

(1) The indigenes were unfamiliar with the standard orthography. With the ban on the teaching of Pidgin as a language in all schools eligible for Government finance and subsidy, and the virtual ban on the use of Pidgin as a medium of teaching literacy and of instruction in general in such schools, which became policy in spite of the wording of the

approval of the use of Pidgin in the Territory as quoted above at the beginning of 3.2.2., the teaching of Pidgin and in Pidgin became restricted to a number of nonsubsidized substandard schools run by various missions in addition to the subsidized English schools under their auspices. Pupils going to such Pidgin schools were quite unlikely ever to reach the standards of general education and proficiency in English as required for employment in Administration and other agencies as translators and writers of Pidgin. This resulted in a situation in which most of the indigenes thus employed had not had any formal training in Pidgin, and had in consequence no proficiency in using the standard orthography though some of them may have been exposed to it in some publications and may have been vaguely familiar with it.

(2) Indigenes employed by Administration and other agencies spoke different dialects of Pidgin and wrote Pidgin in made-up spelling systems of their own, including phonetic and phonological features of their respective dialects in their spelling systems.

(3) Many of the indigenes thus employed had been exposed to nothing but English in their education and training, and tended to include some English spelling habits in their ways of writing Pidgin.

An interesting development in this period has been the rather general respelling of recent English loan words in Pidgin according to their Pidgin pronunciation, in spite of what has been said above under (3).

The third, and late, characteristic feature of the period reviewed here was the modification of the standard orthography by the Lutheran Mission in the light of the views of their own Pidgin experts and of suggestions received from literate indigenes. Some of these suggestions, and the modifications carried out on the basis of them, directly contravened some principles according to which newly created spelling systems were to indicate all phonemic distinctions present in the languages for the writing of which they were to be used. These suggestions were spontaneous on the part of the numerous indigenes making them, and they appeared to lend support to a view that in practical orthographies, phonemic distinctions having a low functional load – this is the case with the above-mentioned modifications suggested by the indigenes – need not be painstakingly indicated.

This modified orthography was used in the Pidgin translation of the New Testament which had a wide circulation and put an extensive, much-read example of this spelling into the hands of tens of thousands of indigenes who were literate in Pidgin.

3.3. Developments since 1969

3.3.1. Spelling Systems

This last period under discussion begins with the impact of the spelling system used in the Pidgin translation of the New Testament making itself felt in view of the wide circulation of the book in indigenous hands, and the large number of copies sold to indigenes. The spelling of Pidgin by many indigenes who had access to the New Testament began gradually to adapt to the New Testament spelling. At the same time, most of the publishers of Pidgin literature, such as the Bible Society, the New Guinea Branch of the Summer Institute of Linguistics, the Christian Leadership Training College, the Creative Training Centre at Nobonob in the Madang District, the large Kristen Pres in Madang, Wantok Publications in Wewak and others, but not the Government Printer and the Department of Information and Extension Services, had largely adopted the spelling used in the New Testament, in part even before the actual appearance of the book.

In recognition of these facts, a renewed effort at standardizing Pidgin spelling was made in November, 1969. Several meetings of over thirty specialists were held with a view to standardizing Pidgin orthography, and a Pidgin Orthography Committee set up under the joint chairmanship of F. Mihalic, the author of the standard orthography Pidgin Grammar and Dictionary (Mihalic 1957), and J. Sievert, one of the main translators and editors of the Pidgin New Testament. The declared aim of this committee was to tidy up the spelling of Pidgin and to convince all publishing houses of the Territory to cooperate voluntarily in the effort. At the meetings which were attended by the heads of seven government departments, three university professors, professional linguists from the Summer Institute of Linguistics, translators, indigenous journalists and broadcasters, four indigenous members of the Papua New Guinea House of Assembly, and various missionaries, the spelling used in the New Testament was declared the norm to follow, and it was agreed to strive for a 'high' Pidgin to be used universally in writing while leaving the spoken dialects alone. The dialect spoken along the entire north coast of mainland New Guinea from Lae to Vanimo was chosen as a standard because it was the one most widely used and understood.

However, as a result of the deliberations at the meeting, it was deemed unwise to resort to a decree for the adoption of the above proposals which were put forward unanimously, though a call for someone in authority to decide officially on the adoption of the proposals was made during the meetings, and appeals for such a recommendation to be made by the members of the House of Assembly present at the meetings directed at them. It was the strong feeling of the meeting that the various departments of the Administration and other agencies involved would find it in their own interest to cooperate voluntarily in this effort.

Subsequently, in 1970, the Orthography Committee made various approaches to government departments and other agencies urging the adoption of the proposed spelling system, and in particular requesting that individuals in departments and other agencies who were engaged in writing, editing, or proofreading Pidgin materials follow it. Authorization was sought from the departments and agencies to promulgate spelling lists and explanatory sheets in them so as to assist in the adoption of the spelling system.

However, the response to these calls and to the proposal directed at the general adoption of the spelling system itself was disappointing, and a number of departments and agencies continued to go their own way in the absence of an official directive.

However, a new edition of Mihalic's Pidgin Grammar and Dictionary appeared in 1971 (Mihalic 1971), and in this the New Testament spelling was used, which gave the public, especially the Europeans, greater access to reference material in this spelling system. Also, other teaching and reference materials published in Papua New Guinea and also outside it (such as Dutton 1973) adopted this orthography which is also used in the ordinary and intensive courses in Pidgin held at the Australian National University in Canberra.

These latter developments have ensured that a new generation of Europeans who study Pidgin seriously as a foreign language will become acquainted with Pidgin in this new standard orthography and more easily accept it without prejudice. Many of these are officials and other persons who are likely to play an active role on the Papua New Guinea scene, and this fact is likely to contribute to the more general acceptance of the new standard orthography in the orbits in which they are expected to be active, and to constitute a counterbalance to the traditional leanings of many Europeans in Papua New Guinea who had 'picked up' Pidgin without actually studying it, and whose uncaring attitudes towards the spelling of Pidgin have been hard to influence.

At the same time, an entirely new development has made itself felt in recent years in the gradual emergence of Pidgin literature in the form of plays, poems, songs, narratives, and stories written by indigenes of generally high, usually tertiary, educational level. Writers of such literature mostly make use of their own dialects of Pidgin, and even in those instances in which the language itself follows standard 'high' Pidgin closely, the spelling systems used by them reflect the local dialects of the writers and deviate strongly from the new standard orthography. This development is perhaps most correctly described as 'indigenous Pidgin dialect literature' and constitutes a trend rather apart from, and complementary to, the development of 'high' Pidgin and the use of the now standard orthography. Being popular among indigenes, this dialect literature constitutes a factor counteracting the general adoption of the new standard orthography by them.

As of now, 'high' Pidgin and its present orthography has been largely limited to use in communications, in the widest sense, by the government, missions, and private business; the literature existing in it, extensive as it may be, consists predominantly of materials written by Europeans or by indigenes under European supervision. 'High' Pidgin, and its orthography, is still waiting for a great indigenous writer or poet to give it full life and to make it a superior model which the indigenes are prepared and willing to accept generally, though the Pidgin New Testament has gone some distance towards this goal.

3.3.2. Factors Influencing Spelling Systems Since 1969

The period under review was characterized at its beginning by a serious effort – by a large group of people from missions, government, the press, the House of Assembly, and institutions concerned with the professional and scientific study of language – to once more attempt a standardization of Pidgin orthography, following the New Testament spelling which has been found to have had a considerable influence upon indigenous spelling habits. Unfortunately, the proposals of the group were not followed by official enforcement, and the recommendations remained largely unheeded in government departments and other agencies, essentially for reasons of individual traditionalism and inertia, and perhaps also for reasons of antimissionary attitudes on the part of some people who looked upon the New Testament spelling as a 'missionary spelling'. At the same time, the subsequent publication of grammars, a large dictionary, and other teaching materials in the new standard orthography, and the utilization of this orthography in the teaching of Pidgin in a number of instances has increased its acceptance among Europeans.

A factor potentially inhibiting the further spread of the acceptance of the New Testament spelling among the indigenous population may be the gradual emergence of an indigenous Pidgin dialect literature, with the writers each utilizing their own spelling systems which reflect their own dialects of Pidgin.

4. FUTURE OUTLOOK

Papua New Guinea is at the threshold of important events: the country is developing rapidly, the indigenes are taking over the reins from the Europeans at an ever increasing rate in anticipation of self-government late in 1973 and of independence at a later date, the influence of Europeans is fading, and, if present, the Europeans of long tradition in the country are moving out of the picture and their places are being taken by new ones who do not bring with them the biased attitudes of the past. In this situation, attitudes towards Pidgin, its standardization, and the standardization of its orthography, are becoming more and more favorable. Its acceptance as a national language of the Papua New Guinea nation seems more and more likely. The present Minister of Education, E. Olevale, has predicted that Pidgin is going to be one of the languages to be used in elementary education in Papua New Guinea.

All this makes a full standardization of Pidgin and its orthography in the near future a likely event, and in many ways imperative. Already thoughts have been voiced on the highest levels that the creation of an institution functioning as a Pidgin Academy concerned with the full standardization of Pidgin grammar, lexicon, and orthography is called for. The present atmosphere makes it seem likely that any recommendations on these lines will receive full official backing and, if necessary, enforcement. It seems, therefore, that at long last, a fully standardized Pidgin orthography can be expected to become a generally accepted reality in the foreseeable future.

BIBLIOGRAPHY

Camden, W. G.
1969 *Dictionary English to Bislama*, mimeographed (Pt. Vila, New Hebrides).
Department of Education
1956 *The Standard Neo-Melanesian (Pidgin) Orthography* (Port Moresby, Territory of Papua and New Guinea: Department of Education).

Dutton, T.
1973 'Conversational New Guinea Pidgin', *Pacific Linguistics*, Series D.12 (Canberra).
Hall, R. A., Jr.
1955a *A Standard Orthography and List of Suggested Spellings for Neo-Melanesian* (Port Moresby: Department of Education).
1955b *Hands off Pidgin English!* (Sydney: Pacific Publications Pty.).
1966 *Pidgin and Creole Languages* (Cornell University Press).
Mihalic, F.
1957 *Grammar and Dictionary of Neo-Melanesian* (Techny, Ill.: The Mission Press, S.V.D.).
1971 *The Jacaranda Dictionary and Grammar of Melanesian Pidgin* (Australia: The Jacaranda Press).
Murphy, J. J.
1943 *The Book of Pidgin English* (Brisbane: Smith and Paterson Pty.).
Wurm, S. A.
1971 'New Guinea Highlands Pidgin: Course Materials', *Pacific Linguistics*, Series D.3 (Canberra).

ROBERT W. YOUNG

Written Navajo: A Brief History

On March 3, 1819, the Congress of the United States acted to establish a 'Civilization Fund' ($ 10,000) designed for the introduction of 'the habits and arts of civilization' among the Indians. This enactment, following up on previous legislation and treaty commitments, laid the foundation for Federal Indian Education and set the scene for development of the policies that guided it across the nineteenth century and well beyond the first quarter of the twentieth century – policies that adhered generally to the goal of Indian acculturation and assimilation into the body politic of the nation.

For more than a century the Federal Government persisted in a fruitless effort to stamp out Indian languages and cultural systems, as a prelude to assimilation – an effort that finally ran its course on the heels of the Meriam Survey, conducted during the period 1926-1928 by the Institute for Government Research. The report of the Meriam Committee, entitled *The Problem of Indian Administration*, described reservation conditions as the study group found them, and urged sweeping changes in Federal Indian policy as well as in the programs carried on or supported by the Federal Government. The Committee took the position that essential changes must include the direct involvement of the Indian communities themselves in defining local needs and finding practical solutions to social and economic problems, coupled with diversification, rather than uniformity, of reservation programs to meet the peculiar requirements of each tribal group. The revolution in Indian administration was set in motion in 1929 with the appointment of Charles J. Rhoads as Commissioner of Indian Affairs, and it gained impetus a few years later, in 1933, with the appointment of John Collier to the post. From 1929 onward Indian languages and tribal cultural systems assumed a respectable status they had not enjoyed for more than a century – a status based on recognition of the fact that Indian languages and cultures constituted the framework within which social and economic planning had to take place.

Prerequisite to effective involvement of many Indian communities, including the Navajo, was the development of improved media for communications between the Federal Government and the tribe, and among tribal members. Improvement of communication media included not only the fostering of tribal governmental organizations, but the use of such readily available tools as the Indian languages themselves, for on many reservations few of the Indian people could speak or understand English.

After a century of almost total insulation against virtually everything that the steady march of knowledge in the social sciences had to offer, the Bureau of Indian Affairs at long last, after 1929, began to apply scientific principles and methods in the development and execution of reservation programs. One such application took the form of utilizing Indian languages in written form as practical tools both for general communication and for educational purposes. Needless to say, the abrupt reversal in Federal policy, that for entire generations had focused on the use of English to the exclusion of native languages, met with strong opposition from the outraged supporters of the historic assimilation effort, both Indian and non-Indian. Nonetheless, the first tentative steps toward the use of written Indian languages were taken in 1934: with the appointment of Willard W. Beatty as Director of Indian Education in the same year, the idea gained a new and powerful champion.

Navajo had been written by ethnologists, linguists, and missionaries for a number of years in a wide variety of orthographic systems for academic and religious purposes. Washington Matthews, the post surgeon at Fort Wingate in the 1880's, devoted much of his time and energy to study of the language and culture of the Navajo. A few years later, near the close of the century, missions began to make their appearance in the Navajo Country. The missionaries were obliged to turn their immediate attention to the study of the Navajo language because without a knowledge of the language they could not communicate with the people they sought to convert.

The Franciscan Order established the first Roman Catholic mission at St. Michaels, Arizona, in 1898, and so energetically did they pursue their study of Navajo language and culture that a mere dozen years after their arrival they published the comprehensive *Ethnological Dictionary of the Navajo Language* (1910) and, two years later, a bilingual dictionary entitled *Vocabulary of the Navajo Language* (1912). For the writing of Navajo, the Franciscans devised a phonemic alphabet that permitted accurate representation of the language, although like other students of the period, they failed to realize that fixed tone is a distinctive feature of Navajo requiring graphic representation.

As by-products of their inquiries into Navajo religion and ceremonialism, the Franciscans painstakingly recorded entire Navajo ceremonies, involving great volumes of text material. In addition, they wrote and published many other documents, including a *Manual of Navajo Grammar* (1926), a series entitled *Learning Navajo* (1940's), and the *Stem Dictionary of the Navajo Language* (1950-1951), as well as religious material. The early Franciscan system of transcription underwent periodic change and, after 1930, the alphabet used by Professor Edward Sapir was adopted in modified form, including the use of diacritics to mark tone.

The Franciscans produced a wide range of materials in written Navajo, but their efforts were largely directed toward a non-Indian audience; they were not motivated by a desire to make the Navajo people literate in their own language.

Likewise, during the first part of the twentieth century, the Presbyterians, the Christian Reformed Church, and other groups developed their own systems for the writing of Navajo and published a variety of religious materials as well as a small phrase book and collection of verb paradigms, the latter written by C. F. Mitchell, and published (1910 and 1932) under the title *Dine Bîzād* [The Navajo Language].

The efforts of the Protestant missionaries were directed primarily at the Navajos themselves and included the development of literacy in Navajo to permit uneducated members of the tribe to read the Bible. However, lack of intercooperation among the various Protestant denominations, coupled with the paucity of reading material in Navajo, posed a constraint in the way of universal literacy.

In 1934, Professor Gladys A. Reichard of Columbia University, a student of Franz Boas, conducted what was known as a Hogan School at Ganado, Arizona. This operation, sponsored by the Bureau of Indian Affairs, was designed to test the feasibility of teaching adult Navajo interpreters to write their own language. Professor Reichard, on a par with contemporary students and interest groups, devised her own individual system for the transcription of Navajo.

At about the same time, in the late mid-1930's, Fr. Berard of St. Michaels Mission was retained by the Bureau of Indian Affairs to prepare Navajo texts for broadcast over a Navajo language radio station that had been established at Window Rock.

Interest in writing Navajo was widespread among early missionaries, ethnologists, and students of language, but motivations and objectives varied, and lack of intercooperation among interested individuals and groups led to a wide diversity of alphabetic systems. To further complicate the problems attendant upon the spread of literacy in the native language, no group was willing to abandon the orthography they had devised, or adopted, in favor of a standard system designed for universal use.

Consequently, when in the 1930's the Bureau of Indian Affairs decided to take a bilingual approach to the education of Navajo children and adults, Dr. Beatty turned to the Smithsonian Institution for expertise in resolving the problem of establishing an independent system for the transcription of Navajo. Motivated, as educators, to teach Navajo children and adults to read and write in both the English and the Navajo language, Bureau planners included in their specifications for the new orthography the requirement that maximum advantage be taken of phonological similarities and analogies between the two languages, applying conventional English alphabetic symbols for the representation of Navajo phonemes wherever possible. In short the specifications called for making written Navajo and written English look as much alike as possible, without sacrificing accuracy and adequacy in transcription.

The existing orthographies had marked the distinctive feature of vowel length in various manners, if at all. By the 1930's the Franciscans and Reichard used a raised period, as in *do·da* 'no'. The Protestant system used by the American Bible Society in *God Bîzād* (*God's Word* – no publication date shown) used a variety of conventions to represent vowel length, depending in part upon the quality of the vowel and the phonological environment. This system consistently used a circumflex to mark short *i*, as in *sîn* 'song'; while long *i* was written simply as *i* in some instances, as *ī* in others. Thus, *adinid* [ádííniid] 'he said', but *hadzī* 'he spoke' [haadzíí']. The macron was generally used with other vowels to mark length, as *łō* [łóó'] 'fish', *sād* [saad] 'word, language'; but in the spelling *hadzī* [haadzíí'], the long vowel *a* is unmarked.

Until the 1930's none of the systems in use on the reservation marked tone, with the result that words distinguished only by this feature were spelled alike; thus, for example, the spelling *at'iṅ* represented both[at'į́] 'he is rich', and [át'į́] 'he did it, it is he'; *dō* was the spelling for both [dóó] 'and', and [doo] 'not'.

For the most part, the then existing orthographies utilized a wide range of special alphabetic symbols. The Franciscan system included, *c*, *ċ*, *č*, *č̇*, *š*, *ž*, *ʒ*, *ǯ*, *γ*, *ł*, *λ*, *ƛ*, *ƛ'*; while the most widely used protestant system contained the letters *c*, *c'*, *ġ*, *ḧ*, *ł*, *ī*, *s̄*, *ṡ*, and *ż*.

Dr. John P. Harrington, a linguist in the Bureau of American Ethnology, was assigned the task of working out a simple, practical alphabet, and producing primer material for use in teaching written Navajo. Harrington was an excellent phonetician, but he had little previous experience in working with Athapaskan languages – the latter was an advantage, inasmuch as he had no previously devised system of Navajo orthography to defend or promote.

In 1937, through the School of American Research in Santa Fe, New Mexico, with which Harrington was affiliated, he was placed in contact with Robert W. Young. Young, then a graduate student at the University of New Mexico, was involved in field work on the Navajo language, jointly with Adolph D. Bitanny, one of Professor Reichard's students. Young and Bitanny used an adapted form of the Reichard alphabet at the time.

In the fall of 1937 Young went to Fort Wingate, on the fringe of the Navajo Reservation, where he continued language work in collaboration with William Morgan (a Navajo co-worker at the Southwestern Range and Sheep Breeding Laboratory). As a result of joint effort, and with the support of Oliver LaFarge, novelist and anthropologist, whose prestige was high at the time, Harrington, Young, and Morgan developed an orthography acceptable to Bureau educators.

A careful analysis of Navajo phonology was made and, as work progressed in the direction of meeting the specifications laid down by the Bureau, it became apparent that the system of writing could be greatly simplified without sacrificing accuracy and adequacy. The simple letter *t* could be assigned to represent the affricate previously written *tx*, or t^x, for example, since *t* was not needed in Navajo to represent an aspirated, voiceless correspondent of voiced (English) *d*. The letter *h* could be assigned to represent two distinct phonemes of Navajo: *x*, a voiceless palatal spirant that occurs only in syllable-initial position, and *h*, a glottal spirant that occurs only in syllable-final position. No conflict or ambiguity arose as a result of the spellings *tó* for *txó* 'water', *teeh* for *txeeh* 'valley', *hosh* for *xosh* 'thorn', or *hah* for *xah* 'quickly'.

Furthermore, for purposes of a practical Navajo alphabet, the need for special symbols could be reduced to a minimum, largely through the use of digraphs, some of which were already familiar features of conventional English orthography. In the new orthography (and in the older Protestant system, as well, to some extent) *ts* = c, *ts'* = ċ, *ch* = č, *ch'* = č̇, *sh* = š, *zh* = ž, *dz* = ʒ, *j* = ǯ, *gh* = γ, *dl* = λ, *tł* = ƛ, and *tł'* =' ƛ (in the Franciscan system).

The Franciscans used a raised period, and the Protestants a macron, to represent vowel length, as noted above, and in the Protestant system the symbol *ṅ* was utilized to indicate that a preceding vowel is nasal – as in *soṅ* [sǫ'] 'star', *łiṅ* [łį́į'] 'horse, pet'.

In the new orthography, doubling of the vowel symbol (as in Finnish) was adopted as a convention for the writing of vowel length, as in *bitoo'* 'its juice' (in contrast with *bito'* 'his water'), and vowel length was consistently written, irrespective of phonological environment – thus the spelling *dooh'ash* 'you two will go', despite the fact that the duration of the vowel in the syllable 'dooh' is much shorter than its duration when the syllable is closed by a stopped consonant, as in *bitoo'* 'its juice'. (Vowel length had often been ignored in environments of the type illustrated above, despite the subtle contrast in such forms as *doh'aash* 'you two are in the act of starting to go', and *dooh'ash* 'you two will go'.)

As a result of the research on Navajo by Professor Edward Sapir, the graphic representation of tone had become a feature of the Franciscan and Reichard systems in the 1930's. Needless to say, use of the macron to write vowel length would have posed an obstacle in the way of simple representation of tone – a spelling such as *hādzī́* for *haadzíí'* would have been needlessly cluttered.

The Franciscan system used an acute accent mark to write high tone (*txó* 'water'), a grave accent mark for low tone on syllabic *n* (*ǹníyá* 'he stopped going'), a circumflex for falling tone (*át'ê·go* 'it being'), and an inverted circumflex for rising tone (*yah ǒ·ya'* 'that you might enter'). The new orthography reduced the number of diacritics for the writing of tone to one, using the acute accent mark alone. High tone could be represented on a short vowel by placing an acute accent over the vowel symbol, as *tó* 'water'; and with a long vowel or diphthong, the diacritical could be written over both vowel symbols, as *díí* 'this', *séí* 'sand'. Low tone was simply unmarked.

With adoption of a doubled vowel symbol to represent length, it was possible to write falling tone by simply writing the acute accent over the first letter only of a doublet, as *naasháago* 'I going about'; and rising tone could be written by placing the acute accent mark over the second element, as *yah oóya'* 'that you might enter'. A similar convention could be used, of course, in writing falling or rising tones on diphthongs and other types of vowel clusters, as *ayóigo* 'extremely'; *bínaaí* 'his older brother'; *náosdza'* 'that I might return'.

The 'nasal hook' was adopted, as in the Sapir-Franciscan system, to represent a nasal vowel, as *łį́į́'* 'pet, horse', *noodǫ́ǫ́z* 'striped', *naadą́ą́'* 'corn' *kǫ'* 'fire'. For a time the use of a tilde for this purpose (as in Portuguese) was considered, but it was decided to reserve the area above the vowel symbol for the marking of tone.

The 'barred-l' (*ł*), as it is called, had been used from the beginning by the Franciscans as well as most other writers of Navajo; after considering the use of *lh* to represent a voiceless lateral, *ł* was adopted by the new orthography.

With these and a few additional modifications, a new orthographic system emerged for the writing of Navajo – a system that, with the addition of an acute accent mark and a nasal hook, can be written on an ordinary English language typewriter (*ł* can be produced by striking a hyphen over an l).

The following passage illustrates the new orthography developed to meet the specifications established by Bureau educators in the late 1930's and early 1940's: *Tádiin dóó ba'ąą ashdla' náháhaiídą́ą́' daats'í t'áá éí Tsééhíłį́ hoolyéegi diné da'ahiisyį́.*

The earliest reading materials produced in the new system included several primers and work books, among them a beginning reader entitled *Shash Yáázh* [Little Bear]. These early materials were never published, however, and the disposition of the manuscripts is unknown.

In about 1935, an interpreters' school was held at Fort Defiance, resulting in a list of anatomical and medical terms written in the Reichard orthography. In about 1940, this document, under the title *Medical Dictionary*, was transliterated into the new orthography adopted by the Government.

In the spring of 1940, Edward A. Kennard and Robert W. Young were employed by the Bureau of Indian Affairs to produce reading and teaching materials in Navajo and in other Indian languages, and to introduce literacy in native languages in the reservation schools. Adolph Bitanny was retained by Navajo Agency as a teacher of literacy, and Willetto B. Antonio was employed at the Phoenix Indian School as a printer.

In 1940, a primer-reader series by J. B. Enochs was translated into Navajo and published under the general title *Diné Yázhí Ba'ałchíní* [Little Man's Family]. It was followed, in quick succession by a reader entitled *Who Wants to be a Prairie Dog*, written by Ann Nolan Clark.

The launching of a literacy program in a language in which there existed no suitable literature presented certain obvious problems that had to be met initially by translating material from English, by mimeographing, and by other expedients.

In 1941 William Morgan joined the Navajo literacy staff, and Dr. Kennard turned his attention to Sioux and Hopi. Young and Morgan produced a book in mimeographed form entitled *Nahasdzáán dóó bikáá' Dine'é baa Hane'* [The World and Its People]. The text was in Navajo and English, on facing pages, and the book included a Navajo-English glossary. This was followed by a four volume series by Ann Nolan Clark, published bilingually in 1940-1943, under the title *Na'nił-kaadí Yázhí* [Little Herder].

In 1942, a new set of bilingual reading materials (*Preprimer*, *Primer*, and *Coyote Tales*), based on Navajo stories, was prepared by Hildegard Thompson, translated into Navajo, and published in mimeographed form with glossaries.

In 1943, Young and Morgan published a sketch of Navajo Grammar and a bilingual dictionary under the title *The Navajo Language* and in the same year an adult level book entitled *Díí K'ad Anaa'ígíí Baa Hane'* [The Story of the Present War]. The latter was a Navajo translation of a book entitled *War with the Axis*, by Chas. McFarlane. Also, in August of 1943, the publication of a monthly Navajo newspaper called *Ádahoo-nílígíí* was launched.

In the following year, 1944, additional teaching materials were produced, including a brochure entitled *The ABC of Navajo* – subsequently republished in 1946 to include an abridged version of *Robinson Crusoe*, and a Navajo-English glossary. This book was designed as an aid to native Navajo speakers who wanted to teach themselves how to read and write.

In the early 1940's the Wycliffe Bible Translators established a field office in Farmington, New Mexico, where they began the task of translating the Bible into Navajo. Convinced of the need for a nonpartisan system for writing Navajo, the Wycliffe translators decided to use the new orthography that had been developed and adopted by the Government. Their influence led many interested groups to join in spreading the 'government system' and in playing an active role in the literacy program. Interested in teaching literacy as well as in Bible translation, the Wycliffe group produced primers and teaching materials, based on the Laubach method, and carried on reading classes at various locations on the reservation. Many of the teaching materials were published by the Bureau of Indian Affairs and made available to schools and Navajo communities.

Following the close of World War II the Navajo newspaper was continued and enlarged. *The Gallup Independent* donated used cartoon matrices for publication with Navajo legends in *Ádahoonílígíí*. At the same time, albeit reluctantly, misssion groups that had declined to abandon their own orthographies for the system adopted by the Government and the Wycliffe translators finally agreed to join forces, but in some instances only after demanding (and obtaining) concessions.

The new orthography used the symbol *gh* to represent a voiced palatal spirant. Before *e* and *i*, *gh* is heavily palatalized, and before *o* it is strongly labialized. Some mission groups that had used the symbols *y* and *w* for the palatal spirant in the environments described above, urged that the Government orthography be modified to eliminate the writing of *gh* where it 'sounded like y or w'. With the agreement of all parties concerned, and in the interest of further broadening support for the new system of writing, the change was effected. As a result, in the late 1940's the spellings *biye'* 'his son', *biyi'* 'inside it', *biwoo'* 'his teeth', and *wolyé* 'it is called', began to appear for *bighe'*, *bighi'*, *bighoo'*, *gholghé*, as the words had previously been written. With this concession, the orthographic system developed by the Government came into general use for practical literacy purposes. Although the Franciscans and individual linguists retained their own systems of writing for scientific purposes, some features of the popular orthography – doubling of the vowel symbol to indicate vowel length, for example – were adopted by scientific writers (e.g. Edward Sapir and Harry Hoijer, *The Phonology and Morphology of the Navaho Language* [*University of California Publications in Linguistics* 50] [1966]).'

The period following World War II was one fraught with many economic problems for the reservation people, a circumstance that generated interest in assembling and carrying out a resource development plan that had taken general shape during the war years in a series of postwar planning conferences. Tribal officials had participated in the conferences, but the rank and file of the Navajo people had little or no knowledge of the proposals that were made. Of these, some were implicit in a formal document presented to the Tribal Council in 1947, setting forth an evaluation of the resource potential of the Navajo Country. Complex and difficult to express in Navajo, the report was translated, explanatory sections were added when necessary, and it was published in *Ádahooníłígíí;* continuing demand for the written translation led to its republication a short time later in brochure form.

With passage of the Indian Claims Act in 1946, the Navajo Tribe became interested in studying the provisions of the 'Naaltsoos Sání' [Old Paper], as the Treaty of 1868 was known, and to satisfy popular curiosity the document was translated, published in bilingual form, and given wide distribution.

During the period 1947-1950, a succession of complex matters were placed before the Tribe for decision. Extemporaneous interpretation was not adequate, for, in many instances, the concepts involved were alien – they could not be TRANSLATED, they could only be EXPLAINED. It was the period during which the Navajo-Hopi Rehabilitation legislation was taking shape in Congress, and the period during which the Department of the Interior was pressing the tribe for adoption of one of three alternative sets of grazing regulations. Written translations and explanations of these matters were widely used in community meetings as an aid in building the popular understanding necessary as a basis for decision making.

A number of old people volunteered to record historical narratives on Soundscriber discs for subsequent transcription and publication. Appearing first in the Navajo language newspaper, the best of these texts were subsequently assembled and republished in *The Navajo Historical Series*. The Series included three separate books, entitled *The Ramah Navajos*, *The Trouble at Round Rock*, and *Selections from Navajo History*, which became available in bilingual form during the period 1949-1952.

At about the same time, Young and Morgan published *The Function and Signification of Certain Navajo Particles*, and a supplement to the 1943 dictionary, under the title *A Vocabulary of Colloquial Navajo*.

Other publications during the 1950's included a translation of the Tribal Council Election Regulations, books on learning English, finding a job, and other themes, authored by the Wycliffe Bible Translators, and, of course, translations of the Bible. In 1958, an additional dictionary of Navajo, written by William Morgan and Leon Wall, was completed and published. Publication of *Ádahooníłígíí*, the Navajo language newspaper, continued until 1957 when it was finally discontinued.

The decade of the 1950's saw Bureau policy swing once again in the direction of assimilation for the reservation people, with heavy emphasis on the teaching and learning of English. The continued use of written Navajo did not appear to be necessary in the new scheme of things; in fact, some of the schools once again discouraged the use of Navajo, even in spoken form.

Over the span of years between 1940 and 1958, a considerable volume of literature had been produced in written Navajo, and an indeterminate number of people (a few thousand, at most) had learned to read in their own language. Nonetheless, the concept of literacy in the native language had not become an institution of Navajo culture; Navajos themselves had not become authors of books and articles in Navajo. The idea of writing had been introduced to the Navajo in exclusive association with the English language at a period when the institutions of Navajo culture, including the Navajo language, were held in low esteem. Consequently, many people looked upon English as the proper language in which to write; in fact, in the early 1940's, some Navajos were opposed to the use of written Navajo and argued that the phonetic values assigned to 'English letters' in writing Navajo were a ridiculous violation of the sounds inherent in the alphabetic symbols.

For a time, in the 1950's, it appeared that the Navajo literacy movement was a dead issue. However, a counterrevolution was quietly taking shape, and by 1960 many young Navajos had awakened to the realization that knowledge of the tribal language and culture – and with it their identity as Navajos – were rapidly slipping away. This realization, voiced with ever increasing frequency at Tribal Youth Conferences in the early years of the decade, led to a reawakening of interest in the Navajo language and the traditional culture and a determination to prevent their disappearance.

Since that time the Rough Rock Demonstration School, the Navajo Community College, the University of New Mexico, the University of Northern Arizona, Brigham Young University, the Massachusetts Institute of Technology, Northwestern University, and other institutions have taken an active interest in the study of the Navajo language and culture, and in the promotion of written Navajo. Once again literature is being produced in the Navajo language, but now with the distinction that the producers of such literature are primarily Navajos.

The Navajo Reading Study, established at the University of New Mexico in 1969 under the direction of Professor Bernard Spolsky and with the support of the Bureau of Indian Affairs and the Ford Foundation, has carried out valuable research bearing on bilingual education for the Navajo and, more importantly perhaps, the Study has brought together a number of Navajo university students who have turned their talents to the writing of textbooks and instructional materials for use in the Navajo schools. Unlike *Little Man's Family*, written in English initially and translated into Navajo in 1940, the Navajo primers and readers of the 1970's are being composed initially in the Navajo language. And finally, supported by a grant from the National Endowment for the Humanities to the University of New Mexico, Drs. Young and Morgan are once again collaborating in the production of a bilingual Navajo/English, English/Navajo dictionary, scheduled for publication in 1977.

Whether or not Navajo will establish itself as a literary language remains to be determined; the possibility is better at present than at any time in the past. And, as the Reading Study Research has clearly demonstrated, use of the Navajo language still has a place in the education of Navajo children: more than 80 percent of the beginners in Bureau schools, and over half of those entering public schools in the Navajo Country still begin their school career speaking only the Navajo language.

Addendum

JOSHUA A. FISHMAN

A Graduate Program in the Sociology of Language

This volume and its companion, *Advances in the Study of Societal Multilingualism*, bring to a close the self-imposed task which I set for myself over a decade ago (1963), during my year as a fellow of the Center for Advanced Study in the Behavioral Sciences (Stanford, California). At that time, while completing *Language Loyalty in the United States* and while in the midst of planning a long range program of empirical and theoretical research, I undertook to develop a graduate training program for the sociology of language, as well as the appropriate texts. At that time neither the one nor the other existed, in the United States or elsewhere. The first issue of this decision (*Readings in the Sociology of Language*) was itself conceived at the Center. Since that time it has been my rare good fortune to be associated for several years with two graduate programs in the sociology of language, one at Yeshiva University in New York and the other at The Hebrew University in Jerusalem, as well as to be associated with a number of others in a visiting capacity of one type or another. These associations have enabled me to define, test, and revise both my graduate training notions as well as the text materials that I prepared or selected to accompany them.

I do not mean to imply by any of the foregoing that yet other and better text materials are not needed in the sociology of language, but, rather, that for the time being I have prepared all that I can (and, perhaps, more than I should) and that others must now step in and contribute where they find gaps in the field.

As Table 1 reveals, my basic notion has been that the sociology of language was itself an interdisciplinary field and, as such, one that needed

Published simultaneously in this volume and in *Advances in the Study of Societal Multilingualism*, vol. II. The Hague, Mouton, 1976.

to be pursued in conjunction with its two parent disciplines, not to mention any one of a number of its other related fields. The American pattern of graduate work, providing as it does for three or more years of full time, broadly guaged and yet rather well-defined study, is of course the underlying (and often unstated) assumption on which a program such as this is based. In the Israeli and, more generally, in much of the European framework of graduate work, it is the master's degree alone which is well-defined while the doctorate is largely left to the individual requirements that professors care to impose on their advanced students. The latter framework is, therefore, typically more specialized in that students have little if any opportunity for interdisciplinary study or research experience during their relatively brief period of study for the master's degree. Nevertheless, via a combination of prerequisite requirements prior to admission to master's work, plus supplementary requirements after admission to doctoral work proper, a program essentially like the American one can also be implemented.

Table 1. *Graduate Training Program in the Sociology of Language*

Core I: *Linguistics*[1]	Core II: *Sociology of Language*[2]
(24 credits)	(24 credits)
Introduction	Introduction
Syntax	Psychology of Language
Phonology	Language Attitudes
Theories of Grammar	Language and National Identity
Field Methods	Language Planning
Comparative	Sociolinguistic Research Methods
Historical	Sociology of Bilingualism
Conversational Analysis	Seminar: Sociolinguistic Theories
Seminar in Linguistics	Seminar: Applied Sociology of Language

Core III: *Sociology*

(24 credits)

Eight courses with emphasis on sociological theory and social research methods, including up to three courses in anthropology, political science, economics and/or history.

1. Including demonstrated reading knowledge of two pertinent foreign languages.
2. Including doctoral seminar (no credit) and two course-related research apprenticeships (no credit) dealing with both sociological and linguistic data.

The rebirth of the sociology of language occurred in the United States at a time of plentiful research funds and training fellowships. As a result, it was relatively painless for universities to offer the specialized and expensive courses and training opportunities upon which it depended. During periods of plenty, interdisciplinary programs are hailed for their experimental, pioneering, and stimulating qualities. Some will even venture that such programs come closer than do traditional departmental approaches to parallelling the 'true state' in the 'real world' of the subject matter or problems to which they are devoted. However, when the fat years are followed by lean ones, as they inevitably seem to be, interdisciplinary problems are the first to be sacrificed. They quickly appear to have no well-established protectors who would claim them as their own natural and legitimate offspring. Universities must be extremely impoverished, indeed, to cut out one department or another, but it takes only a minor budgetary scare to declare an interdisciplinary program to be a luxury. As a result, it is my definite advice that the courses and faculty of programs in the sociology of language must all also have their definite homes in one or both of the parent discipline departments. The courses listed above are all of such a nature as to make such dual citizenship possible and to enrich any 'standard' department of linguistics and/or sociology in the process, by strengthening or offering course work of interest and importance far beyond the limits of sociology or linguistics per se.

The entire enterprise in which I have engaged during the past dozen years has benefited immeasurably from the fact that program building, textbook preparing, and other 'pedagogic' efforts (whether directed at students, colleagues, and/or administrators) were carried on in constant fruitful interaction with basic and applied research. It is, therefore, my strong conviction that students too should be trained in this way, so that study, research, application, and evaluation can be seen and experienced as the necessary continuum that they constitute, rather than as a series of separate and isolated status-related concerns. I have gone out of my way, as a result, whether in connection with *Language Loyalty in the United States*, *Bilingualism in the Barrio*, *Language Planning Processes*, or (currently) *The Sociology of English as a Second Language*, and *The Sociology of Bilingual Education*, to involve as many students as possible in study design, data collection, data analysis, data interpretation, and report writing. I have also tried to be just as helpful as I could with respect to the publication of their joint efforts, often via professional journals and books, or most recently via a journal expressly for student research (*Language Behavior Papers*). It is my view that whatever *I* need in order to facilitate and stimulate my work is also needed by and for my students in order to facilitate and stimulate theirs. We are colleagues in a joint enterprise and that should extend (and it definitely *has* extended) even to the revision of the training program shown above.

It should be the aim of a graduate training program in the sociology of language to develop that field, as well as to cultivate its interdisciplinary ties. Competence in the sociology of language is not something that good linguistics programs or good sociology programs can develop or train for incidentally to their main pursuits. Interdisciplinary fields are not 'picked up' en route to other goals. Indeed, they are harder to master than are corresponding disciplinary fields, precisely because of their broader and less traditional nature.

The view of some linguists that they and their students are qualified to engage in sociolinguistic enterprises because they are 'interested in conversations' or because they have 'studied or taught anthropology', or because they are 'language and area specialists in . . .', is no less ludicrous than would be the claim of sociologists to engage in linguistic (or even in sociolinguistic) enterprises on the basis of such qualifications. After a decade in which I have pursued the sociology of language from one topic to the next, from one discipline to another, and from one continent to another, I am more and more impressed with what remains to be known, and more and more dubious of claims that the field can be theoretically and methodologically mastered or enlightened from a monodisciplinary base or via incidental forays therefrom.

Index of Names

Index of Subjects

Contributions to the Sociology of Language

Edited by Joshua A. Fishman

1. *Advances in the Sociology of Language*
   Volume I: Basic Concepts, Theories and Problems: Alternative Approaches
   Ed. by J. A. Fishman
   1976, 418 pages, 2nd ed. Clothbound
   ISBN: 90-279-7732-1

2. *Advances in the Sociology of Language*
   Volume II: Selected Studies and Applications
   Ed. by J. A. Fishman
   1972, 534 pages. Paperbound
   ISBN: 90-279-2302-7

3. *Multilingualism in the Soviet Union*
   Aspects of Language Policy and its Implementation
   by E. Glyn Lewis
   1972, xx + 332 pages. Paperbound
   ISBN: 90-279-2352-3

4. *Perspectives on Black English*
   Ed. by J. L. Dillard
   1975, 392 pages. Clothbound
   ISBN: 90-279-7811-5

5. *Advances in Language Planning*
   Ed. by J. A. Fishman
   1974, 590 pages. Paperbound
   ISBN: 90-279-2618-2

6. *The Revival of a Classical Tongue*
Eliezer Ben Yehuda and the Modern Hebrew Language
by Jack Fellman
1973, 152 pages. Paperbound
ISBN: 90-279-2495-3

7. *The Political Sociology of the English Language*
An African Perspective (Who are the Afro-Saxons?)
by Ali A. Mazrui
1975, 232 pages. Clothbound
ISBN: 90-279-7821-2

8. *Advances in the Creation and Revision of Writing Systems*
Ed. by J. A. Fishman
1977, XXVIII + 492 pages. Clothbound
ISBN: 90-279-7552-3

9. *Advances in the Study of Societal Multilingualism*
Ed. by J. A. Fishman
1977, in prep. Clothbound
ISBN: 90-279-7742-9

10. *Language and Politics*
Ed. by William M. O'Barr and Jean F. O'Barr
1976, XVI + 506 pages. Clothbound
ISBN: 90-279-7761-5

11. *Universalism versus Relativism in Language and Thought*
Proceedings of a Colloquium on the Sapir – Whorf Hypotheses
Ed. by Rik Pinxten
1976, XIV + 310 pages. Clothbound
ISBN: 90-279-7791-7

12. *Selection among Alternatives in Language Standardization*
The Case of Albanian
by Janet Byron
1976, 160 pages. Paperbound
ISBN: 90-279-7542-6

13. *Black Names*
    by J. L. Dillard
    1976, 114 pages. Paperbound.
    ISBN: 90-279-6702-3

14. *Language Planning for Modernization*
    The Case of Indonesian and Malaysian
    by S. Takdir Alisjabana
    1976, 132 pages. Paperbound
    ISBN: 90-279-7712-7

15. *Issues in Sociolinguistics*
    Ed. by Oscar Uribe-Villegas
    1977, in prep. Clothbound
    ISBN: 90-279-7722-4

16. *Soviet Contributions to the Sociology of Language*
    Ed. by Philip A. Luelsdorff
    1977, in prep. Clothbound
    ISBN: 90-279-7613-9

17. *Acceptability in Language*
    Ed. by Sidney Greenbaum
    1977, in prep. Clothbound
    ISBN: 90-279-7623-6

18. *Towards a Social Grammar of Language*
    by Matthew C. Grayshon
    1977, in prep. Paperbound
    ISBN: 90-279-7633-3

Other volumes are in preparation

MOUTON . THE HAGUE . PARIS

Educational Linguistics/TESOL/ICC
Graduate School of Education
University of Pennsylvania
3700 Walnut Street/C1
Philadelphia, PA 19104